PERIOPERATIVE NURSING

THIRD EDITION

Linda K. Groah, RN, MS, CNOR, CNAA
Service Director Surgery and Intensive Services
Kaiser Permanente Medical Center
San Francisco/South San Francisco

Assistant Clinical Professor
School of Nursing
University of California, San Francisco
San Francisco, California

with two chapters by

Lillian H. Nicolette, RN, MSN, CNOR
Sterilization Systems Specialist
Advance Sterilization Products
Division of Johnson and Johnson Inc.

Perioperative Faculty
Delaware County Community College
Media, Pennsylvania

Appleton & Lange
Stamford, Connecticut

Copyright © 1996 by Appleton & Lange
A Simon & Schuster Company
Copyright 1990 by Appleton & Lange under the title *Operating Room Nursing: Perioperative Practice*
Copyright 1983 by Reston Publishing Company, Inc. under the title *Operating Room Nursing: The Perioperative Role*

All rights reserved. This book, or any parts thereof, may not be used or reproduced in any manner without written permission. For information, address Appleton & Lange, Four Stamford Plaza, PO Box 120041, Stamford, Connecticut 06912-0041.

96 97 98 99 00 / 10 9 8 7 6 5 4 3 2 1

Prentice Hall International (UK) Limited, *London*
Prentice Hall of Australia Pty. Limited, *Sydney*
Prentice Hall Canada, Inc., *Toronto*
Prentice Hall Hispanoamericana, S.A., *Mexico*
Prentice Hall of India Private Limited, *New Delhi*
Prentice Hall of Japan, Inc., *Tokyo*
Simon & Schuster Asia Pte. Ltd., *Singapore*
Editora Prentice Hall do Brasil Ltda., *Rio de Janeiro*
Prentice Hall, *Englewood Cliffs, New Jersey*

Editor-in-Chief: Sally J. Barhydt
Acquisitions Editor: David P. Carroll
Development Editor: Barbara Severs
Production: Andover Publishing Services
Designer: Mary Skudlarek

ISBN 0-8385-7365-7
90000

9 780838 573655

PRINTED IN THE UNITED STATES OF AMERICA

*This third edition
is dedicated to all perioperative nurses
who welcome the opportunity and accept the challenges
to provide quality care to the surgical patient.*

*The material contained in this book is endorsed by
AORN as a useful component in the ongoing
education process of perioperative nurses.*

Reviewers

Colonel Ellen V. Lord, RN, MS, CNOR
US Army (Ret.)
Perioperative Nursing Consultant
Denver, Colorado

Marcia Nidey, RN
Assistant Nurse Manager Post-Anesthesia Care Unit
University of Iowa Hospitals and Clinics
Iowa Cita, Iowa

Patricia Plumb, RN
Supervisor—Sterile Processing
St. Vincent's Medical Center
Bridgeport, Connecticut

Nancy Radoslovich, RN, MA, CNOR
Nurse Manager, Operating Room
Muhlenberg Regional Medical Center
Plainfield, New Jersey

Lois Schick, RN, MN, MBA
Director of SurgiCare One and Emergency Department
Saint Joseph Hospital
Denver, Colorado

Contents

Preface

How will nursing historians describe the decade of the 1990s? The political struggle that is revolving around health care reform has precipitated fundamental changes in the delivery of nursing care. Although organized attempts to legislate change have been unsuccessful to date, the concept of voluntary health care reform has taken on new meaning. Terms and phrases such as delegation, cross training, practice models, unlicensed assistive personnel, noninvasive surgery, lasers, patient-family education, cultural diversity, customer focus, quality improvement, competency-based practice, and cost-effective care describe the surgical patient and/or perioperative nursing. Patients are requesting information about their surgical experience, and perioperative nurses are creating processes and systems to meet patient needs. Enhanced technologies and new treatment modalities have permitted an increase in the number and kinds of surgical procedures that can be performed in ambulatory settings, and these changes have resulted in the development of 24-hour observation units. Operating room nursing has truly evolved into perioperative nursing. The change in the title of this book for its third edition reflects this evolution.

NEW FEATURES

Much of the information in the first and second editions is as relevant today as it was when it was written. Much has changed in this decade, however, in the systems and processes of perioperative nursing. As a result of both the changes in nursing practice and the increased emphasis on the patient as a customer, each chapter of the book has been substantially rewritten. In addition, five chapters have been added to this third edition: Chapter 4, Legal Responsibilities of the Perioperative Nurse; Chapter 15, Physiological and Psychological Needs of Specific Patient Populations; Chapter 16, Ambulatory Surgery; Chapter 19, Improving Organizational Performance; and Chapter 20, Developing Perioperative Clinical Education Programs.

Chapter 1 has been expanded to include descriptions of the new roles for perioperative nurses and a vision of how and where perioperative nursing will be practiced in the next decade. Chapter 2 includes a new emphasis on keeping the operating room environment safe from fire, chemicals, and radiation, and discusses the criteria that must be met in constructing operating rooms in which lasers will be used.

Chapter 3, Management and Leadership of the Surgical Suite, reflects the transition of operating room nurses to professionals who need specific management and leadership skills to function efficiently and effectively in this area of clinical practice. Sixteen major aspects of care—for example, discharge planning, emergencies, fluid balance, medication administration, and physiological monitoring—are identified, with examples of how they can be evaluated according to the standard of care a patient should expect and according to the standards of nursing practice. The chapter also explores the use of unlicensed assistive personnel, and several models of care are studied as potential frameworks for structuring perioperative nursing practice.

Chapter 4 focuses on the legal responsibilities of the perioperative nurse in risk management, liability, malpractice, negligence, and decisions about medical care. Ethical issues and the American Nurses Association Code of Ethics are discussed in relationship to perioperative practice.

Chapters 7 and 8, related to sterilization, disinfection, and other means of limiting operating room contamination, have been updated and include discussions of current concepts, practices, supplies, and the technology enhancements that are recommended to provide a safe environment for both the patient and the surgical team. Chapter 10 describes new techniques used to produce anesthesia and analgesia for the surgical patient, the standards for monitoring patients, and the management of patients receiving intravenous conscious sedation.

In this edition, Chapter 12, Surgical Instruments, details the technologic changes that have had an impact on the care of surgical patients in this decade. An extensive discussion of minimally invasive surgery includes operational assistance with video camera systems. Laparoscopic electrosurgical complications and their prevention are described in depth, as is the clinical use of lasers and laser safety precautions. Throughout the chapter, the most up-to-date surgical instruments are pictured.

All surgical patients are dependent on the nursing care delivered by professional registered nurses. Specific groups of patients, however, present special challenges to the perioperative nurse in planning and providing care. Obese, elderly, diabetic, and pediatric patients are highlighted in Chapter 15, in which these special conditions are related to developing plans of care.

The same standards of care are implemented for all surgical patients in all settings; however, ambulatory surgery patients present specific challenges. Chapter 16 addresses those challenges.

Chapter 17 has been expanded from the second edition to provide perioperative nurses who cross train to the Post-Anesthesia Care Unit (PACU) a broader view of the postoperative care of surgical patients. Current standards for monitoring and managing patients with pain during the immediate recovery period are detailed.

Consistent with the responsibility of perioperative nurses to collect baseline physiological data during presurgical assessments, Chapter 18 addresses the systemic factors that affect wound healing, including nutrition, drug therapies, aging, and radiation therapy. Healthy and malnourished body areas are compared to assist the clinician in identifying patient abnormalities.

Chapter 19 contains an overview of quality improvement and provides examples of how a perioperative program can be developed. The book concludes with a revised chapter on developing perioperative clinical education programs to ensure competent clinical practitioners.

In this edition several lengthy documents to which practitioners will want to refer from time to time have been placed in Appendixes at the end of the text, rather than within a chapter, so as not to interrupt the flow of chapter content.

This book is a text for all levels of perioperative nurses. The novice will find it invaluable in learning about the surgical environment and the basic responsibilities of perioperative nurses. The advanced, expert nurse will find that this edition is a valuable adjunct in planning care for patients with complex nursing problems and in managing the patient's continuum of care throughout the perioperative period.

The author wishes to express appreciation and thanks to all the perioperative nurses who have used this book and provided valuable suggestions for this edition; to Lillian Nicolette who revised Chapter 8, Sterilization and Disinfection, and Chapter 17, Immediate Postoperative Nursing Care; and to Niels Buessem whose editorial assistance was invaluable in producing this third edition.

Linda K. Groah, RN, MS, CNOR, CNAA

PERIOPERATIVE NURSING

NURSING

THIRD EDITION

ONE

The Perioperative Nursing Environment

The Evolution of Perioperative Nursing

Archaeologists have found skulls that date back to 350,000 B.C. with evidence of surgical procedures. The earliest scientific document brought to light on the subject of surgery is the *Edwin Smith Papyrus,* conceived in ancient Egypt about 3000 B.C. In addition to describing clinical methods then in use, it records accurate observations on anatomy, physiology, and pathology.[1]

Hippocrates, "The Father of Medicine," born about 460 B.C., wrote more than 70 books on medicine and surgery. In one book, *On the Surgery,* he discusses the operating room in detail, including how instruments and light were prepared and used. Hippocrates also refers to an assistant when he discusses instrumentation,[2] although it is not known who that other person was. There is little mention of a surgical assistant in the literature until the late 1800s.

■ HISTORY OF OPERATING ROOM NURSING

1873–1900

In 1873, three nursing training schools opened in the United States, patterned after Florence Nightingale's school at St. Thomas Hospital in London. They were Bellevue in New York City, the Connecticut Training School in New Haven, and the Boston Training School (later called the Massachusetts General Hospital Training School) (Figs. 1–1, 1–2). The Bellevue Report of 1875 listed lectures about "Surgical Instruments and Preparation for Operation," "Bandaging," and "Haemostasis."[3]

In *History of Nursing,* James J. Walsh wrote the following regarding the period around 1884:

> The demand for nurses, properly trained, was not felt in the hospitals generally throughout the country until Lister's revolutionary discovery of the value of antisepsis in surgery made it absolutely necessary that nurses should be of such an intellectual calibre and development as would permit them to be trained in the prevention of infection through absolute cleanliness.[4]

In 1889, William H. Welch, pathologist, William S. Halsted, surgeon, and Sir William Osler, physician practicing internal medicine, set up Johns Hopkins University in Baltimore

Figure 1–1. Operating room, Bellevue Hospital, 1870. (The Bettmann Archive.)

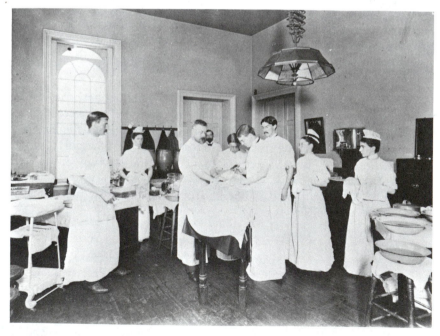

Figure 1–2. Operating room, St. Luke's Hospital, New York, 1880. (The Bettmann Archive.)

to train doctors and nurses. Operating room nursing, identified as an area of specialization, became nursing's first specialty.[5]

During that same year, the Boston Training School added a lecture on bacteriology to the curriculum. In 1891, students were given the responsibility for cleaning and sterilizing instruments for Saturday operations. By 1896, student nurses were sent to assist with Saturday operations.[6]

1900–1920

Soon after the turn of the century, the role and identity of the surgical nurse were radically changed. Advances in anesthesia made it possible to extend operating time and reduce the surgical mortality rate. As more and more surgical procedures were being performed (Figs. 1–3, 1–4, 1–5) graduate nurses were placed in charge of the surgical amphitheaters and student nurses assisted regularly with operations and etherizing.[6]

In 1901, Martha Luce of Boston described the many duties of an operating room nurse, which required knowledge of the principles of asepsis, careful attention to details, and much forethought in preparing supplies.

> The care of the operating room includes dusting with clean, damp cloths; polishing of glass, tables, and utensils; regulation of the temperature and ventilation of the room. In addition to the daily cleaning, it is desirable to use a solution of corrosive sublimate (1 to 3000) before an operation, especially before a Laparotomy, and all the basins to be used

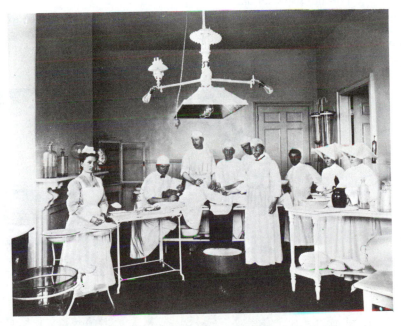

Figure 1–3. Operating room in Mobile, Alabama, 1900. (The Bettmann Archive.)

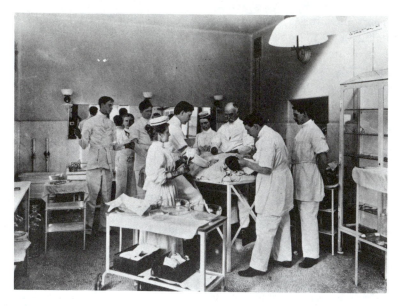

Figure 1–4. Professor Charles McBurney (1845–1913) operating in Roosevelt Hospital, New York, 1901. (The Bettmann Archive.)

for sterile water or any of the antiseptic solutions should be thoroughly cleansed with the same strength of corrosive solution.

The surgeon's retiring room must be kept in perfect order. Gowns, sheets, towels and sponges have to be folded in the regulation way and pinned securely. Gauze sponges of two or three sizes can be made by carefully folding cut gauze in such a way that all the

Figure 1–5. Dr. Halsted operating in Johns Hopkins new ampitheater, 1905. (The Bettmann Archive.)

edges are securely turned in and no sewing is necessary. The sponges are counted before being put in packages.

The instruments for all operations are selected by the surgeon or his assistant, and, with the exception of the knives, are wrapped in cotton cloth for sterilization. The knives are cleaned with soap and water, ether and alcohol (95%). They are wrapped in separate sterile towels and boiled three minutes, but the rest of the instruments are boiled one-half hour in water in which a small amount of bicarbonate of soda has been added.

Most surgeons have individual preferences in the choice of needles, ligatures, etc. and it is the duty of the operating room nurse to acquaint herself with these preferences and to carefully prepare what each requires for his use.

Rubber gloves are tied together in pairs with pieces of cotton bandage on which is marked the wearer's name. A few cots should be included, to be used in case a glove finger becomes punctured.

The operating room nurse is responsible for every detail of the preparation, including the careful instruction of her assistant nurse. If all has been well done, it will prevent awkwardness and delay during the process of the operation.[7]

Leila Clark Woodbury wrote in 1903 that:

Surgical nursing is a subject of such almost unlimited extent that volumes might be written on it. I shall endeavor to give the requirements of a surgical nurse; a brief outline of bacteriology and the relationship this science bears to surgery; the care of the surgical case, and some additional notes of things learned by experience.[8]

One of the areas Woodbury cited dealt with the patient's mental state.

As a rule, the preparations and, perhaps, the unfamiliar surroundings of a hospital tend to make the patient apprehensive and really in a pitiable frame of mind. A good nurse with tact can, by a few cheerful or encouraging words, divert the thought of the patient, or, at least relieve her fears of the ordeal in store for her.[8]

Another area Woodbury identified was economy.

In all parts of her work a surgical nurse who practices economy is doubly valuable. There is no department of nursing where this may be practised to greater advantage than in the care of a surgical case. Many of the materials used in this work are expensive, and a nurse by thought and good judgment may be able to lessen enormously the expense necessary at such a time.[8]

By 1900, surgeons wore sterile scrub suits, and surgical scrubs were performed by all members of the surgical team. Following the scrub, sterile gloves were worn to protect the hands until surgery was started, and then they were removed. In 1905, it was determined that skin could not be sterilized; therefore rubber gloves were worn throughout the procedure. In the same year it was recommended that the instrument nurse wear a sterile gown.

Around 1907, head coverings were advocated; by 1914, surgical masks for surgeons, assistants, and the sterile (surgical) nurse were gaining acceptance.

During these first two decades of the 20th century, the roles of "circulator" and "scrub" nurse emerged. The nurse who remained sterile is referred to in the literature as the scrubbed nurse, suture nurse, washed-up-nurse, sterile glove nurse, tray nurse, instrument nurse, sponge nurse, and setting-up-nurse. The surgeon insisted that this individual be the senior member of the nursing team. By 1910, however, nursing authorities agreed that the nurse who remained unsterile, or who circulated, ran the operating room and, therefore, had to be the senior, more experienced nurse. They also suggested that only a trained nurse, not a student, could fill this role; however, the role of the scrub nurse could be performed by a student if necessary.[9]

1920–1940

It was common for student nurses during the 1920s and 1930s to provide most of the patient care, under the direction of a graduate nurse or senior student. Students were trained in the operating room and expected to function effectively. In many instances, students functioned in the role of circulator after minimal experience. One author in the *American Journal of Nursing* advised that, "The student nurse whose three months' training is completed then continues the work of the non-sterile (circulating) nurse for one month."[10]

Early in this period, no standards or curriculum guides were available to identify how a nurse should be trained. Frequently, the nurse in charge of an area would be the only registered nurse present and would train students in addition to her other duties.

In 1927, the *American Journal of Nursing* published an article, "The Operating Supervisor and Her Qualifications." The operating supervisor was to show ". . . a high sense of responsibility to the patient, the peculiarities of the surgeon, and to instruct young nurses."[11]

In 1929, the National League of Nursing Education (NLNE) included in their standard curriculum a section, "Operating Room Technic," intended as a guide for schools to implement. Nothing in the curriculum was mandatory. Included were 10 hours of instruction in operating room technique and bacteriology and 20 hours in surgical diseases. Aided by this and specific pointers published in nursing journals, head nurses were able to fulfill their teaching assignments.[6]

In 1933, the Subcommittee on Surgical Nursing of the Education Committee of the NLNE outlined a master curriculum plan for an advanced course in operating room technique and maintenance of standards. It was the first attempt by a national organization to standardize the level of nursing care in the operating room, and it served as a model for training during the next decade. The curriculum listed the following objectives[12]:

1. To instruct the student in the relation of the operative procedure to the patient's safety and progress
2. To improve thoughtfulness and skill in the nursing care of patients in the operating room
3. To improve understanding of operating room technique and routines and develop an appreciation of their scientific basis
4. To acquaint the student with the special supervisory problems of the operating room
5. To aid the student in organizing a teaching program in the operating room

The depression in the United States resulted in fewer patients in most hospitals. Consequently, fewer nurses were employed. Many schools of nursing were forced to close due to a lack of financial resources. As a result, the number of graduate and student nurses declined.

1941–1945

When America entered World War II, many nurses left hospital positions to join the armed forces. An acute nursing shortage in the United States resulted. It was necessary for hospitals to train ancillary personnel to take the place of graduate and student nurses. In the operating room, for example, orderlies were used as circulators.[13]

During World War II, corpsmen and nurses in the armed forces were trained to care for the wounded in field hospitals. Because additional training was needed by army nurses assigned to surgery, a 12-week postgraduate course in operating room technique was established at Cushing General Hospital in Framingham, Massachusetts. The course, which included basic principles, such as gowning and gloving, was expanded to cover fluid therapy, including plasma and whole blood transfusions; care of patients in shock or respiratory or cardiac failure; and methods of administering general, spinal, intravenous (IV), or rectal anesthesia.[14]

A new term—operating room technician—referred to personnel who were trained to assist in surgery. The theory, which was usually taught by army and navy nurses, included not only how to function in the scrub and circulating roles but how to serve as an anesthetist and first assistant. In field hospitals, the operating room technician worked under the direction of the surgeon until the nurses arrived. However, on board combat ships where nurses did not serve, the corpsmen ran the operating room.[15]

World War II brought about many changes in how hospitals in the U.S. were organized. Among the changes were the development of centralized sterile and reprocessing departments and the increased use of nonprofessionals to perform tasks formerly identified as nursing responsibilities.

1946–1960

During the immediate postwar years, many hospitals hired operating room technicians who had been trained in the armed forces. Hospital administrators began to question, "In view of the still acute shortage of both professional and practical nurses is it right to utilize, in a definitely technical field, persons who are trained in the bedside care of the sick?"[16]

The nursing literature indicated that operating room technicians were to perform "certain routine duties" under the direct supervision of a graduate nurse and that this would allow the graduate nurse to carry out more complex nursing activities.[17]

Hospitals and adult education programs established training programs to meet the increased demand for operating room technicians. At the same time, nursing educators began to question whether the operating room rotation was essential to the learning experience of student nurses. Despite attempts by some educators, such as Alexander[18] and Shaltis,[19] to prove that the rotation was essential, the general atmosphere of uncertainty limited the development of sound curricula; eventually the rotation was eliminated.

In January 1949 in the midst of these transitions,[17] operating room supervisors from New York City identified the need for an organization to meet routinely to exchange information about their area of specialization. The result of this unprecedented independent nursing meeting was the Association of Operating Room Nurses (AORN). Its primary aims were to:[20]

1. stimulate operating room nurses in other parts of the country to form similar groups
2. become a specific group to pool and share nursing knowledge and technology
3. provide the surgical patient with optimum care through a broad educational program
4. make a body of knowledge available to operating room nurses
5. motivate experienced operating room nurses to share their expertise
6. become an association for the benefit of all professional operating room nurses

The first national conference of AORN was held in February 1954. In 1957, following repeatedly denied requests to affiliate with the NLNE and the American Nurses Association (ANA), AORN became an independent national organization.[20]

1960–1970

In 1960, AORN published the first issue of its official bimonthly journal, *OR Nursing*.[21] With the January-February issue in 1963, its name was changed to the *AORN Journal,* and in 1967 the Association began to publish the journal monthly.

Among AORN's major concerns during the 1960s were the shortage of operating room nurses and how best to use trained paramedical personnel in the operating room.

In 1965, AORN, ANA, and NLN met to recommend standards and guidelines for the selection, instruction, and training of operating room technicians. As an outcome of their decisions, in 1967 AORN published a manual, *Teaching the Operating Room Technician*.[22]

In 1968, an allied association of AORN was structured, the Association of Operating Room Technicians (AORT). During its infancy, this organization was guided by the AORN-AORT Advisory Board; in 1973, AORT became an independent organization,[23] and changed its name to Association of Surgical Technologists (AST). Later, the title of operating room technician changed to surgical technologist.

In 1969, the following definition of professional operating room nursing was adopted:

> Professional nursing in the operating room is the identification of the physiological, psychological and sociological needs of the patient and the development and implementation of an individualized program of nursing care that coordinates the nursing actions, based on the knowledge of the natural and behavioral sciences, to restore or maintain the health and welfare of the patient before, during and after surgical intervention.[24]

The objective of clinical practice of professional operating room nursing was identified: "to provide a standard of excellence in the care of the patient before, during and after surgical intervention."[24]

1970–1980

During this decade, the scope of AORN was expanded from its primary focus on education to providing national standards, official policies, and position statements. One of the first resolutions adopted in 1973 pertained to the necessity of having a registered nurse in the operating room. With the adoption of this resolution, AORN accepted the role of consumer advocate and determined how the functions of registered nurses justify their presence in this critical nursing area. Included in the rationale were the following statements:[25]

The registered nurse has knowledge, experience, and responsibility that prepare her to:

1. Independently assess patient needs.
2. Make collaborative decisions relative to total intraoperative care.
3. Make decisions and take action in emergency situations.
4. Establish and maintain inter- and intradepartmental functioning for continuity of care.
5. Provide for and contribute to patient safety through control of his internal and external environment, biological testing, and product evaluation.
6. Assist the patient to manage anxiety through the application of the principles of biological, physical, and social sciences.
7. Provide efficient patient care in the operating room through organizational skills, preoperative and postoperative visits, and sound principles of management.
8. Conduct and participate in research projects directed toward improvement of patient care through the application of scientific principles.
9. Control hospital costs through budget preparation and implementation.
10. Participate in architectural design of operating suites effecting efficiency and quality in patient care.
11. Participate in supervision and instruction of ancillary and allied health personnel in the operating room.
12. Evaluate and modify the quality of patient care within the operating room.

To validate the outcome of nursing care in the operating room, an ad hoc committee of AORN developed a nursing audit tool, which was published in 1974. It outlined one method of evaluation in which actual patient care is compared with the standards of care defined by departmental policies and procedures.

In 1975, AORN formulated a statement of policy indicating that the circulator must at all times be the professional registered nurse.[26] That same year AORN and ANA collaborated to publish the standards for measuring quality of patient care, *Standards of Nursing Practice: Operating Room.* These standards are directed toward providing continuity of nursing care through preoperative assessment and planning, intraoperative intervention, and postoperative evaluation (see Chapter 5).

Concurrently the Technical Standards Committee of AORN formulated and published *Standards of Technical and Aseptic Practice: Operating Room.*[27] The standards are a guide for developing institutional policies and procedures.

The Standards of Administrative Nursing Practice: Operating Room were published in 1976,[28] and with the previously published standards provided a method for evaluating the quality of nursing administration in the operating room.

In 1978 at the 25th AORN Congress, the House of Delegates adopted the following definition of operating room nursing in its "Statement of the Perioperative Role":[29]

The perioperative role of the operating room nurse consists of nursing activities performed by the professional operating room nurse during the preoperative, intraoperative and postoperative phases of the patient's surgical experience. Operating room nurses assume the perioperative role at a beginning level dependent on their expertise and competency to practice. As they gain knowledge and skills they progress on a continuum to an advanced level of practice.

In 1979, AORN contracted with the Professional Examination Service of New York to offer the first voluntary certification examination for operating room nurses. The purposes of the certification program were to:[30]

1. Demonstrate concerns for accountability to the general public for nursing practice.
2. Enhance the quality of patient care.
3. Identify nurses who have demonstrated professional achievement in providing care for patients during surgical intervention.
4. Provide employing agencies with a means of identifying an individual practitioner's professional achievement.
5. Provide personal satisfaction for practitioners.

1980–1990

During this decade, the health care industry was in the midst of its greatest challenges: increased health care costs, advancements in medical technology, the public's increased knowledge of health care, and the abundant supply of providers and facilities in the health care field. A combination of an oversupply of hospital beds, competition from hospital and nonhospital providers, and the increasing pressures applied by third-party payers stimulated many hospitals to adopt new delivery systems. In pursuing these systems, hospital administrators discovered that ambulatory surgery provided care of equal quality at much lower cost.

The concept of ambulatory surgery was not new. At a meeting of the British Medical Association in 1909, J. H. Nichol, MD reported that he had performed 7,320 operations on an ambulatory basis at the Royal Glasgow Hospital for Children. He reported surgical results for ambulatory patients were as good as those for inpatients.[31]

The advancements in anesthetic and surgical techniques during the 1960s increased the safety of ambulatory surgery. In addition, the surgery was more convenient and comfortable for both the patient and physician, and cost savings were noted. In 1962, the University of California at Los Angeles developed a hospital-based ambulatory surgery program, and in 1970, Wallace Reed, MD and John Ford, MD of Phoenix, Arizona, established the Surgi-Center, a free-standing ambulatory surgery center. By 1983, 239 ambulatory surgery centers had been established, and by 1990 that number had grown to 1,364 centers, with 2.3 million surgeries having been performed.[32] In 1990, 22 million surgeries were performed in the United States of which 13.3 million (60%) were completed on an outpatient basis.[32]

In the ambulatory surgery environment, where contact with the patient is relatively brief, the operating room nurse must have highly refined skills in implementing the nursing process, working with new technologies, and teaching, which involves both the patient and family. The ability to adapt the "Recommended Practices and Standards of Care" in this environment is also important, as is having good organizational skills. Being flexible is essential, as the nurse may be responsible for providing care in all three phases of the perioperative role: preoperative, intraoperative, and postoperative.

The role of the professional operating room nurse expanded into yet another arena, that of the first assistant. In 1980, the AORN House of Delegates adopted a statement on "The Role of the First Assistant." The statement included that in the "absence of a qualified physician, the registered nurse who possesses appropriate knowledge and technical skills is the best qualified nonphysician to serve as the first assistant."[33]

In 1984, that statement was refined and the following definition of the RN First Assistant (RNFA) was adopted:[34]

> The RN first assistant to the surgeon during a surgical procedure carries out functions that will assist the surgeon in performing a safe operation with optimal results for the patient. The RN first assistant practices perioperative nursing, and as a consequence of organized instruction and supervised practice has acquired the knowledge, skills, and judgment that are necessary to assist the surgeon. The RN first assistant practices under the direct supervision of the surgeon during the first assisting phase of the perioperative role. The first assistant does not concurrently function as a scrub nurse.

Inclusion of the first assistant role in perioperative nursing practice provided the momentum for AORN and ANA to collaborate and seek indirect reimbursement from Medicare for these services. Their attempts have been unsuccessful through 1995.

During the 1980s, operating room nurses continued to expand their responsibilities. As this occurred, the AORN Nursing Practices Committee reviewed the Statement of Perioperative Nursing Practice. The 1978 definition of nursing in the operating room was too restrictive because it addressed the individual practitioner rather than the scope of nursing practice in the operating room. The term *perioperative nursing practice* was determined to be more descriptive than the term *perioperative role*. This revised statement was adopted.[35]

Perioperative is an encompassing term to incorporate the three phases of a surgical patient's experience—preoperative, intraoperative, and postoperative. Practice refers to expected behavior patterns and technical activities performed during the preoperative, intraoperative, and postoperative phases.

Perioperative nursing practice is flexible and diverse and includes a variety of nursing roles that incorporate both behavioral and technical components of professional nursing. The scope of practice for an individual perioperative nurse may include, but is not limited to, roles such as scrub person, circulator, manager, educator, and first assistant. The perioperative nurse delivers care through the use of the nursing process, in a manner that is cost effective without compromising quality of care.

Nursing research gained momentum during the 1980s and perioperative nurses conducted clinical research to test the information used in implementing patient care and to validate recommended practices. In 1983 AORN committed itself to support research through education and to earmark funds for projects related to perioperative nursing. A statement adopted in 1988—Policy, Plan, and Priority Statement on Nursing Research—placed a priority on validating through research the current recommended practices for perioperative nursing.[36]

1990s and Beyond

As changes in technology and concerns about health care economics accelerate, the care of perioperative patients continues to shift to settings outside the traditional operating rooms. Laser technology partnered with computers and endoscopic interventions have resulted in a dramatic shift to outpatient surgery. In response to the changes, an AORN conference devised Project 2000 to plan the course of perioperative nursing. Four project teams were identified with responsibility for the following separate but linking projects:

1. To redefine/reconceptulize perioperative nursing
2. To develop a model for the Association's structure
3. To identify new practice models for perioperative nursing
4. To assess the implications of the Healthcare Effectiveness Initiative for perioperative nursing.

The project team to redefine/reconceptulize perioperative nursing analyzed multiple definitions and concepts integral to the delivery of perioperative patient care. By 1994 they prepared a definition of perioperative practice, which included statements of the philosophy of perioperative nursing practice, the goal and scope of practice, and a definition of recipients of perioperative care.[37] As a result of the team's work, specialty assemblies were formed to facilitate national networking of AORN members interested in a subspecialty. The assemblies provide and promote a dynamic network, serve as a forum for communication, identify and explore patient care issues, address current trends and issues, and promote specialized educational programs.

The project team to identify new practice models for perioperative nursing reviewed existing models for their relevancy. They determined that from the selected models of perioperative nursing (team, differentiated practice, nurse extender, professional, independent practice, and case management) each facility should identify the model that best meets the needs of their patient population and the practitioners at the institution. The conclusions of the team indicated that a model must ensure that professional perioperative nursing is rewarded, that quality patient care is provided, and that surgical procedure expenses are reimbursed.

The project team on the Effectiveness Initiative evolved into a task force to establish a minimum data set for describing perioperative nursing. The use of a uniform data base in perioperative nursing will assist in identifying the outcomes in all perioperative practice settings, allow the development of a national and international classification system for perioperative nursing practice, provide a common base for computerized perioperative patient records, and identify the contributions perioperative nurses make to patient outcomes. A uniform classification scheme that supports nursing practice is required to permit identification and analyses of the content, processes, and outcomes of perioperative nursing care. In addition, data collection will support analyzing regional, interhospital, and intrahospital best practices and variations in practice.

Based on the work completed by the project teams, a new mission statement was adopted by AORN's 1994 House of Delegates:

> The Association of Operating Room Nurses, Inc., is the professional organization of perioperative nurses that unites its members by providing education, representation, and standards for quality patient care.[38]

Several recommendations from the project teams were integrated into the Association's 18-month and 3-year strategic planning process.

Several state boards of nursing have incorporated the RN first assistant behaviors in the scope of nursing practice. The core curriculum for the RNFA was published in 1990; the definition of the role was revised by the 1993 House of Delegates to emphasize intraoperative collaboration with the surgeon to promote optimal outcomes for the patient.

Throughout the 1990s, AORN supported social and clinical resolutions and endorsements pertaining to conscious sedation, health care reform, protection of the environment, nursing research, and issues regarding HIV infections.

In 1992 the AORN Foundation was formed with the primary purpose of securing resources, administering assets, and providing funds for education and research. In the same year, the *Standards of Perioperative Nursing* were revised to include *Standards of Clinical Practice* and *Standards of Professional Performance*. The standards apply to all registered nurses providing perioperative nursing regardless of clinical specialty, practice setting, or educational preparation. Activities are related to quality of care, performance appraisal, education, collegiality, ethics, collaboration, research and use of resources.

∎ THE FUTURE OF PERIOPERATIVE NURSING

Technological advances in the areas of lasers, minimally invasive surgery, improved analgesics, and the driving forces of health care economics will continue to have an impact on perioperative nursing practice. The shift to outpatient surgical procedures will continue and the challenges of caring for surgical patients with co-existing diseases will require perioperative nurses to alter the traditional perioperative nursing role. Perioperative nurses will focus on the leadership role of coordinating patient care and facilitating the activities of the patient-directed team. The team of multiskilled care providers will collaborate to achieve expected patient outcomes and "customer" satisfaction. The specific members of each team will depend on patient needs, for example, respiratory therapy, nutritional support, and enterstomal therapy.

As a result of the changes and the complexity of the health care system, an increased number of perioperative nurses will begin to function in roles as independent practitioners. These emerging positions will have both a direct and indirect impact on the practice of perioperative nursing.

Case Managers

The perioperative nurse case manager will be found in many environments that include acute settings, managed-care facilities, home care agencies and insurance companies. The perioperative case manager will assist the surgical patient in negotiating the system, understanding options and services, and taking responsibility for the coordination of services throughout the perioperative continuum.

Nurse Consultants

Perioperative nurse consultants will assume the role of informaticists, experts in various specific areas of perioperative practice such as scheduling, service coordination, sterilization, infection control practices, financial management, and integration of services within and across facilities. Working independently, perioperative nurses will be able to contract their services to acute and ambulatory care facilities, surgical practices, managed care companies, and attorneys' offices for legal expertise.

Sales

Perioperative nurses will be able to use their nursing expertise to function in business as sales associates. Nurses will be employed in sales positions in companies that manufacture perioperative products or market health care services for managed care or health maintenance organizations.

Corporate Clinical Nurse Educators

The alliance between perioperative nursing and the medical manufacturing industry has flourished since the inception of AORN. This relationship has benefited perioperative nurses, industry, and surgical patients, because it has encouraged the involvement of health care providers in all phases of surgical product development. In their role as corporate clinical nurse educators, nurses will continue to fill a void, both in the United States and internationally, when an internal perioperative nurse educator is not available or as an adjunct to the facility educator. Corporate clinical nurse educators will provide educational services in a variety of settings, enhancing the education of perioperative staff nurses and consulting on a variety of issues related to specific perioperative practices.[39]

The work environment of perioperative nurses will no longer be confined to the surgical suite. They will be cross-trained to function in all areas where invasive procedures are performed—any area in a hospital or in a mobile operating room.[40] The mobile van will park at the patient's home, and staff will perform the surgical procedure and return the patient to the comforts of his or her own bedroom for recovery. A monitor will be attached to a cellular videophone at the patient's bedside, allowing the nurse to monitor vital signs and observe the patient from a remote site. The nurse will instruct family members in caregiving strategies and be available via the cellular videophone for communication and consultation. The nurse will also be able to observe wound status via the videophone interactive information system.

Intraoperatively, scrubbing, gowning, and gloving will be rituals of the past. Perioperative nurses will step into environmentally controlled jackets with nonpenetrable hand coverings and hoods. They will then enter chambers that are sterilized by light.[40] The changes will minimize many of the biological and chemical hazards of the workplace. Patient identification and perioperative documentation will be achieved with hand-held computers using bar codes for all routine entries. The patient's medical record will be on the identification card, and universal card readers will allow the record to be read by providers anywhere the patient seeks health care.

Nursing research will play a central role in perioperative nursing as nurses seek to link their role directly to positive patient outcomes. One area of research will focus on exploring expert nursing judgments with the level of demonstrated practice. For example, what does the expert circulating nurse intuitively sense and then do before, during, or after the surgical procedure that affects the patient's outcome? Other research will focus on tasks that can be appropriately delegated to unlicensed assistive personnel. In addition, research is needed that involves the links between staff mix, case complexity, cost of providing care, and outcomes of care. Moreover, substantive data are needed linking the RN first assistant role to cost and patient outcome. Perioperative certification will be a mandatory credential, which will link the consumer of health care to the expert perioperative practitioners.[41]

Approximately 88,000 professional operating room nurses are in the United States. As they pursue excellence in patient care and serve as the surgical patient's advocate, perioperative nurses will continue to be a vital link between technical advances and effective humanistic care in a variety of nontraditional settings.

∎ REFERENCES

1. Zimmerman LM, Veith I. *Great Ideas in the History of Surgery.* New York: Dover Publications; 1967.
2. *The Genuine Works of Hippocrates;* Adams F, trans ed. New York: William Wood & Co; 1929: 7–10.
3. Stewart IM. *Education of Nurses.* New York: Macmillan; 1944.
4. Walsh JJ. *History of Nursing.* New York: P. J. Kennedy; 1929.
5. Clemons B. Lister's day in America. *AORN J.* 1976; 24:47.
6. Metzger RS. The beginnings of OR nursing education. *AORN J.* 1976; 24:80.
7. Luce M. The duties of an operating-room nurse. *Am J Nurs.* 1901;1:404–406.
8. Woodbury LC. Surgical nursing. *Am J Nurs.* 1903;13:688.
9. Van Syckel J. The operating room technique of St. Luke's Hospital, New York. *Am J Nurs.* 1910;10:636.
10. Sister Bertilla M. Operating room routine: The training of students. *Am J Nurs.* 1924;24:380.
11. Lockwood C. The operating supervisor and her qualifications. *Am J Nurs.* 1927;27:97.
12. Advanced course in surgical nursing. *Am J Nurs.* 1933;33:1186.
13. King C. Planning the day's work in the operating room. *Am J Nurs.* 1942;42:396.
14. Poole R. Army course in operating room technic. *Am J Nurs.* 1945;45:270.
15. Danys A. The navy trains operating room technicians. *Am J Nurs.* 1945;45:727.
16. Bell HS. Practical nurses in the operating room. *Am J Nurs.* 1952;52:582.
17. Ferris S. Training operating room technicians pays. *Am J Nurs.* 1955;55:691.
18. Alexander EA. There's a lot to learn in the OR. *Am J Nurs.* 1949;49:584–586.
19. Shaltis LA. Operative aseptic technic in the basic curriculum. *Am J Nurs.* 1949;49:116–118.
20. Driscoll J. 1949–1957: AORN in retrospect. *AORN J.* 1976;24:142.
21. West EJ. Our official journal. *OR Nurs.* 1960;1:23.

22. *The AORN Story.* Denver: AORN; 1973.
23. National AORT advisory board is dissolved. *AORN J.* 1973;18:42.
24. Definition and objective for clinical practice of professional operating room nursing. *AORN J.* 1969;10:44.
25. Delegates approve statements on RN and nursing student in OR, institutional licensure, abortion. *AORN J.* 1973;17:188–189.
26. Delegates approve statements, resolutions of the twenty-second congress. *AORN J.* 1975; 21:1068.
27. AORN standards: OR wearing apparel, draping and gowning materials. *AORN J.* 1975; 21:594.
28. Standards of administrative nursing practice: Operating room. *AORN J.* 1976;23:1202.
29. Operating room nursing: Perioperative role. *AORN J.* 1978;27:1165.
30. Hercules PR, Kneedler JA. *Certification Series Unit 1: Certification Process.* Denver: AORN; 1979.
31. O'Donovan T. Hospital ambulatory surgery in 1980s. *Hosp Health Sev Admin.* 2. 1981;26:21.
32. *Socio-Economic Factbook for Surgery 1994.* Chicago: American College of Surgeons; 1994;52.
33. Association of operating room nurses house of delegates statement on first assisting. *AORN J.* 1980;31:451.
34. Association of operating room nurses taskforce defines first assisting. *AORN J.* 1984;39:403.
35. Association of operating room nurses: A model for perioperative nursing practice. *AORN J.* 1985;41:193.
36. AORN policy, plan and priority statement on nursing research. *AORN J.* 1988;48:437–438.
37. Philosophy of perioperative nursing practice. *AORN J.* 1994;59:1188–1191.
38. Revised Mission Statement. *AORN J.* 1994;59:1171.
39. Nicolette L, Ulmer B. The role of the corporate clinical nurse educator in the changing health care environment. *AORN J.* 1995;61:219–221.
40. Groah L, Howery D. 25 predictions for perioperative nursing. *Nursing 92.* January 1992; 48–49.
41. Bargagliotti L. Perioperative nursing research. *AORN J.* 1989;50:621.

Introduction to the Perioperative Environment

■ DESIGN OF THE SURGICAL SUITE

It is important that the perioperative nurse understand the design and construction of the surgical suite, as understanding will aid in the effective, efficient use of the facilities. To help determine the appropriate number of rooms for a surgical suite, the simple 5% formula is a useful guide. It states that the number of rooms should equal 5% of the total number of surgical beds. Thus, a 200-bed hospital with 100 surgical beds should have 5 or 6 operating rooms. Cystoscopy and endoscopy rooms are not included in this count. Variations on this formula may be determined after a review of seven pertinent factors:

1. Historical data from the preceding 5 years to examine the:
   —number of surgical procedures performed
   —types of surgery performed
   —average length of surgical procedures
   —distribution of inpatient versus outpatient procedures
   —number of emergency surgeries
2. Hours and days of the week that the operating rooms will be available for scheduled surgical procedures
3. Number of critical care beds available for surgical cases
4. Flow of patients, supplies, equipment, and personnel into and out of the area
5. Current and future surgical needs of the community
6. Utilization rate of the existing operating rooms
7. Trends in surgical technology

The utilization rate (item 6 above) is derived by determining the relationship between the actual hours of surgery and the potential hours of surgery that would be performed if all rooms were used 100% of the time during the normal scheduled hours of surgery. A 75% to 80% room use is considered an optimal rate; a higher utilization rate usually justifies additional operating rooms.

∎ DESIGN AND PLANNING OF SURGICAL SUITE COMPONENTS

A surgical suite may be constructed by renovating existing facilities, expanding existing facilities, or constructing a new facility. Construction of the suite will be discussed here in terms of the following three components:

1. traffic patterns
2. surgical support systems (the environment)
3. communication system

Traffic Patterns

The surgical suite should be isolated from the mainstream of corridor traffic in the hospital. Recovery rooms should be adjacent to the suite and easily accessible to central supply, pathology, radiology, the blood bank, and critical care areas. The flow of traffic should be such that contamination from outside the suite is excluded, and within the suite, clean and contaminated areas should be separated.

Traffic control is aided by using a three-zone concept. The three zones are the unrestricted, the semirestricted, and the restricted areas. The unrestricted area includes the patient reception area, locker rooms, lounges, and offices. The semirestricted zone includes the storage areas for clean and sterile supplies, work areas for storage and processing of instruments, and corridors leading to restricted areas of the suite. The restricted zone includes all areas where surgical procedures are performed and unwrapped supplies are sterilized (see Chapter 7).

Locker rooms and lounges are a transition zone between restricted and unrestricted areas for personnel entering the surgical suite. It is preferable that the locker/change area be entered before the surgical lounge. Only individuals authorized to be in the surgical suite should be permitted in the lounge. The traffic plan should reflect this requirement.

Another common mix of traffic is observed in handling supplies. Outside, cartons unloaded directly from delivery trucks must be removed before the contents are delivered to the surgical suite for storage. Therefore, a "staging area" is required where inner cartons or packages are removed from the outer cartons before materials are distributed to the surgical suite. Corrugated cardboard cartons may harbor gas gangrene bacilli, silverfish, or cockroaches, and therefore are not permitted in the surgical suite under any circumstances.

The overall traffic patterns in and out of the suite should be controlled by the central desk personnel. A pass-through window located in this area will reduce the need for traffic to enter the interior corridors of the surgical suite. If the suite is large and has more than one entrance or exit area, the use of closed-circuit television located in the remote areas will assist the central desk personnel in monitoring the movement of supplies and personnel in and out of the suite. The security of the surgical suite, both to guarantee the safety of personnel and to avoid potential loss of supplies and equipment, must be included in the design of all construction in this area.

Cameras placed strategically in each of the operating rooms will allow the control desk to observe progress of the procedure throughout the day. Additionally, they can be used by security when the operating rooms are not occupied to observe the movement of supplies and equipment.

Early in the planning stages, a decision must be made in regard to handling all materials. If the central processing department is located in an area with convenient access to the operating rooms, consideration may be given to moving support functions (i.e., processing of instruments and supplies) to that department. The advantage of central processing supporting the operating rooms is the reduction in the total cost of capital expenditures and maintenance as there is no duplication of equipment (such as ultrasonic cleaners, washer-sterilizers, and cart washers). The disadvantage is that the control of instruments and supplies is removed from the operating rooms, and, therefore, an increase in the inventory of instruments and equipment is often necessary. If the department is not located on the same floor, access may be accomplished via conveyor, monorail, elevator, dumbwaiter, or any combination of these methods. When this method of processing is used, there must be two separate methods of transportation, one to remove contaminated supplies from the operating rooms and one to transport clean and sterile items from the central supply department to the surgical suite. In addition to the initial cost of installing the transport system, routine maintenance costs must be considered as well as an alternative method of transporting supplies and equipment in the event of a malfunction. This system reportedly works well and is cost effective in a surgical suite of less than eight operating rooms.

Supplies prepared outside the surgical suite should be transported to the operating room in closed or covered carts. Soiled items and trash should be contained in a closed impervious system for transportation to the processing or disposal site. If trash and linen are to be picked up at intervals from the surgical suite, a separate room should be constructed for this activity.

Surgical Support Systems (The Environment)

There are four basic designs for surgical suites:

1. Central corridor or hotel plan
2. Double corridor, U-shape, or T-shape plan
3. Peripheral corridor or clean core plan
4. Grouping, cluster, or pod plan

The central corridor plan is effective when only two to four operating rooms are required. In this plan, all the operating rooms and support areas are accessible from a single corridor.

The double corridor plan results in a U-shape or T-shape architectural arrangement and is used in designing 5 to 15 operating rooms.

In the peripheral corridor plan (Fig. 2–1), a corridor surrounds the surgical suite. In the center of the suite is a clean central core where sterile supplies are stored and distributed to the rooms. The surgical team enters the operating room via the clean central core and leaves by way of the peripheral corridor. Patients enter and leave via the peripheral corridor. This plan requires that an elaborate traffic pattern be developed in an attempt to enforce this concept; however, in practice, these patterns are not followed. Valuable storage space is often sacrificed for this design and, the peripheral corridor is frequently used to store equipment and supplies.

The cluster plan of four operating rooms (Fig. 2–2) with a peripheral corridor and a central support area with access to each operating room is widely accepted in designing

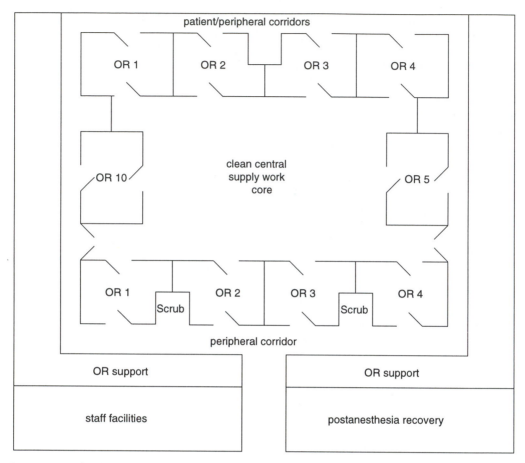

Figure 2–1. Peripheral corridor design. *(Adapted from Chvala C. O.R. supervisor's role in planning the surgical suite. AORN J. 1976; 23(7):1242, with permission.)*

large surgical sites. It is more efficient than the central or double corridor because all operating rooms are in close proximity to the source of supplies. It is the most adaptable to expansion because additional clusters can be added with little disruption to the existing facilities.

With all four designs a holding area for surgical patients may be constructed. Prior to entering this area the patient may be transferred onto an operating room stretcher or surgical table in a vestibular exchange area. This is done on the premise that hospital bacteria may be tracked into the operating room on the wheels of the cart. There is, however, no hard evidence that this practice is a cause of surgical infection.

Preoperative Area. The preoperative area (holding area) is designed to support the patient awaiting surgery. Ideally, it should be a separate room in the surgical suite or immediately

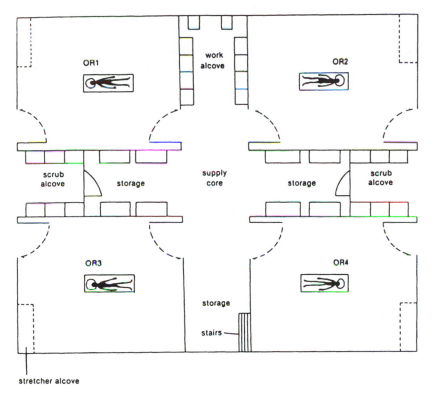

Figure 2–2. Basic modular design. *(Adapted from Chvala C. O.R. supervisor's role in planning the surgical suite. AORN J. 1976;23(7):1243, with permission.)*

adjacent to it. The area should be quiet and restful, away from direct traffic flow, and provide privacy and seclusion. Talk and noise should be kept to a minimum.

The use of music in this area may alleviate a surgical candidate's anxiety.[1] In addition, when patients participate in decision making regarding their care—as, for example, when they may choose what music to listen to—they tend to regain a partial sense of control.[2,3] The preoperative area should be equipped with an emergency cart, drugs, defibrillator, oxygen, and suction devices. Access to the emergency alarm system is essential.

Because increasing numbers of patients are now admitted to the hospital the day of instead of the evening before surgery, the preoperative area has become more important. The nurse in the preoperative area assesses the patient, collecting baseline data that will be important to nurses caring for the patient postoperatively. The assessment includes recording vital signs, noting the conditions or symptoms presented that necessitate surgical intervention, and recording any psychological stresses the patient may be experiencing. Ambulatory surgery patients and/or their significant others may be instructed preoperatively for the postoperative period. The medical record is checked for accuracy, laboratory data are reviewed, and the preoperative checklist is completed. In addition, the patient receives premedication, and the surgical shave preparation, if required, is performed. Other procedures, such as inserting catheters and starting intravenous lines, may also be done in this area.

If effectively managed, a surgical holding area can improve the efficiency of the operating room by reducing the preparation time required once the patient is taken into the operating room. During periods of inactivity, the preoperative area nurse can telephone or visit the previous day's patients to discuss their concerns or impressions regarding the surgical experience.

Interior Design of the Surgical Suite. The design of the surgical suite should allow two, three, or four rooms to share a substerile area and scrub facilities. The standard operating room is rectangular or square of approximately 20 × 20 × 10 feet, to provide a floor space of 400 square feet (approximately 37 square meters). Operating rooms designed for services that require additional equipment, such as cardiac surgery, neurosurgery, or minimally invasive procedures, will require rooms of 20 × 30 × 10 feet, or a floor space of 600 square feet (approximately 60 square meters). Rooms designed for endoscopy and outpatient surgery require only 18 × 18 × 10 feet, or a floor space of 324 square feet (approximately 29 square meters).

Fire-resistant, hard, smooth, nonporous surfaces are used for floors, walls, and ceilings, as these surfaces are easy to clean and not readily adhered to by bacterial particles. Rooms that are to be utilized with lasers must have nonreflective walls and ceilings. The material must be able to withstand repeated washings with germicidal cleaners. The surface should be as free as possible of seams, joints, and crevices.

For many years ceramic tile was used for walls, but because the grouting between the tile was rough and difficult to clean, it was a safe harbor for bacteria. Consequently the use of tile was discontinued. Now, however, a new latex grouting has been developed that is less porous and as a result, less absorbent. Therefore, tile may once again be used in the construction of operating rooms although it is more expensive than other finishes.

Other materials currently used are laminated polyester with an epoxy finish, hard vinyl covering that can be heat-sealed leaving no seams, and panels of ceramic glass sealed to eliminate seams. Stainless steel or Formica guards at corners help avoid damage, as do guard rails on corridor halls. The only color requirement is that it be free from glare. Traditionally, cool pastels have been used, but recently a wide variety of warmer tones have been introduced to complement patient skin tones.

The ceilings absorb sound and are either a polyester film or metal-faced ceiling tile. Floor coverings should be conductive unless a variance is obtained from the appropriate local or state agency. Many institutions are committed to using nonflammable anesthetic agents and, therefore, have obtained the variance. If a variance is not obtained, the floor must comply with standards of the National Fire Protection Association (NFPA). A variety of conductive and nonconductive floor coverings are available, including stone terrazzo, plastic terrazzo, linoleum, asphalt, and a variety of hard plastic materials. Cushioned flooring is more comfortable for the operating room team. The material used should be seamless and able to withstand flooding and wet vacuuming. The color should be such that if a needle is dropped, it will be easily visible. The wall-to-floor junction should be curved or concave to facilitate adequate cleaning. Floors in and around scrub sinks should have a nonslip surface.

Each operating room has recessed cabinets to store supplies. The standard supplies are in the same cabinet location in all operating rooms, with a designated area reserved for special instruments and supplies used for the operations that are usually performed in that room. The cabinets are usually stainless steel with sliding glass doors. All shelves and support areas in the suite should be made of wire. Dust readily accumulates on solid shelving, whereas wire permits air to circulate and consequently, dust accumulation is negligible. One cabinet in the operating room may have a pegboard on which to hang items, such as parts for the surgical table.

An operating room may also have a pass-through cabinet, which is stocked from outside the room with equipment to be used inside. A truck on wheels has a bank of shelves and is moved to a central area for restocking and cleaning. A latch system prevents the inside and outside doors from being open at the same time unless the latch is released. Carts restricted to a procedure or a surgical specialty may be stocked appropriately and moved into the operating room for a specific operation. The movable cart eliminates the need to perform these specific procedures only in designated rooms.

A case cart system may be used if central supply personnel process all the instruments. With this system an enclosed cart containing all the necessary supplies for a specific surgical case is prepared in a remote area and transported to the operating room. Ideally, clean and uncontaminated cart lifts, elevators, or dumbwaiters operate to transport carts between the two departments. At the end of the surgical procedure, the closed cart is returned to the central department where instruments and supplies are reprocessed and the cart is washed. For the system to operate efficiently, physician preference cards and the "pick" lists must be accurate and must be routinely updated. When there is well-developed communication between staff in the central process department and the operating rooms, fewer cabinets are needed in the operating rooms.

Ideally, the operating room should have sliding doors. They eliminate air turbulence created by swinging doors and reduce the potential for microorganisms to become airborne. The sliding doors should be surface mounted to allow for adequate cleaning, and the frame should be at least 5 feet wide. Swinging doors should not open into a corridor and obstruct traffic or decrease corridor width.

Ventilation. To minimize airborne microbial contamination in the operating room, an effective ventilation system is necessary. Currently, 15 air exchanges per hour are required, of which 3 must be fresh air.[4] The air is cleaned by either a bag-filtered or a high-efficiency particulate air-filtered (HEPA) system. HEPA filters can filter 99% of all particles larger than 0.3 micron. The air may need to be modified with an air conditioning system to maintain a temperature of 20° to 24°C (68° to 75°F) and a humidity level of 50% to 55%. Maintaining humidity at this level helps reduce static electricity, prevent an explosion, and reduce bacterial growth. A regular maintenance program is required to monitor HEPA filters for possible leakage and filter loading.

The inlet vent is located at the ceiling; air leaves the room through outlets located in the walls at floor level. The pressure gradient within each operating room is greater than that in the substerile rooms, the scrub area, and the corridors. This 10% positive pressure forces air out of the rooms and prevents air from the support areas from entering the operating rooms. To maintain the positive pressure, the doors of the operating rooms must be kept closed. Air handling systems must be regularly cleaned, inspected, and maintained.

Anesthetists and other operating room personnel are chronically exposed to low concentrations of vapors from volatile, liquid inhalation anesthetic agents, and there is increasing concern that the exposure may be hazardous.

Certain anesthetic gases, such as the halothanes, are not biodegradable beyond the molecular stage and consequently are not filtered out of recirculated air. A scavenging system is therefore necessary to rid the air of escaped gases. One of the following methods may be used: direct passage to the outside from the anesthetic area; aspiration by the air exhaust system of the room; aspiration by a dedicated or shared vacuum system; or by a vacuum pump to the outside.

Laminar air flow or unidirectional flow systems where there are as many as 600 air changes per hour demonstrate substantial reductions in the number of airborne bacteria in the operating rooms. No substantial evidence, however, shows that those reductions translate to a reduced operative-wound infection rate. In addition, the value of the various types of laminar flow is controversial.[5]

Ultraviolet Radiation. Ultraviolet radiation of the operative field during surgery reduces postoperative wound infection in refined clean cases.[6] If ultraviolet radiation is used, protective cream, goggles, and headgear must be used by the surgical team to prevent irritation and potential damage to the eyes and skin. The ultraviolet lights require special care and maintenance to ensure their effectiveness. The intensity must be measured daily with a calibrated meter. The ultraviolet output depends on the temperature, the cleanliness of the lamps, and the humidity level in the room. The lamps must be protected from chilling effects of the ventilation system, and humidity must not exceed 55%, or the effect of ultraviolet radiation declines markedly. The film of grime that collects on the lamps must be removed twice a week.

Lighting. General room illumination is provided by incandescent or deluxe cool white fluorescent lamps. Fluorescent lamps give much less radiant heat than incandescent lamps, and they have a longer life. When fluorescent lamps are used, the fixtures are designed to reduce radio frequency interference to a level that will not interfere with electronic equipment used during surgery. The support lighting should be a uniformly distributed level of 200 footcandles, with provisions for reducing the level.[7]

The surgical light should be a single-post, ceiling-mounted unit (Fig. 2–3). Track lights are not as acceptable because the tracks are inaccessible for cleaning and may harbor microorganisms that are dislodged each time the light is moved. The light should not produce dense shadows that would prevent the surgeon from visualizing the surgical field.

The radiant heat produced must be minimized, both to protect surgically exposed tissue and for the comfort of surgeons and assistants. The approved amount of light should raise the tissue temperature no more than 2° C. The acceptable radiant energy level can be tested by using india ink to paint a 1-cm round spot on the back of the wrist and focusing the light on that spot. If the spot is uncomfortable after one minute, the radiant energy level may be harmful to delicate tissues, such as the brain.[7]

Halogen lights generate less heat than do other types of lights, and the illumination is

Figure 2–3. Single-post ceiling-mounted surgical light. *(Courtesy Skytron, Grand Rapids, MI.)*

stronger. They are, however, more costly and easily damaged by improper handling and power surges. In addition, the color of the light should be near daylight to reduce visual fatigue. The surgical light should be capable of providing a minimum of 2500 footcandles (27 kilolux) directed to the center of a 78-square-inch pattern (195 square centimeters), 8 inches in diameter on a surgical table with the top 39 inches (97 centimeters) from the floor. There should be 500 footcandles at the edge of the circle.[7]

Variable pattern sizes are provided by a focusing control or by moving the light closer to or farther from the surgical incision. Variable voltage transformers or intensity controls provide additional lighting when it is necessary for difficult procedures. The transformers allow selection of any voltage up to 140 volts. The lamp's life is reduced by consistently operating surgical lights above the normal voltage or turning the light on in the high voltage area.

A total lamp failure must be guarded against; for example, multiple lamps in a single lighthead or multiple lightheads may be used. If a single lamp is used, it should be changed routinely to avoid failure during a surgical procedure.

Two-team surgeries may be illuminated with additional lightheads or satellites that extend from the primary mounting.

In rooms designed for lasers, lighting requirements include equipping the rooms for blackouts controlled by the surgeon. When using the microscope's illumination, the support lighting and the OR lights are turned off; the surgeon can control the lights with a foot switch. During a controlled blackout, nondistracting, incandescent lighting should be provided for other team members.

Freestanding portable light and fiber-optic light sources used for a headlight or as part of a sterile instrument must be in accordance with NFPA standards. It must be possible to sterilize a fiber-optic unit used in a sterile field or to encase it in a sterile sleeve. If the light source is to be inserted in the wound, its irradiance should be no more than 25,000 µW/cm.[7]

Headlights are frequently used by surgeons to supplement overhead surgical lights or to provide light from angles that overhead lights cannot achieve. They are particularly useful for seeing into small, narrow, or deep cavities where the beam of light must be parallel with the surgeon's line of sight. Typically, a headlight is mounted on a headband and attached to a cable and a power or light source. The two common styles of headlights are the coaxial and direct. The coaxial type projects a beam forward or down from a location directly between the surgeon's eyes; the direct type projects a beam generally downward from a location on the forehead. Cable size, durability, and ease of maintenance are important factors to consider in evaluating headlights.

X-ray view boxes should be recessed into the wall and located in the line of vision of the surgeon standing at the operating table.

Electrical Requirements. When flammable gases are used by the anesthesiologist, all electrical outlets and fixtures less than 5 feet above the floor must meet explosion-proof code requirements, as identified by the NFPA.

If grounded outlets are installed above the 5-foot level, electrical cords may run down the wall and across the floor to reach equipment, creating a potential hazard for surgical team members who may trip on the cords and fall. Rigid or retractable ceiling service columns in the operating rooms have helped control this hazard. The columns are equipped with a minimum of ten outlets: two vacuums, one compressed air, two oxygen, one nitrous oxide, and four electrical. All outlets should be of the "quick connect" type. Having two columns per operating room increases flexibility in regard to positioning the operating room table.

In addition, a nitrogen control box may be mounted on the wall. Nitrogen is used for power instruments. Because of its volatility, pressure, and flow, nitrogen is controlled manually through the box with gauges that display the line pressure. The nitrogen hookup is a diameter index safety system (DISS), and existing power tools may need to be modified to accommodate the system. Multiple electrical outlets should be located on every wall. Rooms used for minor procedures should have at least four outlets per wall and rooms for other procedures will require as many as 14 duplex outlets per wall. These outlets are in addition to those already identified for use by anesthesia. The outlets should be available from separate circuits to minimize the possibility of blown fuses or faulty circuits shutting off all electricity at a critical moment.

Some lasers have special power requirements. Argon lasers and endoscopic Nd:YAG (neodymium:yttrium-aluminum garnet) lasers frequently require 208-watt to 220-watt three-phase power. In planning operating room construction, it is advisable to install this power in anticipation of future equipment requirements.

For laser safety, lighted "Laser In Use" signs should be mounted on the interior and exterior walls beside every laser room door. A safety interlock system can be installed in a laser room that will automatically shut off power to the laser system when a door to the room is opened during surgery.

In the event that the normal electrical supply source is interrupted, an electrical generator must provide emergency power within 10 seconds to identified areas in the operating room. This usually includes designated outlets in each operating room, the surgical lights, the corridors, and the communication system.

Additional Fixed Equipment. Careful consideration should be given to purchasing additional fixed equipment. In the past few years, it has been in vogue to mount-in the ceiling microscopes, x-ray tubes, image intensifiers, cryosurgery units, and various other pieces of equipment (Fig. 2–4). A disadvantage to having fixed equipment is that when it is repaired or replaced, the operating rooms are unavailable for surgery or the repair must be done on an overtime pay status.

Fixed equipment requiring tracks, such as the surgical lights described above, is a potential source of contamination, as tracks are difficult to clean. Recessing the tracks into the ceiling will minimize the potential for contamination.

Television cameras may be mounted in one corner of the operating room and project an image to a monitor at the control desk. For teaching, television cameras may be mounted on the surgical lights, permitting surgical procedures to be viewed from a remote area.

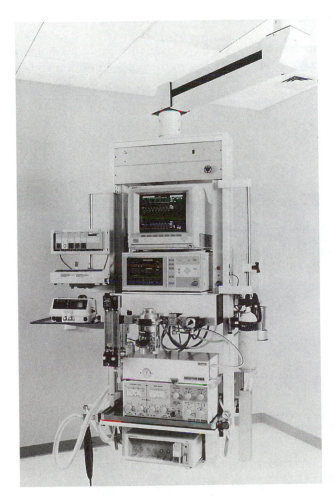

Figure 2–4. Equipment carriers, like this Skyboom Equipment Carrier, provide electrical, gas, and communication services to operating rooms. Support services are provided through gas and electric service boxes and equipment shelves affixed to a rotating single or double arm. (*Courtesy Skytron, Grand Rapids, MI.*)

Two-way video imaging systems may also relay images between the operating rooms and between the ORs and the pathology and radiology areas. Wall screens enable the surgeon to view the results of microscopic sections or x-ray films and to discuss the pathology with consultants. Although the camera and video systems may be a source of contamination, they do eliminate the need for personnel to enter the operating room.

Furniture and Accessory Equipment. Furniture and equipment should be made of a conductive material and have conductive castors or tips. Stainless steel is frequently used in manufacturing furniture for the operating room, as it is durable and easily cleaned. Standard equipment in the operating room includes several items.

Operating Room Table. Operating room tables are movable or they may have a fixed base. The fixed-base table has interchangeable tops to meet the needs of specific surgical specialties (Fig. 2–5). The standard operating room table has three or more hinged sections that can be flexed at the articulating sections of the body. The table can be turned from side to side or moved to accommodate Trendelenburg's or reverse Trendelenburg's positions. Its height is adjustable.

Accessory equipment, such as shoulder braces, knee crutches, stirrups, or leg holders and armboards, is designed to stabilize or brace the patient in the desired position and to

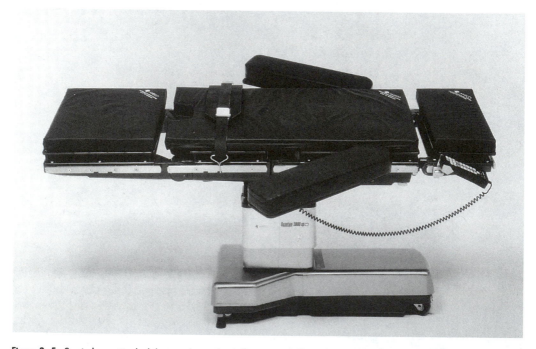

Figure 2–5. Surgical operating bed that may be used with fluoroscopy. Tables are operated manually or electrically and have a brake for stabilization. *(Courtesy American Sterilizer Co., Erie, PA.)*

provide flexibility in positioning patients. Armboards are rigid, fit flush with the table pad, and lock within a 90° radius. The basic head section may be removed and special head rests substituted. A foot extension may be added to accommodate a tall patient. An x-ray penetrable tunnel top may be placed on the operating room table to allow the insertion of x-ray cassette holders at any position along the table. The mattress and armboards are covered with conductive rubber.

Special operating tables (Figs. 2–6A and 2–6B) are available for genitourinary, orthopedic, and ophthalmologic surgery. All are operated manually or electrically and have a brake for stabilization.

Mayo Stand. The base of this stand slides under the operating room table; the rectangular top is used for instruments and sutures that are used during the surgical procedure.

Back Table. This table supplements the mayo stand, providing extra space for instruments, drapes, and sutures that may be required during surgery.

Overhead Table (Gerhardt Table). Various sizes and designs of overhead tables are available. The table combines the mayo stand and back table. It slides over the operating room table and provides a large surface area for the scrub assistant. One advantage of this table is that the scrub nurse never has to turn away from the sterile field.

Ring Stand. The ring stand is covered with a sterile drape, and a sterile basin is placed inside the ring. The basin may be used for rinsing powder from gloves or for rinsing instruments soaked in glutaraldehyde. (The basin must be removed immediately after use; it must not be used as a "splash basin" during surgery.)

Kick Buckets in Wheeled Bases. These buckets are lined with plastic bags and used by the scrub team to discard soiled sponges.

Suction. Each operating room must have at least two sources of suction, one for the anesthesiologist and the other to be used at the operative site. Current construction provides two or more suction sources to the operative site to accommodate two-team surgeries.

Anesthesia Machine. A table or cart for additional drugs and supplies accompanies the machine (Fig. 2–7).

Desk Area. A "desk top" may be built into the recessed cabinets or wall mounted. Current construction also provides a surface area for a computer terminal in each operating room. Computers are used to generate patient changes, maintain current inventory information, and complete intraoperative charting.

Additional Items. Other equipment in the operating room includes poles or hangers for IV solutions; linen and waste hamper frames; stools; standing platforms or steps; and small tables for additional patient preparation.

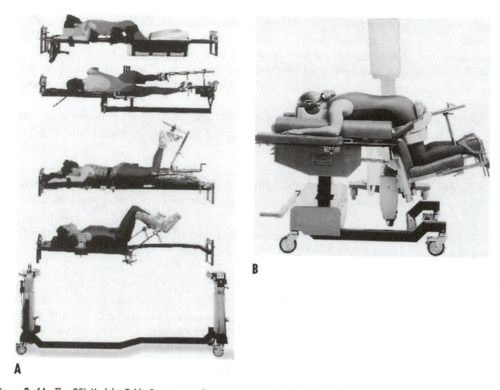

A

B

Figure 2–6A. The OSI Modular Table System provides maximum surgical flexibility with the option of spinal, orthopedic trauma, imaging and pelvic reconstruction, and endourology procedures. The versatility of this system allows a wider range of table utilization by the medical staff. *(Courtesy Orthopedic Systems, Inc., Union City, CA.)* **B.** The OSI Andrews Spinal Surgery Table offers interoperative repositioning of the lumbar spine, decompressed abdomen for improved visualization, and unrestricted AP and lateral views. *(Courtesy Orthopedic Systems, Inc., Union City, CA.)*

Substerile Area and Scrub Room. Two or more operating rooms may be located around a substerile and scrub room area. Sterile supplies may become contaminated by aerosols when members of the surgical team are scrubbing; therefore, the scrub room must be separated from the substerile area. The substerile area may contain cupboards for storing sterile supplies, an autoclave or a washer-sterilizer, blanket-solution-warmer, and a small refrigerator for drugs and solutions. Decentralizing these activities increases efficiency in the operating rooms by decreasing the amount of time team members must travel to a central location. Equipment with open drains, such as a sink or hopper, should not be in the room with a flash autoclave. This equipment should be conveniently accessible, but not connected with the operating room.[4]

Central Processing Area or Workroom. If instruments are processed in the operating room suite, they are decontaminated, prepared, packaged, and sterilized in a central area. The room is divided into a contaminated, or "cleanup," area where all instruments and supplies

Figure 2–7. Anesthesia workstation. Sophisticated cardiovascular monitoring system includes multi-lead ECG and ST segment analysis, two invasive pressure channels, two temperature channels, thermodilution cardiac output with hemodynamic calculations, and monitoring of respirations. (*Courtesy North American Drager Inc. Doylestown, PA*)

are received following surgical procedures, and a clean area, or "instrument room," where instruments are processed in an ultrasonic cleaner and then stored or wrapped for sterilization. Pass-through washer-sterilizers and gravity conveyor belts reduce the need physically to move the instruments from one area to another. The clean area may also contain sterilizers that open into another room—the sterile storage area.

The sterile storage area maintains a stock of sterile gloves, instruments, sponges, catheters, and dressings. Preferably the shelves are freestanding, which allows supplies to be placed on the shelf from one side and removed from the other, rotating supplies automatically. The lowest shelf is 8 inches from the floor and the highest at least 18 inches from the ceiling. All shelves are at least 2 inches from the outside walls.[8]

The size of the sterile storage area will vary with the number of disposable products used. Generally, disposable products require more storage area than do reusable products.

Storage Areas. Architects frequently underestimate the need for storage space. As a consequence, large pieces of equipment, such as image intensifiers, microscopes, and laser machines, may occupy the corridors. In designing new facilities or in remodeling, storage should be located throughout the suite and should exceed the current requirements. Additional storage space is often required for new equipment produced in response to rapidly changing needs and technology.

Housekeeping Facilities. Within the operating room is an area identified for the storage of supplies and equipment used in terminal cleaning. Providing adequate storage for this support service ensures that the equipment is used only within the operating rooms. Rooms should be located at various points in the suite to house hopper sinks for disposing of suction material and equipment required for cleaning between cases.

Music In the Surgical Suite. Music has long been recognized as a form of therapy in managing physical and emotional illness; however, its use in the operating room remains controversial. The disadvantage identified most frequently is the distraction associated with music in the work setting. It is important that each speaker have an on/off switch and a volume control. Patients may wear earphones, thereby eliminating the potential distraction of music for team members. Music may also be played while patients are under anesthesia, as musical vibrations affect the subconscious mind.[9]

Music has the following benefits for patients and personnel:

- A warmer, more pleasant environment is created.
- Music may distract the patient from strange sights, sounds, and treatments.[9]
- For a patient having a regional anesthetic restlessness and the discomfort from positioning muscle strains is lessened and time passes more quickly.
- Headsets muffle extraneous noises, and the patient may be unable to overhear inappropriate conversation.
- The surgical team works in closer harmony because of decreased levels of tension and fatigue.
- Appropriate rhythms may stimulate rapid, coordinated movements.
- The monotony of preparation and cleanup is reduced, contributing to staff morale and efficiency.
- During the recovery period, music may shorten postanesthesia recovery and make it more pleasant.[10]

Research indicates a significant decrease in anxiety from the preoperative to postoperative period among patients who listen to music intraoperatively.[1,11] The philosophies of the operating room committee and the hospital administration concerning the use of music should be discussed before a decision is reached in regard to having music in the surgical suite. If music is incorporated, the most appropriate system is Muzak. Muzak is a centralized system of recorded music that can be connected to the communication system. Guidelines for using the system must be established and communicated to all members of the surgical team. Specific procedures to decontaminate the earphones after each use must be outlined.

Surgical Waiting Room and Signage. Facilities should be provided for relatives and significant others waiting during surgery. Consistent with the philosophy of keeping only essential traffic in the area of the surgical suite, the waiting area is best located one floor above or below the surgical suite. If the area is located on the same floor as the operating rooms, the main entrance into the surgical suite or the recovery room should not be within view, because anxious relatives tend to move into the corridors near these entrances and cause congestion.

Families should be able to get information regarding the progress of surgery or the recovery of the patient. An information desk located in the waiting area should have direct telephone lines with the surgical and recovery areas.

Carefully designed and coordinated signs and directional graphics throughout the operating room suite will greatly enhance the flow of staff, patients, and visitors.

Communication System

A reliable communication system is an important link between the operating rooms and the control desk. The system should differentiate between a routine call and a call requiring emergency assistance. For emergency activation the system should have a foot or knee switch, as well as a hand switch. Each operating unit should be able to control the system so that it can be switched from audible calls to the use of a call light. This variation may be used when patients are awake or if the surgeon requests that the intercom be turned off, as for example during microsurgical procedures.

Each operating room should also have direct communication with the surgical pathology and radiology areas. That link enables direct consultation between physicians in those areas. The substerile area should have an auxiliary intercom system to communicate directly with the recovery room, the central processing area, and the control desk. The control desk should have connections with the blood bank, pathology and radiology areas, recovery room, anesthesia workroom, central processing, holding area, all corridors, operating room administrative offices, and locker rooms and lounges.

Telephone jacks installed in each substerile area enable staff to answer the telephone in multiple locations. This is especially useful when secretarial assistance is unavailable. Depending on the institution, direct telephone lines ("hot lines") may be a valuable connection with the emergency room, intensive care units, or blood bank.

As technology and surgical procedures become more complex, many institutions are installing telephones in each operating room. This allows the surgical team to communicate directly with ancillary areas without going through the control desk.

▌ KEEPING THE ENVIRONMENT SAFE

As the use of flammable anesthetic agents has decreased, the threat of fires and explosions has been reduced to a minimum. Fires, however, may still occur if appropriate actions are not taken.

Fires in the Operating Room

The majority of fires in the operating room ignite on or in the patient. For a fire to occur, the "fire triangle" must be present: a source of heat, a fuel, and an oxidizer. The source of heat is usually electrical equipment, such as an electrosurgical unit (ESU), a fiber-optic light source/cable, a laser, or a heated probe tip. The fuel is anything that will burn, such as linens, dressings, and prepping agents. Ethanol-based prepping agents are volatile and extremely flammable. If these solutions are allowed to pool under the patient, vapors may be generated beneath the drapes. These vapors can then be ignited by heat or sparks from electrical equipment.

Enteric gas is potentially explosive because it contains a high concentration of methane and hydrogen. Precautions must be taken when high energy treatment modalities are performed near the perianal area.[12] Open bottles or basins containing volatile solutions should be closed or removed from the sterile area as soon as possible after use. Most fuels require an oxidizer, such as oxygen or nitrous oxide, to burn. In the OR this can come from the room air or as a byproduct from nitrous oxide.

A patient is at high risk for an airway fire when lasers are used for laryngotracheal procedures. Among the precautions taken are using special laser-resistant endotracheal tubes and the lowest possible concentration of oxygen.

Fire prevention includes controlling heat sources by following the safety guidelines for electrical equipment as identified by the manufacturer. In addition, all electrical equipment should be inspected before use. Outlets and switch plates are checked for damage and cords and plugs for fraying or other damage. The biomedical technician or safety officer should check all equipment before it is used in the operating room.

Managing the source of fuel is essential. Sufficient time is allowed for patient prepping before drapes are applied and the concentration of oxygen is minimized around the patient. If an open oxygen source is used, the drapes must be tented around the patient's head to allow the oxygen to dissipate.

Fire Drills. All perioperative staff must participate in a fire drill at least quarterly. It is recommended that the drill involve all members of the team carrying out a specific assignment. Assignments should include pulling the fire alarm, using fire-fighting equipment, turning off piped-in gases, and unplugging electrical power cords. Videotaping the drill permits team members to critique its effectiveness and correct deficiencies.

Isolated Power Systems

Electrical hazards that continue to exist in the operating room include macroshock and power failures. Equal-potential grounding and isolated power panels are installed in operating rooms to protect patients and personnel from such hazards. The equal-potential grounding system insures that the patient or the personnel and the equipment are grounded to only one ground. Potential voltage differences are thereby eliminated between the patient or personnel and the equipment. Thus shocks will not occur.

The isolated power panels have an alarm that is activated at the 2-milliampere level. This warning system indicates when inadvertent grounding of the isolated circuits has occurred, and it alerts personnel to potential equipment failure or to defective equipment. The panels, which limit the shock that personnel may receive to 2 milliamperes, have been deleted from the NFPA Guidelines due to the controversy regarding cost versus benefits.

Chemical Hazards

Several chemicals identified as potentially hazardous to patients and team members are used in the perioperative areas. They include agents for sterilizing and disinfecting, skin prepping, environmental cleaning, chemotherapy, and tissue preservation. The "right to know" directive of the Occupational Safety and Health Administration (OSHA) states that all employees should be informed of the hazards associated with chemicals in their work setting.[13] Personnel have the responsibility to follow the instructions that are on the containers or included on the Material Safety Data Sheets (MSDS) provided by the manufacturer. The MSDS identify hazards, precautions, signs and symptoms of toxic exposure, first aid treatment for exposure, and guidelines for special handling of the chemical.

Chemicals should be combined only if known safe outcomes are ensured; mixing chemicals can produce unsafe substances. Specific precautions should be observed during the preparation and administration of cytotoxic agents to minimize the spread of contaminants and exposure for both patients and personnel.[14]

MSDS should always be accessible in the surgical suite. A periodic review of chemicals should determine whether a less hazardous chemical could be used.

Radiation Safety

The two types of radiation are ionizing and nonionizing; radiation hazards usually refer to the ionizing type. X-rays, fluoroscopy, image intensifiers, radioactive implants, other therapeutic radiation procedures, and rays from radioactive elements emit ionizing radiation. Exposure to these rays can cause mutation, which may lead to chromosomal aberrations, cell death, cataracts, cancer, or birth defects.[15] Nonionizing forms of radiation are the wavelengths that generally do not alter the body's DNA. They include radio and television microwaves and visible light.

During radiologic procedures the patient and members of the surgical team should be protected from unnecessary exposure to radiation. Pregnant personnel should not be exposed during the first trimester. Lead shields should be placed between the patient and the source of radiation when possible. The ovaries or testes should be protected during x-ray studies of the hips and upper legs. The thyroid should be protected during studies of the upper extremities, trunk, and head. Whenever possible, personnel should leave the room during the exposure period. If that is not possible, leaded aprons and thyroid shields will minimize exposure to scattered radiation. Staff should be positioned behind a lead shield at least 6 feet away from the x-ray tube.[16]

Slings, traction devices, and sandbags should be used to maintain patient position during radiation exposure. Cassette holders should be used to position films. Personnel should not hold the patient unless absolutely necessary and they should avoid exposure to the direct beam. If the patient must be held, radioprotective gloves and leaded aprons should be worn.[17]

The potential for exposure to radiation is greater during fluoroscopy than diagnostic radiography because of increased radiation scatter and exposure time. In addition to the safety measures discussed above, eye protection may be required if personnel stand next to the patient during frequent or long periods of fluoroscopy.[16]

Radiation monitoring devices should be worn by personnel who are in frequent proximity to radiation. Leaded aprons and shields should be cleaned according to the manufacturer's guidelines, and stored flat or hung vertically when not in use. They should not be folded, as that may crack the integrity of the protective material. To ascertain the effectiveness of the aprons and shields, a radiographic test should be done at least once a year.

Patients who have radioactive implants may emit radiation. If they require surgery before the material has decayed to safe levels, personnel may be exposed to radiation. Body fluids and tissue that are removed from patients who have undergone recent diagnostic nuclear medicine studies should be handled according to radiation safety procedures. When patients have radioactive implants placed in the OR, the materials should be kept in a protective, lead-lined container and the capsules or needles handled with forceps. Before the patient is transferred out of the OR, the circulating nurse should notify personnel receiving the patient about the radiation source and its anatomical location. Radiation precautions should be followed during transportation of the patient. Perioperative nursing documentation should include the measures taken to protect patients from direct and indirect radiation exposure.

▌ AMBULATORY SURGERY FACILITIES

Operating rooms and recovery areas in an ambulatory surgery facility will require the same mechanical and electrical support systems that are used in an inpatient operating room. In addition, a business office, examination rooms, toilet facilities, laboratory, x-ray, and admission area are needed. Easy access to the facility is essential, as are adequate parking areas and clearly marked entry points. Sensitive use of building materials, room finishes, color, lighting, furniture, artwork, and plants can contribute greatly to an atmosphere that promotes patient confidence and well-being.

▌ REFERENCES

1. Amodei M, Kaempf G. The effects of music and anxiety. *AORN J.* 1989;50(1):118.
2. Stanley J. Music research in medical/dental treatment: Meta analysis and clinical applications. *J Music Therapy.* 1986;23:28.
3. Evans M, Rubio P. Music: a diversionary therapy. *Today's OR Nurse.* 1994;16(4):17–22.
4. The American Institute of Architects Committee on Architecture for Health, with assistance from US Department of Health and Human Services. *Guidelines for Construction and Equipment of Hospital and Medical Facilities.* Washington, DC: American Institute of Architects Press; 1987:50.
5. McQuarrie D et al. Laminar airflow systems. *AORN J.* 1990;51(4):1046.
6. Hart D, Nicks J. Ultraviolet radiation in the operating room: Intensities used and bactericidal effects. *Arch Surg.* 1961;82:449.
7. Beck WC et al. *Lighting for Health Care Facilities.* New York: Illuminating Engineering Society of North America; 1985:17–22.
8. Garner J. *Guidelines for prevention of surgical wound infections 1985;* Guidelines for the Prevention and Control of Nosocomial Infections. Atlanta, GA: Communicable Disease Center; 1985:6.

9. Halpern S. *Tuning the human instrument.* Belmont, CA: Spectrum Resident Institute; 1978:1.
10. Moss V. Music and the surgical patient. *AORN J.* 1988;48(1):67.
11. Steelman V. Intraoperative music therapy: Effects on anxiety, blood pressure. *AORN J.* 1990; 52(6):1028.
12. Holmes J. A summary of safety consideration for the medical and surgical practitioner. In Apfelberg D, editor. *Evaluation and Installation of Surgical Laser Systems.* New York: Springer Verlag; 1987:69–95.
13. Occupational Safety and Health Administration, Department of Labor. Toxic and hazardous substances, hazard communication standard. Code of Federal Regulations, Title 29, Chapter XVII, Section 1910.1200, 48 FR 53280. Washington, DC: US Government Printing Office; 1983:15–14.
14. Recommended practices for safe care through identification of potential hazards in the surgical environment. In *Standards and Recommended Practices.* Denver: AORN; 1994:174.
15. Goodwin C et al. Nursing Life's guide to hidden hazards on the job: Radiation. *Nursing Life* November–December 1985;5:43–47.
16. Recommended practices for reducing radiological exposure in the practice setting. In *Standards and Recommended Practices.* Denver: AORN; 1995:245.
17. Berger M, Hubner K. Hospital hazards: Diagnostic radiation. *Am J Nurs.* 1983;8:1155–1157.

Management and Leadership
of the Surgical Suite

The management of perioperative nursing practice is the coordination of all functions relating to the nursing care of surgical patients. The title of the individual responsible for leadership and supervision of nursing service varies with the organization's complexity. The person to whom that individual reports also varies. In large, complex environments the title may be nursing director of operating rooms, director of surgical services, or assistant director of nursing services. In smaller or less complex organizations, where the volume of administrative responsibility is less time consuming, the individual may have the title of operating room supervisor or head nurse.

Throughout this text the term *nurse manager* will be used to identify the individual ultimately responsible and accountable for managing the surgical suite, the person who coordinates all the nursing functions related to the care of surgical patients.

In large, complex organizations it has become increasingly popular for the nurse manager of the operating room to report to hospital administration rather than to the vice president of nursing services. When that occurs, the nurse manager must establish communications with other nursing leaders within the institution and maintain an awareness of events and trends in nursing practice.

AORN's "Standards of Perioperative Administrative Practice" are intended to serve as the foundation by which the perioperative setting is organized and administered. The structure standards were developed to guide professionals in administrative roles and to provide direction for evaluating operational systems. (See "Standards of Perioperative Administrative Practice" in Appendix A.)

■ NURSING MANAGEMENT PERSONNEL

Regardless of the size or nature of the setting, every nurse administrator has three major areas of responsibility:

1. Patient care
2. Human resources
3. Operational management

The nurse manager has ultimate responsibility for the overall functioning of the unit, including fiscal management and long-range planning, whereas the operating room supervisor has responsibility for the daily clinical functions of the unit. In large, complex units the assistant supervisor is responsible for specific functions of the unit, such as supervising ancillary personnel, and may function as the administrative head in the absence of the supervisor.

Nursing administrators must collaborate and cooperate if the department is to function effectively and efficiently. The concise performance descriptions which follow will assist this process by identifying lines of authority and responsibility.

Nursing Director, Operating Rooms and Postanesthesia Care

Within the guidelines of institutional philosophy, the nursing director of operating rooms and the postanesthesia care unit has ultimate administrative authority and responsibility for the nursing services provided to surgical patients. The nursing director is accountable for creating a social system that fosters the participation of nursing staff in assessment, planning, implementation, and evaluation of professional practice to ensure safe, efficient, and therapeutically effective nursing care. This includes organizational programming, goal setting, and policy development.

Operating Room Supervisor

The operating room supervisor has 24-hour line responsibility for the operating rooms, including the supervision of clinical nurses, hospital assistants and orderlies, surgical technicians, clerical personnel, and other multiskilled care givers. The operating room supervisor assumes responsibility for the department in the absence of the nursing director.

Assistant Operating Room Supervisor

The assistant operating room supervisor is responsible for ancillary staff in the operating rooms, one or more surgical specialties, and the quality assurance program. In addition, the assistant operating room supervisor assumes 24-hour line responsibility for the operating rooms in the supervisor's absence.

Support Positions

Two additional positions may assist nursing administrators to manage the nonnursing and indirect care activities: supply coordinator and biomedical equipment technician.

The *supply coordinator* is primarily responsible for ordering, receiving, storing, and distributing all supplies used in the operating rooms. In addition, the supply coordinator coordinates services from the following departments: environmental, material, laundry, building management, and purchasing.

The *biomedical equipment technician* installs, inspects, maintains, and repairs equipment used in the operating room. Other responsibilities of the technician include developing and implementing equipment control and safety maintenance programs, conducting educational programs for staff members, and advising the nurse manager on equipment purchases.

Previous operating room experience is a valuable asset in both these positions. The supply coordinator is accountable to the nurse manager; collaboration is essential in purchasing supplies. The biomedical equipment technician may be employed by the clinical engineering department; however, the operating room must take priority over all other responsibilities.

In less complex institutions, these two positions may be combined into one position: a supply and equipment coordinator. When that is the case, the clinical engineer employed by the hospital must be relied upon for maintaining and inspecting all complex medical equipment and instrumentation.

PHILOSOPHY, PURPOSES, AND OBJECTIVES FOR PERIOPERATIVE NURSING

Institutions have a philosophy statement that describes their values and beliefs in regard to patients and employees, the use of resources, and their overall mission. The philosophy of the operating room is consistent with the institution's philosophy and is developed by all levels of departmental personnel. Once developed, the philosophy should be published, and shared with and interpreted to all members of the operating room staff. It is used to orient new employees.

The philosophy is reviewed annually and revised to reflect changes in the hospital's goals and the developments in perioperative nursing practice. An example of a perioperative nursing service philosophy follows (author's note):

> The perioperative nurse has primary responsibility and accountability for the nursing care of patients who are experiencing operative and other invasive procedures. To effectively serve the patient, we will develop individualized plans of care that reflect the patients' ethnic, cultural, and social diversity derived from a nursing assessment. The surgical team will work together with mutual respect and courtesy to blend technical knowledge and professional skills in implementing these plans for cost-effective perioperative patient care. We believe that:
>
> 1. We have as our primary responsibility the assessment of the patients requiring invasive procedures in order to develop, implement, and evaluate comprehensive nursing care guided by professional recommended practices.
> 2. Cost-benefit analysis should precede implementation of recommended practices.
> 3. We have a responsibility to serve as patient advocates and to ensure observation of the Patient's Bill of Rights.
> 4. Perioperative nursing practice is essential to facilitate effective care for the patient having an invasive procedure.
> 5. Patients should have individualized plans of care that reflect their ethnic, cultural, and social diversity.
> 6. Surgical intervention not only alters physiological functions, but may also generate stress, anxiety, and/or discomfort that can disturb individuals, families, and significant others.
> 7. We are responsible for contributing to the continuity of patient care by collaborating with other health care disciplines.
> 8. We are responsible for supporting programs that will enable health care practitioners to provide excellence in patient care.

9. We are responsible for developing an inservice program that will enhance the skills, knowledge, and abilities of our staff.
10. We are responsible for supporting the pursuit of nursing research to improve nursing practice and patient care.
11. We are responsible for developing courteous collegial relationships characterized by mutual respect and understanding.

Purposes

After the philosophy of nursing care is formulated, it is essential to develop a set of purposes. The purposes are defined in greater detail than the articles of the philosophy, and state the activities or actions that will be implemented in accordance with the philosophy. An example of a statement of purposes follows:

- To define and implement a comprehensive nursing care program in the perioperative areas that will assist patients, their families, and significant others to return to their previous level of wellness or to an altered state
- To provide the medical staff with facilities, personnel, and a suitable climate for operative and other invasive procedures

The objectives for nursing care will then determine specifically how the purposes are to be achieved, in what time frame, and by what methods.

Objectives of Nursing Care

Objectives should be reasonable, attainable, and measurable. In identifying objectives, criteria are established to evaluate nursing care. Through constant emphasis on these objectives and their daily use by the administrative and clinical nursing staff members, the nursing care of patients will approximate the kind of care envisioned in the philosophy.

The primary objective of perioperative nursing is to meet individual patient needs in a cost-effective manner without negative outcomes. Implementing the perioperative role is a nurse's primary responsibility. This is accomplished by observing, evaluating, and documenting a patient's pertinent signs and symptoms and initiating appropriate nursing action. The care a patient receives is provided through the collaboration of the nursing and medical staffs. Equipment and supplies are continually evaluated to ensure that cost-effective items are available for operative and other invasive procedures.

To encourage employees to develop a high level of proficiency, educational programs are planned to motivate individuals and enhance their knowledge. An environment conducive to nursing research is fostered, and the results of nursing research are used to initiate change.

▌ POLICIES AND PROCEDURES

Policies are general statements that serve as a guide for the decisions and actions of staff members. The operating room has written policies and procedures that establish authority, responsibility, and accountability. Policies facilitate consistency and the choice of purposeful activity. To implement a policy statement, staff members often carry out a procedure. A procedure, the "how to," is a series of steps required to accomplish a task. Not all policy statements, however, require a procedure.

Policies and procedures are written to protect patients and personnel from injury; to meet local, state, and federal regulations with regard to licensure; to coincide with community standards; and to meet the standards of the Joint Commission on the Accreditation of Healthcare Organizations (JCAHO). They also assist in the development of quality assessment and improvement activities.

Professional organizations may present guidelines for developing institutional policy and procedures. Individual commitment, professional conscience, and the perioperative setting guide a nurse in implementing recommended practices. Variations in practice settings and clinical situations may determine the degree to which recommended practices can be fulfilled.[1]

Policies and procedures are written by appropriate members of the department, and are approved and dated by the nurse manager. The material is usually divided into two sections, administrative and clinical, and is contained in two separate manuals. The manuals are reviewed, revised, and updated annually to reflect changes in technology and perioperative nursing practice. A review of the manuals should also be included in the orientation and ongoing education of personnel, to assist in the development of knowledge, skills, and attitudes that affect the delivery of patient care.

The *administrative* policy and procedure manual should include but not be limited to the following:

Call, guidelines for
Charges, OR
Consent for surgical intervention
Criminal evidence
Disaster plan
   Internal (fire, nuclear material)
   External
Controlled substances
   Dispensing
   Counting
Incident reports
Loaning of instruments and supplies
Operating room rules and regulations
Organizational chart
Orientation of new personnel
Patient charges
Personnel policies
   Attendance
   Continuing education
   Evaluation
   Overtime
   Sick leave
   Parental leave

Leave of absence
Vacation
Philosophy and objectives of perioperative nursing
Preventive maintenance
   Equipment
   Environment
Performance improvement plan
Scheduling of surgical procedures
   Elective
   Urgent
   Emergency
Valuables belonging to patients
Visitors
   Operating room
   PACU
   Preoperative area

The *clinical* policy and procedures manual can be organized according to specific "aspects of care" provided by the perioperative nursing team, such as:

Discharge planning
   Discharge protocol
      Ambulatory Care Unit (ACU)
      Postanesthesia Care Unit (PACU)
Education, patient/significant others
   Preoperative education: Assessment and documentation
Emergencies
   Cardiac arrest procedure
   Checking code carts
   Emergency power source
Fluid balance
Infection control
   Aseptic technique
   Attire, surgical
   Banks
      Blood
      Bone
      Cartilage
      Eye
      Skin
   Bowel technique
   Care of body after death
   Cleaning and maintenance of equipment and environment
   Disinfecting and processing of instruments and supplies
   Donor organ, retrieval
   Draping for invasive procedures

Gowning and gloving
Housekeeping
  End of case cleaning
  Terminal cleaning
Implants, sterilization
Surgical dressings
Surgical shave preparation
Surgical skin preparation
  Patient
  Staff
Sterilization
  Types
  Packaging
  Shelf life
Traffic control
Ultrasonic cleaner
Universal precautions
Interventions: Invasive
  Catheterization, bladder
  Chest tubes
Interventions: Noninvasive
  Nursing care for patients receiving radioactive therapy
  Patient monitoring with pulse oximetry
  Traction
Intravenous therapy
  Venipuncture for peripheral IV therapy
Medication administration
  Administration of medications
  Adult IV administration of drugs
  Care and monitoring of patients receiving conscious sedation/local anesthetic
  Controlled substances
    Dispensing
Nursing process
  Admission to the operating room
  Admission assessment and reassessment of patient care needs
  Ambulatory surgery
  Circulating nurse responsibilities
  Documentation
    Critical paths
    Preoperative nursing care protocol
    Intraoperative documentation
    Postoperative nursing care protocol
    Postoperative evaluation
    Standard care plans
  Scrub assistant responsibilities
  Specimens (collection and disposition)

Pain management
    Epidural catheter removal
    Guidelines for Patient Controlled Analgesia (PCA) Flow Sheet
    Management of patients on PCA
    Pain management standard care plan
Patient Safety
    Arm bands
    Alarm systems
    Counts
        Sponge
        Sharps
        Instruments
    Electrical safety
    Electrosurgical machines
        Grounding
        Hazards
    Lasers, guidelines for use
        Documentation
    Radiation safety
    Tourniquets
    Transportation of the patient to the surgical suite
    X-ray in the surgical suite
Physiological Monitoring
    Estimation and recording of blood loss
Positioning
Skin integrity
Thermoregulation
    Hypothermia machine, guidelines for use
Transfusions
    Administration of blood and blood products

■ ASPECTS OF CARE

Aspects of care are specific categories of perioperative clinical nursing practice. Each aspect of care can be evaluated against two types of standards: a standard of care and a standard of practice (see Table 3–1).

Standard of care statements identify outcomes of patient care when the care is delivered in a competent manner by members of the surgical team. The degree to which patients achieve the desired outcome speaks to the effectiveness of interventions as well as to the quality of care.

Standard of practice statements describe a minimum baseline for professional practice that the nursing staff must meet to ensure that the patient receives quality care, and serve as a guide for nursing practice and as protection for the patient.

The standard of care statements are expected to remain relatively constant. The stan-

TABLE 3–1. ASPECTS OF PERIOPERATIVE CLINICAL NURSING PRACTICE

Aspect of Care	Standard of Care	Standard of Practice

Discharge Planning	Patients/significant others can expect to have the knowledge or resources available to be cared for at home or to be placed at a facility to provide the appropriate level of care which includes:
	  a. education and information
	  b. equipment
	  c. referrals
	  d. postoperative appointments
	In preparation for discharge, the patient can expect that continuing care needs are assessed during the pre-surgical evaluation and that referrals for care will be made by a registered nurse and appropriate other members of the health care team.
		The registered nurse will assess continuing care needs during the presurgical evaluation. The assessment will include the abilities of the patient and/or significant others to manage care needs after discharge. The discharge planning information, including referrals to other clinical disciplines, is documented in the nursing care plan. The RN will:
		  a. assess the patient for anticipated discharge and educational needs during in the presurgery period
		  b. make appropriate referrals
		  c. assess the patient and significant others for ability to learn
		  d. Develop, implement, evaluate teaching plans based on anticipated discharge and education needs
		  e. ensure that the postprocedure appointment has been made

Education: Patient/ Significant Others	Patients can expect that during the perioperative period they will receive education specific to the surgical procedure. Patients and their significant others can expect that they will be included in the teaching/learning process and that they will have an understanding of their health care needs. Patients can expect to be discharged from ambulatory surgery with sufficient knowledge to care for themselves at home.	Registered nurses and/or other members of the health care team will provide the patient and the significant others with education specific to the surgical intervention. The teaching provided will be developed utilizing the nursing process and documented on the medical record. Patient/significant other education will be done by the nursing staff. Registered nurses will base all patient/significant other education on the nursing process, i.e. assessment of physical, social, environmental, self-care, functional, and discharge planning needs. The health care team will provide interpretation to those patients assessed to require this service.
Emergencies	Patients can expect to have timely and efficient responses to any medical emergency.	Team members will demonstrate activation of emergency responses and demonstrate ability to perform in emergency situations according to unit/facility protocol.
Fluid Balance	Patients can expect to have their fluid balance assessed and maintained within normal limits throughout the perioperative experience.	Registered nurses will utilize knowledge of normal physiology and pathophysiology to assess the patient's fluid balance preoperatively and at intervals determined by the patient's condition and procedure. Changes in fluid balance will be reported to the physician in a timely manner.
Infection Control	Patients can expect to cared for in an environment that reduces the risk of acquiring a nosocomial infection. Patients can expect that invasive procedures will be performed in a manner that minimizes risks for infection.	Registered nurses will comply with all infection control clinical guidelines (policies/procedures) and will utilize Universal Precautions throughout the perioperative continuum.

(continued)

TABLE 3–1. *(Continued)*

Aspect of Care	Standard of Care	Standard of Practice
Interventions: Invasive	Patients can expect to have invasive procedures safely conducted with no risk of infection or complications.	Registered nurses will demonstrate proficiency in all procedures related to clinical specialty and will use sterile technique when conducting invasive nursing procedures.
Interventions: Noninvasive	Patients can expect to have nursing interventions appropriately performed with sensitivity to their privacy, comfort, and knowledge needs. Patients can expect to receive noninvasive monitoring as ordered, in a safe and timely manner.	Registered nurses will prepare patients verbally for anticipated nursing care interventions based on clinical guidelines.
Intravenous Therapy	Patients can expect to receive the correct IV solution at the correct rate. Patients can expect to have IV therapy administered according to clinical guidelines.	Registered nurses will administer IV therapy according to the physician's order and clinical guidelines.
Medication Administration	Patients can expect to receive the correct medication in the correct dose, via the correct route at the correct time.	RN/LVNs will demonstrate proficiency in medication administration and knowledge of doses, actions, and side effects of commonly administered medications. Medications will be administered according to physician order, unit/facility policies, procedures and protocols.
Nursing Process Assessment	Patients and their significant others can expect to receive information about the patient's health status and that it will be documented correctly. Patients can expect to be assessed during the presurgical assessment and at appropriate intervals for biophysical, psychosocial, environmental, self-care, educational, and discharge planning factors and to have this assessment documented correctly.	Registered nurses will obtain from patients and their significant others their perspective of the patient's health status and correctly document it. Registered nurses will perform and document patient assessment according to unit standard and patient condition.
Pain Management	Patients can expect to be assessed and treated for pain associated with treatments, procedures, and natural processes occuring during the perioperative period.	Nurses will assess patient comfort and implement nursing/physician orders for pain management, according to clinical guidelines/protocols, and evaluate the effectiveness of interventions.
Patient Safety	Patients can expect to have invasive procedures in an environment which minimizes physical risks, such as biochemical hazards, infectious hazards, or defective equipment. Patients can expect to be free from retained foreign bodies during surgical procedures.	Nursing staff will perform their role functions in compliance with clinical guidelines and organizational safety policies.
Physiological Monitoring	Patients can expect that physiological processes will be maintrained during the perioperative period. Patients can expect to be free of complications associated with the administration of local anesthesia or conscious sedation.	Registered nurses will assess the patient's physiological status according to clinical guidelines and the patient's condition; interventions will be implemented according to clinical guidelines and physician orders. Registered nurses will care for the local anesthesia/conscious sedation patient according to clinical guidelines.

TABLE 3–1. *(Continued)*

Aspect of Care	Standard of Care	Standard of Practice
Positioning/ Skin Integrity	Patients can expect that positioning during surgical intervention will not compromise physiological function, impair skin integrity or cause injury.	The registered nurse will assess and document skin integrity and range of joint motion during the presurgical assessment. The surgical team will position the patient according to clinical guidelines. The circulating nurse will assess and document the patient's skin integrity immediately postoperatively.
Thermoregulation	Patients can expect to have their body temperature regulated during the perioperative period.	Registered nurses will assess the patient's temperature according to clinical guidelines and implement interventions according to physician order and clinical guidelines.
Transfusions	Patients can expect to receive the correctly typed and cross-matched blood and blood products throughout the perioperative experience.	Registered nurses will safely administer blood and blood products to patients according to policy and procedure.

dard of practice statements, however, may change in order to keep pace with innovations in technology or in clinical practice.

▌ UTILIZING A CLINICAL COMPETENCY SERIES

Traditionally, the system of rewarding clinical competency was to move the nurse away from clinical practice and into the administrative role of head nurse. The nurse was required to learn and implement management skills, and the high level of clinical skill was not retained.

A nontraditional approach to staffing that rewards clinical expertise is a clinical series. In this series, the clinical nurse who demonstrates clinical expertise is promoted vertically; the nurse does not move from the clinical setting.

The objectives of the series are:

- to establish career patterns that provide for quality nursing care
- to recognize and place the highly skilled nurse in direct care activities
- to identify levels of nursing competence
- to provide realistic and measurable expectations for practice to guide the evaluation of practice and advancement within the series
- to acknowledge educational preparation of the nurse for the appropriate level of practice
- to enable the nurse to set his or her own goals
- to increase the expertise of the nursing staff by stimulating individual growth and achievement
- to help recruit and retain highly qualified nurse practitioners

Essential to the success of a clinical series is the identification of nonnursing tasks performed by nurses and the subsequent training of assistive personnel to assume those duties. Such tasks include restocking operating rooms, checking sterile supplies for expiration dates, preparing routine and special instruments or supplies for sterilization, and conducting inventories of supplies. Delegating these nonnursing tasks is cost effective and allows nurses to practice nursing.

In developing a clinical series, the depth of knowledge upon which nursing decisions are based, the scope of practice, and the degree of responsibility and accountability for patient care must be identified for each level of practice. The definition of the perioperative role and the continuum (see Chapter 5) on which perioperative nurses function—from basic competency to excellence—comprise the framework for job descriptions.

Therefore, in a five-level clinical series, level one is the student role, and level two includes the operational staff nurses who have basic perioperative skills. The difference in the levels lies in the minimum qualifications for each role and the degree of responsibility and accountability exercised in implementing the behaviors identified in the job description. Level three includes the intermediate practitioner whose professional intraoperative skills have advanced and who has additional responsibilities for patient care within one surgical specialty.

A level four nurse functions as an advanced-level clinician, who may assume a leadership role for one or more surgical specialties. Level five is identified as a clinical specialist, who may be responsible for a continuing education program for the staff, orienting new employees, and acting as a resource person for nurses at the other levels.

Clinical Nurse I

A clinical nurse I is a registered nurse who is closely supervised by a preceptor and works in a controlled patient care situation, performing established nursing procedures for individual patients within an assigned surgical specialty. It is the entry-level classification for a nurse without experience. This level is used only for the duration of the probationary period.

Clinical Nurse II

Under supervision, the clinical nurse II implements established nursing interventions using current clinical knowledge, and provides care for patients with special problems and leadership for other nursing service personnel. This is the operational level for nurses with more than six months work experience.

Clinical Nurse III

Under general supervision, the clinical nurse III provides care for patients in one surgical specialty. Clinical responsibility within the specialty includes teaching, clinical supervision, and evaluating other nursing service personnel assigned to the specialty.

Clinical Nurse IV

Under general direction, the clinical nurse IV develops patient care standards; assesses the health needs of patients; and plans, implements, and evaluates the care of patients in one or more surgical specialty. A nurse at this level uses specialized knowledge and skills for direct patient care, for teaching patients or staff, and for evaluating the clinical performance of nursing service personnel. At this level, limited administrative responsibility is assumed for clinical activity. Clinical nurse IV is a resource person within the organization and may perform duties of lower-level clinical nurses.

Clinical Nurse V

The clinical nurse V may design and conduct educational programs and clinical research. The nurse also assists the clinical nurse IV in evaluating current nursing practice, developing necessary methodologies, and implementing the standards of nursing care. In addition, the nurse provides 24-hour clinical consultation regarding difficult patient management problems, assesses the clinical educational needs of the staff, and implements appropriate educational programs.

Administrative Series

This nontraditional approach to staffing requires reviewing administrative functions and developing an accompanying administrative series. The administrative series should define the roles that require increasing accountability for budget, the size of clinical staff, and the scope of administrative responsibilities. Figure 3–1 is an example of an organizational chart that identifies ways in which the clinical and administrative series can interface.

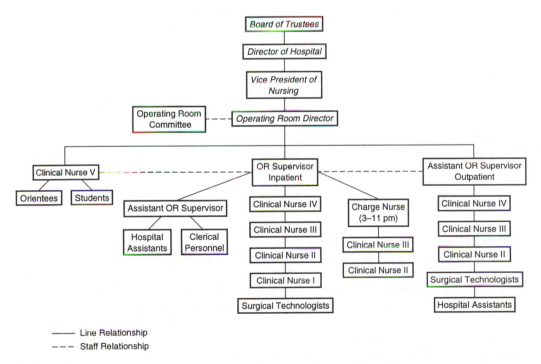

Figure 3–1. Organization chart.

■ OTHER NURSING PERSONNEL

Licensed Practical/Vocational Nurses

Licensed practical/vocational nurses (LPN/LVNs) are qualified by training and experience to take a state board examination for licensure. They may provide nursing care that does not require the skill or judgment that a registered nurse has acquired. Some state practice acts permit LVN/LPNs to administer certain medications. With additional training, they may serve as a scrub person at the operating table. They are not, however, permitted to function independently as a circulating nurse in the OR, although they may assist as a second circulator, working under the direct supervision of a registered nurse.

Unlicensed Assistive Nursing Personnel

Unlicensed assistive personnel (UAP) may assist with delegated patient care according to their level of education, training, and demonstrated competence. In the operating room such personnel include *surgical technologists* and *operating room technicians.* They are accountable to registered nurses and work under RN supervision. If they meet specific educational requirements and pass a certifying examination, surgical technologists may become certified. Certification, however, is not a state license to practice nursing. Surgical technologists are responsible for their own acts, but must function under the supervision of a registered nurse. Current standards of the Joint Commission on Accreditation of Healthcare Organizations (JCAHO) permit surgical technologists to function in the circulating role if a registered nurse is immediately available and the medical record confirms that a qualified RN supervised that activity. On the other hand, surgical technologists are not permitted to administer medications, complete patient records, or carry out direct physician orders regarding treatment.

Surgical technologists are seeking to broaden their role to perform procedures traditionally reserved for surgical first assistants. This proposed role requires that they be directly supervised by the surgeon. Not all state laws, however, currently allow this practice. In addition to the scrub role, surgical technicians may be assigned the tasks of restocking the operating rooms, preparing and selecting supplies and equipment for surgical procedures, routine cleaning and maintenance of equipment, and other related housekeeping tasks.

■ ANCILLARY POSITIONS

Clerical Personnel

As indicated in Chapter 2, communication within the operating rooms is important. Clerical personnel are the key to making the communication system function effectively. They may also be responsible for additional tasks, such as processing patients' charts, maintaining records, preparing reports, and operating computers and fax machines.

Hospital/Nursing Assistant (Orderly)

This group of ancillary personnel are trained to assist the nursing staff with both direct and indirect nursing care activities. Direct care tasks include all the activities that involve contact with the patient, such as assisting with positioning and transporting patients. Indirect tasks include routine housekeeping tasks, such as restocking operating rooms, decontaminating instruments, and preparing supplies and instruments for sterilization.

The unlicensed assistive personnel and ancillary personnel are important components in the staffing pattern of the surgical suite (see Figs. 3–2, 3–3). They provide valuable support to the perioperative nurse and contribute to the care the surgical patient receives.

▮ FUNCTIONS OF THE OPERATING ROOM TEAM MEMBERS

Surgeon

The surgeon is the individual whose primary responsibility is to perform the operative procedure. The surgeon may assist with positioning, preparation, and draping or delegate the responsibilities to the first assistant or perioperative nurses (see Fig. 3–4).

RN First Assistant

The first assistant to the surgeon may be a surgeon, resident, intern, physician's assistant, or nurse. AORN adopted its first official statement on RN first assistants (RNFA) in 1984, and its acceptance by several state boards of nursing has supported the recognition of RNFA behaviors as within the scope of nursing practice. The National Certification Board: Perioperative Nursing, Inc. offered the first examination for certification in 1993. The 1984 position statement was revised in 1993 and delineates the RN first assistant definition, the scope of practice, qualifications, educational requirements, and clinical privileges that must be met by perioperative nurses who practice in that role.

Definition. The RN first assistant at surgery collaborates with the surgeon in performing a safe operation with optimal outcomes for the patient. The RN first assistant must have acquired the necessary specific knowledge, skills, and judgment to practice perioperative nursing. Practice during the intraoperative phase of the perioperative experience is under the supervision of the surgeon. The RN first assistant does not concurrently function as a scrub nurse.

Figure 3–2. Preparing instruments for sterilization.

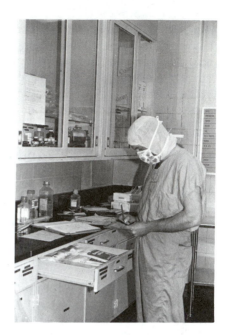

Figure 3–3. Ancillary personnel can be trained to restock the operating rooms.

Scope of Practice. Perioperative nursing is a specialized area of practice. The activities of first assistants are refinements of that practice and executed within the context of the nursing process. Observable nursing behaviors are based on an extensive body of scientific knowledge. These intraoperative behaviors may include:

- handling tissue
- providing exposure
- using instruments
- suturing
- providing hemostasis[2]

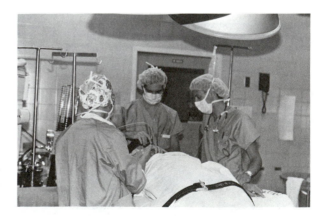

Figure 3–4. Collaborative efforts by nursing personnel and medical staff are essential to effective patient care.

To determine if an RN qualifies for clinical privileges as a first assistant, an approval process must be established by the institution. The process of granting practice privileges includes mechanisms for:

- assessing individual qualifications
- assessing continuing proficiency
- evaluating annual performance
- assessing compliance with relevant institutional and departmental policies
- defining lines of accountability
- retrieving documentation of participation as first assistant
- establishing systems for peer review[2]

Anesthesiologist, Anesthetist

The anesthesiologist is a physician who specializes in administering anesthetic agents. During the surgical procedure, the anesthesiologist administers drugs, fluids, and blood components, and monitors the patient's vital signs.

An anesthetist is a nurse who specializes in anesthesiology.

Scrub Assistant

The scrub assistant may be a nurse or a surgical technologist. In 1988, the AORN House of Delegates adopted a resolution regarding the role of the scrub person.[3] The resolution indicated that the role of the scrub person is an integral part of perioperative nursing practice; therefore, the registered nurse in that role is practicing nursing. The individual who performs the role but is not licensed to practice professional nursing is under direct supervision of a perioperative nurse.

The scrub assistant scrubs his or her hands and arms, dons a sterile gown and gloves, sets up sterile supplies and instruments and hands them to the surgeon or first assistant. Throughout the surgical procedure, the scrub assistant maintains an accurate account of sponges, needles, and instruments. Knowledge of anatomy and physiology is essential to anticipate the surgeon's needs and reduce the amount of time required for the procedure. In addition, the scrub assistant ensures that all team members follow the principles of aseptic technique.

Circulating Nurse

During the intraoperative phase, the circulating nurse coordinates the activities of the room, delegates activities to other team members, implements the nursing care plan, serves as the patient's advocate, and ensures that the environment is safe for the patient. By advocating for the patient, the nurse demonstrates that there is more to caring for a surgical patient than addressing the technical aspects of the role. The nurse supports the patient emotionally prior to anesthesia induction, assists the anesthesiologist with the induction, and throughout the surgical procedure monitors the traffic in the room and keeps an accurate account of urine output and blood loss. The anesthesiologist will use this information to make decisions regarding fluid and electrolyte replacement.

When a procedure is performed with local anesthesia, a second circulating nurse provides continuous emotional support for the patient, administers intravenous narcotics at the surgeon's request, monitors vital signs, and reports abnormalities to the surgeon.

Before the surgical procedure is completed, the circulating nurse completes documentation, informs the postanesthesia care unit (PACU) of special needs, and makes sure that the sponge, needle, and instrument counts are completed. Postoperatively, the circulating nurse accompanies the patient to the PACU, reports to the nurse there about the patient's preoperative status and pertinent information concerning the intraoperative phase, and performs a preliminary evaluation of the patient's postoperative status to determine the outcome of nursing actions.

Preliminary preparation and planning for a surgical procedure may be performed by both the scrub assistant and the circulating nurse. However, from the time the scrub assistant begins the surgical hand scrub to the time that the patient's dressing is applied, the two roles are demarcated. A registered nurse is required for each patient requiring surgical intervention, and perioperative nurses are accountable for the quality of patient care delivered in the OR. Patient care requires accuracy, preparation, prudent judgment, and expert decision making to ensure positive patient outcome.

Delegating Activities.   Perioperative nurses delegate and supervise nursing activities performed by unlicensed assistive personnel. To ensure patient safety, the delegated tasks that are entrusted to nonnurses are consistent with the needs of the patient and the provider's education, training, and skills. The activities that may not be delegated are assessment, diagnosis, outcome identification, planning, and evaluation. The following activities may be delegated:

- opening sterile supplies
- assembling instrument sets
- maintaining equipment
- scrubbing
- transporting patients, supplies, specimens
- prepping patient's skin
- serving as a second circulator
- cleaning
- stocking operating rooms/supply areas
- ordering supplies
- operating equipment
- setting up arterial lines and calibrating cardiac monitors

The perioperative nurse is responsible for the delegated nursing task being performed properly. The following factors must be considered before delegating activities:

- the patient's condition
- complexity of technology and surgery
- predictability of patient outcomes
- level of preparation and education of unlicensed, assistive personnel
- competency of assistant
- ratio of registered nurses to unlicensed assistive personnel, based on patient need
- amount of supervision registered nurses will be able to provide.[4,5]

■ MODELS FOR MANAGING THE PERIOPERATIVE AREAS

Historically, nursing has been part of a bureaucratic hierarchical model. As a management-dominated system, the model dictates policy downward.[6] Management is at the apex of the hierarchical system, and a system of controls limits the independent behavior of the staff nurses at the bottom. Nurses in this type of system experience frustration because they are powerless to effect change.

A variation of the hierarchical model incorporates *participative management*. In organizations with participative management, nurses have increased control over their jobs. They have influence over what they do to achieve their goals, and they participate in making decisions over which management has ultimate control. Input and participation may be withdrawn at any time.

Shared governance is an organizational structure that provides an environment for autonomous staff nurse practice. Members of the organization have an organized, systematic process to govern activities that apply to the practice and processes of all the nurses in the organization. Ownership of decisions stays with the staff nurses; it does not transfer to management.

In some organizations, a blending of the hierarchical and shared governance structures exists. In these situations, the staff nurses independently make decisions in clinical practice; management maintains control over administrative decision making. The concept of shared governance is applicable to any setting where nursing is practiced, and it parallels what is happening in the changing health care industry by providing the framework for resolving issues through consultation and coordination.

■ NURSING CARE DELIVERY MODELS

A model is a tangible, schematic depiction of how something looks or works. Models of nursing care delivery are printed on paper to illustrate how care is given in a specific setting. They usually have one of three foci: patient, institution, or nurse/worker.[7]

The terms most frequently associated with perioperative practice are team nursing, differentiated practice, primary nursing, nurse extender, case management, and private or independent practice. Not all of these examples are models in the truest sense of the definition.

Team Nursing

The two primary tenets of team nursing are (1) a patient-centered philosophy toward nursing care delivery where the health care needs of the individual and the family are met, and (2) an organization of team members that will provide for the efficient delivery of this patient-centered model. Each team has a professional registered nurse serving as a team leader who is responsible and accountable for the nursing care given to a group of patients by team members assigned to their care.

The team assignments are differentiated by function and designed to meet the individual needs of patients and families. The nursing functions are divided into a continuum or spectrum range: assisting functions—simple functions learned through on-the-job training, semiprofessional or technical functions—immediate functions requiring skill and some judgment with technical training required, and complex functions requiring expert skill and judgment represented by the professional registered nurse.

Effective communication is essential to ensure the continuity of nursing care as nursing care plans are individualized, written, and serve as a blueprint for addressing the patient and his or her problems.

Differentiated Nursing Practice

Differentiated nursing practice is an approach to assuring quality care through the most appropriate use of nursing resources. The approach includes a variety of models for the deployment of personnel for practice in which the roles and functions of nurses are defined by criteria. Criteria include but are not limited to education, experience, and competence.

Differentiated practice requires the identification of nursing competencies necessary to serve the recipients of care within a specific practice environment.[8] Differentiated practice models are frequently associated with care managers and critical pathways.

Primary Nursing

Primary nursing is a model in which the staff consists of all registered nurses with responsibility for developing nursing care plans designed to provide physical and emotional support to each patient. Primary nurses are self-directed; they establish priorities and use judgment to meet the patients' needs. They may collaborate with other members of the health care team, such as social service staff. This model has no rigid guidelines, as each patient and nurse is unique.

This model is knowledge based.[9] Knowledge-based work means that the nurse, who is in a practice profession, integrates two sources of knowledge: formal education programs and hands-on practice.[10] The professional component of this model is exercised as the nurse uses judgment about the kind and amount of care a patient will receive. The primary care model evolved into the nurse extender model.

Nurse Extender

The nurse extender is a trained, unlicensed person whose responsibilities range from housekeeping, stocking, and clerical duties to technical tasks, such as scrubbing during surgical intervention. The changing demand for nurses and the changes in financial reimbursement to hospitals motivated the development of programs that prepare nurse extenders to work in partnership with registered nurses. Because of the work that the nurse extender does, the nurse is able to provide nursing services to more patients. In this model, it is imperative that the nurse have the knowledge required to delegate tasks appropriately. The above lists of activities that may be delegated to surgical technicians should assist with these decisions.

Nurse extenders provide an opportunity for nurses to use their knowledge base and judgment to maintain or improve the quality of care, advance autonomy in practice, facilitate the nurse's role in planning and coordinating patient care, reduce the cost of care, educate patients and families, and shorten postoperative stay.

A variation of this model is the patient-focused care model, which relies on cross training, decentralization, and patient care teams. All employees must be directly involved in patient care or support someone who is involved. The teams include both licensed and unlicensed personnel, with the registered nurse accountable for making nursing diagnoses, prescribing care, and evaluating the outcomes of the care. With the explosion of technology and specialization, this model is increasingly used in the perioperative area, as teams can be set up to meet the specific needs of a patient population.[11]

Case Management

Case management is a system of patient care delivery that focuses on achieving outcomes within effective and appropriate time frames and on using resources appropriately. The entire episode of illness is of concern, crossing all settings in which the patient receives care. The document used in this model is referred to as a *critical path,* also called care path, clinical pathway, care map, managed care plan, healing pathway, or target track. A critical path is a management tool used to organize and sequence all care givers' actions and interventions across a time line. The paths are developed by multidisciplinary and interdisciplinary teams (Table 3–2). Their objectives are to improve the quality of care, reduce system inefficiencies, reduce length of stay, reduce overuse of resources, increase predictability, and decrease variation in the treatment process. The critical path may also be an educational tool for care givers and/or patients.

The nurse responsible for developing patient care outcomes and managing the outcomes is the case manager. Nursing case management is considered a second generation of the primary care delivery model. Because not every patient requires that level of intense care, case management is best used for selected patients or populations, as for example, those who:

- are predictably unpredictable
- represent high cost
- have chronically repeated surgical procedures
- have significant variances
- have high-risk socioeconomic factors
- are a high-volume population.[12]

This care delivery system is especially relevant for ambulatory surgery patients, complex surgical patients, and those who require intense care, such as trauma patients or elderly persons.

Private Practice

Autonomy and accountability are the essential framework of the private practice model. It is a philosophic and political position that requires self-governance and self-determination. This includes seeking third-party reimbursement for services. Role differentiation results from mastery of advanced nursing competencies. Practitioners in advanced practice must pay particular attention to the rights and responsibilities of their expanded role, as defined by their state's nurse practice act. Collaboration, particularly during the intraoperative phase, with physicians and other providers is required for the patient to achieve the expected outcomes.

The perioperative nurse in private practice may be an effective provider in a variety of

TABLE 3–2. PERIOPERATIVE CRITICAL PATH FOR TOTAL JOINT PATIENTS

(Average) Total Time in Minutes	(80) 80	(10) 90	(25) 115	(120) 235	(10) 245	(80) 325
Activity/location	Holding area	Preinduction	Induction/prep	Operative procedure	Wake-up	Recovery room
Medication/blood products	IV fluids, IV antibiotics	Epidural for postop pain control, prn	IV/Inhalation anesthetic →, Blood prn	→	Marcan prn, Femoral nerve block prn	Pain medications
Treatment/nursing care	Provide warm blankets, comfort measures, perform chart review & preop interview, start IV, take vital signs, provide patient/family education prn	Position patient on bed, place monitors, assist with induction	Perform skin prep, operative positioning, catheter placement, cautery pad placement, place warming blanket	Open prostheses and other supplies prn, monitor sterile field, perform surgical counts, place drain (surgeon)	Apply dressings, temptek, knee mobilizer prn, abduction pillow prn	Monitor vital signs, provide comfort measures, administer pain meds prn, monitor drains prn, attach and monitor temptek
Documentation	Perioperative nursing record	Intraoperative record, pharmacy charge record, surgical supply record	→	→	→	Recovery room record and log
Invasive procedures	IV		Indwelling catheter prn, intubation	Surgical drains		
DVT prophylaxis						Pneumatic pump, athrombic stockings
Support services				Radiology, prn		Radiology, prn
Consults	Anesthesia interview					

settings, including acute and outpatient facilities—preoperatively, postoperatively, and intraoperatively. A patient's progress may be followed from the decision to have surgery, through activities in every hospital department (diagnostic, surgical, preop and postop, ICU, rehabilitation), and back into the home. A private perioperative nurse practitioner may be a RN first assistant, clinical nurse specialist, nurse liaison, or case manager.

■ NURSE LIAISON ROLE

The nurse liaison role has multiple forms, ranging from the contact person among patient, family, staff, and the organization to one who double-checks such items as correct blood type or medication. The position may be funded by the institution or a group of surgeons; the nurse may be on the staff of an institution or in private practice. Nurse liaison programs ensure that a perioperative nurse serves as the contact among patient, family, and staff during the surgical experience. The nurse is also a patient advocate, assists in managing the anxieties of the patient and family, and protects the patient's rights.

The programs exemplify a change in focus from that of task and technical orientation to one of humanistic caring. As a patient advocate, the nurse liaison recognizes that patients need personal contact and information other than that provided by the surgeon or anesthesiologist.[13] This caring and concern will help the patient to feel safe and secure in a potentially threatening environment, and it will promote positive health outcomes. The patient advocate encourages patient involvement in the plan of care, which allows the patient freedom to make choices.

The role of the nurse liaison is to:

- establish communication between the surgical team and the patient's family and friends
- provide a support mechanism for families under stress
- reinforce the perioperative role of the nurse in promoting holistic health care for the surgical patient and the family
- foster nurses' professional and personal growth
- promote a positive image of the facility to the community it serves

The nurse liaison makes contact with the patient and family prior to surgery. To help allay their fears, the nurse is available to answer questions they may have about surgery. Throughout the day the nurse liaison makes rounds of the ORs, viewing the status of surgical procedures, talking with the surgical teams to help ensure that the family receives accurate information in a timely manner, and checking on the status of patients in the PACU. In addition, the nurse remains up to date regarding cancellations, add-ons, and other changes in the schedule. The nurse can also relay questions and concerns from the family to the surgical team.

The surgical nurse liaison interacts with other departments in the hospital, for example, chaplaincy and social services, to assist the family. In this way, the family may be helped to notify others, arrange for temporary living quarters, or to have home visits made. This role is especially helpful for trauma cases when families are frequently very anxious and confused. Decisions may have to be made quickly and the surgical nurse liaison can assist families to cope.[14]

▌ REFERENCES

1. *Standards and Recommended Practices.* Denver: AORN; 1994:113.
2. AORN official statement on RN first assistants. In *Standards and Recommended Practices.* Denver: AORN; 1994:18–19.
3. House adopts resolution on role of scrub person. *AORN J.* 1988;47(5):1118.
4. Phippen M, Applegeet C. Unlicensed assistive personnel in the perioperative setting. *AORN J.* 1994;60(3):455–457.
5. Abbot C. Intraoperative nursing activities performed by surgical technologists. *AORN J.* 1994; 60(3):382–393.
6. O'Grady T. *Creative Nursing Administration.* Rockville, MD: Aspen; 1986:5.
7. Girard N. Nursing care delivery models. *AORN J.* 1993; 57(2):481.
8. Differentiated Nursing Practice: A Position Statement. New York: National League for Nursing: 1991.
9. Drucker P. *The Age of Discontinuity: Guidelines to Our Changing System.* New York: Harper & Row; 1990:264.
10. Manthey M. Primary practice partners (a nurse extender system). *Nursing Management.* 1988; 19(3):58.
11. Bickler B. Putting patient-focused care into practice. *AORN J.* 1994;60(2):242–245.
12. Girard N. The case management model of patient care delivery. *AORN J.* 1994;60(3): 403–412.
13. Wiseman S. Patient advocacy. *AORN J.* 1990;51(3):759.
14. Donnell S. Coping during the wait. *AORN J.* 1989;50(5):1092.

Legal Responsibilities of the Perioperative Nurse

The professional registered nurse is trained to make decisions that were once beyond the scope of nursing duties. Current standards of nursing education, skill, and expertise qualify the nurse to perform many procedures that once were exclusively the physician's responsibility. Responsibility, however, implies accountability, and in many respects maintaining a high standard of patient care has become as much a legal concern as a moral obligation for all members of the health care team.

Perioperative nursing has changed dramatically in recent years. One factor responsible for the change is specialization. A mistake or inattention by one member of the surgical team that results in injury or death to a patient may confer liability on the entire team: the nurse, surgeon, anesthesiologist, and the hospital.

Another factor involved in the recent change is the trend toward defined standards of nursing practice. Regardless of where nurses practice, they are held to a high level of professional expertise. Traditionally, the legal standard for any health care professional was the standard of care that prevailed within the community; however, now in many states the courts no longer favor the concept of community standard as an adequate criterion for judging the performance of health care professionals.

In addition, the consumer has had a significant impact on the evolving legal picture. Patients today are both medically and legally sophisticated. Daily they may read or hear in the news media about health care issues and about malpractice settlements. Thus, the patient who sustains an injury, even accidently, may turn to the courts for compensation.

Perioperative nurses are particularly vulnerable to charges of negligence in personal injury lawsuits. It is imperative, therefore, that they be informed of the risk management issues associated with their specialty.

■ RISK MANAGEMENT

A risk management program is designed to minimize or reduce negative patient outcomes through the systematic implementation of measures designed to encourage safe, risk-free patient care. A second goal of this program is to protect the financial resources of the facility and care providers. The program is designed to examine every aspect of patient care and to identify actual or potential areas of risk and then ensure that the department has appropriate policies, procedures, and standards of care that are documented and implemented to address those issues. Included in the program is a philosophy that encourages prompt identification of potential new risks and measures to control those risks.

For a surgical suite, the following questions should be addressed in monitoring and evaluating a risk management program:

- Are staff qualified and competent to perform assigned tasks?
- Is the environment safe and does it meet regulatory requirements?
- Does equipment meet current standards and has it been tested and maintained according to manufacturers' recommendations or regulatory guidelines?
- Has staff been trained to use current technologies/equipment?
- Is documentation accurate, complete, and timely?
- Is there a routine review of accidents, injuries and safety hazards?
- What policies and procedures have been developed to prevent and manage risks (for example, sponges, sharps, and instruments counts, positioning, or administration of medication)?
- Is there routine reporting of unusual occurrences or incidents?

Risk Management and Quality Improvement

Risk management and quality improvement programs are closely aligned. Risk management programs focus on the safety of visitors, staff, and patients by:

- identifying and analyzing risks
- developing alternative risk treatment techniques
- selecting the best alternative
- implementing appropriate solutions
- evaluating outcomes

Quality improvement programs, on the other hand, are primarily concerned with issues that do not pose a risk of injury to patients (Chapter 18).

Risk management and quality improvement programs compliment each other. Effective risk management and quality improvement programs can substantially reduce a facility's liability.

■ LIABILITY, MALPRACTICE, AND NEGLIGENCE

Liability is an obligation an individual or corporation has incurred or might incur through any act or the failure to act. Liability may be either criminal or civil in nature. Criminal liability results when a law is violated, for example, when property has been stolen from patients, co-workers, or the facility, or when licensed care givers exceed the scope of practice as defined by the state practice acts. Criminal acts can result in fines or imprisonment. Civil liability is called a tort and is described below.

Negligence is the failure to use ordinary care. It is a careless act or the failure to act or use reasonable precautions. Malpractice is the failure of a professional to meet the standard of care of the profession with the result being harm to another person.

Torts (Civil Liability)

A civil liability is called a tort. It is usually based on fault. It assumes that something was done incorrectly, or that something that should have been done was omitted. This act or omission can be intentional or can result from negligence.

Intentional. An intentional tort always involves a willful act that violates the patient's rights. Such acts include assault and battery, defamation, false imprisonment, invasion of privacy, and the intentional infliction of emotional distress.

Assault and battery occurs when medical or surgical procedures are performed without the patient's consent. Battery also occurs when a consent is obtained for one type of treatment or operation and a substantially different operation is performed. (See the discussion of informed consent later in this chapter.)

Defamation is the wrongful injury to another person's reputation. Written defamation is called libel, while spoken defamation is called slander. A claim of defamation can arise from the inappropriate or inaccurate release of medical information or from untruthful statements about other members of the hospital or medical staff.

Courts have recognized the importance of communications concerning a staff member's performance among supervisory staff within the same organization. These communications are protected by "qualified privilege" when they are made in good faith to the persons who need to know. This means that liability will not be imposed for defamation even if the communication is false as long as it was made without malice. For a communication to be privileged, it must be made within appropriate channels to a person who has a legitimate reason to receive the information.

False imprisonment is the unlawful restriction of a person's freedom, including physical restraints or unlawful detention. Hospital policy should explicitly identify when and how patients may be detained. Hospitals do have the common law authority and responsibility to detain patients who are disoriented, as, for example, after an anesthetic agent is administered for outpatient surgery. This is not false imprisonment, as the patient gave consent for the procedure and expects to be kept from harm by providers while under the effects of the anesthetic.

Invasion of privacy is a violation of the legal right to be free from unwarranted publicity and exposure to public scrutiny, as well as the right to avoid having one's name or private affairs made public against one's will. Hospital staff may be liable for invading a patient's privacy if they divulge information from the medical record to improper sources or if they intrude unwarrantably into a patient's personal affairs. Using a patient's photograph without permission is unwarranted intrusion.

Nurses are required by the laws in most states to disclose to appropriate officials the names of the patients when reporting communicable diseases, wounds of violence, or child or adult abuse. Caution must be exercised to ensure that only those who are required to receive the information receive it.

Intentional infliction of emotional distress is another intentional tort. It includes all conduct that may cause emotional trauma to patients and their families.

Negligence

The most frequent liability claim against health care workers is negligence. To establish liability an injury must have been caused by the negligence. Four elements must be present to establish liability for negligence:

- duty (the obligation to exercise due care)
- breach of duty (a failure to exercise due care)
- injury
- causation (the injury caused by the failure to use due care)

The doctrine of *res ipsa loquitur*, "the thing speaks for itself," is a major exception to the requirement that the above four elements be proven to establish negligence. The doctrine applies when a specific act or an omission cannot be found but the situation would not have occurred unless someone had been negligent. For *res ipsa* to apply five conditions must exist:

- the type of injury would not happen without negligence
- the apparent cause of the injury is the exclusive control of the person or persons being sued
- the person suing could not have contributed to the negligence or voluntarily assumed risk
- evidence of the true cause of the injury is inaccessible to the person suing
- the injury is evident

This doctrine applies to many injuries sustained in the operating room, as, for example, when sponges or other foreign objects are unintentionally left in the body or when nerve paralysis or skin burns are present postoperatively.

Negligence is defined as carelessness, or as the failure to act as a reasonably prudent person would under the same or similar circumstances. It is the failure to use ordinary or reasonable care in performing a task or delivering care to a patient. Ordinary or reasonable care is the care that prudent persons would use to avoid injury to themselves or others in similar circumstances. This is referred to as the *Doctrine of the Reasonable Man*. The duty owed by a professional is that of a reasonable professional, not that of a layman.

To avoid negligence, it is the duty and responsibility of the professional registered nurse to have knowledge and skills to deliver the same level of care as other members of the nursing profession, practicing their profession in the same or a similar locality and under similar circumstances. The professional must act in accordance with community and national standards. Failure to fulfill these duties is negligence.

One way to determine whether or not a person was negligent is to ask: "If persons of ordinary prudence had been in the same situation and possessed the same knowledge, would they have foreseen or anticipated that someone might have been injured by, or as a result of, their actions or inactions?" If the answer is "yes" and if the action or inaction reasonably could have been avoided, then not to avoid it is negligence.

Establishing Liability

Liability may be personal or individual liability, or corporate liability. Corporate liability has two parts: *respondeat superior*, or liability for employees and agents, and *corporate lia-*

bility, which covers the duty owed to patients directly by the facility. If an individual is negligent, both the facility and the individual can be found liable.

Historically, liability arose from negligence imputed to the hospital or physicians because of acts alleged to have been committed by nurses working under a physician's or hospital's direction, supervision and control. The basis for charging one person with another's liability is derived from an English common law maxim decree that a "master must answer for the acts of his servants," or *respondeat superior.* This doctrine imposes liability on the surgeon for all persons in the operating room on a given surgical procedure. Courts, however, have recognized that many procedures performed by members of the team do not need to be supervised by the surgeon.

A *borrowed servant* is an employee who is temporarily under the control of someone other than the employer. Through the borrowed servant rule, the surgeon is liable only for the acts of team members when the surgeon has the right to control and supervise the way in which they (nurses, for example) perform the work. Courts in many states do not apply the doctrine when the nurse continues to receive substantial direction from the hospital through its policies and procedures. Rather, the trend appears to be toward abandoning the borrowed servant doctrine and replacing it with a *dual servant* doctrine. Under this doctrine both the physician and the hospital are liable under *respondeat superior* for the acts of the employee.[1] The law, however, holds that each person is accountable for the consequences of his or her own professional performance. Therefore, the protection frequently associated with the borrowed servant doctrine is not encompassing, and personal liability may result when a nurse does something wrong or fails to do something that should have been done.

Corporations can also be liable for the consequences of breaches of duties owed to the patient, such as maintenance of buildings and grounds, the selection and maintenance of equipment, the proper selection of all staff, a performance review system for the staff, and supervision of all employees.

Temporary agencies that employ nurses and contract with hospitals to provide services are usually liable for the negligent acts of the nurse under *respondeat superior;* however, it is essential that the health care facility carefully select an agency and develop the contract. The contract should include allocation of liability and the responsibility of the agency for maintaining insurance coverage.

▌ STANDARDS OF NURSING CARE

The impact of increased liability on nursing practice is reflected in the growing number of guidelines by which care is rendered to patients. No comprehensive statement of objective professional standards covers every medical judgement that an institution, acting through its employees and agents, is required to make. Professional standards are determined with reference to several sources, such as accrediting agencies, state statutes, credentialing boards, professional organizations, an institution's policies and procedures, expert views in medical literature, and actual practices of health care practitioners.[2] Other standards result from precedents established by court rulings or personal injury lawsuits.

The state licensing board for registered nurses is among the agencies involved in formulating regulations. The legislature in each state empowers the board to protect the public from the unsafe practitioner by means of regulating nursing education, licensure, and practice. To achieve this outcome the board approves schools of nursing, establishes a basic curriculum that must be offered, defines faculty qualifications, and determines what education is equivalent and acceptable for persons who received their nursing education outside the state. The board is also responsible for the development and administration of the state licensing examination that determines whether examinees have the minimum knowledge and competency necessary for safe practice. In addition, regulations are developed to establish criteria that must be met by nurses who wish to be recognized as advanced practitioners of nursing or certified in specialized areas of practice, such as RNFAs.

The boards are directed by the state nurse practice act to take disciplinary action against a licensee for unprofessional conduct, including incompetence and gross negligence, as well as other specified acts. Each board of nursing establishes specific mechanisms of investigation and hearings regarding possible violations. A nursing license can be revoked or a nurse placed on probation or suspended depending on the seriousness of the offense and the findings of the investigations.

It is the responsibility of each nurse to become familiar with the laws of the state where he or she works. The courts have used nurse practice acts or rules and regulations of the boards of nursing as evidence in determining the reasonableness of the nurse's conduct in malpractice suits. A court's finding of liability can be considered by a board of nursing in its determination of a nurse's fitness for continued practice. This interrelationship is increasing as some states require that nurses involved in malpractice actions—even if they are not found liable—be reported to the state licensing board for registered nurses for investigation and possible discipline.

Competence Criteria for Registered Nurses

A registered nurse is considered competent when he or she consistently demonstrates the ability to transfer knowledge of social, biological, and physical sciences when applying the nursing process. The nurse applies the sciences in the following ways:

- Formulates a nursing diagnosis through observation of the patient and interpretation of information obtained from the patient and others.
- Formulates a care plan, in collaboration with the patient, to ensure direct and indirect nursing care that provides for restorative measures and for the patient's safety, comfort, hygiene, and protection.
- Performs skills essential to implementing the care plan and teaches the patient and family how to care for the patient's health needs.
- Delegates tasks to other team members based on the legal scope of practice of the team members and on their preparation and capabilities to perform the tasks.
- Supervises the nursing care delegated to other team members.
- Evaluates the effectiveness of the care plan through observation of the patient's physical condition, behaviors, signs and symptoms of illness, reactions to treatment and through communication with the client and health team members; modifies the plan as needed.
- Acts as the patient's advocate by initiating action to improve health care of the patient or to change decisions that are against the interests or wishes of the patient

and by giving the patient the opportunity to make informed decisions about health care before it is provided.

Supervision/Delegation

The responsibility of the nurse who supervises others is to determine which of the patient's needs can safely be assigned to others, and to make certain that those staff members are properly trained to perform the tasks or to operate the equipment to which they are assigned. Negligence often results from the failure of supervisors to perform the function with which they are charged: that of supervising other staff. Well-defined, documented orientation programs and ongoing credentialing of the staff are essential to ascertain competency. JCAHO requires that staff be competent to perform all assigned duties.

Professional Standards

Professional nursing associations such as AORN and ANA establish standards that provide a basic model to measure the competence of practitioners and the quality of patient care. These standards are broad in scope, relevant, attainable, and definitive. They enunciate for both the practitioner and consumer/public what the quality of nursing care should be. Compliance is voluntary; however, because the standards delineate a competent level of behavior or performance, they should be achieved. For perioperative nurses these include:

1. Standards of Perioperative Administrative Practice (see Appendix A)
2. Standards of Perioperative Professional Performance (see Appendix B)
3. Patient Outcome Standards for Perioperative Nursing (see Appendix E)

In addition to the standards, AORN has developed Recommended Practice Statements that represent optimum, achievable performance in the practice setting. The topics chosen for recommended practices address technical components of perioperative nursing that must be consistently implemented to provide safe patient care. The recommended practices are based on accepted nursing practices, scientific literature, research studies and standards. Regulations and/or standards from other agencies are included in the content or references to provide as much information as possible related to the topic (see specific chapter related to the recommended practices).

■ FEDERAL REGULATIONS

Several federal agencies regulate health care personnel.

- The Department of Health and Human Services incorporates specific requirements that are recognized as the norm for patient care. Hospitals participating in Medicare reimbursement must maintain that level of patient care.
- The Occupational Safety and Health Administration (OSHA) issues and regulates legally enforceable standards for preventing transmission of HIV, hepatitis B virus, and tuberculosis. These standards also include regulations regarding permissible levels of toxic substances in the environment.
- The Environmental Protection Agency (EPA) regulates the use of chemicals for disinfection and sterilization.

- The Federal Food and Drug Administration (FDA) regulates the manufacture, labeling, sale, and use of implantable medical devices and many other products used for patients. The FDA also controls treatment protocols for use of drugs, including antiseptic agents.

Additional standards are set by national, regional, or specialized professional groups.

- The National Fire Protection Association (NFPA) sets standards that reduce potential hazards related to electrical shocks and fires.
- The Association for the Advancement of Medical Instrumentation (AMMI) establishes standards for sterilization, electrical safety, and patient monitoring related to the evaluation, maintenance, and use of medical devices and instrumentation.
- The American National Standards Institute (ANSI) sets standards concerned with exposures to toxic materials and the safe use of equipment, such as lasers.
- The Joint Commission on Accreditation of Healthcare Organizations (JCAHO) establishes standards that pertain to the structure, process, and outcomes of services provided by health care facilities. The standards relate to the optimal quality of care and services that are achievable in the operation of a facility. The Joint Commission evaluates compliance with the standards and reviews clinical outcomes of care as criteria for accrediting a facility. The accreditation process is voluntary.

The net effect of these professional standards, federal regulations, and voluntary guidelines has been to safeguard the patient against injury or mishap. If the standards appear to be excessive to the practitioner, it is important to keep in mind that in addition to promoting patient safety, they protect the professional against potential malpractice.

■ DEPARTMENT POLICIES AND PROCEDURES

The policies and procedures of each institution are developed from federal and state regulations, and professional guidelines. Hospital policies that deviate from national guidelines or regulations or professional standards must be substantiated with scientific principles to withstand legal scrutiny. Perioperative nurses are responsible for knowing and adhering to department policies and procedures and for promptly reporting any observed problems or deviations. The reporting may be verbal but must also be written. See Chapter 3 for more information regarding policies and procedures.

Documentation

The purpose of the patient's health care record (medical record) is to communicate patient care from one health care professional to another. The care provided to the patient must be factually represented. Deficiencies in the record can destroy the credibility of the record and providers. The format for recording information varies among institutions and settings where care is provided. Whatever the format, all entries must:

- be written legibly in blue or black ink
- use only approved abbreviations
- include times, dates, and signatures

- be corrected using a single line drawn through the incorrect notation
- be factual without judgment or opinion
- follow the facility's policy

The health care record is a legal document accepted as evidence of what occurred in the health care setting, and it can be subpoenaed as legal evidence in a trial (see the perioperative documentation discussion in Chapter 5).

Medications and Solutions

Before drugs are transferred to the sterile field, they are checked by the circulating nurse and another team member, preferably the scrub assistant, the surgeon, or the anesthesiologist. All containers on the field with medications and solutions must be identified so that the wrong drug or solution is not inadvertently administered. The name of the medication and the dosage are identified. It is the responsibility of the scrub assistant to hand the correct medication to the surgeon and to state its name and dosage. If during the course of the procedure there is any doubt about the contents of a container with medications or solutions, the circulating nurse disposes of it and replaces it.

All medications and solutions administered on the sterile field or by the circulating nurse must be documented on the patient's health record.

Discharge Policies

Important responsibilities of perioperative nurses are to inform the ambulatory surgery patient of discharge policies and carry out discharge teaching protocols. This responsibility extends beyond the patient-provider relationship. For example, it may include injuries caused or received by patients after leaving the hospital if they did not receive warnings about the effect of treatment on their ability to drive.[3]

The discharge instructions are written and include a warning about the side effects of medications and any nonpharmaceutical elements of the patient's treatment. The instructions should be signed by the patient or guardian and a copy placed in the patient's health care record.

Incompetent Colleagues

Perioperative nurses may encounter colleagues who, they believe, are acting inappropriately or are impaired by either alcohol or drugs. Professionally the nurse must act to protect and prevent the patient from injury. If the situation requires immediate attention, the nurse reports it to the nurse manager or medical director. If the situation does not require immediate attention, it is reported to management, and the nurse actively participates in an investigation to validate the nurse's perceptions.

If following the investigation the nurse believes his or her professional integrity is compromised, the professional advice of an attorney should be sought. The attorney-client privilege protects against disclosure of conversations and allows the nurse access to an objective opinion.[4]

To ensure quality patient care, each facility should have a policy for reporting incompetent colleagues. Such a policy assists perioperative nurses in coping with this ethical and legal dilemma.

Verbal Orders during Surgery

Verbal orders during surgery are both legally and clinically appropriate. If an order is unusual or does not meet the standard of practice, a perioperative nurse must confirm the appropriateness of the order before it is executed. All medications administered intraoperatively must be appropriately documented. Verbal orders are written on the chart by the circulating nurse and initialed by the surgeon postoperatively.

Equipment and Technology

Specialization and advances in the treatment of disease processes have resulted in the development of sophisticated equipment and technology. Concerns related to equipment include the lack of specific safety mechanisms and the use of outdated or inadequate equipment. Perioperative nurses must demonstrate competency in using all equipment for procedures to which they are assigned. The nurse must exercise care in selecting equipment and following the manufacturer's guidelines for proper operation. Competency includes being aware of the hazards associated with the equipment during use.

The facility, as a corporate entity, must provide safe equipment. A biomedical technician or an electrical engineer must be responsible for routine preventive maintenance on all electrical equipment. The equipment is tagged to identify the date of the last maintenance inspection. Computerized equipment maintenance systems are available and enhance this process. Each department must have a procedure for reporting defective or potentially defective equipment.

In 1991 Congress passed the Safe Medical Devices Act, which requires that when a facility becomes aware that a device caused or contributed to a serious patient illness or injury, the facility must file a report within ten days to the manufacturer or, if the manufacturer is unknown, to the FDA. A device is defined as anything used in the treatment or diagnosis of a patient that is not a drug. A serious illness or injury is an incident that is life threatening, permanently impairs a body function, permanently damages a body structure, or necessitates immediate medical or surgical intervention to preclude permanent impairment of a body function or permanent damage to a body structure.

The act includes reporting incidents attributed to user error. The FDA requires that the information provided include who the operator or operators were and the nature of the problem or error that occurred in using the equipment. Another requirement is to identify the user's training in the equipment design, manufacturer's instructions, and hospital policies and procedures.[5]

The procedure regarding new equipment includes defining whose responsibility it is to set up the equipment, developing and implementing protocols for use of the equipment, educating the current staff, educating new staff, providing ongoing instructions in subsequent years, and carrying out maintenance and repairs.

Sales Representatives in the Operating Room

When the physician has a sales representative in the operating room to demonstrate or observe, it must be disclosed to the patient and included in the informed consent. The operating room log and the operative notes reflect the presence and role of the equipment service or sales representative. Institutional policies define the roles and responsibilities of all persons permitted in the surgical suite who are not required to provide direct care to the surgical patient.

■ MEDICAL CARE DECISIONS

Informed Consent

With the exception of life-threatening emergencies where treatment is required to prevent deterioration of the patient's condition, all surgical procedures or diagnostic studies necessitate informed consent. The importance of informed consent has grown with the consumer movement, particularly patient activism. Informed consent, identified as the patient's most important right, is recognized by the JCAHO, the American Hospital Association, the courts, and several state legislatures.

Consent is obtained by the responsible physician in a verbal discussion, a verbal and written process, or by using an audio cassette during a verbal discussion. The informed consent identifies the nature of the ailment, the proposed treatment, the risks, complications, and expected benefits of the treatment. In addition, alternative forms of treatment are discussed. The patient has the right to ask questions or to refuse care, withdrawing consent at any time. The signing of a consent must be witnessed by an appropriate person or persons.

Nurses have the responsibility to obtain informed consent for procedures they authorize or perform in independent or advanced practice roles.

The informed consent is valid until the procedure has been performed or until such time as there are changes in the physician, the circumstances, or in the procedure to be performed. For example, if a patient signs a consent for a specific operation but the diagnostic studies indicate that another procedure should be performed, a new consent must be obtained. Some facilities believe that the informed consent may become "stale" with the passage of time and require that if the procedure is postponed for a period longer than a month, a new consent form should be executed.

Generally, any competent adult older than 18 years must consent to his or her own treatment. Competency is the physician's judgment of a nonsedated patient's ability to comprehend treatment information, deliberate the choices based on his or her individual needs, and communicate his or her decisions.[6]

Incompetent adults must have a conservator, identified by the courts, who may give consent for medical treatment. Patients who are minors may consent to surgical treatment, procedures, or diagnostic studies if they are:

- fifteen years of age, living apart from parent or guardian, and managing their own financial affairs
- on active duty with the United States Armed Forces
- pregnant
- currently or have ever been married

If a patient is unable to write his or her name, a mark must be obtained. The individual securing the consent signs the patient's name; then the patient puts an "X" beneath it. In this situation two people should witness the consent.

Consent by telephone or telegraph may be necessary if the person with legal capacity to consent for the patient is not available. The telephone consent should be witnessed. The person obtaining the consent records and signs it, denoting the exact time and nature of the consent. The witness countersigns and dates the request. During the telephone conversation, the individual giving consent should be instructed to confirm the oral consent by telegram or letter.

Additional informed consents are required if the physician is going to use experimental drugs, chemical agents, or medical devices. In these situations the surgeon completes an investigator's report, which is returned to the supplier of the drug or device.

To take photographs during surgery also requires the consent of the patient or legal guardian. Many facilities have a specific "Consent for Photography" that must be signed.

Voluntary sterilization presents a special responsibility for informed consent. Patients must understand that the procedure will render them permanently unable to father or bear children, and the physician must be certain that patients do not consent to sterilization under "duress, coercion, or deception."[7] When the procedure is paid for with federal funds, facilities must follow appropriate guidelines.

Nursing Implications/Responsibilities. The perioperative nurse's responsibilities include verifying that an informed consent has been obtained from the patient or guardian and addressing any questions or concerns the patient has before surgery. A note regarding the informed consent should appear in the "Progress Notes" written by the responsible physician.

The signing of a consent is witnessed by an employee identified in the hospital policy. The witness has no responsibility to inform the patient about the treatment, only to verify that the signature is the patient's or the legal guardian's. The witness's signature does not imply that the patient has actually given informed consent.

If the patient seeks additional information or expresses reluctance when asked to sign the consent, the nurse should contact the physician rather than attempt to convince the patient to sign the form. The nurse who discovers that a patient has questions or that the consent is not fully informed has the duty and responsibility to preserve and protect the patient's autonomy in making an informed decision or changing his or her decision. If the physician does not respond, the appropriate supervisor or medical director is notified, and they will determine whether intervention is necessary.

Preoperatively, information on the operative consent must be checked for accuracy. The operative consent should identify the procedure to be performed and the operative side if applicable, and it should contain the physician's name and signatures of the patient or legal guardian and a witness. The dates and times of the signatures must also be present. The perioperative nurse can check the consent for accuracy by comparing the proposed procedure and surgeon listed on the patient's operative consent with the physician's order for the procedure. These data should match the information pasted on the OR schedule. If the patient consent does not match the physician's order and the OR schedule, the nurse must resolve any discrepancy before the patient is sedated. The patient's understanding must be ensured as well as the presence of proper instrumentation, time allocation, and surgical team care plan.[8]

Patient Self-Determination Act

The Patient Self-Determination Act requires that hospital personnel inform patients of their legal rights to make medical care decisions, including the right to accept or refuse surgical treatment and to formulate advance directives. This information must be provided in writing at the time of admission.

Advance Directives

Advance directives include documents such as living wills and durable powers of attorney for health care. The act applies to hospitals, nursing homes, home health care agencies, hospice programs, and health maintenance organizations. It does not apply to free-standing ambulatory or office settings.[9]

Living Wills. Living wills allow individuals to specify their treatment wishes in writing. Subject to statutory limitations, living will laws permit individuals to give instructions concerning the use or withdrawal or artificial life support in end-of-life situations. Living will laws often require the attending physician and an additional physician to certify that the patient's condition is not expected to improve before this advance directive can be implemented.

Durable Power of Attorney. A durable power of attorney for health care provides for the appointment of an agent who is empowered to make medical treatment decisions on behalf of an incapacitated adult. The decisions are made according to the patient's wishes, if known, or in the patient's best interests. The scope of the agent's authority is generally broader than that of a living will and usually is not limited to decisions regarding withdrawal of life-support equipment.[10]

The Right to Refuse Treatment

The right to refuse cardiopulmonary resuscitation (CPR) and other life-sustaining therapy was first acknowledged by the American Medical Association in 1977 with the "do not resuscitate" (DNR) order. A dilemma, however, occurs for the anesthesiologist and the patient coming to the operating room; it may be appropriate to suspend DNR orders during the perioperative period, which is consistent with operating room policy that suspends all preoperative orders while the patient is in surgery. The dilemma occurs because patients are more likely to be resuscitated successfully, with no irreversible damage, if arrest occurs during anesthesia. Second, it is often very difficult to distinguish the temporary adverse effects of anesthetic drugs from the consequences of the patient's disease. Adverse events resulting from drug effects are usually easily reversed; at worst, the patient requires life support only until the drug is metabolized.

The suspension of DNR orders for the perioperative period is best done by consultation with the patient, the physician who wrote the DNR orders, and the attending anesthesiologist.[11] Due to the controversial nature of this directive it is important that the institution have a policy regarding DNR orders for patients requiring invasive procedures and/or anesthetic agents.

▌ INCIDENT REPORT/REPORT OF UNUSUAL OCCURRENCE

An incident is any unusual event; it is not consistent with the routine operation of the hospital or the routine care of a patient. It may be an accident or some circumstance that results in actual or potential bodily injury or property damage. The purpose of the incident report is to communicate to the risk-management office and/or the facility's attorney the facts about the incident which may expose the facility to liability for malpractice, personal injury, or property loss or damage.

Incident reports are completed by the staff and physicians whenever an incident occurs that involves patients, visitors, or employees. Incidents include unexpected outcomes of a treatment, falls or injuries sustained by a patient or visitor, alteration in skin integrity, misuse of equipment or supplies, patients leaving a facility against medical advice (AMA), improper consents, loss or damage of patient's personal belongings, loss of narcotics, incorrect equipment counts, and dissatisfaction expressed by the patient or significant others regarding the delivery of care or system breakdowns, such as delays in service or treatment resulting in actual or potential negative patient outcomes.

Traditionally, the incident report is a narrative format completed by the person having first-hand knowledge of the incident. The events are described chronologically, written as statements of facts without interpretation or opinion. A list of witnesses is included. The report usually requires that the unit manager review the report and identify any follow-up action and/or consequences of the incident. The reports are then routed through the appropriate departments and evaluated to determine whether immediate action is required. If not, they are used for statistical analysis of emerging trends or common factors.

Some institutions have designed a form for specific situations, such as wrong counts or medication errors, to replace the traditional unusual occurrence form. The intent is to identify specific information required for high-risk or frequent occurrences.

Incident reports may be subject to discovery or use in a lawsuit. Whether this occurs depends on the purpose of the reports and the laws of the state where the reports are filed. Generally, if a report is prepared for the hospital's attorney for the purpose of obtaining advice on how to handle the incident, the report is protected by the attorney-client privilege. Information obtained by the attorney in anticipation of or in preparation for litigation is also protected.[1]

Each institution will have a policy specifying how unusual occurrences are to be reported and investigated. Perioperative nurses should be familiar with the policies of each institution in which they practice, as deviations may be significant.

The increased liability affecting nursing has increased the awareness of how mishaps can occur and how to prevent them. Important ways for perioperative nurses to prevent mishaps include mastering the skills and guidelines established by professional organizations, observing departmental policies and procedures, and being familiar with equipment. An alert operating room staff is essential; accepted procedures should not be deviated from, and accurate records must be kept of intraoperative activities.

▌ PROFESSIONAL LIABILITY INSURANCE

Professional liability insurance pays for the cost of defending a claim for damages and for any settlement or jury award of damages. Professional liability coverage for nurses is available through many professional and state nursing associations. An *occurrence* policy provides protection for all acts or omissions that occur during the policy period no matter when a suit is brought. A *claims made* policy provides protection for claims that are made during the policy period, regardless of when the act occurred. Most policies written in the 1990s are *claims made* policies. Perioperative nurses should purchase a *tail* policy to protect them when they retire or leave the profession. Coverage is extended to any claims that may result, even if they are not reported until after the policy period is terminated.

Most perioperative nurses are employed by an institution and covered by that facility's policy. However, the employer's policy covers only those actions that the nurse employee performs within the scope of employment. Scope of employment refers to duties performed within the policies and procedures of the institution, within the nurse's job description, and within the employment setting. As perioperative nurses expand their roles to include the RNFA and complex preoperative physical assessments, it is important that nurses be assured that these roles are covered by the institution's liability policy.

It is possible for nurses to be included in their employer's policy and yet be uninsured for actions outside the scope to employment. It is also possible to be underinsured for the risk involved in a particular specialty area.[12]

▋ ETHICAL ISSUES

Ethics is a system of moral principles or recognized rules of conduct. It is defined as a body of knowledge that deals with the concept of morality and with moral problems.[13]
Universal moral principles include:

- autonomy: self-determination
- beneficience: doing good
- nonmaleficence: avoiding harm, preventing harm
- veracity: truth telling
- confidentiality: respecting privileged information
- justice: treating people fairly
- fidelity: faithfulness to promises, duties

The primary goals and values of a profession are explicit in its code of ethics. The ANA Code for Nurses with Interpretive Statements expresses the moral commitment to uphold the values and special ethical obligations of all nurses in the protection, promotion, and restoration of health or prevention and relief of suffering for the dying patient.[14]

Nursing ethics is defined as the analysis of ethical judgments made by nurses.[15] The study of bioethics and nursing ethics is based on ethical theories, principles, and rules that guide ethical analysis and decision making—universal moral principles. The ethical values common to perioperative nursing are fidelity, accountability, virtue, and caring.[16] Fidelity in this context refers to truth and accuracy, which applies because the patient relies on the perioperative nurse both to render professional nursing care throughout the perioperative period and to be the patient's advocate. The perioperative nurse is also accountable to the patient, since the patient's expectation regarding performance, in effect, imposes an obligation on the nurse. The nurse has an unwritten, unsigned "contract" with the patient and has the responsibility to affect the outcomes of patient care. A number of these ethical principles and values have greater significance in some cultures and countries than in others, and perioperative nurses must include these variances in developing individual patient care plans.

Ethical issues, which are difficult to cope with, have an impact on daily practice. Perioperative nurses face unique moral and ethical situations, including such areas as informed consent (how much information is enough), reproductive technologies, organ and tissue transplantation, confidentiality of information, allocation of scarce resources, withdrawal of life-sustaining treatment/equipment, DNR orders, and the question of refusal to treat HIV-infected patients.

To assist perioperative nurses in making ethical decisions, AORN's Special Committee on Ethics added explications for perioperative nursing to ANA's Code for Nurses (see below). This document provides the framework within which perioperative nurses can make decisions and act on behalf of patients. These decisions and actions are based on universal moral principles, and reflect most fundamentally respect for persons.[17]

■ CODE FOR NURSES: AMERICAN NURSES ASSOCIATION

1. The nurse provides services with respect for human dignity and the uniqueness of the client, unrestricted by considerations of social or economic status, personal attributes, or the nature of health problems.
2. The nurse safeguards the client's right to privacy by judiciously protecting information of a confidential nature.
3. The nurse acts to safeguard the client and the public when health care and safety are affected by incompetent, unethical or illegal practice by any person.
4. The nurse assumes responsibility and accountability for individual nursing judgments and actions.
5. The nurse maintains competence in nursing.
6. The nurse exercises informed judgment and uses individual competency and qualifications as criteria in seeking consultation, accepting responsibilities, and delegating nursing activities.
7. The nurse participates in activities that contribute to the ongoing development of the profession's body of knowledge.
8. The nurse participates in the profession's effort to implement and improve standards of nursing.
9. The nurse participates in the profession's effort to establish and maintain conditions of employment conducive to high-quality nursing care.
10. The nurse participates in the profession's effort to protect the public from misinformation and misrepresentation and to maintain the integrity of nursing.
11. The nurse collaborates with members of the health professions and other citizens in promoting community and national efforts to meet the health needs of the public.

Perioperative nurses can think through ethical problems by asking, "To whom am I most accountable?" Nurses are responsible and accountable for professional standards and must ask the question, "How can I conduct myself professionally to protect my patients from harm?" Maintaining this focus will assist the professional registered nurse in making the right decision at the right time.

▮ REFERENCES

1. Rhodes A, Miller R. *Nursing and the Law, 4th ed.* Rockville, MD: Aspen; 1984:116.
2. Macdonald M et al. *Health Care Law: A Practical Guide, 2nd ed.* New York: Matthew Bender; 1990:11.02(3).
3. Murphy E. Healthcare workers face increasing liability to the driving public. *AORN J.* 1989; 50(6):1320.
4. Murphy E. Legal aspects of whistle-blowing. *AORN J.* 1989; 49(2):482.
5. The Safe Medical Devices Act of 1990. Public Law 101–629.
6. Feutz S. Nursing and the Law. Eau Claire, WI: Professional Education Systems; 1989:39.
7. Southwich A. *The Law of Hospital and Health Care Administration, 2nd ed.* Ann Arbor, MI: Health Administration Press; 1988:441.
8. Newhouse R. Physician, nursing facility implications of informed consent. *AORN J.* 1993; 57(2):508.
9. Murphy E. Advance directives and the patient self-determination act. *AORN J.* 1992;55:270.
10. Fade A. Advance directives: Keeping up with changing legislation. *Today's OR Nurse.* 1994; 16(4)23–26.
11. Martin R. et al. Consistent guidelines to manage patients designated do not resuscitate in the operating room. *Surgical Rounds.* 1993;4:309–311.
12. Kemmy J. Professional liability insurance coverage for perioperative nurses. *AORN J.* 1992; 56(3):526–530.
13. Davis A, Aroskar M. *Ethical Dilemmas and Nursing Practice, 3rd ed.* Norwalk, CT: Appleton & Lange; 1991:1–2.
14. ANA Code for Nurses with Interpretive Statements. Kansas City, MO: American Nurses Association; 1985:4.
15. Veatch R, Fry S. *Case Studies in Nursing Ethics.* Philadelphia: WB Saunders; 1987:1.
16. Reeder J. Secure the future: a model for an international nursing ethic. *AORN J.* 1989;50 (6):1303.
17. ANA code for nurses with interpretive statements—explications for perioperative nursing. In *Standards and Recommended Practices.* Denver: AORN; 1995:39.

Implementation of Perioperative Nursing Practice

■ PERIOPERATIVE NURSING PROCESS

Perioperative nursing practice is based on Schlotfeldt's definition of nursing:

> Nursing is an independent, autonomous, self-regulating profession with the primary function that of helping each person attain his highest possible level of general health. The practice of nursing focuses on assessing people's health status, assets and deviations from health, and on helping sick people to regain health, and the well or near-well to maintain or attain health through selective application of nursing science and use of available nursing strategies.[1]

Perioperative nursing, as stated earlier, involves the preoperative, intraoperative, and postoperative phases of the surgical patient's experience. Operating room nurses enter the specialty at a basic competency level and gradually increase their level of excellence with additional decision making, knowledge, skills, and education (Fig. 5–1).

The nurse interacts with the preoperative patient in the admission area and surgical unit and, postoperatively, with the patient in the home or clinic setting (Table 5–1). During the intraoperative phase, nursing activities are confined to the location of the invasive procedure. Essential to the continuity of care is the nurse's collaboration with the patient about his or her needs and then assisting and supporting the patient to meet those needs.

The nursing process is a systematic approach to nursing practice using problem-solving techniques. It is a dynamic and continuous process. To effectively implement the six components of the nursing process—assessment, diagnosis, outcome identification, planning, implementation, and evaluation—perioperative nurses should:

- base nursing practice on principles and theories of biophysical, physiological, behavioral, and social sciences
- extend the geographical boundaries for operating room nursing practice beyond the surgical suite
- continuously update knowledge and skills by applying new knowledge generated by research and by changes in the health care delivery system and patient populations

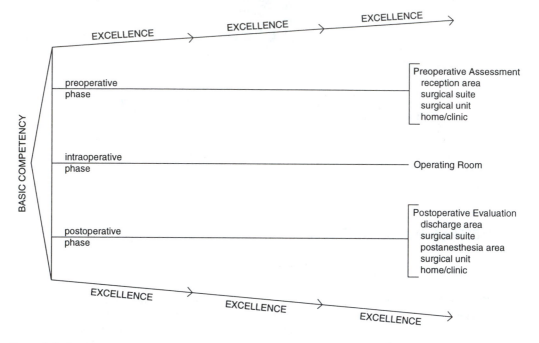

Figure 5–1. Perioperative nursing practice: a continuum. (*From 1994 Standards and Recommended Practices. Denver: AORN. 1994:61.*)

- determine the plan of care by considering the patient's needs, the nurse's competence, and the resources available
- ensure patient and family participation in identifying needs, assessing nursing intervention outcome, and determining perception of surgery

The nursing process framework was used to develop the "Standards of Perioperative Clinical Practice" (Table 5–2). The standards are used to measure the quality of perioperative nursing practice. Inclusion of the nursing process expands the focus from task orientation to a dynamic professional specialty that uses theories and concepts derived from the biologic, natural, and behavioral sciences.

▌COMPETENCY MODEL

AORN used the nursing process as the framework for a Competency Model for perioperative nursing practice.[2] The model can be used to gain information about:

- position descriptions
- performance appraisals

TABLE 5–1. EXAMPLES OF NURSING ACTIVITIES IN PERIOPERATIVE NURSING PRACTICE

Preoperative Phase	Intraoperative Phase	Postoperative Phase

Preoperative assessment
Home/clinic
1. Initiates initial preoperative assessment
2. Plans teaching methods appropriate to patient's needs
3. Involves family in interview
Surgical unit
1. Completes preoperative assessment
2. Coordinates patient teaching with other nursing staff
3. Explains phases in perioperative period and expectations
4. Develops a plan of care
Surgical suite
1. Assesses patient's level of consciousness
2. Reviews chart
3. Identifies patient
4. Verifies surgical site
 	
Planning
1. Determines a plan of care
 	
Psychological support
1. Tells patient what is happening
2. Determines psychological status
3. Gives prior warning of noxious stimuli
4. Communicates patient's emotional status to other appropriate members of the health care team
	Maintenance of safety
	1. Assures that the sponge, needle, and instrument counts are correct
	2. Positions the patient
	  a. Functional alignment
	  b. Exposure of surgical site
	  c. Maintenance of position throughout procedure
	3. Applies grounding device to patient
	4. Provides physical support
	Physiological monitoring
	1. Calculates effects on patient of excessive fluid loss
	2. Distinguishes normal from abnormal cardiopulmonary data
	3. Reports changes in patient's pulse, respirations, temperature, and blood pressure
	
	Psychological monitoring
	(prior to induction and if patient conscious)
	1. Provides emotional support to patient
	2. Stands near/touches patient during procedures/induction
	3. Continues to assess patient's emotional status
	4. Communicates patient's emotional status to other appropriate members of the health care team
	Nursing management
	1. Provides physical safety for the patient
	2. Maintains aseptic, controlled environment
	3. Effectively manages human resources
		Communication of intraoperative information
		1. Gives patient's name
		2. States type of surgery performed
		3. Provides contributing intraoperative factors (i.e., drain, catheters)
		4. States physical limitations
		5. States impairments resulting from surgery
		6. Reports patient's preoperative level of consciousness
		7. Communicates necessary equipment needs
		Postoperative evaluation
		Recovery area
		1. Determines patient's immediate response to surgical intervention
		Surgical unit
		1. Evaluates effectiveness of nursing care in the OR
		2. Determines patient's level of satisfaction with care given during perioperative period
		3. Evaluates products used on patient in the OR
		4. Determines patient's psychological status
		5. Assists with discharge planning
		Home/clinic
		1. Seeks patient's perception of surgery in terms of the effects of anesthetic agents, impact on body image, distortion, immobilization
		2. Determines family's perceptions of surgery

From *A model for perioperative nursing practice, 1994 Standards and Recommended Practices.* Denver: Assoc. Operating Room Nurses; 1994:60.

- staff orientation and development
- peer review
- clinical ladders
- developing standards of care
- developing departmental policies and procedures
- outlining courses for generic curriculum
- monitoring accountability in the care of a surgical patient (quality assurance)
- preparing for certification/recertification exam

TABLE 5–2. STANDARDS OF PERIOPERATIVE CLINICAL PRACTICE

Standard I
The perioperative nurse collects patient health data
Standard II
The perioperative nurse analyzes the assessment data in determining diagnoses
Standard III
The perioperative nurse identifies expected outcomes unique to the patient
Standard IV
The perioperative nurse develops a plan of care that prescribes interventions to attain expected outcomes
Standard V
The perioperative nurse implements the interventions identified in the plan of care
Standard VI
The perioperative nurse evaluates the patient's progress toward attainment of outcomes

From Standards of Perioperative Clinical Practice. 1994 Standards and Recommended Practices. Denver: Assoc. Operating Room Nurses; 1994: 91–93. Used with permission.

In the model (see Appendix H), 18 competency statements are listed along with criteria for measuring each competency. Examples provided in the competency statement, although not comprehensive, are suggestions for how the criteria, or expected behaviors, can be accomplished and documented.[3]

Basic competencies are expected of all practicing perioperative nurses and should be attained within a specific time frame, such as 6 to 12 months. After meeting these expectations perioperative nurses progress to become advanced- and expert-level practitioners.

The perioperative advanced practice nurse (APN) is a registered nurse with a graduate degree in nursing and specialized knowledge and skills in the care of clients and families undergoing operative and invasive procedures. The following illustrates one particular competency of the perioperative APN. A complete listing appears in the advanced practice competency statement (see Appendix I).

- The perioperative APN conducts comprehensive health assessments and demonstrates autonomy and skill in diagnosing and treating complex responses of clients (patient, family, and community) to actual and potential health problems related to the operative or other related procedures.
- The perioperative APN formulates clinical decisions to manage acute and chronic illness by assessment, diagnosis, and prescribing treatment modalities, including pharmacological agents.
- The perioperative APN promotes wellness.
- The perioperative APN integrates clinical practice, education, research management, leadership, and consultation into a single role.
- The perioperative APN functions in a collegial relationship with other nurses, physicians, and others who influence the health environment.[4]

▌ PHASES OF THE PERIOPERATIVE ROLE

The preoperative phase begins when the patient is scheduled for surgery and ends when anesthesia is induced. Then the intraoperative period begins; it ends when the patient is transported to the recovery room or to the inpatient unit if the recovery room is not required. Finally, the postoperative period extends through the recovery period to a follow-up home or clinic visit.

Preoperative Phase

During the preoperative phase, the perioperative nurse assesses the patient to collect data that will be used in making judgments and predictions about the patient's response to illness or changes in the life processes (Fig. 5–2). The assessment may be done in the admission area, surgical suite, surgical inpatient unit, clinic, physician's office, patient's home, or on the telephone. The assessment is critical in establishing a nursing diagnosis and predicting outcomes of nursing intervention.

When assessment is performed in the preoperative area or surgical suite, the information obtained is entered in the patient's record and discussed with the surgeon, the anesthetist, and the patient. Information is limited due to the patient's medication and the time available. When preoperative assessment is performed outside the confines of the surgical suite or on the telephone, however, the nurse has an opportunity not only to collect data but to provide information to the patient and family about the surgical experience.

Preoperative assessment includes collecting data, formulating nursing diagnoses, identifying expected outcomes, and documenting findings.

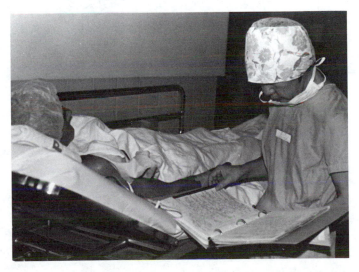

Figure 5–2. Perioperative nurses can collect information about the patient immediately prior to surgical intervention by reviewing the chart and talking with the patient.

Collecting Data. Initially, the perioperative nurse collects baseline data about the patient that will be used to develop an individual care plan. Subjective and objective data will assist in evaluating the patient's responses throughout the perioperative period.

Sources of data include the patient's record, other health team members, the patient's family or close friends, and the patient. Data is obtained from the patient by means of interview, observation, and examination. If the patient's record is available, the perioperative nurse reviews the nursing history, medical history (including surgical), laboratory data, diagnostic studies, surgical consent, current medications, allergies, and progress notes (Fig. 5–3).

The nurse relates the data collected to the proposed surgical procedure. Discussions with other personnel, such as the team leader or the primary care nurse, may reveal additional information about the patient, including his or her response to hospitalization and the impending surgical procedure. An interview with the patient and family permits the nurse to validate or clarify information obtained from other sources. In addition, during an interview the nurse may learn from the patient or observe signs and symptoms of anxiety. Cognitive, motor, and physiologic indications of anxiety are listed below.

During an interview, the perioperative nurse assesses the patient's perceptions and expectations of the surgical experience. The nurse establishes an environment of trust and support, thereby enabling the patient to express concerns and questions about the impending surgery. Open-ended questions facilitate dialogue with patients and their families. Appropriate questions are:

- What is your understanding of the surgical procedure?
- You said you were upset about surgery tomorrow. Would you like to tell me about it?

Figure 5–3. Reviewing the chart on the surgical unit provides a more accurate assessment of the patient.

- I hear frustration in your voice. Would you like to talk about it?
- You say you're concerned about your family. What do you mean?

The questions should be clear, brief, simple, logical, and purposeful and presented on the patient's level of understanding.

The nurse must also be alert to nonverbal communication, which may provide information about the patient's psychosocial condition. In addition, nonverbal communication may modify or contradict what the patient is saying and give clues to unexplained emotions. Nonverbal communication may consist of facial expressions, body gestures, muscle tension, rate of breathing, and tone of voice.

During preoperative assessment the nurse focuses on the following factors as they relate to the surgical experience: sociocultural status, mental-emotional status, physical assessment, and educational needs of the patient.

Sociocultural Status. The sociocultural assessment includes, but is not limited to, the following patient data:

- language barriers/patterns of communication
- cultural superstitions associated with illness, specifically surgical intervention
- spiritual requirements, i.e., visit by clergy, religious mementos, concerns about death
- use or abuse of alcohol and/or other drugs
- ethnicity
- sexuality
- occupation
- economic concerns
- family, friends, significant others, i.e., their location, whether they will be a source of support or a patient responsibility during recovery, and what they see as the role and responsibility of professional care givers

The United States is experiencing an influx of refugees, and attention must be given to the issues of cultural diversity and their implications for nursing care. Concepts important to cross-cultural nursing care are listed in Table 5–3.

The complex whole of culture includes the knowledge, beliefs, art, morals, laws, customs, and other capabilities and habits acquired by members of a society. A culture represents ways of perceiving, behaving, and evaluating the world. Culture is learned, beginning at birth, by means of language acquisition and socialization. It is an adaptation to specific environmental conditions, yet it is a dynamic, ever-changing process.[5]

A culture defines diet, language, communication patterns, religion, history, family life process (e.g., sexuality, child rearing, health care practices, rituals of life and death), social interactive patterns, and values.

An ethnic group is a social group within a cultural and social system that has particular traits, including religious, linguistic, and ancestral.[6] Examples of the hundreds of ethnic groups in the United States are Hawaiians and persons of German, Italian, or African descent.

Everyone living in America belongs to the American culture, *and* they belong to subcultures. Examples of subcultures are the Amish, Mennonites, and Gypsies.

Transcultural (ethnic) nursing care is the nurse's effective integration of the patient's ethnic cultural background into the nursing process. Table 5–3 will assist the nurse in planning cross-cultural care.

Family Support. Family support and involvement in patient care are associated with successful patient coping and crisis resolution. The specific needs of families during hospitalization must be included in the perioperative nurse's plan of care. Informational needs were found by Carmody and coworkers to be of the highest priority among families in the perioperative period. They reported that a family needs to:

- speak with the surgeon once surgery is completed
- know the probable outcome of the patient's illness
- know what to do to help the patient after surgery
- know beforehand what to expect on the day of surgery
- have explanations given in terms that are understandable
- feel that hospital personnel care about the patient[7]

Silva identified that among spouses whose mates had had major surgery, the experience produced:

- moderate to high anxiety
- altered time perceptions during the intraoperative phase
- disruption in lifestyle
- feelings of isolation from the health care team[8]

Families provide better support for patients if they are well informed about the patient's disease, are coping with the stressors of hospitalization and surgery, and are not experiencing a personal crisis. Support provided to families by perioperative nurses can prevent the onset of a crisis event that may have a negative impact on the patient's recovery. Two essential components of perioperative nursing competency are including the family in the preoperative assessment phase and providing a family waiting area where the circulating nurse or surgical nurse liaison may telephone with reports about the surgery. A family waiting area also provides a consistent location where the surgeon may find the family.

Mental and Emotional Status. Surgical intervention is stressful; therefore, assessing the mental and emotional status of a surgical patient has particular significance. Patients experience and express anxiety in many ways. Their motor activity may change and they may tremble or they may have cognitive changes, such as an exaggerated startle response or inability to concentrate. Anxiety may also be manifested in physiologic signs and symptoms, such as shortness of breath or a feeling of being smothered. Anxiety may be based on an incomplete understanding of a procedure and consequently, exaggerated fears. Patients should be encouraged to ask questions about the invasive procedure, and perioperative nurses must answer in terms the patient can understand. The nurse may need to repeat and rephrase information until the patient comprehends and retains it.

(*Text continued on page 97*)

TABLE 5-3. CULTURAL VARIATIONS RELATED TO HEALTH CARE*

Ethnic/Culture Group	Social Network	Nutritional Patterns	Health Beliefs and Practices	Folk Medicine and Healers	Unique Illnesses
Afro-Americans	Strong kinship bonds; several generations may live in one household. Strong religious beliefs. This is an important source of psychological support in dealing with stresses associated with illness.	"Soul food" named from a feeling of kinship among the Afro-Americans. Salt pork as a seasoning is key to vegetables, especially black-eyed peas, chicken and pork. Food is usually boiled or fried.	Relates to Afro-American belief about life and nature of being. God sends illness as punishment for sin. Life is a process rather than a state. All things living or dead influence each other. Health is harmony with nature, whereas illness is a state of disharmony. Traditional Afro-Americans view health, mind, body and spirit as one entity.	Roots, herbs, potions, oils, powders, tokens and rituals are important. Predominately "self-treatment" is used under the direction of the "old lady" spiritualist, voodoo priest and root doctors.	Sickle cell anemia, hypertension, dermatities (keloids, vitiligo), socioenvironmental diseases
Latin-Americans	Close family ties. Courtesy and respect shown toward elderly and adults. Value modesty and privacy. Retain first language and take pride in speaking and reading Spanish. All family members must approve surgical procedures.	Food is a form of socialization and consists of what they can afford. Usually corn, beans, potatoes, rice, green bananas, and chilies.	Family planning is not discussed and birth control is not used. Diseases are related to spiritual punishment, hot/cold imbalances, witchcraft, dislocation of human organs, natural disease and mental/emotional origin. They use herbs and prayers to promote wellness.	Use herbs and potions as stimulants. Copper bracelets used to treat rheumatoid arthritis. Folk healers are (Curandero) spiritualist, folk chiropractors, midwives, and herbalist.	Anemia in females Parasites, lactose intolerance, lead poisoning, tuberculosis, diabetes, obesity, and high infant mortality related to malnutrition

(continued)

*Author's Notes.

91

TABLE 5–3. *(Continued)*

Ethnic/Culture Group	Social Network	Nutritional Patterns	Health Beliefs and Practices	Folk Medicine and Healers	Unique Illnesses
Filipino Americans	Family has high value. Interdependency among family members stressed. Resources pooled with entire family. Children encouraged to develop modesty, industry and respect toward elderly. Family in constant company of ill member.	Hot and cold concepts influence diets. Mothers believe that what they eat affects their baby's health. Diet is influenced by religion. Rice, fish, and vegetables are staples.	Diseases attributed to natural and supernatural causes. Overwork, excessive exposure to cold heat, rain, anxiety, excessive eating and poor living conditions contribute to illness. Curses come from spirits, dead, witches, evil people. Must suffer in silence.	Flushing, heating, and protection are important concepts. Flushing is to rid the body of debris. Heating means that hot and cold in the body must balance. Religious articles are worn to drive evil forces away.	Hyperuricemia, Coccidioidomycosis Cardiovascular-renal disease Diabetes mellitus Tuberculosis Cancer of the liver
American Indian	Extended family very important and has economic as well as a social function. Family plays a significant role during illness. Many tribes are matrilineal and this requires that decisions for surgery or treatment be discussed with the elder female family members. Medical pluralism. Seek physician for immediate cause of illness and native healer for ultimate cause.	Corn, squash, and beans. Corn is used in religious ceremonies. Navajo women drink blue cornmeal gruel after childbirth. They believe that it will increase the supply of milk. Food restrictions are frequently followed for 1 year after delivery of a child. Some individuals do not eat certain foods for cultural and religious reasons.	Health is defined as a person's state of harmony with nature and the universe. If an individual harms himself, he also harms the earth. Forces that prevent individuals from achieving harmony put them in a vulnerable and unhealthy state. All ailments have a supernatural aspect. Many individuals carry objects to guard against witchcraft. Technical medicine is not part of harmony. In death, save all body parts, including umbilical cord, so body passes on in its entirety.	There are 6 types of medicine men: 1. Positive role: can transform self into another from 2. Good & evil: can perform negative acts against the enemy 3. Diviner and diagnosticians: can diagnose, define cause, and indicate cure but cannot implement treatment 4. Specialist medicine person: can implement treatment 5. Care for the soul: takes care of the spiritual needs	High infant mortality Trachoma Tuberculosis Alcoholism Diabetes mellitus Liver disease Heart disease

| Chinese Americans | Close family ties with extended family are very prevalent. Traditionalists have a tendency to cluster around Chinatown. Chinese heritage is preserved. Children are taught to respect elders and have filial piety toward parents. Women are taught to keep their place in the family. They are not an asset but a liability to the family. | Rice, tofu, soup, and Chinese vegetables. Food is usually stirfried. Soy sauce is used as condiment. | Chinese medicine is based on the theory of Yin/Yang and the 5 elements. Healing is aimed at reestablishing the balance. Health practices emphasize moderation to avoid excesses that bring on illness. The concept of disease is based on wind and poison. Wind enters the body and causes illness. Poison is used to describe disease conditions. | 6. Singers: cure by song and laying on of hands

Herbalists, acupuncturists, and bone setters are all important. Herbs are used to balance the body and prevent illnesses. Soups and teas are used to increase energy, sedate the "hot" condition, and tone the "cold" condition. | Lactase intolerance
Alcohol intolerance
Tuberculosis
Dermatitis |
| Japanese Americans | The individual is seen in relation to the group. The extended family includes the work group, neighborhood and community. Behaviors and all aspects of life are interwoven within the group. | Tea, fish, vegetables beef, pork, and poultry. Soy sauce, monosodium glutamate and miso sauce are used as condiments. Diet is low in total fat, cholesterol, animal protein and sugar; high in CHO and salt. Very rich in linoleic acid. | Disease is thought to be caused by individual coming into contact with polluting agents such as blood, corpses, and skin diseases. Herbal purgatives are used to cleanse the body. Health is achieved through harmony and balance between self and society. | Acupuncture, acupressure, massage and moxibustion are used to restore the flow of energy by the use of needles, pressure, or heat at strategic locations along the affected meridians. Natural herbs are also used to help restore equilibrium to the body. | Alcohol intolerance
Lactase deficiency
Hypertension
CVA
Cancer of the esophagus, stomach, liver and biliary system
Ulcers
Colitis
Psoriasis |

(continued)

TABLE 5–3. *(Continued)*

Ethnic/Culture Group	Social Network	Nutritional Patterns	Health Beliefs and Practices	Folk Medicine and Healers	Unique Illnesses
	Outsiders are not brought in to help solve problems as the group feels responsible for the members. Worship ancestors and think about the past.		Disharmony with society or not taking care of the body results in disease.		
Vietnamese Americans	Strong family-centered culture. Emphasis on harmony in social relations. Family interests are first over individuals. There is no word for "I" in their language. Kinship system is patrilineal but females are not relegated to a low status; they share in major decisions.	Rice and fish cooked in pungent sauce called nuoc man. Vegetables, fruits, spices, noodle soups, sweets made from rice gluten and coconut. Drinking during meals is rare. Naps follow the noon meal.	Diseases are caused by natural and physical phenomena. Belief that life has been predisposed toward certain events by cosmic forces; therefore, they use astrology and fortune telling to determine these forces. They also believe that mental illnesses are caused by bad spirits that must be exorcised by a sorcerer. Concept of Yin/Yang is also important.	Health depends on maintaining a balance of bodily elements. Cure is dependent on restoring the balance. Foods and illness are believed to be related to hot and cold. Women avoid eating some hot and cold foods during pregnancy so the body's balance is not disturbed and they will not be susceptible to illness. They also avoid visiting shrines believed to be inhabited by bad spirits due to affects on the unborn child.	Tuberculosis Intestinal parasites Anemia Malnutrition Skin diseases Malaria Hepatitis Dental problems

Gypsies	Highly seasoned. High in salt and sugar. Meats high in fat (pork/beef). Tobacco use high.	Hospitalization very turbulent—fear of being away from other Gypsies. Therefore, members gather to support the sick. Hospitals are considered to be polluted. Seek "important" (well-known) physicians. Distrust in "free" clinics. Family elders may try to shield patient from facts of illness. When death occurs they freely scream, pull out clumps of hair, and hurl their bodies against the wall and floor. Refuse autopsy.	Healers are generalists or specialists. Generalists have powers from supreme being. They use talismans, magic cloths, prayers and Sino-Vietnamese medical practices. Specialist treat certain ailments and particular patients. Wise female is the elder administrator. Complex set of values containing evil spirits and demons. Special saints are for good luck. Traditional remedies are administered with a ceremony and include: • Mold/algae for hemorrhage or epilepsy • Love potions of menstrual blood • Alopecia ointment of hog lard and chryscrobin • Garlic compresses • Tea with crushed strawberries	Hypertension Diabetes Occlusive coronary or peripheral vascular diseases Elevated triglycerides or cholesterol Obesity
Romany language spoken. Close-knit family and ethnic unit. Extended families live together. Marriage between second cousins is ideal. After marriage couple lives with groom's parents. First-born grandson raised by paternal grandparents. Strong wanderlust contributes to lack of formal education. Maintain private society with an internal moral code and legal system. Home dominated by male. Woman's role to encounter outside world.				

(continued)

TABLE 5–3. *(Continued)*

Ethnic/Culture Group	Social Network	Nutritional Patterns	Health Beliefs and Practices	Folk Medicine and healers	Unique Illnesses
	Very distrustful of non-Gypsies (Gaje).		Very wary of medical personnel; will change physicians frequently if experience is unfavorable. "Crisis care": use emergency facilities freely. Poor preventive or follow-up care. Share medications with family. Few immunizations or pre-natal care. Body below waist is considered "polluted," especially women. Menstruating women may not prepare food. Upper body is "pure." Measles called "God's Rose."		

Anxiety reactions range from mild nervousness to panic. *Mild anxiety* usually results in heightened sensitivity to environmental stimuli and an overall alertness. *Moderate anxiety* may be marked by decreased attentiveness and physical signs such as tremulousness, sweating palms, dry mouth, and restlessness. *Severe anxiety* can disturb thought processes and one's ability to make decisions and act. *Panic* usually refers to severe, acute anxiety; signs and symptoms include rapid heart rate, palpitations, shortness of breath, dizziness, gastrointestinal upset, fear of dying, or a feeling of unreality.[8]

The following is a useful checklist of signs and symptoms of anxiety:

Cognitive
- Difficulty in concentrating
- Feeling "on edge"
- Insomnia
- Irritability
- Poor eye contact
- Startle response, exaggerated

Motor
- Fatigue
- Movements extraneous
    Foot shuffling
    Hand/arm movements
- Pacing
- Restlessness
- Speech
    Stuttering
    Rapid
    Voice quivering
- Trembling, twitching, feeling shaky

Physiological
- Chills
- Dry mouth
- Dizziness or lightheadedness
- Flushed appearance
- Frequent urination
- Gastrointestinal upset
- Hot flashes
- Palpitations or increased heart rate
- Pupil dilation
- Shortness of breath, feeling of being smothered
- Sweating or clammy hands

In communicating with anxious patients, nonverbal behavior is very important. A calm, interested, helpful perioperative nurse who listens empathetically and offers appropriate reassurance is frequently the most effective treatment for a patient's anxiety.

Identifying a patient's preoperative status establishes an appropriate data base to compare the patient's mental status postoperatively.

- Mental status: Is the patient alert, drowsy, disoriented, semiconscious, comatose?
- Orientation: How is the patient oriented to time, people, place?
- Level of anxiety: Is the patient short of breath, sweating, agitated?
- Coping mechanisms: How is the patient coping verbally and nonverbally?
- Concept of body image: Is rejection of body possible due to impending surgery?
- Relationships: What are the patients relationships with family, friends, and members of the health care team?

Physical Assessment. Physical assessment includes observing the patient's appearance; it may require a systematic "hands-on" examination. Areas of concern include, but are not limited to, the following assessments:

Mobility/Limitations

- Skeletal
    Limited range of joint motion
    Joint replacement
    Amputations
    Prosthesis
    External fixation devices (casts, traction)
- Muscular
    Paralysis
    Muscle tone
    Neurological reflexes
    Contracture

Sensory Impairments (Identify Bilateral or Unilateral)

- Acuity of vision
    Glasses
    Contact lens
    Glaucoma
    Blind
    Unusual discharge
- Acuity of hearing
    Hearing aid
    Lip reading
    Sign language
    Unusual discharges
- Speech patterns
    Aphasic
    Hoarseness
    Tracheostomy
    Laryngectomy
- Areas of tactile concern

Paresthesia
Hyperesthesia
Anesthesia
Pain

Cardiopulmonary Status. Assessment of cardiopulmonary status has nursing implications for all surgical patients in regard to their transport and positioning preoperatively and postoperatively. Assessment of cardiopulmonary status has additional specific implications for the cardiovascular patient:

- Vital signs
- Labile pressure
- Quality of pulses
- Quality of breath sounds
- Perfusion to extremities
- Pacemaker present
- Angina
- Arrhythmias
- Cyanosis
- Syncope
- Edema
- Dyspnea
- Orthopnea
- Cough (productive or nonproductive)
- Smoking history
- Respiratory obstruction (pharyngeal or pulmonary)
- Endotracheal tube
- Pressure lines

Gastrointestinal Status

- Nausea or vomiting
- Gastritis
- Nasogastric tube
- Gastrostomy
- Bowel incontinence
- Ileostomy
- Colostomy

Genitourinary Status

- Bladder incontinence
- Urinary catheter
- Suprapubic catheter
- Ureteral catheter
- Anuria

- Oliguria
- Kidney transplant
- Dialysis
- Nephrostomy
- Ureterostomy
- Ureteral or vaginal discharge

Metabolic-Endocrine Dysfunction

- Diabetes
- Hypoglycemia
- Adrenal
- Pituitary
- Thermal regulatory

Nutritional Status

- Time of last food or fluid intake
- Body structure and size
- Dietary customs
- Current nutritional status
- Fluid and electrolyte status

Skin and Appendages

- Color
- Turgor
- Temperature
- Integrity
- Rashes
- Abrasions
- Bruises
- Infection

Immunologic Status

- Total lymphocyte count
- Allergic reactions to
  Food
  Environmental agents
  Blood transfusions
  Anesthetic agents
  Medication

Information Needs. During an interview with the patient, the perioperative nurse explains the preoperative, intraoperative, and postoperative routines associated with the impending surgical procedure (Table 5–4). In addition, the nurse assesses the patient's knowledge

TABLE 5–4. GUIDELINES FOR PREOPERATIVE ASSESSMENT

1. Introduce yourself
2. Identify for the patient the purpose of the assessment
   a. To obtain information that will be helpful in planning care in the operating room
   b. To answer questions and concerns about the surgical experience
3. Determine the patient's general knowledge of the intended surgery and the need or desire for additional or supplemental information
4. Explain the routine for the day of surgery
   a. Absence of food or fluid
   b. Premedication
   c. Time to arrive at the hospital
   d. Transportation to operating room (i.e., time and mode)
   e. Location and anticipated length of wait prior to being taken into the operating room
   f. Special skin preparations
5. Familiarize the patient with what he or she will see and experience in the operating room
   a. Operating room lights and table
   b. Accessory equipment
   c. Temperature of the room
   d. Intravenous fluids
   e. Blood pressure cuff
   f. Electrocardiogram monitoring
6. Tell the patient, family, and significant others
   a. Time to arrive at the hospital
   b. Where they should wait during surgery
   c. Restaurant facilities
   d. Anticipated length of time in the operating room and the recovery room
7. Explain the postanesthesia care
   a. Location of PACU
   b. Purpose of the PACU
   c. Routines of postanesthesia care (i.e., vital signs, checking dressings)
   d. Identify anticipated dressings, drains, catheters, packs, casts, traction
   e. Time and date of postoperative appointment
8. Discuss any relevant physical problems with the patient to determine the focus of the intraoperative care plan (visual or hearing alterations, joint or muscle immobility)
9. Discuss postoperative activities and identify teaching and learning needs
10. Formulate a written assessment and individual nursing care plan
    a. Discuss relevant information with the unit nurse
    b. Make an entry on the patient's chart that a preoperative assessment was completed
    c. Formulate a nursing diagnosis, identify expected outcome, and plan nursing interventions
11. Other considerations
    a. Establish an atmosphere of confidence and a climate of acceptance
    b. Give the patient ample opportunity to ask questions or verbalize concerns
    c. Be aware of nonverbal communication
    d. Allow the patient to decide if family or significant others should remain during the interview
    e. Avoid conflict, judgment, or instilling false encouragement
    f. Determine the patient's level of comprehension and use appropriate language; avoid jargon
    g. Write individual care plan after leaving patient

deficits. What is the patient's understanding of the proposed surgical procedure? What is the patient's ability to verbalize questions, concerns, and needs? What additional teaching and learning needs does the patient have?

Preoperative teaching of the ambulatory surgical patient helps the patient to perceive that the facility is concerned with his or her well-being; hence, the patient is more likely to comply with preoperative routines. Preoperative education helps patients and families to manage stress and apprehension that they may be experiencing. It also provides information about postoperative activities and how to cope with potential and actual problems after returning home.

In addition to one-on-one instruction, many facilities conduct tours of the unit. Role-playing with pediatric, elderly, and mentally or physically handicapped patients is a very effective method of education. Booklets and audiovisual materials written at the eighth-grade level are also excellent tools to assist with the teaching and learning process of all surgical patients.

Formulating a Nursing Diagnosis. After data are collected, the nurse analyzes it and sorts out what information is pertinent to the surgical experience. Then, based on the interpretation of data concerning the patient's needs and health status, the nurse formulates one or more nursing diagnoses.

A nursing diagnosis is a clinical judgment about individual, family, or community responses to actual or potential health problems/life processes. It is derived from collected data and is the basis for selecting the nursing interventions directed to achieve outcomes for which the nurse is accountable. A patient problem is actual or a potential risk. Actual, or concrete, diagnoses reflect an alteration in the patient's functioning, and nursing actions must be planned and implemented to assist the patient during the perioperative period. For example, a patient's response to the perioperative experience may be altered by deafness, joint immobility, or inability to speak English.

Risk Factors. A nursing diagnosis may identify a patient at risk for problems that do not actually exist but may develop in a vulnerable individual or family member. The diagnosis is supported by risk factors that contribute to increased vulnerability. The risk factors appear to have a patterned relationship with the nursing diagnosis. They are described as *associated with, related to,* or *contributing to.* Appropriate nursing actions can modify, or diminish, the risk. Examples of risk factors that may be modified by nursing intervention are:

- Impaired skin integrity related to use of an electrosurgical unit
- Positioning injury related to immobilization and/or anesthesia
- Anxiety reaction related to change in health status/fear of surgery, etc.
- Fluid volume deficit associated with excessive blood loss

Currently accepted nursing diagnoses that have particular relevance for the surgical patient are listed below. For easy reference, the list may be written on 3-by-5 cards or on the back page of the nursing documentation record.

- Activity Intolerance
- Adjustment, Impaired

- Airway Clearance, Ineffective
- Anxiety
- Body Temperature, Risk for Altered
- Bowel Incontinence
- Cardiac Output, Decreased
- Communication, Impaired Verbal
- Confusion, Acute
- Confusion, Chronic
- Coping, Defensive, Ineffective
- Denial, Ineffective
- Dysreflexia
- Energy Field Disturbance
- Environmental Interpretation Syndrome, Impaired
- Family Coping: Compromised, Disabling, Ineffective
- Family Process: Alcoholism, Altered
- Fear
- Fluid Volume Excess or Deficit, Risk for
- Gas Exchange, Impaired
- Grieving, Anticipatory, Dysfunctional
- Growth and Development, Altered
- Hopelessness
- Incontinence, Functional, Reflex, Stress, Total, Urge
- Infection, Risk for
- Injury, Risk for
- Knowledge Deficit (specify)
- Management of Therapeutic Regimen:
  Families: ineffective
  Individual: ineffective, noncompliance (specify)
- Memory, Impaired
- Nutrition, Altered
  Less than body requirements
  More than body requirements
- Oral Mucous Membrane, Altered
- Pain, Chronic
- Parental Role, Conflict
- Perioperative Positioning Injury, Risk for
- Peripheral Neurovascular Dysfunction, Risk for
- Physical Mobility, Impaired
- Powerlessness
- Self-Care Deficit
  Bathing/Hygiene
  Feeding
  Dressing/Grooming
  Toileting
- Self-Esteem, Chronic Low, Situational Low, Disturbance

- Sensory/Perceptual Alterations
- Sexuality Patterns, Altered
- Skin Integrity, Impaired
- Skin Integrity, Risk for Impaired
- Spiritual Distress
- Sustain Spontaneous Ventilation, Inability to
- Swallowing, Impaired
- Thermoregulation, Ineffective
  Hypothermia
  Hyperthermia
- Thought Processes, Altered
- Tissue Integrity, Impaired
- Tissue Perfusion, Altered
- Urinary Elimination, Altered
- Urinary Retention

Asking questions of the patient, family, or other health care providers may help to validate a diagnosis. The nurse may consider the following questions:

- Is the data base sufficient, accurate, and developed from some concept of nursing?
- Does the synthesis of data demonstrate a pattern?
- Is the nursing diagnosis based on scientific nursing knowledge and clinical expertise?
- Does the nursing diagnosis lend itself to independent nursing actions?
- Would other qualified practitioners formulate the same nursing diagnosis based on the data?

Formulating Patient Outcomes. After nursing diagnoses are formulated, the perioperative nurse identifies the desired patient response or outcome specific to the actual or potential problem. The patient, his or her significant others, and the perioperative nurse collaborate to identify expected outcomes. The outcomes, derived from the diagnoses, are specific and have a time frame for achievement. They must also be attainable and include measurable criteria to determine if the expected outcome is a result of the nursing interventions.

After the outcomes are identified, they are prioritized, communicated to the appropriate team members, and documented.

Factors that may be considered when formulating outcomes are:

- Absence of infection
- Maintenance of skin integrity
- Absence of adverse effects through proper use of safety measures related to positioning, extraneous objects, and chemical, physical, and electrical hazards
- Maintenance of fluid and electrolyte balance
- The knowledge that the patient and significant others have of the physiologic and psychologic responses to surgical intervention
- Participation of the patient and significant others in the rehabilitation process

Long-term goals reflect the maximum level of health the patient will be able to achieve, and they reflect the nursing activities that will occur over a long period. Examples of long-term goals for the surgical patient are:

- Establish a positive self-image, e.g., following amputation of a leg, radical mastectomy, laryngectomy
- Verbalize concerns and feelings about change in lifestyle, e.g., following abdominoperineal resection, coronary artery bypass, gastric resection

Documentation. The fourth and final step of assessment is documentation. It is essential that the nursing diagnosis be recorded as well as relevant data obtained from the patient, the record, and other health care team members. That information will provide a framework for the next step of the nursing process—planning patient care.

Documentation is critical in all phases of the perioperative role; therefore, it will be discussed in detail at the end of this chapter.

Developing a Plan of Care. The perioperative nurse is accountable for developing a plan of care that prescribes interventions directed at achieving expected outcomes. In developing a plan, activities are identified that are within the scope of the nurse's responsibility; that are based on current nursing practice; that consider the Patient's Bill of Rights;* and that are realistic. The activities must be specific to avoid misinterpretation; information should include who is to perform the activities, when, and where.

According to the Standards of Perioperative Clinical Practice, the plan includes, but is not limited to, the following specific interventions:

- providing information and supportive perioperative teaching specific to the surgical intervention and nursing care
- identifying the patient
- verifying the surgical site
- verifying operative consent and procedure and reports of essential diagnostic procedures
- positioning the patient according to physiological principles
- adhering to the principles of asepsis
- providing appropriate and properly functioning equipment and supplies for the patient
- providing comfort measures and supportive care for the patient
- monitoring environmental safety
- evaluating outcomes of identified interventions
- communicating intraoperative information to significant others and the health care team to provide continuity of care

Communicating the nursing care plan to the patient, family, significant others, and appropriate health personnel is essential for successful implementation of the plan. Other health personnel may be informed during team conferences or a change of shift report.

*Statement on the Patient's Bill of Rights, American Hospital Association, October 21, 1992, Chicago, IL.

Communication may be with the individual staff person assigned to participate in the patient's care or in written nursing care plans that are available to appropriate staff members.

Perioperative Nursing Care Plans (Standard Care Plans/Models of Care). Standard care plans, or models of patient care, are defined as nursing care plans written for a group of patients with common predictable problems resulting from their diagnosis or condition. The components of standard care plans are the same as those of the individual care plan: nursing diagnosis; expected outcomes; nursing interventions; and evaluation of outcomes.

Four approaches may be taken in developing standard care plans, or models, for a surgical patient:

1. surgical procedure, e.g., total hip replacement, kidney transplant, abdominal hysterectomy (see Table 5–5)
2. intraoperative position of the patient, e.g., lithotomy (see Appendix I-1), lateral, prone
3. age of the patient (Appendix I-2)
4. type of anesthesia (Appendix I-3)

The third model, age of the patient, is based on the patient's age as well as any attendant physiological and psychological needs relevant to planning surgical intervention.

By combining the appropriate care plans, predefined nursing diagnoses are identified and a plan of care that describes interventions is available. The plans may be part of the permanent record or a notation may be made on the patient's chart identifying the standard care plans that were implemented.

Surgeon Preference Cards. Another valuable tool in planning for surgical procedures is the surgeon preference card. It lists the specific requests and preferences of each surgeon for each surgical procedure. The card also identifies type of skin preparation, position, method of draping, special supplies, instruments, sutures, and dressing required for a given surgical procedure (Table 5–6). Each card is routinely revised to reflect changes in the surgeon's requests and preferences.

Intraoperative Phase: Implementing Interventions

Implementing the intraoperative patient care plan begins when the patient is transported into the operating room; it is completed when the patient is transported to the recovery room. The focus of this phase is to consider the individual's dignity and desires. The interventions are consistent with the established plan of care and enable continuity of nursing care.

Using the plan of care as a guide, the perioperative nurse may supervise others in carrying out the plan or implement the prescribed nursing actions by providing direct care.

To determine who will perform nursing activities, the following factors are considered:

- assessment of the patient's needs and condition
- complexity of the patient's condition

(*Text continued on page 110*)

TABLE 5–5. MODEL OF PATIENT CARE FOR: ABDOMINAL HYSTERECTOMY

Nursing Diagnosis	Patient Outcome	Nursing Actions	Schedule for Evaluation

1. Risk of anxiety related to unfamiliar environment and/or impending surgery	1a. Ability to cope with anxiety
	b. Verbalizes basic understanding of surgical procedure
	c. Understands preoperative and postoperative activities
		1a. Assess patient's perception of surgical procedure—note degree of anxiety, denial, depression
		b. Assess support systems
		c. Explain events of day of surgery with rationale
		  1. Preoperative: n.p.o., premedication, time of transportation to OR, time of surgery, holding area, shave-prep, OR environment (i.e., lights, equipment), anticipated length of surgery
		  2. Postoperative: Recovery room location and activities, anticipated length of stay, pain, pain medication, Foley catheter, dressings, vaginal drainage of blood
		d. Encourage patient to verbalize concerns and questions
		e. Communicate to surgeon any unresolved concerns or questions the patient may have
			Preoperatively
			
			24–48 hours postoperatively

2. Risk of musculoskeletal discomfort, nerve damage, or circulatory and respiratory compromise related to improper positioning	2a. No musculoskeletal discomfort b. No nerve damage c. No compromise in circulation or respirations d. Skin integrity maintained	2a. Place safety strap above knees, over blanket b. Pad all boney prominences c. Align extremities anatomically d. Instruct Hospital Assistant to have shoulder braces padded and available e. Provide anesthesiologist with free access to airway and IV lines f. When position of OR table is adjusted, check toes and feet for pressure areas	24–48 hours postoperatively
3. Possible unwarranted anxiety about sexual appeal or activity related to misinformation or superstitions regarding hysterectomy	3. Misinformation and superstitions replaced with accurate information	3a. Provide support and information regarding sexual concerns b. Dispel superstitions and myths about outcome c. Encourage patient to verbalize concerns	Preoperatively

(continued)

TABLE 5–5. *(Continued)*

Nursing Diagnosis	Patient Outcome	Nursing Actions	Schedule for Evaluation
		d. Alert surgeon and other team members to patient's concerns	
4. Risk of loss of dignity related to excessive exposure	4. Dignity maintained	4a. Limit exposure of patient only to area needed for surgical procedure	Intraoperatively
5. Risk of damage to skin related to pooling of antiseptic solution under the patient	5. No skin damage	5a. When prepping the patient, place towels along patient's trunk to absorb excess solution b. Remove towels when prep is complete	Recovery room, 24–48 hours postoperatively
6. Risk of urinary tract infection related to insertion of Foley catheter	6. No urinary tract infection	6a. Follow procedure for insertion of Foley catheter b. Connect to straight drainage c. At all times, keep urinary drainage bag below level of patient's bladder	24–48 hours postoperatively
7. Risk of skin damage related to improper placement of electrosurgical ground plate	7. Skin integrity maintained Absence of: Burns Bruises Blisters Redness	7a. Cover plate evenly with conductive substance b. Place plate as close as possible to incision site c. Check connection of inactive cord to plate and electrosurgical unit d. Set controls to appropriate setting	Recovery room, 24–48 hours postoperatively
8. Risk of foreign body left in patient related to surgical incision	8. Absence of foreign body	8. Instruments, sponges, and needles counted according to procedure	Intraoperatively
9. Risk of wound infection related to contamination during intraoperative period	9. Wound free of infection Absence of: Edema Redness Tenderness Heat Pain Exudate	9a. Ensure compliance with principles of asepsis b. Report noncompliance with principles of asepsis on appropriate form	24–48 hours postoperatively
10. Risk of fluid imbalance related to n.p.o. and loss of body fluids	10. Body fluids maintained within normal limits	10a. Monitor urine output b. Estimate blood loss on sponges and in suction c. Communicate to anesthetist d. Check on blood availablity	Intraoperatively 24–48 hours postoperatively
11. Risk of decrease in body temperature related to surgical exposure	11. Normal body temperature maintained	11a. Limit eposure of patient to area required for surgical procedure	Recovery room

TABLE 5–5. *(Continued)*

Nursing Diagnosis	Patient Outcome	Nursing Actions	Schedule for Evaluation
		b. Place thermal blanket on OR table	
		c. Provide anesthesiologist with blood/fluid warmer as needed	
		d. Place warm blanket on patient at end of procedure	
12. Anxiety of significant others related to lack of communication regarding patient's progress	12. Reduce anxiety and/or able to cope with anxiety	12a. Inform patient's significant others when surgery has started	Postoperatively
		b. Inform of any unusual delay	
		c. Inform when patient goes to recovery room	

TABLE 5–6. SURGEON PREFERENCE CARD

Surgeon: Dr. C. Rocky
Procedure: Abdominoperineal Resection
Skin prep: 1% Iodine
Suture and needles:
Ties: 2-0, 3-0, 4-0, 18" Silk & Dexon
    2-0, 3-0, 4-0, Silk (D-Tach)
    2-0 Silk 30"
    2-0 Dexon 27"
Pelvic floor: 0 Chromic (T-12)
Colostomy: 4-0 Dexon (CE-4) $\times$ 4
Peritoneum: #1 Chromic (T-12)
Fascia: #1 Dexon—Large Mayos
Subcutaneous: 4-0 Dexon (CE-4)
Skin: Stapler or Steristrips
Anus: #2 Ticron—Retention
Perineum: 0 Dexon—Large Mayo
      4–0 Dexon (CE-4)
Supplies:
    Hernia tape x 3
    Wound protector
    Magnetic mat
    Catheter plugs $\times$ 2
Dressings:
    Telfa, 4 $\times$ 4s, Benzoin, paper tape, Colstomy Bag, Fluffs, Male patient: Fuller Shield. Female patient: T-Binder.

Glove size: 8
Patient position: Supine then lithotomy
Drapes: Towels, towel clips
    Lap sheet
    Half sheet
    Perineal sheet
Instruments:
    Basic instrument set
    Major retractor pan
    GI specials
    Israels $\times$ 2
    Wertheim clamps x 4
    Peans $\times$ 6
    Straight Jones clamps $\times$ 4

Drains: Abramson sump x 1
        Penrose drains $\frac{1}{2}$" $\times$ 6

- complexity of technology and proposed surgical intervention
- predictability of patient outcomes
- knowledge, skill, and expertise of team members
- amount of supervision the perioperative nurse will be able to provide

Scientific knowledge, interpersonal skills, research, and past experience are employed by the nurse to continuously monitor the patient's response to nursing activities. The nurse is alert to changes in the patient's psychologic and physiologic status, as they may require identifying new diagnoses, revising outcomes, and modifying the care plan.

The implementation phase is concluded when all the identified nursing actions have been implemented and documentation completed.

Postoperative Phase: Evaluation of Patient Outcomes

Patient care may be evaluated in the recovery room, on the unit, in the clinic, the physician's office, or the patient's home. Evaluating the patient somewhere other than the PACU allows participation and feedback from the patient, the family, and significant others.

The goals of postoperative evaluation are to:

- assess the effectiveness of interventions in relation to outcomes
- assess the patient's current status and revise the diagnoses, outcomes, and plan of care as appropriate
- discuss goal achievement with the patient, family, and significant others
- address any concern or question that the patient, family, or significant others may have regarding the perioperative period

In conducting postoperative evaluation, the nurse examines the patient's record for signs and symptoms and observes the patient. Through interviews with the primary care nurse, the patient, family, and significant others, the nurse will gain information about nursing practice and the level of goal achievement.

If identified patient outcomes were not achieved, the nurse must question why. Were all data collected? Were the nursing diagnoses appropriate? Were the outcomes realistic? Were the appropriate resources available? The plan must then be revised in collaboration with other health personnel, the patient, family, and significant others. The nurse documents on the patient's chart or care plan the level of goal achievement and any new nursing diagnoses, patient outcomes, and nursing activities.

Introspection is the final step in implementing the perioperative role, and the nurse judges the level of his or her practice. *What could I have done to provide more effective and efficient patient care?*

▌ DOCUMENTING PERIOPERATIVE NURSING CARE

To help ensure continuity of care and to validate the nursing care rendered, perioperative care—preoperative, intraoperative, and postoperative—must be documented.[9] The perioperative plan of care, including assessment, planning, implementation, evaluation, and expected outcomes, is documented. Not only is continuity of care enhanced, so too is communication with other team members about the patient during the perioperative period.

Written records demonstrate responsibility and accountability for nursing practice: the patient's actual/potential problems are identified; nursing strategies are recorded; and outcomes, as evidenced by the patient's responses, are documented. The record compares desired patient outcomes with the those achieved by the patient. It must also reflect ongoing evaluation throughout the perioperative period, alterations in the plan of care, and the patient's response to all nursing interventions. An example of perioperative care documentation is the multi-part form in Fig. 5–4.

Documentation is a comprehensive means for retrieving information in the event of legal action and for identifying data for quality improvement programs. In addition, the documentation of perioperative nursing provides a data base for research on the perioperative role.

The recording of perioperative nursing care varies from institution to institution and from inpatient to outpatient facility. It may be done in the nurse's notes, the progress notes, or a special form designed to encompass the perioperative role. Documentation forms for ambulatory surgery patients consist primarily of a checklist that encompasses the preoperative, intraoperative, and postoperative phases of the surgical experience.

Traditional Narrative. In the traditional narrative, referred to as source-oriented charting, entries are made on the nurse's notes in chronological order. An example of this format is:

> 4/22/95 10 A.M.: Mr. Brown admitted to OR from holding area. Anesthetized on stretcher, turned and transferred to OR table, and placed in prone position. Body rolls placed longitudinally from acromioclavicular joint to the iliac crest. Arms extended upward on arm boards. Pillow placed under feet. Safety strap placed 2 inches above knees. Ground plate for electrosurgical unit 212 position on left buttock. Skin prepped and painted with iodophor solution.—J. Coleman, RN

POMR. If problem-oriented medical records (POMR) are used, the nurse documents data in the nurse's notes or the progress notes. Essential to POMR charting is a list of patient problems. Each problem is defined, labeled, and numbered, and narrative notes are related to each problem. New problems are numbered and titled as they are identified by any member of the health care team. An example of POMR charting is:

> 4/22/95 10 A.M.
> 3. Painful right shoulder: Instruct transport team to provide adequate support for right shoulder and arm during transport to operating room. Provide additional support and padding when positioning for surgical procedure. Notify anesthesia and recovery room of positioning requirements.—J. Coleman RN 6. Shortness of breath: More pronounced when patient is lying flat. Keep head of bed elevated. Notify transport team and recovery room.—J. Coleman, R

SOAPIE. The concept of POMR has evolved into the SOAP, or SOAPIE, model. This six-part model consists of:

- Subjective data, which involve the health status of the patient and how he or she views it and feels about it

- Objective data, which include the physical and laboratory findings as well as observations of the patient
- Assessment, which is comprised of a nursing diagnosis/patient problem, a statement of the desired patient outcome, and evaluation criteria to assess degree of goal attainment
- Plan, which defines the activities necessary to assist the patient to achieve the desired goal
- Implementation, which defines how the nursing actions were carried out and by whom
- Evaluation statement, which contains the patient's degree of goal attainment as a result of the nursing actions

The SOAPIE system may be written in the nurse's notes or the progress notes. In some institutions, the nurse's orders are written on a combined physician/nurse's order sheet. An example of the SOAPIE format is:

4/22/95   1 P.M.
- S   "I had a stroke last year."
- O   Right-sided weakness. Difficulty in moving right arm and leg. Altered sensory perception on right side.
- A   Altered sensation on right side to touch and pain. Altered mobility due to left cerebrovascular accident (CVA). Safely transported to OR and positioned for surgery; adequate personnel to assist in transfer and positioning; extremities on right side positioned in proper alignment with boney prominences padded. No further nerve damage or areas of ischemia will occur.
- P   Obtain additional personnel to assist in transfer from bed to OR stretcher and from OR stretcher to OR table. Provide support to right side while transferring. Use foam padding under heels; pad and protect right arm and elbow with towels when positioning. Support right leg in proper alignment with sandbags.
- I   Transferred to OR stretcher without difficulty or untoward incidents by transportation team. Lifted onto OR table with extra support to right side. Foam padding positioned under heels. Towels placed under right arm and elbow. Right leg supported with sandbags in proper alignment.
- E   No complaints of discomfort during transfer. No evidence of further damage or ischemia. Body alignment maintained.—J. Coleman, RN

Charting by Exception. Charting by exception (CBE) was developed as a response to problems identified in traditional chronological narrative charting. Among the concerns were that the trends in patient status were not obvious, abnormal data were obscured by normal data, and nurses' notes were cumbersome and lengthy. The CBE system is a multifaceted approach to planning care. Orders for the patient's care plan are derived from four sources:

- nursing diagnosis–based care plans
- protocols and incidental orders
- standards of nursing practice
- physician's orders

The sources are both independent and interdependent nursing functions and encompass everything that nurses do for their patients.

The underlying philosophy of the CBE format is to chart only significant findings or exceptions to norms. Once the patient care plan is established, the completion of orders is documented in this exception format until a revision in the plan is required.

Synopsis. In all formats, it is essential that the patient's record reflect preoperative assessment, the planning carried out by the perioperative nurse, the care delivered by members of the surgical team, and the outcome.

Intraoperative documentation should include, but not be limited to, the following:

- Perioperative plan of care, including assessment, planning, implementation, evaluation, and expected outcomes
- Persons providing care; name and title of person responsible for the entry
- Evidence of patient assessment on arrival to the perioperative suite, including level of consciousness, psychosocial status, and baseline physical data
- Patient's overall skin condition on arrival and discharge from the perioperative suite
- Presence and disposition of sensory aids and prosthetic devices accompanying the patient to surgery; prosthetic devices are defined as artificial substitutes for body parts, such as arm, leg, eye, dentures, hearing aid, or wig
- Patient's position, supports, and/or restraints used during the surgical procedure
- Placement for the dispersive electrode pad and identification of electrosurgical unit and settings
- Placement of temperature control devices and identification of unit recording time and temperature
- Placement of electrocardiographic or other monitoring electrodes
- Medication, irrigations, and solutions administered by the registered nurse
- Specimens and cultures taken during the procedure
- Skin preparation, solution, area prepped, and any reactions that may have occurred
- Placement of drains, catheters, packings, and dressings
- Placement of tourniquet cuff and person applying it, the pressure, time, and identification of unit
- Placement of implants (the tissue, inert or radioactive material inserted into a body cavity or grafted onto tissue, manufacturer, lot number type, size, and other identifying information)
- Surgical item counts
- Time of discharge, disposition of patient, method of transfer, and patient status
- Intraoperative x-rays and fluoroscopy
- Wound classification
- Other direct patient care issues that are pertinent to patient outcomes

Using the criteria identified in the expected patient outcomes and in the patient's responses to the nursing activities, the patient's record should reflect an ongoing evaluation of perioperative nursing care, the patient responses to nursing interventions, and all other direct patient care issues that are important to patient outcomes.

■ REFERENCES

1. Schlotfeldt M. Planning for progress. *Nurs Out.* 1973;21(12):766–769.
2. A model for perioperative nursing practice. In *Standards and Recommended Practices.* Denver: AORN; 1995:69.
3. Competency statements in perioperative nursing. In *Standards and Recommended Practices.* Denver: AORN; 1995:73–85.
4. Perioperative advanced practice nursing. *AORN J.* 1995; 61(1).
5. Andrews M, Boyle J. *Transcultural Concepts in Nursing Care, 2nd ed.* Philadelphia: JB Lippincott; 1995:10.
6. Spector R. *Cultural Diversity in Health and Illness, 3rd ed.* Norwalk, CT: Appleton & Lange; 1991:52.
7. Carmody S et al. Perioperative needs of families. *AORN J.* 1991; 54:(3)566.
8. Silva M et al. Caring for those who wait. *Today's OR Nurse.* 1984; 6:26–30.
9. Recommended practices for documentation of perioperative nursing care. In *Standards and Recommended Practices.* Denver: AORN; 1995; 151–153.

PREOPERATIVE (ALL PATIENTS)

DATE	TIME	☐ PREOPERATIVE ASSESSMENT PRE-COMPLETED ☐ CHANGE IN STATUS DOCUMENTED IN NURSE'S NOTES ☐ ASSESSMENT DAY OF SURGERY	☐ PREADMISSION ASSESSMENT REVIEWED ☐ NO CHANGE IN PT STATUS

PATIENT PREPARATION   Wt _____ Ht _____ Age _____

PREOPERATIVE CHECKLIST	✓	NA
PREVIOUS CHART(S)		
CONSENT, SURGICAL		
CONSENT, STERILIZATION		
ANESTHESIOLOGY EVALUATION		
H & P		

CONSULT	N/A	ORDERED/DATE	ON CHART
☐ C.Cath Report			
☐ Preg			
☐ RH Factor Done			
☐ CBC			
☐ Chemistries			
☐ COAG			
☐ Other			
☐ EKG			
☐ X-Ray			

ALLERGIES: ☐ NKDA   Allergy Bracelet: ☐ Y ☐ N

NPO Since: _____ ☐ MID ☐ AM ☐ PM

AM Meds Taken: ☐ Yes ☐ No ☐ N/A ☐ Meds: _____

Make-up/Nail Polish Removed: ☐ Yes ☐ No ☐ None

Dentures Removed: ☐ Yes (Location: _____) ☐ No ☐ None

Glasses/Contacts Removed: ☐ Yes ☐ No ☐ None   Voided: ☐ Yes ☐ No

Jewelry Removed: ☐ Yes ☐ No ☐ None

Valuables: ☐ None ☐ Yes ☐ Family ☐ To Safe   ☐ Catheter: Time: _____

☐ Declined Safe   Describe: _____   ID Bracelet: ☐ Yes ☐ No

VITAL SIGNS	B/P	P	R	O₂Sat	RA	T

PARENTERAL FLUIDS

TYPE	AMOUNT	NEEDLE	SITE	TIME STARTED

IV INSERTED BY: _____ ,RN

PRE-OP MEDICATION

DRUG	AMOUNT	METHOD/SITE	TIME	GIVEN BY	EFFECT

BLOOD AVAILABILITY IN BLOOD BANK	NO. OF UNITS

TYPE: ☐ AUTO ☐ D.D. ☐ RANDOM

TED stockings: ☐ YES ☐ NO ☐ N/A

BELONGINGS TO: ☐ HELD ACU

☐ FLOOR RM _____ ☐ PACU ☐ FAMILY

NURSE'S NOTES: _____

☐ **Patient Urgent/Emergent Add On**

☐ **Patient Scheduled A.M. Admit**

SIGNATURE _____ , RN   ☐ **Patient Unscheduled Postoperative Admit**

POSTOPERATIVE (HAS patients only)

Time Admitted: _____   **Level of Consciousness:** ☐ Awake ☐ Drowsy ☐ Other: _____

From: ☐ OR ☐ PACU ☐ CCL ☐ Radiology ☐ P.R. ☐ Other: _____

MEDICATIONS	TIME	DRUG/AMOUNT	METH/SITE RESPONSE	RN	TIME	DRUG/AMOUNT	METH/SITE RESPONSE	RN

☐ ACU /☐ PACU NURSE'S NOTES:	TIME	B/P	P	R	T	DRSG. PULSE	TIME	B/P	P	R	T	DRSG. PULSE

DISCHARGED FROM: ☐ ACU ☐ PACU VITAL SIGNS:	B/P	P	R	T	O₂Sat	RA

DISCHARGE CRITERIA

			INTAKE/OUTPUT	TOT. AMT.
☐ Vital signs stable x 3	☐ No excessive bleeding/discharge	☐ Discharge instructions given Type: _____	IV	
☐ Nausea, vomiting, dizziness minimal or absent	☐ Alert & oriented	☐ Responsible adult escort present	PO	

☐ Airway reflexes intact, able to
  swallow liquids
	☐ Voided (As per Standard)
	☐ Post-op pain mild or absent
		☐ Discharge
		  Time: _____
			TOTAL	

☐ Absence of respiratory distress	☐ D/C medication dispensed	☐ Wheelchair ☐ Amb ☐ Other	URINE	
	PHYSICIAN RESPONSIBLE FOR DISCHARGE		EMESIS	
D/C Criteria Met (Sign): _____ , RN		_____ , MD		

Figure 5—4. Perioperative Services Flow Sheet. Courtesy Kaiser Permanente.

OR RN ASSESSMENT

Nurse's Admission Record Reviewed: ☐ No Change In Status   ☐ Change In Status; Please review OR Nurse's Notes

Date: _____   Signature: _____

ALLERGIES NOTED? ☐ Yes ☐ No
1. _____
2. _____
3. _____

	ID BAND	CONSENT	PATIENT, SURGEON & CONSENT AGREE ON OPERATIVE SITE
ASA: _____	☐ YES ☐ NO	☐ YES ☐ NO	☐ YES ☐ RIGHT ☐ LEFT ☐ OTHER

PREP: ☐ N/A ☐ Povidone-Iodine Scrub/paint ☐ Hibiclens Scrub ☐ Iodine Tinct ☐ Duraprep ☐ Alcohol ☐ Other:

Pre-op shave: ☐ None Site: _____ Done by: _____ Prep site: _____ Applied by: _____

Procedure: _____

Positioning: ☐ Supine ☐ Prone ☐ Lithotomy ☐ Lateral ☐ Rt ☐ Lt ☐ Other _____

Padding: ☐ Yes ☐ No Type _____ Location _____

Urinary Catheter: Type _____ Size _____ Balloon _____ cc Inserted by: _____

Urine: ☐ Clear ☐ Yellow ☐ Cloudy ☐ Sediment ☐ Clots ☐ Dark Amber ☐ Drainage Bag ☐ Urimeter

ESU Biomed #	☐ Coag _____ ☐ Cut _____	☐ N/A
ESU Biomed #	☐ Coag _____ ☐ Cut _____	☐ N/A
Bipolar Biomed #	☐ Coag _____ ☐ Cut _____	☐ N/A
Argon Biomed #	☐ Coag _____ ☐ Cut _____	☐ N/A
K Thermia Biomed #	Temp (Cel./F.) _____	☐ N/A
☐ Laser _____ watts Biomed #		☐ N/A
Tourniquet: Biomed #		☐ N/A
Tourniquet Pressure _____ mmHg Location		
☐ Padded	Total Tourniquet Time	
Time Up	Time Down	
Time Up	Time Down	

R   L   L   R

Safety Strap 1
Ground Plate 2
Tourniquet 3
EKG Leads x
Other Devices 4
Type:
_____
_____
_____
_____

MEDICATION(S)/IRRIGATION(S)/CONTRAST MEDIA

DRUG	AMT/DOSE	METHOD/SITE	TIME	MIXED/GIVEN BY	RESPONSE (IF ANY)

DRAINS/PACKS	TYPE/SIZE	SITE	DRAINAGE (APPEARANCE/AMT)
Drain(s)/Wound Suction			
Catheter(s)			
Pack(s)			
Wound Dressing			

Cast(s): ☐ N/A ☐ Short Leg ☐ Long Leg ☐ Short Arm ☐ Long Arm ☐ Splint ☐ Elevated on Pillow: ☐ Yes ☐ No

Ground Pad Removed: ☐ Yes ☐ No Condition Pad Site: ☐ Normal ☐ Red Comments: _____

OR NURSE'S NOTES: _____
_____
_____

RN SIGNATURE	RN SIGNATURE

OR TRANSFER NURSING ASSESSMENT

For Vital Signs and/or IV Fluids See Anesthesia Records | TO: ☐ PACU ☐ CVICU ☐ ICU ☐ ASU ☐ Other

TRANSPORTED VIA	BLOOD UNITS	NEUROSTATUS
☐ Gurney ☐ Bed ☐ Crib ☐ Other ☐ V//C	Whole Blood _____ FFP _____ Cryo _____ Packed Cells _____ Platelets _____	☐ Awake & Responsive ☐ Sedated & Responsive ☐ Anesthetized, Intubated

O₂ _____ L/M   Accompanied on transport by: 1. _____, RN 2. _____, MD 3. _____, CRNA

☐ NP ☐ Mask   Report given to PACU nurse: ☐ Yes ☐ No ☐ Verbal ☐ Written Given to _____ RN

Figure 5—4. Perioperative Services Flow Sheet. *(Continued).*

POSTANESTHESIA CARE UNIT (PART 1)

Procedure _____   Date _____ Time _____ Report From _____ Report To _____

_____   Type of Anesthesia: ☐ Spinal ☐ IV Sedation ☐ Regional Block
☐ General ☐ Epidural ☐ Local Type: _____

Airway: ☐ None ☐ Oral ☐ Nasal ☐ ETT ☐ Trach   Breath Sounds: _____

O₂ Therapy: ☐ None ☐ N/C ☐ Mask ☐ T-piece _____ L/Min. _____ %   ☐ Other: _____

Medical Hx/OP Notes

_____
_____
_____

PACU Monitoring Equipment

☐ Pulse Oximeter Central Line
☐ Dinamap   ☐ PA Cath
☐ Cardiac Monitor ☐ CVP
☐ Art Line   ☐ ²/₃ Lumen

Additional Equipment

☐ Hyperthermia Blanket
☐ Hypothermia Blanket
☐ Warming Lights
☐ Sequential Antiemboli Hose
☐ Other: _____

Dressings/Pads
Condition on admission to PACU

_____
_____
_____

LAB WORK/X-RAY

TIME	TYPE	RESULTS	NOTIFIED

ALDRETE SCORING

	IN	0.5°	1°	1.5°	2°	2.5°	3°	3.5°	4°	OUT

CONSCIOUSNESS
Awake and oriented 2
Drowsy and oriented, or awake and disoriented 1.5
Responsive to verbal stimuli 1
Responsive to noxious stimuli 0.5
Nonresponsive 0

RESPIRATORY
Normal airway; normal respirations; no adventitious breath sounds: awake ..2
Normal airway; normal respirations; no adventitious breath sounds: asleep 1.5
Labored respirations; oral/nasal airway 1
Apnea or airway maintained by ET tube 0

CIRCULATORY
BP and P ±20% of preanesthetic levels 2
BP and P ±20-35% of preanesthetic levels 1.5
BP and P ±35-50% of preanesthetic levels 1
BP and P ±50% of preanesthetic levels 0

COLOR
Pink mucous membranes 2
Pale or jaundiced mucous membranes 1.5
Dusky mucous membranes 1
Cyanotic mucous membranes 0

ACTIVITY
Full sensory and motor function x 4 2
Full motor return with nearly complete sensory return;
  < 10mm Hg Δ BP from supine to 90° sitting position 1.5
Sensory and motor block with decreasing level 1
Sensory and motor block with stable level, or no spontaneous movement ...0

Ventilator: _____ ☐ N/A

TIME	F₁O₂	T.V.	SIMV	PEEP	TIME	pH	PCO₂	PO₂	HCO₂	BASE EXCESS	O₂SAT

MEDICATIONS

TIME	DRUG	AMOUNT	METHOD/SITE	RESPONSE	GIVEN BY

NURSING ASSESSMENT NOTES

_____
_____
_____
_____
_____
_____
_____
_____
_____
_____
_____

Figure 5–4. Perioperative Services Flow Sheet. *(Continued).*

Note: Part 2 of PACU document is not included here.

PREOPERATIVE PLAN OF CARE

Standards of Care For:

1. _____   3. _____

2. _____   4. _____

Additional Nursing Diagnosis: ☐ None 1. _____ 2. _____

Nursing Interventions: ☐ None 1. _____

Outcomes: ☐ Met ☐ *Not met _____ Initials: _____

*Comments: _____

_____

_____

_____

_____

INTRAOPERATIVE PLAN OF CARE

Standards of Care For:

1. _____   3. _____

2. _____   4. _____

Additional Nursing Diagnosis: ☐ None 1. _____ 2. _____

Nursing Interventions: ☐ None 1. _____

Outcomes: ☐ Met ☐ *Not met _____ Initials: _____

*Comments: _____

_____

_____

_____

_____

POSTOPERATIVE PLAN OF CARE

Standards of Care For:

1. _____   3. _____

2. _____   4. _____

Additional Nursing Diagnosis: ☐ None 1. _____ 2. _____

Nursing Interventions: ☐ None 1. _____

Outcomes: ☐ Met ☐ *Not met _____ Initials: _____

*Comments: _____

_____

_____

_____

_____

DISCHARGE PLANNING NEEDS:
☐ See Nursing Admission Assessment Discharge Planning

SIGNATURE BANK

INITIALS	SIGNATURE	TITLE

Figure 5–4. Perioperative Services Flow Sheet. *(Continued).*

Controlling Infection

SIX

Evolution of Asepsis and Microbiology Review

▮ HISTORICAL REVIEW OF ASEPSIS

Among the many very early references to asepsis and surgery was the Code of Hammurabi, established about 1800 B.C. It was a collection of laws set up to identify legal practices in Babylonia; it also listed the penalties that had to be paid by unsuccessful surgeons. For example, if a patient lost an eye because of faulty surgery, the surgeon's eye was taken out.

Hippocrates (460–370 B.C.) recognized the importance of cleansing his hands prior to performing surgery, and he used boiling water for irrigating wounds. He forbade wounds to be moistened with anything except wine unless the wound was on a joint. "Dryness is more nearly a condition of health, and moisture more nearly an ally to disease. A wound is moist and healthy tissue is dry."[1]

Marcus Terentius Varro (117–26 B.C.), one of Caesar's physicians, stated in *Rerum Rusticarum*, "Small creatures, invisible to the eye, fill the atmosphere, and breathed through the nose cause dangerous diseases." Ambroise Pare (1517–1590), among the first physicians recognized as a surgeon, proved that tying blood vessels was a better method of stopping hemorrhages than cauterizing with hot oil or a hot iron. He also recognized the importance of keeping wounds clean.

In 1546, Fracastorius published *De Contagione* in which he stated his beliefs that diseases were spread by direct contact, touching objects touched by an infected individual, or airborne transmission. Fracastorius's observations were validated in 1683 when Anton van Leeuwenhoek developed the microscope.

The theory of spontaneous generation persisted until Louis Pasteur (1822–1895), a French chemist, disproved the doctrine and proved that fermentation, putrefaction, infection, and souring are caused by the growth of microbes. These "germs," he said, were carried by the air and could be destroyed by heat or other means. On April 30, 1878, members of the Academie de Medecine heard Pasteur's lecture on the germ theory:

> If I had the honour of being a surgeon, convinced as I am of the dangers caused by the germs of microbes scattered on the surface of every object, particularly in the hospitals, not only would I use absolutely clean instruments, but, after cleansing my hands with the greatest care and putting them quickly through a flame, I would only make use of

charpie, bandages, and sponges which had previously been raised to a heat of 130° to 150° C; I would only employ water which had been heated to a temperature of 110° to 120° C. All that is easy in practice, and, in that way, I should still have to fear the germs suspended in the atmosphere surrounding the bed of the patient; but observation shows us every day that the number of these germs is almost insignificant compared to that of those which lie scattered on the surface of objects, or in the cleanest ordinary water. Historically, physicians had attempted to prevent infections associated with a specific disease such as puerperal fever. As early as 1773 Charles Wite of Manchester, England insisted on strict cleanliness and ventilation of the lying-in room (delivery room).[2]

In 1843, Oliver Wendell Holmes of Boston advised his students and obstetricians who had been working in the dissecting room to wash their hands and change their clothes before attending a confinement. In 1849, Ignaz Semmelweis of Vienna insisted that all students coming from the postmortem or dissecting rooms wash their hands in a solution of chloride of lime before entering the lying-in wards. The result was dramatic; deaths fell from 15% to 3% and then to 1%.[3] An English surgeon, Lord Joseph Lister (1827–1912), developed a theory that if he could prevent airborne organisms from gaining access to a wound, infection would be prevented. Lister wrote:

> But when it had been shown by the researchers of Pasteur that the septic property of the atmosphere depended, not upon the oxygen or any gaseous constituent, but on minute organisms suspended in it, which owed their energy to their vitality, it occurred to me that decomposition of the injured part might be avoided without excluding the air, by applying as a dressing some material capable of destroying the life of the floating particles.[1]

Lister experimented with carbolic acid, which was being used to combat sewage odors. He used it to soak dressings, sponges, and instruments and to spray the environment.

As a result of these experiments, routine nursing preparations for surgery were as follows:

> No. 8 Ward in which the operation was performed was purified two days previously with sulphur fumes. Subsequently, walls and floors washed with 1:20 carbolic lotion and two carbolic sprays were turned on for 2 hours immediately previous to the operation. The patient was also prepared for the operation by being dieted on milk for two days previous to operation. All instruments were soaked in 1:20 carbolic lotion and warm 1:40 was used throughout for sponges, etc.[3]

These antiseptic techniques earned Sir Joseph Lister the title, Father of Antiseptic Surgery.

In 1882 Robert Koch, a German bacteriologist, and his assistant, Wolffhügel, introduced steam sterilization, and thus surgery took the form of a mixed antiseptic-aseptic technique.[3]

The surgeon scrubbed up; towels were treated by steam heat; some instruments were boiled; sharp instruments, such as scissors and scalpels, were still soaked for twenty minutes in carbolic; hands, face, and hair went uncovered; antiseptics such as carbolic and mercuric chloride were freely used. An improved apparatus for steam sterilization was introduced around 1890 by Ludwig Lautenschlagen, a German pharmacologist, working with two surgeons, Ernst von Bergmann and Ernst Schimmelbusch. This apparatus enabled almost pure aseptic technique.

A covering for the hands was first suggested in 1843 by Dr. Thomas Watson; however, it was not implemented until 1885 when J. von Mikulicz-Radecki wore cotton gloves. The modern rubber glove was introduced by William Stewart Halsted of Johns Hopkins Hospital, Baltimore, in 1894. He also introduced caps to cover the hair. Gauze face masks were first worn by either Mikulicz or the French surgeon Paul Berger in 1896 or 1897. Masks were not generally used for many years, as some surgeons believed that silence was enough to prevent droplet infections. The operating room gown appears to have originated in Italy in the mid-1800s.

Aseptic technique has evolved since Lister introduced the use of carbolic acid. The basic objective, however, remains unaltered: to prevent infection by eliminating microorganisms.

▮ PRINCIPLES OF BACTERIOLOGY

Bacteria are single-celled microorganisms that are measured in microns. One bacterium measures 1/25,400 of an inch, 1/1,000 of a millimeter, or 2 microns in length; and 0.5 micron wide. Under optimum conditions, bacteria divide on the average of every 20 minutes; therefore, 1 million new cells may be produced in 10 hours from a single bacterium. Disease-producing bacteria are identified as pathogenic.

Bacteria occur in three distinct shapes: cocci, bacilli, and spirilla (Fig. 6–1). Cocci are ball-shaped and are found as a single cell or group of cells. Bacilli are rod-shaped and may occur as a single cell or in chains. Spirilla are shaped like a corkscrew and always are a single cell.

Bacteria are also classified by their reaction to a gram stain. Distinct physical and chemical differences have been demonstrated between the cell walls of gram-positive and gram-negative bacteria. The cell wall of gram-positive bacteria appears as a single, homogeneous, dense layer, almost twice as thick as the wall of the gram-negative bacteria, whereas the cell wall of the gram-negative organism appears to be composed of several individual layers and is chemically more complex. The reaction of the bacteria to the gram

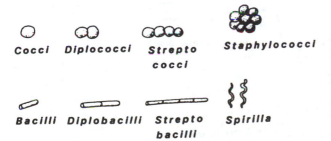

Figure 6–1. Bacteria have three distinct shapes; cocci, bacilli, and spirilla. When they occur in pairs they are called diplococci or diplobacilli. When they form chains, streptococci or streptobacilli. When cocci form irregular clusters, they are called staphylococci.

stain is not related to the pathogenicity of the organism, but it is important in choosing drug therapy.

Bacteria Cell Structure

The cytoplasm of the bacterial cell is surrounded by a thin membrane called the cytoplasmic membrane. The nuclear structures in the chromatinic area are chromosomes, nucleoids, and chromatin bodies.

Surrounding the cytoplasmic membrane is the cell wall. The cell wall gives the bacterium its characteristic shape (i.e., cocci, bacilli, spirilla) and like the cytoplasmic membrane is semipermeable (Fig. 6–2).

Many pathogenic bacteria secrete a third layer of material that covers the cell wall and increases their virulence. This layer is the capsule, or slime layer. The thickness of the capsule varies; in some species of bacteria it can be twice as thick as the cell itself and in others, barely detectable. The chemical composition of the capsule is polysaccharides and proteins and sometimes mucinlike material.

The capsule is a protective layer that resists the action of certain defense mechanisms in the human body, such as phagocytosis or the bactericidal activity of body fluids.

The bacterium may be propelled by a threadlike appendage called the flagellum. The number of flagella and their position on the bacterium vary with the species. Flagella, however, are not the only means by which bacteria move. Some species "crawl" over a surface by waves of protoplasmic contraction. Almost all the spiral bacteria and about half the species of bacilli are motile, whereas most cocci are nonmotile.

Bacteria in their active state are vegetative. A few bacteria, however, are able to develop a specialized structure called a spore. When a certain period arrives in the life cycle of these organisms, the vegetative cell disintegrates releasing a highly resistant dehydrated bit

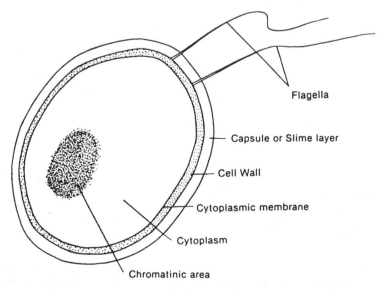

Flagella

Capsule or Slime layer

Cell Wall

Cytoplasmic membrane

Cytoplasm

Chromatinic area

Figure 6–2. Structure of a bacteria cell.

of protoplasm—the spore. A spore is so resistant that it can survive prolonged exposure to drying, heat, chemical disinfectants, and other unfavorable conditions. The protoplasm within a bacterial spore can remain alive for many years. As long as environmental conditions are adverse to the growth of the bacterium, the spore will remain a spore. When, however, the proper conditions for growth occur (for example, if the spore is introduced into the human body through a wound), the wall splits, a vegetative cell emerges, and the bacterial cell begins to reproduce. *Clostridium tetani,* which produces tetanus, and *C. perfringens,* which results in gas gangrene, are spore-producing bacteria.

Conditions Influencing Bacterial Growth and Reproduction

Temperature. The optimum temperature for growth and reproduction varies for different types of bacteria. Thermophilic bacteria function best in an environment at 140° to 190°F (60° to 90°C). For mesophilic bacteria 98.6°F (37°C) is optimum, and psychrophilic bacteria function best from 39° to 50°F (4° to 10°C). Most bacteria that are pathogenic to human beings are mesophilic.

Food or Nourishment. Bacteria require nutrients for both protoplasm synthesis and energy.

Moisture. Moisture is important for bacteria to grow and multiply, as water is the means by which dissolved nutrients enter the cells and the wastes leave. The absence of moisture, however, does not necessarily kill microorganisms.

Oxygen. Most microorganisms grow best in air that has oxygen. Facultative bacteria can live and reproduce with or without oxygen. Aerobic bacteria must have free oxygen; anaerobic organisms can live only in the absence of oxygen.

Environmental pH. Most pathogenic bacteria grow best in a neutral pH; however, some will grow and reproduce in an acid pH, in some cases, in a pH as low as 1 or 2.

Normal Flora

Microorganisms that ordinarily inhabit areas of the human body are referred to as the normal flora. They do not produce disease unless they are transferred somehow to an environment within the body that is conducive for them to cause infection. For example, *Escherichia coli* is part of the normal flora of the large intestine. If the organism, however, contaminates the urinary tract during a bladder catheterization, a urinary tract infection will result. Similarly, staphylococci are part of the normal flora of the skin; however, when the integrity of the skin is disrupted, staphylococci may enter the body and cause infection.

The type of flora present in various body areas depends on the temperature, pH, moisture, and nutrients.

Infectious Properties of Bacteria

Infection results when the body or a part of it is invaded by a pathogenic agent that, under favorable conditions, grows and multiplies producing injurious effects. An undesirable host-parasite relationship is established.

Pathogens may enter the body through the respiratory or digestive tract, the blood, genitourinary system, skin, or mucous membranes. Organisms exit the body in secretions from the respiratory tract and in feces, urine, blood, mucus, and substances from infected areas, such as pus or other discharges from wounds and boils.

Pathogens may be transmitted by either direct or indirect contact. Direct transmission occurs when there is body contact with an infected person. Indirect transmission may occur by means of contaminated droplets, dust, water, blood, insects, equipment, and infected persons or carriers. One of the predominant sources of indirect transmission are the hands, which, when contaminated with pathogens, serve as a vehicle for cross-contamination.

Many pathogenic bacteria secrete substances that contribute to their virulence. *Endotoxins* are present inside the bacterial cell and are released only after the cell's death and disintegration. Some clinical symptoms that may be attributed to the release of endotoxins into the bloodstream are fever, weakness, lethargy, hypotension, irreversible shock, and death.

Other injurious substances are *exotoxins* which are secreted by a living bacterium and released into surrounding tissue. The microorganisms do not have to die to release exotoxins; for example, *C. botulinum,* which causes food poisoning, and *C. tetani,* which results in tetanus, are two examples of bacteria that produce exotoxins.

In addition, there are several substances secreted by various bacteria that assist in the breakdown of body tissue and the spread of disease within the host. These substances include hemolysins, leukocidins, hyaluronidase, streptokinase, coagulase, and collagenase.

Mycobacterium tuberculosis, a non-spore-forming aerobic bacillus, was a leading cause of death in the early 1900s. Drugs were developed to fight tuberculosis (TB) and were effective for the many decades. This trend was reversed recently, however, and from 1985 to 1992 more than 50,000 cases of TB were reported in excess of projections.[4] The increase is attributed to a new strain of the tubercle bacillus referred to as multidrug-resistant tuberculosis (MDR-TB). The higher incidence is attributed to individuals who have immigrated from countries where tuberculosis is common, nosocomial transmission to patients and health-care workers due to inadequate isolation precautions in known and unknown cases, and simultaneous infection with the human immunodeficiency virus. Among the reported MDR-TB cases, 90% occurred in HIV-infected patients.[5]

The Centers for Disease Control and Prevention (CDC) and the Occupational Safety and Health Administration (OSHA) have published guidelines for preventing the spread of TB and other airborne diseases. Two key elements are ventilation and appropriate face protection. The room where surgical procedures are performed must have a minimum of 12 air exchanges per hour. The room must also have negative pressure to prevent TB particles from being blown out of the room when the door is opened. Members of the surgical team must wear a particulate respirator designed with a proper face-seal fit to screen particles down to 0.4 to 0.6 mμ.[6]

■ NONBACTERIAL INFECTIONS

With the expanded use of steroids, immunosuppressive agents, and multiple antibiotic agents, the incidence of fungal and viral infections has steadily increased.

Fungi

Fungi are much larger, considerably more complex, and more highly organized than bacteria. Among the pathogenic fungi there are two categories of molds and yeast: the first group infect only skin, hair, and nails (the dermatophytes), and the second group infect deeper organs of the body, as well as the skin. Most diseases caused by systemic fungi are very difficult to treat, as they do not respond well to antibiotic therapy.

Viruses

Viruses are much smaller than bacteria, ranging from 20 to 250 mμ. Unlike bacteria, viruses multiply only within living cells. Viruses may be in the air, on surfaces of equipment, or in dirt, but they cannot multiply until they invade living tissue.

HBV. One virus of concern to the perioperative nurse—hepatitis-B (HBV)—causes infectious hepatitis and serum hepatitis. It remains the major infectious occupational health hazard in the health care industry. The principal mode of transmission of these two diseases is oral ingestion or parenteral injection of fecal- or blood-contaminated food or water, or contact with blood or blood products contaminated with the hepatitis virus. The virus may be in blood or feces without previous or current signs or symptoms in the host. A safe, effective vaccine to prevent HBV infection is available. All health care workers exposed to blood and body fluids are encouraged to receive it.

HIV. Of primary concern is the virus that causes acquired immunodeficiency syndrome (AIDS). Human immunodeficiency virus (HIV) weakens and eventually destroys the body's immune system. The body is left vulnerable to opportunistic infections caused by a variety of organisms, such as *Pneumocystis carinii*.

Malignancies, such as Kaposi's sarcoma (KS) and central nervous system lymphoma, also develop as the result of HIV infection. It is also demonstrated that HIV directly infects cells of the nervous system, leading to encephalopathy, meningitis, myelopathy, and peripheral neuropathy.

The HIV is fragile and normally must live inside a human body to survive. The virus is transmitted in an infected person's blood, semen, or vaginal fluids. Infected fluid may be introduced directly into the bloodstream of another person, or the organism may enter through mucous membranes or a break in the protective surface of the skin. Contacting unbroken skin is not sufficient exposure to transmit infection.

Groups at high risk for AIDS include homosexual or bisexual men, intravenous drug abusers, recipients of contaminated blood or blood products, heterosexual partners of HIV-infected persons, and children born to infected mothers. Table 6–1 identifies the types of surgical procedures AIDS patients may require. Viruses pose a hazard to all health care workers unless appropriate procedures are instituted.

■ DEFENSE MECHANISMS

The body's first line of defense against infection includes intact skin, mucous membranes, and membrane secretions. For example, cilia on the mucous membranes of the respiratory

TABLE 6–1. COMMON SURGICAL PROCEDURES IN AIDS PATIENTS

Diagnostic procedures
  Tissue biopsies

Supportive procedures
  Placement of long-term indwelling intravenous catheters for TPN or antimicrobial therapy

Emergencies
  Intraabdominal complications
  Evaluation of acute abdomen for:
    Peritonitis secondary to cytomegalovirus enterocolitis and perforation
    Gastrointestinal bleeding associated with non-Hodgkin's lymphoma or Kaposi sarcoma
  Biliary surgery for acute cholecystitis and acute cholangitis related to infection with cryptosporidiosis and cytomegalovirus
  Resection, bypass, or colostomy for acute gastrointestinal perforations related to cytomegalovirus infection, cryptosporidiosis candidiasis, and
    necrotic lymphoma
  Splenectomy for splenomegaly or thrombocytopenia

Pulmonary complications
  Chest tube placement related to spontaneous pneumothorax

From Davis J. Acquired immunodeficiency syndrome, from Care of Surgical Patient. *Eds., Wilmore et al. New York: Scientific American; 1993:2, 7.*

tract help move microorganisms to the exterior; the acid pH of mucous secretions in the vagina limits the growth of microorganisms; tears remove pathogenic bacteria; and the acid pH of the urethra coupled with the outward flow of urine defend the urinary tract against invading organisms.

Phagocytes are the second line of defense. Phagocytic cells include leukocytes of the blood, macrophages in tissues throughout the body, and the fixed phagocytes of the reticuloendothelial system. Leukocytes remove debris (including bacteria) by phagocytosis. Macrophages, on the other hand, pass through a variety of tissues to the site of an injury. They, too, are capable of phagocytosis. Cells of the reticuloendothelial system are in the liver, spleen, bone marrow, lungs, and lymph nodes. The remove bacteria and other material from circulating fluids.

Antibodies are the third line of defense in the body. They are formed in response to antigens. Antibodies are immunoglobulins, and each reacts with the antigen that stimulated its production. Antibodies function in a variety of ways. Some react with bacteria, making them more susceptible to phagocytosis; others cause lysis of bacterial cells. An antibody that develops in response to a virus neutralizes the virus.

∎ INFLAMMATORY RESPONSE

A surgical incision causes an inflammatory response. Signs of acute inflammation are discoloration, swelling, heat, and pain. Discoloration and heat are caused by the increased blood in the injured area. Vessels dilate to accommodate the blood supply. Swelling results from the dilated vessels and the increased pressure from tissue fluids. The swelling causes pressure on nerve endings, which, along with the incision, produces pain.

If no bacteria are present, inflammation is followed by healing. If bacteria are present, however, tissues provide the necessary environment for infection to occur. Subsequently, the process of phagocytosis begins. The exudate around the infected area contains fibrin, and as connective tissue cells multiply, the area becomes walled off. Pus forms—a mass of dead white blood cells, tissue, blood, tissue fluids, and dead and living bacteria. The pus and necrotic tissue within the walled-off area form an abscess.

If the walling-off process is incomplete, large amounts of poisonous products may be absorbed into the bloodstream. If only toxins are absorbed, the condition is toxemia; if bacteria are also present, it is a septicemia. Bacteria in the bloodstream may localize at points away from the original injury, and secondary abscesses result.

■ CLASSIFICATION OF SURGICAL INFECTIONS

Infection may develop spontaneously in the home or community. As many as 30% to 40% of patients admitted to a surgical service may have home-based infections, that is, acute appendicitis, acute cholecystitis, acute diverticulitis with perforation and peritonitis, foreign bodies, and animal bites. Such infections are effectively treated with antibiotics.

Infection may also occur during an individual's hospitalization; it is hospital acquired, or nosocomial. Most often the infections result from microbial invasion by virulent, antibiotic-resistant microorganisms. Invasion may follow surgical intervention; diagnostic procedures, such as arteriography; or therapeutic procedures, such as bladder catheterization, tracheostomy, or intravenous therapy.

The bacteria frequently associated with nosocomial infections are *Escherichia coli, P. aerogenes,* enterococci, *Proteus, Pseudomonas aeruginosa, Enterobacter, Klebsiella, Staphylococcus aureus, Candida, and Serratia.* Table 6–2 identifies some of the most common bacteria that result in surgical infections.

Risk factors that increase a surgical patient's vulnerability to wound infections include malnutrition, immunosuppression, diabetes mellitus, cancer, morbid obesity, infections at other sites, being older than 65 years, an incision site that is especially accessible to pathogens, and intraoperative breaks in aseptic technique.

When infection occurs consideration must be given to the sterility of instruments, drapes, and surgical technique. Airborne contamination is a variable that must also be considered. The most effective method of assessing overall aseptic practices in the operating room is to monitor the occurrence of wound infections among surgical patients.

Operative wounds are categorized as follows:

Category 1. A *clean wound* is a nontraumatic, uninfected operative wound that does not require entering the respiratory, alimentary, or genitourinary tract or the oropharyngeal cavity. Clean wounds are made under aseptic conditions. Usually, a clean wound is primarily closed without drains. Reported infection rates are 1% to 5%.

Category 2. *Clean contaminated wounds* include operative wounds in which the respiratory, alimentary, or genitourinary tract or oropharyngeal cavity is entered without unusual contamination; wounds that are mechanically drained; or wounds in which there are only

TABLE 6–2. COMMON PATHOGENS RESULTING IN INFECTIONS

	Normal Flora/Location	Infection	Prevention and/or Control of Infection[b]
Bacterial Infections[a]			
I. Aerobic Bacteria			
A. Gram-positive Coccus			
1. *Staphylococcus aureus*	Skin, hair Naso-oro-pharynx	Boils (furuncles) Wound infection Pneumonia Urinary tract infection Septicemia	1) Strict aseptic technique 2) Hand washing 3) Isolation of infected persons 4) Disinfection of all discharges
2. *Streptococcus pyogenes*	Nose Nasopharynx	Cellulitis Puerperal fever Wound infections Urinary tract infection	1) Strict aseptic techniques around wounds 2) Hand washing 3) Disposal of all discharges 4) Environmental sanitation 5) Adequate ventilation with appropriate air changes
3. *S. pneumoniae*	Nose Naso-oro-pharynx	Lobar pneumonia Conjunctivitis Peritonitis Meningitis	1) Exclusion of infected persons or carriers from the surgical suite 2) strict adherence to aseptic technique 3) Environmental sanitation 4) Hand washing
B. Gram-negative Coccus			
1. *Neisseria gonorrhoeae*	Genitourinary tract Rectum, mouth Eye	Gonorrhea Pelvic inflammatory disease Septicemia Conjunctivitis	1) Environmental sanitation 2) Early diagnosis and treatment including all contacts
2. *N. menigitidis*	Nose Oro-pharynx	Meningitis Pneumonia	1) Identification of carriers 2) Environmental sanitation 3) Strict adherence to aseptic technique 4) Hand washing
C. Gram-negative Bacillus			
1. *Escherichia coli*	Large intestine Perineum	Septicemia Inflammation of the liver and the gallbladder Urinary tract infection Peritonitis	1) Hand washing 2) Strict aseptic technique during bladder catherization 3) Isolation of bowel contents and instruments during large bowel resection
2. *Serratia*	Urinary tract	Deep wound infection	1) Hand washing 2) Disinfection of equipment 3) Environmental sanitation 4) Proper cleaning of housekeeping equipment
3. *Pseudomonas aeruginosa*	Intestinal tract Skin Soil	Wound infections Urinary tract infection Burns	1) Use aseptic technique when handling wounds and burns 2) Proper disposal of contaminated materials 3) Environmental sanitation

(continued)

TABLE 6–2. *(Continued)*

	Normal Flora/Location	Infection	Prevention and/or Control of Infection[b]
4. *Salmonella typhosa*	Intestinal tract	Typhoid Fever	1) Isolation 2) Disinfection of feces and urine 3) Sanitary control of food, water, and sewage disposal 4) Hand washing
5. *S. shigella*	Intestinal tract	Bacillary dysentery or shigellosis Gastroenteritis Septicemia	Same as for *S. typhosa*
6. *Hemophilus influenzae*	Respiratory tract	Bacterial meningitis Acute airway obstruction	1) Disinfection of respiratory secretions
D. Gram-positive Bacillus			

1. *Mycobacterium tuberculosis*[c]	Respiratory tract
	Urine (occasionally)
	Lymph nodes
		Tuberculosis
		  Peritonitis
		  Meningitis
		  Lungs
		  Bone
		  Skin
		  Lymph nodes
		  Intestinal tract
		  Fallopian tubes
		  Endocarditis
			1) Early diagnosis and treatment
			2) Environmental sanitation
			3) Disposal of all discharges from respiratory tract
			4) Disinfection and sterilization of contaminated equipment
			5) Isolation of individual with active infection
			6) Proper air exchanges
			7) HEPA respirator masks

II. Microaerophilic Bacteria			
A. Gram-positive Coccus			
1. *Hemolytic streptococci, alpha type*	Respiratory tract	Abscess in gums or teeth Subacute bacterial endocarditis Meningitis	1) Identification of carriers 2) Adherence to aseptic technique 3) Proper handling of contaminated masks 4) Exclusion of personnel with upper respiratory infection from operating room 5) Hand washing
2. *Nonhemolytic*	Respiratory tract	Endocarditis Urinary tract infection	Same as for *Hemolytic* (alpha)
III. Anaerobic Bacteria			
A. Gram-positive Coccus			
1. *Peptococcus*		Abscess of skin or of respiratory and intestinal tract	1) Strict aseptic technique
2. *Peptostreptococcus*	Vagina (premenopausal)	Abscess of respiratory and intestinal tract Septic abortions	1) Strict aseptic technique

(continued)

TABLE 6-2. *(Continued)*

	Normal Flora/Location	Infection	Prevention and/or Control of Infection[b]
B. Gram-positive Bacillus			
1. *Clostridium perfringens*	Soil	Gas gangrene (rare)	1) Strict aseptic technique
2. *C. novyi*	Dust	Food poisoning (common)	2) Cleansing of all wounds by irrigation with copious amounts of solution to eliminate extraneous material and necrotic tissue
3. *C. septicum*	Manure		
4. *C. histolyticum*	Human feces		
	Vagina		
5. *C. tetani*	Soil	Tetanus (lockjaw)	1) Tetanus toxoid
	Dust	Surgical tetanus	2) Tetanus antitoxin
	Feces		3) Sterilization of all instruments and dressings
C. Gram-negative Bacillus			
1. *Bacteroids species*	Nasopharynx	Wound infections	1) Strict aseptic technique
	Intestinal tract	Rectal, brain abscess	2) Environmental sanitation
	Vagina	Endocarditis	3) Hand washing
		Osteomyelitis	4) Plaster casts should be bivalved or removed outside the operating room
2. *Fusobacterium*	Nasopharynx	Anaerobic infections of brain and respiratory tract	1) Strict aseptic technique
	Intestinal tract	Vincent's angina (trench mouth)	2) Good dental hygiene
		Cellulitis	

Nonbacterial Infections

IV. Fungi			
A. *Candida albicans*	Respiratory Gastrointestinal Female genital tracts	Moniliasis or thrush	1) Avoid disturbance of normal microbial flora
V. Viruses			
A. *Hepatitis A*	Water contaminated by human sewage Shellfish from naturally contaminated sources Blood, urine Food prepared or handled by infectious persons who practice poor hygiene	Infectious hepatitis	1) Vaccine 2) Sanitary disposal of sewage 3) Use disposable syringes and needles on infected persons 4) Exercise care in handling syringes, needles, and instruments used on infected persons 5) Sanitary food processing 6) Enforce good hygiene with all food-processing personnel (i.e., hand washing) 7) Gamma globulin immunization within 2 weeks
B. *Hepatitis B*	Blood Saliva Other body fluids Feces	Serum hepatitis	1) Hand washing 2) Use disposable presterile needles and syringes whenever possible

TABLE 6–2. *(Continued)*

	Normal Flora/Location	Infection	Prevention and/or Control of Infection[b]
			3) Nondisposable items must be terminally sterilized or disinfected following use
			4) Careful disposal of contaminated syringes, needles, knife blades, and suture needles
			5) Wear gloves when handling contaminated items
			6) Vaccine
			7) Scrub nurse must exercise care not to puncture own skin with needles or knife blades
			8) Gamma globulin immunization within 7 days
C. *Human Immunodeficiency*	Blood Saliva Semen Cerebrospinal fluid Tears Amniotic fluid Pericardial fluid Peritoneal fluid Vaginal secretion Synovial fluid Pleural fluid Saliva (dental procedures) Any body fluid visibly contaminated with blood	AIDS	1) Wear gloves when touching blood saliva or mucous membranes 2) Wear masks and protective eyewear when splashing of blood or saliva is likely 3) Do not recap needles 4) Nondisposable items must be terminally sterilized or disinfected following use 5) Impervious gowns or plastic aprons should be worn during procedures that are likely to generate splashes of blood or body fluid 6) Careful disposal of contaminated syringes, needles, knife blades, and suture needles 7) Team members should refrain from all direct patient care when they have exudative lesions or weeping dermatitis 8) Scrub nurse must exercise care not to puncture own skin with needles or knife blades 9) Follow institutional policy after any exposure
D. *Cytomegalovirus (CMV)*[d]	Body fluids Blood products Transplanted organs/bone	Lymphadenpathy Enteritis Pneumonitis Chorioretinitis	1) See above for AIDS

[a]Bacterial infections may be mixed (e.g., aerobic and anerobic microoganisms, gram-positive and gram-negative microorganisms, and synergistic microorganisms).
[b]Strict handwashing technique is the most important precaution in the prevention and the control of infections.
[c]Immunocompromised patients have high susceptibility for *Mycobacterium tuberculosis*. Examples of these patients are: AIDS, geriatrics and oncology patients.
[d]See above for AIDS.
From *Occupational exposure to blood-borne pathogens. Final Rule.* Fed. Reg. *1991;56:64175.*

minor breaks in technique, such as glove puncture. Reported infection rates are 3% to 11%.

Category 3. *Contaminated wounds* include open, fresh traumatic wounds; operations with a major break in sterile technique (e.g., open cardiac massage, gross spillage from the GI tract); and incisions encountering acute, nonpurulent inflammation such as cholecystitis or wounds made in or near contaminated or inflamed skin. Reported infection rates are 10% to 17%.

Category 4. *Dirty or infected wounds* include old traumatic wounds and those involving clinical infection or perforated viscera. The definition of this classification suggests that the organisms causing postoperative infection are present in the operative field before surgical intervention. Infection rates are frequently greater than 27%.

Antibiotic Prophylaxis

The prophylactic use of antibiotics to prevent wound infection has become common practice. Several studies demonstrate its effectiveness in selected surgical procedures.[7,8] Antibiotic prophylaxis, however, can fail even when its indication is proven. Failure may occur if an inappropriate agent is used or if it is administered inappropriately.[9]

An inappropriate prophylactic agent may be one in the drug regimen to which the infecting organism is resistant, or it may be the wrong antibiotic. Garibaldi showed that 73% of the patients in a study who received antibiotics perioperatively developed wound infections from organisms that were resistant to the antibiotic that was administered.[10]

Inappropriate administration, the other reason for prophylactic failure, refers specifically to the timing of administration. Classen[11] demonstrated that prophylactic antibiotics are most effective if given during the 2-hour period before the incision is made. Patients who received antibiotics more than 3 hours after the incision was made had a wound infection rate more than 5 times that demonstrated among patients who received antibiotics within 2 hours of surgery. A high rate of wound infection is also associated with administering a drug more than 2 hours before surgery. This study showed that to reduce the risk of infection, high levels of antibiotics must be in the bloodstream and tissues at the time of incision.[11]

The circulating nurse must call the surgical unit or the preoperative area to ensure that the prophylactic antibiotics are administered at the appropriate time for the maximum effectiveness.

■ REFERENCES

1. Zimmerman LM, Veith I. *Great Ideas in the History of Surgery.* New York: Dover; 1967; 21, 464.
2. Vallery-Radat R. *The Life of Pasteur.* Trans RL Devonshire. New York: Doubleday; 1926;255.
3. Cartwright F. *The Development of Modern Surgery.* New York: Thomas Crowell; 1968;48, 63–64, 80.
4. Daugherty J et al. Prevention and control of tuberculosis in the 1990s. *Nurs Clin North Am.* 1993; 28:599–611.
5. Hutton M, Polder J. Guidelines for preventing tuberculosis transmission in health care settings: What's new? *Am J Infect Control.* February 1992; 20:25–26.
6. Pugliese G. TB respirators: What's required and what isn't. *Materials Management.* 1994; 3:(4)30–35.
7. Shapiro M. Perioperative prophylactic use of antibiotics in surgery: Principles and practice. *Infect Control.* 1982; 3:38–40.

8. Kaiser A. Antimicrobial prophylaxis in surgery. *N Engl J Med.* 1986; 315:1129–1138.
9. Bryant J. Perioperative antibiotic prophylaxis: The importance of timing. *Today's OR Nurse.* 1992; 14(10):8.
10. Garibaldi R et al. Risk factors for postoperative infection. *Am J Med.* 1991; 91:1585–1635.
11. Classen D et al. The timing of prophylactic administration of antibiotics and the risk of surgical wound infection. *N Engl J Med.* 1992; 326:281–286.

SEVEN

Limiting Contamination Sources
in the Operating Room

■ SOURCES OF CONTAMINATION IN THE OPERATING ROOM

During the intraoperative phase, the safety of the patient is the primary focus of the perioperative nurse. One of the most important safety concerns in the operating room is preventing infections by limiting the source of contamination.

The primary sources of bacterial contamination are:

- The surgical team (their health, hygiene, and attire)
- Air circulation
- Environment (the OR's design, sanitation, and equipment)
- Supplies used during surgical intervention
- The patient

■ PREVENTION AND CONTROL OF INFECTION

The Surgical Team

Written policies regarding the attire of surgical team members and the potential health hazards that the staff present will help minimize the effects of large numbers of potentially pathogenic bacteria on the skin and hair and in the respiratory tract. These bacteria present on surgical team members are a source of infection for the surgical patient.

All members of the surgical team and other support personnel in the surgical suite should be free of transmissible bacterial infections. Of primary concern are upper-respiratory tract infections; skin lesions, such as carbuncles, furuncle, and dermatitis; unhealed wounds; and infections of the mouth, eyes, or ears. Personnel exhibiting signs or symptoms of these conditions should be excluded from the surgical suite.

Personal hygiene is important in controlling infections. Hair is a source of bioparticulate matter and should be washed frequently, and always after a haircut. A daily bath or shower is recommended; however, because the greatest amount of skin debris and microorganisms is shed immediately after bathing, personnel should bathe or shower a few hours before changing into operating room attire. Frequent handwashing is an important means of controlling the spread of infections and must be carried out by all personnel before and after patient contact, even when gloves are used, and after handling equipment or other potentially contaminated items.

Staff should have a physical examination when they are employed and annually thereafter. As stated in the Occupational Safety and Health Administration Bloodborne Pathogen Standards, it is the employer's responsibility to provide surgical team members with a hepatitis B vaccination within 10 days of their employment. If employees decline the vaccination, they must sign a declination form.[1]

Occupational Exposure to Bloodborne Pathogens

In 1991 OSHA published the "Final Rule on Occupational Exposure to Bloodborne Pathogens." This regulation provides full legal force to universal precautions: employers and employees must treat blood and body fluids as infectious. Meeting these requirements is not optional. Universal precautions are essential to prevent illness, chronic infection, and even death.[2] The regulation specifies that health-care workers must not get blood or other potentially infectious materials on their skin, hair, eyes, mouth, mucous membranes, or personal clothing. In complying, employers must implement strategies to protect their employees. Personal protective equipment (PPE) must be used when it is reasonably anticipated that skin, eye, mucous membrane, or parenteral contact with blood or other potentially infectious materials may result in the performance of duties. The duration, frequency, or amount of exposure is not relevant. An exposure incident is an event in the performance of an employee's duties when a contaminant makes specific contact with eyes, mouth, or other mucous membranes or nonintact skin. Nonintact skin is defined as having dermatitis, hangnails, cuts, abrasions, or chafing. An exposure incident also includes parenteral contact, such as occurs with human bites and needle sticks that break the skin.[1]

To comply with the OSHA regulations, each facility must establish an exposure control plan (ECP), which lists the job classifications in which some or all of the employees have occupational exposure, as well as the tasks and procedures performed by these employees where exposure may occur. In addition, compliance is achieved by requiring personal protective equipment, universal precautions, engineering controls, work practice controls, and housekeeping protocols.

Personal Protective Equipment (PPE)

Personal protective equipment includes special clothing, not necessarily impervious, or equipment worn to protect one from occupational exposure to blood or other potentially infectious materials. An employee's skin, eyes, mouth, or other mucous membranes, personal clothing, and undergarments should be protected from contamination. In the perioperative areas, PPE includes gloves, gowns, laboratory coats, face shields, masks, eye protection, and resuscitation devices. OSHA standards require that all PPE be removed prior to leaving the surgical suite.[1] In addition to the above personal protective equipment, head covers and shoe covers are also removed (shoe covers are not always worn). Contamination does not have to be visible to necessitate removal of the protective item.

If PPE is penetrated by any contaminated material, such as blood, the item must be removed immediately, or as soon as feasible. It is the responsibility of employers to launder, repair, replace, or dispose of all PPE at no cost to the employee.

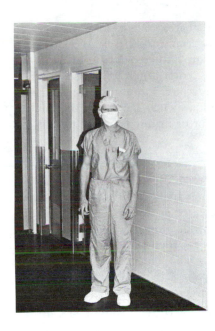

Figure 7–1. Proper operating attire.

Scrub Attire. Proper scrub attire is made of a cool, flame-resistant fabric that meets or exceeds the NFPA standards. Name tags are included in the attire, which should be worn by all members of the surgical team, support personnel, and visitors in all areas of the surgical suite.

Scrub attire consists of a two-piece pant suit. The sleeves must be short enough to permit adequate scrubbing above the elbow (Fig. 7–1). The top should be tucked inside the pants to prevent contamination as personnel move about the suite and to decrease dissemination of bacterial shedding from the thoracic and abdominal skin of the wearer. Wearing trousers decreases dispersal of bacteria-carrying particles from the skin. Pants should have tight cuffs or ankle closures. Circulating nurses and anesthesiologists should wear jackets to prevent shedding from bare arms and to protect forearms form contamination with blood and bloody fluid splashes. The jackets should be buttoned to prevent excessive air movement and contamination when moving around the sterile field.

When pants are donned, shoes should be removed; care must be exercised not to drag the pants along the floor. The wearer gathers the trouser legs in one hand and pulls each on without the trouser leg touching the floor.

Scrub attire should be changed daily or when it becomes visibly soiled or wet. It is discarded or placed in a laundry hamper after use, not hung or put in a locker to wear at another time. Mailhot and colleagues identified that bacterial counts were higher when scrub clothes were removed before lunch, stored in a locker, and donned after lunch.[3] Operating room attire should be transported and stored in closed carts.

Surgical attire should be worn only inside the surgical suite. If it becomes necessary to leave the area before changing, the scrub attire may be covered by a clean gown tied in the back at the neck and waist. Research has demonstrated that cover gowns provide some protection to certain areas of scrub attire.[4] No conclusive correlation has been established, however, between using a cover gown or changing scrub clothes before reentering the suite and the rate of surgical wound infection. Therefore, cover gowns are not cost effective and their use should be carefully considered by each facility. Jumpsuits with shoe coverings and appropriate headgear may be used by individuals when they enter the semirestricted areas of the surgical suite to perform minor repair or maintenance. Jumpsuits are not permitted in restricted areas.

Masks. Surgical masks are worn at all times in the restricted areas of the surgical suite, including areas where sterile supplies or scrubbed persons are located. Conversing and breathing without a mask results in droplet nuclei entering the air and settling on horizontal surfaces. With proper conditions for growth and reproduction, the bacteria multiply, become airborne, and may be deposited on sterile items or in the wound.

Surgical masks are air-purifying devices designed to filter out particulate, including bacteria, viruses, and fungi, from exhaled breath. The patient is thereby protected from the wearer's flora. The masks filter out particles 5 μ or larger with 99% efficiency. Studies have shown that potential airborne biohazards in the operating room could place operating room personnel at risk.

An aerosol is particulate formed from the disintegration of solid or liquid material in the matrix of air. In the surgical area, types of aerosol include dust, fumes, or mist, such as that created by powered tools, and smoke created by lasers and electrosurgery machines. Components of the smoke contain particles of carbonized tissue, blood, live DNA virus, and carcinogens. The risks of exposure to surgical smoke include infection and chronic irritation of skin, lungs, and mucous membranes.

Viruses range in size from 0.003 to 0.05 μm and bacteria from 0.3 to 13.0 μm. Thus, the standard surgical mask does not afford protection when an inhalation risk is perceived. In these situations, a respirator designed to seal to the face and control the wearer's inhalation exposure to airborne contaminants (including *Mycobacterium tuberculosis*), as small as 0.3 μ should be worn (see Chapter 6).

Surgical masks have many design features. Some have protective layers of special material that reduce the risk of fluid penetration. Some have a special fog filter to reduce eyeglass fogging; others a see-through visor to protect the eyes from splashing, spraying, or splattering blood or other infectious material. When applying the mask, it must be secured so as to prevent venting on the side. A metal strip is adjusted to conform with the nose, assisting in a proper fit and preventing fogging of eyeglasses. Masks should not be left to hang around the neck or be put into a pocket for future use, as bacteria collected from the nasopharyngeal airway will contaminate scrub attire.

Surgical masks are disposed of after each surgical procedure. When removing a mask, only the strings are handled. Due to the excessive contamination, care must be exercised not to touch the filter portion of the mask.

Goggles. Goggles must be worn by members of the surgical team to protect their eyes. Face shields should be used whenever power saws, drills, or irrigation is used. The OSHA

Standards require that eyeglasses or goggles have side shields to protect from lateral splashing. Routine cleaning of the goggles is essential immediately following each case.

Surgical Gowns. Surgical gowns and gloves, originally worn by surgical team members to protect the patient, now are also worn to protect personnel from the blood and body fluids of patients. The OSHA Standards state that protective clothing must prevent blood or other potentially infectious materials from reaching the skin or clothing. The type of material or fabric that should be used in the manufacture of the gown is not specified, however. Universally accepted methods of testing a fabric's level of fluid resistance have not been established.[6] Gowns that are impervious to liquids in a laboratory situation may not in practice be effective. The stretching and shearing of fabric that occurs in the OR reduces protection from liquid penetration. Surgical gowns that are available exhibit varying resistance; the only complete protection found in one study was plastic reinforcements or an impervious apron under the surgical gown.[7]

One study indicated that surgical gowns should be impervious to liquids, especially over the arms and anterior trunk.[8] One option is to wear an extra pair of sleeves over the gown. Heavy strikethrough occurs most frequently on the cuffs and sleeves worn by surgeons and first assistants during deep cavity surgery, when the forearms are exposed to moist laparotomy sponges, and when there is surface abrasion of the gown's forearm; damage to the gown's fiber structure results.

Reinforced surgical gowns are more costly than the standard gown, but are not required for all team members. One study suggested that OR attire be determined according to the team members' roles, the blood loss estimated, and the length of the procedure (Table 7–1).

Gloves. Gloves will also protect team members from exposure to the patient's blood, body fluids, and mucous membranes. Types of gloves include disposable surgical gloves, examination gloves, and reusable utility gloves. Disposable gloves are made of vinyl, natural latex, synthetic rubber, or polyethylene. It is important that they meet the FDA standards for protective gloves and that the correct type of glove is used for the task to be performed. Latex gloves provide a better barrier than vinyl gloves and should be used when a barrier to blood and fluids is required over an extended period of time. Vinyl gloves are appropriate and economical; they may be used, for example, when the circulating nurse counts sponges. Disinfecting agents may cause vinyl gloves to deteriorate and moisture may soak through by capillary action (wicking); reusable utility gloves are advocated for tasks such as end of case cleaning.

For staff members allergic to latex, alternatives, such as hypoallergenic gloves, glove liners, or powderless gloves, must be available.[1] All latex substitutes are not equally impermeable to blood-borne pathogens and care must be exercised when choosing substitutes. Gloves must be changed as soon as possible when they become torn or punctured, and hands must be washed when gloves are removed. Reusable utility gloves can be disinfected and reused if they have no signs of deterioration, which would compromise their barrier function.[1] Wearing two pairs of gloves provides additional protection to the scrub team, resulting in a 60% to 80% decrease in inner-glove perforation and visible-glove contamination.[9] Cut-resistant glove liners and puncture-resistant gloves are also available. The liners

TABLE 7–1. SUGGESTED ATTIRE FOR SURGEON, FIRST ASSISTANT

Operative site	Estimated blood loss/duration of procedure		
	<100mL/<2 hr	100–500 mL/2–4 hr	>500 mL/ > 4 hr
Head/neck	Standard gown	Reinforced gown/boots	Reinforced gown/boots
Chest	Standard gown	Reinforced gown	Reinforced gown
Abdomen	Reinforced gown	Impervious gown	Impervious gown/boots
Perineum	Reinforced gown	Impervious gown	Impervious gown/boots
Extremity	Standard gown	Reinforced gown/boots	Impervious gown/boots

Note:
- All trauma requires impervious gown and boots.
- Transurethral resection of the prostate (TURP) requires specialty gown and boots.
- Boots should be knee-high disposable footwear.
- Scrub person always wears standard gown.
- Other assistants wear one level less protection than surgeon or first assistant.

Adapted from Hubbard S et al. Reducing blood contamination and injury in the OR. AORN J. 1992;55 (1):199, with permission.

are made of polymer fibers or a metal mesh. Some are disposable and others may be sterilized with steam or ethylene oxide. Gloves do not prevent needle-stick injuries; however, evidence has been reported that gloves may provide some protection. Gerberding, for example, found a significant reduction, up to 50%, in the amount of blood on a needle as it passed through a latex or vinyl glove because of the wipe-off effect of the material.[10] The most common locations of injuries caused by a sharp instrument are, in the order of occurrence, the index finger and the thumb followed by the other digits.[11] Research indicates that there is a barrier loss as the length of the surgical procedure increases. The physical characteristics of gloves may change due to body heat and contact with fat or other physiologic fluids.[12]

Latex Sensitivity. Latex allergy is a significant problem for some patients and surgical team members. The FDA reports that 6% to 7% of all surgical personnel are sensitive to latex.[13] Allergic reactions are classified as local and systemic (anaphylactic). The American College of Allergy and Immunology has indicated that the following groups of individuals appear to be at risk:

- patients (particularly children) with myelomeningocele and/or a history of chronic or recurrent instrumentation of the genitourinary tract
- patients receiving barium enemas via a latex balloon tip catheter
- patients involved in manufacturing latex gloves or catheters
- health care personnel and others who wear gloves and become sensitized, including individuals with histories of eczematous reactions to some brands of gloves.[14]

The majority of patients who develop latex hypersensitivity have histories of allergic conditions, such as hay fever. It is important that every patient be asked about any unexplained allergy they might have experienced before they undergo a procedure that involves contact with latex. Any patient who has a history of rashes, itching, hives, rhinitis, swelling, eye irritation, or asthmatic symptoms after touching a balloon, rubber gloves, or any object that contains latex is at risk for anaphylaxis. According to the College, anaphylactic events rarely occur in health care providers or other workers who report a history of only mild eczema caused by latex gloves. A history, however, of severe or worsening eczema induced by latex gloves or work-related conjunctivitis, rhinitis, asthma, or urticaria may indicate allergic sensitization and an increased risk for more severe reactions in the future.[14]

The anaphylactic reaction is characterized by hypotension, tachycardia, increased airway pressure with bronchospasm, and generalized erythema. In most cases, it is necessary to end the surgical procedure because of the patient's unstable condition.

If a suspected or actual allergic reaction occurs, the patient and family should receive appropriate literature explaining all the signs, symptoms, and risk factors for latex allergy. The information should recommend that the patient consider immunology testing to confirm sensitivity. The patient should wear an allergy identification bracelet and carry epinephrine to treat accidental exposure reactions.[15]

The following five techniques are recommended to protect patients at risk for latex-sensitive reactions:

1. Latex-sensitive patients should be protected from unintended exposures in the same manner as drug-sensitive patients. Hospital protocol regarding allergies should be observed, including an allergy wristband.
2. All products and medical procedures that come into direct patient contact or are used by health-care personnel must be reviewed for possible latex content. A master list of items safe to use on sensitive patents should be available in each surgical suite. Manufacturers should be consulted about their specific products to determine if the products contain latex and whether a latex-free alternative is available (Table 7–2).
3. For elective surgical procedures, physicians should refer patients with myelomeningocele to centers that have latex-free surgical suites. Physicians should evaluate patients with histories that suggest a high risk of anaphylaxis and treat them appropriately before surgery.
4. Health-care personnel who show signs of latex contact dermatitis or latex hypersensitivity should avoid continued exposure to natural latex products and use either synthetic latex or nonlatex substitutes.
5. Hands should be washed immediately after removing gloves to eliminate latex proteins from the skin and prevent latex protein transfer to mucous membranes of the eyes, nose, or mouth. Handwashing after glove removal also prevents transfer of latex proteins to other surfaces where they may be contacted by latex-sensitive individuals.[15]

Skin Care. In an attempt to reduce the latex allergens transferred to their hands, team members may unwisely use protective hand creams before donning gloves. The practice has negative ramifications both for the gloves acting as a barrier and for the person wearing the gloves.

TABLE 7–2. COMMON ITEMS CONTAINING LATEX AND ALTERNATIVE NONLATEX PRODUCTS

Latex Items	Nonlatex Alternatives
Catheters	Silastic catheters
Blue paper towel drape with adhesive	Cloth towels
Blood pressure cuff tubing	Rolled cotton batting on areas of contact with patient's skin
Self-adhering tape	Plastic tape, paper tape
Esmarch bandages	White cotton ace
IV bag and burrette rubber stopper	Do not puncture with needle
IV tubing rubber stoppers	Three-way stopcocks on IV tubing
Face masks with elastic bands	Other types of surgical mask
Medication vial rubber stoppers	Remove rubber stoppers to withdraw medication
Mouth gags	Silastic mouth gag
Penrose drain	Nonlatex glove for IV tournequet, Jackson-Pratt drain, vessel loops for vessels, tendon retraction
Rubber bands	Vessel loops, small pieces of nonlatex gloves
Rubber shods or suture bolsters	Cut pieces of silastic catheter
Syringes with rubber plungers	No premixed medications
Tourniquet cuff tubing	Rolled cotton batting on areas of skin contact
Urine drainage system port	Prevent any patient contact; cover with tape

Adapted from Young M et al. Latex allergy. AORN J. 1992:56(3):496–497, with permission.

It is unacceptable to use sterile petrolatum ointment on the hands after the surgical hand scrub, before donning sterile gloves. A hydrocarbon-based lubricant, such as petrolatum or oil, will penetrate the latex, causing it to swell and act as a plasticizer. Plasticizers change the physical characteristics of the polymer, including its elasticity, tear resistance, and dimensional stability.[12] While water-based lubricants do not affect the physical properties of the latex, they may not produce the desired effect. Beezhold and coworkers found that the use of hand creams before donning gloves increased the amount of latex protein that was transferred from gloves to the hands of the wearer.[16] Before surgical team members use an ointment or emollient, the manufacturer of the glove should be contacted for specific information regarding changes that may occur to the physical characteristics of the glove.

Other Protective Measures

Head Coverings. Hair, if not completely covered, can be a source of bacteria and cause wound infections. Therefore, all personnel entering the semirestricted and restricted areas of the surgical suite must wear a covering over all head and facial hair, including sideburns and neckline hair. It should be donned before scrub attire to prevent hair and dandruff from collecting on the attire.

The scrub cap or surgical hood must be clean and lint-free and made of a fabric that meets or exceeds the standards of the National Fire Protection Association. Bouffant and hood-style head covers are preferred. Skullcaps are inadequate and should not be worn in the surgical suite. Caps made of net or crinoline should not be worn either, as they permit dandruff and hair fallout.

Reusable head coverings are acceptable if they are laundered after each use in the hospital's laundry facility. Ensuring proper laundering procedures is one reason OSHA advocates having contaminated PPE remain in the employer's control. Home laundering could lead to migration of contaminants outside the work environment.[1]

Footwear. Surgical shoes should be covered if the probability is high that contamination with blood or other potentially infectious materials will occur. Shoe covers, however, should not be required, as no controlled clinical studies indicate that the covers prevent or reduce surgical wound infections. Studies have shown that there was no significant difference in floor contamination when ordinary shoes, clean shoes, or shoe covers were worn. In another study, Copp and colleagues found that unprotected street shoes transferred a considerable number of bacteria onto a study area in the OR, and that they could be reduced by staff wearing OR-restricted shoes or shoe covers. The study, however, did not examine whether the bacteria on street shoes were directly related to wound infections.[5] No strong theoretical rationale supports the use of shoe covers or indicates that the benefits expected from them are cost effective. The primary reason, then, for protective foot attire is to facilitate sanitation. If covers are worn, they are removed before leaving the surgical area and removed when they become torn, wet, or soiled.

If explosive anesthetics are used within the surgical suite, conductive shoe covers must be worn. When applying these shoe covers, a black carbon strip is placed inside the sock in contact with the bottom of the foot. Conductivity should be checked before entering the surgical suite and at frequent intervals throughout the day. If appropriate measures of conductivity do not occur immediately, a few drops of water in the bottom of the shoe will help achieve the proper measurement.

When choosing footwear, the kind of equipment used in the surgical suite is an important consideration. Necessary reaction times are another factor. Because most of the equipment is very heavy and emergency situations require quick responses, canvas shoes and clogs are not recommended for the surgical suite. Clogs do not provide the ankle support and stability required for efficient, safe functioning within the environment. Shoes should be easy to clean and have enclosed toes and heels to minimize injuries.

Unnecessary Adornment. Rings, watches, and necklaces are reservoirs for bacteria and should be prohibited in the surgical suite. Earrings that dangle outside the scrub hat may fall into the sterile field; necklaces may contaminate the front of the sterile gown if not confined.

Universal Precautions

Medical histories and examinations cannot reliably identify all patients infected with HIV or other blood-borne pathogens; blood and body-fluid precautions should be consistently used for all patients. This approach, recommended by the Centers for Disease Control and Prevention (CDC), is referred to as universal blood and body-fluid precautions, or universal precautions. It should be used in the care of all patients, particularly those in emergency situations where the risk of blood exposure is increased and the infection status of the patient is usually unknown.[1]

Precautions in the surgical suite include:

1. All personnel, including the circulating nurse, should routinely use appropriate barrier precautions to prevent skin and mucous-membrane exposure when contact with blood or other body fluids of any patient is anticipated.
2. Gloves should be worn for touching blood and body fluids, mucous membranes, or nonintact skin of all patients; for handling items or surfaces soiled with blood or body fluids; and for performing venipuncture and other vascular access procedures.
3. Masks and protective eyewear or face shields should be worn by all personnel during procedures that are likely to generate aerosolization or splashing of fluids.
4. Impervious gowns or plastic aprons should be worn during procedures that are likely to generate splashes of blood or other body fluids.
5. Hands and other skin surfaces should be washed immediately and thoroughly if contaminated with blood or other body fluids. Hands should be washed immediately after gloves are removed.
6. Sharp items (needles, scalpel blades, and other sharp instruments) should be considered potentially infective and should be handled with extraordinary care to prevent accidental injuries.
7. Hands should not be used in place of retractors.
8. Surgeons and first assistants may use a thimble on the index finger of the nondominant hand to prevent injuries while suturing.
9. Broken glassware that may be contaminated must not be picked up directly with the hands. A dust pan with tongs or forceps should be used in the operating rooms. A brush or broom may be used in the PACU.
10. Disposable syringes, needles, scalpel blades, and other sharp items should be placed in puncture-resistant containers located as close as is practical to the area in which they are used. To prevent needle-stick injuries, needles should not be recapped, purposefully bent, broken, removed from disposable syringes, or otherwise manipulated by hand. Disposable syringes and needles are preferred; only needle-locking syringes or one-piece needle-syringe units should be used to aspirate fluids from patients.
11. To minimize the need for emergency mouth-to-mouth resuscitation, mouthpieces, resuscitation bags, and other ventilation devices should be available for use in areas where the need for resuscitation is predictable.
12. Team members who have exudative lesions or weeping dermatitis should refrain from all direct patient care and from handling patient-care equipment until the condition resolves.
13. All specimens of blood, body fluids, or tissue should be put into a container with a secure lid to prevent leaking during transport. Care must be used to prevent contamination of the outside of the container. The use of a self-sealable plastic bag de-

signed with an outside pouch to hold the requisition serves as an excellent method of containing tissue specimens.

14. All soiled linen should be handled as little as possible. It should be placed and transported in bags that prevent leakage.
15. Waste should be disposed of as indicated by the state and local health departments regarding the disposal of infectious waste. Table 7–3 presents requirements for handling medical waste.
16. Eating, drinking, smoking, and personal grooming are permitted only in designated areas.

ENGINEERING AND OTHER WORKPLACE CONTROLS

Air Circulation

Three sources of airborne organisms may be present in the operating room: air delivered to the room through the ventilation system; surgical team members; and aerosolization from lasers, electrosurgery machines, and surgical powered tools. As described in Chapter 2, an effective ventilation system, properly maintained, can minimize contamination.

Microorganisms collect on horizontal surfaces, such as the floor, countertops, and equipment. Air turbulence created by excessive numbers of people in the operating room, swinging doors, or shaking of linen may cause bacteria to settle on the sterile field or in the wound. Educating the staff and establishing a policy to control traffic and visitors within the operating room will assist in controlling airborne microorganisms.

TABLE 7–3. REQUIREMENTS FOR HANDLING MEDICAL WASTE

	Mandatory		Voluntary		
Item	State	OSHA	EPA	CDC	JCAHO
Formal education/training	X	X	Ltd.	X	X
Sharp boxes	X	X	X	X	X
Biohazard labels	X	X	X	X	X
Written program	X	X	0	X	X
Infection control	X	X	0	X	X
Hazard communication	X	X	0	X	X
Vaccination	X	X	0	0	X
Personal Protective Equipment	X	X	0	X	X
Universal precautions	X	X	0	X	X
Waste disposal	X	X Ltd.	X	X	X

Ltd. = Limited
X = Yes
0 = No
Adapted from Fay M et al. Medical waste: the growing issues of management and disposal. AORN J. 1990:51(6)1506.

Smoke Evacuators

The components of smoke from electrosurgery machines and lasers contain particles of carbonized tissue, blood, live DNA virus, and known carcinogens. The potential risks of exposure to surgical aerosols include infection and chronic irritation of skin, lungs, and mucous membranes. An evacuation system may protect patients and perioperative personnel from inhaling the smoke generated during electrosurgery and from inhaling the plume associated with laser use.[17] When the CO_2 laser is used, the laser beam is absorbed by water in the tissue and converted into heat. Rapid boiling results, increasing the pressure in cells until they explode or vaporize. The high temperature created at the laser site carbonizes protein and other organic matter within the cell and causes gaseous hydrocarbons to form. The carbonized cell fragments, water vapor, and hydrocarbons are released in the smoke plume.[18] While further research must be performed to determine the actual magnitude of smoke exposure from electrosurgery, preliminary findings suggest that the potential for bacterial and viral contamination of electrosurgical smoke is similar to that generated by lasers.[19]

A freestanding smoke evacuator system with a high-efficiency filter decreases the risk of smoke and plume inhalation. Using wall suction lines to exhaust smoke plume is not recommended.[20] If the central vacuum system is used, the particulate matter in the smoke plume can compromise the system and, over time, decrease or destroy suctioning capability throughout the system. As more and more particles are retained in the system, airflow resistance increases, which decreases suction capabilities.[18] Mechanical smoke evacuator systems contain one or more particulate filters to remove carbonaceous particles from the suctioned smoke plume. A charcoal filter may be used to absorb the gaseous hydrocarbons contained in the smoke. The filtered air is then recirculated back into the environment through a vent in the evacuator machine. The smoke evacuator efficiency is determined by the system's ability to capture the smoke plume at the point of generation and by the particle size for which filtration is specified.[17] The placement of the evacuator suction tubing should be as close to the source of the smoke as possible to maximize smoke capture and enhance visibility at the surgical site.

Methyl Methacrylate

Methyl methacrylate (MMA), or bone cement, is a mixture of liquid and powder polymers. It is used to hold metal or synthetic prostheses in place, for example, during total joint replacements. It is the responsibility of the scrub assistant to mix the chemical at the sterile field just before use. The vapors released during mixing irritate the eyes and respiratory tract. The fumes, in high concentrations, may also cause drowsiness. Animal studies and cytogenetic studies have shown that exposure to MMA may be mutagenic, carcinogenic, and hepatotoxic.

A scavenging system may reduce the occupational hazards posed by handling MMA. The system collects the vapor during mixing and then exhausts it to the outside air or absorbs it through activated charcoal.

In addition, to prevent skin irritation, two pairs of latex gloves should be worn while the cement is in use, since the chemical can diffuse through a single pair of gloves.

Environmental Design

As indicated in Chapter 2, the design of the surgical suite and the use of specific building materials will have an impact on the effectiveness of housekeeping procedures.

Cracks and crevices harbor microorganisms and should be eliminated during construction or controlled with proper maintenance. When operating rooms are undergoing renovation or construction, patients must be protected from airborne contaminants by impervious barriers constructed between the surgical suite and the construction area. Of primary concern are fungi. Spores accumulate with dust and may result in aspergillosis infections. Sheetrock walls are preferable to taped plastic drapes that can be pushed aside. Construction materials should be transported during off-hours, and the site should be thoroughly cleaned before transporting patients through the area.

The Joint Commission on Accreditation of Healthcare Organizations identifies interim safety measures that must be carried out during the construction and remodeling of an occupied building. They include, but are not limited to, training staff, removing debris, and monitoring construction activities.

■ HOUSEKEEPING PROTOCOLS

Management and Disposal of Medical Waste

Of all medical waste, 20% percent is infectious. Another 5% consists of toxic, corrosive, flammable, reactive, or radioactive materials, and is classified as regulated waste. The remaining 70 to 75% of medical waste is usually less contaminated than household waste.[21] Medical waste is generated by clinics, nursing homes, blood banks, laboratories, and physician and dental offices. Hospitals, however, are the major producers; operating rooms produce more than other departments. Waste from the operating room includes sharps, microbiological cultures, pathological or anatomical waste, human blood and blood products, patient drapes, bloody sponges, gowns, gloves, body parts and tissue, bandages, casts, catheters, and other items used in the care of the surgical patient.

The Environmental Protection Agency (EPA) has broadly defined infectious waste as waste capable of producing an infectious disease,[22] though an acceptable method of treating various waste products has yet to be established. Diseases that are potentially transmissible in infectious waste include hepatitis B, non-A non-B hepatitis, HIV disease, malaria, syphilis, enteric diseases, and tuberculosis. Treatments usually employed to decontaminate medical waste include heat (such as incineration, autoclaving, and microwaving), chemicals (hypochlorite, chlorine dioxide), and radiation (gamma ray, electron beam).

Some states have adopted their own health and environmental standards for handling, packaging, transporting, and disposing of waste. Because no firm guidelines are in place, hospitals must determine which wastes constitute a biological hazard and establish their own waste management program. These programs involve:

1. Forming a waste management team with the authority to implement an internal program that meets the EPA requirements
2. Identifying what waste poses a hazard of infection
3. Educating staff regarding what waste poses a significant infection hazard

4. Using containers that confine, contain, and identify infectious waste for transportation, such as red plastic bags and rigid, leak-resistant containers
5. Establishing an effective enforcement system that identifies individuals and departments that do not follow established guidelines

Most noninfectious, unregulated medical waste is placed in landfills; most infectious waste from hospitals is incinerated. Among hospitals, 67% use on-site incinerators, 16% use autoclave systems and landfills, and approximately 15% have off-site treatment facilities.[23]

Perioperative nurses must be alert to the need to segregate potentially infectious material from clean waste at the point of generation to reduce the cost associated with processing the material. Throughout the surgical suite, color-coded, labeled bags may be used to visually segregate infectious waste from noninfectious waste.

To decrease supply waste, custom, packs may be used that eliminate the need for outer wrappers on many items contained within the pack. In addition, when reviewing current and new products or materials, consideration must be given to the by-products of the item. Industry should be encouraged to use more biodegradable materials in the manufacture of items used for surgical patients.

Sanitation of Equipment and the Environment

The environment of the surgical suite cannot be sterilized; however, through appropriate disinfection of floors, furniture, surgical lights, and equipment, the transmission of pathogenic organisms can be prevented.

Cleaning the surgical suite may be the responsibility of the housekeeping department, hospital assistants, or both. When responsibility is shared, hospital assistants are usually responsible for the end-of-procedure cleanup and the housekeeping department for the terminal cleaning. If any portion of the cleaning is delegated to the housekeeping department, it is imperative that the nurse manager and executive housekeeper together determine the routine procedures to be used to clean the surgical suite. To effectively implement the cleaning program, housekeeping employees and hospital assistants must be instructed and trained in the cleaning procedures and their rationales.

Prior to the day's first scheduled surgical procedure, all horizontal surfaces, including furniture, countertops, equipment, and surgical lights, are damp-dusted with a hospital-grade disinfectant. During the surgical procedure, perioperative personnel are responsible for confining and containing contamination to the area around the sterile field. All surgical procedures are considered contaminated.

When scrubbed, perioperative personnel are responsible for the correct use and maintenance of instruments throughout the procedure. The following techniques are consistent with this concept and help control cross-contamination:

1. Sponges are discarded into a plastic-lined kick bucket.
2. The circulator uses an instrument or disposable gloves when counting sponges or needles and when receiving any item passed from the sterile field.
3. If an area becomes contaminated by organic debris, such as blood, the area should immediately be cleaned using a tuberculocidal hospital-grade disinfectant or a 1:10 dilution of household bleach, which is prepared daily. This procedure will prevent the tracking of organic debris throughout the surgical suite.

4. A surgical instrument that falls to the floor is picked up by the circulator, wearing disposable gloves, and placed in a pan containing a hospital-grade disinfectant. It remains there until the case is completed. This procedure prevents organic debris from drying and becoming airborne. If the instrument is needed to complete the surgical procedure, it is washed prior to being sterilized.

At the conclusion of the surgical procedure, the scrub has several responsibilities:

1. Linen is removed from the patient and placed in an impervious laundry bag. Laundry bags and containers must be color coded and labeled with biohazard signs.
2. All gross blood and other debris are removed from the surgical instruments. All instruments are disassembled and box locks or hinges opened before they are placed on perforated trays in preparation for reprocessing. By placing delicate and special instruments in a separate pan, additional protection is provided, which will prolong the life of the instruments.

    If a washer-sterilizer is not available, one of the following alternative procedures may be carried out after instruments are carefully washed and rinsed:

    a) Place instruments in a perforated tray and autoclave at 270°F (132°C) for 3 minutes or at 250°F (121°C) for 15 to 20 minutes, or

    b) Collect instruments in a watertight basin; transfer them to a pressure steam sterilizer; cover with a 2% solution of trisodium phosphate. Sterilize for 30 minutes at 270°F (132°C) or for 45 minutes at 250°F (121°C) to 254°F (124°C). Use fast exhaust for drying.

3. Suction tips and other instruments that have a lumen are irrigated with water to prevent obstruction with organic material. Disposable suction tubing is recommended due to the difficulty encountered in cleaning the lumen of reusable suction tubing.
4. All knife blades and needles are disposed of in a puncture-resistant container so that they will not be a potential source of injury and contamination to support personnel. Knowing how trash is disposed of (compactor, incinerator, or as landfill) and what the local regulations are will influence which procedure is used to dispose of items from the operating room.
5. All disposable items are put in impervious containers.
6. All linen items, soiled or not, are placed in an impervious hamper bag to be laundered.
7. All solutions are suctioned out of the basins, and the items are dried for terminal sterilization.
8. The circulator disconnects suction tubing from the wall to avoid contamination of the wall outlet. The contents of the suction container should be disposed of in a hopper while it is flushing. Adding a commercial garbage disposal to the hopper will help dispose of blood clots and bone chips.

    If a hopper is not available, the suction contents are decontaminated with a proper disinfectant before disposal.

    If glass suction bottles are used, they must be washed and terminally sterilized after each case.

9. Items that require gas sterilization are cleaned and then wiped with a detergent germicide before transporting them to a workroom or central supply department for reprocessing.
10. The scrub assistant then removes his or her gown and gloves and closes the case cart, or covers the table contents by touching the clean ends of the table drape. The table or cart is then removed from the operating room.

Instrument Decontamination

The potential hazard of direct contact with the virus of serum hepatitis or AIDS is ever present when handling contaminated surgical instruments. Consequently, instruments are decontaminated using a five-step process: soaking, prerinsing, washing, rinsing, and sterilizing.

In the decontamination area of the workroom or central supply department, instruments are soaked in an enzyme solution for a minimum of 2 minutes. Effective soaking removes all visible debris except for ointments and, in most situations, is an acceptable alternative to manual cleaning.[24]

Instruments are removed from the solution and rinsed under running water, preferably with a power spray to thoroughly remove the enzymatic solution. Cannulated items are rinsed by forcing water or air through the openings to determine whether the items are free of soilage.

If it is necessary to use a brush to clean the instruments, the brush must be kept below the water level to prevent the dissemination of microorganisms in aerosols and droplets. Personnel should wear a plastic apron, protective eyewear, gloves, and a mask when performing this task. Adequate ventilation is essential because the enzymatic product may cause redness or irritation to the skin, mucous membranes, or eyes.

The instrument washer-sterilizer is generally used for mechanical cleaning (Fig. 7–2). For the washer-sterilizer to perform at maximum effectiveness, however, organic debris must not be permitted to dry in serrations, box locks, or ratchets of the instruments. To prevent drying, instruments must be wiped, rinsed, or soaked during the surgical procedure. Soaking instruments, such as intestinal clamps, rongeurs, and bone rasps, in cold water immediately after use facilitates the cleaning process.

The washing process in the washer-sterilizer is accomplished by means of a vigorously agitated detergent bath. A combination of high-velocity jet streams of steam and air develop a violent underwater turbulence (Fig. 7–3). During the washing phase, water temperature rises to 63°C to 68°C (145°F to 155°F). The detergent solution disengages the blood, grease, and tissue debris from the instruments and carries it to the surface. As the heated water expands in the chamber, the level rises, and the released soil and scum overflow into the waste line. The automatic program control then activates the steam-inlet and water-outlet valves. Steam is admitted into the top of the chamber, forcing the wash water out through the bottom drain. Steam under pressure floods the chambers, and the temperature of 132°C (270°F) is maintained for not less than 3 minutes. Then the steam is exhausted through an automatic condenser exhaust and an audible signal indicates that the washer-sterilizer is ready for unloading.

If a washer-sterilizer is not available, instruments should be soaked in an enzyme solution, washed in warm water with a moderately alkaline low-sudsing detergent, thoroughly

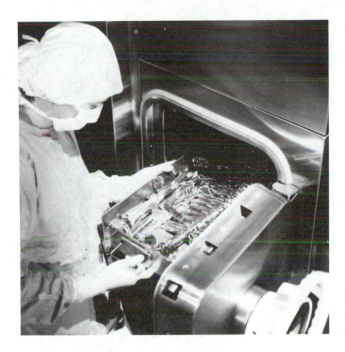

Figure 7–2. Loading a washer-sterilizer with all instruments open or on a stringer. *(Courtesy American Sterilizer Company, Erie, PA).*

cleaned, and then rinsed with hot water. Rinsing with hot water is essential because the residual heat will assist in the rapid drying of the instruments.

Water spotting and discoloration of instruments may occur for various reasons, such as when the water has a high mineral content and the instruments are allowed to dry slowly. Remaining moisture may also cause rust. Water spotting may also occur if the drying cycle in the autoclave is faulty. The valves and gaskets on the autoclave should be checked for proper fit. In addition, steam supplies to hospital sterilizers may contain inorganic impurities, such as rust or particles from the inside of the pipes. When these impurities are deposited on instruments they can cause stains. Wet steam will cause wet packs and contribute to staining of the linen. Removing these solids and liquid impurities from steam through an in-line steam filter will eliminate these problems.

Installing new sterilizers or repairing old sterilizers or plumbing may contribute to instrument stains. To prevent mineral deposits due to new plumbing, the autoclave should be run empty for 100 cycles prior to autoclaving instruments. The wrong detergent may also cause spots, stains, or discoloration on instruments. If instruments have a yellow-brown discoloration, it indicates that the detergent has an incorrect pH. Detergents should be neutral (a pH of 7). Moreover, random corrosion and pitting result from blood, debris, or both left on the instrument too long after use. Patterned pitting occurs when a chemical indicator comes in contact with instruments, particularly in "flash" sterilization. Indicators and other paper should not touch instruments. Laundry residue from cloth wrappers or chemicals released from paper wrappers may also discolor instruments.

Following terminal decontamination, the instruments may be placed in the ultrasonic cleaner.

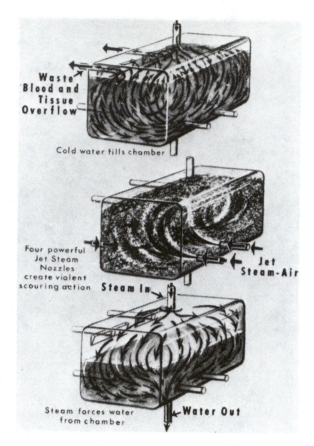

Figure 7–3. Cleaning of instruments is accomplished by means of a vigorously agitated detergent bath. The combination of high-velocity jet streams of steam and air develops violent underwater turbulence. (*From Perkins JJ* Principles and Methods of Sterilization in Health Sciences, *2nd ed., 1978. Springfield, IL: Charles C Thomas, with permission.*)

Ultrasonic Cleaning of Instruments

The ultrasonic cleaner helps maintain surgical instruments in proper working condition by removing debris from the box locks and serrations. It is the final step in processing instruments. Dissimilar metals, such as copper, brass, and stainless steel, are not combined in the ultrasonic unit, as cleaning dissimilar metals causes ion transfer resulting in etching and pitting. Chrome-plated instruments are not put in the ultrasonic cleaner, as they may be damaged by mechanical vibrations, which cause flaking.

Ultrasonic is the term used to describe a vibrating wave of frequency above that of the upper-frequency limit of the human ear; it generally embraces all frequencies above 15,000 cycles per second. The process of cleaning instruments is called cavitation.

Cavitation occurs when sound waves passed through water create cavities ranging in size from submicroscopic to large. These minute bubbles expand until they are unstable and then collapse. The implosion (bursting inward) generates minute vacuum areas on the instruments that are responsible for the cleaning process. During cavitation, the binder that adheres the organic debris to the instrument is dislodged, dispersed, or dissolved.

Some of the debris rises to the surface of the solution, while heavier debris settles to the bottom of the tank.

After cleaning, the instruments must be rinsed under pressure to remove residual debris and detergent. The instruments are then dried at 88°C (190°F).

The ultrasonic cleaner does not decontaminate or sterilize and must not be used as a substitute for the washer-sterilizer. If instruments are not decontaminated prior to being placed in the ultrasonic cleaner, the solution will serve as a reservoir for microorganisms with subsequent cross-contamination.

The effectiveness of the ultrasonic cleaner may be measured by rubbing pencil lead into the porous surface of a ceramic ring. The ceramic ring is then placed with the porous side up in a tray, and the ultrasonic cleaner is turned on for 1 minute. If more than 75% of the lead is removed, the cleaner is functioning appropriately.

Lubricating Instruments

Detergents used in the washer-sterilizer and the ultrasonic cleaner remove the lubricant from stainless steel. Therefore, all instruments with movable parts should be lubricated after every cleaning. The water-soluble lubricate, frequently referred to as a milk bath, is antimicrobial and does not contain any toxic components. Residuals left on the instruments are not harmful to the patient, and for maximum effectiveness, the lubricating solution must not be rinsed or wiped off the instruments.

The lubricant provides a protective coating, which reduces instrument rusting, staining, and corrosion; it improves instrument function, reduces the growth of bacteria, and allows penetration of steam. In addition, the amount of organic debris that adheres to the stainless steel is reduced when the instruments are used in subsequent procedures, making them easier to clean. The lubricant must be water-soluble to allow steam penetration, have a neutral pH, and contain high amounts of surfactants to dissolve the protein material in box locks.

Inspecting and Sorting Instruments

After instruments are processed, they are sorted and inspected before being stored or placed in sets. Each instrument is examined for cleanliness and proper working condition. Hinged instruments are checked for stiffness and alignment of jaws and teeth. Sharp instruments, such as scissors and chisels, are checked for dents and chips and their sharpness verified; plated instruments are observed for chips, sharp edges, and worn spots. At the first sight of damage or malfuntioning, instruments are removed from circulation and repaired.

Stiff instruments should not be oiled, as steam sterilization will not effectively penetrate the oil. Stiffness is frequently due to foreign matter that has accumulated in the box lock. It usually does not occur when instruments are routinely processed in the ultrasonic cleaner. To relieve stiffness and regain smooth functioning, a small amount of a water-soluble grinding compound, available from instrument manufacturers, may be worked into the box lock by opening and closing the instrument several times.

For instruments that require lubrication, such as air drills, manufacturers offer silicone oil compounds or oil in water preparations that do not inhibit sterilization by autoclaving.

▌ MAINTAINING A STERILE FIELD

As discussed in Chapter 6, intact skin is an excellent barrier to microbial invasion. Any skin break, such as a surgical incision, results in a potential port of entry for microorganisms. Therefore, any item that comes in contact with the surgical incision must be sterile, that is, free of living microorganisms. Aseptic technique prevents contamination with microorganisms.

All members of the surgical team must be aware of the technique. As the patients' advocates, perioperative nurses must constantly be aware of what is occurring in and around the sterile field. They, as well as other members of the team, must exercise professional judgment and be willing to take the risk of pointing out known or suspected violations of the technique and of initiating corrective action. To perform this role effectively, it is essential that perioperative nurses have a thorough knowledge of the principles of aseptic technique and implement them.

Principles of Aseptic Technique

• *All Items Used within a Sterile Field Must Be Sterile.* A sterile field is created by placing a sterile towel or sheet over an unsterile surface. The sterile field is maintained by not permitting an unsterile item to come in contact with the field. Once a sterile drape is positioned, it cannot be moved or shifted.

Sterile items are stored in clean areas free from moisture. They must remain sterile until they are opened for use. Before opening a sterile package, the circulator must check for proper packaging, the integrity of the package and seal, the expiration date, and the appearance of the sterilization indicator.

Before removing items from the autoclave, the graph or printout must be checked to ascertain that the proper temperature was achieved for the appropriate amount of time. *If there is any doubt about the sterility of an item, it is considered unsterile.*

• *The Edges of Sterile Containers Are Not Considered Sterile Once the Package Is Opened.* Often, the boundaries between sterile and unsterile are not easily identified, and the perioperative nurse must exercise professional judgment in making these determinations.

When opening a large item, such as a linen pack, it is placed on a flat surface with the end flaps extended. The outer wrapper is then cuffed so that the circulating nurse avoids contact with the sterile contents by keeping all fingers under the cuff. To open the other side of the pack, the circulator must move to the other side of the table. If the wrapper is used to drape the table, the margin begins at the table edge.

In opening smaller items, the ends of the flaps are secured in the hand so they do not flip back and contaminate the contents or the sterile individual (Fig. 7–4). A 1-inch safety margin is standard on package wrappers.

On peel-back packages, the inner edge of the heat seal is the sterile boundary. The scrub nurse must remove items from these packages by lifting them straight up and not allowing the contents to slide over the edge. Sharp or heavy objects should always be presented to the scrub nurse or opened on a separate surface. Sterile items should not be "tossed" onto a sterile field, as they may roll off the edge or become contaminated, thereby increasing the cost of the procedure.

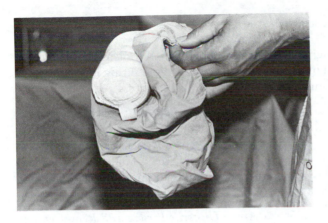

Figure 7–4. To prevent contamination, the ends of the flap are held so that they do not flip back and contaminate the contents of the package.

When the cap is removed from a sterile liquid, it is considered contaminated and may not be replaced on the bottle. The contents of the bottle must be used or discarded. When pouring from a bottle, the solution is poured in a steady stream so that it does not splash out of the container (Fig. 7–5). In addition, care must be exercised to prevent the solution from running over the unsterile part of the bottle, dripping onto the sterile field, and contaminating it.

To receive solutions, the scrub nurse moves the container to the table's edge or holds the receptacle so the circulator does not reach over the sterile field.

- *Gowns Are Considered Sterile in Front from Shoulder to Table Level. Sleeves Are Sterile to 2 Inches above the Elbow, to the Stockinette Cuff.* Wraparound gowns that cover the back may be sterile when they are first put on; however, because the back of the gown cannot be continuously observed, it is not considered sterile. The stockinette cuff is not considered sterile, as it is an area where moisture collects and, therefore, not an effective microbial barrier. The stockinette cuff should be covered by sterile gloves at all times. The neckline and shoulders are also considered unsterile.

Gloved hands should be kept in sight, at or above waist level. Arms should not be

Figure 7–5. The receptacle is moved to the edge of the table and the sterile solution is poured in a steady stream to prevent splashing.

folded with the hands tucked in the axillae because the hands may become contaminated with perspiration.

Scrub nurses should avoid changing levels (for example, from a footstool to the floor) and should not sit or lean against an unsterile surface. The only time sitting is acceptable is when the surgical procedure is performed from the sitting position.

• *Draped Tables Are Sterile Only at Table Level.* The sterile field on the back table or a "prep" table is limited to the top of the table. Any item falling over the edge is considered contaminated and cannot be brought back into the sterile field.

The same principle applies to the draped patient; however, the boundaries are less distinct. The perioperative nurse must exercise astute observation and professional judgment when interpreting sterile areas versus unsterile areas on the draped patient.

• *Sterile Persons and Items Contact Only Sterile Areas; Unsterile Persons and Items Contact Only Unsterile Areas.* The sterile members of the surgical team contact only sterile areas and sterile items. The unsterile members should not touch the sterile field, reach over it, or permit unsterile items to touch it. When opening a sterile item, the hands of the circulator should be positioned to avoid accidental contact with the scrub nurse or the sterile field. This safety margin can be created by using a cuff created by the sterile wrapper or by using a sterile instrument as an extension of the hand. A sterile instrument may be used for one transfer and is then considered contaminated.

When opening a sterile package, the scrub nurse opens the near side first (so the gown is protected) and the far side last, whereas the circulator opens the far side first and the near side last to prevent reaching over a sterile field.

During a case, provided that the status of the operative procedure permits, if items need to be flashed and the substerile item meets the appropriate physical configuration, the scrubbed person may leave the sterile field to retrieve the items from the autoclave. A second method of retrieval is to use a flash sterilization pan with a detachable handle. Without placing any portion of the arm into the sterilizer, the circulator attaches the cool, unsterile, detachable handle to the outside of the flash pan. The pan is then removed from the sterilizer using the handle and transported to the scrubbed person at the sterile field. The pan is held out to the scrubbed person who takes the sterilized item out of the pan without touching the unsterile handle. The pan should never be placed on any portion of the sterile field. If this type of pan is not available, the circulator can put on sterile gloves and, not reaching into the sterilizer, lift the pan from the sterilizer, touching only the front of the pan. The pan is carried to the scrubbed person, who removes the item from the pan. The pan should not be placed on the sterile field.

• *Movement within or around a Sterile Field Must Not Cause Contamination of the Sterile Field.* Sterile team members stay close to the sterile field; they do not wander about the room or leave it while in sterile attire. When sterile persons change positions, they move back-to-back or face-to-face, maintaining a safe distance from each other and the sterile field.

Unsterile team members circulate around the sterile area but do not come in direct contact with it. They maintain at least 1 foot of distance from the sterile field, always facing it and never walking between two sterile fields.

- *A Sterile Barrier That Has Been Permeated Must Be Considered Contaminated*. The integrity of drapes and gowns must be inspected before use and continuously during surgical intervention. When liquids soak through linen from the sterile to unsterile surface, "strikethrough" occurs. When that occurs, the barrier must be replaced or reinforced. Nonwoven and certain treated woven materials are more resistant to strikethrough. However, under abrasive conditions or prolonged exposure, strikethrough will occur in all materials.

Any sterile item that becomes damp or wet is considered contaminated. When items are removed from the autoclave, they must be permitted to dry before they are placed on a cold surface. This prevents condensation of steam, which would contaminate the item.

When a sharp instrument, such as a towel clip, perforates a barrier's sterile surface, the points of the instrument are contaminated and it may not be relocated.

- *Items of Doubtful Sterility Are Considered Unsterile*. When a sterile item wrapped in a pervious wrapper, such as muslin, is dropped on the floor, contaminated air may enter the package from the force of the fall. Therefore, the wrapped item is considered unsterile.

When dropped, items packaged in impervious wrappers are less likely to become contaminated. If the integrity of the package is maintained, the item is considered sterile and safe for immediate use.

Sterile fields are set up immediately prior to surgical intervention and must never be left unguarded. They should not be set up and then covered for later use, as it is impossible to remove the cover sheet without contaminating the field. If a surgical case is canceled or delayed, the field is considered contaminated and a new setup prepared.

It is not acceptable to use "splash basins" to rinse gloved hands. It is difficult to maintain the sterility of these basins, as they provide a potential breeding ground for the microorganisms that have been removed from the gloves.

■ END-OF-CASE CLEANUP

The built-in central wet vacuum pickup system is the method of choice for cleaning the floor between surgical procedures. To use it requires plugging a hose-and-wand into a wall outlet. A central system is quiet and eliminates any possibility of bacteria contaminating the air. In addition, equipment setup and cleanup time is reduced.

If the system is not available, the desired results may be achieved using a portable wet vacuum machine with a bacterial filter and a pump-type garden spray can to dispense a detergent disinfectant. Cleaning solutions must never be sprayed around analytical equipment, such as blood gas analyzers, as the aerosolized compounds may affect the equipment and result in sensitivity and status errors.

If a wet vacuum system is unavailable, a two-bucket technique with detergent germicide in both buckets can be used. If this technique is used, a clean mophead is used for each operating room and the buckets cleaned prior to storage at the end of each day.

It is important that a clean mophead and fresh decontaminating solution be used for each procedure. Soiled mops and buckets of solutions in which soiled mops have been rinsed are potential breeding grounds for bacteria. Soiled mops and solution standing in the department is not consistent with good infection control practices. When the same mophead and solution are used repeatedly throughout the day, bacteria may be transported from room to room and throughout the entire surgical suite.

With all of these techniques, it is only necessary to clean a 3- to 4-foot perimeter around the OR table. It is important, however, that the OR table be moved to check for any sponges or instruments that may be under the table. The area cleaned in between cases should be expanded to meet the level of contamination present following the procedure. Brooms should not be used in the surgical suite due to the air turbulence they create.

All personnel involved in cleaning within the surgical suite must wear utility gloves and eyewear to protect themselves and assist in preventing cross-contamination.

End-of-case cleanup involves the following steps:

1. All horizontal surfaces of furniture, equipment, and countertops are cleaned with a detergent germicide.
2. Walls and doors are spot-cleaned.
3. To avoid cracking the heat filters, the surgical light is cleaned after it is cooled. A detergent disinfectant is recommended by the manufacturer. Some disinfectants leave a residue and will reduce the amount of light available for use.
4. The operating room table is cleaned with a detergent disinfectant. Because organic debris tends to accumulate where sections of the table come together and under the mattress pad, all surfaces must be exposed and cleaned.
5. All equipment used for the surgical procedure is wiped with a detergent disinfectant and returned to the proper storage area.
6. After the floor is sprayed or wet down with the detergent disinfectant, the furniture is moved to one side of the room. Moving the operating room table and other equipment through the solution serves as a method of decontaminating the castors. The floor is then cleaned by one of the previously discussed methods.
7. The linen and trash bags are closed and then moved to the appropriate area for disposal.

During the day, the hallways and the substerile and scrub rooms should be mopped with a detergent disinfectant. The frequency will be determined by the number of cases and personnel in the surgical suite.

Doormats placed at the entrance to the surgical suite soaked in an antiseptic solution are not effective in reducing bacterial population. Mats soaked with an antiseptic solution do not affect the bacterial count of cart wheels or shoe soles that traverse them. The antiseptic solution requires a minimum contact time of at least 30 seconds to be effective.

▐ TERMINAL CLEANING

At the completion of each day's surgical schedule, all operating rooms and scrub and substerile areas are terminally cleaned. A chemical disinfectant and mechanical friction are used in the cleaning process.

1. Surgical lights including the tracks are cleaned.
2. All other fixed and ceiling-mounted equipment is washed.
3. All furniture including the wheels and casters are washed.
4. The face plates of all vents are wiped.
5. Doors of cabinets and operating room doors around handles and push plates are wiped.
6. All horizontal surfaces including tops of counters, autoclaves, solution warmers, and other fixed or recessed shelves are wiped.
7. Floors are machine scrubbed, and the solution is picked up with a wet vacuum or a clean mop that has been sterilized. The mop is used for only one room. The solution should remain wet on the floor for at least 5 to 10 minutes.
8. Kick buckets are washed and sterilized.
9. Scrub sinks are washed, and the spray heads of faucets are removed for sterilization.
10. Soap dispensers should be washed and sterilized prior to being refilled.
11. All support areas in the surgical suite should be scrubbed daily. In the sterile storage area, care must be taken not to contaminate any sterile items.
12. Transportation and utility carts are cleaned with a detergent disinfectant after each use; terminal cleaning includes the wheels and the casters.

Following terminal cleaning, all cleaning equipment is disassembled, cleaned with a detergent disinfectant, dried to prevent the growth of microorganisms, and inspected for proper function.

Weekly Cleaning

In addition to daily terminal cleaning, the following steps are taken at the end of each week:

1. All cabinet shelves are cleaned with a detergent disinfectant.
2. Air-conditioner grills and ducts are vacuumed.
3. Transportation and utility carts are steam cleaned.

To evaluate the effectiveness of cleaning procedures, rodac plates may be used. The bacteriologic count on the unused surface of the floor 12 hours after cleaning and disinfecting should be less than 5 organisms per square centimeter. If the count is above that, the cleaning procedure should be reviewed and the equipment observed for appropriate maintenance.

■ REFERENCES

1. Occupational exposure to bloodborne pathogens: Final rule. *Fed. Reg.* Dec. 6, 1991;56: 64132–64177.
2. United States Department of Labor. Occupational Safety and Health Administration, 91–618. *U.S. Department of Labor News.* Dec. 1, 1991; 1.

3. Mailhot C et al. Cover gowns: Researching their effectiveness. *AORN J.* 1987; 46(3):482–490.

4. Copp G, Malhot C, Zalar M et al. Covergowns and the control of OR contamination. *Nurs Res.* 1986; 35(5):267.

5. Copp G, Slezak L, Dudley N, Malhot C. Footwear practices and OR contamination. *Nurs Res.* 1987; 36(6):366–369.

6. Belkin N. The challenge of selecting an appropriate protective gown. *Today's OR Nurse.* 1994; 16(4)5.

7. Smith J, Nichols R. Barrier efficiency of surgical gowns: Are we really protected from our patients' pathogens? *Arch Surg.* 1991; 126:756.

8. Hubbard M et al. Reducing blood contamination and injury in the OR. *AORN J.* 1992; 55(1):200.

9. Jackson M, McPherson D. Blood exposure and puncture risks for OR personnel. *Today's OR Nurse.* 1992; 14(7):8.

10. Gerberding J. Invited Presentation. Third International Conference on Nosocomial Infections. Atlanta, GA: Centers for Disease Control; July 31–August 3, 1990.

11. Wright J et al. Mechanism of glove tears and sharp injuries among surgical personnel. *JAMA.* 1991; 266:1669.

12. Fay M, Dooher D. Surgical gloves: measuring cost and barrier effectiveness. *AORN J.* 1992; 55:(6)1511.

13. Food and Drug Administration. *Medical Alert Bulletin.* Washington, DC: U.S. Food and Drug Administration; March 29, 1991:2.

14. College of Allergy and Immunology Task Force on Latex Hypersensitivity. *Interim Recommendations to Health Professional and Organizations Regarding Latex Allergy Precautions.* Palatine, IL: American College of Allergy and Immunology, May 1992; 1–5.

15. Young M et al. Latex allergy. *AORN J.* 1992; 56:(3)490.

16. Beezhold D et al. The transfer of protein allergens from latex gloves. *AORN J.* 1994; 59:(3)612.

17. *Standards and Recommended Practices.* Denver: AORN; 1994:145, 193.

18. Fogg D. Clinical issues. *AORN J.* 1990; 52(2)408.

19. Sawchuk W et al. Infectious papillomavirus in the vapor of warts treated with carbon dioxide laser or electrocoagulation: Detection and protection. *J Am Acad Dermatol.* 21 July 1989; 41.

20. ECRI General purpose surgical laser smoke evacuation systems. *Technology for Surgery.* April 10, 1990; 1–5.

21. Fay M et al. Medical waste. *AORN J.* 1990; 51(6)1494.

22. Standards for Tracking and Management of Medical Waste. Final Rule. *Fed. Reg.* 1989; 54(56):12326–12395.

23. Rutala W et al. Management of infectious waste by U.S. hospitals. *JAMA.* 1989; 262:1640.

24. Kneedler J, Darling M. Using an enzymatic detergent to prerinse instruments. *AORN J.* 1990; 51:(5)1332.

EIGHT

Sterilization and Disinfection

Lillian H. Nicolette

Intense pressure to control and contain health care costs makes it necessary for health care professionals to weigh the cost-benefit ratio of what has been described as "hallowed" practices that are usually immune from criticism."[1] Today's health care professional responsible for or involved with sterilization and disinfection in the practice setting is confronted with an increasing range of challenges. The responsibility for the delivery of safe, cost-effective care is of primary importance in making sure this is done from an environmentally safe perspective. Within the past decade, the Occupational Safety and Health Administration (OSHA) regulations for the use of ethylene oxide (ETO) and handling infectious waste have forced the practitioner to look at these practices with more concern and realism. No longer can devices simply be placed in a gravity displaced sterilizer for a 30-minute cycle. Although the basic tenets of sterilization and disinfection have not changed, the establishment of stringent requirements, as well as controlling and monitoring processes and cost, has increased many times.[2]

With the major advances in sterilization technology, it is important that the perioperative practitioner understand the relationship between sterilization and patient outcomes. According to the AORN "Recommended Practices for Sterilization in the Practice Setting," the creation and maintenance of an aseptic environment has a direct influence on patient outcomes. One of the major responsibilities of the perioperative nurse is to reduce the risk to the patient of acquiring a nosocomial infection, as well as providing a safe environment. Measures to minimize or reduce the risk of surgical wound infections include the provision of instrumentation, supplies, and equipment free of contamination at the time of use.

▋ SCIENTIFIC PRINCIPLES OF STERILIZATION

Sterilization by definition is a process intended to remove or destroy all viable forms of microbial life, including bacterial spores, to an acceptable sterility assurance level. Proving that a particular item is sterile can be quite difficult. Even if the item is immersed in culture media and incubated for a period of time and subsequently shows no evidence of microbial growth, it may still be possible that some organisms have survived. One issue to consider in rendering an object safe for handling is the bioburden associated with the item. Bioburden is best defined as the microbiological load or bioload (i.e., the number and type of contaminating organisms in or on an item prior to decontamination). For example, the automated steam sterilization cycle is established to kill a total of 10^6 microbes per sterilized item. Subsequently, an item with a more than 10^6 bioburden cannot be sterilized in one cycle without the exposure period being increased.[3]

However, the term *sterile* is not absolute because microorganisms die logarithmically. The logarithmic order of death infers that the same percentage of living bacteria die each minute. This means that complete sterilization is never attained. For example, assume that an item is contaminated with 1 million cells. After 1 minute of a given sterilization process, 90% or 900,000 cells would be killed and 100,000 would survive. After the second minute, 90,000 would be killed and 10,000 would survive. After the third minute, there would be 1000 survivors (see Figs. 8–1, 8–2, and Table 8–1). The rate at which bacteria die is expressed as the *D* value. The *D* value refers to the decimal reduction time *(DRT)*. This is the time required at any constant temperature to destroy 90% of the population of organisms, or the time required for the survivor curve to traverse one log cycle.

If an item is cleaned properly in a clean, controlled environment by personnel using proper handwashing techniques, a bacterial count of less than 10^6 may be achieved. Thus, these items can be sterilized in a routine manner. Since absolute sterility cannot be achieved, the goal in the practice setting is to reduce the number of microbes to the lowest possible number. In a healthy individual, 1 million bacteria are necessary for most infections to occur. However, some exceptions do occur. For example, it takes only one mycobacterium tuberculosis organism to reach the lung and cause active tuberculosis. The number of organisms needed to cause an infection is also dependent on the virulence of the microbe and the susceptibility of the host. Fewer organisms are needed to cause an in-

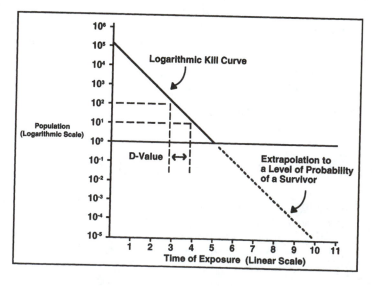

Figure 8–1. Bacterial survival curve.

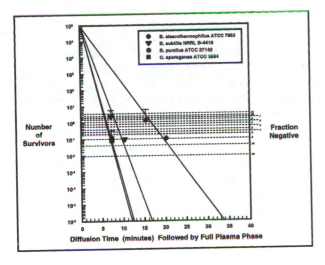

Figure 8—2. Kill curve by sterility method.

fection when the patient is immunocompromised (such as the debilitated individual on chemotherapy, patients with HIV, or very elderly and pediatric patients). Sterilization may be achieved by chemical or physical processes. Chemical agents commonly used in the health care practice setting are ETO, activated glutaraldehyde, and peracetic acid. The physical methods are ionizing radiation, dry heat, low-temperature hydrogen peroxide plasma, ozone, and saturated steam under pressure. The degree of sterilization achieved by any of these methods is directly related to the preparation and the packaging of the supplies.

TABLE 8–1. EXAMPLE OF THE INACTIVATION OF A BACTERIAL POPULATION

Initial Bacterial Count	Bacteria Killed in 1 Minute	Final Bacterial Count	Logarithm of Survivors
1,000,000	900,000	100,000	5
100,000	90,000	10,000	4
10,000	9,000	1,000	3
1,000	900	100	2
100	90	10	1
10	9	1.0	0
1.0	0.9	0.1	−1
0.1	0.09	0.01	−2
0.01	0.009	0.001	−3
0.00	0.0009	0.0001	−4

▮ DECONTAMINATION

Decontamination is the most critical step in breaking the cycle of cross-infection between patient and patient and between patient and the health-care worker. To select the appropriate decontamination procedure requires knowledge of the available processes as well as knowledge related to material compatibility of the individual item to be processed. An item can potentially be rendered safe to handle by proper cleaning to physically remove all contaminants. Decontamination can be the use of manual and automated methods as well as the use of chemical agents. Items to be sterilized should be decontaminated in a controlled environment, utilizing universal precautions. The physical design for separating decontamination and processing procedures, ventilation, temperature, humidity, appropriate use of protective attire for personnel, and cleaning procedures should be controlled to ensure appropriate presterilization processing. Cleaning efficiency can be significantly affected by today's many complex surgical devices (i.e., certain types of endoscopic instrumentation). Manufacturer's written instructions should be obtained and used for all devices used in the perioperative practice setting.[4]

▮ PREPARATION OF ITEMS FOR STERILIZATION

The preparation of instruments and supplies consists of a sequence of steps once the device has been decontaminated. Some of these include:

- All articles must be clean and dry and inspected for cleanliness and functionality. Any debris, such as grease, dirt, or blood, will inhibit contact by the sterilizing agent and prevent sterilization, or it may cause the item to require a longer exposure time.
- The sterilizing agent must contact all surfaces of an item. Surgical instruments and supplies should be prepared and packaged so their sterility can be achieved and maintained to the point of use.
- The box locks or hinges on all instruments should be opened and detachable parts disassembled. Instruments can be strung on pins or racks. Rubber bands should not be used to hold instruments together.
- Instruments should be sterilized in trays with perforated bottoms, mesh bottoms, or specially designed containers. This type of process should be used to allow adequate circulation of the sterilizing agent. The Association for the Advancement of Medical Instrumentation (AAMI) provides guidelines for the weight and density of sets and muslin packs. Instruments packaged individually should have the tips protected to avoid damage and possible perforation of the packages.
- To adequately sterilize items with lumens, such as catheters, tubing, needles, and some endoscopes, the lumen must come in contact with the sterilant. The design of complex surgical devices with multiple parts may prevent surface contact of the sterilant. These instruments may require additional exposure times. In the case of steam, distilled or demineralized water should be placed in the lumen prior to packaging. The water will become steam as the temperature rises, and the air in contact with the internal surface of the lumen will be displaced. Steam cannot penetrate

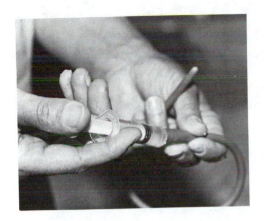

Figure 8–3. All items with a lumen must be flushed with distilled water prior to steam sterilization.

from the outside of many lumens because the lumen acts as a diffusion restricter (Fig. 8–3). All reusable tubing should be packaged in such a way that kinks are avoided. The reuse of single-use items (i.e., different types of tubing and catheters) must follow the manufacturer's written instructions.

- There have been many advances in barrier materials used in the practice setting. (Barrier materials will be discussed later in this chapter.) If a reusable barrier material is used, the manufacturer of the reusable fabric must be able to provide the laundry with recommended formulations for the fabric reprocessing. Resterilization of woven materials without laundering may lead to superheating and could be a deterrent to achieving sterilization. AAMI provides guidelines for the weight and density of reusable textiles. Reusable textiles must be routinely inspected by the appropriate departments. Multiple processings may eventually diminish the life and protective barrier qualities of the material.
- Prior to sterilization, reusable wrappers and drapes must be carefully inspected for defects, linting, holes, and stains. Because of the strength of new reusable fabrics, the need for patching is greatly reduced. Criteria for reusable barrier repairs should be established before a reuse program is in place.
- Rubber sheeting and materials such as Esmarck bandages should not be folded or rolled tightly, as the sterilant may not penetrate the rubber. Such materials should be covered with a piece of muslin or polypropylene wrap and rolled loosely.
- Wood should not be steam-sterilized, as heat drives lignocellulose resin (lignin) out of the wood. This resin may condense onto other items in the sterilizer, and if these items come into contact with an individual, a tissue reaction may occur. Wood based materials should only by sterilized according to the manufacturer's written instructions.

▌ PACKAGING SYSTEMS

The objective of utilizing packaging is to ensure sterility of packaged contents and to keep items sterile following the sterilization process until they are presented for patient use. Sterile packaging should be suitable for the type of sterilization method used. According to the AORN Recommended Practices on Selection and Use of Packaging Systems, the following criteria should be used in the perioperative practice setting:

- provide a barrier for the specific item being sterilized
- provide an adequate seal integrity and be tamperproof
- provide an adequate barrier to particulate matter and fluids
- withstand physical conditions of and be compatible with the sterilization process
- permit adequate air removal
- allow penetration and removal of the sterilant
- protect package contents from physical damage
- resist tearing and puncturing
- be free of holes or tears
- be free of toxic ingredients
- be low linting
- allow for ease of aseptic presentation
- have a positive cost-benefit ratio
- be used according to the manufacturer's written instructions.

The following types of packaging available today have been greatly improved over the past:

- Textiles (woven)
- Nonwoven material
- Pouch Packaging
- Protective Packaging
- Rigid Container Systems

Textiles

The word linen has been traditionally used in the health-care environment and has had several different definitions. Historically, linen material (woven flax) was recognized as a highly protective covering. Over the years, muslin, which is more sturdy and cost-effective, began to be used. The advantages of muslin include reproducible performance depending on the quality of the product. Maintaining sterility until point of use is more difficult with textile products because of the open weave. Muslin also absorbs moisture, therefore creating a pathway for wicking and the introduction of microorganisms. The reality is that once muslin is wet, it loses its barrier properties. Currently, reusable packaging has evolved from muslin to the current 100% polyester continuous filament, which is considered durable to laundering and has fluid repellent properties. Muslin is considered suitable for steam dry heat and for ETO sterilization. It is important that we identify and quantify the advantages and disadvantages of all packaging systems.

Woven wrappers are manufactured in a variety of sizes, and it is important that the correct size be used. Wrappers that are too small will not adequately cover and protect the items, and too large a wrapper will be bulky and difficult to handle when opening the item. When wrapping items in woven material, they may be wrapped sequentially in the two wrappers with all corners of the wrapper folded in. A small cuff on the first fold of the fabric over the contents provides a safety margin when opening the item. Pressure-sensitive tape is used to secure the packages as it indicates that the item has been exposed to the sterilization cycle. Woven packaging should be maintained at room temperature (i.e., 18°C to 22°C) and at a relative humidity of 35% to 70%.

The textile packaging wrapper is not the absolute microbial barrier. Selection of a single or double wrapper should be made according to the item being processed, the packaging properties, barrier quality, consideration for aseptic presentation, and the manufacturer's written instructions. A program should be designed and implemented to monitor reusable products throughout the process. Packaging materials should be checked for correct contents, folding, and placement. Canvas or other heavy woven fabrics are not suitable for sterilization as the thread weave does not allow penetration of steam, gas or any of the new technologies on the market. Product evaluations and selections should be completed on all new products used in the perioperative practice setting.

Nonwoven Packaging Materials

There are a variety of nonwoven packaging materials available today. *Nonwoven* refers to the manufacturing process used to produce a fabric-like quality material through other than a weaving process. Nonwovens are commonly referred to as "disposables." Nonwovens have been very effective in the perioperative practice setting for providing an adequate barrier. These packaging materials are discarded after use, eliminating the labor-intensive activities associated with reusable materials. The variety of nonwoven products has significantly increased since their early introduction. A major problem with older generation nonwovens was memory, which created difficulty in aseptically delivering a sterile product to the surgical field. The advantages of using a nonwoven (disposable) system are that nonwovens provide excellent microbial barriers, are low linting, and, with new materials such as polypropylenes, are tear resistant. Although the main disadvantage in the past had been memory, today the total cost of maintaining and disposing these materials is the main concern for perioperative managers and practitioners.

Pouch Packaging

Pouch packaging has gained increased popularity as a packaging method. There are basically two types of pouch packaging available on the market:

- paper/plastic that may be used for steam and ETO
- tyvek® and mylar®, which is more durable and can be used in ETO and hydrogen peroxide plasma sterilization

Pouches are available in rolls, bags, or pre-cut sizes that are presealed on three sides or are able to be heat sealed. When using a heat seal, it is advisable to use a double seal as this offers an extra margin of safety. Plastic pouches should be spot-checked for pinholes. Double-pouch packaging can be used to facilitate aseptic presentation of multiple small items to the sterile field and reduce sharp penetration of the package. During sterilization using double-peel packages, the paper portions should be placed together to insure sterilant penetration, air removal and drying or aeration. Expansion of air within the package may cause rupturing of the peel pouch.

Peel pouches (see Fig. 8–4) should open without tearing, linting, shredding, or delaminating. When there is a faulty mechanical function of the pouch, contamination of the

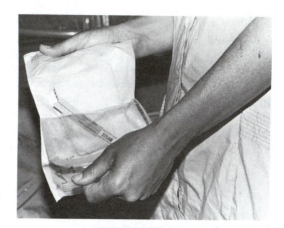

Figure 8–4. Peel pouch packages allow aseptic presentation of sterile items.

sterile contents will occur. Peel pouches used in a sterilization process should be of a design that is recommended by both the packaging and the sterilizer manufacturer. The peel packaging should be compatible with the sterilization process, permit sterilization of all contents, and maintain sterile integrity until opened.

Protective Packaging Materials

Protective packaging offers the advantage of being impervious to environmental contamination and assisting to protect the package until needed. Polyethylene is used for dust covers on textile (woven) and nonwoven packages. The sterility maintenance cover is a 3-mil-thickness plastic bag used for the protection of a sterile instrument set or item. This cover, applied immediately after sterilization, protects the sterility of the product. Handling of items should be minimized to prolong the sterility of the item.

Nylon film is not acceptable for any sterilization process. In gas sterilization, nylon does not allow the gas to penetrate. In steam sterilization, the moisture cannot escape from the package and as a result the package remains wet.

Rigid Sterilization Containers

Rigid sterilization containers offer an alternative packaging methodology for surgical instrumentation. Rigid containers offer a variety of features to package, sterilize, protect, and store instrument sets. These systems are made of a variety of materials, such as heat-resistant plastics, plastic-metal combinations, stainless steel, and anodized aluminum (see Fig. 8–5).

Rigid containers have filter systems and/or valve systems that need to be secured and in proper working order subsequent to sterilization. Perforations in the lid and the bottom surface are covered with steam-permeable, high-efficiency bacterial filters. The filters most commonly used are made of a nonwoven material. Most containers have a two-basket system to allow for better care and handling of instruments. The dual basket system further minimizes set-up time.

The manufacturers of rigid container systems vary in their recommendations related to the types of sterilizers where these systems may be used. Gravity displacement sterilization is generally not recommended because of the difficulty in air removal. To compensate for this slow air removal an extended sterilization exposure time is necessary.

Figure 8–5. Rigid container system. (*Courtesy Johnson & Johnson Medical, Inc., Arlington, TX.*)

Containers used for prevacuum steam or ETO sterilization are generally found to provide an adequate method for sterile processing. With any type of system, the containers need to be properly positioned for penetration of the sterilant. Rigid container packaging systems should be sterilized using a dedicated load. Sterilization exposure times should be based on the manufacturer's data and written instructions. Rigid containers offer a sterility assurance since this type of packaging is puncture resistant, cannot be abraded or torn, and is easily stacked. Each packaging system should be looked at for cost-effectiveness, efficiency, and patient safety. The AORN "Recommended Practices for Product and Medical Device Evaluation and Selection" should be consulted.

Labeling

All items should be labeled prior to sterilization. Proper labeling is necessary for quality assessment and improvement processes, inventory control, and stock rotation. Labeling information should include a description of the contents, the initials of the individual packaging the item, and the lot-control number. The lot-control number indicates the sterilizer used and the cycle or load number. This facilitates the identification and retrieval of supplies when the biological monitors or mechanical control monitoring devices demonstrate improper function during the sterilization cycle. Pencils or markers used to label packaging systems should be indelible, nonbleeding, nontoxic, felt-tip pens or very soft lead pencils.

Shelf Life

Shelf life is the length of time a package may be considered sterile and safe for use. Shelf life is considered to be event-related rather than time-related and depends on several factors, including:

- Type and configuration of packaging materials used
- Number of times a package is handled before use
- Number of personnel who may have handled the package
- Storage on open or closed shelves
- Condition of the storage area (cleanliness, temperature, humidity)
- Use of dust covers and method of sealing

A heat seal is a more secure method of closure and extends the shelf life. There should be written policies and procedures for how shelf life is determined and for how it is indicated for the product. The probability of a contaminating event occurring increases over time and with increased handling. If sterile packages are handled and stored properly, many packaging materials will maintain sterility for indefinite periods of time. Additionally, the use of dust covers will assist in the maintenance of shelf life.

▌ HISTORICAL DEVELOPMENT OF STERILIZATION

The research of Robert Koch (1843–1910), a German bacteriologist, on the disinfecting properties of steam and hot air marks the beginning of the science of disinfection and sterilization. Koch demonstrated that moist heat was a more effective method of sterilization than dry heat because of its greater penetrating powers.

In 1881, Koch and his associates developed the first nonpressure flowing-steam sterilizer (Fig. 8–6). It consisted of a metal cylinder in which water was heated through the bottom by a gas flame. The steam that resulted sterilized the items placed on shelves above the water.

In 1885, Schimmelbusch used the first steam sterilizer for the sterilization of surgical dressings, and in 1888, Hugo Davidsohn first demonstrated the use of boiling water as a method of sterilizing surgical instruments.

Other advances in the development of sterilization were made by Von Esmarch and Max Rubner. Von Esmarch emphasized the importance of using saturated steam containing the maximum amount of water vapor in steam sterilization. Max Rubner demonstrated that the bacterial effect of steam is diminished in proportion to the amount of air present in the sterilizer.

In 1888, the Kay-Scheerer Company of New York produced the first steam sterilizer with a steam-tight radial-locking-arm door.

The effect of formaldehyde gas as a disinfectant was identified in 1888. J. J. Kinyoun,

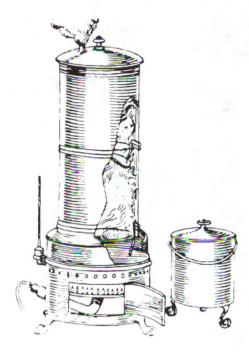

Figure 8–6. Nonpressure steam-type sterilizer devised by Robert Koch and his associate in 1880–1881. It was used by the German for intermittent or fractional sterilization of media. (From JJ. Perkins, Principles and Methods of Sterilization in Health Sciences, *2nd ed. 1978. Springfield, IL: Charles C Thomas, with permission.*)

an American biologist, discovered that greater penetration of formaldehyde could be achieved if the process was combined with steam.

During the early 1900s, sterilizers were designed for operation by a vacuum system of control. This system consisted of partial evacuation of air from the sterilizing chamber obtained by means of a steam ejection or vacuum attachment. The purpose of the evacuation was to assist in the displacement or removal of air from the chamber to insure penetration of the items by steam.

In 1915, the gravity process of eliminating air from the chamber of the sterilizer was introduced through the efforts of W. B. Underwood. This sterilizer used the concept that, as pressure was built up in the chamber from the incoming steam, it would force air out through a drain located in the front and the bottom of the chamber. The drain emptied into a pail on the floor. The efficacy of this sterilizer was entirely dependent upon the individual operating the equipment.

In 1933, the American Sterilizer Company introduced the first pressure steam sterilizer with a thermometer, located in the discharge outlet at the bottom of the chamber (Fig. 8–7). The addition of the thermometer refined the process of sterilization and led to the development of high-vacuum, high-temperature steam sterilizers.

▌ STEAM STERILIZATION

Steam sterilization is the oldest and most cost-effective method of sterilization available in today's health-care facilities. Moist heat in the form of saturated steam under pressure is

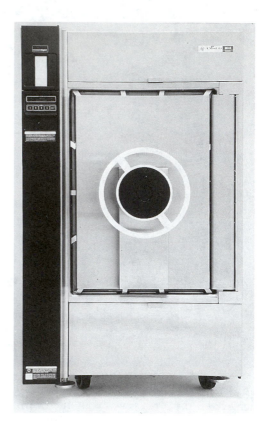

Figure 8–7. Modern steam sterilizer. (*Courtesy American Sterilizer Company, Erie, PA.*)

the most economic, efficient, and rapid method of sterilization. It destroys resistant bacterial spores and leaves no toxic residues. The components necessary for sterilization to occur by this method are heat, steam, pressure, and time. Heat independent of the other agents will destroy microorganisms; however, with the addition of moisture (steam) the time required for microbial destruction is reduced. The addition of pressure causes the steam to rise to a higher temperature. For example, in steam sterilization, water is heated to boiling, 100°C (212°F) and then converted to steam. As the pressure increases, the temperature is elevated (that is, 15 lbs of pressure at 250°F, 27 lbs of pressure at 270°F, and 30 lbs of pressure at 274°F). The time required to kill microbes varies with the size and the physical characteristics of the items being sterilized (load), the type of sterilizer, cycle design, bioburden, and packaging.

Death of microorganisms by moist heat is the result of denaturation and coagulation of the protein within the bacterial cells. Steam at the proper temperature for the proper amount of time must penetrate every fiber and all surfaces of the items for sterilization to occur. Therefore, it is essential that all air be eliminated from the chamber as air blocks the steam from penetrating the items to be sterilized.

The two types of steam sterilizers currently available in most health care facilities are the gravity displacement sterilizer and the prevacuum or high-vacuum sterilizer.

Sterilizers are constructed of a rectangular or round chamber surrounded by an outer shell. The space between the two forms a jacket. Steam fills the jacket that surrounds the chamber. The material used in the construction is void of crevices and is resistant to the corrosive and erosive action of steam and water and other solutions. A safety steam-lock door is located at the front of the chamber.

When the door of the sterilizer is closed, the steam enters the inner chamber of the sterilizer at the back and is deflected upward. By gravity the air goes to the bottom of the chamber and is forced out through a discharge outlet at the bottom. The discharge outlet has a screen that serves as a filter to prevent lint and sediment from entering the waste line. The temperature gauge for the chamber is located in the air discharge line, below the screen, as this is the coldest point in the chamber. When the proper temperature has been reached, the sterilization cycle begins. When the proper time has elapsed, the steam is exhausted from the chamber and the cycle is completed.

Gravity Displacement Sterilizers

Gravity displacement sterilizers are operated at 250°F, 270°F, or 274°F. The entire length of the cycle depends on the size and the physical characteristics of the item being sterilized. Sterilizers vary in design and performance characteristics, so cycle parameters should always be verified against the sterilizer manufacturer's written instructions. Phase I (come-up) time is when saturated steam is admitted into the chamber. The steam pushes the air out of the drain as it fills the chamber. The pressure and temperature inside the chamber rise until the preset temperature is reached. Phase 2 (exposure) time is when the sterilizer maintains the temperature by periodically removing cooled steam through the drain and replacing it with fresh steam at the top. This process continues until the sterilization time is completed. Phase 3 (come-down) time is when the timer reaches the end of the sterilization cycle time, the steam valve is shut off, the drain opens, and the steam is exhausted from the chamber. Phase 4 (drying) time is when atmospheric pressure is reached within the chamber, at which point drying begins. After this drying phase, which helps prevent wet packs, a signal indicates that the cycle has been completed.[5]

Before removing items from the steam sterilizer, the printed reading must always be checked for the appropriate time and temperature parameters. Table 8–2 indicates the exposure period for items frequently sterilized in gravity displacement sterilizers. At the conclusion of the steam sterilization cycle, even after appropriate drying times have been reached, items may still retain some steam vapor. Touching sterile items at this vulnerable

TABLE 8–2. EXPOSURE TIMES FOR STEAM STERILIZATION

Load Contents	Exposure Time		
	Gravity (250°F)	Gravity (270–274°F)	Prevacuum (270–274°F)
Wrapped/containerized instrument sets	30 min.	15 min.	4 min.
Wrapped basins	30 min.	15 min.	4 min.
Wrapped textiles	30 min.	25 min.	4 min.

stage could result in compromising the barrier properties of some packaging materials. If the packing material is breached by this liquid, the item should be considered contaminated. For all items to be placed in a gravity displacement sterilization cycle, the operator should consult the instrument and sterilizer manufacturer's written instructions.

Flash Sterilization

Although most instruments or items are processed by the wrapped method when using steam sterilization, in urgent situations it may be necessary to steam sterilize an item for immediate use.

Originally, the flash steam sterilization process was developed for the emergency processing of a single dropped instrument in the operating room setting. The cycle has more recently been used for the routine processing of items that are not prepackaged.

Flash sterilization (see Table 8–3 for exposure times) should be carefully selected to meet special clinical situations. It should be used only when there is insufficient time to sterilize an item by the preferred prepackaged method or when the surgical suite has been specifically designed to incorporate flash sterilization of instrumentation, such as when the steam sterilizer opens into each operating room and when decontamination facilities are designed accordingly. When performed correctly, flash sterilization is a safe and effective process for the sterilizing of medical devices for use in contact with compromised tissue or the vascular system.

Items processed by means of this cycle must always be used immediately, since sterility assurance cannot be maintained. The transferring of sterile products from the sterilizer to point of use can create a compromised product; closed container systems are available for transporting instruments. The key is to carefully consider the ways in which an item may actually become contaminated en route from the sterilizer to the patient and to eliminate as many situations as possible. It is essential that health-care personnel properly carry out the complete reprocessing of instrumentation when flash sterilization cycles are used.[6]

Flash sterilization at the point of use will continue to remain a viable safe option in the perioperative practice setting. It is the responsibility of the perioperative nurse to insure that the sterilization methods used are safe and efficacious for both the patient and the health-team members.

Prevacuum/High-Vacuum Sterilizers

The prevacuum or high-vacuum sterilizer differs from the gravity displacement sterilizer in the manner in which air is eliminated from the chamber and the load. In a prevacuum cycle, a vacuum pulls most of the air and the load contents from the sterilizer chamber out through the drain in the bottom front floor of the sterilizer. As the air is evacuated, "con-

TABLE 8–3. EXPOSURE TIMES FOR GRAVITY DISPLACEMENT "FLASH" STERILIZATION

Load Contents	Exposure Time (270–274°F)
Nonporous items	3 min.
Porous items	10 min.

TABLE 8–4. EXPOSURE TIMES FOR PREVACUUM "FLASH" STERILIZATION

Load Contents	Exposure Time (270–274°F), minutes
Nonporous items	3
Porous items	4

ditioning steam" is injected into the chamber, thus diffusing the air in the space surrounding the items. Conditioning the load insures fast heating to the sterilizing temperatures. At the completion of the steam cycle, a vacuum cycle exhausts steam from the chamber and air is admitted through a bacteria-retentive filter to relieve the vacuum, to return the chamber to atmospheric pressure, to remove moisture, and to cool the load. The prevacuum sterilizer operates at 270°F–274°F (Table 8–4).

Steam under pressure may not be used on heat-sensitive items, oils, ointments, and powders, and it should be used according to manufacturer's instructions.

The steam sterilizer must be loaded to allow the passage of steam through the load from the top of the chamber at the back toward the front to the discharge line. This requires that the sterilizer not be overloaded as this would inhibit complete penetration of the materials with the moisture and heat from the steam.

Linen packs should be placed on their sides on the carrier cart or sterilizer rack, leaving space for air and steam circulation. Basins and solid bottom trays are placed on edge to permit air and steam circulation and to allow moisture to drain freely. Large packs should be placed on the bottom shelf of the loading cart, with smaller items on the shelf above. If a load is a mixture of porous and nonporous items, the nonporous items should be placed on the bottom shelf to prevent the condensation from dripping onto the surface of the porous items.

When items are nested, such as basin sets, they should be separated with an absorbent towel or other wicking material to facilitate the passage of steam to all surfaces and to allow for adequate drying. Surgical instrument trays with mesh bottoms may be placed flat on a carrier shelf or sterilizer rack to allow the steam and moisture to adequately circulate through the tray (Fig. 8–8).

Solutions must be sterilized separately, and the manufacturer's written instructions for sterilization should be followed.

When the sterilization cycle is completed, the door should be opened and the contents permitted to cool and dry. Placing warm, moist articles on a cold surface will cause condensation, both within the package and from out of the air, and prior contamination of the items. Sterilizer function should be monitored with mechanical, chemical, and biological indicators to meet all monitoring standards.

Implants

Implants require special handling before and during sterilization. Therefore, it is important that these items be clearly labeled so that they can be appropriately processed. Implants should not be flash-sterilized because of the possible consequences to the patient. A minimally contaminated device placed in an avascular environment could increase the risk

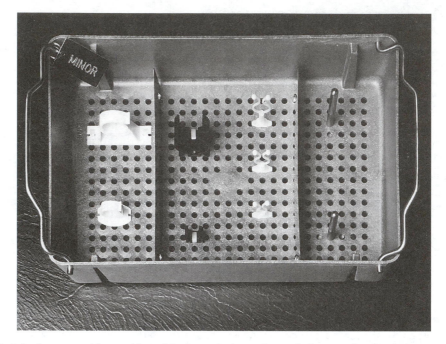

Figure 8–8. Sterilization tray. (*Courtesy Advanced Sterilization Products, a division of Johnson & Johnson Medical, Inc., Irvine, CA.*)

of patient injury and infection. Careful assessment, planning, packaging, and inventory management in cooperation with implant manufacturers can eliminate the need to flash sterilize these items. Implantable items should be sterilized with a biological monitoring device, and the item should not be implanted until the indicator has a negative reading. Practitioners should quarantine implantable devices and await the outcome of biological monitoring before releasing items for patient use. If the indicator is found to be positive, the surgeon should be notified immediately.[7] Most manufacturers do supply implants already sterilized.

Routine Maintenance of Sterilization Processes

The manufacturer of the sterilizer provides written instructions for daily inspection and cleaning of all equipment. Examples of items requiring daily cleaning are door gaskets, loading carts, recording charts and pens, the chamber drain screen, the internal chamber, and the external surfaces. Periodic inspection and cleaning reduce the frequency of sterilizer malfunction and prevent the buildup of residue from the steam line on items being sterilized.

During the weekly cleaning, the strainer located at the front of the autoclave should be flushed based on the manufacturer's instructions. This weekly flushing of the discharge system will keep the drainline free of clogging substances, such as grease and resins. If these substances are allowed to accumulate, there may be some problems with the discharge of air and condensation from the chamber.

■ DRY-HEAT STERILIZATION

Dry-heat sterilization is used only when direct contact of the material with saturated steam is impractical or unattainable. Dry-heat sterilization is used only for specialized purposes in modern health care facilities. In this method of sterilization, organisms are destroyed by oxidation. This requires two basic parameters: high temperatures and long exposure periods. Dry heat is used effectively on powders, petroleum ointments and gauze, anhydrous oils, greases, and other substances that would be damaged by steam, or that are insoluble in water than therefore not permeated by moist heat. (An example in the practice setting is the use of talc in thoracic surgery). Since dry heat does not exert a corrosive effect on sharp instruments or erode ground glass, it can also be used on cutting instruments, needles, and syringes.

The effectiveness of dry heat depends on the penetration of heat through the object to be sterilized. Thus, the nature of the material, the method of preparation and packaging, and the loading of the sterilizer are important factors in determining the time and the temperature relationships. The time-temperature ratios for dry-heat sterilization should be determined according to the instructions of the manufacturer of the items being sterilized as well as of the sterilization manufacturer.

■ IONIZING RADIATION

Some items purchased from manufacturers as sterile items have been sterilized by ionizing radiation. The principal types of radiation plants are the cobalt-60 gamma-ray emitters and high-energy electron accelerators. The most commonly used type is the cobalt 60, as it produces gamma rays capable of penetrating bulk objects, such as cartons ready for shipment.

Currently, ionizing radiation is used only by industry due to the high initial cost and the size of the facility required. Sterilization by this method is reliable, requires less energy, and is relatively inexpensive to maintain.

■ CHEMICAL STERILIZATION: ETHYLENE OXIDE

ETO was invented and discussed by C. A. Wurtz in 1859 as a room fumigant. In 1929, H. Schrader and E. Bossert discovered that ethylene oxide possessed bactericidal properties, and in 1956, ETO was first used in hospitals as a sterilizing agent.

ETO is most commonly used to sterilize heat- and moisture-sensitive items. ETO is provided to end users for health care processing in a weight-to-weight mixture of ETO and inert diluent gases. The most widely used diluent is CFC 12 (dichlorodifluoromethane). ETO is commercially available as a highly flammable liquid, explosive in air. For this reason, ETO was mixed with carbon dioxide or fluorocarbons (Freon) to reduce its explosive and flammable potential. Due to environmental changes 100% ETO sterilization in health care facilities is now being used (Fig. 8–9). The main advantages of using 100% ETO are:

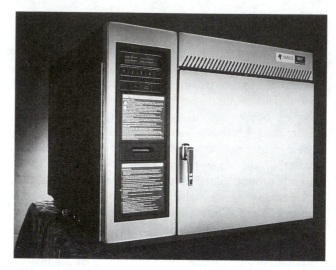

Figure 8–9. Modern 100% ETO gas sterilizer. *(Courtesy American Sterilizer Company, Erie, PA.)*

- the elimination of the use and dependence on CFC's
- safety features that reduce or minimize the potential for occupational exposure to ETO
- increased productivity and efficiency over 88/12 mixtures

ETO is an alkylating agent that, under the right parameters, results in microbial death. ETO chemically interferes with the nucleic acids and alters the metabolic and reproductive processes of the microbial cell, resulting in inactivation or death of the cell. The rate at which the destruction of the organisms occurs appears to be related to the rate of diffusion of the gas through the cell wall and the availability or accessibility of the cell's nucleic acid to react with ethylene oxide.[8]

ETO is a sterilizing agent known for its hazardous and toxic nature. All ETO sterilizer and aeration equipment should be exhaust-ventilated to the outside of the building, away from pedestrian traffic, other work areas, and air intake vents. Symptoms of ETO exposure are nausea, vomiting, headache, irritation of the respiratory passage and eyes, drowsiness, weakness, and lack of coordination.

In 1984, the Occupational Safety and Health Administration established a 50-fold reduction in the permissible limit for occupational exposure to ETO. This reduction was made because of ETO's carcinogenic and reproductive hazards. The permissible limit was set at one part per one million parts of air (1 ppm). This was determined as a time-weighted average (TWA) exposure over an 8-hour period of time. In 1988, OSHA established an additional limit for exposure to ETO as 5 ppm averaged over a sampling period of 15 minutes. To achieve this excursion level, institutions may need to implement the following engineering controls:[9]

- Implement a postvacuum purge at the end of the sterilization cycle
- Install a local exhaust above the sterilizer chamber door
- Implement an exhaust system to the outside of the building

- Locate the sterilization area in an isolated area under negative pressure
- Implement 6 to 10 air exchanges per hour in the sterilization area
- Install conveyors from the sterilizer chamber to the aeration area[10]

Health-Care Worker Monitoring

To monitor compliance with the OSHA regulations, employers are required to perform breathing zone sampling by a method that is accurate to a confidence level of 95% for airborne concentrations of ETO at the excursion level of 5 ppm. Samplings should represent 15-minute exposures associated with job tasks that are most likely to produce exposures above the excursion level in each area, for each job classification, and for each shift. Monitoring of the individual who would be most likely to receive the greatest exposure is sufficient to meet the regulation.[10] The frequency of monitoring will depend on the results obtained. There are six possible combinations of time-weighted-average and short-term exposures that will dictate monitoring needs of the health-care worker (Table 8–5).

Activities such as changing ETO tanks and cleaning the sterilizers may result in short-term, high exposures; the employees performing these tasks should wear respirators for additional protection.

The process of sterilization with ETO is more complicated than with steam, dry heat, hydrogen peroxide plasma, or peracetic acid. In addition to the time and the temperature required for steam and dry heat, the concentration of ETO and moisture are important to gas sterilization.

Temperature ranges from 120° to 140°F (49° to 60°C) are most frequently used in ETO sterilizers. The temperature is an important factor in the sterilizing efficiency of ETO as it affects the destruction of microorganisms by enhancing the penetration of ETO through the cell wall. An increase in temperature results in the required exposure time being decreased.

The appropriate concentration of ETO is essential in gas sterilization. The recommended concentration is 450 mg/L. Higher concentrations up to 1000 mg/L may be

TABLE 8–5. ETHYLENE OXIDE EXPOSURE REQUIRING MONITORING

Exposure	Required Monitoring
Below the action level at or below the excursion level	No monitoring required
Below the action level and above the excursion level	No time-weighted-average monitoring required; monitor short-term exposures four times per year
At or above the action level, at or below the time-weighted average, and at or below the excursion level	Monitor time-weighted-average exposures two times per year
At or above the action level, at or below the time-weighted average, and above the excursion level	Monitor time-weighted-average exposures two times per year, and monitor short-term exposures four times per year
Above the time-weighted average and at or below the excursion level	Monitor time-weighted-average exposures four times per year
Above the time-weighted average and above the excursion level	Monitor time-weighted-average and short-term exposures four times per year

Time-weighted average = 1 ppm averaged during an 8-hour period.
Excursion level = 5 ppm averaged during a 15-minute sampling period.
From Occupational exposure to ethylene oxide, final standard. Fed Reg. April 6, 1988, with permission.

used, and exposure periods are then reduced to about one-half. Concentrations greater than 1000 mg/L do not appreciably affect exposure times.

Moisture is important to the sterilizing efficiency of ETO. The optimum humidity levels are 20% to 40%. A humidity level lower than 20% or higher than 65% reduces the sterilizing properties of ETO.[11] The moisture content of microbial cells is also important in gas sterilization, as dry or desiccated organisms are more resistant to the penetration of ETO. To avoid dehydration of organisms, the relative humidity in the area where the items are packaged for sterilization should be maintained at 50% or more.

The amount of time required for gas sterilization is directly related to:

- Sterilant concentration
- Relative humidity
- Porosity of the item
- Packaging of the item
- Bioburden
- Temperature
- Exposure time

Adherence to the manufacturer's guidelines in operating the ETO sterilizers is critical to the effectiveness and the efficiency of this hazardous method of sterilization.

Ethylene oxide can be used to sterilize endoscopic instruments, plastic items, rubber items, delicate instruments, cameras, sutures, electrical cords, pumps, and motors. Exposure of glass vials of solution will result in only the outside of the vial being sterile, as ETO does not penetrate glass.

ETO may not be used on some acrylic plastic materials, medications, and pharmaceuticals as it will alter the chemical composition of these types of items.

Preparation of Items for Gas Sterilization

Subsequent to packaging, all items must be clean and dry. Wet items will remain wet, and the water may unite with ethylene oxide to form ethylene glycol and ethylene chlorohydrin. These substances are not eliminated by aeration and may result in toxic reactions in patients and personnel.

In loading the gas sterilizer, an attempt should be made to sterilize full loads of items having common aeration times. The sterilizer must be loaded so the gas can circulate freely to penetrate the entire load. Items should be loaded so they do not trap air, pool water, nor contact the chamber wall. Overloading should be avoided. Items should be placed in baskets or carts to minimize operator exposure when the load is transferred from the sterilizer to the aerator.

Aeration Cycle

Items sterilized with ETO must be properly aerated in a mechanical aerator. When a combination sterilizer/aerator unit is used, both cycles must be completed before the items are removed. When using a separate aeration unit, items should remain on the sterilizer cart or in a non-ETO absorbent basket during transportation. If a cart or table is used, it should be pulled rather than pushed during transfer, and this process should be completed as quickly as possible. Pulling rather than pushing the cart during the transfer process directs the flow of ETO-containing air away from personnel. Metal and glass that are unwrapped

TABLE 8–6. MECHANICAL AERATION*

Air Changes Per Hour	Temperature	Time
4	50°C (122°F)	12 hours
4	60°C (140°F)	8 hours
12–25	Room temperature 18–22°C (65–72°F)	7 days

*Aeration time depends on the type of ETO sterilization system used.

do not require aeration; all other items must be aerated. If it is necessary to handle individual items or any ETO absorbent material before the aeration cycle is completed, butyl rubber gloves should be worn by the health-care worker to provide protection. If rubber gloves are worn, they should be placed in the aeration cabinet after use to reduce environmental contamination.

The specific aeration time depends upon the composition and the porosity of the sterilized items, the type of ETO sterilization system used, the packaging material, the intended use of the items, the temperature of the aerator, and the air flow rate. Specific aeration written recommendations should be obtained from the manufacturer on all items requiring gas sterilization. In the absence of such recommendations the guidelines in Table 8–6 may be used as a model.

If ambient aeration is used, the ventilation in the room must be maintained at a negative pressure and ventilated outside the building. Access to the room should be restricted to persons needed to operate the area, and storage of other supplies in this area is prohibited. Inappropriate aeration of items sterilized by ETO have resulted in the following outcomes for the patients and health-care workers: facial burns from anesthesia face masks, laryngotracheal inflammation from endotracheal tubes, and blood hemolysis from tubing used in hemodialysis and cardiopulmonary bypass. ETO should not be used on any item that can be sterilized by a different process.

■ LOW TEMPERATURE HYDROGEN PEROXIDE PLASMA STERILIZATION

One of the most recent technological advances in sterilization is low temperature hydrogen peroxide plasma sterilization. This process utilizes low temperature gas plasma to achieve rapid, low temperature, low moisture sterilization of medical and surgical items (Table 8–7). Low temperature gas plasma consists of a reactive cloud of ions, electrons, and neutral atomic particles that is produced through the action of either a strong electric or magnetic field.

In physics, plasma is considered the 4th state of matter in relationship to solids, liquids and gases. It composes 99% of the atmosphere. An example of plasma is neon lights and the aurora borealis. Peroxide plasma technology has the potential for displacing many uses of both steam and ethylene oxide sterilization. Generally, the gas plasma process rapidly destroys a broad spectrum of microorganisms, including gram-negative and gram-positive vegetative bacteria, mycobacterium, yeast, fungi, lipophilic and hydrophilic viruses. Upon completion of this sterilization process, no toxic residuals remain on the

TABLE 8–7. ATTRIBUTES OF PLASMA STERILIZATION

Rapid sterilization <75 minutes

Dry process

No toxic residuals

Low temperature

No aeration required

Items can be packaged

Easy installation-just plug in

sterilized items, making it safe for both patients and health-care workers. This system has a front panel indicating the cycle stages and elapsed time and provides a paper printout for confirmation of the cycle and documentation of the process (Fig. 8–10). A schematic of the plasma cycle phase is shown in Fig. 8–11.

Preparation of instrumentation for sterilization includes cleaning and decontamina-

Figure 8–10. Hydrogen peroxide plasma sterilization system. (*Courtesy Advanced Sterilization Products, a division of Johnson & Johnson Medical, Inc., Irvine, CA.*)

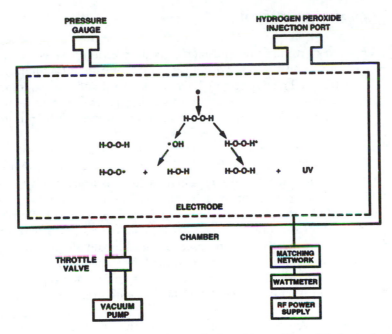

Figure 8–11. Hydrogen peroxide plasma sterilization: plasma cycle phase. (*Courtesy Advanced Sterilization Products, a division of Johnson & Johnson Medical, Inc., Irvine, CA.*)

tion procedures, reassembly, wrapping with a nonwoven polypropylene wrap or Tyvek®- Mylar® pouches. Supplies for use in this type of processing are biological and chemical process indicators, trays, and pouches. These items are used in the same fashion as those for steam and ETO sterilization processes.[12]

■ OZONE STERILIZATION

Ozone has been used in treating drinking water and liquid sewage treatment for several years, but has also been proposed as a vapor sterilant for medical devices. Ozone is a gas that is normally found in the air in very small concentrations and quantities. It is made up of various molecular structures that have 3 atoms of oxygen, O_3 as opposed to O_2. Ozone is produced by ionizing oxygen, disassociating some of the O_2 molecules into "singlets" of oxygen, or mon-atomic oxygen. When these singlets collide with another oxygen molecule, tri-atomic oxygen O_3 is formed. The chemical makeup of this ozone therefore consists of O_2 with a loosely bonded 3rd oxygen atom that is readily available to attach to, and oxidize additional molecules. OSHA does require monitoring, and the OSHA 8-hour time-weighted average in the United States is 0.1 ppm. Although, the FDA has granted limited application of ozone sterilization, it is not frequently seen used in today's health-care facilities.

■ LIQUID CHEMICAL STERILIZATION

The need for appropriate sterilization and high-level disinfection has been emphasized in the literature recently as it relates to the decontamination of patient care items. According to both the Association of Practitioners in Infection Control and Epidemiology and the Centers for Disease Control, it is unnecessary to sterilize all patient-care items. Hospital policies and procedures must dictate whether cleaning, disinfection, or sterilization is indicated on the basis of the items' intended use.

A solution of activated aqueous glutaraldehyde in a 2% concentration is the most common liquid agent that is used in today's health-care settings. It is currently used as a high-level disinfectant and chemosterilizer. Glutaraldehyde is noncorrosive, nonstaining, and safe for all instruments that can be immersed in a chemical solution. When glutaraldehyde is used as directed by the manufacturer, it can destroy all forms of microbial life, including bacterial and fungal spores, tubercle bacilli, and viruses. Two percent activated aqueous glutaraldehyde is most frequently used on flexible and rigid endoscopic equipment because it does not damage lenses or the glues of instruments with lenses.

When using a liquid chemosterilizer, the item must be free of bioburden and totally immersed in the solution. Wet items will dilute the concentration of the sterilant. All surfaces of the item must be in contact with the sterilant.

After items are removed from the liquid sterilant, they should be thoroughly rinsed with sterile distilled water to avoid tissue damage. It takes approximately 10 hours to successfully sterilize an item by this method.

Most cold sterilizing solutions are effective for a specific period of time. Therefore, it is essential that the manufacturer's instructions be followed when preparing the solution and in calculating the expiration date.

Peracetic Acid

Automated equipment utilizing peracetic acid as a liquid sterilant has become popular over the last several years. Peracetic acid is an effective sterilizing agent that is not considered to leave residuals on medical devices if they are properly rinsed. This process can be considered harmful, in that it uses a toxic chemical that can cause serious injury if not properly handled, neutralized and rinsed. These types of solutions are corrosive, but newer systems use various types of anticorrosive solutions as buffers for sterilization use. If items are sterilized in an automated system, they should be used immediately. These items are wet after being processed in cassette or container systems that are not hermetically sealed; subsequently they are prone to contamination. If a device is not to be used immediately, then it needs to be reprocessed immediately prior to use. The manufacturers of automated devices need to provide written instructions not only for use but for storage and packaging requirements.

Differences of opinion exist within the scientific community about how liquid peracetic acid systems should be chemically and biologically monitored. Therefore, it is the responsibility of the perioperative nurse manager to establish policies and procedures related to the use and implementation of this type of sterilization methodology.

Items that are to be sterilized or disinfected should follow the Spaulding classification system, as outlined by the CDC. This classification is used by infection control practitioners and others when selecting methods of disinfection and sterilization. Items are placed in one of three specific categories (See Table 8–8):

1. *Critical.* Items that enter sterile tissue or the vascular system are considered critical and must be sterile.
2. *Semicritical.* Items that come in contact with nonintact skin or mucous membranes are considered semi-critical and should receive a minimum of high-level disinfection.
3. *Noncritical.* Items that come in contact only with intact skin are considered noncritical items and should receive intermediate-level or low-level disinfection or cleaning.

When evaluating the types of liquid chemosterilizers, only those products whose product labels indicate that they are registered as a sterilant by the United States Environ-

TABLE 8–8. CLASSIFICATION TABLE

Devices	Spaulding Processes	EPA Products
Critical	Sterilization	Sterilant/disinfectant
surgical instruments	Sporicidal chemical; prolonged contact	
cardiac & urinary catheters		
implants		
scalpels & needles		
Semicritical	High level disinfection	Sterilant/disinfectant
flexible endoscopes	Sporicidal chemical; short contact	
laryngoscopes		
respiratory therapy equipment		
anesthesia equipment		
ET tubes		
thermometers		
Noncritical	Intermediate level disinfection	Hospital disinfectant with label claim for tuberculocidal activity.
bed pans		
blood pressure cuffs		
crutches		
linen		
stethoscopes	Low level disinfection	Hospital disinfectant without label claim for tuberculocidal activity.
tabletops		
floors		

Modified and adapted from Favero, MS, Bond, WW. Chemical disinfection of medical & surgical materials. In: Block SS, ed. Disinfection, sterilization & preservation. 4th ed. Philadelphia: Lea & Febinger 1991, 627.

mental Protection Agency (EPA) and cleared for marketing by the FDA should be considered as sterilizing agents.

▌ STERILIZATION MONITORING PROCESSES

A sterilization process monitoring device, or chemical indicator, should be used on each package to be sterilized, including items being flash sterilized. If the monitoring device is not visible from the outside of the package, a separate process indicator should be used on the exterior of the package.

The chemical indicator is usually a strip treated with a sensitive dye or chemical that changes color or its physical status when conditions for sterilization have been met. The conditions for steam sterilization are time, temperature, and moisture. For gas sterilization, the conditions are time, humidity, gas concentration, and temperature. Conditions for hydrogen peroxide sterilization are time, phases, exposure to sterilant, and temperature.

Although process monitors do not verify that sterilization has been achieved, they do indicate when items have been exposed to the physical conditions within the sterilizing chamber, or when procedural errors or equipment malfunctions have occurred. When sterile packages are opened, perioperative personnel should check the indicator prior to handling the item or to placing it on the sterile field, to ensure that these conditions were met. The purpose of the external process monitor is to differentiate between processed and nonprocessed items. The process monitor should be clearly visible on the outside of every package to be sterilized. If the interpretation of the external and/or the internal process monitor suggests inadequate processing, the item should not be used.[13]

Pressure-sensitive tape on the outside of the package indicates when items have been exposed to the physical conditions of the sterilization cycle. There are various types of tape, specifically designed for the type of sterilization process being used. Pressure-sensitive tape may change in color if stored in an area of high temperature, high humidity, or exposure to the sterilant.

In all prevacuum sterilizers, a Bowie-Dick type test should be conducted once every 24 hours, randomized throughout the week, to identify operational variables. The commercially available Bowie-Dick test is designed to detect residual air in the sterilizer chamber, which would prevent steam contact with items in a load and, therefore, interfere with sterilization. This is only applicable to prevacuum or high-vacuum sterilizers.

The test pack should not be processed with other items. To perform the test, four pieces of autoclave tape, 8 inches long, are crisscrossed on a cotton huckaback towel; towels are then folded and stacked one on top of another until the stack measures 10 to 11 inches (25 to 28 cm). The pack is then wrapped and placed in the lower front area of the sterilizer, and the cycle is run. Uniform color changes on the autoclave tape indicate the complete elimination of air from the test pack. If the steam supply to the sterilizer was turned off, a minimum of 30 minutes is required between turning on the steam and running the test pack.[14]

Mechanical control monitors should be used to verify time, temperature, pressure, and cycle recordings, based on the type of sterilization system used. Controlled time-temperature documentation should be maintained on each sterilization system. Monitors provide actual assessment of the sterilization cycle conditions and a permanent record for the health-care facility. Recordings of parametric data should be used to ascertain that the sterilization system functioned within the design parameters. It also records the load number and the duration of each exposure. If the exposure periods are greater or less than prescribed, or if the cycle or temperature was not reached, there is a record of this malfunction. This provides evidence on which to act in correcting discrepancies. The printout should be checked after each sterilization cycle and should be changed daily or more often as required by the manufacturer's written instructions.

Mechanically controlled charts are not available on all ETO sterilizers. When they are present, they should be changed daily and used as a reference during and after the cycle to check the effectiveness of the unit.

Sterilizer efficacy should be monitored by utilizing a biological monitoring device. There are commercially available biological monitors using spores that are highly resistant to gas, steam, and hydrogen peroxide sterilization. *Bacillus stearothermophilus* is used for steam sterilizers and *Bacillus subtilis* for ETO, dry-heat, and hydrogen peroxide plasma sterilization. The spores are available in ampules, capsules, or strips. Each of the biologic control units contains a strip to be sterilized and a control strip to be sterilized. Two biological indicators and one internal chemical indicator, or a biological test pack and a chemical indicator, separated from each other, should be placed in the center of a pack or load as recommended by the sterilizer manufacturer. The biologic test pack is placed near the bottom front of the steam and hydrogen peroxide plasma sterilizer or in the middle section of the gas sterilizer. When the cycle is compete, the test indicator is removed from the pack and sent with the control indicator to the laboratory for evaluation.

Self-contained biological indicators are commercially available to monitor all types of sterilization processes. They contain both the spore strip and the growth media and can be incubated in the perioperative suite.

Biological testing should be performed at least weekly on steam and dry-heat sterilizers. Hydrogen peroxide plasma sterilizers should be monitored daily, and each cycle of an ethylene oxide sterilizer should contain a biological monitor. Whenever possible, results of biological and chemical monitoring should be known before using a device.

If the results of the bacterial monitoring are positive, the sterilizer should be taken out of service until it is inspected by a qualified individual, the sterilizer retested, and negative biological results obtained. All items processed during the interval of time from when the biological monitoring was performed to when the positive results were obtained should be considered unsterile. They should be retrieved and reprocessed according to the institution's policies and procedures.

The effectiveness of the aeration chambers can be monitored by using a rubber or plastic device that absorbs ETO. When the device absorbs the gas, it changes color; when the indicator is placed in an aerator, the color will fade to indicate that safe levels of ETO have been reached. There are two types of indicators: one for polyvinyl chloride items (as these items require the longest aeration), and one for all other items.

Preventive maintenance should be performed on a scheduled basis by a qualified individual. Proper periodic inspections, maintenance, and replacement of components subject to normal wear are necessary to insure and maintain proper functioning of the sterilizer. The efficiency and the accuracy of gauges, charts, graphs, steam lines, and drains should be tested regularly. Following any repairs and preventative maintenance inspections, a test pack with a biological monitor and a Bowie-Dick test should be run and negative results obtained before the sterilizer is used.

Records are kept on all sterilizers and retained for a specific period of time indicated by the local, state and federal regulations, along with an established guideline from the institution's risk manager. Accurate and complete records are required for process verification and are useful in equipment malfunction analysis. A sterilizer record system should contain the following information:

- Sterilizer identification number
- Load number
- Contents of each load
- Date
- Cycle numbers
- Duration and temperature of sterilizing phase (recording chart)
- Identification of the operator
- Results of biological and chemical monitoring
- Bowie-Dick test results on prevacuum sterilizers
- Record of repairs
- Record of preventive maintenance

Commercially Packaged Sterile Items

There are many surgical items used in perioperative patient care that are commercially available to health-care facilities and that are marketed as *presterile,* or single-use devices. Before purchasing these items, it is important to carefully examine the package. The package should have wide margins that allow easy hand gripping. The package should be the appropriate size; too small a package may result in the item falling out of the package when it is opened, and too large a package will take up excessive storage space. The outer edges of the package must not touch the sterile product, and the nurse must have complete control of the product at all times during the opening process.

Manufacturers of single-use devices culture and quarantine the items until the results of the cultures validate the sterility in the manufacturing facility. These supplies may be packaged with inner and outer envelopes that are mechanically sealed. This method of packaging makes it almost impossible for normal biologic contaminants to gain access to the interior of the package. The sterility should be maintained as long as the package remains intact. However, as noted previously in this chapter, sterility is event-related. Therefore, the condition of storage, the amount of handling, the type of packaging material, or the use of additional external dust-type covers will affect the sterility maintenance.

Perioperative nurse managers should emphasize the importance of establishing par levels of single-use items. Supply levels should be evaluated routinely and adjusted according to the changes in the surgical case load. Single-use items *should not* be resterilized unless specific manufacturer's written instructions are obtained. It is very difficult for a health-care facility to establish a quality control process to insure that a product meets the same use specifications each and every time it is sterilized. Subsequently, the health-care facility also takes on an additional liability if the original manufacturer does not provide written instructions for reuse of the item.

▮ DISINFECTANTS

Disinfection is the process by which most pathogenic agents or disease-producing microbes, excluding bacterial spores, are destroyed by either physical or chemical means. Disinfectants are liquid chemical compounds used on inanimate objects, such as furniture, floors, walls, equipment, and some heat-sensitive items. An antiseptic is a chemical substance that prevents growth either by inhibiting or destroying microorganisms. These agents are used primarily for topical application to the skin and the mucous membrane. There are some chemical compounds that may be used as both disinfectants and antiseptics.

Disinfectants and antiseptics are identified as *bacteriostatic* or *bactericidal*. Agents that are bacteriostatic act by inhibiting growth. However, when the agent is removed, the cells will resume normal multiplication. Bactericidal agents kill bacteria. Sporicides, virucides, and fungicides are agents that kill spores, viruses, or fungi, respectively. Microorganisms differ in their resistance to chemicals. Most vegetative bacteria are susceptible to chemical compounds, tubercle bacilli and nonlipid viruses are significantly more resistant, and bacterial spores are highly resistant.

For disinfectants or antiseptics to affect microorganisms, they must act on some vital part of the cell structure. Some agents alter the membrane of the cytoplasm. This membrane is easily injured by substances that reduce surface tension. Other chemical agents can react directly with certain enzymes, the nucleus, or structural proteins, such as the cell wall. Certain chemical compounds are effective against one type of organism and not another.

Important factors to be considered in using the disinfection process are:

- Number of microorganisms
- Amount and kind of organic debris
- Concentration of the disinfectant being used
- Temperature of the solution

The larger the number of organisms contaminating the skin or inanimate object, the longer it takes for the germicide to destroy them. Organic matter, such as blood, feces, and tissue, inhibits the efficiency of the germicide by absorbing the germicide molecules and deactivating them. The proper concentration of the disinfectant will depend on the material to be disinfected and the manufacturer's guidelines. Higher concentrations will effect the bactericidal activity. Most chemical compounds will be bacteriostatic in low-level concentrations and become bactericidal in high-level concentrations. An increase in temperature will accelerate the rate of the chemical reaction. Table 8–9 identifies some of the commonly used chemical disinfectants.

TABLE 8–9. COMMONLY USED CHEMICAL DISINFECTANTS

Agent*	Microorganism Destroyed and Time Required; " = Minutes	Mechanisms of Action	Practical Use	Usefulness Disinfectant	Usefulness Antiseptic	Precautions
Mercurials	Weak bacteriostat	Oxidation combines with proteins	None	None	Poor	Unpleasant odor, tissue reactions on skin and mucous membrane; personnel must wear gloves when using agent.
Phenolic compounds	Bactericidal—10" Pseudomonacidal—10" Fungicidal—10" Tuberculocidal—20"	Surface active—disrupts membrane Inactivates enzymes Denaturation of proteins	Walls, furniture, floors, equiopment	Good	Poor	
Quaternary ammonium compounds ("quats")	Bactericidal—10" Pseudomonacidal—10" Fungicidal—10"	Surface active—disrupts cell membrane Inactivation of enzymes Denaturation of proteins	Limited hospital use as these do not destroy gram-negative pathogens and tubercle bacilli	Fair	Fair	Neutralized by soap; active agent is absorbed by gauze and fabrics thus reducing strength.
Chlorine compounds	Most gram-negative bacteria pseudomonas Virucidal	Oxidation of enzymes	Spot cleaning of floors and furniture	Good	Fair	Inactive in presence of organic debris, unpleasant odor, corrosive to metal.
Iodine compounds (iodine + detergents = iodophors)	Bactericidal—10" Pseudomonacidal—10" Fungicidal—10"	Oxidation of essential enzymes	Dark-colored floors, furniture, walls	Good	Good	Iodine stains fabrics and tissues; may corrode instruments. Inactivated by organic debris.

Agent	Activity / Times	Mode of action	Use			Comments
	Tuberculocidal—20" with minimum concentration of 450 ppm of iodine					
Alcohol (usually isopropyl and ethyl alcohol 70–90% by volume.)	Bactericidal—10" Pseudomonacidal—10" Fungicidal—10" Tuberculocidal—15"	Denaturation of proteins	Spot cleaning Damp dusting equipment	Good	Very good	Inactivated by organic debris; becomes ineffective when it evaporates. Dissolves cement mounting on lensed instruments and fogs lenses. Blanches floor tile.
Formaldehyde (Aqueous Formalin, 4% or 10%)	Bactericidal—5" Pseudomonacidal—5" Fungicidal—5" Tuberculocidal—15" Virucidal—15"	Coagulation of proteins	Lensed instruments	Fair	None	Irritating fumes, toxic to tissue; rubber and porous material absorb the agent.
Alcohol Formalin (8% formaldehyde and 70% isopropyl alcohol)	Tuberculocidal—10" Virucidal—10" Sporicidal—12 hours	Coagulation of proteins	Instruments	Good	None	Dissolves cement mounting on lensed instruments; toxic to tissue, irritating fumes.
Glutaraldehyde**	Vegetative microorganisms—5" Tubercle bacilli—10" Spores—10 hours	Denaturation of proteins	Disinfection of instruments in 10". Useful for lensed instruments. Effective liquid chemosterilizer in 10 hours.	Good	None	Unpleasant odor, tissue reaction may occur; instruments must be rinsed well in distilled water.

*Follow manufacturers' recommendations regarding optimal temperature of solution.
**Chemical indicator is available to test efficacy of solution.

■ STERILIZATION TECHNOLOGY AND THE PERIOPERATIVE NURSE'S ROLE

As new sterilization technologies are introduced for use in the perioperative practice setting, it is very important that the practitioner strictly follow the manufacturer's instructions for the operation and maintenance of the equipment. As perioperative nurses, we should also be aware of the occupational hazards that the sterilant may pose to the patients, the environment, and ourselves. Selection of new sterilization and disinfection technologies should follow the AORN "Recommended Practices for Product and Medical Device's Selection and Evaluation" along with the associated APIC guideline. When evaluating and selecting new sterilization technologies, the following questions can be a useful guide when determining whether the technology is appropriate for your practice setting:

- What is the regulatory status (EPA, FDA, OSHA, DOT) of the product?
- What specifically can and cannot be sterilized?
- How can the sterility of a device be maintained?
- How is the sterilization/disinfection process monitored?
- How complex is the process to use and operate?
- What is the cost factor associated with purchasing a new product?
- What impact does the sterilization/disinfection process have on the surgical set composition?
- What are the future trends in processing? Will point-of-use processing continue to increase? Will centralization continue to decrease? And will the surgical services departments continue to manage the sterilization lines?

Using these types of questions will assist the perioperative nurse and manager in selecting and using sterilization and disinfection products conducive for their practice setting.

■ REFERENCES

1. Panel of experts considers a list of eight sacred cows. *OR Manager.* 1990; 6:13.
2. Reichert MM, Young JH. *Sterilization Technology for the Health Care Facility.* Gaithersburg, MD: Aspen Publications; 1993:11.
3. Perkins JJ. *Principles and Methods of Sterilization in Health Sciences.* Springfield, IL: Charles C Thomas; 1982:33, 213.
4. Association for the Advancement of Medical Instrumentation. "Good Hospital Practice: Steam Sterilization and Sterility Assurance," in *AAMI Standards and Recommended Practices, Sterilization.* Arlington, VA: AAMI, 1993: 11.
5. American Society for Healthcare Central Service Personnel of the American Hospital Association. "Training Manual for Central Service." Chicago, IL: AHA Publication: 1993: 124.
6. Recommended Practice on Sterilization in the Practice Setting. Denver: AORN, 1995.
7. Association for the Advancement of Medical Instrumentation. "Good Hospital Practice: Flash Sterilization for Patient Care Items," in *AAMI Standards and Recommended Practices.* Arlington, VA:1995.
8. Perkins JJ. *Principles and Methods of Sterilization in Health Sciences.* Springfield, IL: Charles C Thomas; 1982:214–215.

9. Occupational exposure to ethylene oxide. Final standard. *Fed Reg.* 1988; 53(66):11414
10. Occupational exposure to ethylene oxide. *Fed Reg.* 1983; 48(78):17285
11. Association for the Advancement of Medical Instrumentation. "Good Hospital Practice: Ethylene Oxide Sterilization and Sterility Assurance," in *AAMI Standards and Recommended Practices.* Arlington, VA;1995:9.
12. Jacobs PT. Plasma sterilization, Journal of Health Care Materials Management, Vol. 7, No. 5, July 1989, 49.
13. Association for the Advancement of Medical Instrumentation. "Good Hospital Practice: Steam Sterilization and Sterility Assurance," in *AAMI Standards and Recommended Practices.* Arlington, VA;1995:19.
14. Association for the Advancement of Medical Instrumentation. "Good Hospital Practice: Steam Sterilization and Sterility Assurance," in *AAMI Standards and Recommended Practices.* Arlington, VA;1995:22–23.

THREE

Intraoperative Care

NINE

Preparation of the Patient
and Surgical Team Members

▮ ADMITTING THE PATIENT TO THE SURGICAL SUITE

The information obtained by the perioperative nurse during the preoperative assessment is conveyed to the individual responsible for transporting the patient to the surgical suite. Such information may include the appropriate method of transportation, unusual patient problems such as impaired mobility, alterations in sensory perceptions or emotional status, and any individual patient requests, such as wearing a prosthesis to the surgical suite. Children are encouraged to bring a favorite toy or "security" blanket to the surgical suite to help minimize their anxiety.

The stretcher used to transport a presurgical patient is equipped with side rails, a safety strap, and an IV pole. It should have the capability of being manipulated so that a patient may be transported in Trendelenburg's position. In some institutions, the primary care nurse will accompany the patient to the surgical suite or the holding area and give a report to the perioperative nurse.

The operating room nurse greets the patient by identifying himself or herself and then identifies the patient by asking, "What is your name?" This question precludes errors that may occur if a patient were asked, "Are you Mrs. Brown?" Patients who have received a premedication may be drowsy or disoriented and respond inappropriately to the latter question. The patient's name is verified by checking the patient's name and identification number on his or her identification bracelet and chart. Correct identification is everyone's responsibility, and it should not be assumed that someone else has correctly identified the patient.

Following the identification process, the perioperative nurse checks the completeness of the chart and the preoperative checklist. The preoperative checklist includes the information about presurgical patients that is required by hospital policy. The checklist is completed by the unit nurse before the patient is transported to the surgical suite and is then verified by the operating room nurse when admitting the patient. Several specific points must be ascertained using the checklist:

1. Patient's identification on ID band, chart, and addressograph card, and name on surgical schedule

2. Patient allergies
3. The results of laboratory tests required by hospital policy; tests usually include hemoglobin, hematocrit, urine analysis, chest x-ray, and electrocardiogram for patients older than 40 years
4. Recording of the physician's completion of a patient history and physical examination
5. The time that the patient last ate or drank
6. The patient's wearing of devices, such as eyeglasses, contact lenses, artificial hair or eyelashes, dentures, or hearing aid, or having implants, such as pacemakers, intraocular lens, or total joint replacement
7. Preoperative medication and its effects noted by the unit nurse; the perioperative nurse also observes patient for signs and symptoms of adverse effects of the preoperative medication
8. Specific preoperative orders, such as a surgical shave, the need for a plaster cast to be bivalved or removed, or medications to be administered, such as eye drops
9. A signed consent for surgery form that is witnessed and dated; information of the operative permit must agree with the site and side listed on the surgical schedule; perioperative nurses should be familiar with the state and hospital requirements regarding who may sign the consent and who may witness the consent (see Chapter 4)

Following the admission procedure, the patient may have an IV inserted, a surgical shave performed, or a cast bivalved or removed. The cast saw is not used in the operating room as the plaster dust becomes airborne and contaminates the sterile field. During such activities, the patient is never left unattended. The perioperative nurse supports the patient by explaining the procedures and why they are necessary. Noise in the environment is kept to a minimum. When preoperative routines are completed and the operating room is prepared, the patient is transported into the operating room.

▌ PREPARATION OF THE SKIN

The surgical scrub and preoperative skin preparation of patients minimize the number of microorganisms in the area of incision. Chemical disinfection of the skin is called degermation.

The skin has two layers: epidermis and dermis. The epidermis is constantly worn away and replaced with cells from the dermis. The thickness of the dermis varies in different parts of the body. For example, it is thicker on the soles and the palms than on the eyelids or forehead. The dermis is composed of blood vessels, lymphatics, nerves, the secreting portions of sebaceous and sweat glands, and hair follicles (Fig. 9–1).

The bacteria of the skin are identified as transients and residents. Transient microorganisms are held in place by sweat, oil, and grime. They can easily be removed with soap and water and mechanical scrubbing. Resident bacteria, on the other hand, adhere to epithelial cells and extend downward between cells into the hair follicles and glands.

Among the common resident bacteria are *epidermis,* aerobic and anaerobic diph-

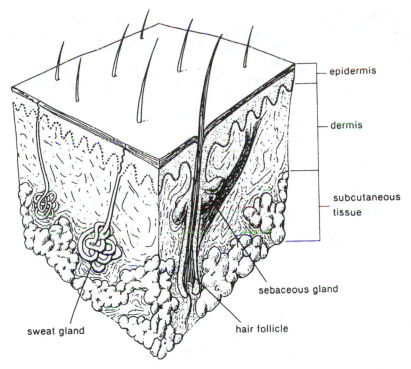

Figure 9–1. A section of human skin.

theroid bacilli, aerobic spore-forming bacilli, aerobic and anaerobic streptococci, and gram-negative rods of intestinal organisms. They are modified by the presence of hair; folded skin surfaces; excessive secretions of sweat and sebaceous glands; their proximity to mouth, nose, anal, or genital regions; and the nature and condition of the clothing worn. Resident microorganisms are considered permanent residents of the skin and are not readily removed by mechanical friction.

The antiseptic agents used in skin preparation and the surgical scrub reduce transient organisms, but they do not penetrate deeply into the dermis. The mechanical action of scrubbing and the rising with water are important in degerming the deeper layers of the dermis, but a portion of the resident flora remain. While surgical gloves are worn, the diminished resident flora is replenished from the deeper skin layers. Therefore, care must be exercised to avoid glove puncture and to change gloves immediately if punctures do occur. The knife, needle, or instrument that caused the puncture is removed from the sterile field.

The objectives of the surgical scrub and skin preparation of patients are to:

- remove soil and transient microbes from the skin
- reduce the resident microbial count to a subpathogenic level with the least amount of tissue irritation
- inhibit rapid rebound growth of microbes[1,2]

Soaps and Detergents

Soaps reduce surface tension, and dirt, oil, and microbes become enmeshed in the lather and are removed during the washing process. Detergents also reduce surface tension. They appear to exert their antiseptic effect by disrupting membranes and denaturing proteins. Detergents that have a positive charge are called cationic detergents, and those with a negative charge, anionic. Soaps and detergents can be combined with antimicrobial agents to form antiseptics, which are used in preoperative skin preparation or surgical scrubs.

Antiseptic Agents

The criteria that an antiseptic soap or detergent should meet include:

1. Acting rapidly
2. Having a residual effect ·
3. Reducing resident microorganisms
4. Containing a nonirritating antimicrobial preparation
5. Inhibiting rebound growth of microbes
6. Affecting a broad spectrum of microbes
7. Being nontoxic

The antiseptic of choice is 4% chlorhexidine gluconate (CHG) because it has immediate, persistent, residual antimicrobial properties. The 2% product has an equivalent antimicrobial effectiveness when it is used on a regular basis. In some studies the 2% solution demonstrated less irritation potential to the hands than the 4% chlorhexidine gluconate formulation.[3]

The iodophors have effective, immediate, and persistent antimicrobial properties, but they do not have significant residual effects. Iodophors are a good alternative for individuals who cannot tolerate CHG.[4]

Hexachlorophene 3% combined with a soap is a bacteriostatic agent active against gram-positive organisms, but it has only minimal activity against gram-negative microorganisms. It is not sporicidal or tuberculocidal and requires a cumulative action for maximum effectiveness.

The Federal Drug Administration has limited the use of hexachlorophene to physician prescription due to the serious toxic hazards that may accompany its continued use. Research findings indicate that hexachlorophene used in bathing newborns could to some extent be absorbed into their circulation, causing permanent brain damage. With these findings and the predominance of gram-negative nosocomial infection, hexachlorophene 3% should have very limited use as an antiseptic agent.

Parachlorometaxylenol (PCMX) is available in concentrations up to 3.75%, but the products are not acceptable for surgical hand scrubs.[4] They are very mild on the skin, but their immediate and persistent effects are minimal and they have no residual antimicrobial effects.

Alcohol preparations in concentrations of 60% to 90% have repeatedly demonstrated superior antimicrobial activity when compared with detergent-based preparations. They, however, are not widely used for scrubbing, as they act as a defatting agent and dry the skin.[5] Some alcohol preparations have emollients added to minimize this disadvantage.

Ethyl alcohol 70% may be used as a degerming agent. It is effective against *M. tuberculosis* and vegetative forms of other bacteria, but it does not destroy spores. Other disinfectants are sometimes dissolved in alcohol resulting in a tincture with additional disinfectant properties, as well as increased grease solvency. A major disadvantage remains its drying effect with repeated use.

Alcohol foam is available in convenient dispensers that can be mounted at any site or on carts. Using the foam does not require that the surgical team member leave the patient or that the hands be dried. It is, therefore, an excellent resource for the anesthesia carts. The main deficiency of the foam is that it does not remove dried blood or other excretions that require handwashing.[6]

Iodine 1% is an effective germicidal agent, as it kills bacteria, fungi, viruses, and spores. Its use, however, is limited because it stains fabric and causes skin burns and tissue irritation.

Dispensers. Receptacles used to dispense antiseptics are washed and dried thoroughly before refilling to prevent the growth and spread of potentially harmful microorganisms. Disposable containers are discarded when empty.

Defatting Agents. For some selected surgical procedures, such as plastic surgery, a defatting agent, such as Freon TF, is used. Freon TF emulsifies the residue from soaps and removes remaining skin oils, which permits the surgeon to make identifying marks without the lines being distorted by the skin oils.

Preoperative Skin Preparation of Patients

Preoperative skin preparation of patients begins with cleaning the skin around the operative site to remove superficial soiling and transient flora. The cleaning may be accomplished by:

- a shower or bath before a patient arrives at the facility
- washing the operative site on the surgical unit or in the preoperative area
- washing the operative site in the operating room before applying the antimicrobial agent

Removing Hair. Removal of hair from the operative site is not necessary unless the hair interferes with the surgical procedure. Hair rarely needs to be removed from children. Similarly, the head and neck of female patients seldom require that hair be removed. Some surgeons advocate hair removal to ensure that the site is clean and to prevent hair from gaining access into the wound where it would act as a foreign body or carry bacteria.

Shaving. When shaving is ordered by a physician, it should be done less than 2 hours before the surgical procedure, as there is evidence that the length of time between the shave and the operation is critical and has a direct effect on the infection rate. Shaving destroys some natural integumentary defenses and may produce multiple superficial lesions containing exuded tissue fluids that favor or contain bacterial growth (Table 9–1).

The area to be shaved is determined by the site of the incision and the nature of the

TABLE 9–1. MODEL OF PATIENT CARE FOR PREOPERATIVE SHAVE PREPARATION

Nursing Diagnosis	Patient Outcome	Nursing Actions	Schedule for Evaluation
1. Risk of inappropriate preoperative shave performed on patient	1. Appropriate shave performed	1a. Check patient's identification band with chart b. Confirm site and side of surgical procedure by comparing consent and OR schedule c. Check physician's orders for type of shave or check standard skin preparation manual	1. Preoperatively
2. Risk of infection related to cross-contamination	2. No infection related to cross-contamination	2a. Wash hands prior to contact with patient b. Wear plastic disposable gloves while performing shave c. Wash hands at end of the procedure	2. 24–48 hours postoperatively
3. Risk of anxiety related to having body shaved	3a. Ability to cope with anxiety b. Ability to verbalize questions and concerns	3a. Explain procedure to patient in a reassuring professional manner b. Answer questions and concerns using terminology the patient understands	3. During shave procedure
4. Risk of loss of dignity related to excessive exposure	4. Dignity maintained	4a. Limit exposure of patient only to area needed for adequate shave b. Provide for privacy while performing the shave	4. During shave procedure
5. Risk of discomfort from the procedure	5. Minimal discomfort	5a. Maintain proper body alignment b. Use additional supports if indicated c. Place extra linen or waterproof pad under and around area to be shaved d. Use warm water e. Use wet method of shaving f. Shave hair in direction it grows g. After completion of prep check with patient to ascertain that he or she is: Comfortable Warm Dry	5. During shave procedure and immediately following the procedure
6. Risk of abrasions and rashes related to shave procedures	6. Skin integrity maintained	6a. Provide for adequate lighting b. Check area to be shaved for any abnormal skin conditions (i.e., lesions, allergies, irritations); if present check with surgeon before proceeding with shave c. Maintain an awareness of skin irregularities such as warts and moles d. Document abnormal findings e. Maintain an awareness of the anatomical area to be prepped, exercising special precautions on boney prominences f. Alert surgeon to any untoward effects of the shave following the procedure	6. Immediately following the shave

operation. A wide area around the incision is usually prepared to allow for extension of the incision and placement of tubes and drains. In orthopedics, the area prepared usually includes the joint above and the joint below the incision.

Unusual circumstances, such as traumatic injuries, may require that the patient be shaved in the operating room. Shaving there, however, should not occur routinely, as loose hair may be deposited on the sterile field. An area outside the operating room, such as the preoperative area, is preferable if it affords privacy and adequate lighting.

The wet method of shaving is mandatory, as it facilitates hair removal, minimizes skin trauma, and prevents dry hair and debris from becoming airborne. To avoid soiling the linen and the patient's gown, waterproof pads or towels are placed under the area to be shaved. The razor should be disposable or one that can be terminally sterilized following the procedure.

Disposable vinyl gloves, soap, and warm water are used. The skin is lathered well with gauze sponges or a disposable scrub sponge. As the patient's skin is held taut with one hand, the hair is shaved in the direction that it grows. Hair is periodically removed from the razor by rinsing it in water. Extreme care must be exercised to avoid cutting the skin or shaving over a bony prominence.

Cotton-tipped applicators may be used to clean the umbilicus; scrub brushes are effective in cleaning hands and feet; and a disposable nail cleaner may be used to clean under the nails. When shaving the head, electric hair clippers are effective.

When the shave is completed, the area is rinsed well with water to remove loose hair and soap residue. The area is then dried. Adhesive tape will help remove hair that adheres to the skin or linen. Hands should be washed immediately after the procedure to avoid cross-contamination.

Items used in shaving are either disposed of or cleaned and terminally sterilized. The head on electric hair clippers is removed from the body, washed under running water, and autoclaved. The body of the clippers is wiped with a disinfectant.

Depilatories.   A safer method of removing hair is using depilatory creams, provided the patient is not sensitive to them. The depilatory is applied to the skin for a time specified in the manufacturer's directions. It is then wiped off, and the skin is thoroughly rinsed and dried.

A manual should be available that describes routine preoperative skin preparations that are approved by the surgeon; it will facilitate the shaving process and serve as a guideline in choosing the appropriate skin preparation for a particular surgical procedure (Fig. 9–2).

When mechanical scrubbing of a site is done in the operating room, it is usually completed after the patient is anesthetized and positioned on the operating room table. The pooling of solutions under the patient may cause a skin burn or irritation due to the chemical reaction between the laundry detergent and antimicrobial scrub solution. To prevent skin irritation, waterproof pads or additional linen may be used under the patient and discarded at the end of the scrub procedure.

Using a clean scrub set, the operative site is scrubbed with 4 × 4 sponges and an antimicrobial solution. The routine procedure is to begin at the site of the incision and proceed to the periphery (Fig. 9–3). Firm pressure is exerted in circular strokes. The sponge is

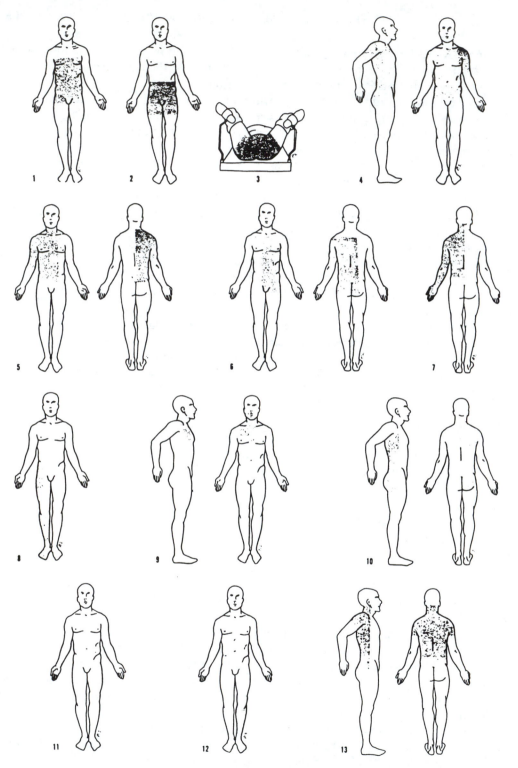

Figure 9–2. Standard skin preparations.

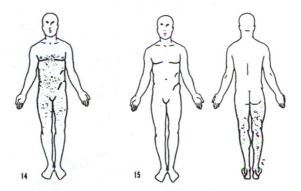

Procedure	Figure #	Procedure	Figure #
Abdominal hysterectomy	1	Graft—skin	Check chart
Abdominal perineal resec-			for orders
tion	1, 3	Hand surgery	11
Adrenalectomy	1	Hernia, inguinal	2
Adrenalectomy—posterior		Hip total joint	8
approach	10	Laminectomy cervical	13
Amputation—leg	8	Laminectomy lumbar	10
Ankle	12	Laparotomy	1
Aortic aneurysmectomy	14	Laryngectomy	9
Aortic valve	4	Mandibular resection	9
Appendectomy	1	Mastectomy	5
Arm—forearm	7	Mediastinal exploration	4
Axillary dissection	5	Mitral valve	4
Brachial duct cyst	9	Nephrectomy	6
Carotid artery	9	Porto-caval shunt	14
Cholecystectomy	1	Rectal fistulectomy	3
Coronary artery bypass	15	Shoulder surgery	7
Crainotomy	Check chart	Sympathectomy lumbar	6
	for orders	Thyroidectomy	9
Esophageal diverticulec-		Thoractomy	6
tomy	9	Vaginal hysterectomy	3
Esophagotomy	9	Varicose vein ligation	
Foot surgery	12	(unilateral)	8

Figure 9–2. Continued.

discarded when the periphery is reached, and the scrubbed area is rinsed and dried. A fresh sponge is then used; a soiled sponge is never brought back over the area scrubbed.

If the site to be prepped includes an area of high bioburden, such as an external stoma, the area may be isolated with a plastic drape or it may be scrubbed last. Traumatic wounds may require irrigation to dislodge and rinse out debris. The amount of irrigation will depend on the site and the size of the wound.

Following the mechanical scrub, a broad spectrum, nontoxic antiseptic agent may be applied using a sterile or no-touch technique. Which agent is selected is based on patient sensitivity, incision location, and skin condition. The antimicrobial residue left on the skin

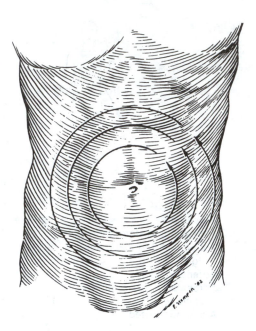

Figure 9–3. The scrub begins at the site of the incision and proceeds to the periphery.

prevents microbial growth during surgery. The antiseptic solution is allowed to dry before drapes are applied to increase the effects of the agent and decrease the potential for fire when using electrosurgery or lasers.[7] The technique used is consistent with that described for the mechanical scrub. Seeding the surgically manipulated tissue with the patient's own normal flora may result if the antimicrobial solution is not appropriately applied.

Surgical Hand Scrub

The surgical hand scrub is performed before donning a sterile gown and gloves. Although a hand scrub does not render the skin sterile, it does reduce the number of microorganisms if performed effectively (Fig. 9–4). Consequently, if gloves are perforated during the surgical procedure, fewer microorganisms are released into the wound.

A reusable or disposable scrub brush or sponge is used for the surgical hand scrub. There is no evidence that the brush offers any advantage over the sponge.

If reusable brushes are used, they must be sterilized in a container that permits removal of a single brush without contaminating other brushes. The decision to use a reusable or a disposable scrub brush is based on economic factors. Cost analysis should include the amount of labor required to clean and process reusable brushes.

Nail cleaners should be metal or plastic and must be sterilized between uses. Orangewood sticks are not acceptable because they cannot be sterilized.

Some disposable brushes are impregnated with an antimicrobial scrub agent. As indicated earlier in this chapter, the antimicrobial scrub solution of choice is 4% chlorhexidine gluconate. A nonmedicated scrub soap followed by application of an alcohol-based hand cleanser is used for individuals with skin sensitivity to other antimicrobial agents.[3]

Surgical hand scrubs may employ the time method or the stroke count method. In

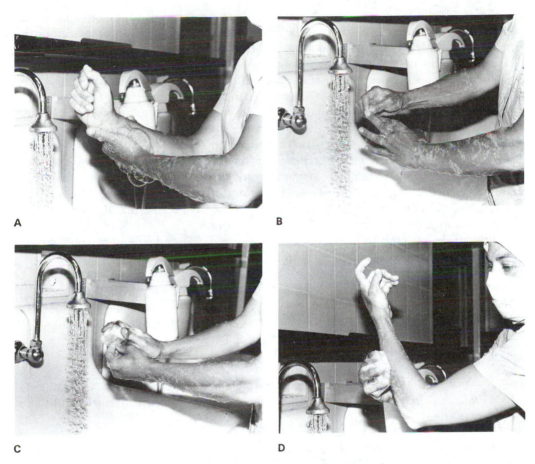

Figure 9–4. Surgical scrub technique. **A.** Hands and arms are lathered to 2 inches above elbow. **B.** Clean the nails and the subungual area with a nail cleaner. **C.** Hold the brush perpendicular to the nails and scrub the fingertips. **D.** Using a circular motion, scrub all sides of the forearm to 2 inches above the elbow.

the time method, the fingers, hands, and arms are scrubbed for a prescribed time that is consistent with the scrub agent manufacturer's written recommendations. Studies indicate that there is no significant difference in the 3-, 4-, and 5-minute scrubs.[8,9]

In the stroke count method, a prescribed number of strokes are used on each surface of the fingers, hands, and arms. To the nails, 30 strokes are applied; on other areas of the hands and on the arms up to 2 inches above the elbow, 20 strokes are applied. To ensure adequate cleaning, the fingers are considered to have four sides. Each side, including the webbed area between the fingers, is scrubbed using firm pressure in a circular motion. The arm is divided into thirds; using circular strokes, each one third is scrubbed up to 2 inches above the elbow.

The stroke count method, unlike the time method, ensures that all skin surfaces are exposed to the same amount of mechanical scrubbing and germicidal solution.

Before a hand scrub is begun, all personnel should check their hands and arms for abnormal skin conditions. The skin must be free of abrasions and cuts, because microorganisms are frequently on skin inflamed from minor trauma or dermatitis.

Nails should not extend past the fingertips. When circulating, long fingernails may scratch patients during the process of moving and positioning them. Nails are also a reservoir for microorganisms. In addition, long fingernails contribute to gloves tearing.

Cuticles should be in good condition. Under the stress of a good mechanical scrub, nail polish easily cracks and peels, thereby providing microscopic niches where microbes can breed.[10] If nail polish is worn, data suggest that it should be worn no longer than 4 days before changing. Artificial or acrylic fingernails are not proven to increase the risk of surgical infection. Higher numbers of gram-negative microorganisms, however, have been cultured from the fingertips of personnel wearing artificial nails, both before and after handwashing. In addition, fungal growth occurs frequently under artificial nails because of moisture trapped between the natural and artificial nails.[11]

Prior to hand scrub, the surgical head covering is adjusted to ensure complete hair coverage, and the mask is tied securely to prevent venting at the sides. Eyeglasses are adjusted for comfort and proper fit to avoid fogging of the lenses. Scrub shirts should be tucked into trousers to prevent clothing from getting wet and to reduce the risk of scrubbed hands and arms brushing against loose garments and becoming contaminated.

The procedure for the surgical hand scrub should be written and posted in the scrub room area. The procedure includes the following steps:

1. Remove all jewelry from hands and arms.
2. Turn on the water and adjust to comfortable temperature.
3. Check to see that the foot pedal for the soap dispenser is convenient and that it works.
4. Wet hands and forearms.
5. Using an antimicrobial soap or a detergent, lather the hands and arms to 2 inches above the elbows. This washing will loosen surface debris and remove the gross contamination.
6. Rinse hands and arms so that water flows off at the elbows. Arms are flexed with the fingertips pointing upward.
7. If a prepackaged scrub brush is used, the brush and nail cleaner are removed from the package. The brush is held in one hand and is used to clean the nails and the subungual area of the free hand. If a disposable nail cleaner is unavailable, a sterile reusable metal or plastic cleaner may be used. The reusable cleaner must be disposed of in the appropriate location so that it may be resterilized.
8. Rinse hands.
9. If the brush is impregnated with an antimicrobial soap or a detergent, wet it and begin the scrub procedure. If the brush is not impregnated, the soap or detergent is applied to the hands. The timed scrub method or stroke count method is then used.
10. Turn off water, discard brush, proceed to operating room holding hands and arms up and away from scrub clothes.
11. If during the scrubbing procedure the hands or arms inadvertently touch some part of the sink, add 10 strokes to that area of skin to correct the contamination.

Procedure for the timed scrub (10 minutes):

1. Left hand — 1 minute
    Left arm and elbow — $1\frac{1}{2}$ minutes
    Rinse hand, arm, and brush

    Repeat process for right hand

2. Left hand — 1 minute
    Left arm up to 2 inches above elbow — 1 minute
    Rinse hand, arm, and brush

    Repeat process for right hand

3. Left hand — $\frac{1}{2}$ minute
    Rinse hand and brush

    Repeat process for right hand

Procedure for the stroke count method:

1. Left hand and arm:

Nails	—30 strokes across nails, rinsing fingertips after 10 strokes to remove dislodged soil
Fingers	—30 strokes to all sides of each digit and web spaces
Hand	—20 strokes to palm and back of hand
Arm	—Using a circular motion, scrub all sides of the forearm to 2 inches above the elbow, with 20 strokes to all surfaces
Rinse	—Flex the arm at the elbow and rinse from fingertips to elbow, allowing water to run off elbow; rinse the brush or sponge

Repeat process for right hand and arm

2. Left hand and arm:

Nails	—30 strokes across nails
Fingers	—20 strokes to all sides of each digit and web spaces
Hand	—20 strokes to palm and back of hand
Arm	—Scrub all sides of the forearm to 2 inches above the elbow, with 20 strokes to all surfaces
Rinse	—Rinse hand, arm, and brush thoroughly

Repeat process for right hand and arm

Subsequent hand scrubs are as rigorous as the initial method because microorganisms can multiple rapidly in the warm, moist environment of a gloved hand.[12]

Drying Hands and Arms. Hands and arms must be thoroughly dried with a sterile towel to prevent contamination of the sterile gown by organisms on the skin and scrub attire.

To avoid contamination of the sterile field, a gown package is opened on a small table for the scrub nurse. It contains one gown and one or two towels. Without dripping water on the sterile field, the scrub nurse grasps a towel and lifts it straight up and away from the sterile field. The hands and the arms are kept up and away from the scrub clothes. The nurse bends slightly forward to prevent the towel, as it is unfolded, from touching the scrub clothes.

If two towels are used, one towel is used for each hand and arm. The towel is unfolded and the hand is thoroughly dried. Then using a rotating motion, the forearm and the elbow are dried, and the towel is discarded.

If one towel is used, one half is used for each hand and arm (Fig. 9–5). The towel is unfolded, and the hand is dried thoroughly. Then, using a rotating motion, the forearm and the elbow are dried. With the dried hand, grasp the dry unused end of the towel, and repeat the process on the second hand and arm. Discard the towel. In both these techniques, once the towel has been moved from the hands up to the elbow, the towel is considered contaminated and must not come in contact with the dried portion of the hand or the arm. Care must be taken not to let the edges of the towel touch the front of the scrub clothes.

▮ GOWNING AND GLOVING

Gowning

The gown is folded so that the scrub nurse can put it on without touching the outer side with bare hands. The inside front neckline of the gown is visible after the towels have been removed. The procedure for donning a gown follows:

1. Lift the folded gown upward from the sterile package, and step back from the table.
2. Grasp the gown at the neckline and allow the gown to unfold with the inside of the gown toward the wearer. The outside of the gown must not be touched with bare hands.
3. Simultaneously the hands are slipped into the armholes, holding the hands at shoulder level and away from the body.
4. The circulating nurse may assist the scrub nurse by reaching inside the gown and pulling the inside seam. If the closed-gloving technique is used (Fig. 9–6), the gown is pulled on leaving the sleeves extended beyond the hands approximately 1 inch. If open-gloving technique is used, then the hands are extended through the cuffs of the gown (Fig. 9–7).

(Text continues on page 215)

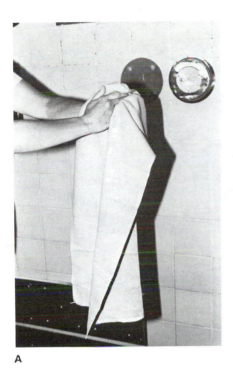

A

B

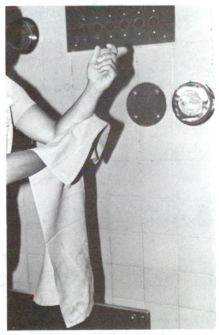

C

Figure 9–5. Drying with one towel. **A.** Dry one hand and arm using one half of the towel. **B.** The dried hand grasps the unused end of the towel. **C.** Dry the second hand and arm.

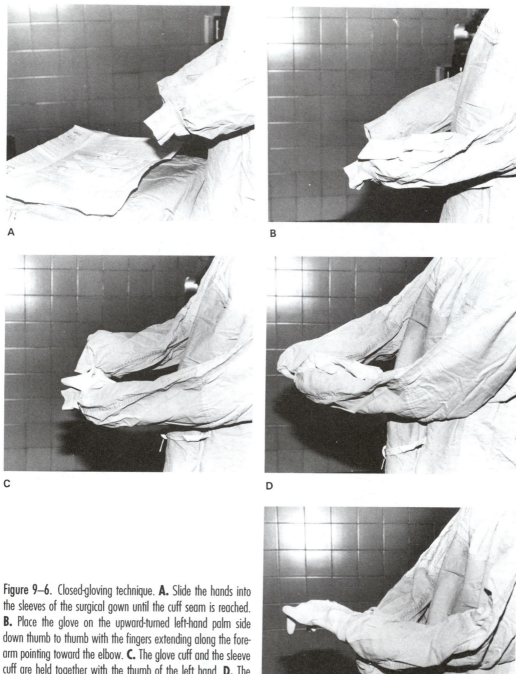

Figure 9–6. Closed-gloving technique. **A.** Slide the hands into the sleeves of the surgical gown until the cuff seam is reached. **B.** Place the glove on the upward-turned left-hand palm side down thumb to thumb with the fingers extending along the forearm pointing toward the elbow. **C.** The glove cuff and the sleeve cuff are held together with the thumb of the left hand. **D.** The right hand stretches the cuff of the left glove over the opened end of the sleeve. **E.** As the fingers are worked into the glove, the cuff is pulled up onto the wrist.

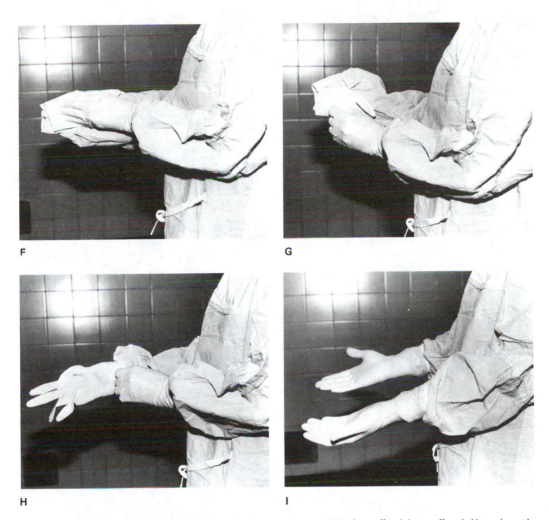

Figure 9–6. Continued. **F.** The right glove is positioned in the same manner. **G.** The glove cuff and sleeve cuff are held together with the thumb of the right hand. **H.** Fingers of the right hand are worked into the glove, and the cuff is pulled up onto the wrist. **I.** Gloves are adjusted to ensure appropriate fit.

5. The circulating nurse ties or snaps the back of the gown, at the neck and the waist, touching only the ties or snaps. The gown is adjusted by grasping at its bottom edge and pulling down, which eliminates the blousing or ballooning effect sterile gowns frequently develop.

6. If a wraparound gown is used after the scrub nurse is gloved, the front ties are untied and the sterile gown may be wrapped in one of the following ways:
   a) The tie attached to the back on the right is handed to another gowned and gloved team member who remains stationary. The scrub nurse pivots to the

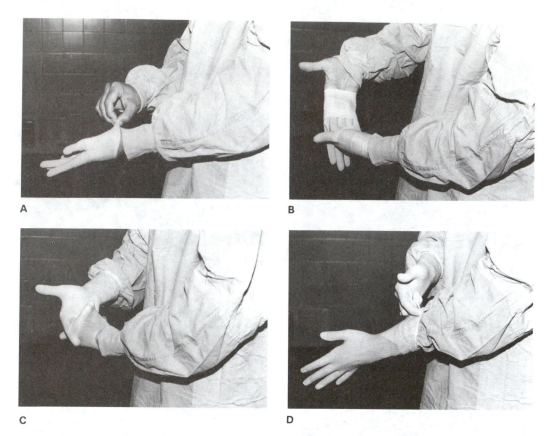

Figure 9–7. Open-gloving technique. **A.** Pull the glove onto the left hand leaving the cuff of the glove turned down. **B.** With the gloved left hand, slide the fingers inside the cuff of the right glove. **C.** Place the fingers of the gloved right hand under the folded cuff of the left glove. **D.** Rotate the arm and pull the cuff of the glove over the gown.

left, which brings the flap over the back of the gown, and the gown is tied in the front.

b) If other members of the team are not gowned and gloved, a Kocher or Allis clamp may be snapped to the end of the tie and the instrument handed to the circulating nurse. While the circulating nurse remains stationary, the scrub nurse turns to the left, bringing the flap around. The circulating nurse releases the instrument, and the scrub nurse takes the tie and ties the gown. If this method is used, the instrument must be placed in an appropriate place so that it will be included in the instrument count.

c) If disposable gloves are used, the inner wrapper, if it is cardboard, may be used to tie the gown. The scrub nurse places the end of the tie in the center crease of the glove wrapper, folds the wrapper over, and hands the wrapper to the circulating nurse. While the circulating nurse remains stationary, the scrub nurse turns to the left and takes the tie from the glove wrapper, being careful not to touch the wrapper or the circulating nurse, and ties the gown.

Donning Sterile Gloves

Suggested procedures for closed and open gloving follow.

Procedure for Closed Gloving. For the scrub nurse, the closed method of gloving is preferred because it is not possible for the bare hand to contact the outside of the glove (Fig. 9–6).

1. Slide the hands into the sleeves of the gown until the cuff seam is reached; the hands must not touch the cuff edges.
2. With the right hand, which is covered by the fabric of the sleeve or the cuff, pick up the left glove.
3. Place the glove on the upward-turned left hand, palm side down, thumb to thumb, with fingers extending along the forearm pointing toward the elbow.
4. The glove cuff and the sleeve cuff are held together with the thumb of the left hand.
5. The sleeve-covered right hand stretches the cuff of the left glove over the open end of the sleeve.
6. The sleeve-covered right hand grasps both the cuff of the glove and the gown; as the fingers are worked into the glove, the cuff is pulled up onto the wrist.
7. The right glove is put on in the same manner with the help of the gloved hand.

Procedure for Open Gloving. The open-gloving technique is used before performing sterile procedures (such as bladder catheterization or insertion of an IV cutdown) or when both gloves must be changed without assistance during a surgical procedure (Fig. 9–7).

1. Slide hands into the gown all the way through the cuffs of the gown.
2. Pick up the cuff of the left glove using the thumb and the index finger of the right hand.
3. Pull the glove onto the left hand, leaving the cuff of the glove turned down.
4. With the gloved left hand, slide the fingers inside the cuff of the right glove, being careful to keep the gloved fingers under the folded cuff.
5. Pull the glove onto the right hand avoiding inward rolling of the cuff. Then, by rotating the arm, the cuff of the glove is pulled over the gown.
6. Place the fingers of the gloved right hand under the folded cuff of the left glove, rotate the arm, and pull the cuff of the glove over the gown.

Assisting Team Members with Gowning and Gloving

The scrub nurse is responsible for assisting members of the surgical team to don the sterile gowns and gloves (Figs. 9–8, 9–9).

1. The scrub nurse opens the towel and places one end over the outstretched hand of the other team member.

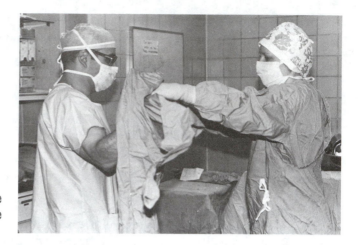

Figure 9–8. Gowning another person. The scrub nurse makes a protective cuff of the neck and shoulder area.

2. The gown is picked up by the neck band and unfolded.
3. The scrub nurse makes a protective cuff of the neck and shoulder area, turns the inner side of the gown toward the person being gowned, and places the gown on the outstretched arms.
4. Once the other team member has placed his or her hands in the sleeves, the scrub nurse releases the gown. The circulating nurse assists in pulling it on by touching only the inside of the gown.
5. In gloving team members, the right hand is always gloved first. The glove is picked up under the everted cuff.
6. The palm of the glove is held toward the other team member.
7. The glove is stretched to open it.
8. The scrub nurse holds the thumbs out or protects them under the cuff of the glove to keep them from coming in contact with the bare hands of the other team member.

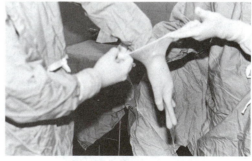

A   B

Figure 9–9. Gloving another person. **A.** The scrub nurse holds her thumbs out to prevent them from coming in contact with the bare hands of the other team members. **B.** Team member assists in donning second glove.

9. As the other team member slides a hand into the glove, the scrub nurse exerts firm upward pressure, making certain that the gloved hand does not go below the waist.
10. The glove cuff is pulled over the cuff of the gown.
11. The procedure is repeated for the left glove.
12. If a wraparound gown is used, the scrub nurse holds the tie as the other team member turns.

Regloving

If a member of the surgical team, other than the scrub nurse, perforates or contaminates a glove during the surgical procedure, the circulator grasps the outside of the glove and pulls the glove off inside out. The scrub nurse then regloves the team member as previously indicated.

If the scrub nurse needs to change gloves, the options are to:

- remove both gown and gloves
- have another member of the team assist in regloving
- use the open-glove technique

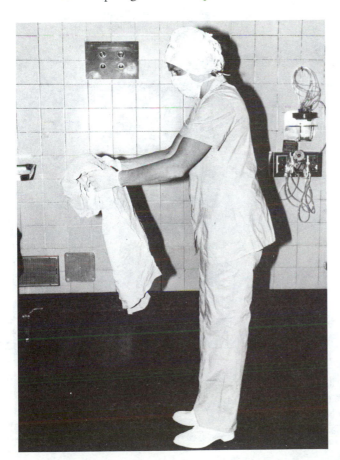

Figure 9–10. Removing soiled gown. The gown is rolled and deposited in the linen or waste hamper.

Closed gloving cannot be used to reglove, because once the hand passes through the cuff of the gown, the edge of the cuff is contaminated; therefore, the outside of the new glove would be contaminated.

Dangers of Powder

In manufacturing, glove surfaces are usually prelubricated with an absorbable dry starch powder to facilitate donning the gloves and to prevent adhesion of the glove surfaces. Immediately after gloving, however, before touching instruments or other sterile items, the glove powder must be removed. This is necessary because the starch commonly causes iatrogenic diseases, such as granulomas or periotonitis, and can be responsible for serious postoperative morbidity and complications. Glove powder is a foreign body; until it is broken down by the body, it incites an inflammatory response, delays healing, carries allergens, and possibly lowers the inoculum of bacteria necessary to cause infection.[13] Powder is removed from the gloves by thoroughly wiping them with a sterile wet towel. Using a

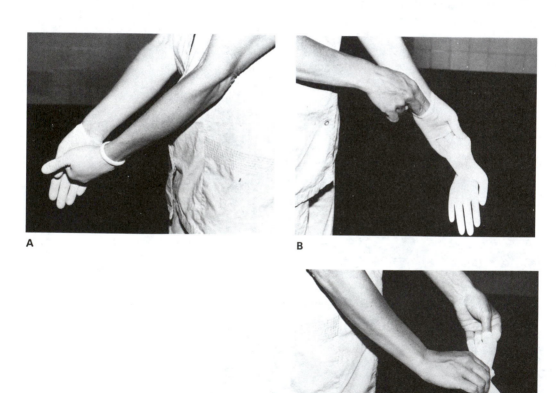

A

B

Figure 9–11. Removing soiled gloves. **A.** Grasp the right rolled glove cuff with the left hand and invert the glove as it is pulled from the right hand. **B.** The fingers of the right hand are then placed inside the cuff of the left glove. **C.** The glove is inverted as it is removed.

C

"splash" basin is strongly discouraged, as it is necessary to exert friction to remove the powder, and the particles of starch clump in the basin.

Latex gloves can be coated on the inside with a hydrogel lubricant to facilitate donning without the potential hazard of the glove powder.

Removing Soiled Gown and Gloves

At the conclusion of the surgical procedure, the gown and the gloves are removed in a manner that avoids cross-contamination of the arms, hands, and scrub clothes. The following steps are followed:

1. The front tie is untied by the scrubbed member of the team.
2. The back neck and waist ties are released by the circulator.
3. The gown is removed by grasping the gown at the shoulders and pulling it over the gloved hands, turning the gown inside out. Care is taken not to touch the scrub clothes (Fig. 9–10).
4. When the gown is removed, it is folded with the contaminated surface on the inside. Then it is rolled up and deposited in the linen or waste hamper. Rolling the gown will ensure that cross-contamination will not soak through the laundry bag.
5. Gloves are removed by grasping the right rolled glove cuff with the left gloved hand and inverting the glove as it is pulled from the right hand (Fig. 9–11).
6. The fingers of the right hand are then placed inside the cuff of the left glove, along the palm of the hand; the glove is inverted as it is removed.

If the gloves are removed before the gown, the contaminated gown would then be pulled off over the bare hands—causing the hands to become contaminated. Gown and gloves are never worn outside the operating room and must be removed before the surgical dressings are applied.

▌ REFERENCES

1. Recommended practices for skin preparation of patients. In *Standards and Recommended Practices*. Denver: AORN; 1995:255–259.
2. Recommended practices for surgical hand scrubs. In *Standards and Recommended Practices*. Denver: AORN; 1995:185–190.
3. Paulson D. Comparative evaluation of five surgical hand scrub preparations. *AORN J.* 1994; 60(2):255.
4. Aly R, Maibach H. Comparative antimicrobial efficacy of a 2-minute surgical scrub with chlorhexidine gluconate, povidone, iodine and chlorxylenol sponge brushes. *Am J Infect Control.* 1988; 16:173–177.
5. Larson E et al. Alcohol for surgical scrubbing? *Infect Control Hosp Epidemiol.* 1990; 11(3):142.
6. Beck W. Alcohol foam has a place in the clinical arena. *AORN J.* 1989; 50(1):158.
7. Larson E. Guidelines for use of topical antimicrobial agents. *Am J Infect Control.* 1988; 16:262.
8. O'Shaughnessy M et al. Optimum duration of surgical scrubtime. *Br J Surgery.* 1991; 78:685–686.
9. Hingst V et al. Evaluation of the efficacy of surgical hand disinfection following a reduced application time of 3 instead of 5 min. *J Hosp Infect.* 1992; 20:79–86.

10. Baumgardner C. Effects of nail polish on microbial growth of fingernails: Dispelling sacred cows. *AORN J.* 1993; 58(1):84–88.
11. Pottinger J. Bacterial carriage by artificial versus natural nails. *Am J Infect Control.* 1989; 17:340–344.
12. Larsen E, Goldmann D. Hand washing and nosocomial infections. *New Eng J Med.* 1992; 327:120–122.
13. Ellis H. The hazards of surgical glove dusting powders. *Surgery, Gyn & Ob.* 1990; 171:521.

Anesthesia

■ HISTORICAL INTRODUCTION TO ANESTHESIA

Historians have documented that people have consistently sought relief from pain and suffering. Mandragora wine was given by the ancient Greeks and Romans as an anesthetic agent and it remained in use through the 12th century. In the *Annals of the Later Han Dynasty,* performing surgery with the assistance of a "bubbling drug medicine" is mentioned. The medicine, an effervescent powder added to wine, produced numbness and insensibility. The powder may well have been opium.

"Sleeping apples," or sponges impregnated with potions and extracts from plants and herbs, were also used to produce sleep. The extracts included juices of the unripe mulberry, spurge flax, mandragon, and ivy; hyposcyamus (scopolamine); lettuce seed; the shrub of hemlock; and opium. In the sunlight, this mixture was soaked up by a sponge. The sponge was then applied to the nostrils until the patient fell asleep.[1] The ancients, however, did not understand the strength of their potions; patients were often overdosed and killed.

Intoxication with alcohol, compression of the carotid arteries to induce unconsciousness, and hypnotism were all tried as a means of producing anesthesia and frequently failed. When appropriate anesthesia was not available, patients were strapped to the operating table or were restrained by friends or members of their family.

Lanney, Napoleon's chief military surgeon, noticed that a partially frozen soldier had a higher pain threshold, so he used the numbing effects of cold to amputate limbs painlessly on the battlefield.

In 1772, Joseph Priestley first prepared an impure form of nitrous oxide and, in 1800, Sir Humphry Davy published the results of his research on the properties of nitrous oxide. Although he suggested that it was capable of eliminating physical pain and that it probably could be used in surgical operations, no one used Davy's research for producing anesthesia. Nitrous oxide became a scientific plaything labeled "laughing gas" because of the giddy laughter induced by the agent.

Ether entered medicine as a treatment for lung disease; it was inhaled from a saucer. The effects of excessive ether became known, and parties called "ether-frolics" were held; sometimes guests passed out from the effects of ether. When Dr. Crawford Long of Jefferson, Georgia, witnessed the frolics, he administered ether to one of his patients in 1842 and, as was his intent, prevented the pain of surgery. He, however, did not publish his results until 1849.

Dr. William Thomas Green Morton, an American dentist, is identified as the pioneer of surgical anesthesia. In October 1846 at the Massachusetts General Hospital in Boston, Dr. Morton administered ether anesthesia while Dr. John Collins Warren removed a tuberculous gland from the neck of an unconscious patient. At the completion of the procedure, Dr. Warren asked the patient to describe what he felt. The patient replied, "It felt like someone was scratching my neck."[2]

Chloroform was being used medicinally when Sir James Simpson of Edinburgh introduced it as an anesthetic agent* in 1847. For the next 60 years, chloroform became the most widely used anesthetic agent. It was more pleasant to inhale than ether, and more powerful. Consequently, it was easier to administer successfully. When it was found that chloroform caused more deaths, its use as an anesthetic agent was discontinued.

Until late into the 20th century, most anesthetics were administered through a mask placed over the nose and mouth. The anesthetic was either dropped directly onto the mask or vaporized by means of a hand bellows (Fig. 10–1). Nitrous oxide was administered through a rubber mask and sometimes mixed with the vapor of ether or chloroform. These methods made surgery on the head and neck difficult and dangerous; there was always the possibility of an obstructed airway due to the relaxation of muscles and the

---

*The name for the drugs that cause complete or partial loss of feeling was proposed by Dr. Oliver Wendell Holmes. The term *anesthetic* came from the Greek term meaning "without sensation." The loss of feeling became known as anesthesia. The specialty is called anesthesiology. A physician trained in anesthesia is an anesthesiologist, and a nurse trained to administer certain types of anesthetics is an anesthetist.

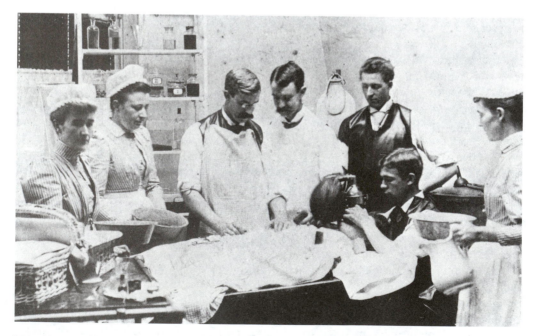

Figure 10–1. Anesthesia being administered with the surgical team ready for action, 1880. Bellevue Hospital, New York. (*The Bettmann Archive.*)

tongue falling back into the throat. To avoid an obstructed airway, in some surgical procedures the surgeon performed a tracheostomy through which a tube could be inserted for anesthesia.

Sir William Macewen devised the idea of passing a tube through the mouth, between the vocal cords, into the trachea. The anesthetic agent could then be administered directly into the trachea without the fear of obstruction from the tongue. The tubes of silver or gum elastic could be bent to the desired angle but would retain their shape when inserted. On July 5, 1878, the first endotracheal anesthesia was administered.[2]

The continued development of anesthetic agents and techniques has not only freed patients from pain, it has also prolonged operating time, allowing the surgeon to refine and expand surgical techniques.

■ ANESTHESIA

Anesthesia is the partial or complete loss of sensation with or without the loss of consciousness. It may occur as a result of disease or injury or the administration of a drug or gas. The two broad types of artificially induced anesthesia are general and regional. *General anesthesia* produces unconsciousness in the patient; *regional anesthesia* causes a loss of feeling in some area of the body that requires monitored anesthesia care (MAC). In MAC cases, the local anesthetic is administered by the surgeon; however, the anesthesiologist evaluates the patient preoperatively, administers preoperative medication, monitors the patient during the surgical procedure, and transfers the patient to the postanesthesia care unit.

The method of administering anesthesia and which agents will be used are determined after reviewing the patient. One tool used to evaluate the patient's risk for anesthesia is the physical status classification (Table 10–1). The following patient factors are included:

TABLE 10–1. PHYSICAL (P) STATUS CLASSIFICATION OF THE AMERICAN SOCIETY OF ANESTHESIOLOGISTS*

Status	Definition	Examples
P1	Normal, healthy patient	No physiologic, psychologic, biochemical or organic disturbance
P2	Patient with mild systemic disease	Cardiovascular disease with minimal restriction on activity. Hypertension, asthma, chronic bronchitis, obesity or diabetes mellitus
P3	Patient with severe systemic disease	Cardiovascular or pulmonary disease that limits activity. Severe diabetes with systemic complications. History of myocardial infarction, angina pectoris, or poorly controlled hypertension
P4	Patient with severe systemic disease that is a constant threat to life	Severe cardiac, pulmonary, renal hepatic, or endocrine dysfunction
P5	Moribund patient who is not expected to survive without the operation	Surgery is performed as a last recourse. Major multisystem or cerebral trauma, ruptured aneurysm, or large pulmonary embolus

*Also referred to as ASA class.
Based on ASA 1995 Relative Value Guide. Printed with permission of the American Society of Anesthesiologists. A copy of the full text can be obtained from ASA, 520 N. Northwest Highway, Park Ridge, Illinois 60068-2573.

- Physical and mental status
- Age
- Coexisting disease
- Concurrent drug therapy
- Previous allergic reactions to drugs
- Previous anesthesia experience
- Preference

Other influences on selection of method and agent include:

- Site and duration of proposed surgical procedure
- Use of electrocautery
- Surgeon preference
- Expertise of the anesthesiologist

The administration of anesthesia begins with the preoperative medication.

Preoperative Medication

Preoperative medications are given to allay preoperative anxiety, decrease respiratory tract secretions, reduce reflex irritability, relieve pain, and lower the body's metabolism so that less anesthetic is required. In general, patients with a high metabolic rate require higher doses of medication; these patients are heavy smokers, alcoholics, those with hyperthyroid activity, and those who are toxic or emotional. Conversely, debilitation and age usually reduce the need for medication and increase the side effects. The side effects include confusion, restlessness, decreased respirations, hypotension, nausea, vomiting, or uncomfortably dry mouth and lips.

To ensure adequate drug action, the medication is administered 45 to 60 minutes before induction of anesthesia or as ordered by the anesthesiologist. The drugs of choice are barbiturates, narcotics, and anticholinergics. Patients medicated preoperatively must be assessed and continually observed during the preoperative period.

Barbiturates. Barbiturates may produce reactions that range from mild sedation to general anesthesia. They are classified by their duration of action:

- ultrashort (10 to 15 minutes duration)
- short to intermediate (1 to 6 hours duration)
- long acting (duration of up to 1 day or more)

Pentobarbital (Nembutal) and secobarbital (Seconal) are used as preoperative medications. Doses range from 50 to 200 mg and depend on the route of administration. These drugs provide good sedation with minimal respiratory or circulatory depression and rarely cause postoperative nausea and vomiting. However, as preoperative medication barbiturates have a duration of action that is too long for most purposes and their use may result in transient psychoses, disorientation, and agitation in the elderly. Therefore, benzodiazepines are more frequently used.

The benzodiazepines are effective preoperative medications because they possess excellent anxiolytic and amnesic properties. Diazepam (Valium), 10 mg, provides sedation and tension relief without circulatory depression. Diazepam is frequently administered before local anesthesia because of its anticonvulsive properties. Convulsions are a rare but potential problem with the systemic absorption of local anesthetic drugs.

Midazolam hydrochloride (Versed) may be administered as a preoperative medication. It is potent and can cause severe respiratory depression. Dosage of Versed must be carefully adjusted according to individual requirements, including age, body weight, physical and clinical status, underlying pathologic conditions, and the nature and duration of the procedure. Versed has a rapid onset with a short duration of effect. It produces more amnesia and less sedation than Valium and infrequently causes nausea, vomiting, or emergence excitement in the recovery period.

Lorazepam (Ativan) is used in doses of 2 mg to 4 mg and has good antiemetic action. It is usually given intravenously for the amnesic properties.

Narcotics. The narcotics primarily used are morphine, in a dose of 5 to 15 mg, and meperidine hydrochloride (Demerol), 50 to 100 mg. Both provide good preoperative sedation and are useful for patients experiencing pain or when painful procedures are anticipated prior to the induction of anesthesia. For short surgical procedures, narcotics administered preoperatively decrease excitement and restlessness due to pain immediately postoperatively. They, however, may prolong emergence from anesthesia. Narcotics depress the respiratory and circulatory systems, decrease gastric motility, and may produce nausea and vomiting.

Anticholinergics. Atropine and scopolamine are given preoperatively to reduce secretions and block vagal transmission. The usual dose is 0.2 to 0.6 mg. These drugs depress the parasympathetic nervous system; therefore, the heart rate is increased. The increase counteracts the bradycardia that may occur as a result of (1) stimulating the carotid sinus and vagus nerve and (2) traction on the extraocular muscles or the intraabdominal viscera. These drugs may cause a rise in the body temperature, especially in children. Scopolamine promotes amnesia and, postoperatively, it may produce restlessness, irritability, and disorientation in elderly patients.

Glycopyrrolate (Robinul) is a synthetic anticholinergic agent. The desired effects are the same as those of atropine and scopolamine, but glycopyrrolate decreases oral secretions more effectively. It is believed that this drug does not cross the blood-brain barrier and is less likely to cause confusion and other adverse reactions of the central nervous system (CNS). It also reduces the volume and acidity of gastric secretions.

General Anesthesia

General anesthesia is a drug-induced depression of the CNS characterized by analgesia, amnesia, and unconsciousness, with a loss of reflexes and muscle tone. The effects of general anesthesia are reversible when the drug is eliminated. General anesthetic agents may be administered by inhalation or IV injection.

The exact way that general anesthetic agents produce their effect is not known. It is known, however, that the agents are carried by the blood to all body tissues and that their chief effect is on the brain. In the brain, the anesthetic agent interrupts the activity of the nerve cells, which temporarily cease to function. Sensory impulses are not carried to the

CNS; thus, the patient feels no pain. The CNS is no longer capable of issuing motor discharges; therefore, the patient cannot move parts of the body.

The two most critical periods of general anesthesia are at the time of induction and emergence from anesthesia. During the induction phase the circulating nurse may apply cricoid pressure to the patient's neck. Cricoid pressure compresses the esophagus between the vertebrae and trachea and reduces the risk of aspiration during intubation. The nurse should maintain pressure until intubation has been accomplished, the cuff on the endotracheal tube inflated, and bilateral breath sounds verified. If the patient begins to vomit while pressure is being exerted, the pressure should be released immediately and the patient's head turned for suctioning. Cricoid pressure applied during active vomiting could cause esophageal rupture.

The four stages of general anesthesia and appropriate nursing actions are identified in Table 10–2.

Anesthesia Machine. Perioperative nurses should be familiar with the anesthesia machine (Fig. 10–2) and know how to connect it, how to administer oxygen to and ventilate a patient. The anesthesia machine is connected to a source of gases, either from the high-pressure tanks attached to the machine or piped from a central hospital source. In either situation, the end of each connector must be designed so that it is impossible to connect it to any source other than its own, which is labeled. To further guard against accidents, cylinders containing anesthetic gases and their fittings and outlets are color coded. The color for oxygen is green, nitrous oxide is blue, and cyclopropane is orange.

The anesthesia machine permits the administration of inhaled gases in known, controlled mixtures of oxygen and the anesthetic agent. Using a mask or endotracheal tube, inhalation gases may be administered by an open, semiclosed, or closed system. In the open system, the patient inhales anesthetic agents and oxygen from the anesthetic machine and then exhales through a valve directly into the atmosphere. Water vapor and heat are lost, and high flows of gases are necessary for this method.

In the semiclosed system, the patient exhales gases into the atmosphere, or the gases are mixed with fresh gases and the patient rebreathes the mixture. In this system, the gases pass through a chemical (CO_2) absorber; there, granules of the hydroxides of sodium, calcium, or barium absorb moisture and carbon dioxide from the exhaled gases. As the granules become saturated with the carbon dioxide, they change color.

Both the open and semiclosed methods of administering anesthetic gases allow waste gases to enter the atmosphere and should not be used because of the potential health hazards of exposure to trace concentrations of waste anesthetic gases.

The closed system permits rebreathing of exhaled gases. It is a circular arrangement consisting of an anesthetic agent, a reservoir bag, a chemical absorber, an expiratory overflow valve, and two conducting tubes (elephant hoses) connected to a face mask or an endotracheal tube. Valves in the conducting tubes allow the gases to flow in one direction only. This prevents the rebreathing of exhaled gases before carbon dioxide has been removed by the chemical absorber.

When manually compressed, the reservoir bag forces air into the patient's lungs. This is the standard way a patient is assisted with ventilation.

TABLE 10–2. THE FOUR STAGES OF ANESTHESIA

Stage	Biologic Response	Patient Reaction	Nursing Action
I Relaxation	Amnesia Anlagesia	Feels drowsy and dizzy Exaggerated hearing Decreased sensation of pain May appear inebriated	Close OR doors Check for proper positioning of safety belt Have suction available and working Keep noise in room to a minimum Provide emotional support for the patient by remaining at his or her side
II Excitement	Delirium	Irregular breathing Increased muscle tone and involuntary motor activity; may move all extremities May vomit, hold breath or struggle (patient is very susceptible to external stimuli such as a loud noise or being touched)	Avoid stimulating the patient Be available to protect extremities or to restrain the patient Be available to assist anesthesiologist with suctioning
III Operative or surgical anesthesia	Partial to complete sensory loss Progression to complete intercostal paralysis	Quiet, regular thoraco-abdominal breathing Jaw relaxed Auditory and pain sensation lost Moderate to maximum decrease in muscle tone Eyelid reflex is absent	Be available to assist anesthesiologist with intubation Validate with anesthesiologist appropriate time for skin scrub and positioning of patient Check position of patient's feet to ascertain they are not crossed
IV Danger	Medullary paralysis and respiratory distress	Respiratory muscles paralyzed Pupils fixed and dilated Pulse rapid and thready Respirations cease	Be available to assist in treatment of cardiac or respiratory arrest Provide emergency drug box and defibrillation Document administration of drugs

Future Anesthesia Machines. Innovations based on additional computer control are in the developmental stage. They include computerized delivery systems, record keeping, and monitoring. Computer processed, physiologically based feedback control of anesthesia machines includes on–off devices, a minimal number of moving parts, and fixed orifices or flow regulators. Volatile anesthetics are injected rather than vaporized into the gas mixture, thereby eliminating many constraints based on requirements for temperature and flow compensation. Electronic microprocessors monitor the patient and the anesthetic delivery system and provide the information to the clinician.

The complexity of anesthetic administration has dramatically increased. Automated record keeping and direct transcription of physiologically monitored values onto an anesthesia record have been evolving since 1980. The data collected directly from the patient via respiratory gases, anesthesia machine settings, blood oxygen content, blood flow and

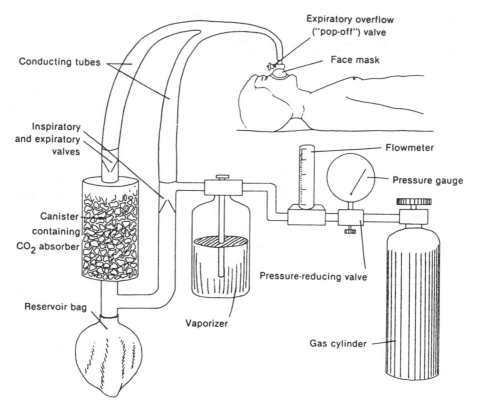

Figure 10–2. Components of an anesthesia machine.

organ function, integrated with alarm systems and artificial intelligence, will contribute to a self-editing, learning function of the automated anesthesia record-keeping systems.

Monitoring

The purpose of monitoring is to identify specific measurements that cannot be quantified precisely by the senses and to provide ongoing analysis of the integrity of life support equipment. The goal is to be acutely aware of the patient's condition, to treat changes rapidly, and to keep the patient stable.

Several safety features have been incorporated into anesthesia machines to avoid or reduce hazards of malfunction or operator errors. These features help the anesthetist to avoid or rapidly correct conditions that could lead to hypoxia, cardiac arrest, or arrhythmias. The American Society of Anesthesiologists (ASA) recommends and the Joint Commission on Accreditation of Healthcare Organizations requires an oxygen monitor in the breathing system to detect hypoxic gas mixtures due to component failure, incorrect setting, or insufficient oxygen flow.

Monitors with alarms protect patients from excessive pressure and warn of changes in patient respiration or the onset of unsafe operating conditions. Exhaled-volume monitors with properly adjusted alarms can be used to detect leaks and disconnections. Monitors measure the level of carbon dioxide in exhaled gas, which indicates the adequacy of pulmonary circulation and ventilation. The carbon dioxide monitor can also indicate when the trachea has not been intubated. Moreover, the monitor helps identify the presence of leaks and disconnections, as a failure to properly ventilate the lungs will result in a major change in exhaled carbon dioxide levels.

Pulse oximeters, a noninvasive means of monitoring the oxygen saturation of hemoglobin in the blood (SaO_2), are emerging as part of the standard of care during anesthesia. An oxygen monitor, however, is still required for early detection of a hypoxic gas mixture.

Intravascular Pressure Monitoring. Invasive pressure-monitoring systems are used intraoperatively and postoperatively. The pressures they monitor include: peripheral arterial, pulmonary wedge via Swan-Ganz catheters, heart chamber, umbilical artery, intrauterine, and intracranial.

An electronic, direct pressure-monitoring system consists of a fluid-filled catheter that is designed so that one end is placed in the intravascular space where fluid pressure is to be measured and the other end is connected to an electronic pressure transducer. The transducer converts fluid pressure into electric signals that are displayed on a monitor. To ensure accurate pressure measurement the system must periodically be calibrated and the catheter and tubing must be kept free of blood clots and other obstructions that prevent free transmission of pressure waves. The catheter and tubing are flushed to prevent blood clots from forming at the time of the cannula. Flushing can be continuous, using a device to deliver a constant flow of flush solution, or intermittent, using a syringe and stopcock. The syringe and stopcock invade a closed system and are discouraged.

Among the types of invasive pressure monitoring, intravascular is the most common. Bacteremia is the most frequent infectious complication reported with this monitoring. Bacteremia can occur from contamination of fluid and monitoring components external to the skin or from infection of the catheter insertion site. Pressure monitoring systems should be assembled in the simplest arrangement possible. Sterile items, including disposable domes and lines, are kept in their sterile wrapping until needed. These items and the transducer should not be assembled hours before the time of actual need, even to prepare for a possible emergency. Similarly, systems are never filled with flush solution and stored, as microorganisms inadvertently introduced into the solution at the time of assembly can rapidly multiple during storage. Flush solutions should not contain glucose, because it supports the growth of many microorganisms.[3]

Intraoperative Neural Monitoring. Intraoperative neural monitoring is used during surgical procedures to determine whether nerve impulses are being conducted at normal levels. This monitoring helps prevent iatrogenic damage and serious complications. The three general types of neural monitoring include:

- *electroencephalography* to monitor brain metabolism
- *evoked potentials* that detect specific brain responses to stimuli
- *nerved conduction studies* that detect provocation of specific nerves

The quality of intraoperative neural monitoring can be affected by the temperature of irrigation fluids, electrical noise from equipment, patient movement, and the quality of contact between electrodes and the patient. Cold irrigation fluids cause nerve impulses to slow and may be misinterpreted as decreased neural functions. Electrical equipment that can cancel monitoring signals includes electrosurgery units, cell-saver devices, heating blankets, and blood warmers. Positioning such equipment as far as possible from a patient's electrodes and ensuring that ESUs are grounded will help counteract electrical interference. Proper positioning prior to the surgical procedure will minimize patient movements that cause electrode wires to move and create electrical artifacts.

Following the procedure the electrodes are removed. If a gel or paste was used to attach the electrodes to the skin, it is cleaned with a damp cloth. Needle electrodes should be disposed of as is any other sharp device. Reusable needles are decontaminated, repackaged, and gas sterilized.[4]

Inhalation Anesthetic Agents

Inhalation anesthetics, which are delivered through a mask or endotracheal tube, enter and exit through the lungs. Some are gases and others volatile liquids that evaporate easily to produce vapors that may be inhaled. The anesthetic is transferred from inspired gas through the pulmonary alveoli into arterial blood and then to the brain. Adequate respiratory rate and depth are necessary during the induction phase. Any condition that interferes with the smooth flow of gases into and out of the lungs causes prolonged anesthesia induction and recovery time. The rate of blood flow to a tissue affects how rapidly the anesthetic agent is delivered to the tissue and when saturation is reached. Vessel-rich tissues such as brain, heart, kidneys, and liver have a rapid uptake of anesthetics. In adipose tissue, the uptake is slow due to decreased perfusion despite high solubility of anesthetics in the tissue.

Gaseous Agents. *Cyclopropane* is a colorless, sweet-smelling, flammable, explosive gas. It is a very potent anesthetic gas with rapid induction and emergence times. Cyclopropane may cause respiratory depression. It may cause cardiac arrhythmias by sensitizing the myocardium to a catecholamine such as epinephrine. Due to its explosive nature, cyclopropane is rarely used.

Nitrous oxide is a colorless, odorless, nonexplosive, nonirritating gas with rapid induction and recovery periods. Except for short procedures, it is a relatively weak anesthetic agent that requires the addition of other agents. Too high a concentration of nitrous oxide can produce hypoxia.

Waste Anesthetic Gases. Research results are mixed and controversial concerning the occupational hazards of long-term exposure to trace concentrations of waste anesthetic gases. These health hazards include the increased likelihood of spontaneous abortions and reproductive difficulties among females working in the operating room, and congenital defects in their children. In addition, nitrous oxide may depress the function of important enzyme systems in the human body and thus have widespread interference with normal bodily functions. Until this issue is resolved, waste anesthetics must be scavenged appropriately. Four methods of scavenging waste anesthetic gases are identified in Chapter 2. In addition, the anesthesia machine is checked daily for leaks and scheduled routinely for preventive maintenance and repairs. To ascertain the effectiveness of the gas control program, periodic air monitoring should be conducted to measure the level of waste gases present in each operating room.

Volatile Agents. Volatile anesthetic agents are liquids that are easily vaporized and inhaled. The most commonly used are halothane (Fluothane), enflurane (Ethrane), methoxyflurane (Penthrane), desflurane (Suprane), and isoflurane (Forane)—all halogenated compounds with a sweet odor. They are nonflammable liquids that require a special vaporizer for administration.

Halothane provides a smooth induction and rapid emergence with little excitement. It is nonirritating to the respiratory tract and produces minimal nausea and vomiting postoperatively. Halothane depresses the cardiovascular systems, resulting in hypotension and bradycardia. It can sensitize the myocardium to produce cardiac arrhythmias. The use of epinephrine as a local injection for vasoconstriction may aggravate or precipitate the arrhythmias.

Due to halothane's depressant effect on the hypothalamus, shivering may occur in the immediate postoperative period.

Some evidence indicates that halothane may cause liver damage in some patients and that subsequent exposures may result in severe or fatal jaundice. Therefore, most anesthesiologists avoid using halothane on patients requiring multiple surgical procedures.

Enflurane provides rapid induction and emergence with minimal nausea and vomiting. It is nonirritating to the respiratory tract during induction. It reduces ventilation and decreases blood pressure as the depth of the anesthesia increases. The cardiac rate and rhythm remain relatively stable. Enflurane produces adequate muscle relaxation for intraabdominal procedures.

Methoxyflurane is a potent drug that provides slow induction and long emergence with some nausea and vomiting. It is an excellent muscle relaxant and provides good analgesia at low concentrations. Methoxyflurane causes minimal sensitization of the myocardium to catecholamine. The breakdown products of methoxyflurane are toxic to the kidney; therefore, this agent is limited to surgical procedures of short duration.

Desflurane is a methyl ethyl ether that facilitates a quicker induction and emergence period than either enflurane and isoflurane. Induction occurs within seconds with a slight reduction in blood pressure while the heart rate and rhythm remain stable. Patients respond to commands within minutes after the agent is discontinued. Because it offers good cardiovascular stability with quick induction and rapid recovery, desflurane is ideal for elderly persons having ambulatory surgery.

Isoflurane provides rapid, smooth induction without stimulating excessive secretions. Emergence is rapid. The cardiovascular system remains stable, and the myocardium is not sensitized to catecholamine. Isoflurane provides good muscle relaxation. No renal or hepatic damage is evident. A greater incidence of coughing, breath holding, and laryngospasm results from using isoflurane than from using other volatile agents.

Ether, one of the oldest anesthetic agents, is a colorless, volatile liquid with a pungent odor. It is one of the *safest* anesthetics for patients because there is a wide margin between the concentration adequate for surgical procedures and the concentration that produces respiratory and circulatory depression. However, induction and emergence are long. Ether also causes postanesthesia nausea, vomiting, and urinary retention. It is very irritating to the skin, mucous membranes, lungs, and kidneys, and because it is highly flammable and explosive, ether is rarely used as an anesthetic agent.

Intravenous Anesthetic Agents

Intravenous drugs are frequently used as anesthetics and/or to supplement inhalation agents. Unlike the inhalation agents that can be removed by ventilating the lungs, IV agents must first be metabolized and then excreted from the body. The IV drugs cannot be removed or their action stopped once they are injected. This technique of induction is frequently requested by patients as it is rapid and pleasant.

Total intravenous anesthesia (TIVA) is a technique whereby hypnosis, analgesia, and muscle relaxation can be achieved without the use of any potent volatile anesthetic vapors or gases. TIVA has gained popularity as drugs have been developed and technological advances in infusion pumps have occurred.

Infusion pumps make possible accurate delivery of intravenous drugs to a predetermined plasma concentration. The aim of intravenous drug administration is to achieve and maintain a plasma-blood receptor concentration sufficient for the desired effect. This is best achieved with a variable-rate continuous infusion because it avoids the inappropriately high and low plasma levels that occur with intermittent bolus doses.[5]

Most infusion pumps have the capability to infuse fluids and medications epidurally, intra-arterially, and subcutaneously, as well as intravenously. This feature is a function of the infusion delivery pressure. Most pumps are capable of giving both boluses and constant-rate infusions. The delivery rate of a bolus may vary with the pump model and the syringe size. Pumps are designed strictly for intraoperative administration of specific intravenous anesthetics using preprogrammed templates. These templates attach to the face of the pump and are capable of modifying the pump and its readout display. Magnets in each template trigger switches in the pump. The pump microprocessors then read the activated switches and program the pump rate and the readout of the drug dose appropriately and accurately. This allows a wide variety of drugs of different concentrations to be used without the risk of potentially dangerous calculation errors.

Barbiturates are often used for IV inductions. The barbiturates act directly on the central venous system, producing a reaction ranging from mild sedation to unconsciousness; little pain relief is provided. The principal barbiturate used is the ultra-short-acting thiopental (Sodium Pentothal). In addition to being used for inductions, thiopental is used to supplement nitrous oxide during short procedures and as a hypnotic during regional anesthesia. It has a rapid onset of action, producing unconsciousness in 30 seconds. Depending on the amount and the rate of injections, thiopental is a potent depressant of respirations. It can also depress the cardiovascular system, resulting in varying degrees of hypotension. An anesthesia machine and oxygen should always be available to assist or control ventilation.

Narcotics may also be used to supplement inhalation agents. The most commonly used narcotics are morphine, meperidine hydrochloride (Demerol), and fentanyl citrate (Sublimaze). The use of narcotics during surgery results in good postoperative analgesia; however, morphine and meperidine hydrochloride depress the respiratory system, and impaired ventilation may be a major problem during the recovery phase.

Fentanyl citrate is a synthetic narcotic with a potency 80 to 100 times greater than morphine. Its duration of action is shorter than that of morphine or meperidine; therefore, the period of impaired ventilation is shorter too. Fentanyl may cause muscle rigidity and profound respiratory depression. Circulatory depression is less common; hypotension and bradycardia may occur after rapid IV administration of the drug.

An altered state of consciousness called neuroleptanalgesia is produced by the combination of a narcotic analgesic, such as fentanyl, and an antiemetic, such as droperidol. This combination is used as a preoperative medication and for patients undergoing diagnostic or therapeutic procedures.

Innovar is a combination of the narcotic fentanyl citrate and the tranquilizer droperidol (Inapsine). It may be used in small doses as a preoperative medication or in larger doses during surgery to supplement nitrous oxide or a regional anesthesia. It produces a general quiescence and excellent analgesia with a lower incidence of postoperative nausea and vomiting. Innovar has a long duration of action. Consequently, during the postoperative period, patients must be observed for respiratory depression, hypoventilation, apnea, and hypotension.

Ketamine hydrochloride is a dissociative anesthetic drug, a type of drug that selectively interrupts associative pathways in the brain. Given intravenously or intramuscularly, ketamine results in a rapid onset of a trancelike, profound analgesic state without respiratory depression or the loss of muscle tone, thus protecting the airway. The cardiovascular system is stimulated with an increase in heart rate and blood pressure.

Ketamine hydrochloride is excellent for diagnostic or short surgical procedures or to supplement weaker agents, such as nitrous oxide. It is administered to children intramuscularly because anesthesia occurs within 3 to 5 minutes.

During recovery from ketamine hydrochloride, patients may experience unpleasant dreams, hallucinations, or distorted images, and may act irrationally. These reactions are seen more often in adults than children and can be reduced by minimizing the stimulating effects of light, noise, touch, or movement until the patient awakens naturally.

Propofol (Diprivan) is a sedative-hypnotic drug that can be used both for induction and maintenance of general anesthesia. A single IV injection produces loss of consciousness within 40 seconds while patients are awake, responsive to verbal commands, and fully oriented in less than 8 minutes after it is discontinued. Patients ambulate earlier, ingest fluids, and eat sooner than with standard anesthetic agents. The drug, therefore, has advantages in an outpatient setting. Adverse reactions include hypotension and apnea. The drug should be used with caution in elderly, debilitated, and hypovolemic patients and in those in Status P3 and higher (see Table 10–1).

Tranquilizers and nonbarbiturate sedatives are used for induction and as adjuncts to other anesthetic agents. Their use permits the administration of lower doses of other agents. The most commonly used tranquilizers include *diazepam, midazolam (Versed), and droperidol (Inapsine)*. Diazepam provides sedation and amnesia and reduces anxiety and apprehension. Adverse reactions are excessive sedation, respiratory depression, preoperative or postoperative nausea, and vomiting. Droperidol has good antiemetic and sedative properties. The most common side effects are hypotension and reflex tachycardia.

Midazolam, a potent sedative, is never administered in a set dose; it must be individualized. Small doses of the drug are administered slowly, over a period of at least 2 minutes. Then, at least 2 to 3 minutes are allowed to elapse so that the patient's response to the drug may be fully evaluated. A total dose of more than 5 mg is rarely necessary.[6] If the drug is used with other narcotics, the dose of midazolam is decreased by 25% to 30%. Midazolam has a more rapid onset of action than diazepam with sedation occurring within 3 to 5 minutes after intravenous injection.[7] Midazolam has a shorter duration of action, usually less than 1 to 2 hours following injection. Following the administration, patients experience anterograde amnesia. This is an important advantage for patients who may experience significant discomfort during a local anesthetic injection.

Midazolam is frequently administered for conscious sedation and as an adjunct to local anesthesia. When conscious sedation occurs, patients have slightly slurred speech and diminished verbal communication. They are also relaxed, cooperative, and can easily be aroused from sleep. Administered properly for conscious sedation, midazolam decreases the patient's fear and anxiety and permits rapid return to ambulation, which is important for outpatient procedures.[6] Signs of overdose include severely slurred speech, unarousable sleep or somnolence, confusion, impaired coordination, diminished reflexes, drop in respiratory rate, variations of pulse and blood pressure rates, and coma. Patients who are extremely apprehensive or agitated or who have essential hypertension may experience hypotensive episodes after an intravenous injection of the medication (see the section on "Management of Patients Receiving IV Conscious Sedation" at the end of this chapter).

Neuromuscular Blocking Agents

Neuromuscular blocking agents are used to provide muscle relaxation during surgery or to facilitate passage of an endotracheal tube. These drugs exert their action on the striated muscles of the body by interfering with the impulses that occur at the motor end plate, the point where a motor nerve fiber connects with a muscle fiber. The two types of muscle relaxant drugs are depolarizers and nondepolarizers.

Depolarizing Agents. Depolarizing agents produce a neuromuscular block by depolarizing the membrane of the motor end plate. When these drugs are administered, the muscle fiber acts as though acetylcholine was released and the muscle contracts, or twitches. The drug remains attached to the muscle fibers and prevents the repolarization necessary for another contracture to occur. The action is characterized by muscle fasciculation and potentiation of the maximum twitching; thus, the muscle remains relaxed. The effects of depolarizing agents can be reversed with atropine or Robinul (glycopyrrolate).

The most frequently used depolarizing agent is succinylcholine chloride (Quelicin, Anectine). It is a rapid-acting drug with a duration of 3 to 5 minutes. It is, therefore, frequently used for intubation. When longer periods of relaxation are required, it may also be administered by a continuous intravenous drip solution.

Patients who receive depolarizing muscle relaxants often complain of overall muscle soreness followed surgery, which is related to the severe fasciculation.

Nondepolarizing Agents. Nondepolarizing muscle relaxants inhibit the effect of acetylcholine at the neuromuscular junction, but they do not cause depolarization of the motor end plate. Tubocurarine (Curare), pancuronium bromide (Pavulon), gallamine triethiodide (Flaxedil), atracurium (Tracrium), vercuronium (Norcuron), and rocuronium bromide (Zemuron) are all nondepolarizing agents.

Reversing the effects of nondepolarizing agents can be accomplished by administering neostigmine (Prostigmin) or tensiton (Endrophonium), which allows acetylcholine to accumulate at the neuromuscular junction.

The onset time of tubocurarine is 3 to 5 minutes and its duration of action is 20 to 60 minutes. It frequently causes hypotension and bronchospasms. Tubocurarine is potentiated by certain anesthetics such as halothane, enflurane, and methoxyflurane and by some antibiotics.

Pancuronium bromide is longer acting than tubocurarine and about five times as potent. It causes hypertension and tachycardia.

Gallamine triethiodide has a slightly shorter duration of action than tubocurarine, but it does not cause hypotension or bronchospasm. Gallamine triethiodide affects the vagus nerve and can produce tachycardia and hypertension.

Atracurium and vercuronium have no significant cardiovascular effects. Atracurium results in a slight release of histamine, whereas vercuronium has no influence on histamine production.

Rocuronium is highly selective for the neuromuscular junction. It produces no blockade of autonomic ganglia and has a low potential for histamine release, thus contributing to cardiovascular stability. Its duration of action is intermediate; the onset of action is more rapid in pediatric patients and slower in geriatric patients. The drug is eliminated by the hepatobiliary route and the action is prolonged in patients with hepatic dysfunction. The anesthesiologist maintains an awareness of the amount of paralysis by applying a nerve stimulator to the ulnar nerve at the elbow or the wrist and by observing the absence of contractions or the diminished strength of the hand muscles.

Balanced Anesthesia

Balanced anesthesia is a term applied to anesthesia produced by the combination of two or more drugs (e.g., a barbiturate administered intravenously for induction, nitrous oxide and morphine for analgesia, and a muscle relaxant to provide additional relaxation of the muscles).

Malignant Hyperthermia

Malignant hyperthermia is a complication of general anesthesia that occurs in 1 out of 15,000 children and in 1 out of 100,000 adults.[8] It is characterized by a rapid elevation of temperature as high as 42.8°C to 44°C (109°F to 111°F). The complication occurs when anesthetic agents such as halothane, methoxyflurane (Penthrane), cyclopropane, or succinylcholine are administered to a susceptible patient. The patient has a genetic skeletal muscle defect that allows the anesthetic to trigger a sudden increase in the intracellular calcium ion concentration. The increased calcium sets off a series of biochemical reactions that increase the patient's metabolic rate, eventually liberating heat. Muscle contractures also increase, liberating more heat.

The most consistent, early symptom is tachycardia. Other symptoms include increased skin temperature; mottling of the skin with or without cyanosis; dark blood in the operative field; hypotension; diaphoresis; and excessive heat in the chemical (CO_2) absorber and in the reservoir bag on the anesthesia machine. Muscle rigidity and cardiac arrhythmias usually follow. There are elevated levels of creatine phosphokinase, serum potassium, and myoglobin. If malignant hyperthermia is not treated immediately and correctly, the hypermetabolic state progresses causing irreversible organ damage or death.

Early diagnosis is essential. Treatment involves terminating the surgical procedure, discontinuing the anesthetic agent, hyperventilating the patient with 100% oxygen, and administering dantrolene sodium (Dantrium) 2.5 mg/kg either by direct IV injection or continuous rapid infusion. Dantrium interferes with the release of calcium ions within muscle fibers and, therefore, interrupts the cycle. Additional treatment may include surface cooling with bags of ice or a cooling mattress, irrigating the wound with cold saline solution, administering iced intravenous solutions and sodium bicarbonate, inserting a Foley catheter to monitor urinary output, inserting a CVP and a arterial line or Swan-Ganz catheter. Additional drugs to have available include procainamide, 50% glucose, insulin, and sodium bicarbonate.

After the patient is out of danger, he or she is transferred to the PACU or ICU for observation. Monitoring continues because symptoms of malignant hyperthermia may recur as late as 72 hours after the patient has an initial positive response to treatment.

Genetically, malignant hyperthermia is an autosomal dominant gene affecting 50% of the offspring. It is more common among males and frequently occurs in individuals with subclinical or clinical myopathy, numerous drug allergies, or a family history of unexplained surgical deaths.

Hypothermia and Anesthesia

Hypothermia is an imbalance between heat generation and loss within the body; it is defined as a core body temperature of less than 30°C. The tympanic membrane is an accurate indicator of core temperature. Maintenance of temperature depends on the balance between heat production and heat loss. Because anesthetics and sedative-hypnotic drugs, especially barbiturates, impair the ability of the hypothalamus to respond to demands for adjustment, patients assume the temperature of the environment. The elderly, infants, and cachexic, bleeding, burned, and paraplegic patients lose heat quickly and rewarm slowly. Surgical procedures or conditions that place a patient at high risk to develop significant hypothermia are major vascular, trauma, and transurethral resections.

Return to normothermia is 50% slower following regional anesthetic techniques than after general techniques. Because heat loss continues until the anesthesia block recedes, monitoring of temperature continues in the PACU until movement returns.

Hypothermia has physiologic consequences. Vasoconstriction, the body's adaptive response to cold, shunts circulating blood centrally to protect essential organs. Some anesthetic drugs block vasoconstrictive reflexes and allow further heat loss. Muscle relaxants inhibit shivering and prevent the body's attempt to rewarm itself. As the patient rewarms, vasodilation may be accompanied by profound hypotension, hemodynamic instability, and cardiac arrhythmias. Significant hypothermia can delay awakening and clearance of narcotics, barbiturates, benzodiazipines, and muscle relaxants administered during the anesthetic period. Aminoglycocide antibiotics potentiate the effect of nondepolarizing agents; administration should be deferred until the patient is warm.

Postanesthetic shivering (PAS), another adaptive body reflex, increases muscle activity to generate energy and heat, causing pain hypoxia and acidosis. Oxygen consumption can increase 400% to 500% during postanesthetic shivering.

Monitoring a patient's temperature provides information regarding the actual value as well as trends in the temperature. Rectal, oral, or axillary temperatures are useful; however, the most meaningful values are obtained from an esophageal or tympanic membrane probe.

Providing warm blankets, thermal mattresses, forced air warming systems, and warmed, humidified oxygen are intraoperative nursing measures to increase a patient's core temperature.

■ CLEANING AND PROCESSING ANESTHESIA EQUIPMENT

Anesthesia equipment that comes in contact with mucous membranes, blood, or body fluids is terminally cleaned, disinfected, or sterilized before it is used for another patient. Disposable, single-use equipment is difficult to reprocess safely and should be discarded appropriately. These items are designed and manufactured for a single use and represent a potential hazard to the patient if they are reprocessed due to residual toxicity and potential malfunction of the item. Manufacturers' written instructions for reuse must be followed.

All personnel handling anesthesia equipment must observe universal precautions at all times (see Chapter 7).

Preparation and Care of Reusable Supplies

The anesthesia hoses, mask, and breathing bag must be terminally cleaned and thoroughly dried before high-level disinfection or sterilization. The cleaning and packaging of anesthesia equipment should be consistent with the discussion in Chapter 7. Currently, most of the material used in the manufacture of these items will withstand steam sterilization. If sterilization is not possible, these items should receive a minimum of high-level disinfection.

Microbial growth contaminates the inspiratory and expiratory valves on anesthesia machines. Because soda lime is not effective as a filter or a bactericidal agent, each time it is changed the absorbers and valves must be cleaned according to the manufacturers' instruction. Most absorbers are heavy, difficult to remove, and made of material that excludes heat sterilization; therefore, a sterile, single-use absorber and valve system is recommended.

The anesthesia ventilators are disassembled and all parts that have been exposed to the patient are steam sterilized. Ancillary equipment, such as endotracheal tubes, stylets, laryngoscope, and airways, becomes grossly contaminated and immediately after use is placed in a receptacle designated for contaminated items. These items are not placed on top of the anesthesia machine.

The top of the anesthesia machine is cleaned with a detergent germicide after each patient use. All other exterior surfaces and the drawers are cleaned once every 24 hours.

Blood pressure cuffs and tubing are cleaned and decontaminated with a disinfectant solution, when contaminated or at the end of the day.

As discussed in Chapter 6, handwashing is one of the most important controls in reducing cross-infection. Members of the anesthesia team should wash their hands before and after each case. If handwashing facilities are not readily available or handwashing is not feasible, OSHA guidelines on blood-borne pathogens indicate that it is necessary to provide antiseptic hand cleaners, which include alcohol-based rinses, foams, and impregnated paper wipes. Following the uses of these products, washing with soap and water is done as soon as feasible.[9]

▌ REGIONAL ANESTHESIA

Regional anesthesia temporarily interrupts the transmission of nerve impulses to and from a specific area or region by blocking the passage of sodium across the nerve membrane. Fast sodium channels are enzymes that normally facilitate the rapid passage of sodium across nerve membranes; local anesthetics act by binding to these enzymes and consequently blocking sodium passage. Motor function may or may not be involved, but the patient does not lose consciousness. The extent of the anesthetized field depends on the site of application, the total volume administered, and the drug's concentration and penetrating ability.

Regional anesthetics may be used for patients when a general anesthetic is contraindicated or less desirable. The advantages of regional anesthetics are:

- The technique is simple and a minimal amount of equipment is required.
- The drugs are nonflammable.
- Less nausea and vomiting occur postoperatively.
- Less bleeding occurs when a vasoconstrictor is used.
- Bodily function is less disturbed; thus, the regional anesthetics are excellent for surgical procedures performed for outpatients.
- They can be used when general anesthetics are contraindicated (recent ingestion of food or cardiac or pulmonary dysfunction).
- They can be used for procedures in which it is desirable to have the patient awake and cooperative.
- They are less expensive than general anesthesia.
- They can be used when an anesthesiologist is not available.
- They do not pollute the environment.

The disadvantages of regional anesthetics are:

- Many procedures are too complex for regional anesthetics.
- They are difficult to administer to the very young patient and to patients who are emotionally unstable.
- They cannot be used if skin infection or sepsis is near the site of injection.
- Patients are awake and may become apprehensive due to the sights and sounds of the operating room.
- The drug cannot be controlled once it is injected.
- Local and general complications may occur.

If complications occur, they are usually due to overdosage, accidental intravascular injection, or the administration of a normal dose to a sensitive patient. The normal dose is determined by the area to be anesthetized, the vascularity of the tissues, the individual's tolerance, and the technique of anesthesia. The lowest dose that is necessary to provide effective anesthesia is administered. Table 10–3 outlines the general characteristics and recommended maximum doses of the commonly used solutions for infiltration and topical anesthesia.

The local complications of regional anesthetics include urticaria, edema, inflammation, abscess, necrosis, and gangrene. Inflammation and abscess usually result from a break in sterile technique at the time of local injection. Necrosis and gangrene may result from vasoconstriction in the area of the injection. Hypersensitivity reactions in some patients may be due to the preservatives used in many of the local anesthetics.

To constrict blood vessels and reduce bleeding, vasoconstrictive drugs may be added to local anesthetic agents. Vasoconstrictors also slow drug absorption, thereby minimizing toxic reactions but prolonging the operating time. The addition of a vasoconstrictor is contraindicated when it is injected in the fingers, toes, penis, or urethra. These drugs should be used cautiously in patients with a cardiac condition because the vasoconstrictor may be absorbed in sufficient quantity to increase heart rate or arrhythmias.

The signs and symptoms of a systemic toxic reaction due to the overdose of a regional anesthetic are manifested by central nervous system (CNS) stimulation, followed by CNS and cardiovascular depression. The first signs are restlessness, excitement, incoherent speech, headache, dizziness, blurred vision, metallic taste, nausea, vomiting, tremors, convulsions, and increased blood pressure and pulse with an increased respiratory rate. Treatment includes establishing an airway, administering oxygen, and sedating the patient with a fast-acting barbiturate. If the toxic reaction goes untreated, unconsciousness, hypotension, apnea, and cardiac arrest will result.

Sterile technique is used to administer a local anesthetic, and resuscitation equipment must be available. Resuscitation equipment includes a patient cart with the option of Trendelenburg's position, suction, oral airways, oxygen, bag and mask for ventilation, and drugs, such as vasoconstrictors and barbiturates.

Techniques of Administering Regional Anesthesia

The techniques used to apply drugs to the nerves include topical anesthesia, local infiltration, nerve blocks, and spinal anesthesia.

Topical Anesthesia. A local anesthetic agent is applied directly on the surface of the area to be anesthetized. The method is frequently used on the respiratory passages prior to intubation or for diagnostic procedures, such as laryngoscopy, bronchoscopy, or cystoscopy. The onset of action is 1 minute and duration is 20 to 30 minutes. Collapse of the cardiovascular system may occur following application of a topical anesthetic to the respiratory tract.

Local Infiltration. In local infiltration, the drug is injected into the subcutaneous tissue surrounding the incision, wound, lesion, or area to be manipulated. An advantage of this technique is that the drug may affect only the skin, or the local anesthetic may be adminis-

TABLE 10–3. DRUGS USED FOR LOCAL ANESTHETICS

	Cocaine	Novocaine (Procaine) (Hydrochloride)	Lidocaine (Xylocaine) (Hydrochloride)	Tetracaine (Pontocaine) (Hydrochloride)	Mepivacaine (Carbocaine) (Hydrochloride)	Bupivacaine (Marcaine) (Hydrochloride)	2-Chloroprocaine (Nesacaine) (Hydrochloride)
Topical concentration	Eye 1% Other 4%–10%	Ineffective	Eye 0.5% Other 4%	Eye 0.5% Other 1%–2%	Eye 0.5% Other 1%–2%	Not used	Not used
Onset (minutes)	Immediate	2–5	0.5–1.0	10–20	3–5	5	6–12
Duration (minutes)	30–60	15–30	120	120–240	30–120	120–180	15–30
Maximum dose	200 mg		200 mg	50 mg	500 mg		
Infiltration concentration	Not used	0.25%–1.0% 2.0, 10%	0.5%–2%	0.05%–0.1%	0.5%–2%	0.25%–0.75%	1%, 2%, 3%
Onset (minutes)		5–15	3–5	10–20	5–10	5–10	5–10
Duration of action (minutes), plain		45–60	30–60	90–120	150–240	90–120	30–60
Duration of action (minutes) with epinephrine 1:200,000		60–90	45–90	140–180	240–320	140–180	45–90
Maximum dose, plain		1000 mg or 15 mg/kg	300 mg or 6–8 mg/kg	50–100 mg or 3 mg/kg	500 mg or 6–8 mg/kg	175 mg or 4–6 mg/kg	1000 mg or 15 mg/kg

tered into deeper organs or structures. A disadvantage is that a large amount of drug must be administered to anesthetize small areas.

Intravenous Regional Anesthesia. Intravenous regional anesthesia may be used for surgery below the level of the elbow or knee. Before the local anesthetic is administered into a vein in the limb, the surgeon exsanguinates the limb using an elastic bandage or pneumatic tourniquet. Venous circulation in the limb must be completely blocked to prevent the local anesthetic from causing systemic toxicity. Tourniquet pressure is released slowly so that only 15% to 30% of the drug is released into the systemic circulation. If the pressure is released abruptly, peak levels occur in about 30 seconds. Serum levels of local anesthetic using this technique usually are less than the levels obtained when a block of the brachial plexus or a lumbar epidural block is used. For intravenous regional anesthesia, the volume as well as the concentration of the local anesthetic is important in determining the level of anesthesia.[10]

Nerve Blocks. A nerve block is achieved by injecting the local anesthetic agent into or around the individual nerves or nerve bundles that supply a specific area. Nerve blocks are used to prevent pain or relieve chronic pain, to identify the cause of pain, and to increase circulation in some vascular diseases.

The nerve blocks most frequently used in operative procedures involve the brachial plexus; cervical plexus; intercostal nerves; and radial, ulnar, and digital nerves.

Field Block. Regional anesthesia produced by a series of subcutaneous injections over a nerve is called a field block. This type of anesthesia is useful in surgery involving the fore-arm, scalp, or anterior abdominal wall.

Caudal and Epidural Blocks. When a local anesthetic solution is injected into the epidural space through the sacral hiatus and caudal canal, the technique is termed *caudal block*. Injection of an anesthetic solution into the epidural space through the interspaces of the lumbar, thoracic, or cervical spine is termed an *epidural block*. Epidural anesthesia differs from spinal anesthesia in that it requires a larger dose, which may result in high blood levels of local anesthetic. Local anesthetic is removed from the epidural space rapidly because of blood flow in the area; a continuous infusion is sometimes necessary to maintain adequate anesthesia.

After confirming proper placement of the catheter, the anesthetist secures it and administers a regional anesthetic. The choice of drug is based on the expected length of the operation and the degree of muscle relaxation required. The catheter may be left in place postoperatively, and additional injections administered for vasodilation or analgesia.

A local anesthetic, narcotic, or steroid may be administered by continuous infusion, or the anesthetist may administer intermittent bolus doses. The patient's blood pressure and respiratory status must be closely monitored; an apnea monitor may be ordered for the first 12 to 24 hours after surgery.

Pregnant patients require significantly smaller doses of local anesthetics, due to vascular changes related to pressure on the vena cava.

Spinal Anesthesia

Spinal anesthesia is achieved by injecting an anesthetic agent into the cerebrospinal fluid. The agent is then absorbed by the sensory, motor, and autonomic nerve fibers, and nerve transmissions are blocked. Injection is through one of the spaces between lumbar 2 (L2) and the sacrum (S1), most frequently between L3 and L4. Because the spinal cord usually ends at L1 or L2, puncturing at that level or above may cause damage to the spinal cord.

The level of anesthesia depends on the following factors:

- drug dose and concentration
- volume injected
- site and rate of the injection
- specific gravity of the solution (may be increased by adding 10% glucose)
- cerebrospinal fluid pressure
- length of the vertebral column
- position of patient during the injection and immediately after

For the injection, the patient may sit on the edge of the operating table with arms resting on the thighs, feet on a stool, and chin resting on the chest. Or the patient may be in the flexed lateral (fetal) position. Both positions straighten the natural curvature of the spine and widen the intervertebral spaces to facilitate insertion of the spinal needle.

The spread of the anesthetic agent is influenced by the specific gravity of the solution and the patient's position immediately after the injection. The level of analgesia is usually fixed within 15 to 20 minutes and no longer influenced by position changes.

Spinal anesthesia is low-spinal, midspinal, and high-spinal anesthesia. The low spinal (saddle block) involves the sacral nerves (S1-5) and provides adequate anesthesia for diagnostic and surgical interventions in the perineal and anal regions. The midspinal is used for surgical procedures below the level of the umbilicus (T-10), such as appendectomies and herniorrhaphies.

The high spinal reaches the nipple line (T-4). Immediately following injection of the drug, the patient's head is lowered until the desired height of anesthesia is reached. The anesthesiologist must watch the level of anesthesia very carefully, as intercostal paralysis and respiratory insufficiency may occur. The high spinal may be used for surgical procedures that involve the stomach and biliary tract. Hiccups and nausea frequently occur in the high spinal, especially following vagus stimulation and manipulation of the viscera during the surgical procedure.

Although spinal anesthesia produces excellent analgesia and relaxation for abdominal and pelvic procedures, its most important side effect is hypotension. Hypotension is caused by a preganglionic block of the sympathetic fibers, resulting in vasodilatation and reduction in venous return to the heart. The treatment usually consists of administering oxygen and intravenously administering vasopressors.

A spinal headache may occur 24 to 48 hours postoperatively if the dura mater does not seal following extraction of the needle and cerebrospinal fluid leaks into the epidural space. With the leakage, cerebrospinal pressure is decreased and stress is put on nerves between the cranium and brain. Treatment for a spinal headache is bed rest, hydration, and sedation, and in severe cases, a blood patch graft. A blood patch graft consists of an epidural injection of 10 ml of the patient's blood, which plugs the leak.

Nursing Concerns for Patients Receiving a Regional Anesthetic

The perioperative nurse assists the anesthesiologist to assemble and set up the equipment necessary for regional anesthesia. During the procedure, the nurse observes the anesthesiologist for breaks in technique. Physical and emotional support is given to the patient by staying close by, providing words of encouragement, and assisting with the position required for the regional nerve block (Fig. 10–3). Touch is especially important to a patient having a local anesthetic. It reassures the patient that the nurse is present and concerned about the patient's comfort and safety (Table 10–4).

In the absence of an anesthesiologist, for example, when local infiltration is done, the circulating nurse is responsible for monitoring and documenting the patient's vital signs every 15 minutes and before administration of a local anesthetic agent or analgesic. Intraoperative care also includes initiating oxygen therapy and administering intravenous fluids when clinical findings warrant action. All changes in the patient's condition are reported to the surgeon. Documentation includes vital signs and a list of IV fluids and medications administered.

At the beginning of these surgical procedures, two nurses must be assigned to circulate, one to monitor the patient and the other to assist sterile members of the team. After the incision is made and the procedure is proceeding, only one circulator may be required.

The scrub assistant for a local infiltration procedure should label all drugs on the sterile field and maintain an accurate record of the amount of each drug injected during the course of the procedure. Departmental policies and procedures should define what drugs

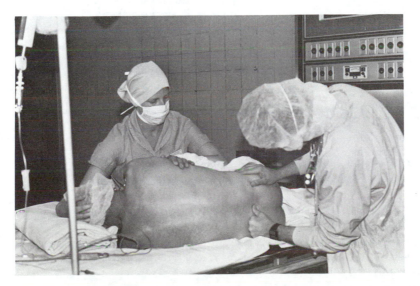

Figure 10–3. The perioperative nurse provides physical and emotional support to patients having regional anesthetics.

TABLE 10–4. PATIENT CARE PLAN FOR REGIONAL ANESTHESIA/CONSCIOUS SEDATION EVALUATION

Nursing Diagnosis	Patient Outcome	Nursing Actions	Schedule for Evaluation
1. Risk for anxiety related to unfamiliar environment and/or impending surgery	1. Ability to cope with anxiety	1a. Explain preoperative and intraoperative activities b. Encourage patient to verbalize questions and concerns c. Stay with patient and provide support d. Provide nonverbal support by touching patient	Preoperatively Intraoperatively 12–24 hours postoperatively
2. Risk for fear of pain	2. Pain controlled	2a. Encourage patient to verbalize discomfort b. Discuss with patient availability of pain medication	Intraoperatively
3. Risk for altered sensory perceptions related to preoperative medication	3. Able to respond appropriately and to follow directions	3a. Maintain quiet atmosphere b. Post sign on door "Patient Awake" c. Turn off auditory intercom	Intraoperatively 12–24 hours postoperatively
4. Risk for loss of dignity related to excessive exposure and lack of personal care	4. Dignity maintained	4a. Limit exposure of patient only to area required for surgical procedure b. Call patient by name c. Only pertinent team members permitted in room	Intraoperatively 12–24 hours postoperatively
5. Possible discomfort related to position	5. Comfortable position	5a. Position patient anatomically b. Flex table slightly at knees to reduce strain on back muscles c. Place pillow under knees d. Pad all boney prominences e. Pad wrists with webril prior to restraints being applied f. Ask patient about position	Intraoperatively 12–24 hours postoperatively
6. Risk for contamination of wound related to patient inadvertently touching wound	6. No wound contamination	6. Apply padded clover leaf hitch arm restraints	Intraoperatively
7. Risk for alteration in body temperature related to temperature of operating room	7. Body temperature maintained within normal limits	7a. Apply warm blankets b. Use warm solutions c. Limit skin exposure to area required for surgical procedure d. Ask patient about body temperature	Intraoperatively
8. Possible adverse reaction to local anesthetic agent related to sensitivity to agent or overdose	8. Avoid or minimize cardiovascular and respiratory compromise	8a. Two nurses assigned to circulate b. Check chart for allergies c. Obtain baseline vital signs before surgery	Intraoperatively

(continued)

TABLE 10–4. *(Continued)*

Nursing Diagnosis	Patient Outcome	Nursing Actions	Schedule for Evaluation
		d. Monitor amount of local anesthestic administered	
		e. Use electrocardiograph to monitor patient for cardiac arrhythmias	
		f. Monitor and record vital signs as indicated or at least every 15 minutes and before and after medication	
		g. Communicate changes to surgeon	
9. Risk for lack in continuity of care related to patient returning to primary care nurse/inpatient unit	9. Continuity of care	9a. Inform primary care nurse what procedure was performed	Immediate postoperative
		b. Vital signs	
		c. All medications administered	
		d. Amount of IV fluids infused	
		e. Estimated blood loss	
		f. Location of any drains or packs	
		g. Type of dressing	
		h. How the patient tolerated the procedure	
Ambulatory Patients			
10. Risk for latent adverse reaction or side effects to local anesthesia or surgical procedure	10. Adverse reaction and side effects treated appropriately	10a. Observe patient for minimum of 30 minutes postoperatively prior to discharge	Immediate postoperative
		b. Alert patient and significant others to signs and symptoms of adverse reaction and how to respond appropriately	
		c. Validate postoperative instructions by requesting verbal feedback	
		d. Provide dietailed written instructions to reinforce verbal instructions	
		e. Give patient and significant others telephone number of operating room surgeon and emergency room; instruct patient to call regarding any questions or concerns	
		f. Obtain telephone number where patient can be reached for postoperative phone call in 24 hours	24 hours postoperatively

(continued)

TABLE 10–4. *(Continued)*

Nursing Diagnosis	Patient Outcome	Nursing Actions	Schedule for Evaluation
11. Risk for ineffective breathing pattern related to altered levels of consciousness	11. Maintain effective breathing pattern with respiratory rate, patterns, and quality within normal range	11a. Assess patient's reaction to conscious sedation agent b. Monitor respiratory rate, pattern, quality and O_2 saturation c. If signs of dyspnea occur, open airway d. Administer O_2 per face mask at 8–10 L/min as ordered e. Suction as needed f. Elevate head of bed as procedure permits	Intraoperatively
12. Risk for lack of knowledge related to poor recall	12. Patient/family/significant other able to explain and discuss specific postoperative instructions	12a. Complete patient teaching prior to the administration of amnesic medications b. Provide detailed written instructions that reinforce verbal instructions and serve as a reference to the patient or caregiver at home c. Include family/significant other in patient teaching	Preoperatively PACU 12–24 hours postoperatively
13. Risk for altered cardiac output related to drug effect on myocardium	13a. No signs or symptoms related to shock b. No reports of chest pain	13a. Monitor cardiac rate and rhythm b. Monitor vital signs c. Report changes to physician d. Administer all conscious sedation medication with caution e. Observe for changes in tissue perfusion: cyanosis, low oxygen saturation, mottled skin, clamminess	Intraoperatively

may be administered by the perioperative nurse and the level of monitoring skills that are required.

■ MANAGEMENT OF PATIENTS RECEIVING IV CONSCIOUS SEDATION

Intravenous conscious sedation is produced by administering pharmacologic agents. A patient under conscious sedation has a depressed level of consciousness, but retains the ability to independently and continuously maintain a patent airway and respond appropriately to physical stimulation and verbal commands. It is within a registered nurse's scope of practice to manage the care of patients receiving conscious sedation if the nurse is familiar with basic life support and airway management, including bag and mask ventilation.[11]

One health care provider (RN, LVN, or physician) should have the primary responsibility of monitoring the patient's vital signs and level of consciousness during the entire procedure. That individual should not have other responsibilities that would leave the patient unattended or compromise continuous monitoring. A qualified anesthesia provider or physician will select and order the medication to achieve IV conscious sedation.

Before the drug is administered, a baseline patient assessment is completed. Vital signs, oxygen saturation, and responsiveness to verbal and physical stimuli are assessed. The availability of appropriate transportation to be used following the procedure is verified during the preprocedure assessment, and the patient is given written discharge instructions, including the names and telephone numbers of persons to contact in an emergency.

When IV conscious sedation is used, the following equipment and medications must be immediately available:

Blood pressure monitor
Cardiac rhythm monitor
Crash cart
Electrical outlets
    Connection to emergency power system
Masks
Medications
    Mazicon (flumazenil)
    Narcan (naloxone)
Nasal cannula
Oxygen source
    Oxygen administration equipment
Pulse oximeter
Rescuscitation bag, self-inflating
Suction source
    Catheters
    Suction tubing

Monitoring and Documentation during the Procedure

The objective of monitoring a patient during the procedure, as well as during the recovery phase, is to ensure the adequacy of ventilation, oxygenation, and circulatory function. The physiologic measurements include, but are not limited to, respiratory rate, oxygen saturation, blood pressure, cardiac rate and rhythm, and level of consciousness. Responsiveness to verbal and physical stimuli should be assessed 5 minutes after a drug is administered and at least every 15 minutes thereafter.

Documentation includes recording vital signs and responsiveness to verbal and physical stimuli; time and dose of medications administered; abnormal ECG rhythms; blood pressure 20% below or above baseline; oxygen saturation less than 95%; respiratory rate less than ten breaths per minute; and any other complication.

When the procedure is completed, the patient must be monitored and vital signs assessed as during the procedure. Patients may be returned to their preprocedure level of care and monitoring. Before discharge outpatients must ambulate with minimal assistance, tolerate fluids by mouth, be awake and alert to surroundings, and be accompanied home by a responsible adult.

Because drugs that are used for conscious sedation produce memory lapses, postoperative instructions are reviewed prior to the procedure with the family and/or significant others. Instructions should include what to observe if benzodiazepine resedation occurs (e.g., slurred speech, unarousable sleep, difficulty with respiration). The patient should be told that medications may impair memory and judgment for a period of time. The nurse should also tell the patient that for 24 hours after the procedure the following activities should be avoided: consuming alcoholic beverages or nonprescription drugs, operating machinery, making crucial decisions, or doing anything that requires being alert.

The policies and procedures of each department should include adverse events that are reported as an "unusual occurrence." These incidents may include:

- administration of a reversal agent
- assisted ventilation
- oxygen saturation dropping below 80% for any period or to less than 90% for 2 minutes
- vital signs deviating more than 20% from baseline

■ REFERENCES

1. Zimmerman L. *Great Ideas in the History.* New York: Dover; 1967:103.
2. Cartwright F. *The Development of Modern Surgery.* New York: Thomas Crowell; 1968:48, 226.
3. Soule B, ed. *The APIC Curriculum for Infection Control Practice,* Volume II. Dubuque, IA: Kendall Hunt Publications; 1988:665.
4. Pearlman R, Schneider P. Intraoperative neural monitoring. *AORN J.* 1994; 59(4):841–849.
5. Glass P et al. Intravenous anesthetic delivery. In: Miller R, ed. *Anesthesia.* New York: Churchill Livingstone; 1990:367–388.
6. Watson D. Safe administration of midazolam. *AORN J.* 1991; 53(1):163.
7. Barnhart E, ed. *The Physicians's Desk Reference,* 49th ed. Oradell, NJ: Medical Economics Co.; 1995:2066–2069.
8. Beck C. Malignant hyperthermia. *AORN J.* 1994; 59(2):367–390.
9. Occupational exposure to bloodborne pathogens. Final rule. *Fed Reg.* December 6, 1991; 56:64117.
10. Benz, J. Injectable local anesthetics. *AORN J.* 1992; 55(1):280.
11. Position statement on the role of the RN in the management of patients receiving IV conscious sedation for short-term therapeutic, diagnostic or surgical procedures. *AORN J.* 1992; 55(1): 207–208.

Positioning and Draping

■ POSITIONING

The circulating nurse is responsible for coordinating the efforts of the team members in positioning the surgical patient. Due to preoperative medication and anesthetic drugs, the patient's normal defense mechanisms cannot guard against joint damage and/or muscle stretch and strain. Knowledge of anatomical structures and physiological functioning are imperative so that the circulating nurse can ensure patient safety and comfort.

The proper patient position must provide for:

1. Optimum exposure of the operative site
2. Access for the anesthesiologist to maintain the patient's circulatory and respiratory functions
3. Access for the administration of IV solutions
4. Protection of neuromuscular and skeletal structures
5. Minimal interference with circulation
6. Physiological alignment
7. Comfort and safety for the patient
8. Preservation of the patient's dignity

The desired patient outcomes related to positioning are:

1. Skin integrity is maintained
2. No injury related to positioning

Nursing Considerations

During preoperative assessment, the perioperative nurse will evaluate the patient's size, nutritional status, and skin condition and identify any existing respiratory, skeletal, or neuromuscular limitations such as rheumatoid arthritis, joint replacements, or emphysema. The nurse should use a systematic skin evaluation tool (e.g., Braden, Norton scales) to assess and document the skin status on all patients who are at risk for pressure ulcer development.[1] Following the preoperative assessment, an individual patient care plan is developed for the specific procedure. The plan may include nursing orders regarding the number of personnel required for transportation (Fig. 11–1), the appropriate mode of transportation, and the appropriate patient position during transportation.

The surgeon's preference card will determine the appropriate position for the proce-

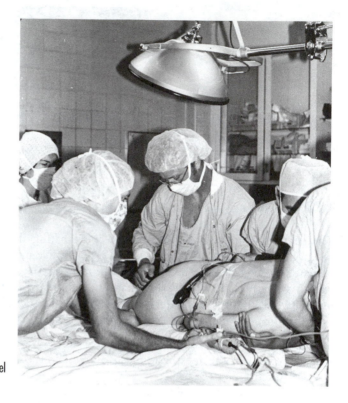

Figure 11–1. Sufficient numbers of personnel are required to safely position a patient.

dure. This card can be used as a guide in selecting the necessary equipment and the positioning aids and in determining the number of personnel required to achieve the position. All the equipment used to position patients should be checked for proper functioning and completeness prior to the patient's arrival in the operating room. Communication and collaboration between all team members is essential to ensure positive patient outcomes during this period.

Factors that influence the actual time at which the patient is positioned are the site of the operation, the age and size of the patient, the anesthetic technique, and if the patient experiences pain on moving. If the patient is going to be placed in the prone position, the anesthesiologist may want to anesthetize the patient on the transportation vehicle and then move the patient to the operating room table while turning the patient to the prone position. Frequently, the anesthesiologist or the circulating nurse will hold a child during the induction phase and then place the child on the operating room table. If the patient experiences pain on moving (as in the case of accident or trauma victims), the anesthesiologist may elect to anesthetize the patient on the transportation vehicle to prevent additional pain.

When transferring the patient to the operating table, it is important for the patient's safety that the transportation vehicle and the operating room table be the same height and both be locked. Two people must be in attendance when transferring the patient to the operating room table. The transportation vehicle is placed next to the operating room table with one person on each side to assist the patient in the move. The patient should be told that the table is narrow and that a safety strap is being placed across his or her legs as a reminder of this fact. The safety strap should be placed 2 inches above the knee immediately after the transfer. The strap should be applied snugly but must not restrict venous circulation or exert pressure on the nerves. The patient must never be left unattended; at least one member of the nursing staff must be present in the operating room at all times.

One of the most frequent comments from patients in regard to the operating room concerns the temperature. Every effort should be made by the perioperative nurses to provide a warm, comfortable environment. In readiness for the patient's arrival into the operating room, the operating room table may be covered with a blanket from the solution warmer; the blanket is then removed just prior to the patient being transferred to the operating room table. Additional blankets may then be placed over the patient, and a pillow offered for additional comfort.

Risk for Injury Related to Perioperative Positioning

During surgery, patients are immobile and, if anesthetized, are unable to perceive the discomfort of prolonged pressure. They are not able to reposition themselves to relieve pressure areas. The period of immobility extends throughout the entire perioperative period, and therefore a patient who is most normally at high risk for pressure ulcer development is placed at high risk.[2] When the patient has other risk factors, such as those identified in Table 11–1, the probability of skin breakdown is exacerbated during surgery.

Patients with urinary incontinence should be assessed and a plan implemented to ensure that the patient is kept dry during the operative or invasive procedure. If the procedure is expected to last more than 2 hours, consideration should be given to inserting a Foley catheter. If the procedure is less than 2 hours, urinary absorption pads may be adequate to keep the patient dry.

A pressure ulcer is defined as any lesion caused by unrelieved pressure, which results in damage of underlying tissue.[3] Pressure ulcers usually appear over bony prominences and are graded or staged according to the degree of tissue damage observed. There are four

TABLE 11–1. FACTORS PREDISPOSING PATIENTS TO DISRUPTION IN SKIN INTEGRITY

1. Age extremes	12. Liver failure
2. Obesity	13. Incontinence
3. Anemia	14. Hypovolemia
4. Diabetes mellitus	15. Immobility
5. Infections	16. Vascular insufficiency
6. Fever	17. Low serum albumin
7. Cardiopulmonary disorders	18. Poor oxygenation
8. Emaciation	19. Steroid therapy
9. Poor tissue perfusion	20. Immunosuppressive drugs
10. Moisture from draining wound or diaphoresis	21. Radiation therapy
11. Dependent edema	22. Chemotherapy

stages of pressure ulcers; each one represents increased tissue damage. Nursing intervention during the perioperative period is directed toward prevention of a Stage I ulcer unless the patient presents with a Stage II, III, or IV ulcer already present. In these three stages the ulcer is treated as an open wound during surgical intervention.

> Stage I: This stage is characterized by non-blanching erythema of intact skin. Reactive erythema should not be confused with Stage I pressure ulcers. Reactive erythema normally can be expected to last for one-half to three-quarters as long as the duration of the pressure that occluded blood flow to the area; after this time, reactive erythema disappears.[3]

If repositioning the patient is necessary after the induction of anesthesia, it is performed with care and the patient is lifted into position rather than rolled or pulled to avoid shearing forces and friction. Shearing occurs when the skin remains stationary and the underlying tissue shifts, causing subcutaneous blood vessels to become kinked or stretched. This obstructs blood flow to and from the areas supplied by those vessels and contributes to the development of pressure sores. When the position of the operating table is changed, the weight of the patient's torso tends to move the tissues attached to the bony structures with the patient; however, due to friction between the linen and the skin, the dermal layers tend to stay in a fixed position and the patient's skin is susceptible to injury.

In the supine position, skin destruction is likely to occur in the sacral area, where the blood supply to the posterior tissue exits the well-anchored deep fascia into the looser subcutaneous fascia. Angulation occurs, and thrombosis of the vessels with ischemic ulceration may result. Friction occurs when a patient is pulled or pushed across a coarse surface such as linen. This results in epidermal damage that significantly lowers the perpendicular pressures necessary to produce breaks in skin integrity.

Many intrinsic and extrinsic variables are associated with pressure ulcer development; however, the intensity and duration of pressure are the critical components in the etiology of pressure ulcers.[4] Tissue insults precipitated by pressure may occur during surgery. Perpendicular pressure (tissue compression) is an unavoidable consequence of gravity that occurs during positioning and affects capillary pressure.

Alopecia caused by prolonged immobilization of and pressure on the head has occurred following surgical intervention. It occurs early in the postoperative period as edema and a very painful seroma of the occipital scalp, followed by ulceration and transient or permanent localized hair loss. The position of the patient's head should be rotated a few degrees to the left or right by the anesthesiologist every 30 minutes to avoid alopecia.[5]

Pressure may occur when a member of the surgical team inadvertently leans or rests on the patient. This additional pressure added to the patient's own weight may result in the development of pressure ulcers. The scrub person and the circulating nurses must monitor the position of all team members during surgery and remind them not to lean on the patient. Another factor believed to contribute to the development of the sacral pressure ulcer is deeply planted retractors that exert pressure inside to outside.[6]

Normal capillary pressure ranges between 23 to 30 mm Hg. When there is more pressure on the capillaries than in them, capillary circulation slows and blood flow in the microvasculature is obstructed. Unless the external pressure is relieved, hypoxic tissue damage will result.

The tissue of any patient, whether supine, prone, or lateral, is under sufficient pressure to develop pressure injuries. A relationship exists between pressure, surface area, and time. Pressure and surface area are inversely proportional; the greater the surface area, the lower is the pressure. If pressure is dissipated over a broad surface it is less likely that skin breakdown will occur. An inverse relationship also exists between time and pressure: the longer the time that pressure is exerted on tissue, the less pressure it will take to cause ischemic changes.

The following pressures are sufficient to cause tissue ischemia in a supine patient[5]:

- 20–40 mm Hg—at the occiput
- 30 mm Hg—at the spine
- 40–60 mm Hg—at the sacral area
- 30–45 mm Hg—at the heels
- 30–40 mm Hg—at the costal margins and knees (prone)

Pressure injuries can occur anywhere. The ischium, sacrum, and trochanter account for 60% of all skin ulcers. The lower leg, pretibial, malleolus, and heel comprise an additional 17%. The remainder of ulcers involve all other body surfaces (e.g., chin, occiput, shoulder, scapula, wrist).[7] Two hours is the longest period of time that pressure should go unrelieved, particularly during vascular procedures.[3] Without disrupting the surgery, nursing care provided by the circulator should include shifting or moving the extremities to relieve pressure and allow the cells to receive oxygen. Massaging bony prominences to stimulate blood and lymph flow and to avert pressure ulcer formation is not well established; there is evidence suggesting that it may lead to deep tissue trauma.[3]

The relation between sustained pressure during a surgical procedure and the development of a pressure ulcer is not always evident. The pressure exerted deep in the tissue is greater than the pressure at the skin surface so the tissue damage is not always visible until after the pressure is relieved.

Additional Risks for Injury

Pressure areas are attributable to known physiological responses unique to the surgical environment; however, they are frequently erroneously described as "burns." Several factors in the OR can cause an injury, and until the cause is determined the injury should be referred to as a lesion. The following can be the source of lesions in the surgical patient: electosurgical unit, hypothermia unit, cryosurgical unit, lasers, pooling of prep solutions, residual ethylene oxide, and alcohol. Electrical currents may produce a burn alone or in combination with chemicals if the liquid undergoes electrolysis.

Disruption to the skin integrity may appear up to 1 to 3 days postoperatively and can be identified by these characteristics:

1. The skin appears as a reddened area resembling a burn.
2. The area progresses to an ecchymotic area that resembles a bruise.
3. The skin blisters or peels, exposing the partial thickness skin layers.
4. Necrosis develops with full thickness loss of skin, and invasion of deeper tissues that may involve the fascia, muscle, and bone.

Operating Room Tables

As discussed in Chapter 2, a variety of operating room tables with accessory equipment designed to stabilize or brace the patient in a specific position are available. The perioperative nurse must be familiar with the mechanics of all the tables and the attachments available within the surgical suite. The most common table accessories are:

1. Anesthesia screen
2. Armboards—these can be positioned parallel to the table to provide extra width for obese patients
3. Headrests
4. Kidney braces
5. Lateral armboards
6. Shoulder braces
7. Stirrups
8. Table extension—this can be used as an extension of the table for tall patients or placed perpendicularly to the table and padded to support the feet

Additional items that will assist in effective positioning are:

1. Blankets
2. Davis roller
3. Draw sheet (lift sheet)—A double-thickness sheet is placed under the patient's trunk; the arms are placed between the flaps, and the top flap is brought down over the arm and tucked under the mattress. This positions the arm in the correct anatomical position and prevents the elbow and fingers from resting on the edge of the table.
4. Doughnut—A doughnut is used for surgical procedures on the head and face. It is made in the shape of a doughnut, using towels or foam, and then covered with webril. The head rests in the center portion, which prevents the head from rolling. If the head is turned to one side or the other, the doughnut protects the ear and the superficial nerves and blood vessels of the face.
5. Elbow pads or protections
6. Laminectomy rolls (body rolls/bolsters)—These rolls consist of a solid roll of cloth or foam rubber about 6 inches in diameter and 18 inches long.
7. Pillows
8. Protective padding (sheepskin, polyurethane foam, felt, gel floatation, alternating pressure mattresses). Egg crate mattresses are flammable and should not be used in the OR.
9. Sandbags
10. Surgical Positioning System (Vac-Pak) (Fig. 11–2)—This system consists of soft pads filled with tiny plastic beads; the patient is positioned on the pads, suction is attached to the pads, and as the air is evacuated the pads become firm, thus maintaining the patient's position. At the end of the procedure, the valve is released, air enters the pad, and it becomes soft.
11. Tape
12. Towels

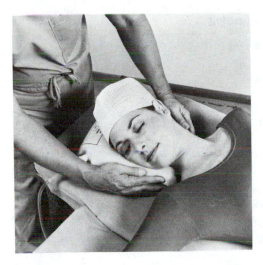

Figure 11–2. Surgical Positioning System. To maintain the patient's position, this system requires air to be evacuated. *(Courtesy Olympic Medical Corp., Seattle, WA.)*

Conventional operating table pads are not capable of adequately protecting against pressure sores. The use of a full-length silicone gel pad has proven effective in preventing serious pressure injuries in surgical procedures lasting longer than 2 hours. Their effectiveness past 10 hours has not been tested. The silicone pads do not offer complete protection but extend the time that pressure can be tolerated.

One disadvantage of the silicone gel pad is that warming or cooling the patient may prove difficult, since the hypothermia blanket must be placed under the gel pad. Prewarming or precooling the gel pad prior to placing the patient on it will help alleviate this problem preoperatively but does not solve the problem during the intraoperative phase when rapid warming or cooling is required.

There are a number of different positions used for surgical intervention. Each of these positions has specific criteria that must be met to protect the patient from any untoward effects as a result of improper positioning. Table 11–2 delineates guidelines for nursing actions in positioning all patients.

Common Surgical Positions and Nursing Considerations

Supine or Dorsal Recumbent. In the supine position, the patient lies flat on the back, head in line with the body, arms secured at the side or one arm extended on an armboard with palms down, and legs are straight with feet slightly separated and uncrossed (Fig. 11–3A). If the arm is positioned at the side and tucked under the draw sheet, fingers and elbows should be placed close to the body. This will ensure that they do not rest on the table edge or that a team member does not inadvertently lean on the patient's arm. Small pillows or towels may be placed under the head and the lumbar curvature to assist in maintaining anatomical alignment. Small pillows can also be placed under the patient's legs superior to the popliteal space. The pillow must not be placed directly behind the knees because it may cause pressure in the popliteal space and disrupt or interrupt the blood supply. Pressure in the popliteal space can also injure the common perineal nerve that runs through

TABLE 11-2. GUIDELINES FOR NURSING ACTIONS IN POSITIONING ALL PATIENTS

1. The anesthetized patient is never moved without checking with the anesthesiologist.
2. To prevent damage to the brachial plexus, arms are never abducted beyond 90°.
3. Legs must not be crossed as this creates pressure on blood vessels and nerves.
4. Body surfaces should not be in contact with one another.
5. Hands and feet should be protected and not allowed to hang off the table.
6. The patient should not be touching any metal part of the table. If the elbow rests on the table edge, ulnar nerve damage may result.
7. Patient exposure is limited to the area required for the surgical procedure.
8. If the patient is conscious, all activities as well as the rationale should be explained.
9. The instrument table, the mayo stand, or other equipment should not be in contact with the patient's toes or legs.
10. During the surgical procedure if the mayo stand, instrument table, or operating table is moved, the patient must be checked for pressure points.
11. Movement of the anesthetized patient is done gently and slowly. Turning the patient too quickly may cause circulatory depression.
12. To ensure the patient's safety, adequate numbers of personnel must always be present when positioning the patient. The patient is lifted into position, never pushed or pulled, to avoid stretching or shearing the skin.
13. When moving an anesthetized patient, the anesthesiologist guards the endotracheal tube and protects the patient's head and neck.
14. The position must not obstruct any catheters, tubes, or drains.
15. Team members should be reminded not to lean on the patient.
16. If the surgical procedure is unilateral, the consent form and the x-ray films should be checked and the proper side exposed.
17. If the surgical procedure is on an extremity, such as an amputation, both extremities should be exposed for comparison.
18. Check pulses in all extremities.
19. All equipment used in positioning patients is padded and terminally disinfected after use.
20. The patient's position is documented as part of the intraoperative nursing notes.

this area. The safety strap is placed 2 inches above the knees. The feet are supported by a padded foot extension to prevent foot drop and to protect the feet from the weight and the pressure of the drapes.

Vulnerable pressure points that may require additional padding include: occiput, scapula, olecranon, sacrum, ischial tuberosity, and calcaneus (Fig. 11-3B). When the head is turned to one side, a special headrest should be used to protect the ear and superficial nerves and blood vessels of the face. The eyes should be protected from corneal abrasions or irritation by applying an eye patch or eye shield.

Trendelenburg. The Trendelenburg position is used for operations on the lower abdomen where it is desirable to tilt the abdominal viscera away from the pelvic area for better exposure. It is also used in some surgery on the extremities to assist in hemostasis. To prevent pressure on the perineal nerves and phlebitis, the patient is positioned in the supine position with the knees over the lower break of the table. The operating room table is tilted downward so the patient's head is lower than the feet (Fig. 11-4). Well-padded shoulder braces assist in maintaining the patient's position. The shoulder braces are positioned away from the neck and against the acromion and the spinous process of the scapula, rather than the soft tissue, to avoid injury to the brachial plexus. The upward displacement of the ab-

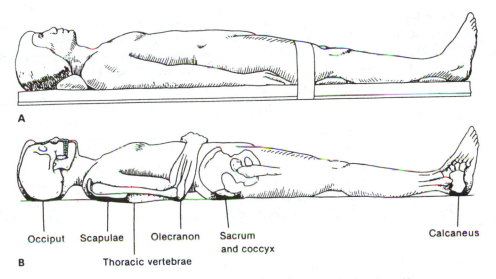

A

B

Occiput   Scapulae   Olecranon   Sacrum   Calcaneus
                                     and coccyx
              Thoracic vertebrae

Figure 11–3. A. Dorsal or supine position. **B.** Potential pressure points in supine position.

dominal viscera decreases the movement of the diaphragm and interferes with proper respiratory exchange. This position is contraindicated in patients with increased intracranial pressure as lowering the head and thorax increases intrathoracic pressure, contributing to an increase in intracranial pressure.

When the patient is in the Trendelenburg position, blood pools in the upper torso and the blood pressure increases; when the patient is returned to the supine position, he or she may become hypotensive. Movement from this position must be slow to allow the heart time to adjust to the change in blood volume. The leg section should be raised first to reverse the venous status in the legs and then the entire table leveled. A modification of this position is used in hypovolemic shock.

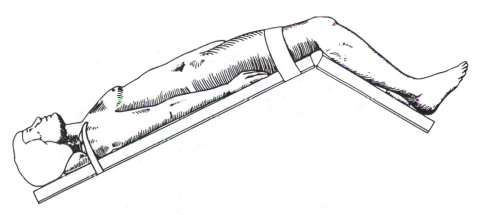

Figure 11–4. Trendelenburg position.

Reverse Trendelenburg. In the reverse Trendelenburg position, the head is raised and the feet are lowered (Fig. 11–5). This position is used for upper-abdominal surgery and for head and neck surgery. When used for abdominal surgery, it facilitates the movement of the abdominal viscera away from the diaphragm and therefore provides better visualization of the biliary tract. In head and neck surgery, it aids in hemostasis. The patient is positioned in the supine position with a well-padded footboard in place and the safety strap in position. A second safety strap may be needed for additional stability. Small pillows placed under the knees and the lumbar curvature will assist in making the patient comfortable. The head may be hyperextended by lowering the table headpiece or by placing a sandbag or a rolled towel under the patient's shoulders. If the reverse Trendelenburg is going to be used for an extended period of time, antiembolectomy stockings will aid in the venous return. In this position, blood pools in the lower extremities, and caution must be exercised in returning the patient to the supine position as the cardiovascular system may become overloaded.

Sitting or Modified Fowler's. The patient is positioned over the break in the table; the footboard is placed perpendicular to the table to support the feet (Fig. 11–6A). The backrest is elevated, the knees are flexed, and the patient's arms rest on a pillow placed in the lap. The shoulders are supported with tape to prevent hyperextension, and the safety strap is positioned 2 inches above the knees. Antiembolectomy stockings will assist in venous return. Areas that may require additional padding include: sacrum, ischial tuberosities, posterior knee, calcaneus, and medial malleolus (Fig. 11–6B). A potential problem associated with

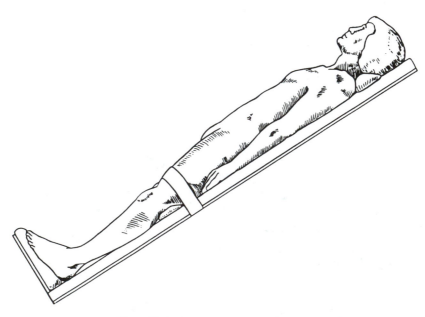

Figure 11–5. Reverse Trendelenburg position.

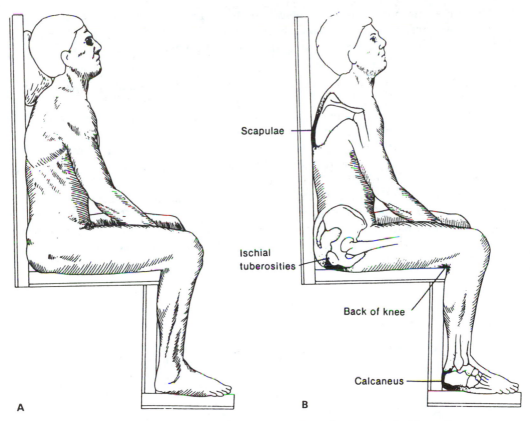

Figure 11–6. **A.** Sitting or modified Fowler's position. **B.** Potential pressure points in sitting position.

prolonged pressure on the ischial tuberosities is sciatic nerve damage. Special care should be given to the eyes to prevent injury.

Air embolism is a threat in any surgical position where a negative gravitational pressure gradient exists between the operative site and the right atrium. The sitting position is an example. A right-atrial catheter is inserted to assist in diagnosing and treating air embolisms. The following stages of the procedure are particularly critical points at which air embolisms may occur:

- When muscles are being dissected free from the occiput
- When bone is being removed
- When dura is being tacked up
- When a vascular tumor bed is entered

The scrub nurse should respond with a copious amount of irrigation, wet sponges, cottonballs, cottonoid, and absorbable gelatin sponges soaked in saline. This will allow the irrigation solution to be aspirated rather than air. If bone work is being performed, bone wax will assist in closing the hole.

The circulating nurse should act quickly to assist the anesthesiologist, while making certain that the scrub nurse does not exhaust any supplies. The anesthesiologist will attempt to aspirate the embolized air via the right-atrial or pulmonary artery catheter.

Lithotomy. The lithotomy position is used in surgical procedures requiring a perineal approach. The patient is positioned in a supine position with the buttocks near the lower break of the table to prevent lumbosacral strain (Fig. 11–7A). Cotton or flannel boots are placed over the feet to provide additional warmth and to contain any shedding of the epidermis from the feet. If the patient is to remain in the lithotomy position for more than 2 hours, a pneumatic compression device should be applied. This will decrease the pooling of blood and help prevent deep vein thrombus formation.

A pneumatic compression device consists of an air pump, connecting tubes, and extremity sleeves. By inflating and deflating the sleeves, this device enhances blood flow and venous return in the deep veins, preventing venous stasis. It also helps to prevent thrombosis as enhanced blood flow increases fibrinolytic activity. Pneumatic compression also increases femoral venous flow rates and augments muscle pump evacuation of blood. There

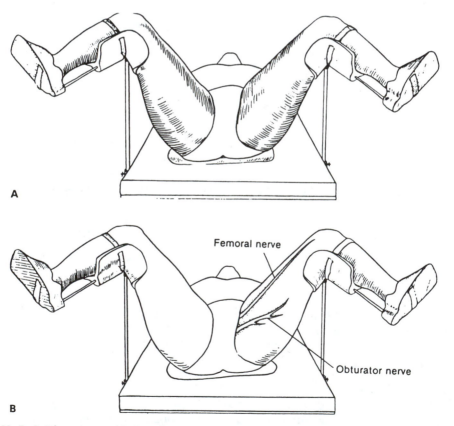

Figure 11–7. **A.** Lithotomy position. **B.** Nerve damage may occur to the femoral and obturator nerves in the lithotomy position.

are two types of pneumatic compression devices: intermittent and sequential. The intermittent compression device has a single chamber sleeve that fits over the entire leg and is connected through tubes to a small pump that applies 30 to 120 mm Hg of pressure. When the sleeve inflates, the pressure accelerates interstitial movement, mainly in the venous system, pushing fluid from the leg toward the heart. During deflation the venous vessels fill with fluid. Inflation and deflation alternate from one leg to the other on a preset time cycle. The sequential compression device has a sleeve with several chambers and the pump delivers 45 to 65 mm Hg of pressure that moves incrementally up the leg. The first chamber inflates and holds, then the second chamber inflates and holds, until all the chambers inflate and hold. The entire sleeve then deflates. A complete cycle can take from 75 seconds to 5 minutes, depending on the device.

An assessment of the patient's legs and feet should be performed before and after the devices have been applied. This should include checking the peripheral circulation, pedal pulses, skin color, and temperature. Care must be exercised when applying the devices to ensure that the sleeve of the pneumatic compression device hasn't become wrinkled or that it is too tight as this could create pressure areas. After applying the sleeve two fingers should fit between the sleeve and the leg.

Pneumatic compression devices are contraindicated in patients who have leg ischemia caused by arterial occlusive disease, massive edema of the legs, extreme leg deformities, arterial ischemia, inflammation or severe phlebitis, trauma, severe arteriosclerosis, congestive heart failure with leg or pulmonary edema, local skin disorders (infections, recent skin grafts, lesions, or ulcers), or thighs measuring more than 26 inches around.[8]

Stirrups are placed on the table at the same height and at an outward angle. The height is adjusted to the length of the patient's legs. After the patient is anesthetized, two members of the surgical team simultaneously place the legs in the stirrups to avoid back strain and hip dislocation.

Nursing actions are directed toward prevention of damage to superficial veins and nerves on the medial and lateral aspects of the thigh and the knee. Unpadded or misplaced stirrups can damage the saphenous and perineal nerves and predispose the patient to venous thrombosis. The most prevalent problem is peroneal nerve damage on the lateral aspect of the knee, which can cause foot drop. Excessive pressure on the femoral and obturator nerves in the groin may cause sensory disturbances to the inner aspects of the leg (Fig. 11–7B).

Team members must be cautioned about leaning on the inner aspect of the patient's thigh, which may accentuate external rotation or flexion of the hip joint. If a self-retaining retractor is utilized, the surgeon should be reminded to release tension on the lower pelvic blades at regular intervals to prevent prolonged compression.

If stirrups are used with popliteal knee support, they must be well padded so there is an even distribution of the thigh and leg weight. This will prevent thrombosis of the superficial vessels from occurring.

In the lithotomy position, most of the weight rests on the sacrum; to avoid pressure, additional padding may be required for lengthy procedures. A small lumbar pad will help reduce strain.

To prevent damage to the digits when raising or lowering the bottom portion of the table and to prevent peripheral nerve damage, the arms are placed on armboards positioned parallel to the table or are positioned loosely over the patient's abdomen and supported with a sheet or the patient's gown.

In this position, circulatory pooling occurs in the lumbar region. Venous flow may be reduced because of interference with lung expansion due to the pressure of the thighs on the abdomen and the pressure of the abdominal viscera against the diaphragm. Blood loss during surgery may not immediately produce clinical symptoms due to the pooling in the lumbar area. However, when the legs are lowered, 500 to 800 mL of blood may drain from the lumbar area into the legs, causing severe hypotension. When surgery is completed, the patient's legs must be lowered simultaneously and slowly returned to the normal supine position.

Prone. The prone position is used for surgical procedures on the posterior surface of the body (Fig. 11–8A). Induction of general anesthesia and intubation of the patient frequently occurs in the supine position on the transportation vehicle. After the anesthesiologist indicates that the patient may be moved, the patient is turned carefully onto the abdomen with the lumbar spine over the center break of the table. Four team members are used in turning the patient prone and in the return to supine, as it must be done gradually and slowly to allow the patient's cardiovascular system to adjust to the change in position. Rapid turning of the patient can result in hypotension. Patients with limited cardiac and respiratory reserves may not be able to tolerate the prone position if any additional respiratory or hemodynamic insult occurs.

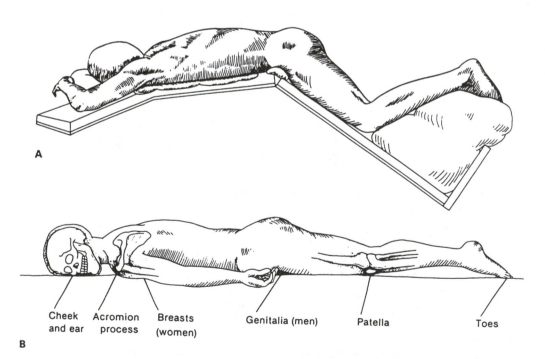

A

B

Cheek and ear   Acromion process   Breasts (women)   Genitalia (men)   Patella   Toes

Figure 11–8. **A.** Prone position. **B.** Potential pressure points in prone position.

In this position diaphragmatic movement is severely restricted, which limits tidal volume. Ventilatory assistance is almost always necessary in this position. The patient must be positioned to allow unrestrained abdominal movement for respiratory effort and to prevent pressure on the inferior vena cava. This can be accomplished by placing two large body rolls longitudinally from the acromioclavicular joint to the iliac crest. This allows the diaphragm to move freely and the lungs to expand. Women's breasts should be placed laterally to reduce pressure on them and male genitalia should be checked after final positioning to ensure they are positioned between the legs and free from pressure.

All headrests must be well padded and special care must be taken to prevent damage to the ears, the eyes, and the superficial nerves and blood vessels of the face.

The arms are placed at the patient's side or are placed on padded armboards with the arms extended outward and upward, palms down, with elbows slightly flexed to prevent overextension of the shoulder. The feet are elevated off the table with a pillow to prevent plantar flexion and pressure on the toes and to aid venous return by offering a slight incline to the lower extremities. Additional padding may be required on the shoulder girdle, olecranon, anterior superior iliac spine, patella, and dorsum of the foot (Fig. 11–8B). The safety strap is positioned 2 inches above the knees.

Jackknife or Kraske's Position. The patient is placed in the prone position with the hips over the table break and the table is flexed at a 90° angle, raising the hips and lowering the upper portion of the body (Fig. 11–9). The arms are placed on padded armboards with the arms extended outward and upward, palms down, and elbows slightly flexed. A small towel roll placed under each shoulder will protect the brachial plexus. Padding should be placed under the patient's hips to relieve pressure on the anterior superior iliac spine and

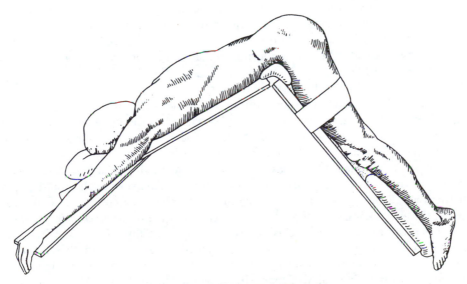

Figure 11–9. Jackknife or Kraske's position.

male genitalia. A pillow is placed under the lower legs and the ankles to prevent pressure on the toes. The safety strap is positioned across the thighs.

When this position is used for rectal procedures, hemorrhoid straps assist in optimum exposure and visualization. Hemorrhoid straps are wide strips of adhesive tape applied to both sides of the buttocks, at the level of the anus a few inches from the midline; they are pulled tight and fastened to the underside of the table.

The same principles in regard to turning the patient in the prone position apply to the jackknife position.

Lateral. The lateral position is used for surgical procedures on the kidney, the chest, or the upper ureter. The patient is anesthetized in the supine position and then positioned by four team members on the unaffected side, with the back close to the edge of the mattress. The shoulders and hips must be turned simultaneously to prevent torsion of the spine and great vessels. The lateral position is referred to as left or right according to the side on which the patient has been placed. In the right lateral position, the patient lies on the right side with the left side uppermost. This prepares the patient for a procedure on the left side. This position is also referred to as lateral recumbent, lateral decubitus, or Sims' position.

Positions for Kidney Procedures. When used for kidney procedures, the flank region is positioned over the kidney elevator, so that the area between the twelfth rib and the iliac crest will be elevated when the table is flexed and the kidney elevator raised (Fig. 11–10A). The patient's feet and head are in dependent positions, which encourages venous pooling and leads to hypotension. Respiratory effort is compromised because of the pressure on the lateral chest wall. This position may also create a mediastinal shift and rotation of the heart. Cardiac output may be decreased because of decreased venous return. The lower leg is flexed and the upper leg is straight, with pillows positioned between the legs to minimize the pressure and the weight from the upper leg to the lower leg. Pillows between the knees also assists in facilitating venous drainage in the lateral position. To prevent peroneal nerve damage to the lower knee, additional padding may be required to prevent compression against the OR bed. The ankles and the feet should be protected from pressure and foot drop (Fig. 11–10B).

The position is maintained by using sandbags, pillows, rolled blankets, or well-padded kidney braces; the short kidney brace is positioned at the back, and the long brace is attached in front of the patient. Adhesive tape is placed across the hip and shoulder and secured to the underside of the table for additional support. As in the prone position, female breasts and male genitalia should be free from compression or pressure.

The upper arm is placed on a raised armboard, and the lower arm is flexed near the face on the mattress (or a double armboard may be used). An axillary roll should be placed under the lower axilla to assist in chest expansion, to prevent compression of the scapula and brachial plexus. Radial pulses should be checked frequently to assess adequacy of circulation since the axillary and brachial arteries may be partially compressed by a poorly placed axillary roll and/or from the weight of the shoulder girdle and chest. The safety strap is positioned across the hip for stabilization. The entire table is tilted downward so the operative area is horizontal; the upper shoulder, the hip, and the ankle are in a straight line.

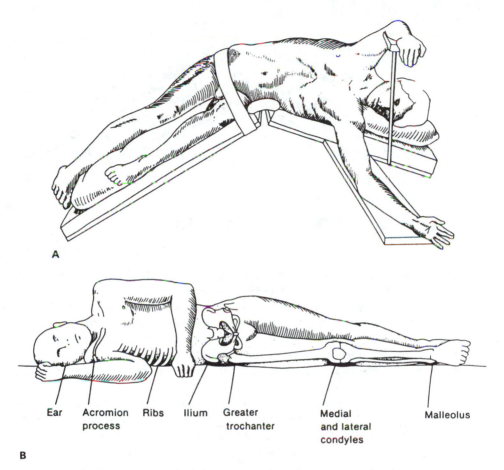

A

B

Ear   Acromion   Ribs   Ilium   Greater   Medial   Malleolus
      process   trochanter   and lateral
                                           condyles

Figure 11–10. **A.** Lateral or kidney position. **B.** Potential pressure points in lateral position.

Positions for Chest Procedures. In chest procedures the legs may be positioned in three ways: the lower leg may be flexed and the upper leg straight, or both legs may be flexed, or the upper leg may be flexed and the lower leg straight. In all three of these positions, pillows are placed between the legs, and the ankles and the feet are protected from pressure (Fig. 11–11).

The lower arm is slightly flexed and positioned in front of the patient on an armboard and the upper arm is positioned over the head to elevate the scapula from the operative site and to separate the intercostal spaces. A rolled sheet or towel placed between the patient and the mattress, below the level of the axilla, will relieve pressure on the dependent arm and allow chest movements. The patient's head is supported on a pillow.

The body is stabilized with the use of braces, sandbags, and body rolls. If braces are used, they should be well padded; the front brace should be positioned between the xyphoid and the umbilicus, the back brace in the lumbar area. Adhesive tape placed across the upper hip and fastened to the table on both sides assists in stabilization.

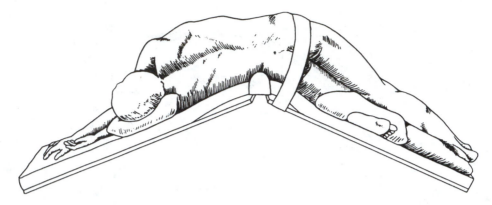

Figure 11–11. Lateral or chest position.

Circulation in the lateral position is compromised due to blood pooling in the lower limbs; as much as one unit of blood can pool in the legs. Lateral flexion can cause venous obstruction by occluding the inferior vena cava when the kidney elevator is raised. The combination of vena caval obstruction and pooling of venous blood in the legs can cause a severe drop in the patient's blood pressure. Prolonged positioning in the lateral position can result in significant pooling of blood in the legs and cause a relative volume deficit. The addition of IV fluids during the procedure can cause fluid overload when the surgical team returns the patient to the supine position.

Due to the weight of the body on the lower chest pulmonary compliance is reduced, which makes ventilation difficult. Morbidly obese patients or patients with large abdominal masses are especially prone to caval compression during lateral positioning because of the weight of the abdomen on the inferior vena cava and the aorta.

▌ DRAPING

The purpose of draping is to provide a sterile operative field by placing drapes over the patient, leaving only a minimum area of skin exposed around the site of the incision.

Criteria for Surgical Drapes

Surgical drapes should establish an effective barrier eliminating the passage of microorganisms between nonsterile and sterile areas. Draping material should be resistant to blood and aqueous fluid, abrasion resistant, lint-free, sufficiently porous to eliminate heat buildup, and should meet or exceed the requirements of the National Fire Protection Association. In addition, the drapes should be memory-free, possess a high degree of drapability, and be penetrable by gas or steam for sterilization.

The types of drapes available are reusable woven or disposable nonwoven materials and plastic adhesive skin drapes. The woven materials are made of muslin (140 to 160 thread count) and cotton (280-plus thread count) with special waterproofing treatment.

Nonwoven materials are made of processed cellulose fibers either alone or in combination with reinforcements of various types including polymeric films.

The components of a draping system are towels, sheets in various sizes, fenestrated drapes, specialty drapes (eye, peroneal, thyroid, chest sheets), and mayo stand covers. The drapes must be of adequate size to drape the patient without proximity to the floor. Non-perforating towel clips should be used on all surgical drapes.

Reusable Drapes

The basic requirements for reusable surgical drapes are the same as those described in Chapter 8 (Packaging Materials) for wrappers. Woven drapes must be checked for defects, lint, and stains. Inspection must be done over an illuminated table. Defects are patched with a vulcanized heat-seal patch.

Muslin with a thread count of 140 to 160 per square inch is available as surgical drapes. Muslin drapes do not retard the passage of fluids, and this results in migration of bacteria to the operative site. If the drapes become wet during the surgical procedure, they must be covered with another layer of draping material. The perioperative nurse must exercise caution in the number of layers of linen placed over the patient as excessive layers will interfere with heat dissipation from the patient's skin through the drapes.

Cotton with a thread count of 280-plus per square inch can receive a special water-proofing treatment that provides a barrier to liquids and abrasions for up to 75 washing-sterilizing cycles and uses. Due to this limitation, a system of accounting for the number of uses of each drape must be implemented. Processing of reusable drapes must be according to the manufacturer's guidelines.

Disposable Drapes

Disposable or "paper" drapes refer to those made of nonwoven material designed for one-time use. They can be manufactured with either absorbent or nonabsorbent properties. The nonwoven drapes are adaptable to lamination and bonding, which results in moisture repellency. Disposable drapes are compact, lightweight, permeable to air, and lint-free and are available in presterile form in packs or as single-wrapped items.

Some disposable drapes tend not to conform as well as linen on areas around the face, the head, and the extremities. In addition, solvents and volatile liquids tend to penetrate the drapes. Table 11–3 contrasts the properties of woven and nonwoven materials.

Literature is available to support both nonwoven and woven materials as surgical drapes. The nurse manager will incorporate these studies into an analysis of the departmental needs in determining whether woven or nonwoven drapes will be used. Areas to be included in the analysis are the total cost of repair and replacements, the cost of inspection and delinting, the type and condition of laundry equipment, the amount of storage space available, pilferage of woven items, and the adequacy of the laundry service including the length of time that elapses before soiled linen is washed. To assure that the blood protein is removed, a period of 11 hours is suggested as the maximum amount of time that should elapse. Additional areas to be explored are the acceptability of the items to the users, an analysis of the impact nonwovens would have on the waste system, and the concerns of the ecologist in using nonwovens.

TABLE 11–3. PROPERTIES OF WOVEN VERSUS NONWOVEN SURGICAL DRAPES

Properties	Woven (140–160)	Woven (280+)	Nonwoven
Bacterial filtration	Low	High (up to 75 washings)	High
Fluid strikethrough	Immediate	Resistant	None
Wicking	Immediate	Resistant	None
Air permeable	Yes	Yes	Yes
Linting	Sheds lint	Sheds lint	Lint-free
Size of pack	Bulky	Bulky	Compact
Weight of pack	10–12 lbs	10–12 lbs	3–5 lbs
Fenestration	Fixed	Fixed	May be enlarged
Drapability	Excellent	Excellent	Some limitations
Shelf life*	Indefinite	Indefinite	Indefinite—provided conditions of sterility are maintained
Quality control inspection required	Yes	Yes	Random checking prior to use
Pentrated by gas or steam for sterilization	Yes	Yes (check manufacturer guidelines for time–temperature heat profile)	Presterile
Meets NFPA requirements	Yes	Yes	Yes

*Shelf life is event related.

Custom Packs

Custom procedure packs have gained wide acceptance for cases performed in high volume or when quick turnover time is essential. A custom pack is a vendor-supplied collection of disposable surgical supplies, assembled in predetermined sequence, aseptically wrapped, sterilized, and delivered as requested by the institution. The principal reason for these packs is to assist in reducing the nonrevenue set-up time and, therefore, increase the time available for revenue-producing surgical procedures. Analysis by the OR manager regarding "cost reductions" and setup time is essential prior to implementation of a custom pack program.

Procedure-Based Packs

This concept builds on the custom procedure packs by providing products for the preoperative, intraoperative, and postoperative phases of the patient's surgical procedure. The concept is designed to deliver a large percentage of products that are required for a specific procedure through a single vendor order number. The products, including the end of case cleaning items, are delivered in a container that can be utilized to dispose of waste at the end of the case. The start-up of this system may be tedious and time consuming as it does require a commitment to standardization of supplies. However, it does reduce the need for labor-intensive activities surrounding the procurement and distribution of supplies and the departmental picking of supplies, and it reduces in-house sterilization. The resources utilized to support these activities can be allocated to the delivery of direct patient care.

TABLE 11–4. GUIDELINES FOR NURSING ACTIONS IN SURGICAL DRAPING

1. The skin around the incision must be dry before drapes are applied.

2. Sufficient time should be allowed to observe proper technique and application of the drapes.

3. Sterile drapes should be handled as little as possible; shaking linen should be avoided.

4. The drapes are carried folded to the operating room table. To avoid contamination of the front of the gown, care must be taken to maintain an appropriate distance from nonsterile areas (Fig. 11–12).

5. Drapes should be held high enough to avoid touching the nonsterile areas of the table.

6. To protect the sterile gloved hands, form a cuff from the drapes or towels

7. When placing drapes, never reach across the nonsterile area of the operating table to drape the other side; go around the table.

8. If a drape is incorrectly placed, it should be discarded. The circulating nurse will remove the drape without contaiminating other drapes or the operative site.

9. If the drape falls below waist level, it should be discarded because the area below the waist is considered unsterile.

10. A towel clip that has been placed through a drape or to the patient's skin is considered contaminated. It must not be repositioned during the procedure.

11. Draping is always done from a sterile area to an unsterile area, draping the nearest area first.

12. The area around the incision is draped first and then the periphery.

13. Whenever sterility is in doubt, consider the drape to be contaminated.

14. Drapes should be placed over the patient and over all furniture and equipment in the sterile field.

Plastic Adhesive Drapes

Plastic adhesive drapes are available in various sizes and configurations for surgical draping. The plastic drapes may be applied directly to the dry skin prior to draping or over the sterile drapes. When applied over the sterile drapes, plastic drapes assist in holding them in place, thus eliminating the need for skin towels and towel clips. The incision is made through the plastic drape; the cut edges remain adherent to the skin and keep the surgical

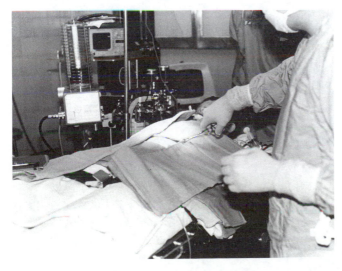

Figure 11–12. To avoid contamination of the front of gown, care must be taken to maintain an appropriate distance from nonsterile areas.

incision sealed off from the migration of bacteria. The drapes are clear, allowing visibility of the patient's skin; they conform to irregular body surfaces; and they may be used to wall off contaminated areas such as a colostomy, the anus, and infected wounds.

Three sterile team members can effectively apply a large plastic drape. Two members stand on opposite sides of the operating room table holding the drape about 12 inches above the patient. The third member removes and discards the backing, holding the drape taut; and the first two members lower the drape until it touches the patient's skin surface. The third member uses a towel to smooth the drape out, starting in the center and moving to the periphery (Table 11–4).

Plastic adhesive drapes should be removed carefully from patients, particularly those with fragile skin, to prevent denuding of the skin.

▌ REFERENCES

1. Perioperative nurse translation of the AHCRP clinical practice guidelines. In *Standards and Recommended Practices*. Denver: AORN; 1995:60.
2. Vermillion C. OR acquired pressure ulcers. *Decubitus*. 1990; 3(2):26–30.
3. *Clinical Practice Guidelines: Pressure Ulcers in Adults: Prediction and Prevention*. Rockville, MD: US Department of Health and Human Services; 1992.
4. Bergman-Evans B, Cuddigan J, Bergstrom N. Prediction and prevention of pressure ulcers. *Today's OR Nurse*. 1994; 16(6):33–39.
5. Gendron F. *Unexplained Patient Burns: Investigating Iatrogenic Injuries*. Brea, CA: Quest; 1988:170, 173, 238.
6. Campbell K. Pressure point measures in the operating room. *J Enterostomal Therapy*. 1989; 16(3):119–124.
7. Gendron F. Burns: Occurring during lengthy surgical procedures. *J Clin Engineering*. 1980; 5:19.
8. Bright L, Georgi S. How to protect your patient from DVT. *Am J Nursing*. 1994; 12:30.

TWELVE

Surgical Instruments

Archaeologist have found skulls dating back to 350,000 B.C. that show evidence of one of the first surgical interventions to be performed—trephining. An opening was chiseled through the skull of a patient "to release demons." An ancient toolmaker sharpened flints and made the crude hammers necessary for these procedures. Sharpened animal teeth were later used for bloodletting and to drain abscesses.

The surgical instruments used in the United States from 1776 to 1826 were imported or made by American artisans under the direction of a surgeon. The surgeon used the services of steel workers, coppersmiths, silversmiths, needle grinders, sewers of leather, glassblowers, and spinners of silk and hemp to design and manufacture instruments, which were crude and expensive.

> The cutlers who made and sold knives kept small assortments of surgical instruments and changed their shop signs from "Cutler and Scissor Grinder" to "Cutler and Surgical Instrument Maker." Thus, began the physicians' supply houses and surgical instrument making in America.[1]

During the early 1800s, the physicians' principal tools were their eyes, ears, and keen observation. Kitchen and pen knives doubled as scalpels, and table forks were used as retractors. Federal records disclose that three of four operations during the Civil War were amputations, and the carpenter's saw worked as well as a forged instrument. The use of ether and chloroform as anesthetic agents in 1846 brought with it new surgical procedures and, consequently, new ideas and demands for surgical instruments.

In the late 19th and early 20th centuries the demand for smaller, more delicate instruments increased. German silver, brass, and steel that could withstand repeated sterilization replaced the wood, ivory, and rubber formerly used on instrument handles. Stainless steel developed in Germany during World War I was a superior material for surgical instruments.

■ MANUFACTURE

Currently, most surgical instruments are made of stainless steel. They are manufactured in the United States, Germany, France, and Pakistan. However, because no standards are established for instrument manufacturing, the quality of instruments may vary among manufacturers. Instruments must be examined before purchase to ascertain their quality. A well-made instrument when properly cared for will last at least 10 years.

Steels capable of stainless qualities are compounds of iron, carbon, and chromium. Some also contain small amounts of nickel, magnesium, and silicone. The classification and the type of steel, such as 410, 416, 420, depend on the amounts of carbon and chromium used.[2] The subsequent processing determines the degree to which the steel is "stainless."

Recently, titanium alloy has been used in the manufacture of surgical instruments. It has quickly developed a reputation for having unique characteristics and advantages over traditional stainless steel:

- titanium does not collect a magnetic charge, ensuring that needles will not cling to needle holders
- titanium is up to 45% stronger than stainless steel and 50% lighter
- titanium is highly resistant to staining, pitting, and rusting.

Instruments may be finished in one of three ways: polished; satin, or dull; and black, or ebonized. Because the bright polished finish reflects light and may cause eye fatigue, the satin, or dull, finish is used more frequently. Glare is eliminated and eye fatigue decreased. Instruments with this finish should always be used when taking photographs or filming surgical procedures. The black, or ebonized, finish is used during laser surgery to prevent deflection of the laser beam.

Surgical instruments are very expensive. New instruments and replacements constitute a sizable portion of the operating room's annual budget. Instruments, however, can enhance the skill of a surgeon or compromise a surgical procedure. The successful outcome of a procedure may be directly related to instrument design, quality of manufacture, and care. The ideal surgical instrument becomes an extension of the surgeon's hand and expertise. It must have a tactile responsiveness that expresses the nature of the tissue to the surgeon's hand. Understanding the function, design, and proper care and handling of instruments will complement the nurse's ability to affect the outcome of the surgical procedure for the patient in a cost-effective manner.

Instruments are manufactured in a wide variety of sizes and shapes in four main categories: sharps, clamps, graspers, and retractors.

Sharps

Sharp instruments include scalpels, scissors, bone cutters, rongeurs, chisels, osteotomes, saws, curettes, and dermatomes. They are designed to incise and dissect tissue and bone. Scalpel handles have one end for attaching a disposable blade. This allows the blade to be changed at intervals during the procedure. To prevent lacerations, blades should be applied and removed with a needle holder, touching only the dull side of the blade.

Scissors, an essential component of all surgical procedures, must cut tissue cleanly without chopping or tearing it. They are manufactured in various sizes, the blades are curved or straight, and the tips may be blunt or sharp (Fig. 12–1). Heavy scissors (such as the curved mayo scissors) are used on heavy tough tissue, and the lighter Metzenbaum scissors are used to dissect delicate tissue. Straight mayo scissors, frequently called suture

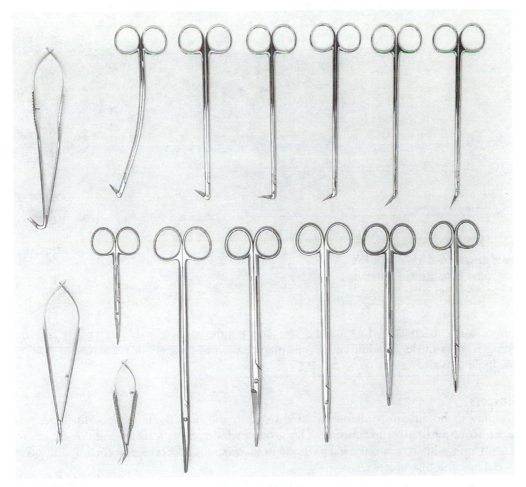

Figure 12–1. Scissors are designed in a variety of lengths, blade styles, sizes, and angles to adapt to all types of body tissue and suture. Use of the appropriate scissors for the task is important. *(Courtesy Scanlan International, Saint Paul, MN.)*

scissors, are used to cut sutures. When the procedure is being performed in a cavity, 9-inch scissors and scalpels are used to allow visualization and better control of the dissecting site.

Clamps

Clamping instruments are most frequently used to compress blood vessels and other tubular structures to control bleeding and maintain hemostasis by occluding the flow of blood. The grasping ends of these instruments have serrations that are meshed to prevent the clamp from slipping off a blood vessel (Fig. 12–2).

Vascular clamps have special jaws designed to minimize trauma to delicate blood vessels and to keep the clamp in position without biting into the vessel while the surgeon resects or repairs the structure (Figs. 12–3 and 12–4). The clamp's size, pressure, and jaw

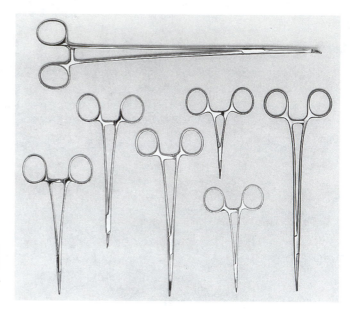

Figure 12–2. Clamps of various sizes are used to compress blood vessels and to hold or manipulate tissue. *(Courtesy Scanlan International, Saint Paul, MN.)*

surface are chosen according to the size and condition of the blood vessel, and the strength of its pulse. In addition, clamps may be used as graspers or retractors to hold or manipulate tissue.

Graspers

Grasping or holding instruments are used to grasp and hold tissue or bone for dissection or retraction or to assist in suturing. This group includes tissue forceps (Fig. 12–5), tenacula, rib approximators, stone forceps, bone holders, sponge forceps, towel clips, and other special holding instruments.

Tissue forceps are also known as pickups and are used to grasp or pick up tissue when dissecting, suturing, cauterizing, or exploring tissue. A specific forceps is designed to grasp suture needles. Well-designed forceps should be perfectly balanced and produce precise

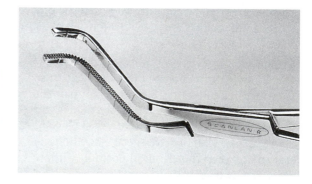

Figure 12–3. This vascular clamp is designed for full occlusion of peripheral vessels such as internal carotid arteries in adults or larger vessels in children such as the renal arteries. The longer ratchet permits gradual clamping and release. The double row of Cooley jaws creates a noncrushing surface for delicate tissues. *(Courtesy Scanlan International, Saint Paul, MN.)*

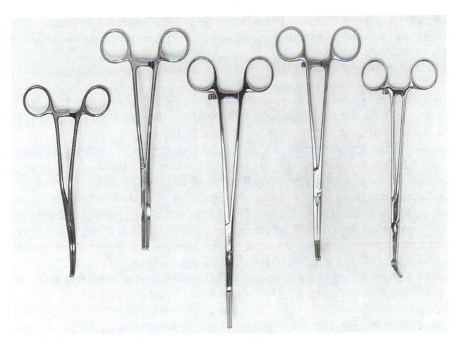

Figure 12—4. Large aortic and multipurpose clamps are designed with angles in the shanks and jaws for deep, partial, or total occlusion of the vessel or structures such as bronchial tree. *(Courtesy Scanlan International, Saint Paul, MN.)*

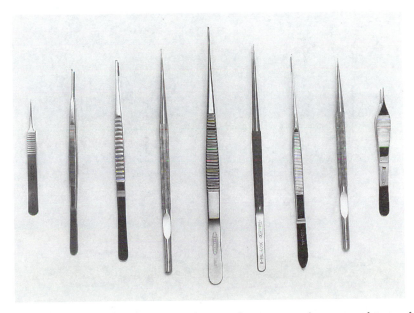

Figure 12—5. Tissue forceps are available in many sizes and patterns of tips to accommodate any type of tissue or function. *(Courtesy Scanlan International, Saint Paul, MN.)*

nonslip handling of delicate tissue. These instruments are of different lengths and available with or without teeth. Forceps with teeth are used on thick or slippery tissue; forceps without teeth, on delicate thin tissue.

Tenacula are designed with a sharp point and are used to pierce an organ, such as the uterus, to facilitate retraction or dissection.

Towel clips are available as nonpiercing or piercing clamps. Mostly they are used to hold the drapes in place or to clip towels or sponges to the edges of the wound. Piercing clamps damage both linen and tissue, and their use is discouraged.

Sponge forceps are most often used to hold gauze sponges, although they are also used to hold tissue. A 4 × 4 sponge may be folded in thirds, placed on the sponge stick, and then be used for prepping, retracting tissue, and absorbing fluids.

Needle holders, or needle drivers, are designed to hold and pass suture through tissue. They give the surgeon complete control of the needle for precise handling. The needle holder must grasp the suture needle securely, yet not damage it. Inappropriate or damaged needle holders can scratch or burr a needle, and consequently inhibit suturing and damage tissue. Needle holders must have smooth box locks so that suture is not snagged or cut when performing an instrument tie, and they must have a smooth opening and closure of the locking mechanisms for ease of handling (Fig. 12–6 and 12–7). Diamond jaw needle holders have a tungsten carbide insert to prevent rotation of the needle. The longitudinal groove in the jaw releases tension and prevents flattening of the needle. Needle holders must be frequently repaired or replaced, as grasping and holding needles shortens the life of the instrument. One of the advantages of the diamond jaw needle holder is that

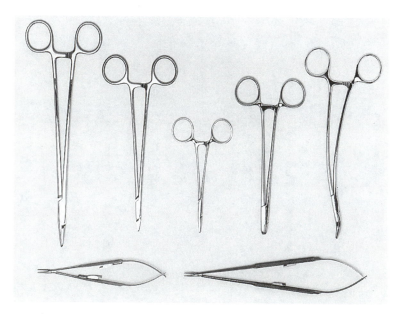

Figure 12–6. Needle holders must be appropriate for the size of the suture needle as well as the surgical procedure. *(Courtesy Scanlan International, Saint Paul, MN.)*

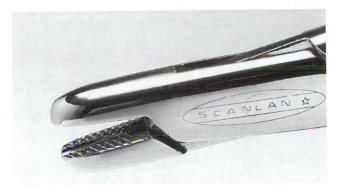

Figure 12–7. Sternum needle holder. The short, heavy jaws of this needle holder permit ease of passing large sternal wire needles and easy twisting for closure. *(Courtesy Scanlan International, Saint Paul, MN.)*

the inserts can be replaced as often as required, thus decreasing the expense of replacing the entire instrument (Fig. 12–8).

Several special holding forceps have tips or jaws designed for use on specific tissue. Allis and Allis-Adair forceps, frequently used in perineal surgery, have multiple sharp teeth that do not crush or damage tissue. A Kocher or Ochsner clamp has one sharp tooth and is used on tough heavy tissue. The Babcock forceps has a curved fenestrated jaw without teeth and is used on delicate tissue, such as the intestine or ureter.

Retractors

Retractors are used to assist in visualization of the operative field (Fig. 12–9). They are designed to provide the best exposure with minimal trauma to surrounding tissue. Retractors come in various sizes with the blade usually at a right angle to the handle. The width and the length of the blade and whether it is sharp or dull depends on where the retractor is used. A malleable retractor is made of a special stainless steel that permits repeated bending and shaping by the surgeon without hardening the metal. Self-retaining retractors have a frame to which blades may be attached, or they may consist of two blades held apart with a ratchet.

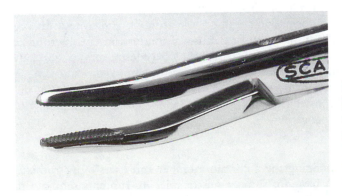

Figure 12–8. The angle of the shanks and jaw of this needle holder allows the surgeon to reach and maneuver needles from the atrial approach to the cuspid valves. The tungsten carbide inlay firmly holds large needles, preventing slippage or rotation. *(Courtesy Scanlan International, Saint Paul, MN.)*

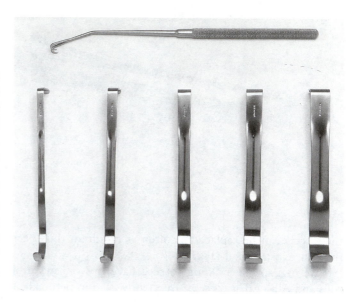

Figure 12–9. These dual-end retractors combine the gentle curve of a Deaver-style retractor for gently retracting large structures with the right-angled, shallow field Army-style retractor on the opposite end. These retractors are available in a variety of widths for a wide range of surgical applications. The Mitral Hook is used to retract the valve leaflets or annulus in mitral valve surgery. The angled shaft of the long hook gives good exposure to the left ventricle from a left atrial surgical approach. *(Courtesy Scanlan International, Saint Paul, MN.)*

▌ HANDLING OF INSTRUMENTS

When handing instruments to the surgeon, the following guidelines are useful:

- Scalpels are always handed to the surgeon so that he or she has control of the handle.
- All curved instruments are handed so that the curve of the instrument is in the same direction as the curve of the surgeon's palm. The scrub assistant holds the instrument by the hinged area so that the surgeon can view the tips.
- When mounting needles on a needle holder, the needle must point in the direction it will be used, which depends on whether the surgeon is right- or left-handed.
- Retractors are handed so the surgeon can grasp the handle of the retractor.

Familiarization with Instruments and Inventory

New personnel will be helped to learn about instruments through the use of a card file. The file may include the following information about each instrument: a picture of the instrument, the vendor's name, order number, principal use of the instrument, method of sterilization, and cost. Grouping the instruments within the card file by surgical specialty and by instrument set or special trays will add clarity to the learning process.

Access to the instrument room or instrument cupboards is controlled to prevent pilferage and indiscriminate use. An instrument inventory is conducted at least annually to assess the effectiveness of inventory control.

Instrument Selection

Standard basic instrument sets containing the minimum number and types of instruments will facilitate instrument counts. A basic instrument set includes instruments required to open and close the incision and provides the majority of other instruments needed to complete the surgical procedure. Table 12–1 identifies a basic major instrument set appropriate for use in the following surgical specialties: gynecologic, genitourinary, vascular, and general. Basic sets should be assessed at regular intervals to identify instruments that need to be added or deleted.

Proper selection of additional instruments is based on information obtained during the preoperative assessment and includes the age and the size of the patient, the selected surgical approach, the anatomy, the possible pathologic condition, and the surgeon's preferences.

Surgical instruments represent a major investment in all surgical facilities. The proper selection, use, and processing of instruments have a direct influence on the resources allocated for replacement and repair costs. The scrub assistant and the circulating nurse are accountable for the proper management of these resources.

Instrument Counts

Instruments are counted during all surgical procedures to ensure patient safety and to prevent loss of the instruments. Toward this goal, instruments are assembled in a predetermined manner with all instruments accounted for. The scrub assistant and the circulating nurse verify the count in the operating room before the surgical procedure is begun. Instruments added during the case are added to the count sheet by the circulating nurse. Another instrument count is taken before the cavity is closed and at the time of permanent

TABLE 12–1. BASIC MAJOR INSTRUMENT SET

Sharps		Forceps		Clamps		Retractors	
#4 Knife handle	2	6" Thumb forceps	2	Large towel clip	6	Loop	2
#7 Knife handle	1	6" Tissue forceps	2	Small towel clip	12	USA	2
Straight mayo scissors	1	8" Thumb forceps	2	Short needle holder	2	Vein	2
Curved mayo scissors	1	8" Tissue forceps	2	Long needle holder	3	Small Richardson	2
7" Metzenbaum scissors	2	10" Thumb forceps	1	Providence	6	Medium Richardson	2
9" Metzenbaum scissors	1	Adson forceps	2	Straight Kelly	6	Large Richardson	2
				Curved Kelly	6	Narrow Deaver	2
				Mayo	8	Wide Deaver	2
				Kocher	6	Harrington	1
				Allis	4	Balfour with blade	1
				Short Babcock	2	Narrow Crile	1
				Long Babcock	2	Wide Crile	1
				Long straight Kelly	6		
				Long curved Kelly	6		
				Mixter	6		
				Pean	6		
				Sponge forceps	4		

relief of the scrub assistant. The final instrument count is not taken until the wound is closed and the surgical drapes removed.

Instruments broken or disassembled during the procedure are accounted for in their entirety. If a count is incorrect, the surgeon is notified, a search is made for the item, and appropriate measures are taken (e.g., an x-ray of the patient is taken before he or she leaves the operating room) and documented by the circulating nurse according to hospital policy.

■ GUIDELINES FOR THE CARE OF INSTRUMENTS

The following are guidelines to observe in the care of instruments:

1. Instruments are used only for the purpose for which they were designed.
2. Instruments are handled gently. Sharp and delicate instruments are placed in a separate tray for terminal cleaning.
3. Instruments are open during sterilization so that steam can penetrate the box locks.
4. During a surgical procedure, instruments are frequently soaked, rinsed, or wiped off. Instruments with lumens are irrigated with sterile water to prevent them from becoming obstructed with organic material.
5. Instruments must not be soaked in saline, as the sodium chloride will increase rusting and discoloration.
6. All instruments with removable parts are disassembled after use to expose all surfaces for terminal sterilization.
7. Following a surgical procedure, instruments are soaked in an enzymatic detergent solution for a minimum of 2 minutes. Next the instruments are processed through a washer-sterilizer and then a sonic cleaner to ensure adequate cleaning. Detergents should be noncorrosive and low sudsing with a pH close to neutral (see Chapter 7).
8. Abrasives, such as steel wool and scouring powders, are not used, as they will scratch and remove the finish on the metal, thus increasing the possibility of corrosion.
9. Instruments are checked after each use. Those that are damaged or stiff are repaired or replaced.
   a. Forceps and hinged instruments are inspected for alignment of the jaws and teeth.
   b. The tips of clamps must be even, and when the instrument is held up to the light fully closed, no light is visible between the jaws.
   c. Clamps are closed on the first rachet, held by the box lock, and tapped lightly against a countertop; if the clamp springs open, it is faulty.
   d. Heavy scissors, such as mayos, should cut through four layers of gauze at the tips; delicate scissors should cut through two layers.
   e. Needle holders are checked with a needle in place; if the needle can be moved easily by hand, the needle holder needs repair.
   f. Chrome-plated instruments are checked for chips, sharp edges, and worn areas.
   g. Chisels, osteotomes, and gouges are sharpened on a routine rotation; care must

be exercised not to hit the edges of these instruments against each other or other instruments.

10. Stiff instruments are treated with a water-soluble lubricant. Oils form a bacteria-protecting film and prevent sterilization.

11. Instrument milk is used routinely as preventive maintenance.

12. Instruments are marked with an electroetching device or a laser rather than a vibrating marker to avoid hairline cracks. All markings are on the shank of the instrument to avoid fracturing the box lock. The date of purchase is indicated on the instrument so that the life of the instrument can be properly assessed. It may also assist in identifying defects associated with manufacturing.

■ INSTRUMENTS FOR SPECIAL USES

Microsurgery Instruments

Lightweight metals such as titanium and tungsten carbide are now used in the manufacture of microsurgery instruments. These lightweight, high-strength materials provide sharper cutting edges and are easier for the surgeon to manipulate. They are more corrosion resistant than stainless steel. Titanium and tungsten carbide, however, will corrode if not properly cared for.

Microsurgical instrument trays safely position and secure instruments (Fig. 12–10). The trays are usually lined with finger mats (posts) constructed of polyfoam, silicone, or Teflon to prevent direct contact between instruments. Contact between instruments during storage, use, or processing can cause sufficient damage to require repair or replacement.

When instruments are on the mayo stand, the tips should be elevated in the air by placing a rolled towel under the handles. Protective guards are left on until the surgeon is ready to use the instruments. During use, the instruments are cleaned only with nonfibrous sponges to avoid damage to the delicate tips.

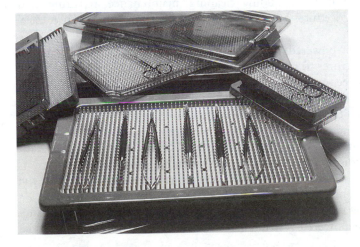

Figure 12–10. Microsurgical instrument trays are designed to safely position and secure instruments. (Courtesy Scanlan International, Saint Paul, MN.)

At the end of the procedure, the gross soil is removed from the instrument with a soft toothbrush. The instrument is placed back into the instrument tray and terminally processed in the washer-sterilizer and ultrasonic cleaner. Prior to storage, instruments must be thoroughly dried, especially the tips and the box locks, to prevent corrosion. Compressed gas or a hot air blower may be used. If hand drying is required, a chamois is preferable, as it will not leave lint on the instrument. Following the cleaning process, the tips are checked with a magnifying glass to detect any defects.

Air-Powered Tools

During the past quarter century, air-powered instruments have been used successfully in neurosurgery, orthopedic, dental, plastic, and reconstructive surgeries. The instruments are powered by compressed air or compressed dry nitrogen (99.97% pure) and controlled with a foot pedal or hand switch. The instruments are used for cutting, shaping, and beveling bone; taking skin grafts; and for dermabrading.

The bone instruments, used to cut or remove bone, have a rotary, reciprocating, or oscillating action. The rotary action is used to drill holes and insert screws, wires, or pins. The reciprocating cutting action is from front to back; the oscillating action is from side to side.

All blades and attachments must be seated properly before activating the instrument. They are always tested for proper working condition before being given to the surgeon. When air-powered instruments are used on bone, saline solution is dripped from a plastic bulb syringe by the scrub assistant or the first assistant to cool the bone and wash away the particles.

High-speed burrs used in conjunction with metal suction tips generate a dispersion of very fine metallic particles into the soft tissue adjacent to the operative area. Although the particles by themselves do not have immediate clinical effects, they may have a deleterious effect if the patient requires further magnetic resonance imaging (MRI) studies of the area; the particles cause a distortion defect in the image analogous to a starburst configuration. Therefore, plastic suction tips should be used for high-speed burrs or drills.

It is important that all personnel associated with using these instruments understand all aspects of their proper surgical use, including cleaning, maintenance, repairing, and sterilization. Critical to these procedures are the manufacturer's directions for use, care, cleaning, and lubrication.

Some air will leak from all air-powered instruments; the amount varies from instrument to instrument and from manufacturer to manufacturer. This exhausting of propellant gas is an important consideration in recommending cleaning procedures and sterilization exposure times. If the air-powered instrument is internally bacteriologically contaminated, direct wound infection is possible from the forward exhaust of the gas during the operation.

Air-powered instruments and air hoses are decontaminated immediately after use according to the manufacturer's instructions. The air hose should remain attached to the instrument during cleaning and disassembled prior to sterilization. These items are not immersed in water or placed in an ultrasonic cleaner, as damage may result if water enters the internal mechanism of the instrument or hose.

Lubrication, if specified by the manufacturer, is an essential step for the proper functioning and sterilization of air-powered instruments. The instrument must be activated after being lubricated to ensure dispersion of the lubricant. The powered instruments are then disassembled and packaged for steam sterilization with a prevacuum cycle. The prevacuum cycle allows rapid air removal and steam penetration into internal portions of the air-powered instrument. Sterilization of powered surgical instruments using ethylene oxide gas is done only according to the manufacturer's instructions. There is no evidence that ethylene oxide properly sterilizes the internal mechanism of the instruments, and there is concern that the gas does not readily diffuse through the lubricants.

Flash sterilization should be used only in emergencies, and the manufacturer's recommendations for sterilization times must be closely followed. With proper care and maintenance, air-powered tools have an indefinite life span.

Electrically Powered Tools

Dermatomes, drills, and saws may also be powered electrically. The motors must be explosionproof and have sparkproof connectors. The anesthesiologist is alerted to the use of equipment that requires an electrical motor because these units are not used in the presence of a flammable anesthetic agent. With the switch in the off position, equipment with a motor must be plugged into the electrical outlet before anesthesia begins and must not be removed until after the anesthetic agent is discontinued.

As with air-powered tools, it is important that the hospital staff carefully follow manufacturers's directions for use, care, cleaning, and lubrication. The motor must not be immersed in any liquid, the power cord and the foot pedals must be cleaned following each use, and cords must be removed from the outlet by grasping firmly on the plug, not by pulling on the cord. All power cords and plugs are checked prior to each use for any crack or break.

Fiberoptic Cables

Fiberoptic cables are made of high-refractory optical glass and contain many hundreds of tiny fibers. The fibers transmit light from the light source to an instrument. To avoid unnecessary damage to the cables, they must not be pulled or stretched. This requires that the cables be long enough to allow adequate slack when in the operating position. Only nonperforating or plastic towel clips are used to secure the fiberoptic cables to the drapes.

The light source is turned on with the rheostat at the lowest setting and then turned up slowly to avoid blowing out the bulb. If the cable and the optics are in good condition, a medium position should provide the required brightness for the examination. Bulbs will deteriorate and give less light before they burn out. The consistent need to turn the light source above the normal setting may be an indication that the bulb needs to be replaced. If the illuminator does not have a built-in second standby lamp, an extra bulb should be available in the operating room.

The light sources should not be allowed to remain in contact with the drapes for prolonged periods during the procedure, as the heat from light cords may cause the drapes to burn.

After the procedure is completed, the circulating nurse turns the rheostat to zero and lets the fan run 2 to 3 minutes to cool the bulb. If the light cable is left on for an extended period, it may burn a hole in the drapes and result in the patient's being burned.

The cable should be removed from the illuminator by grasping the stainless steel ferrule and pulling firmly. If the cable is yanked from the illuminator, the fibers will break.

Fiberoptic cables are washed by hand in a mild detergent with warm water, rinsed, air-dried, and checked for light transmission and breakage of fibers. The cable is checked for broken fibers by directing one end of the cable to a light and observing the opposite end; black spots indicated broken fibers. If 25% or more of the fibers appear black, the cable needs to be repaired or replaced.

For sterilization, the cable should be coiled loosely, placed in a sterilizing case, or wrapped according to departmental procedure. Some fiberoptic cables may be steam sterilized; however, this may reduce the life of the cable. All fiberoptic cables may be sterilized with ethylene oxide. Cables should withstand 12 months of normal use without noticeable deterioration.

Endoscopes

Personnel must follow universal precautions when handling and processing contaminated endoscopes, endoscopic accessories, or related equipment. Endoscopes and related instrumentation should be inspected, tested, used, and processed according to design and manufacturer's written instructions to reduce or minimize adverse patient outcomes. These tasks are carried out at all stages of handling; for example, prior to use, during the procedure, immediately after use, prior to cleaning, after rinsing, after drying, and prior to disinfection or sterilization. Poorly functioning or broken equipment delays the procedure, increasing risks of infection and patient injury.

Scopes that enter normally sterile areas of the body should be sterilized before each use. If this is not feasible, they should receive high-level disinfection.[3]

Each piece of endoscopic equipment should be assigned an identification number for documentation of inspections and tracking of patient and equipment problems.[4] In addition to the routine documentation discussed in Chapter 5, endoscopic procedures should have a permanent log that indicates the identification number and type of endoscopes, accessory instruments, the person processing each endoscope, the results of the inspection process, and the results of the leak test for fiberoptic endoscopes.

Nonlensed Endoscopic Instruments. Laryngoscopes, bronchoscopes, and esophagoscopes consist of a tubular instrument with a removable light carrier. They are powered by using a battery cord or fiberoptic cable and power or light source. These instruments are very delicate. The accidental dropping of an instrument, handling the instrument with forceps, or placing a heavier instrument on a lighter one may result in dents or scratches, requiring repair or replacement.

These instruments are cleaned immediately following the procedure to prevent the formation of encrustations and clogged channels. They are soaked in an enzymatic detergent and washed in a mild soap solution using a soft brush. A water pistol with interchangeable nozzles, which can be attached to any water faucet or air outlet, will assist in cleaning and drying the interior of the instrument. The instruments do not contain any optics; therefore, autoclaving is the preferred method of sterilization.

Lensed Endoscopic Instruments. Endoscopic instruments that contain lenses require special care and handling to ensure their safe and efficient operation. To prevent scratching and potential injury to the patient, the instruments are never handled with another instrument.

They are handled one at a time and picked up by the proximal end, the eyepiece. On a sterile setup, the instruments are placed in the center of the table to prevent them from rolling off the table's edge. Excessive bending, loosening, or removal of the eyepiece is avoided.

To clean instruments, they are disassembled, flushed with an enzymatic detergent solution, and washed in warm or tepid water with an appropriately sized soft brush and a water pistol. The water pistol helps clean small channels, holes, and hinges. Plastic pans are used for the disinfecting process to avoid the reaction of metal with the disinfectant and to prevent scratching the instrument's surface.

The proximal and distal lenses are cleaned with 70% isopropyl alcohol on a cotton applicator or sponge. After the instrument is cleaned and dried, the lenses are checked for visual clarity. A "half moon" but otherwise clear view could indicate that the instrument has a dent on the outside sheath. Fogging and loss of image result from condensation within the optical system.

After rinsing with water, the endoscopes are rinsed with 70% to 90% ethyl or isopropyl alcohol and air is forced through the channels to facilitate internal drying. This will decrease bacterial contamination of the endoscopes during storage. The scopes are stored vertically in a protected area to prevent damage, or they are placed in perforated metal containers with towels folded loosely around each one to prevent direct contact between the scopes during processing and storage.

For these instruments to operate efficiently and effectively, it is important that the manufacturer's guidelines be followed regarding the proper sterilization procedure. Some of the lensed instruments are autoclavable; however, even under ideal conditions, heat and pressure during a steam autoclave cycle will reduce the life of any optical system. Ethylene oxide gas sterilization may be used on all lensed instruments if they are thoroughly dried before packaging. Aeration should be in accordance with the sterilizer manufacturer's instructions.

An alternative to ethylene oxide gas sterilization is high-level disinfection in 2% glutaraldehyde for 45 minutes. The 45-minute soak time ensures 100% mycobactericidal activity. The instrument is then rinsed and dried.

Fiberoptic endoscopes are tested for pressure leaks according to the manufacturer's instructions following each use and prior to immersion in a liquid. The leak testing identifies interstitial space damage to the endoscope, which requires repair to prevent additional damage. In addition, contaminants could enter the interstitial space, increasing the potential for infection.[3]

■ MINIMAL ACCESS SURGERY

Minimal access surgery has developed rapidly over the past few years fueled by emerging technology and competition among vendors of instrumentation to support the procedures. The major advantages of minimal access surgery are:

- shorter hospital stay
- decreased postoperative pain
- less restriction of activity postoperatively

The major disadvantage is that the time required to complete these procedures is frequently longer than that required for the open method due to limited visualization of anatomy. Consequently, the patient is anesthetized longer and the perioperative costs of these procedures may be higher than those of conventional open methods.

Patient selection for minimal access procedures is critical to the success of the procedure. Risks include injury to internal structures, such as a punctured bowel or bladder, and injury to the deep or large blood vessels. If any of these complications occur, the laparoscopic procedure will need to be converted to an open procedure with little delay. The patient, therefore, is prepped and draped for a laparotomy, but with instruments and supplies to support an open procedure available in the room. If the surgeon has not contaminated the sterile field, for example, placed his eye directly on the eyepiece of the scope, redraping and repreping are not required.

Special attention must be given to positioning these patients, as the procedures require that the OR table be rotated laterally and placed to accommodate Trendelenburg to displace the patient's intracavity organs. This positioning enhances visibility for the surgical team, but does create the potential for patient injury if proper positioning devices are not used (Chapter 11).

Minimal access surgery employs four categories of instruments and equipment for the procedures:

- laparoscope with fiberoptic cable and light source
- video camera system
- instruments to assist with exposure
- instruments for hemostasis, dissection, and tissue removal

Laparoscope

The laparoscope is a lensed endoscope that is inserted through a small abdominal incision. Surgery is performed through one or more tubular sleeves that are passed through the abdominal wall at strategic locations within the view of the laparoscope.

Video Camera System

The images projected by the laparoscope's viewing area are very small and must be projected and enlarged to allow the surgeon to see adequately and perform the procedure safely. This is accomplished with a video camera system (VCS), which transmits the images viewed through the laparoscope to the video screen. The surgeon operates by viewing the screen; the scrub assistant anticipates the surgeon's needs by watching the image.

The three components of the system are the camera, control unit, and monitor. The camera has two parts: the endocoupler and the charged coupled devices (CCDs). The endocoupler contains the optical lenses, the focusing adjustment, and the coupling for gripping the endoscope.

The charged coupled devices are chips that produce the unprocessed video signal. Cameras may have one, two, or three chips; those with fewer chips are smaller; however, the color and image quality is inferior to the three-chip cameras. Three-chip cameras are necessary to use with microscopes, because the high magnification requires additional resolution.[5]

Many cameras are not compatible with lasers, especially neodymium:yttrium-aluminum-garnet lasers (Nd:YAG), or with CO_2 systems. The intense laser beam can damage the CCDs in unprotected cameras. The camera is used on the sterile field and, therefore, must be sterilized, according to the manufacturer's guidelines. Care must be exercised not to point the camera toward any high-intensity light source, such as the operating room lights, as permanent damage to the light-sensing element may result.[5] Troubleshooting suggestions for solving camera malfunctions are identified in Table 12–2.

The camera control unit allows the operator to adjust the image for color and light

TABLE 12–2. TROUBLE-SHOOTING PROBLEMS OF VIDEO CAMERA SYSTEMS

Problem	Possible Causes	Solutions
No power	Power switch off	Turn power on
	Power cord not plugged in	Plug cord in
	Circuit breaker tripped	Check circuit box
No picture	No power	Check above
	Equipment sequence incomplete	System will not work unless all components have power
		Check all components
	Camera placed on dark surface	Turn face of camera up
No sound	Microphone batery dead	Replace battery
	Microphone switch off	Turn switch on
	Audio cables incorrectly connected	Connect VCR audio "out" to monitor "in"
Poor light	Light bulb blown	Replace light bulb
	Fiberoptic light cable damaged	Replace cable
	Camera light sensor picking up glare from instruments	Reposition instruments
Foggy picture	Tissue or condensation on lens	Place tips of scope in warm water
	Smoke	Use suction
Picture will not focus	Cracked scope or camera lens	Send scope out for repair
	Coupling between eyepiece of scope and camera endocoupler loose	Tighten
Picture grainy	Loose cable connections	Tighten all cables
	Cable not grounded	Remove any cables not in use
Colors unnatural	Camera not white balanced	Follow procedure for white balancing
	Camera white balanced with filter on "off white" object used to white balance camera	Remove filter
		Use white object to white balance
	Monitor unbalanced	Use color bar switch on control unit or set to "reset"
Record button will not engage	No tape in VCR	Put tape in. Depress "record" and "play" simultaneously
Insufflator alarm sounds	CO_2 tubing blocked	Check tubing—crimped? stopcock turned off?
CO_2 leakage	CO_2 tubing blocked	Check tubing
	Stopcock partially closed	Open fully
	Incorrect size or faulty seals	Check size and seals
	Sleeve incorrectly reduced	Check reducer

Adapted from Fuller, J. Surgical Technology Principles and Practice, 3rd ed. (Philadelphia), W.B. Saunders, 1994. With permission.

intensity. It also connects the camera to the video monitor and the screen. The level of light required for a given procedure is related to the size of the cavity into which the scope is placed. Units that produce levels of light sufficient for surgical procedures can cause drapes to scorch or smolder and, therefore, should never be placed on the drapes for extended periods.

Video images can be recorded with a VCR, a video printer (Mavigraph), and a videodisc. The Mavigraph prints a hard copy that may be placed on the patient's chart; the other two systems store the image for retrieval at a later date.

The monitor is the screen component of the video camera system. It is usually a 20-inch screen with a higher resolution than the camera to ensure clarity. The monitor is mounted securely on a cart to avoid the unit's being knocked or bumped off the cart (Fig. 12–11).

The control unit and monitor should be kept clean and free of dust. Solutions should never be placed on top of the control unit as they may accidentally spill or be splashed onto the unit. All cables, connections, and cords should be routinely inspected for their integrity and stored to prevent kinking or bending.

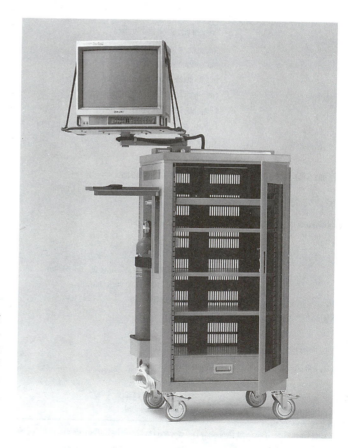

Figure 12–11. The video endoscopy cart makes working with video endoscopy equipment easier and more convenient. It features a sliding articulating arm that allows a TV monitor to be extended to either side of the cart, at any angle, making it ideal for procedures such as laparoscopic cholecystectomies. (Courtesy Sharn Inc., Tampa, FL.)

Instruments to Assist with Exposure

To prevent injury to abdominal structures during minimal access surgery and to facilitate visualization, the surgeon inflates the peritoneal cavity with carbon dioxide using a insufflation (pneumoperitoneum) needle. When carbon dioxide is used for insufflation, end tidal CO_2 is closely monitored due to the increased risk of hypercarbia. The patient is also observed for subcutaneous emphysema.[6] Hypothermia can also result from CO_2 insufflation, as heat loss from CO_2 is known to occur at a rate of 0.3°C per 40 to 50 L of infused gas.[7]

Insufflator equipment includes a disposable hydrophobic filter to prevent gas cylinder contaminants from flowing through the insufflator into the operative cavity. It is important that the filter be compatible with the insufflator so that it will not interfere with flow rate. Contaminants flow more readily when the volume of gas in the cylinder is low; therefore, replacing the cylinder before the gas level is low helps prevent contamination of the sterile field.[8] Cylinders with nonferrous internal surfaces or surfaces incapable of creating residual material, which may escape during the gaseous phase of delivery, may prevent the transfer of particulate matter.

The level of gas remaining in the cylinder may be monitored by tracking the number of times the cylinder is used and weighing the cylinder prior to each use.

When a pneumoperitoneum is established, the surgeon passes one or more trocars and sleeves through the abdominal wall. The trocar is then withdrawn, leaving the sleeve, through which the laparoscope or other instruments are passed. The instruments are used for cutting, dissection, suctioning and hemostasis. Trocars are available in variety of sizes and may be reusable or disposable. The disposable trocars are generally sharper than reusable ones, and their valves more efficient in preventing the escape of gas. The choice of size depends on the diameter of the laparoscope and instruments to be used for the procedure.

Instruments for Hemostasis, Dissection, and Tissue Removal

Hemostasis is achieved during laparoscopic surgery primarily by electrocautery, laser, or both. During electrosurgery tissue injury may occur outside the view of the scope because of three different types of "stray" energy: insulation failure, capacitive coupling, and direct coupling.

An unrecognized defect in the insulation surrounding the active electrode may lead to the undetected delivery of 100% of the ESU energy to a site outside the view of the scope. Repeated use of instruments may lead to insulation failure due to cracking of the insulation. Defects may be too small to be seen, even under a magnifying lens. Breaks in insulation may create an alternate route for the current to flow, and if the current is concentrated, significant patient injury may occur (Fig. 12–12).

In capacitive coupling, electrical energy is transferred through intact insulation into other nearby conductive materials. Some degree of capacitive coupling occurs with all standard monopolar electrosurgical instruments. Whether the "stray" energy of capacitive coupling causes clinical injury depends on the total amount of energy that is transferred by the capacitance, and the concentration of the current, or power density, as it makes its way back to the patient ground pad. The capacitive coupling or transfer of the current through

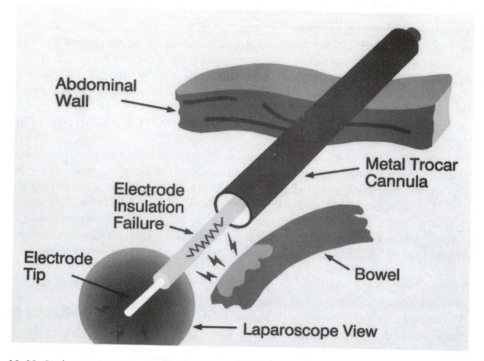

Figure 12–12. Breaks in insulation can create an alternate route for the current to flow. If this current is concentrated, it can cause significant injury to the patient. *(Courtesy Valleylab, Boulder, CO.)*

insulation is an induced current that occurs because of the electromagnetic field around an activated electrode.

The radio frequency (RF) current flowing intentionally through the active electrode, return electrode, and wires induces unintended RF currents on nearby conductors. The process, referred to as the capacitance effect, occurs without any direct electrical contact or breaks in the insulation[9] (Fig. 12–13).

An effective way to deal safely with the electrosurgical current that capacitively couples to the operative scope is to use a nonconductive, nonmetal, trocar sleeve either with or without plastic stability threads. The tissue of the abdominal wall in contact with the sleeve is of sufficiently large surface area that the portion of electrosurgical current that capacitively couples to the operative scope is continuously discharged safely to the abdominal wall with no burning of the tissue.[10]

Direct coupling refers to the condition where the activated electrode touches other metal instruments, especially the laparoscope within the abdomen, creating a situation whereby the energy can be transferred (coupled) directly from the electrode to the laparoscope (e.g., the bowl along its shaft) to tissue[9] (Fig. 12–14). To prevent this potential injury, a metal cannula without plastic stability threads may be used.

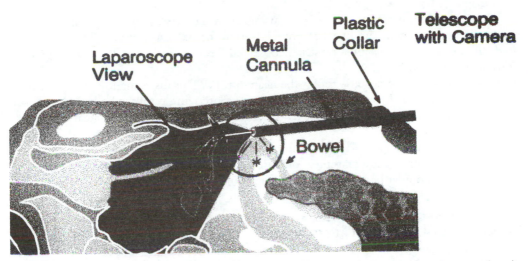

Figure 12–13. The capacitively coupled current may build up and exit to adjacent tissue on its way to the patient return electrode. *(Courtesy Valleylab, Boulder, CO.)*

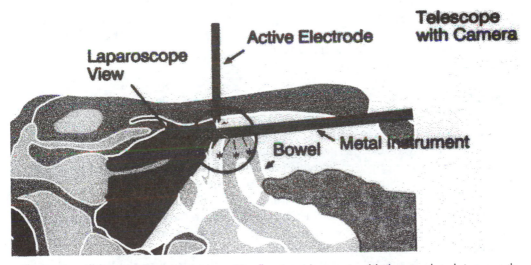

Figure 12–14. Direct coupling occurs when the user accidentally activates the generator while the active electrode is near another metal instrument. *(Courtesy Valleylab, Boulder, CO.)*

Some surgeons prefer using the laser during laparoscopic surgery as it provides a more precise area of treatment and may prevent inadvertent tissue destruction. When the laser is used, all safety precautions must be strictly observed (see the section on laser safety precautions later in this chapter).

Another type of hemostatic tool is the heater probe. This instrument generates heat at its tip to cauterize small vessels and is excellent for cauterizing capillary beds such as those on the surface of the liver. It does not use electric current as the source of heat; therefore, arcing is not a danger.

Dissection, clamping, and cutting instruments are available in a variety of types and sizes. These instruments are extremely delicate and must be handled carefully. Disposable instruments are popular because they retain their cutting edge and do not require cleaning and reprocessing.

Learning the Skills of Minimal Access Surgery

Minimal access surgery involves difficult techniques and not all surgeons are able to master the skills. The techniques are taught in laboratories, many sponsored by manufacturers, and then applied in the clinical setting. Most facilities require that surgeons produce a certificate indicating that they have attended one of these courses. In addition, a specific number of cases must be monitored/proctored by an appropriate physician before the surgeon may independently perform minimal access surgery.

Before performing the surgery, team members should do a "dry run," which will familiarize them with the room layout, equipment, and instrumentation. Technology concerns may be addressed at this time rather than when a patient is on the operating room table, thus saving valuable time and resources.

▌ LASERS

LASER is an acronym: Light Amplification by Stimulated Emission of Radiation. The laser is a device that converts electrical energy to light energy. The light that the laser produces is unique, characterized by very desirable properties; it is impossible to obtain the light by any means other than the laser. Light waves stimulate molecules to generate additional light waves, which if allowed to continue will generate millions of similar waves until an intense beam of light is created. The reaction of this light to biologic tissue varies according to absorption propensities, power settings on the laser, time of exposure, and size of the target tissue.

When a laser beam strikes tissue, one of four reactions occurs: the beam is absorbed, reflected, scattered, or transmitted. Only beams that are absorbed will affect tissues.

Laser Technology

Absorption. Absorption occurs when the beam is strongly absorbed by the target with little or no scatter and tissue damage is precisely confined. Laser beams are absorbed by tissue according to the pigment content of the tissue. For example, melanin and hemoglobin absorb the wavelength of argon lasers. The laser may be used to coagulate small blood vessels because its blue-green beam is absorbed by the red pigment of hemoglobin.

Reflection. The laser beam is reflected when it hits a shiny metal instrument or a mirror and the direction of the beam is changed. Laser light can intentionally be reflected in this manner to impact hard to reach areas. Because this type of reflection presents a safety concern, the light must be controlled at all times.

Scattering. Scattering occurs when the beam's heat is widely diffused in tissue; the light has a wider effect than appears on the surface of the tissue. The Nd:YAG laser beam is not absorbed well by tissue and has considerable scattering effect.

Transmission Transmission occurs when the laser beam penetrates tissue with minimal effect, passes through the tissue, and impacts the underlying tissue. For example, the argon beam passes through the eye's clear vitreous and is absorbed by the hemoglobin in the blood vessels behind of the eye.

How Lasers Operate

The effects of laser beams on tissue are vaporization (cutting and tissue evaporation) and coagulation (hemostasis and necrosis). When the laser beam touches tissue, the laser energy is absorbed heating the water in the cell. Intracellular protein is destroyed. As the temperature rises, intracellular water turns into steam and carbon. The cell membrane ruptures from the increased pressure and cellular debris and plume (laser smoke) are released from the tissue. The degree of damage to adjacent tissue, which is also heated, depends on the duration of its exposure to the laser.[11]

All lasers have the three following components:

- an active laser medium (liquid, solid, gas, or a semiconductor)
- an excitation, or pumping, mechanism
- a resonant cavity

The excitation mechanism gives the atoms in the lasing medium additional energy. The mechanism may be an electrical discharge current running through a gas, another laser stimulating the medium, a flash lamp, or a chemical reaction with the medium itself.

The resonant cavity is the tube containing the lasing medium with a mirror at each end. The mirrors reflect the protons back through the medium, stimulating the release of protons and amplifying the light. The totally reflecting mirror on one end and the partially reflective mirror on the other end of the cavity must be precisely aligned to create beams with parallel axes (Fig. 12–15).

The types of laser are gas, solid, semiconductor, excimer, solid state, and dye. They are also distinguished by the functional or biophysical reaction created in the target tissue. The two types of reactions are thermal dissolution and photodynamic destruction. To treat patients, the thermal reactive types are used. They include the carbon dioxide, argon, krypton (KTP), and Nd:YAG lasers.

Lasers have different modes of operation: continuous wave, pulsed wave, or Q-switched. In the continuous mode the laser beams are constant and the power delivered to

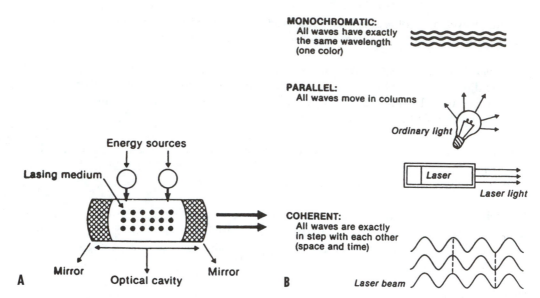

Figure 12–15. Laser. **A.** Main components of a laser. **B.** Basic characteristics of a laser. *(From Fuller, J. Surgical Technology: Principles and Practice, 3rd ed. Philadelphia, W. B. Saunders, 1994. With permission.)*

the tissue does not vary. Pulsed wave lasers produce beams in small bursts that can be controlled by the user. Both the continuous wave and pulsed wave lasers may be operated in a Q-switched, or giant pulse, mode. To achieve the giant pulse mode an optical element is placed in the resonant cavity, allowing the energy level to build up. When the shutter is opened, a giant pulse is released with a resulting brief, powerful burst.

Laser beams may be delivered by either direct optic or fiberoptic systems. Direct optic systems use mirrors and lenses to direct laser beams. The highly collimated beam emerges from the laser, travels through articulated arms (hollow tubes and mirrors connected in a manner that maintains the alignment of the laser beam), and is focused at a specific spot.

On the other hand, fiberoptic systems consist of thin, flexible fibers that carry optical energy along their paths. They produce a less coherent laser beam than a direct optic system. This divergent beam is refocused with a lens placed at the end of the fiber. The sharpness of focus depends on the size of the optical fiber.

Types of Lasers

Gas Lasers. The CO_2 *laser medium* is a combination of helium, nitrogen, and carbon dioxide. The beam is invisible to the human eye. A helium-neon laser beam is used in conjunction with the CO_2 beam to permit the surgeon to see where the CO_2 beam will be in contact with the tissue. The CO_2 *laser* beam is absorbed by water and thus it reacts with all tissue. The amount of water in the tissue determines how rapidly the beam is absorbed. For example, fat tissue absorbs the beam quickly, whereas bone takes a long time to absorb the beam. For that reason, the laser is generally not used for bone resections. The carbon dioxide laser beam can be finely focused to make precision cuts, or defocused to perform epithelial peeling of superficial skin lesions.

The *argon laser* produces a visible blue-green beam that is readily absorbed by blood, red-brown tissue, and melanin. The argon beam is not absorbed by clear or translucent tissue and, therefore, passes through the cornea, vitreous, and lens of the eye without creating a thermal effect.

Solid State Laser. The *neodymium:yttrium-aluminum-garnet laser* has crystals that are similar to artificial diamonds. The beam is infrared and thus invisible to the human eye. This laser uses a spot beam of helium-neon to locate the Nd:YAG beam. The thermal energy of the Nd:YAG laser is nonspecific, as it is absorbed by both pigmented and nonpigmented tissue. It has the greatest penetration depth of all lasers, making it ideal for deep tissue coagulation and vaporization.

Liquid Dye Lasers. The active medium in the dye laser is an organic dye dissolved in an alcoholic solvent in a specific molar concentration. The solution is placed in a small-diameter glass tube and illuminated by a flash-lamp or another laser. By using different types of dyes these lasers can be tuned over a wide wavelength and the laser beam can be matched to the individual lesion. These lasers are used in conjunction with photoactive drugs in photodynamic therapy and in diagnostic procedures, such as spectroscopy (Table 12–3).

Nursing Care of the Patient Requiring Laser Intervention

The nursing process discussed in Chapter 5 is the standard of care that applies to the patient requiring laser intervention. Of particular concern during the assessment phase is de-

TABLE 12–3. TYPES OF LASERS

Laser Medium	Wavelength (Microns)	Significant Properties and Action	Medical Use	Delivery System
Argon	0.48	Absorbed by pigment tissue (red-brown) Coagulation, sealing	Ophthalmology Dermatology Gastroenterology Otology	Hollow tube with mirrors or fiberoptic cable
Dye	630	Photosensitizing	Photodynamic therapy for cancer	Fiberoptic cable
Nd:YAG	1.06	Nonspecific absorption Deep coagulation	Gastroenterology Pulmonology Ophthalmology Urology Gynecology	Fiberoptic cable
CO_2	10.6	Highly absorbed by water Vaporization, coagulation, sealing, drilling	Gynecology Rhinolaryngology Neurosurgery Dermatology	Hollow tube with mirrors Fiberoptic cable

termining body size, the patient's perception of the technology, and the patient's knowledge of the treatment, as well as preoperative instructions. Body size is important, as deviations from standard-size instruments and equipment may be required. The patient's perceptions regarding laser surgery and the procedure that is planned are assessed. At this time, ample time remains to answer questions, address concerns, and clarify misperceptions regarding the treatment. In addition to routine preoperative instructions, patients are instructed regarding any special precautions they should take related to the use of the laser. For example, patients having laser therapy above the shoulder area should be instructed not to use hair spray before the procedure, as the spray is highly flammable.

Postoperatively the patient should receive written discharge instructions that are specific to the laser procedure, as well as conventional instructions.

Laser Safety Precautions

In addition to the intraoperative planning and nursing actions implemented during conventional invasive treatments, the use of lasers requires implementing several safety measures to protect the patient and surgical team members from injury. The following precautions are AORN's Recommended Practices for Laser Safety in the Practice Setting.[12]

- The room identified for laser use should have adequate amperage to meet the power requirements of the specific laser. Failure to provide significant power can trip the circuit breakers that serve other rooms.
- "WARNING" signs should be displayed at all entrances to the areas where lasers are used. The sign should be designed according to the American National Standards Institute, Inc. and the American National Standards for the Safe Use of Lasers. A pair of protective glasses may be hung next to the warning sign outside the room for persons to put on before entering the laser area.
- All viewing windows in the rooms where the lasers are used should provide adequate protection specific to the laser wavelength.
- The laser key should never be left *in the laser* during storage. Controlled access to the laser key must be maintained.
- When the laser is set up and not being used, the controls should be set to "standby," "wait," or "disable" to prevent inadvertent activation.
- The foot pedal should be operated only by the surgeon when the laser is being used, not by the assistant or scrub person. Assistants should activate all other pedals such as the bipolar or electrosurgery unit. If the surgeon must use other pedals, such as the microscope, that pedal should be placed behind him or her.
- Dull, ebonized, or nonreflective anodized instruments should be used near the laser site to decrease the amount of direct laser beam reflection and beam scatter.
- Patients and team members should be protected from inhaling the plume and noxious fumes associated with lasers; a mechanical smoke evacuator system that has a high-efficiency filter is used (see Chapter 7). Instruments that assist in evacuating smoke, such as speculums with a second portal for suctioning or endoscopes with additional evaluation portals, should be used.
- High-filtration surgical masks for laser use should be worn during procedures that produce plume.

- Laser-safe eye protection with appropriate wavelength and optical density should be worn by all team members. Each type of laser requires a different type of eye protection; therefore, it is important that glasses be labeled to protect against improper use.
- The patient's eyes and eyelids should be protected from the laser beam. If the patient is awake he or she should wear appropriately labeled eye wear. The anesthetized patient's eyelids should be closed and taped, or closed, covered with saline-moistened pads or other nonflammable material, and taped. For procedures immediately around the eye or on the eyelid, protective eyeshields or scleral shields are used.
- Flammable or combustible anesthetics, prep solutions, drying agents, ointments, plastic resins, or plastics should not be used near the laser site. The intense heat of the laser beam can ignite combustible-flammable solids, liquids, and gases. Prep solutions that are allowed to pool can retain laser heat and burn tissue.
- Only moistened, reusable or disposable fabrics, and/or laser-retardant drapes are used to drape the operative site.
- When thermally intensive lasers are used, exposed tissues around the operative site should be protected with saline- or water-saturated towels or sponges. The solution absorbs or disperses the energy of the beam in areas not intended for laser application; therefore, the towels are remoistened periodically to ensure proper protection. An irrigating syringe filled with sterile saline should always be available. Saline may be needed to cool the thermally involved tissue directly.
- When a laser is used in the rectal area, a wet pack may be inserted into the rectum to provide a tamponade that will prevent the escape of methane gas from the rectum into the surgical area causing an explosion. If a sponge is used for this pack it must be included in the count to prevent its being inadvertently left in place following surgery.
- A basin of water or saline should be readily available in case of a fire within the sterile field. A halon fire extinguisher should also be available for laser fires to prevent harm to the optics or delicate circuits of the laser.
- During laser surgery involving the aerodigestive tract, laser-safe endotracheal tubes are used. The endotracheal tube cuff should be inflated with saline and protected with wet gauze sponges.

Safety is the most critical factor in the use of any type of laser. A comprehensive laser safety program should include a safety committee with one person assuming the responsibilities of laser safety officer. A member of the team must be available for all laser procedures in addition to the scrub assistant and the circulating nurse. The laser team member is responsible for keeping the laser on inactive status when it is not actually being used, adjusting the laser modes and pulse durations as directed during the procedure, and ensuring that all the policies and procedures for safe practice are adhered to by all team members.

Following the completion of a case, the laser team member and the scrub assistant are responsible for disassembling and cleaning the appropriate parts, checking their functioning, and storing the laser in the appropriate location.

Laser instruments require protective processing. Caution must be taken to prevent striking them together or tumbling them excessively in their containers. To maintain the refractive safety features, it is essential that care be taken to avoid scratching and pitting the instrument's surface. The instruments should be kept in sterilizing trays that have protective inserts.

In addition to routine documentation, laser safety is important to record for medical-legal reasons. Documentation may be in a laser log or part of the intraoperative patient notes. It should include the type of laser used, the operator's name, type of procedure, power settings, time of exposure, the mode of exposure (continuous, pulse, auto-repeat), and all safety precautions and patient protective activities taken during the procedure.

∎ REFERENCES

1. Crawford M. Surgical instruments in America. *AORN J.* 1976; 24(1):152.
2. Use and care of endoscopes. In *Standards and Recommended Practices.* Denver: AORN; 1995:163–167.
3. Rutala W. APIC guidelines for selection and use of disinfectants. *Am J Infect Control.* 1990; 19:99–117.
4. Recommended practices for endoscopic minimal access surgery. In *Standards and Recommended Practices.* Denver: AORN; 1995:169–174.
5. O'Connell W. Video technology. *AORN J.* 1992; 56(3):442–454.
6. Williams M, Murr P. Laparoscopic insufflation of the abdomen depresses cardiopulmonary function. *Surg Endos.* 1993; 7:12–16.
7. Ott D. Laposcopic hypothermia. *J Laparoendosc Surg.* 1991; 1:127–131.
8. ECRI. Entry of abdominal fluids into the laparoscopic insufflators (abstract). *Hazard.* 1992; 21:180–181.
9. Voyles C, Tucker R. Education and engineering solutions for potential problems with laparoscopic monopolar electrosurgery. *Am J Surg.* 1992; 164(7):57–62.
10. Ball K. Laser versus electrosurgery: What to use in laparoscopy. *Minimally Invasive Surgical Nursing.* 1994; 8(1):19–20.
11. Ball K. *Lasers: The Perioperative Challenge,* 2nd ed. St. Louis: C. V. Mosby; 1994.
12. Recommended practices for laser safety in the practice setting. In *Standards and Recommended Practices.* Denver: AORN; 1995:211–215.

THIRTEEN

Hemostasis

▮ INCISION SITES

The most important factors determining where an incision is to be made are the patient's diagnosis and the pathology the surgeon expects to encounter. Other important considerations are maximum exposure, ease of extending the incision, ease of closure, minimum postoperative discomfort, maximum postoperative wound strength, and cosmetic effect. In emergencies, the ease and speed of entering the affected area is a factor. Figure 13–1 indicates frequently used incision sites and the types of surgical procedures for which each is used.

▮ HEMOSTASIS

Hemostasis is the arrest or control of bleeding. It occurs by the natural clotting of blood, by artificial means, or by a combination of the two. Hemostasis during surgical intervention is essential to prevent hemorrhage, facilitate visualization of the surgical field, and promote wound healing.

Natural Physiologic Hemostasis

Blood clotting is a defense mechanism whereby the soluble blood protein, fibrinogen, is changed into the insoluble protein, fibrin. Exactly how it occurs is not known, but five known blood components take part in the reaction: prothrombin, factor V, thromboplastin, calcium, and fibrinogen. The data below demonstrate the basic chemical reactions in blood clotting.

$$\text{Prothrombin} + \text{``Factor V''} \xrightarrow{\text{(Thromboplastin, CA}^{++})} \text{Thrombin}$$

$$\text{Fibrinogen} \xrightarrow{\text{(Thrombin)}} \text{Fibrin}$$

Basic chemical reactions in blood clotting: Prothrombin and Factor V react with thromboplastin and calcium ions in the blood to form thrombin; thrombin unites with fibrogen to form fibrin.

Platelets adhere to the endothelial lining of a blood vessel when the lining becomes "roughened" by cutting or bruising. The platelets start to disintegrate. Thromboplastin is

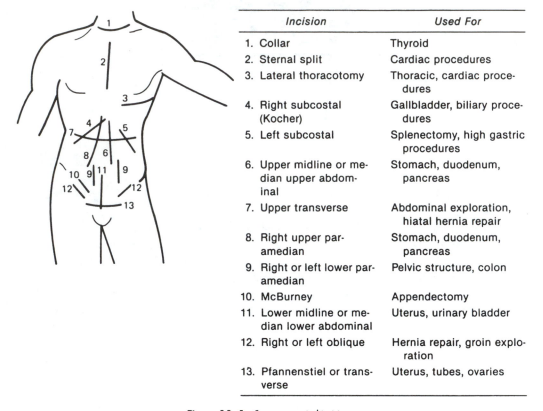

Incision	Used For
1. Collar	Thyroid
2. Sternal split	Cardiac procedures
3. Lateral thoracotomy	Thoracic, cardiac proce-dures
4. Right subcostal (Kocher)	Gallbladder, biliary proce-dures
5. Left subcostal	Splenectomy, high gastric procedures
6. Upper midline or me-dian upper abdom-inal	Stomach, duodenum, pancreas
7. Upper transverse	Abdominal exploration, hiatal hernia repair
8. Right upper par-amedian	Stomach, duodenum, pancreas
9. Right or left lower par-amedian	Pelvic structure, colon
10. McBurney	Appendectomy
11. Lower midline or me-dian lower abdominal	Uterus, urinary bladder
12. Right or left oblique	Hernia repair, groin explo-ration
13. Pfannenstiel or trans-verse	Uterus, tubes, ovaries

Figure 13–1. Common surgical incisions.

released from disintegrating platelets and the injured tissue cells. The thromboplastin enters the blood and forms thrombin.

Prothrombin and factor V, both globulins, are formed by the liver. Vitamin K catalyzes the synthesis of prothrombin. Because vitamin K is fat-soluble, its absorption depends on the presence of adequate amounts of bile in the intestinal tract. Patients with bile duct obstructions or liver diseases may not synthesize enough prothrombin, and a bleeding tendency results. These patients may receive an injection of vitamin K preoperatively.

Fibrinogen, also a globulin, is formed by the liver. Only in rare instances of extreme liver damage is fibrinogen so deficient that clotting is hindered. Calcium ions come from ingested foods; blood always contains enough calcium to catalyze the clotting reaction.

Artificial Methods of Hemostasis

Instruments. Clamping the end of a bleeding vessel with a hemostat is the most common method of achieving hemostasis. It stops the flow of blood until the vessel is ligated (tied) or pressure applied. The vessel may be ligated with a free tie or a suture ligature (transfixion suture). A suture ligature is accomplished by pushing a needle holder with a needle and suture material through a piece of tissue and then tying the suture around the vessel's end.

Pressure. Manual pressure may be applied directly on small vessels to delay bleeding until the blood begins to form a clot. When sponging an area with a gauze sponge or sponge stick, light pressure applied and released helps in identifying the source of bleeding.

Heat. Heat speeds up the clotting mechanism by dilating the vessels and allowing more blood to get to the area. Platelets and tissues are thereby stimulated to liberate more thromboplastin.

Bonewax. Bonewax (refined beeswax) is used to control bone marrow oozing. It is frequently used in neurosurgery and orthopedic surgery. Pieces of bonewax are rolled into balls and handed to the surgeon for application to the bone.

Ligating Clips. Ligating clips (small clips made of tantalum or stainless steel) are used to ligate arteries, veins, or nerves. Serrations across the wire prevent them from slipping off the vessel. The clips are various sizes with applicators and are also used to mark biopsy sites and tumor margins. This allows visualization of the x-ray film to detect postoperative complications and to observe the size of the tumor.

Tourniquets. Tourniquets are used on the extremities to prevent the flow of blood to a designated area, thereby conserving the patient's blood volume and creating a bloodless field. Following the release of the tourniquet, the bleeding must be controlled.

Tourniquet systems consist of compressed air or gas from a portable canister, tank, or piped-in system. The portable systems are mounted on stands or IV poles. Recent tourniquet technology includes an automated computerized microprocessor that performs self-calibration, displays elapsed inflation time, and has an audible alarm that signals when predefined parameters are not met.

The manufacturer's guidelines must be followed in applying the tourniquet. Prior to applying the tourniquet, the patient's skin may need to be protected with a stockinette or cotton padding; the tourniquet is then applied directly over the padding. Some tourniquet technology does not require padding, as it interferes with the Velcro and reduces the effectiveness of the closure. Selection of the proper tourniquet cuff is determined by the patient's age, anatomy, and medical condition. Proper fit entails measuring the circumference of the limb and selecting a cuff length that allows overlap. The ideal overlap is 3 inches; the maximum is 6 inches. If the ends overlap too much they will roll or wrinkle the underlying soft tissue and increase the pressure to the area of overlap. The shape of the limb also is a consideration. A contour cuff may be more appropriate than a straight cylindrical cuff on a tapered limb that is muscular or obese because patient comfort would be enhanced and the risk of sheering would be reduced.[1]

As wide a cuff as possible is selected, as a wide bladder occludes blood flow at a lower pressure. The potential for nerve damage is affected by the width of the cuff in relation to the size of the limb, the amount of soft tissue between the cuff and nerve, and the degree and duration of cuff pressure. On an upper extremity, the tourniquet cuff should be placed proximal to the extremity because more of soft tissue is in this area to provide padding for underlying nerves and blood vessels. A tourniquet applied to a lower extremity should be applied to the proximal third of the thigh to avoid vulnerable neurovascular structures.

To drain venous blood from the limb, the extremity is elevated and wrapped with a rubber bandage; the tourniquet is then rapidly inflated. Inflation pressure depends on the patient's age, systolic blood pressure, and limb circumference, and on the width of the cuff. The minimum pressure that will produce a bloodless field is an appropriate guideline. In an average adult this pressure may be 50 to 75 mm Hg above the patient's systolic pressure for an upper extremity and 100 to 150 mm Hg above systolic pressure for a lower extremity.

Complete exsanguination prolongs pain-free tourniquet time. Rapid inflation of the cuff will occlude arteries and veins simultaneously and avoid return of blood to the limb. Thus, superficial veins are not filled before the arterial blood flow is occluded.[2] A rubber bandage is not used for a patient with a traumatic injury or a patient who was recently in a cast. Thrombi, if present, could become dislodged and result in emboli. Exsanguination is done without using an elastic bandage if infection is present or a painful fracture or amputation due to a malignancy has occurred.[3] The use of a pneumatic tourniquet is contraindicated for patients with vascular disease or poor peripheral circulation.

There is no rule stating how long a tourniquet may be safely inflated. Use of the tourniquet is always kept to a minimum. If it is kept on too long, tourniquet paralysis may result. Other complications of prolonged tourniquet time include tissue damage and compartment syndrome. The duration of tourniquet time is determined by the patient's age and the presence or absence of vascular disease in the limb.[2] For an average healthy adult younger than 50 years, it is preferable not to leave the tourniquet inflated on an arm longer than 1 hour, or on a thigh longer than 1 to 2 hours.[3] If the operation requires more time, the tourniquet is deflated for 10 minutes, and the limb exsanguinated again before reinflation. The circulating nurse should inform the surgeon of the tourniquet time at regular intervals.

Documentation in the patient's record of tourniquet use should include: cuff location and pressure, time of inflation and deflation, skin and tissue integrity under the cuff before and after tourniquet use, assessment and evaluation of the entire extremity, name of person who applied the cuff, and identification or serial number and model of the specific tourniquet.

When prepping patients with tourniquets, care must be exercised to prevent solutions from leaking under the tourniquet, as a chemical skin burn may result.

Tourniquet gauges should be checked for accuracy according to the manufacturer's guidelines. During use, the gauge should be clearly visible and checked frequently, as nerve damage may result from either excessive or insufficient tourniquet pressure.

After each use the cuff and bladder should be cleaned, dried, and rinsed according to the level of contamination, following the manufacturer's guidelines. If blood or other body fluid comes in contact with the cuff, an enzymatic detergent is used to remove blood. The cuff should then be washed, dried, and sterilized.

If the bladder is removed, care must be taken to prevent introducing water into the bladder through the ports, as water in the port can result in microbial growth. Subsequent deflation of wet bladders may cause minute droplets of water to be forced back into the tourniquet-regulating mechanism.[2] All the connecting tubing should be wiped with a hospital-grade chemical germicide and dried prior to storage.

Thrombostat. Thrombostat (thrombin, USP) is an enzyme extracted from dried beef blood. It unites with fibrinogen to accelerate the coagulation of blood and to contain capillary bleeding. It is supplied as a powder and may be applied on the surface of bleeding tissue as a solution or powder. Solutions are prepared in sterile distilled water or isotonic saline just prior to use, and they are appropriately labeled. The solution may be placed in a syringe and used as a spray by attaching a cannula or spray nozzle to the syringe.

Thrombostat may also be applied using an absorbable gelatin sponge. The sponge is immersed in a solution of Thrombostat, and the scrub assistant kneads the sponge to remove trapped air and facilitate saturation of the sponge. The saturated sponge is applied to the bleeding area.

Thrombostat must never be injected or allowed to enter large vessels because extensive intravascular clotting may occur.

Gelatin Sponge. A gelatin sponge (Gelfoam) is made from a specially cured gelatin solution beaten to a foamy consistency, dried, and sterilized. The sponge is dipped in saline or a solution containing epinephrine or Thrombostat and then placed on the bleeding area. Fibrin is deposited in the interstices of the sponge, and the sponge swells as it absorbs 45 times its own weight in blood. Because the gelatin sponge increases in size with absorption of blood and clot formation, unwanted pressure may be exerted in a confined space, for example, during neurosurgical procedures. In such cases, the scrub assistant asks the surgeon if the sponge will be left in place. If the sponge is left, documentation on the intraoperative record should include the site and approximate size of the sponge. When the gelatin sponge is implanted, it will be absorbed in 20 to 40 days.

A gelatin sponge is not used in the presence of infection, biliary drainage, or intestinal spillage, because the sponge may provide a focus for later infection. It is not used in closing skin edges because it may interfere with wound healing.

Gelatin sponges are available as compressed sheets, powder, film, and a cone. The cone is specifically made to work with the Foley catheter to control postprostatectomy bleeding. The cone may be left in the prostatic bed after the Foley catheter is removed. The sheets may be cut to the appropriate size without crumbling.

Absorbable gelatin sponges and powder products cannot be resterilized. They are stored at room temperature, and the opened unused portions discarded at the end of the surgical procedure.

Oxidized Cellulose. Oxidized cellulose (Oxycel, Surgicel) is a specially treated gauze or cotton that is placed directly over the bleeding area. It absorbs an amount of blood seven to eight times its own weight and forms coagulum. The hemostatic activity results from the coagulum and the pressure of the swelling cellulose.

The hemostatic effect of oxidized cellulose is greater when it is applied dry; therefore, it is not moistened with water or saline.

Oxidized cellulose may be left in situ, as it is absorbed in 7 to 14 days with minimal tissue reaction. When it is used to help achieve hemostasis around the spinal cord or the optic nerve and its chiasm, it must always be removed when hemostasis is achieved, as the swelling of the cellulose could exert unwanted pressure on these structures. When used on bone it must also be removed, as it may interfere with bone regeneration. When it is applied to surface wounds, the oxidized cellulose product may cause a burning and stinging sensation due to its low pH.

Opened, unused oxidized cellulose must be discarded because resterilization results in the physical breakdown of the product.

Microfibrillar Collagen Hemostat. Microfibrillar collagen hemostat (MCH) is an absorbable topical hemostatic agent prepared from purified bovine dermis collagen. It achieves hemostasis by the adhesion of platelets and the formation of thrombi in the interstices of the collagen. MCH does not interfere with bone growth and is an excellent product to use to control oozing from vascular anastomotic sites. Because MCH adheres to wet gloves and instruments, dry, smooth forceps are used to apply the powder or sponge directly to the source of bleeding. It is then necessary to apply pressure over the site with a dry sponge. How long the pressure is applied will vary with the force and severity of bleeding. After several minutes, the excess MCH should be teased away. If breakthrough bleeding occurs, more of the substance may be applied.

An alternative method of applying MCH involves cutting off the tip of a syringe, removing the plunger, packing the syringe two-thirds full with MCH, and then replacing the plunger. The contents are then compressed, yielding a wafer of MCH. MCH can be inserted between a fold of oxidized regenerated cellulose to form a sandwich, thereby enabling easier delivery of MCH to the bleeding site. MCH may be left in place and is usually absorbed within 84 days of implantation.

MCH should not be spilled on nonbleeding surfaces, as it may increase the rate of adhesion formation. In addition, MCH is not to be used with autologous blood salvage units.

Because MCH may not be resterilized, unused portions are discarded.

Instat. Instat is a hemostat material that is an absorbable collagen sheet of bovine dermal origin. It conforms to bleeding surfaces but does not adhere to gloves or instruments when wet with blood. Hemostasis is usually achieved in 1 to 4 minutes. Adverse reactions include adhesion formation, allergic reactions, and foreign body reactions. When used in contaminated wounds Instat may enhance infection.

Helistat. Helistat is an absorbable collagen sponge made from the bovine deep flexor tendon. Its mode of action and adverse reactions are the same as Instat. An additional adverse effect is that it reduces the bonding strength of methylmethacrylate when used to attach prosthetic devices to bony surfaces. Collagen sponges are not used in skin closure.

Styptic. A styptic is an astringent that arrests bleeding. One category of styptics includes chemicals that constrict blood vessels. Two examples are epinephrine and tannic acid.

Epinephrine may be added to a local anesthetic agent to prolong the drug's action and to decrease bleeding when the incision is made. Epinephrine 1:1000 may also be used to soak gelatin sponges prior to applying them to bleeding surfaces.

Tannic acid is a powder used on the mucous membranes of the nose and throat to control capillary bleeding.

Sponges. Sponges of various sizes are used to control capillary oozing, wall off the viscera, and keep tissue moist. When sponges are used to control capillary oozing, they are moistened with hot saline, placed on the tissue, and pressure is applied. When used to wall off the viscera, it is essential that the scrub assistant maintain an accurate account of the number used to ensure that all sponges are removed prior to the closure. This may be accomplished by setting aside an equal number of empty suture packs or instruments. Gauze 4 × 4 sponges may be unfolded into single thickness and used for "blunt finger dissection" in the perineal area, or they may be folded into 2 × 2 squares and used on a sponge forceps. Because these sponges can easily be lost in the wound, they are not used as free sponges in large wounds.

Compressed rayon or cotton "patties" with strings are commercially available in assorted sizes (Fig. 13–2). They are used to sponge delicate tissues, such as the spinal cord or brain. Before the patties are used, they are moistened in saline and excess moisture is pressed out between the fingers. If the patties are cut, they must be accounted for in their entirety during the sponge count.

Cotton-filled gauze balls or heavy cotton tape is available for dissection or to absorb fluids. These sponges are always used on a sponge stick or a Pean clamp.

All sponges and patties used on the operative field must be labeled x-ray detectable or radiopaque. Sponges are manufactured with a small radiopaque insert sewn into the material, or they are impregnated with a radiopaque substance such as barium sulfate. Radiography can then be used to locate sponges or patties.

Each size and type of sponge should be kept separate from the other sponges and from the linen to prevent their being inadvertently carried into the wound. X-ray detectable sponges are never used for dressings.

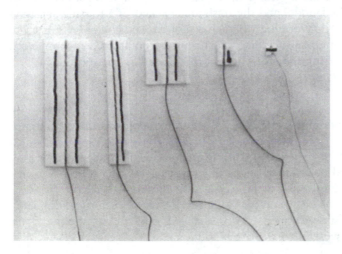

Figure 13–2. Compressed rayon or cotton patties are available in assorted sizes with strings.

Sponge count. The scrub personnel and circulating nurse count all sponges before an operation. The scrub person separates each sponge and counts audibly with the circulator who records the number and type of sponges on the count sheet or count board. Sponges placed on the sterile field during the surgical procedure are counted and recorded following the procedure. If the package does not contain the appropriate number of sponges, the sponges are handed off the sterile field, placed in a bag, and marked with the number. Some institutions may require that they be immediately removed from the room.

As the surgical procedure progresses, soiled sponges are discarded into a polyethylene-lined kick bucket. A sponge forceps or disposable gloves are used to handle the soiled sponges. The discarded sponges are then secured in a clear polyethylene bag according to the type and the number contained in the original package. The bags are then placed in an area of the room where the anesthesiologist observes the contents to ascertain the patient's blood loss. As the sponges are bagged, they are subtracted from the count sheet on the board. When sponges are used to pack a wound, the scrub person should inform the circulator of the number used so that the number can be recorded with the sponge count.

The first count of closure occurs when the surgeon begins to close the incision. All soiled sponges are discarded for the circulating nurse to count and bag; the sponges remaining on the field are then counted audibly by the scrub person and the circulator. The number of sponges bagged or in the kick bucket and the number remaining on the sterile field should equal the initial count plus any sponges added during the surgical procedure.

If the count does balance, the circulating nurse informs the surgeon, "The first count is correct." The second count begins with the skin closure and uses this same procedure. If the count is correct, the surgeon is informed, and the count is documented on the intra-operative nurse's note.

A third count is performed when a body organ (such as the bladder or the uterus) is opened but not removed. This count is taken before closing the organ.

Linen and waste containers are never removed from the operating room until all counts are completed.

If the count is inaccurate, a recount of all sponges not bagged is performed. If the count remains incorrect, the circulating nurse opens all the bags and recounts the discarded sponges. If necessary, the laundry and the trash are checked. If a missing sponge is not found, an x-ray is required to determine whether or not the missing sponge is in the patient. If the sponge is not found, an incident report must be completed, documenting all the steps taken to find the missing sponge. The report is signed by the surgeon and circulating nurse.

Weighing Sponges. Weighing sponges is one way to assess blood loss and to accurately identify the amount of blood that needs to be replaced. Sponges are routinely weighed for pediatric, elderly, and critically ill patients, and during extensive surgical procedures. A scale calculated in grams is used to weigh sponges; 1 g equals 1 cc. The scale platform is covered with wax paper or plastic sheeting to protect it from contamination.

Each type of sponge is weighed dry, and that weight is posted in each operating room or attached to the scale. If the sponges are used dry, the weight of the dry sponge is subtracted from the blood-soaked weight to calculate blood loss.

If the sponges are used wet, the weight of the wet sponges should be calculated for each case because varying amounts of solution will be removed by each individual when wringing out the sponges. One of each type of sponge is wrung out by the scrub person and handed off the field for the circulating nurse to use as a baseline weight. The weight of the wet sponge is then subtracted from that of the blood-soaked sponge to determine the amount of blood in the sponge. Sponges are weighed frequently, because when they dry out they do not accurately reflect the blood loss.

To assess the amount of blood lost in suction, the irrigating solution used is subtracted from the total amount of liquid in the suction bottle. In addition, the amount of blood on the drapes is estimated and added to the total. The total blood loss is kept accurately and recorded in the full view of the anesthesiologist and the surgeon.

While accurate accounting of blood loss is essential, one of the goals in surgery is to minimize blood loss. The invention of the Bovie unit (electrosurgery) allowed surgeons to perform more extensive surgery while minimizing the loss of blood.

▌ ELECTROSURGERY

In the 1920s, as surgical techniques began to expand, an electrosurgical unit was developed in the United States that incorporated grounded technology; a grounded generator took grounded wall current and increased the frequency. When the current entered the patient's body, it was assumed that the patient-return electrode would be the path of least resistance to ground; however, the patient could be touching several grounded objects, such as the OR table or EKG electrodes. If one of these objects is more conductive than the patient-return electrode, the current will select it as the pathway to ground, at which point current concentration may lead to an alternate-site burn. With current division, the current completes the circuit to ground whether it travels the intended electrosurgical circuit to the patient-return electrode or to an alternate site. Patients are exposed to the risk of alternate site burns because the current always follows the easiest, most conductive path; ground itself, not the generator, completes the circuit, and an operating room offers many alternative routes to ground.

In the 1970s, solid-state electrosurgical units became available. They use transistors, diodes, and rectifiers to generate the current. Most electrosurgical units (ESU) are now isolated generators, and the circuit path goes from the active terminal through the pencil, out through the dispersive, or ground, pad, and back to the ESU. The isolated generator isolates the therapeutic current from ground by referencing it within the generator circuitry. The generator, therefore, not ground, completes the electrosurgical circuit and eliminates many of the hazards inherent in a grounded system, for example, current division and alternate-site burns. Removing the ground as a reference for transformers isolates one circuit from another to achieve isolated output. High-radio-frequency current is used rather than low, because the low-frequency current would stimulate muscles and nerves and could electrocute a patient.

Return-electrode monitoring (REM) was recently developed to protect patients from burns due to inadequate contact of the return electrode. Pad site burns are caused by increased impedance at the return-electrode site. REM-equipped generators actively monitor the amount of impedance at the patient-pad interface. When impedance reaches an un-safe level, the generator is deactivated and audible and visual alarms occur before an injury results. For this safety feature to be active, the unit must utilize an REM-compatible pa-tient-return electrode.

In electrosurgery, high-frequency electrical current is passed through an active elec-trode tip and destroys tissue by heating it to a point at which cells burst. ESUs can vary the level of electrical power that they generate. Therefore, the units can be used to control bleeding by causing coagulation at the surgical site and to combine cutting and coagula-tion.

The electrosurgical generators produce a variety of electrical waveforms. As the wave-form changes, the effects on tissue change. If a constant waveform, for example "cut," is used, the surgeon is able to vaporize or cut tissue. Cutting divides tissue with electric sparks that focus intense heat at the surgical site over a very short period of time. Vapor-ization of tissue results. When the generator produces an intermittent waveform, such as "coagulation," the electrical cycle is reduced. This interrupted waveform produces less heat, and instead of tissue vaporization, a coagulum is produced. Electrosurgical fulgura-tion—sparking with the coagulation waveform—coagulates and chars the tissue over a wide area. The cycle time is only about 6% and therefore less heat is produced. The result is a coagulum rather than cellular vaporization.

Electrosurgical desiccation occurs when the electrode is in direct contact with the tis-sue, and is achieved most efficiently with the cutting current. By touching the tissue with the electrode, the current concentration is reduced. Less heat is generated and no cutting occurs. The cells dry out and form a coagulum rather than vaporize and explode.

Although the electrosurgical units are effective in cutting and coagulating blood ves-sels, they do significant tissue damage. If they are used extensively and a large amount of coagulated tissue is present, sloughing may occur and interfere with wound healing.

Active Versus Inactive Electrodes

The appropriate functioning of the electrosurgical unit depends on two electrodes: the ac-tive and the inactive, or ground. The tip of the active electrode is small and current density is high; as surface temperature increases, the tissue is burned. The inactive electrode, on the other hand, is large and current density small; little heat is generated.

The tip of the active electrode may be a blade, ball, loop, or needle that fits into a pencil-shaped handle; or it may be a suction tip. The smaller the electrode used, the higher is the current concentration. Therefore, the tissue effect may be the same using a smaller electrode, even though the power setting is reduced. The active electrode, activated by a hand control or foot switch, introduces the electrical current into the patient's body. The inactive, or dispersive, electrode provides the electrical current with a return path to the electrosurgical unit.

When the active electrode is not in use, plastic holders are available. They help avoid the problem of drapes inadvertently igniting if the unit is accidently activated.

Newer electrosurgical units have built-in warning systems known as contact quality monitoring systems that continuously monitor the return path from the patient to the generator. An alarm sounds if the quality of the return path has deteriorated to a level haz-ardous to the patient. The unit is deactivated if unit malfunction is suspected. Older units do not have these warning systems and the perioperative nurse must make sure that the plate is in proper contact with the patient. Safety precautions must be observed and instituted to ensure the safe use of all electrosurgical units.

The active electrode may be disposable or reusable. If it is to be reused, the cable must be examined for cracked or frayed insulation and the handpiece inspected for damage after each use. The active electrode and the cable are checked for electrical continuity. During use, the tip must be clean and free from dried blood and tissue.

Several forms of inactive or ground electrodes are available: reusable metal plates, disposable foil plates, and self-adhesive plates. If a reusable metal plate is used, the ground cable must be inspected for broken, frayed, or damaged insulation and for maintenance of electrical continuity. Cables that are spliced or taped or have cracked insulation must not be used.

If the cable is designed for permanent attachment to a ground plate, the connection must be firm. The use of alligator clips for ground plate attachments is unacceptable. The surface of the metal plate must be flat, free from cracks or creases, clean, and free from corrosion.

The reusable metal plate and the disposable foil plate require that a conductive gel be applied to reduce tissue heating at the point of electrode contact. Only gels designed for electrosurgery should be used. The electrolyte gel is spread completely and evenly over the conductive surface. Missed spots may cause burns, and too thin a coat may dry out during a lengthy surgical procedure.

Another type of disposable inactive ground plate is foil covered with a foam pad impregnated with an electrolyte gel. The inactive electrode is usually referred to as a ground pad or plate. Generally, this type of inactive ground plate is flexible and self-adhering. It provides more uniform contact with the patient and presents fewer pressure points.

Pressure points due to bony protuberances can be grounding hazards, as the pressure exerted at those sites may cause increased current density that results in "hot spots." Electrosurgical current tends to heat at the small, low-resistance area created by the pressure point, and a burn may result.

Electrosurgical Burns

The greatest hazard in using the electrosurgical unit is a radio-frequency electrical burn, which may be first, second, or third degree, depending on the exposure time.

Most burns result from a concentration of current that overheats the tissue to the point of necrosis. The damaged tissue of an electrosurgical burn is hard and has a translucent tan color. Blanching of the skin may show immediately postoperatively; however, the injury may not develop fully for about 24 hours. The lesion usually has a red rim and is very painful to the touch. The necrosed area eventually blackens to form a typical eschar. Unlike burns associated with noxious liquids, electrosurgical burns do not heal well and may require debridement and skin grafting.

Improper placement of the inactive, or ground, electrode accounts for most burns associated with electrosurgical units. The dispersive pad should be placed as close as possible to the surgical site; however, placing it over a fleshy area is more important. If two ESUs are used, each pad should be as close to the respective surgical site as possible. If the patient is not in adequate contact with this electrode, the current will find other paths to ground through ECG electrodes, stirrups, the operating room table, towel clips, or any other conductive material in contact with the patient. In such an instance, too much current flows through too small an area and the temperature rise is excessive, resulting in a burn. Electrocardiogram electrodes should be placed as far as practical from the active site.

The circulating nurse is responsible for applying the inactive electrode to the patient, and it is important to be knowledgeable about electrosurgery to prevent injury to the patient.

Guidelines for Preparing to Use an Electrosurgical Unit

1. Explosive anesthetic gases are contraindicated for procedures using electrosurgery.
2. Flammable skin preparations must dry thoroughly and the fumes dissipate before activating the electrosurgical unit. Flammable agents, such as alcohol and tinctures, may ignite when the electrosurgical unit is used.
3. Be familiar with the unit and how to connect all the cables. Know where the operating manual is located.
4. Place the electrosurgical unit where stress on the cables is avoided and where personnel will not trip over the cables.
5. Check the site where the dispersive pad will be placed on the patient and remove hair that may prevent good adhesion of the pad. Avoid scar tissue, areas of bony protuberance, and the area over an implanted metal prosthesis.
6. Whenever possible, eliminate patient contact with any device that offers a potential alternate return path for the electrical current (i.e., OR table or towel clips).
7. Inspect the electrical plug and cord, the foot switch cord, and all electrical connections for damage.
8. Test all safety features (lights, activation, sound).
9. In using electrosurgical units designed for a specific purpose, such as laparoscopy or other endoscopic procedures, follow the manufacturer's guidelines.

Guidelines for Using Ungelled Pads

1. Apply a smooth, even film of electrolyte gel over the entire plate.
2. Select a site for the ground plate that is muscular, clean, and dry and as close as possible to the operative site. Avoid bony protuberances, sites where fluids might pool, skin folds, scar tissue, areas of excessive adipose tissue or hair, and sites to be x-rayed. The electrode must contact the patient's bare skin in an area with a good blood supply.
3. Lift or turn the patient to position the plate. Do not slide the plate under the patient.
4. Avoid having insulators, such as drapes, to come between the plate and the patient.
5. In surgical procedures with excessive fluid runoff, the foot pedal is placed in a plastic bag.

Guidelines to Follow During Use of the Electrosurgical Unit

1. Confirm the power settings with the surgeon before the unit is used.
2. Set the volume loud enough to hear when the unit is activated.
3. Operate the generator at the lowest effective power setting. If the surgeon repeatedly requests higher than normal power settings, check the ground plate and the

connections of the active and inactive electrodes; during urologic procedures, make certain that a nonconductive irrigation solution is being used.

4. If the patient is repositioned or moved during surgery, recheck the position of the ground plate and the connection of the cable.
5. The unused active electrode should be positioned so that accidental activation of the unit will not harm the patient or the surgical team members or burn the drapes.
6. If the surgical procedure is long and a reusable metal or a disposable foil plate is used, check to ensure that the gel does not dry out; if necessary, regel the electrode.
7. Do not use the top of the generator as a storage area. Solutions may leak inside and damage the unit.
8. The unit is activated only when the active electrode touches tissue.
9. Electrocardiogram monitoring and pulse oximetry may be affected while the ESU is in use.[4]

Guidelines to Follow after Electrosurgical Unit Use

1. Turn all dials to the off position.
2. Disconnect the power supply cord first and then the active and inactive electrode cables.
3. Remove the ground plate and inspect the site for skin damage. If a self-adhering pad was used, remove it carefully, peeling it back slowly to avoid denuding the skin.
4. Wipe the generator and all reusable parts with a disinfectant; do not immerse or pour fluid over the electrosurgical unit.
5. Remove all gel and foreign material from the reusable metal ground plate and wipe dry.
6. Store the foot switch appropriately, with the electrical cord coiled.

Maintenance

Routine preventive maintenance is performed and documented. The generator is checked to confirm power output versus control settings. All connections for active and ground electrodes are tested for secure fit. Foot switches and electrical cords are checked for fraying or breaks, internal connections are tightened, and spark gaps are changed if needed. If isolation circuits have alarms, they are checked for appropriate function, and the unit receives a routine electrical safety check.

Pacemakers and Electrosurgery

Electrosurgery can disrupt the operation of pacemakers, particularly external-demand pacemakers, which tend to be more susceptible to electrical interference. Unlike implanted pacers, the external-demand pacemakers are not shielded by body fluids.

Most pacemakers are subject to interference; however, they are designed to be inhibited during use of the ESU. A bipolar cautery unit should be used on patients with pacemakers, as the current does not flow through the patient.

In addition to the previously discussed precautions taken for electrosurgery, follow these steps for patients with a pacemaker:

1. Make sure that the distance between the active electrode and the ground plate is as short as possible and that both are as far as possible from the pacemaker.

2. Place electrosurgical cords and cables as far as possible from the pacemaker and leads.
3. Monitor the patient's ECG continuously during the procedure.
4. Ensure that a defibrillator is available in the operating room.
5. Postoperatively evaluate the pacemaker for proper function.

It is also important that the surgeon use short activation periods so that the heart can be paced normally between activations.

Argon Beam Coagulator

The argon beam coagulator (ABC) provides radio-frequency coagulation from an ESU generator that is capable of delivering monopolar current through a flow of ionized argon gas. A noncontact form of coagulation is created. A large, raw bleeding surface may be coagulated rapidly with a thin eschar. Less rebleeding occurs. The coagulator is advantageous when performing surgery on the liver, spleen, and kidneys. The beam penetrates approximately one half as far as a standard ESU, and the beam is not activated until the tip is within 1 cm of the target surface. The result is that less tissue is destroyed and healing is faster.

The gas beam is room temperature and thus will not ignite materials such as linens, gloves, or sponges. There is less smoke plume with the ABC when compared with a standard ESU. The ABC uses a gas cylinder that must be checked prior to each case and turned off at the end to prevent gas leakage. The safety concerns common to ESUs also apply to the argon beam coagulator.

Bipolar Electrosurgical Units

The bipolar unit uses forceps for coagulation. One side of the forceps is the active electrode, the other is the inactive electrode, or ground. Therefore, this unit does not require a ground plate. The current flows only between the tips of the forceps, not through the patient. The bipolar unit is controlled with a foot switch and provides precise hemostasis without stimulation or current spread to adjacent structures.

Heated Scalpel

A heated steel scalpel may be used to seal small vessels as it cuts, resulting in less tissue damage than when the spark-gap or solid-state electrosurgical units are used. The heated scalpel is electrically insulated from the patient. No electric current passes through the patient's body; therefore, a ground pad is not required and the risk of electrical burns is eliminated.

The unit does require that the surgeon develop a different technique than is used with a conventional scalpel or with the electrosurgical unit. Incisions must be made slowly and through thin layers of tissue to eliminate the need to "go back" over the area to coagulate bleeding vessels.

Documentation Regarding the Electrosurgical Unit

During preoperative assessment, all abnormal skin lesions are identified and documented on the preoperative assessment form. This documentation will ensure that the lesions identified preoperatively are not confused with lesions acquired during the intraoperative period.

Placement of the ECG monitoring pads and other electrical equipment used for the patient is recorded, as these devices, as well as the ESU, can be a source of intraoperative patient burns.

The brand name of the electrosurgical unit, the serial number, the settings used, and the location of the ground plate are documented on the intraoperative nurse's notes.

If a skin lesion is observed postoperatively, a full investigation of the injury and a report of the findings are required. The electrosurgical dispersive pad, the active electrode, and the unit must be impounded and not used for another patient until the biomedical technician can inspect all items for possible malfunction. A Defective Device Report is completed and sent to the safety officer. Depending on hospital policy, an incident report may be required.

In 1991 Congress passed the Safe Medical Devices Act. This act requires that when a facility becomes aware that a device caused or contributed to serious illness or patient injury, the facility must file a report within 10 days to the manufacturer, or to the FDA if the manufacturer is unknown. A device is defined as anything used in treatment or diagnosis that is not a drug. A serious illness or injury is an incident that threatens life, that results in permanent impairment of a body function or permanent damage to a body structure, or that necessitates immediate medical or surgical intervention to preclude permanent impairment of function or permanent damage to a body structure.

The law includes reporting user error. The FDA requires that the following information be provided:[5]

- Names of the operator or operators
- Nature of the problem
- Error that occurred in using the equipment
- User's training related to equipment design
- Manufacturer's instructions
- Hospital's policies and procedures

INDUCED HYPOTENSION

Hypotension may be induced and controlled by the anesthesiologist to reduce blood loss and provide a bloodless field. It is frequently used in total hip replacement and vascular surgery to control oozing and in neurosurgery for vascular tumors and cerebral aneurysms. It is also used when compatible blood is not available or when receiving blood transfusions is contrary to a patient's religious beliefs.

To prevent damage to vital organs during induced hypotension, adequate oxygenation of the heart, liver, kidneys, and lungs is essential. Complications of induced hypotension are coronary thrombosis, anuria, and reactionary hemorrhage.

INDUCED HYPOTHERMIA

Hypothermia may be used to lengthen the period of circulatory interruption, ischemia, or hypoperfusion. Decreasing the body's temperature decreases cellular metabolism; therefore, the need for oxygen is reduced and bleeding is decreased. Hypothermia may be light, $37°C$ to $32°C$ ($98.6°F$ to $89.6°F$); moderate, $32°C$ to $26°C$ ($89.6°F$ to $78.8°F$); deep, $26°C$ to $20°C$ ($78.8°F$ to $68°F$); or profound, $20°C$ ($68°F$) or below.

Induced hypothermia may be achieved by surface or internal cooling, or extracorporeal circulation. Surface cooling can be accomplished with thermal blankets (temperature control unit), packing the patient in ice, or immersing the patient in an ice bath. When surface cooling is used, nursing care measures are directed at preventing frostbite by wrapping the extremities in cotton sheeting or towels.

Thermal blankets, placed under or over a patient, cool (or warm) according to the temperature of fluid circulating through them. Internal cooling is achieved by irrigating with cold fluids or placing ice packs around internal organs. Moderate and profound hypothermia are accomplished through the heat exchange device of the heart–lung machine.

During hypothermia, the body's cellular activity drops below basal metabolic rates, decreasing cellular oxygen requirements. Decreased respirations and CO_2 retention lead to acidosis (decreased pH values).

Hypothermia depresses the cardiac output, lowers blood pressure, causes cardiac dysrhythmia, and decreases cerebral, hepatic and visceral blood flow. Decreased renal blood flow results in decreased glomerular filtration, and subsequently, a rise in blood urea nitrogen and creatinine levels. Dehydration follows decreased water absorption. Other concerns are disturbance of blood coagulation, downward drift of patient temperature, and pressure areas from the thermal blankets.

Urinary output, the electrocardiogram, and body temperatures are carefully monitored during hypothermia. A nasopharyngeal temperature probe reflects the brain's temperature, an esophageal probe monitors the heart's temperature, and a rectal probe monitors core temperature. The location of all temperature probes must be checked when the patient is repositioned. During hypothermia appropriate reductions must be made in the delivery of anesthetic agents. Results of blood gas analyses performed during the cool state require conversion to normal temperature.

Because many anesthetic agents are metabolized in the liver and hepatic blood flow is decreased, the recovery phase may be prolonged. Decreased cerebral blood flow may also cause the patient to be confused and disoriented in the PACU.

The patient is rewarmed slowly to prevent vasoconstriction and shivering. Shivering increases oxygen requirements by 400% to 500%; without an appropriate increase in cardiac output, metabolic acidosis—"rewarming shock"—will occur. Rewarming is accomplished in the immediate postoperative phase using the heat exchange device of the heart–lung machine, warm blankets, thermal blankets, humidified oxygen heat lamps, or convective warming therapy. When a thermal blanket is used, a sheet is placed between the blanket and the patient. After moving the patient onto the blanket, the blanket is checked to ensure that no creases or folds are present that would concentrate heat in one area. The temperature of the heating fluid must be constantly monitored and never allowed to exceed $42°$ C. Convective warming is a system that directs a gentle flow of warm air across the patient using a warming cover.

Thermal burns or pressure necrosis may occur in patients when thermal blankets are used. Most of these injuries occur during lengthy surgical procedures that include extracorporeal circulation or cross-clamping of the aorta. In some cases, excessive temperature may be the cause; the pattern of the burns matches the pattern of the tubing in the thermal blanket. These injuries tend to be concentrated where pressure is the greatest, such as over the sacrum.

Injuries have also occurred when the unit was not used in the heating mode. In these cases of prolonged immobility, prolonged pressure on subcutaneous blood vessels obstructs the blood flow to the tissues, resulting in tissue necrosis.

The use of hypothermia is documented on the intraoperative nurse's notes and includes all nursing care measures instituted. If a temperature control unit is used, the brand name, serial number, and the temperature at which the unit was set, as well as the patient's temperature, are charted.

Routine inspection, preventive maintenance, and user education and observation during use are essential to ensure safe operation of temperature control units.

Investigating a Skin Lesion

When a skin lesion occurs, it is important to avoid the tendency to assume that a particular device, such as the electrosurgical or temperature control unit, was at fault. The injury is referred to as a "skin lesion" rather than a burn, and all possible causes of the injury are investigated. Its location, size, and shape are evaluated. If the lesion is relatively large and either an irregular or symmetrical shape around skin folds or body crevices, the possibility of a liquid or chemical burn should be considered. If the lesion is located on a surface where they may have been pressure, a pressure sore is considered. A thorough investigation is done as soon as possible.

If an electrosurgical burn is considered, all staff members involved in placing and checking the ground pad should be interviewed. The electrosurgical unit is removed from service and checked by the biomedical engineer or the manufacturer's representative. If the area is noted immediately following surgery, the active electrode and the ground plate are saved and sent with the generator for investigation.

If the lesion appears to be associated with a temperature control unit, the unit and the thermal blanket are removed from service and examined for appropriate function by the biomedical engineer.

Color photographs of the lesion taken as soon as it is discovered and periodically as it heals will assist in identifying any characteristic patterns of skin destruction and may help identify the causative mechanism.

The written report should include all the facts discovered during the investigation and recommendations for preventing similar occurrences.

▋ BLOOD REPLACEMENT

Blood for a transfusion may be homologous blood, designated (directed) blood, or autologous blood.

- Homologous blood: blood collected from donors for transfusion to another individual; labeled "volunteer donor"
- Designated blood: blood collected from a donor designated by the intended recipi-

ent; must meet all the requirements for homologous blood, including negative results for transfusion-transmitted disease markers
- Autologous blood: blood collected from the intended recipient either prior to planned surgery or during surgery

Whole Blood

Whole blood is used to treat acute, massive blood loss; it provides the oxygen-carrying properties of red blood cells and the volume expansion of plasma. Acute loss of as much as one third of the patient's total blood volume can often be managed with crystalloid solutions, colloid solutions, or both. The signs and symptoms the patient may exhibit that suggest whole blood is required include acute massive blood loss with hypertension, tachycardia, shortness of breath, pallor, and low hemoglobin/hematocrit. In a nonbleeding adult, one unit of whole blood should increase the hematocrit by 3% and hemoglobin by 1 g/dL. Rapid infusion of whole blood can result in congestive heart failure.

Packed Red Blood Cells

Packed red blood cells have 90% of the plasma removed and a special solution added that contains a preservative that increases the shelf life and decreases viscosity. Packed red blood cells may be appropriate in acute or chronic blood loss with tachycardia, shortness of breath, pallor, low hemoglobin/hematocrit, or fatigue. They are not used for volume expansion, to enhance wound healing, or to improve general well-being.

Washed or Frozen Red Blood Cells

Washed or frozen red blood cells are administered to prevent recurrence of febrile, non-hemolytic transfusion reactions such as urticarial and anaphylactic reactions, caused by donor white blood cell antigens reacting with the recipient's white blood cell antibodies. Washing the blood removes 80% to 95% of the white blood cells and all the plasma. Removing the plasma lowers the potassium level of the blood, which is an additional advantage for neonatal patients as hyperkalemia interferes with the contraction of skeleton and smooth muscles and can result in bradycardia or cardiac arrest. Washing requires an additional hour of processing, and the unit must be transfused within 24 hours.

Irradiated Blood

Blood products can be exposed to a measured amount of radiation, thereby rendering the donor lymphocytes incapable of replication. The product carries no radiation risk to the person administering the transfusion or the recipient. Irradiated blood products are used to prevent posttransfusion graft-versus-host disease in recipients. Irradiated blood products are indicated for patients with Hodgkin's or non-Hodgkins's lymphoma, acute leukemia, congenital immunodeficiency disorders, or for low birth weight neonates, or patients receiving intrauterine transfusions or bone marrow transplants.

Platelets

To control or prevent bleeding associated with a deficiency in platelet number or function, platelets may be administered. Patients with such a deficiency may exhibit petechiae, gum bleeding, ecchymoses, blood in the urine, blood in the stool, or low platelet counts. The therapy prevents or resolves bleeding due to thrombocytopenia or platelet dysfunction. One unit of platelets should raise the peripheral platelet count if the underlying cause of thrombocytopenia is resolved or controlled.

Fresh Frozen Plasma

Fresh frozen plasma (FFP) is administered to increase the level of clotting factors in patients with a demonstrated deficiency. Plasma is frozen within 6 hours of collection to preserve all the clotting factors. It is thawed in the transfusion service before it is sent to the operating room and must be used within 24 hours of thawing. Storing it after 24 hours results in the loss of the clotting factors.

Colloid Solutions

Albumin and plasma protein fraction (PPF) are colloid solutions that expand volume in shock and massive hemorrhage. They may also be used to treat acute liver failure, burns, and hemolytic disease in the newborn by maintaining adequate blood pressure and volume support.

∎ TRANSFUSION REACTIONS

Signs of transfusion reaction in an unconscious patient include weak pulse, fever, hypotension, hemoglobinuria, increased operative bleeding or oozing at the surgical site, tachycardia, bradycardia, and oliguria/anuria. When a reaction occurs, the transfusion should be stopped immediately. The blood bag with attached blood administration set and labels are sent to the transfusion service along with blood and urine samples. Documentation of the transfusion reaction should be completed according to facility procedure.

Blood Warmers

Rapid, massive infusion of cold blood components may result in arrhythmias and cardiac arrest. A preventive measure is to warm blood in an approved in-line warmer, which may be a temperature-monitored water bath in which coiled plastic tubing is immersed or electrically heated plates through which blood tubing passes. The warmer must have an audible and visual alarm system as the upper acceptable limit for warming blood is 38° C. A unit of blood that has been warmed but not used must be discarded. It is not acceptable to hold a blood bag under hot tap water, to immerse it in an unmonitored water bath, or place it in a microwave oven.

∎ AUTOLOGOUS BLOOD TRANSFUSION

Concern about HIV transmission has heightened awareness of the complications of blood transfusion and caused an increased interest in autologous transfusion. Autotransfusion, or autologous transfusion, is reinfusing a patient's own blood rather than relying on banked stores of homologous blood. Currently, four autologous techniques are available:

- predonation of blood
- recycling blood during surgery
- hemoconcentration (blood dilution)
- postoperative collection for retransfusion

In the *predonation* program, blood is collected from the patient and banked several weeks before elective surgery. If the patient is an acceptable homologous donor, unused products may be transfused to other patients.

Intraoperatively, if the blood lost is not contaminated by bacteria or tumor cells, it may be salvaged and *recycled* for transfusion. To transfuse this blood, collection must be sterile and the blood not allowed to clot. It is placed in a suitable container for administration. Intraoperative salvate systems are of two types—those that transfuse the salvaged product without further treatment and those that "wash" it by saline suspension and centrifugation. If washing is not used, care must be taken to avoid excessive dilution of the product with surgical irrigants and to prevent hemolysis caused by vigorous suction. Aspirated thrombin preparations and microfibrillar collagen sponges may not be removed completely from the blood during the washing process. Manufacturers of some products (Avitene) warn that blood salvage in the area where these products are used is contraindicated.[6] Pharmaceutical companies must be contacted to review what products can be used during the blood salvage technique.

Hemoconcentration is used for patients undergoing open heart surgery. The patient's blood is usually diluted preoperatively with crystalloid or colloid solutions to extend its volume to accommodate the additional volume of the heart–lung bypass circuit. After that is done, the patient's blood may be centrifuged to remove the added liquid volume while preserving the cellular components.

Postoperatively, blood can be collected sterilely from mediastinal or chest drainage and transfused. Anticoagulation is not required because the blood is defibrinogenated and does not clot.

Autotransfusion is considered the safest transfusion option for surgical patients.[7] It offers a safeguard against serious transfusion reactions and offers the patients whose religious beliefs will not allow them to receive transfusions of banked blood a viable alternative.

Cryoprecipitated Fibrinogen

Concentrated autologous and donor-directed blood can also be used to procure fibrinogen that aids in hemostasis. Cryoprecipitated fibrinogen concentrate is prepared by thawing fresh-frozen plasma and recovering the cold precipitate, which is warmed and transferred under sterile conditions to a sterile bottle. The fibrinogen is then refrozen for storage. Prior to use, the component is warmed to 37°C and applied topically with thrombin to the surgical site via a syringe or aerosol dispenser. Cryoprecipitated fibrinogen assists in the control of hemostasis, tissue sealing, and wound healing.

▮ REFERENCES

1. Recommended practice for use of pneumatic tourniquet. In *Standards and Recommended Practices.* Denver: AORN; 1995: 227.
2. Tourniquet Safety Home Study. Dover, OH: Zimmer Inc; 1991: 6.
3. Edmonson A, Crenshaw A. *Campbell's Operative Orthopaedics*, 8th ed. St. Louis: C.V. Mosby; 1992: vols. 1, 2.
4. Moak E. Electrosurgical unit safety. *AORN J.* 1991; 53 (3):749.
5. The Safe Medical Devices Act of 1990, Public Law 101–629.
6. Transfusion Therapy Guidelines for Nurses. Washington DC: National Institute of Health. Publication no. 90–2668, September 1990.
7. Johnson G, Bowman R. Autologous blood transfusion. *AORN J.* 1992; 56 (2): 285.

Wound Closure

▮ A HISTORICAL PERSPECTIVE

Ligatures have been devised from various materials beginning as far back as 3000 B.C. Some of the materials used over the centuries by different civilizations have been animal sinews, dried gut, dried tendon, strips of hide, horsehair, human hair, bark fibers, and textile fibers of various kinds.

Among the more exotic methods of suturing skin was the use of the Sauba ant. In the historical publication, "Surgery Through the Ages," the technique is described as follows:

> An ant is set on the margin of the open wound and promptly sinks its claws into the wound. The edges are then drawn together and the rear claws of the ant grip the other side of the wound. The insect is then beheaded and the shriveling of its body draws together the edges of the cut. The ant, even in death, will not release its grip.[1]

Another unusual method of skin closure was practiced by the Masai and Zulu Africans.[1] The witch doctors, in addition to their incantations and voodoo, sutured open wounds by inserting tiny sharp slivers of wood on each side of the edges of a cut. They then used a bast, which is the phloem or inner bark tissue of plants, to draw the slivers together. The bast was tied forming a suture line. Following suturing, the wound was bandaged with leaves purported to have medicinal properties.

The first recorded use of surgical gut is found in the writings of Galen, about A.D. 200. The Arabian surgeon Rhazes in his writings in A.D. 600 contributed to the misnomer, kitgut. The material used for the surgical gut, derived from the intestines of sheep, was first used as a string on a small instrument called a kit. Thus, the term "kitgut" evolved. Because a small cat is called a kit, the word "catgut" replaced "kitgut."

Through the years various materials were used, including during the 1800s buckskin, parchment, and kid, but the most satisfactory was gut fabricated from tanned intestines of sheep and steer.[1]

During the 1800s when a surgeon used sutures, the ends would be left long and dangling from the wound. The sutures were thought to be the cause of postoperative pus and infection. Secondary hemorrhages from abscess and sutures prematurely sloughing out was another common complication. It was not until 1867 that Lister answered the problem of contamination by spraying sutures with carbolic acid.

The development of asepsis and general anesthesia (1842) provided the necessary information for surgeons to perform new surgical procedures. Thus, the need developed for better suture material and advanced suturing techniques.

An important step came with Lister's promoting chrome treatment of catgut to delay its absorption in tissues and thus contribute to the longer-lasting strength of sutures.

Following the use of carbolic acid, heat was used to sterilize sutures; and in 1902, Claudius introduced sterilization by chemical treatment with potassium iodide. By 1901, sterile surgical gut was available in boilable glass tubes. These tubes were wrapped in muslin and placed in the instrument sterilizer to be boiled with the instruments for each case. In the 1920s, the packaging of sutures changed to nonboilable tubes. The operating room nurse washed the tubes in green soap and placed them in a glass jar containing a formaldehyde solution, which sterilized the exterior of the tubes. The fumes of the solution were irritating, and many individuals developed allergic reactions. More important, the solution was not effective against the hepatitis virus.

Efforts to improve the package and the sterilization process continued, and in 1956 the precursor of today's package was introduced: a double plastic envelope. The outer envelope could be opened and the inner package containing the suture delivered safely to the sterile field. This system eliminated the use of formaldehyde, saved time, was safer, and reduced shipping costs. In a few years all manufacturers adopted the sterile dry-pack system, and the basic system is still used.

Regulating Standards and Sutures

In 1820, a group of physicians created a nonprofit organization to establish a United States Pharmacopeia (USP) that would include all substances and preparations they believed of substantial worth in medical practice. Until 1906, the standards included in the USP were followed voluntarily; then on June 30, 1906, the U.S. government passed the Pure Food and Drug Act. The standards were those of the USP and the *National Formulary (NF),* a publication of the American Pharmaceutical Association. Federal law now required that drug preparations conform to these standards if the label carried the USP or NF reference.

As of 1937, sutures were included in the USP, and standards and tests for suture size, diameter limits, and tensile strength were indicated. In addition, the standards cover suture packaging, labeling, needle attachment, dyes, and sterility.

The diameter of each suture strand must fall within the minimum and maximum limits for the gauge. The tensile strength is measured on the basis of the knot-pull strength. The minimum knot-pull strength is specified for each size and type of suture.

Knot-pull strength is the force that can be applied to the free ends of a suture, tied with a surgical knot around rubber tubing of $\frac{1}{4}$-inch diameter, before the suture breaks. For example, for size 3/0 surgical gut, the diameter limits are 0.30 to 0.339 mm, with a minimum tensile strength of 1.25 kg. Size 0 surgical gut (which is larger) has diameter limits of 0.40 to 0.499 mm, with a minimum tensile strength of 2.77 kg.

In 1976, the Medical Device Amendment to the Food, Drug and Cosmetic Act of 1938 gave the Federal Food and Drug Administration regulatory control over all medical devices. In the amendment, a device is an instrument, apparatus, implement, machine, contrivance, implant, in vitro reagent, or other similar or related article, including any component, part, or accessory, that is:

1. Recognized in the USP
2. Intended for use in the diagnosis, cure, mitigation, treatment, or prevention of disease
3. Intended to affect the structure or any function of the human body

The legislation classified all devices into one of three categories based on the extent of control necessary to ensure the safety and effectiveness of the device. The three categories are:

*   *Class I, General Controls:* Simple medical devices are included; requirements are that the company follow good manufacturing practices and report information to the FDA regarding the safety, efficacy, and proper labeling of these devices.
*   *Class II, Performance Standards:* These devices require performance standards that ensure the items are safe, effective, and labeled correctly. Sutures, which previously did not require a New Drug Application prior to marketing, are included in this category.
*   *Class III, Premarket Approval:* These devices are life sustaining, life supporting, or implanted in the body, or they present a potential unreasonable risk of illness or injury. Devices classified in this category are required to apply for premarket approval. All new materials manufactured for use as a suture will be Class III.

Although the FDA had been involved with the efficacy of synthetic absorbable sutures, it was not until 1976 that the Medical Device Amendment required manufacturers to submit proof of suture safety and efficacy prior to marketing. USP minimal standards remain voluntary; however, the USP standard must be met if the product label indicates that the sutures conform to these standards.

▮ CLASSIFICATION OF SUTURE MATERIAL

Sutures have two primary purposes: to occlude the lumen of blood vessels and to approximate wound edges until healing is complete. Suture material is classified as absorbable and nonabsorbable.

Absorbable sutures are digested by body enzymes or hydrolysis. They first lose strength, and then gradually disappear from the tissue. The minimal standard for absorbable surgical suture is defined in the United States Pharmacopeia, Twenty-second Revision (UPS XXII), and is presented below:

> Absorbable Surgical Suture is a sterile strand prepared from collagen derived from healthy mammals, or from a synthetic polymer. Its length is not less than 95.0 percent of that stated on the label. Its diameter and tensile strength correspond to the size designation indicated on the label, within the limits prescribed herein. It is capable of being absorbed by living mammalian tissue, but may be treated to modify its resistance to absorption. It may be impregnated or coated with a suitable antimicrobial agent. It may be colored by a color additive approved by the Federal Food and Drug Administration.[2]

The USP requirements for diameter and tensile strength are different for surgical gut and synthetic absorbable sutures. For example, on 2/0 surgical gut, the limits are 0.35 to 0.399 mm, with a minimum tensile strength of 2.00 kg.; size 2/0 synthetic absorbable suture has diameter limits of 0.30 to 0.0339 mm, with a minimum tensile strength of 2.68 kg.

Sutures that are not affected by enzyme activity or absorption in living tissue are classified as nonabsorbable material. Nonabsorbable sutures become encapsulated in fibrous tissue during the healing process and remain embedded in body tissues unless they are surgically removed. The USP XXII provides the following description of nonabsorbable surgical sutures:

> Nonabsorbable Surgical Suture is classed and typed as follows: Class I Suture is composed of silk or synthetic fibers of monofilament, twisted, or braided construction. Class II Suture is composed of cotton or linen fibers or coated natural or synthetic fibers where the coating forms a casting of significant thickness but does not contribute appreciably to strength. Class III suture is composed of monofilament or multifilament metal wire.
>
> Nonabsorbable Surgical Suture is a strand of material that is suitably resistant to the action of mammalian tissue. Its length is not less than 95.0 percent of that stated on the label. Its diameter and tensile strength correspond to the size designation indicated on the label, within the limits prescribed herein. It may be nonsterile or sterile. It may be impregnated or coated with a suitable antimicrobial agent.
>
> Nonabsorbable Surgical Suture may be modified with respect to body or texture, or to reduce capillarity, and may be suitably bleached. It may be colored by a color additive approved by the Federal Food and Drug Administration.[2]

Monofilament suture is a single strand of material that is noncapillary and designated by USP as type B. Multifilament suture consists of more than one strand held together by spinning, twisting, or braiding. All multifilament sutures have a certain capillarity, which means that fluid is soaked into and along the thread. The USP identifies multifilament as type A suture. The capillarity can be reduced by coating the thread with silicone or paraffin. Type A sutures elicit a higher degree of tissue reaction.

The diameter (size or gauge) of suture is designated in descending sequence from No. 5, 4, 3, 2, 1, 0, then 2/0, 3/0, and so on, down to 11/0. Size 5 is the heaviest material and 11/0 the smallest diameter suture. Less tissue reaction occurs with smaller diameter sutures.

Absorbable Suture Material

Natural Absorbable Sutures (Surgical Gut).
Except for specialized uses, surgical gut has been abandoned. Surgical gut, formerly called catgut, comes from the submucosa of sheep intestine or the serosa of steer intestine and is about 98% collagen. The intestines are first washed and stripped of all impurities. The collagen is stretched and slit into long ribbons, inspected for color and condition, and then identified for either plain or chromic gut.

Chromic surgical gut resists tissue enzymes for a longer period than plain gut because it is subjected to a "tanning" process called chromicizing. Tanning may be done to either the ribbons before they have been twisted or spun into strands, or to the finished strand. The diameter of the strand depends on the number and width of ribbons it contains. Plain gut strand is twisted or spun in the same manner but is not chromicized.

After the strands are dried, they are polished and ready for needles to be attached or for packaging. Surgical gut is packaged in an inner packet in a small amount of conditioning fluid to maintain pliability.

Surgical gut should be handled only when it is moist; therefore, it should remain in the package until it is needed. It is handled as little as possible; excessive handling or running gloved fingers up and down the strand can cause fraying. Gut is straightened when it is removed from the packet with a steady gentle pull. Needle-suture combinations are straightened in the same manner except the strand is grasped about 2 inches from the needle attachment to avoid stress on the needle-suture junction.

If surgical gut is opened and prepared in advance, for individual ties, for example, it is stored in the folds of a dry towel and moistened in cool saline solution or water for 4 to 6 seconds before handing it to the surgeon. If gut is soaked for a longer period, it will absorb moisture, swell, and lose tensile strength.

Surgical gut is absorbed by phagocytosis, which results in varying degrees of inflammatory reaction. The rate of absorption is influenced by the following factors:

- Plain gut absorbs more rapidly than chromic gut.
- Gut is absorbed more rapidly in the presence of infection and proteolytic enzymes in the gastrointestinal tract.
- Surgical gut is absorbed much more rapidly in serous or mucous membrane than in muscle tissue.
- In undernourished, debilitated, anemic, or elderly patients, surgical gut may be absorbed faster than desired.

Additional disadvantages of surgical gut include:

- It is inconsistent in absorption and has poor tensile strength compared with synthetic absorbable sutures.
- The knot security is poor.
- It must be packaged moist for pliability.
- It is difficult to handle because is has memory.

The only advantage to surgical gut is that it is absorbable. Due to its many disadvantages, researchers experimented with a more acceptable absorbable suture. In the early 1960s, reconstituted extruded collagen was developed but abandoned, except for specialized uses, due to problems with absorption. It was not until 1971 that a superior absorbable suture, Dexon, was available. It is made from a polymer of polyglycolic acid and creates minimal tissue response.

Synthetic Absorbable Sutures. Synthetic polymers are extruded to form monofilament and braided, coated, or uncoated absorbable sutures. The sutures are absorbed by hydrolysis, a process whereby the polymer reacts with water to cause a breakdown of the molecular structure. The byproducts of this metabolism are excreted by the urinary, digestive, and respiratory systems; therefore, tissue response is very mild.

Absorption time and tensile strength are not affected by infection, the inflammatory process, or proteolytic enzymes in the gastrointestinal tract. The tensile strength of synthetic absorbable sutures exceeds that of surgical gut of a comparable diameter and compares favorably with most nonabsorbable sutures. These sutures are particularly useful in tissues where slow healing is anticipated, such as the fascia, or where extended wound support is desirable, as in elderly patients, and an absorbable suture is preferable.

Packages of synthetic absorbable sutures show an expiration date; therefore, the stock must be rotated.

These sutures are packaged and used dry. They must not be soaked or dipped in water or saline. The material hydrolizes in water; thus excessive exposure to moisture will reduce the tensile strength.

Polyglycolic acid suture (Dexon S) is a synthetic polymer of glycolic acid constructed of fine filaments to provide optimal handling properties and increased tensile strength. Dexon S is also available as Dexon Plus, which is coated with poloxamer 188, an inert surfactant, excreted in the urine. The surfactant becomes slick in contact with body fluids for smooth passage of the suture through tissue. The suture requires two or three additional throws in knot tying, and ends must be cut longer than uncoated material. The coating virtually disappears from the suture site within a few hours, which may strengthen knot security.

Polyglactin 910 (Vicryl) is a copolymer of lactide and glycolide available coated or uncoated. Vicryl is coated with polyglactin 370 and calcium stearate, which provide a nonflaking lubricant for smooth passage of the suture through tissue and precise knot placement. This absorbable coating does not affect suture absorption rate or tensile strength.

Monofilament absorbable sutures have also been developed. One is a copolymer of glycolic acid and trimethylene carbonate (Maxon) and the other is extruded from the polyester poly (p-dioxanone) PDS and PDS II. These monofilament sutures are easier to tie, and the material passes through tissue with less resistance than braided suture, permitting the surgeon to use a running closure and save time at the close of the procedure. In addition, concern has always been expressed that with infection, bacteria could migrate through the interstices of braided suture.

All absorbable suture, including synthetic, is contraindicated when extended or prolonged approximation is required.

Nonabsorbable Metallic Sutures

Stainless Steel. Stainless steel sutures are made of a ferrous alloy wire. It is available as a monofilament or twisted multifilament stainless steel suture. Stainless steel wire has the greatest tensile strength of any suture material. It is inert, nonmagnetic, and electropassive in tissue fluids. It is useful in the presence of infection when minimal tissue reaction is desired, and when slow healing is anticipated. It is often used for secondary repairs of wound disruption, eviscerations, and tendon repairs, and as retention sutures.

Because stainless steel wire kinks easily, rendering it useless, special handling techniques are required. Care must be exercised in handling the ends of the suture to avoid tearing gloves. Only wire scissors are used to cut stainless steel sutures.

In addition to the USP definitions of ranges in diameter size, stainless steel wire is frequently identified by the Brown and Sharp (B & S) scale for diameter (i.e., No. 40, No. 35). Table 14–1 identifies wire diameter equivalents in USP and B & S gauges.

When a prosthesis is implanted, it is important to know the composition of the metal. If it is made of Vitallium, titanium, or tantalum, stainless steel sutures must not be used to close the wound, as two different kinds of metals create an unfavorable electrolytic reaction.

Silver Wire Sutures. Silver wire, available as a monofilament, has antibacterial characteristics and a high tensile strength. It is soft, pliable, and easier to handle than stainless steel. Silver wire is available only in size 7 swaged to a large needle for closure after dehiscence.

Natural Fiber Nonabsorbable Surgical Sutures

Silk Sutures. Surgical silk sutures are made from the thread spun by silkworm larvae when making cocoons. The raw silk is degummed and bleached before being braided or twisted together to form a multifilament suture strand.

When wet, surgical silk loses up to 20% of its tensile strength. To reduce its capillarity and improve its handling characteristics, surgical silk is treated with silicone or paraffin, which may cause tissue reaction. Silicone is physiologically inert and therefore provokes less tissue reaction than does paraffin.

The tensile strength of silk is stronger than cotton; however, it is not as strong as comparable sizes of synthetic materials. Silk loses substantial tensile strength 90 to 120 days after implantation; therefore, it is not used if long-term support is vital, for example, in suturing a vascular prosthesis or a heart valve.

Silk is contraindicated in the presence of infection or contamination, and in the biliary or urinary tract. It is frequently used in the eye, gastrointestinal tract, brain, cardiovascular system, and as a skin closure.

TABLE 14–1. WIRE DIAMETER EQUIVALENTS

Steel Size	Equivalent B & S Gauge
7	18
5	20
4	22
3	23
2	24
1	25
0	26
00	28
000	30
4–0	32/34
5–0	35
6–0	38/40

Virgin Silk Sutures. Virgin silk suture is bleached but not degummed or treated for capillarity. It is available in 8/0 or 9/0, white or dyed black. It is primarily used in ophthalmic surgery.

Cotton Sutures. Cotton sutures are made by twisting long, staple cotton fibers into a smooth multifilament strand, which is smoother, more uniform in diameter, and stronger than ordinary cotton thread. Cotton sutures are weaker than silk, but moistening cotton before use increases its tensile strength by 10%. Moistening also reduces the tendency of surgical cotton to cling to gloves.

Cotton sutures are used in repairing the fascia, brain, and thyroid gland, and in the serosal layer of gastrointestinal anastomosis.

Like silk, cotton sutures are contraindicated for wounds known or suspected to be contaminated.

Synthetic Nonabsorbable Sutures

Technological advances in producing synthetics for surgical needs have decreased the use of natural fibers, cotton and silk, and increased the use of synthetic nonabsorbable sutures. The synthetic materials are polyesters and polyamides, originally developed for the textile industry. Synthetic fibers cause less tissue irritation than natural fibers, have a higher tensile strength, and retain their strength in tissue. Braided synthetic fibers are capillary, as are natural fibers. To reduce capillarity, a coating may be applied to the twisted or braided thread or to the individual fibers before twisting or braiding.

Nylon Sutures. Nylon is made of a polyamide derived from coal, air, and water. It is available as a monofilament or a multifilament. Like silk, multifilament nylon is tightly braided and treated to prevent capillary action. When treated, it handles like silk, but is 40% stronger, passes more smoothly through tissue, and produces less tissue reaction than silk.

Nylon may be used in all tissue where cotton and silk are used. Like silk, nylon is not used if long-term support is vital.

Monofilament nylon may be clear, blue, black, or green. Because it is very smooth and inert, it is used for general skin closure and plastic surgery procedures. Monofilament nylon can be extruded in gauges as fine as 11/0 and is used in ophthalmic microvascular and peripheral nerve repairs.

Polyester Sutures. Surgical polyester fiber, Dacron, is made from a polymer of polyethylene terephthalate. The raw material is first produced as pellets, which are melted and extruded into filaments. The filaments are stretched and braided into a multifilament suture strand. Treated and untreated forms are available.

Untreated polyester is rough and stiffer than treated and tends to drag through the tissue. Treating polyester suture aids in handling and smooth passage through tissue. Polyester sutures are considered to have the highest tensile strength of all the synthetic nonabsorbable sutures. They retain high tensile strength after prolonged implantation and produce minimal tissue reaction. This material is used when extended approximation is required, such as implanting heart valves, vascular grafts, and revascularization procedures.

Polyester sutures may be treated with one of three materials: silicone, Teflon, and polybutilate.

Silicone is physiologically inert and becomes liquid at a low temperature, allowing it to vulcanize to the Dacron strand without a bonding agent.

Polytetrafluoroethylene (Teflon), on the other hand, requires a high temperature to become liquid. Therefore, it is applied to the Dacron suture in a solid dispersion that requires a bonding agent, or it is impregnated into spaces in the braid of the polyester fiber strand. Minute particles of this coating may flake off the strand, producing foreign body granulomas.

Polybutilate was developed specifically as a surgical lubricant. This material adheres strongly to the braided polyester fiber and decreases drag through the tissue.

Polybutester Suture (Novafil). Compared with other synthetic polymers, Novafil is more flexible and elastic, which is a physiologic advantage in apposing wound edges. Novafil is a monofilament synthetic material available in clear or blue. It is indicated for approximation in all types of soft tissue except neural and those involving microsurgery.

Polypropylene Sutures. Polypropylene is made from a linear hydrocarbon polymer extruded into smooth monofilament strands. It is available clear or pigmented with cyan blue. Because it is smooth, it passes through tissue or vascular prostheses with minimal drag. Polypropylene has a high tensile strength that is retained during extended periods of implantation; therefore, it is an acceptable substitute for stainless steel in situations where strength and nonreactivity are required. It causes minimal tissue reaction.

Polypropylene suture may be used when delayed or retarded healing is anticipated, in the presence of infection, and when extended support is required, such as during cardiovascular surgery.

The method of packaging polypropylene is vital because it has memory. When removed from some types of packages, it has a tendency to kink and is therefore difficult to handle.

▌SUTURE PACKAGING

Suture packages protect the sterile suture from contamination and permit the suture to be extracted from the package ready for immediate sterile use.

Sutures are packaged in a double envelope. The suture is sealed inside the primary envelope, which is then placed in an outer peel-package cover. The unit is then sterilized by ethylene-oxide gas or by cobalt 60 irradiation and packaged in boxes, each containing one to three dozen envelopes. To simplify identifying different types of material, a color code appears on the envelopes and the boxes of the suture material.

Each envelope and box contain all the information required by the USP /trade name, generic name, size, color, length, number of sutures in the package, needle description, suture construction (braided, twisted, monofilament), coating material used, catalogue number, date of manufacturing and/or date of expiration, and an indication that the suture meets USP standards.

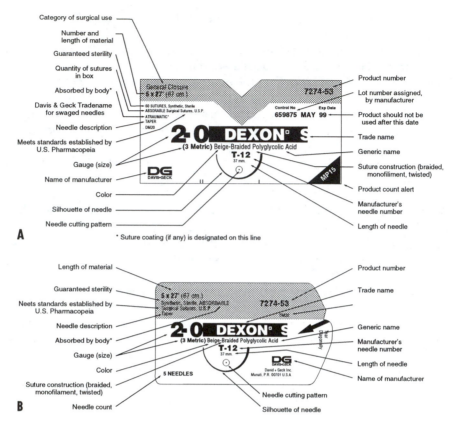

Figure 14–1. **A.** Suture box label information. **B.** Packet label information. (*Courtesy Davis and Geck, Wayne, NJ, with permission.*)

It may be more efficient and cost effective to use prepackaged, custom suture packs based on type of procedure or layer of tissue for the opening and closing. In that way time is saved during setup, inventory and distribution are reduced, waste is reduced, charges are simplified, and the circulating nurse has more time to spend with the patient.

To transfer the sterile primary suture packet to the field, the circulating nurse peels apart the outer wrapper exposing the sterile inner package for the scrub assistant to retrieve (Fig. 14–2). Only in an emergency are sutures flipped onto the sterile field, because in flipping the sutures the field may inadvertently become contaminated by the circulating nurse's hands extending over the sterile surface.

▌ Surgical Needles

Surgical needles are made of a special steel alloy with a high carbon content. Properly balanced heat treatment and tempering permit the wire to acquire the necessary firmness but retain its elasticity to avoid breakage under heavy strain. Various sizes and shapes of needles are formed; the thickness depends on the diameter of the wire. Reusable eyed needles

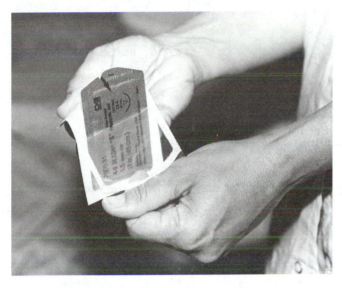

Figure 14–2. Opening suture package. The circulating nurse peels apart the outer wrapper exposing the sterile inner package for the scrub assistant to retrieve.

were formerly the most popular; however, during the last two decades they have been replaced with disposable eyed needles and needle-suture combinations.

All suture needles have three basic components: the point; the body, or shaft; and the eye. The body, or shaft, is straight or curved (Fig. 14–3). The various curvatures are $\frac{3}{8}$, $\frac{1}{2}$, and $\frac{5}{8}$ circle. Variations include $\frac{1}{4}$ and 160° for ophthalmic surgery. Needle points are tapered (noncutting), cutting, and blunt (Fig. 14–4).

Points of the Needle

Tapered needles do not have a cutting edge; they are used for tissue offering little resistance, for example, the intestines and peritoneum. These needles tend to push the tissue aside as they pass through, rather than cutting it.

Conventional cutting needles have a triangular point with two edges in the horizontal plane and one edge in the vertical plane following the inner curvature of the needle. In a

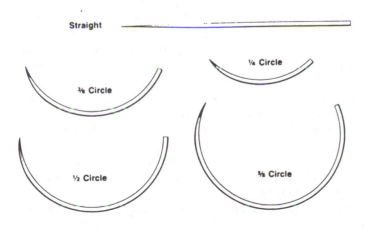

Figure 14–3. Surgical needles vary in shape, size, type of point, body, and how suture is attached (swaged or threaded). (*Courtesy Davis and Geck, Wayne, NJ, with permission.*)

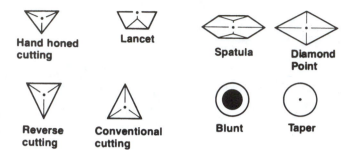

Figure 14–4. Needle cross sections. (Courtesy Davis and Geck, Wayne, NJ, with permission.)

reverse cutting needle, the sharp edge follows the outer curvature of the needle; on cross section it appears as an upended triangle. Cutting needles are used in tough tissue, such as skin and tendons.

Another variation of a cutting needle is a spatula. *Spatulas* have a somewhat flattened needle shaft ending in a spatulate point, with the cutting edge in the horizontal plane. These needles are primarily used in ophthalmic surgery.

A *trocar needle* has a highly sharpened point and tapered body. It provides cutting action with the smallest hole as it penetrates tissue. These needles are useful in tough tissue, such as cartilage.

A *straight needle* with a sharpened triangular blade used for skin closure without a needle holder is called a Keith needle.

A *blunt needle* terminates in a rounded end. This type of needle is used for suturing the liver or kidney, where neither cutting nor piercing is required.

A *rounded needle* is becoming more frequently used, as it passes easily through muscle and fascia but not through gloves and skin.

Eye of the Needle

The eye of the needle, where the suture attaches, may be round, oblong, or square. Needles are threaded from the inside curvature with 2 to 3 inches of suture pulled through the eye. A single twist of the double strand near the needle will lock the suture and help prevent it from pulling out of the needle.

French eye, or spring-eye, needles have a split from the inside of the eye to the end of the needle through which the suture is drawn. To thread a french eye, place the needle in a needle holder. With the needle holder in the left, or nondominant, hand and 3 inches of the suture secured by fingers of that hand, use the right, or dominant, hand to bring the suture strand over the top of the spring and down into the eye of the needle (Fig. 14–5). French eyes are used with fine sizes of suture material.

Which needle eye is appropriate depends on the area being sutured, the type of tissue, the diameter of the suture material, and the surgeon's preference. The diameter of the needle should be about the same size as the suture. Eyed needles may be reused or disposed of. If they are reused, the needles must, after each use, be cleaned and checked for burred points and eye damage. Dull or burred points may cause tissue damage, and defects in the eye will cut the suture material during threading. Prepackaged disposable needles are available and eliminate this time-consuming task.

Eyed needles cause tissue trauma due to the excessive bulk created by the needle and

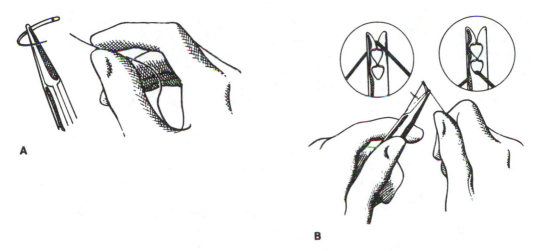

Figure 14–5. **A.** If eyed needle is threaded from inside curvature, take care to avoid pricking glove on sharp needle point. **B.** Holding suture strand taut with left hand, bring strand down over top and string into eye. Pull through about 3 inches. (*Courtesy Davis and Geck, Wayne, NJ, with permission.*)

the two suture strands passing through the tissue. For this reason many surgeons prefer atraumatic needles.

Atraumatic Needles

When the needle and suture are one continuous unit, it is referred to as a swaged, or atraumatic, suture. The diameter of the needle matches the size of the suture as closely as possible.

Atraumatic suture is available with single- and double-armed needle attachments. The needles on double-armed suture may be dissimilar and are designed for a specific surgical procedure, such as a tendon repair. Double-armed suture is frequently used in cardiovascular surgery when the surgeon wants to approximate tissue on both sides from a midpoint in the suture.

A modification of atraumatic sutures is the suture-release needle. It detaches from its suture by means of a light tug. These needles are used in bowel anastomoses and general closure when rapid placement of interrupted sutures is desired.

Needles such as those used in ophthalmic and plastic surgery require additional manufacturing techniques. Using special equipment, the needles are polished and hand honed under magnification. The needle ends are drilled and carefully matched to the diameter of the suture, and the surface of the needle undergoes a special process to permit easier penetration through tissue.

▪ PREPARING SUTURES

The surgeon's preference card will designate the type of suture to be used for each surgical procedure. A minimal amount of suture is prepared before the procedure to eliminate waste and control costs.

Sutures are prepared in the order of use. First, sutures will be used to ligate, or tie off, bleeding vessels. These sutures may be handed as a free tie, placed in the end of an instrument for a deep tie, or on a needle for a suture ligature. Nonneedled suture material is placed in a "suture book," a fan-folded towel with suture ends extending for visualization and rapid extraction (Fig. 14–6). The largest size is placed in the bottom fold, and the smallest in the top fold. The suture is pulled from the book toward the operative field to prevent contamination.

The scrub assistant is careful to avoid damage to sutures during handling. Crushing or crimping with surgical instruments, such as a needle holder or forceps, is avoided, except when grasping the free end of the suture for an instrument tie.

Suture for ligating is available in precut lengths, continuous ties on radiopaque ligating reels, or standard lengths that can be cut to meet the requirements of the surgical procedure.

For large blood vessels, the surgeon may request a suture ligature or a stick tie. It may be a swaged suture or a taper-point eyed needle threaded with suture.

The size of the needle holder depends on the size of the needle and the location of the area to be sutured. A small needle requires a needle holder with fine jaws. When the area to be sutured is deep inside a cavity, a longer needle holder will be needed than that used in superficial areas.

The needle is placed at approximately one-third the distance from the swaged or eyed end of the curved needle to its point (Fig. 14–7). The needle holder is never clamped over the swaged area, as it is the weakest needle area. The needle holder is closed to the first or second ratchet.

The needle holder is handed to the surgeon with the point of the needle down, directed toward the surgeon's thumb, and ready for immediate use. The free end of the suture is held in one hand while passing the needle holder with the other hand. The free end of the suture is handed to the first assistant; it must be allowed to drag across the sterile field.

Figure 14–6. A "suture book."

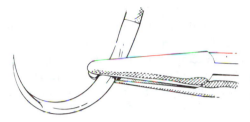

Figure 14–7. Clamp the needle holder approximately one-third the distance from swage or eye to point of needle. (*Courtesy Davis and Geck, Wayne, NJ, with permission.*)

To assist in identification, atraumatic suture may be armed, placed on a needle holder, and left in the package until it is needed (Fig. 14–8).

Safe Handling

Suture needles must be handled with extraordinary care to prevent accidental injuries to members of the scrub team. The following guidelines will be helpful:

1. Load the needle onto the needle holder directly from the package.
2. Used sterile needles are passed from the needle holder directly into the needle counter.
3. Contaminated needles are passed off the sterile field into a specimen container.
4. The needle is removed from the suture before tying the suture.
5. A magnet or tape is used when picking up needles from the floor.
6. Needles that are loaded on a needle holder and sitting on the mayo stand or back table are stored point down to avoid snagging gloves.
7. Surgeons and RNFAs may want to use a thimble on the index finger of the non-dominant hand to prevent injuries while suturing.

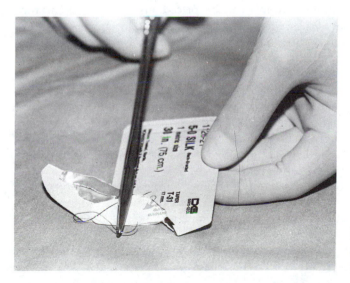

Figure 14–8. Atraumatic suture may be armed and left in the package until it is needed.

Needle Counts

The scrub assistant and the circulating nurse count needles in the operating room three times: before the beginning of the operation, before closure begins, and when skin closure is started. The scrub assistant maintains an accurate account of all needles by handing them to the surgeon on an exchange basis. Needles must never be left free on the sterile field, as they may be inadvertently dragged into the incision. Any needle broken during the procedure must be accounted for in its entirety. If the final needle count is incorrect, the surgical drapes and floor are searched. If the needle is not found, an x-ray is required to determined whether the missing needle is in the patient. If the needle is not found, an incident report must be completed and signed by the circulating nurse and surgeon.

Disposable needle count pads are available commercially. Because the pads are expensive, guidelines should be established for their use. For example, when fewer than 20 needles are used on a surgical procedure, a needle pad is not required; with more than 20 but less than 50 needles, a small-size pad is used; and when more than 50 needles are used, a large needle pad is appropriate.

▌ SUTURE TECHNIQUES

The primary suture line refers to the line of sutures used to approximate the edges of the incision during healing by first intention. An interrupted or a continuous suture technique may be used.

Interrupted sutures are placed and tied separately. If one suture breaks, the entire suture line is not disrupted; therefore, there is less opportunity for infection to spread to other interrupted sutures.

A *continuous, or running, stitch* is one suture that approximates the edges from one end of the incision to the other, and is tied only at the ends of the suture line. If a break occurs at any point in the suture, the entire suture line is in danger of disruption.

Both interrupted and continuous sutures can be placed in several different ways. Some of the most common types of suture techniques are illustrated in Figure 14–9.

Buried sutures are placed under the skin. A *purse string suture* is one suture stitched around a lumen, drawn tight, and tied to close the lumen. This stitch is used when inverting the stump of the appendix.

Subcuticular stitches are short lateral stitches taken beneath the epithelial layer of the skin. The suture comes through the upper layer of the skin at each end of the incision. The suture is drawn tightly enough to hold the skin edges in approximation and leaves a minimal scar. If a nonabsorbable suture is used, it is removed by cutting off the knot and pulling the strand through the length of the incision. Using an absorbable suture eliminates the risk of trauma and breakage during removal.

Traction sutures are used to hold tissue out of the way during the surgical procedure. A heavy, nonabsorbable suture may be placed through the tissue, such as the tongue, and then retracted to the side. Dacron or cotton umbilical tape may be put around large vessels or tendons to retract them out of the way.

A *mattress suture* is placed through the tissue from one side of the wound to the

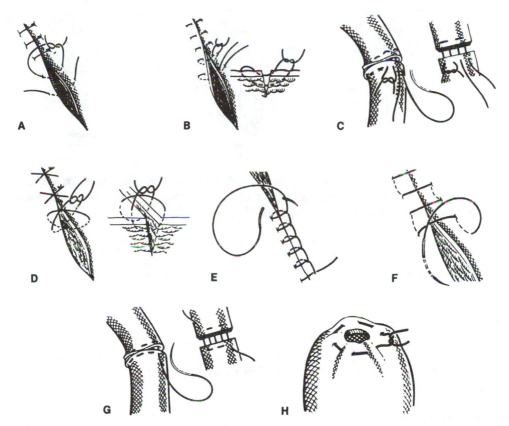

Figure 14–9. A. Interrupted skin closure. **B.** Interrupted vertical mattress. **C.** Horizontal mattress. **D.** Figure-of-8 mattress. **E.** Continuous skin closure (lock stitch). **F.** Continuous inverting mattress. **G.** Continuous everting mattress. **H.** Purse string. (*Courtesy Davis and Geck, Wayne, NJ, with permission.*)

other, then back through the tissue again. Most of the suture is buried; a small loop on one side of the incision and the knot on the other are visible on the skin.

When the wound appears to require additional support beyond that provided by the primary suture line, a secondary suture line—referred to as *retention, stay, or tension, sutures*—may be used (Fig. 14–10).

Heavy, nonabsorbable sutures on large cutting needles are placed from the fascia to the skin on each side of the primary line. Closure of the primary suture line is completed, and the stay sutures are then tied.

Each retention suture may be threaded through a short length of rubber or plastic tubing (bolster, bumper, boot) to protect the skin and suture line. The heavy sutures are prevented from cutting into the skin and suture line.

Retention sutures are frequently used when slow healing is anticipated due to obesity, malnourishment, carcinoma, or infection. They may also be used to prevent wound disruptions when postoperative stress on the primary suture line is anticipated due to cough-

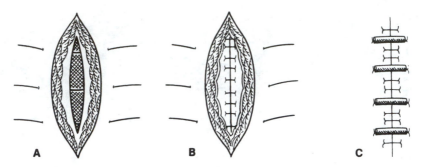

Figure 14–10. **A.** Retention sutures may be placed from inside the abdominal cavity through all layers to the skin, or **B.** the peritoneum may be closed first and retention sutures passed from fascia through skin. **C.** Bolsters often are used to protect skin from pressure of heavy retention sutures. (*Courtesy Davis and Geck, Wayne, NJ, with permission.*)

ing, vomiting, and straining. In addition, retention sutures are used for secondary closure following wound dehiscence or evisceration.

Suturing Drains
Drains may be placed in the wound to prevent the accumulation of blood and serum. These drains are frequently sutured to the skin with a nonabsorbable material so they will not slip in or out of the wound. Tubes placed in an organ or duct are sutured in place with an absorbable suture.

Stapling Instruments
Stapling instruments, which mechanically close tissue, are used for ligation and division, resection, anastomosis, and skin and fascia closure. The instruments are used in thoracic, abdominal, and gynecologic surgeries, and may be a disposable or reusable item.

Tissue manipulation and handling are reduced by the mechanical application of the instrument and the staples produce an even, airtight, leakproof closure. The instruments fire from sterile, preloaded, disposable cartridges, either a single staple or simultaneously one or two straight lines of multiple staples. Each instrument is designed for specific tissue, that is, fascia, bronchus, gastrointestinal tract, blood vessels, or other tubular structures.

The staples are shaped like a capital "B" and are noncrushing; thus, nutrition is able to pass through the staple line to the cut edge of the tissue. Healing is promoted and the possibility of necrosis reduced. The staples are essentially nonreactive, thereby reducing tissue reaction and infection. An anastomosis in which staples are used appears to function sooner than one in which manual technique is employed.

The surgeon is responsible for choosing the appropriate instrument and is instructed outside of the operating room regarding its proper use and function. Inappropriately placed staples are much more difficult to correct than manually placed sutures.

The nursing personnel must know how to assemble the instrument. Inappropriately assembled instruments may misfire. The reusable instruments are cared for in a routine manner. After use they are disassembled, terminally sterilized in the washer-sterilizer, and

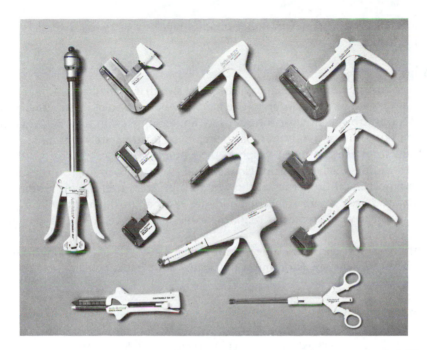

Figure 14–11. Disposable stapling instruments (*Courtesy, United States Surgical Corporation, Stamford, CT.*)

placed in the ultrasonic cleaner. They are lubricated and then steam sterilized (completely disassembled) according to the manufacturer's recommendations.

The preassembled, disposable instruments, of course, do not need assembling, cleaning, or repairing (Fig. 14–11). For economic reasons, it is important that the stapling instruments not be opened until the surgeon identifies the instrument and cartridge required for each procedure.

A variety of disposable skin staples are commercially available for the approximation of skin edges. All the staplers implant stainless steel staples in varying size cartridges and widths. Wide staples are easier to use, as they span a wider area before closing and thus assist in everting skin edges. Regular-width staples require more careful approximation and eversion of skin edges. The length of the incision will determine which size cartridge is used.

Skin stapling is the fastest method of skin closure, and skin staples have a low level of tissue reactivity. Their use may significantly shorten operating room time, reduce blood loss, and shorten postoperative hospitalization. They are removed 5 to 7 days postoperatively.

Skin Clips

Skin clips are made of noncorroding metal and may be used for skin closure or for securing towels to the skin. They are steam-sterilized and may be used if infection or drainage is present. They are applied quickly. Postoperatively, skin clips create more discomfort than suture material or skin staples. Another disadvantage is that they leave a larger scar than other skin closures.

Skin Strips

A reinforced micropore surgical tape with an adhesive that immediately adheres to the skin has been developed for skin closures. The tape may be used to close superficial lacerations in conjunction with subcuticular sutures or with interrupted skin sutures. When used with interrupted skin sutures, the sutures may be removed postoperately within 32 to 48 hours, and the skin strips will continue to support the wound.

The ease with which skin strips close wounds varies, depending on the anatomic site and the biomechanical properties of the wound site. Areas over a joint require additional support from sutures, whereas linear wounds are easily approximated using strips. Areas of the body with excessive secretions (e.g., the axilla, palms, and soles) discourage tape adherence.

Adhesive skin strips are available in widths of $\frac{1}{8}$, $\frac{1}{4}$, and $\frac{1}{2}$ inch, and lengths from $1\text{-}\frac{1}{2}$ to 4 inches. The strips may be cut to meet the needs of the patient.

▮ References

1. Riall, CT. Surgical and medical devices and their origins. *J OR Res.* 1981; 2:35.
2. *Pharmacopeia Twenty-second Revision.* Rockville, MD: United States Pharmacopeial Convention; 1990:769.

FOUR

Specific Populations and Settings

FIFTEEN

Physiological and Psychological Needs of Specific Patient Populations

All surgical patients are dependent on the nursing care delivered by the professional registered nurse. While the outcomes of care are identified and predicted for all patients, those individuals with specific physiological and psychological needs represent special challenges. The perioperative nurse who understands the special needs of these individuals will greatly enhance their perioperative experience and ensure positive outcomes by planning and providing patient care plans related to their needs. Included in this patient population are the obese, the elderly, the diabetic, and the pediatric patient.

■ OBESE PATIENTS

An obese surgical patient has specific nursing care needs that must be met during the perioperative period.

A person with an abnormally high proportion of body fat (adipose tissue) relative to lean body mass is designated as obese. Even though a patient is obese, a protein deficiency or other metabolic disturbances, such as hyperlipidemia, may be present. Morbid obesity occurs when weight exceeds 100 pounds over the ideal weight for a specific height. For this group of patients, thromboembolism is the most common cause of perioperative death.[1]

An obese patient has an increased tendency toward concomitant disease and, therefore, a decreased life expectancy. Ideally, obesity and malnutrition should be corrected prior to any invasive procedure that is not of an emergency nature, and treatment adjusted for concomitant conditions, such as hypertension and diabetes mellitus.

The severely obese patient faces an increase in surgical risk for every pound of excess weight. Many authorities indicate that an additional 25 miles of blood vessels are required to supply 30 pounds of excess fat. These additional vessels place a strain on the patient's heart, as the blood volume, cardiac output, heart size, and pulmonary ventilation all increase accordingly. The patient often cannot withstand the additional stress of surgery.

The concomitant conditions obese patients frequently suffer from are hypertension, atherosclerotic cardiovascular disease, and metabolic problems, such as diabetes mellitus. The hypertension may cause vascular changes in the kidneys that ultimately affect the elimination of protein wastes and the maintenance of fluid and electrolyte balances. In addition, the obese patient is at risk for aspiration and aspiration pneumonia, because gastric emptying time is decreased and the acidity of gastric contents is increased.

Anesthesia Management
Because intravenous access may be difficult on the obese patient, a venous cutdown may be necessary prior to the induction of anesthesia.

Anesthetic induction time is prolonged in obese patients due to the difficulty in ventilating the patient and the subsequent lower intraalveolar concentrations of anesthetic gases. Airway maintenance may also be difficult due to increased neck and chest bulk, which makes intubation difficult or impossible. As a result, mask ventilation may be required during a general anesthesia. After the patient is anesthetized higher concentrations of anesthetic agents will be required to compensate for the continued uptake of the agent by adipose tissue. Because anesthetic agents are stored in the adipose tissue and metabolized slowly, these patients are often still anesthetized when taken to the recovery area. The patient must be maintained on a respirator until the anesthetic washout is complete. It is important that the obese patient not be removed from the respirator or extubated prematurely.

Surgical Technique
Adipose tissue impacts the technical aspects of surgery and frequently extends surgical time. Adipose tissue is relatively avascular. Consequently, fewer white blood cells, fibrocytes, and nutrients are available for wound healing.

To achieve adequate exposure of the surgical site the incision in an obese patient is usually larger than normal and requires more than a normal amount of retraction to extend the layers of fatty tissue. Extra-long instruments and large retractors are required to facilitate the surgical procedure. The prolonged, excessive traction may result in an incisional hernia developing postoperatively.

The large instruments and extra retraction traumatize subcutaneous tissue and increase the patient's risk for wound complications. The larger incision and the excessive intraabdominal fat make closing the incision more difficult; frequently an increased amount of dead space results after suturing. The dead space and trauma to adipose tissue increase the risk of postoperative infection. Closed wound drains are frequently used to remove accumulated fluids and obliterate dead spaces.

Obese patients have an increased incidence of thrombophlebitis and thromboembolisms. The increase is related to the patient's relative immobility and the pressure on pelvic veins and the vena cava, resulting in venous stasis in the lower limbs. Thus, care must be taken when transferring the patient to the OR bed and in positioning the patient. Anticoagulants may be given prophylactically to decrease the potential for thromboembolic complications.

Nursing Implications
Nursing interventions are planned to reduce stress on the patient's cardiovascular, respiratory, and musculoskeletal systems during the perioperative period. Positioning the patient will require additional assistance. Psychological support is also important. Every effort is

made to maintain the patient's dignity and promote a sense of self-worth by having the proper-size patient gown, chair, transportation vehicle, and OR table available when it is required.

To decrease the potential for wound infection, a patient is instructed to shower each day for several days prior to surgery. Washing is concentrated on the intertriginous zones, particularly in the inframammary folds and under the large apron of abdominal fat. Preoperative preparation of the skin will decrease bacterial colonization (see Chapter 9).

Obesity also causes strain on joints and ligaments, leading to chronic joint pain. Osteoarthritis may limit the mobility of the spine and joints and require modifications in routine positions. Extra padding and positioning devices will be required to prevent pressure areas and bruises. In positioning the electrosurgical ground pad, care must be exercised to ensure that overlapping skin folds are not in contact with the pad as this tissue could be burned.

Postoperative Concerns

The obese patient is also more susceptible to postoperative pulmonary complications. Because the efficiency of respiratory muscles is decreased by obesity, coughing and deep breathing may be considerably more difficult for these patients. The excessively thick chest wall and abdominal adipose tissue impede diaphragmatic descent, which may result in hypoventilation and subsequent oxygen deficiency. Therefore, pulmonary complications, such as hypoxemia and atelectasis, develop more frequently in obese patients. Aggressive pain management is essential. Controlling pain will help the patient to move more easily and breath adequately postoperatively.

Postoperative instructions should highlight wound care, including symptoms of infection, and maintenance of a nutritious diet.

▌ ELDERLY PATIENTS

Over the past three decades average life span has steadily increased and led to a shift in the population's age distribution. Persons older than 65 years are predicted to account for more than 20% of the total U.S. population by the year 2020.[2] More elderly patients will require surgical treatment. Indeed, it is estimated that half of persons older than 60 will require surgery sometime during their remaining years. This is projected to increase the number of geriatric operations 130% by the year 2001.[3]

Knowledge of the aging process is evolving. Physical changes resulting from this process include systemic effects such as tissue deterioration, slowed cell division and atrophy, impaired homeostasis, a decline in the efficiency of the immune system, and decreased neuromuscular responses.

The normal physiological changes of aging that have an impact on wound healing are:

- the decreased rate of cellular replacement
- circulatory changes
- decrease in the inflammatory response
- decreased skin sensitivity
- slowed epithelialization of the wound (see Chapter 18)[4]

Aging and surgical risk are not clearly associated. Cardiovascular and pulmonary complications, however, cause the majority of deaths among elderly surgical patients. Therefore, these two body systems are carefully assessed preoperatively, monitored intraoperatively, and evaluated postoperatively. Similarly, careful preoperative assessment of an elderly patient's neurologic status provides valuable baseline data for postoperative comparison.

Table 15–1 identifies the physiologic effects of aging and the related perioperative nursing interventions. Aging, however, is a process unique to each individual, which necessitates that each patient preoperatively have a comprehensive physical and psychosocial assessment (Chapter 5). The preoperative assessment is essential to collect baseline data, establish a nursing diagnosis, and predict outcomes. The preoperative data will assist staff to recognize significant changes intraoperatively and postoperatively.

General Appearance

A decrease in height of several inches can occur as a result of bone deterioration in the spine. With age, the proportion of lean to fat tissue changes, and fat shifts from the extremities to the center of the body. The change in fat distribution may result in an older person appearing overweight. Determining accurate height and weight is essential for calculating the proper dosage of medications and anesthetic agents.

Nutritional Status

Assessment includes a review of the nutritional status and eating habits of the patient. Malnutrition may result from inadequate intake, poor digestion or absorption, and from increased nutritional need. Protein, calorie, mineral, and vitamin deficiencies are types of malnutrition. Protein-calorie malnutrition (PCM) is one of the most common nutrient deficiencies. It also is referred to as protein energy malnutrition, marasmus, or cachexia.[5]

In the elderly, protein-calorie malnutrition is most likely caused by acute and chronic disease, and vitamin deficiencies result from poor diet. Mineral deficiencies are usually secondary to drug use. It is common for elderly patients to have more than one type of nutrient deficit, ranging from mild to severe[6] (see Table 15–2).

Thermoregulatory Mechanism

One serious complication of surgery and anesthesia among the elderly is inadvertent, intraoperative hypothermia that can advance rapidly to a life-threatening situation. Hypothermia is defined as a core body temperature below 36°C (96.8°F).

The elderly have limited cardiovascular reserves, slower autonomic responses, decreased heat production, loss of fat and subcutaneous tissue, degenerative changes in their thermoregulating mechanism, and a decreased metabolic rate. All of these factors impact the production and conservation of body heat. For each decrease of 1° in body temperature, the basal metabolic rate falls 6% to 7%. Hypothermia, therefore, can occur rapidly. The thermoregulating mechanism may be further impaired by anesthetic agents or trauma.

Nursing Interventions

Maintaining body temperature preoperatively and intraoperatively is key to preventing postoperative hypothermia. The following factors promote heat loss from patients during surgery:

(Text continues on page 352)

TABLE 15–1. PHYSIOLOGIC EFFECTS OF AGING WITH RELATED PERIOPERATIVE NURSING INTERVENTIONS

Changes	Significance of Changes	Nursing Interventions
Cardiovascular system		
The number of elastic fibers in the heart decreases, resulting in rigidity. The cardiac wall and the endocardium thicken. The valves of the heart become rigid.	Cardiac output decreases; heart rate decreases and contractility of heart muscles is reduced. Cardiac reserve decreases.	Assess for hypoxemia, shock, and cardiac failure. Minimize the number of stressors. Administer oxygen as needed.
In the arterial system, the concentration of collagen increases and individual fibers stiffen. The walls thicken, and calcium and cholesterol accumulate in the vascular walls.	Peripheral resistance increases and peripheral circulation decreases.	Assess for thrombosis formation. Initiate measures for preventing venous thrombosis: —antiembolic stockings —sequential compression device
Sympathetic and parasympathetic nervous supply to heart decreases.	Ability to increase cardiac output decreases.	Assess for hypotension and shock. Decrease the number of stressors. Protect from falls related to orthostatic hypotension. Monitor blood loss, provide visualization of sponges and suction canister. Check on availablity of blood. Intraop—blood gases and electrolytes will be required.
Conduction of impulses may become blocked due to anatomic changes in conduction system and ischemia.	Interrupted conduction impulses cause dysrhythmias.	Assess for cardiac dysrhthmias.
Respiratory system		
Cross-linkage in collagen and elastic fibers around alveolar sacs increases; air spaces dilate; the number and size of alveolar pores increase, and lung tissue becomes less elastic.	Vital capacity of lung decreases about 25%; total lung capacity decreases minimally. Forced expiratory volumes and maximum breathing capacity decrease. Residual volume and functional residual capacity increase. Reduction in number of alveoli can result in decreased diffusion surface for oxygen and carbon dioxide. Blood oxygen level decreases; cerebral oxygenation decreases. Inadequate elimination of carbon dioxide, combined with deterioration in renal and hormonal function, leads to electrolyte imbalances.	Assess baseline parameters. Monitor respiratory status for failure. Administer oxygen as needed. Postop encourage mobility, unless contraindicated. Preop teaching to include coughing and deep breathing. Institute patient safety measures. Monitor patient for electrolyte imbalances.
Costal cartilages calcify. Thoracic skeletal deformities occur, postural changes occur, and intervertebral disks of thoracic spine degenerate.	Rib mobility decreases; chest wall compliance decreases; anteroposterior diameter may increase, and the exchange of air between lungs and environment decreases.	Encourage pulmonary hygiene to prevent pulmonary infections. Assess for pulmonary infection. Monitor for hypoxia postop.

(continued)

TABLE 15–1. *(Continued)*

Changes	Significance of Changes	Nursing Interventions
Muscle tone decreases as does sensitivity to stimuli.	Cough reflex diminishes.	Assess for respiratory infection.
Epithelium dries and atrophies.	Ciliary mechanism becomes less effective.	
Neurological system		
The number of neurons decreases and they are infiltrated by lipofuscin and fat.	Losses occur in sensory functions; i.e., tactile sense decreases and pain tolerance increases. Intellectual ability remains stable.	Protect patient from pressure sores and other skin and joint damage. Talk with patient as an adult, not a child.
The nerve fibers degenerate and decrease in number.	Reaction time slows due to decrease of conduction velocity of impulse through peripheral nerves. Prone to delirium and altered mental status while in hospital.	Provide ample time for decisions. Implement safety measures. Orient frequently.
Genitourinary system		
Anatomical narrowing and loss of vessels occurs, and vasoconstriction is persistent.	Renal blood flow decreases.	Assess for shock. Anesthesia and surgery significantly depress renal blood flow and glomerular filtration rate. Renal blood flow may not return to normal for 5 hours after surgery.
The amount of connective tissue between the apices of the pyramids of the kidney decreases; the number of functionally intact glomeruli diminishes.	Glomerular filtration decreases; effective plasma flow decreases, as does reabsorption time.	Monitor for side effects of drugs since drug excretion is often reduced or prolonged. Monitor for transient mental dysfunction.
	The ability of the kidney to form ammonia is impaired.	Monitor fluid and electrolyte balance.
Gross anatomical change leads to retention and stasis of urine and loss of power to sterilize urine.	Bladder capacity decreases. The sensation of the need to void may be absent or occur only when the bladder is almost full to capacity. Urinary frequency occurs and the residual volume increases.	Assess for urinary tract infection. Insert indwelling catheter with caution. Assist with voiding as needed.
Prostate enlarges.	Normal urinary flow is obstructed.	Monitor fluid and electrolyte balance.
Gastrointestinal system		
Diminished taste buds, loss of teeth, and loss of the grinding surface of molars.	Poor appetite and inability to eat can result in malnutrition.	Postop teaching; encourage intake of nutritious, appealing meals. Refer to dietician or home health nurse. Have dentures available immediately postop.
Hydrochloric production decreases.	Pernicious anemia develops due to absence of intrinsic factor in gastric secretions.	Assess for pernicious anemia, i.e., anorexia, soreness of the tongue, fatigue, and malnutrition.
Gastric mobility decreases.	Constipation occurs.	Identify normal pattern of bowel elimination.

TABLE 15-1. *(Continued)*

Changes	Significance of Changes	Nursing Interventions
		Monitor patient's bowel sounds preopertively/ postoperatively. Postop: encourage increased activity, fluid intake, and discuss effects of sedatives and narcotics on GI activity.
Decrease in saliva production and esophageal peristalsis.	Difficulty in swallowing as mouth may be excessively dry.	Postop: offer ice chips, mouth swabs, and other moistening measures. Monitor for aspiration.
Blood flow to liver is reduced, decreasing drug detoxification.	Drug toxicity.	Assess for side effects of drugs.
Musculoskeletal system		
Bone resorption increases. Muscle mass decreases. Joints degenerate.	Brittle bones, tendency for fractures increases. Muscle strength, endurance, and agility decrease. Joints become stiff.	Position patient on OR bed carefully. Move patient gently. Place pillow under knees and head.
Integumentary system		
Epithelial cells thin; this leads to prominence of bony markings.	Risk of pressure sores increases	Implement measures to prevent pressure areas. Lift patient to avoid shearing force.
Mitosis slows. Increased vascular fragility causes reduced vascularity.	Wound healing is delayed.	Postop: promote wound healing via discussion of nutrition and wound care.
Subcutaneous fatty layers thin; collagen and elastic fibers regress, and epithelial layer shrinks.	Skin becomes dry and inelastic; patient's susceptibility to cold environmental temperatures increases. Bruise easily.	Use paper tape on dressings or an appropriate alternative. Implement measures to prevent pressure sores. Do not use skin turgor as an indicator of hydrational status, i.e., elevation of mucous membrane, laboratory studies, urinary output. Keep patient warm; prevent damage to skin.
Sweat glands decrease in number, which prevents patient from sweating freely.	Susceptibility to heat exhaustion increases.	Monitor patient's temperature.
Melanocytes decrease.	Skin pale.	Assess for signs of anemia; do not confuse with pallor.
Sensory system		
Cochlea undergoes degeneratiive changes. Eardrum thickens, decreasing sound transmission.	Hearing is diminished. Difficulty hearing high-pitched sounds, and gradual loss of hearing.	Speak clearly, slowly, and in a normal tone while standing in front of the patient. Keep extraneous noise to a minimum. Encourage patient to wear hearing aid to OR. Leave in place during local procedures and replace in PACU if patient has a general anesthesia. Have paper and pencil to write instructions as needed.

(continued)

TABLE 15–1. *(Continued)*

Changes	Significance of Changes	Nursing Interventions
Elasticity of the lens decreases.	Eyesight is diminished.	Encourage patient to wear glasses to OR. Focus high-intensity light on the area to be seen. Postop ambulation: prevent patient from falling; provide adequate support.

- low ambient temperature of the operating room
- anesthetic agents
- positioning and skin preparation
- a long procedure in which a large body cavity is entered

As the body is exposed to cold temperatures, blood is shunted away from peripheral body parts to the head. Because the head lacks fat deposits and vasoconstriction capability, heat loss from the head can be as much as 25% to 60% of the total body heat loss. As the body attempts to conserve body heat by constricting peripheral vessels, the skin may appear mottled and feel cold.

To prevent heat loss place a warm blanket or a heating/cooling blanket on the OR table, increase the ambient temperature of the operating room, cover the patient with warm blankets, and put a head covering on the patient. Infrared lights and reflective materials placed over the patient will assist in retaining body heat. Wound irrigating fluid, blood, and intravenous solutions should be warmed. Anesthetic gases may be humidified and warmed before they are administered.

Intraoperative delays may result in extended exposure and must be prevented. Having all supplies assembled prior to surgery will assist in preventing delays.

Postoperative Care

Postoperative nursing care of the hypothermic elderly patient is continuing the measures that were implemented intraoperatively. Temperature monitoring is a high priority. Wet linen is changed to ensure the patient's warmth and comfort. Placing warm plastic containers of saline near the groin or axilla provides additional heat for the patient. Wrapping the containers in a towel helps prevent burns to the thin, fragile skin of the aged.

Rewarming an elderly patient must occur slowly. If it is done too rapidly, many complications are possible, including hypoxia, acid-base disturbances, pulmonary edema, pneumonia, dehydration, hyperglycemia, and acute tubular necrosis.

Signs of hypothermia in a conscious patient are frequently misdiagnosed. They include apathy, listlessness, slurring of speech, and disorientation.

Response to Medications

Geriatric patients tolerate many medications poorly, because their ability to detoxify and excrete drugs is reduced. Narcotics and sedatives interact with anesthetics and must be administered judiciously.

TABLE 15–2. COMMON NUTRITIONAL DISORDERS OF THE ELDERLY

Condition	Contributing Factors	Symptoms	Diagnostics
Chronic protein-calorie malnutrition (PCM)	anorexia malabsorption disorders protein-losing enteropathy cancer paralysis chemotherapy radiation therapy end-stage renal or hepatic disease depression/isolation	wasted appearance loss of lean body mass loss of subcutaneous fat brittle hair ridged or banded nails dermatoses of lower legs apathy weakness	protein <6g/dL albumin <3.2 g/dL hemoglobin <12 g/dL TLC <800 upper-arm circumference <29.3 cm (male) <28.5 cm (female) ferritin <15 mg/dL total iron binding capacity <250 g/dL transferrin <30% low weight for height no response to skin tests
Protein malnutrition (kwashiorkor)	burns (severe) blistering dermatoses cancer renal disease with massive albuminuria (may be secondary to toxicity from mercurial diuretics)	edema delayed wound healing loss of lean body mass (patient may appear obese)	protein <6g/dL TLC <800 upper-arm circumference <29.3 cm (male) <28.5 cm (female) low weight for height

Iron deficiency	blood loss secondary to hemorrhage from:
	  1. tumors of the GI tract
	  2. esophageal varices of alcoholism
	  3. ulcers related to use of anti-inflammatory agents
	  4. anticoagulant use
		pallor
		weakness
		dyspnea
			hemoglobin <12 g/dL
			hematocrit <37 g/dL

B12 deficiency	malabsorption due to:
	  1. lack of intrinsic factor
	      partial/total gastrectomy
	  2. loss of ileal absorption site
	    a. regional enteritis
	    b. ileal resection
	    c. radiation enteritis
	  3. drugs
	    a. colchicine
	    b. neomycin
	  4. hypothyroidism
	  5. liver disease
		weakness
		numbness/tingling
		dyspnea
		tachycardia
		hypotension
		pallor
		sore mouth/tongue
			B12 levels <200 pg/mL
			megaloblasts in bone marrow and peripheral blood
			Schilling test with <8% absorption of radioactive B12

Folate deficiency	low intake of food sources of folate
	  green leafy vegetables, liver, fortified cereals
	drugs
	  a. phenytoin
	  b. phenobarbital
	  c. cholestyramine
	  d. sulfasalazine
	  e. methotrexate
		confusion
		loss of memory
		symptoms similiar to B12 deficiency
			megaloblasts in bone marrow
			blood serum folate <5 g/dL

(continued)

TABLE 15–2. *(Continued)*

Condition	Contributing Factors	Symptoms	Diagnostics
Thiamine deficiency	alcoholism gastric carcinoma hemodialysis	Wernicke-Korsakoff syndrome (in alcoholics) ptosis of eyelids nystagmus ataxia weakness	history of alcohol abuse abatement of symptoms with thiamine administration

From R. Collinsworth. *Determining nutritional status of the elderly surgical patient: Steps in the assessment process.* AORN J. 1991;54 (3):626–627.

Because elderly patients frequently self-medicate with over-the-counter drugs and do not consider the medication important in their history, it is important to ask specifically about such drugs. Several of these medications may have a significant impact on the patient's fluid and electrolyte balance or cause drug-related complications and must be included in the assessment documentation.

The effects of various medications in the elderly include:

- Propranolol hydrochloride and diazepam cause excessive drowsiness and adverse drug reactions, including bradycardia and heart block, twice as often in the very elderly as in middle-aged people.
- Digitalis or its derivatives cause digitalis toxicity because of electrolyte changes that occur in major surgery.
- Nitroglycerin, taken during the night or during exercise, causes people with angina to be poor surgical risks.
- Highly acidic nonsteroidal anti-inflammatory medication, such as piroxicam, causes displacement of other medications because it is bound to plasma proteins.
- Concurrent use of anticoagulant and anti-inflammatory medications may result in displacement of anticoagulants, and bleeding may result due to more anticoagulant in active form.

Fat-soluble drugs, such as thiopental sodium, have a prolonged duration because they are absorbed by body fat, which decreases with aging. In addition, as the total amount of intracellular water decreases and liver and kidney function decreases, there is a potential for increased concentration and an extended life for all medications. Therefore, patients are monitored continuously during the entire perioperative period for hypoxia.

General anesthesia and some drugs may cause transient mental dysfunction in an elderly patient. Labels, such as senile or demented, are avoided in describing the behaviors of a geriatric patient because other providers may modify their interaction with the patient based on this observation of transient behavior. Possible etiologies for altered mental status among elderly patients include:

Pneumonia
Diabetes
Hyperthyroidism
Vitamin B12 deficiency
Decrease in RBC
Hypoxia
Fecal impaction
Elevated/decreased temperature
Bladder distention
Dehydration
Acute blood loss
Restraints
Intubation

Drugs
  Tranquilizers
  Sedatives
  Cardiovascular drugs
  Antidepressants
  Digitalis
  Diuretics
  Antihypertensives
  Antiemetics
  Narcotics
  Anesthetic agents

Cognitive Abilities

The psychological assessment, including cognitive, affective, and intellectual behaviors, is a significant component of the overall assessment of an elderly patient. Considerations include:

- socioeconomic, the patient's needs postoperatively and the support network available
- the patient's home environment and his or her ability to manage activities of daily living
- assessment of the family's or spouse's ability to provide competent care following discharge

Age-related intellectual changes in an older adult are best identified in the three-stage model of memory defined by Murdock.[7]

1. Sensory memory. The fleeting perceptions of the visual, auditory, olfactory, and tactile senses are information received by the senses for an extremely brief moment. Visual memory lasts about 1/2 to 1 second, auditory memory about 2 seconds, and it does not pass into primary memory.[8]

2. Primary memory. Primary memory, or short-term memory, includes what is passed on by the sensory information if it is not deleted by decay or subsequent stimuli. It is also brief storage and is frequently referred to as "What I have in mind."[8]

3. Secondary memory. Long-term memory includes all that is known.

The elderly have sensory changes in seeing and hearing, but sensory memory does not appear to change with age. Primary memory is brief but appears to play an important part in learning. Retrieval and speed of recall are less in older adults, but there is no great loss in primary memory with age.[9]

Research of secondary memory reports substantial changes with age. It is thought that with age, defects develop in both acquisition and retrieval of new information. Memory failure seems to occur most frequently in older adults with physical or emotional needs that interfere.

Older adults usually function in crystallized intelligence, which considers the person's past experiences, disease processes, education, learning, and lifestyle. Crystallized intelligence consists of mental abilities, such as information content, verbal comprehension, social intelligence, and number facility.

The implications of this research for perioperative nurses is that older adults can learn; however, to retain information they may need to have smaller amounts given to them frequently.

Preoperative Teaching

Perioperative nurses must ensure that when older patients return home following surgery they are able to act as autonomously and independently as possible. Therefore, preoperative teaching is a priority, and sufficient time must be allocated for this activity. Traditional approaches and various visual aids may require modification for use with the older patient population.

The nurse's attitude toward an elderly surgical patient is a significant component in the interaction that occurs between the two. Because of stereotypes and myths, some nurses have negative attitudes toward elderly people and unconsciously distort their intended messages.[10]

Nonverbal negative behavior may include avoiding eye contact, appearing rushed, pacing, looking out the door, frowning, furrowing eyebrows, turning away when the patient is speaking, and leaning away during interactions. An elderly patient usually perceives such behavior as resentment or indifference and it inhibits the development of a trusting nurse-patient relationship.[11]

Touch is very important to an older patient. A nurse's gentle touch transmits caring and concern. For the patient it can ensure a feeling of security and set the tone for interaction.

Learning cannot proceed if the elderly patient has unmet needs. These needs must be a priority of the perioperative nurse when planning education during the presurgical and postsurgical periods. If patients have anxieties, fears, or worries, memory deficits become more pronounced and it is more difficult to comprehend and retrieve information that may be vital to their welfare. Relaxation techniques, with progressive muscle relaxation, increase an elderly patient's ability to learn. Any pain that a patient has is dealt with before beginning a teaching session.

Teaching is done in a quiet environment. Environmental distractions and background noise greatly interfere with hearing when presbycusis is present. Too many stimuli from outside sources interfere with a patient's ability to concentrate and motivation to learn.

Internal memory strategies employed to counter secondary memory deficits may include rehearsal, imagery, categorization, the use of mnemonics, and practice.[8] External memory aids include notes, calendars, reminders from other people, and articles or items that trigger memory. Visual aids are extremely important because of the elderly patient's hearing degeneration, which may adversely affect communication and understanding. In addition, because of retrieval problems all preoperative and postoperative discharge instructions are written in large print and should be given to the patient to take home. A magnifying glass should be available to help a patient read instructions or consent forms.

Assessing the patient's understanding of information is important. Encouraging questions, obtaining frequent feedback of key points, and observing return demonstrations will provide opportunities to correct misunderstandings and facilitate retention of information. The perioperative nurse must be sensitive to signs that a patient is becoming overwhelmed with information and either stop the flow of new information or slow communication.

Additional time in the holding area should be allocated for an elderly patient to become oriented to the surgical environment, get undressed, put clothes away, and secure personal belongings, such as eyeglasses or hearing aids.

Before going to the operating room, the patient should void to prevent bladder distention or incontinence during the surgical procedure. Whenever possible, an elderly patient should be allowed to take dentures, a hearing aid, or eyeglasses to the operating room. These sensory aids frequently help the patient follow directions and maintain some control over the situation.

When technique permits, a surgical mask should not be worn when talking to the patient. The mask muffles the voice, and the patient may need to read lips. An assistive listening device (e.g., a PockeTalker) may be used to transmit environmental sounds from a microphone to headphones that the patient wears. These devices may be worn in the preoperative area, the preanesthesia area, and the PACU.[11]

Aging is a universal process that for each individual is genetically determined, environmentally modulated, and event dependent. For a geriatric surgical patient the following nursing diagnoses must be carefully considered:

- Risk for infection
- Risk for fluid volume deficit
- Risk for anxiety reaction
- Risk for positioning injury
- Risk for confusion
- Risk for impaired skin integrity
- Sensory/perceptural alterations; visual and auditory

The perioperative nurse may enhance the quality of a major event—surgical intervention—by providing individualized care to the elderly patient.

▌PATIENTS WITH DIABETES MELLITUS

Undergoing surgery is particularly stressful for diabetic patients. Even persons with well-controlled diabetes mellitus may have problems related to the stress of surgery, fluid and nutritional changes, and altered physical activity. Diabetics are also prone to infection and the surgical incision opens a new portal for infectious agents. Wound healing is delayed due to circulatory and metabolic changes (see Chapter 18).

To minimize these problems, patients with diabetes require specific preoperative and postoperative care. Clinical care varies depending on whether the patient has insulin-dependent (Type I or IDDM) or noninsulin-dependent diabetes (Type II or NIDDM) and on whether the surgery is elective or emergency.

The goal of preoperative care for Type I diabetic patients is to regulate the diabetes; weeks may be required to stabilize the condition. On the other hand, Type II patients may require little preparation. Most are managed on diet alone or with oral hypoglycemic medication.

Implications for Nursing Care

A variety of treatment plans may be prescribed for a patient with diabetes mellitus. The anesthesiologist and surgeon determine the regimen based on the severity and type of diabetes, the length and type of surgery, and the presence of other diseases.

Preoperative laboratory tests may include fasting and postprandial blood sugar, urinalysis for sugar and acetone, complete blood count, blood urea nitrogen, serum electrolytes, EKG, and a chest x-ray. A one-hour preprocedure blood sugar may be requested to prevent the patient's developing hypoglycemia during surgery. If blood sugar level is low, the patient will require an intravenous infusion of 5% glucose in water before anesthesia is induced.

The diabetic patient is usually scheduled for morning surgery so that the patient's diet and insulin regimen are interrupted by NPO as little as possible. The procedure should be canceled or delayed only after consulting with the anesthesiologist and surgeon.

Intraoperatively, if the patient is undergoing major surgery or has moderate or severe diabetes, 1000 ml of 5% glucose in saline or water is administered intravenously. To cover the IV glucose, one half of the patient's normal daily dose of insulin is usually given.

Continuous monitoring of blood glucose levels is essential throughout the perioperative period and may be accomplished by using "point of testing" equipment. The glucometer accurately measures blood sugar and may be kept in the OR or PACU. The glucometer must be calibrated according to the manufacturer's directions and nurses should periodically demonstrate competency in performing the tests. Both the competencies and the calibrations are documented.

Postoperatively the goals of intervention include:

- stabilize the patient's condition
- reestablish control of the diabetes
- prevent wound infection
- promote wound healing

All possible measures are taken to prevent nausea and vomiting, because they will interrupt the patient's ingestion of food. A change in intake would require an adjustment in drug therapy or an extended hospitalization.

Prior to discharge, a patient will need instruction about drug and dietary management. Diabetic retinopathy may make it difficult for a patient to read medication labels or written postoperative instructions. Peripheral neuropathy may decrease a patient's hand movement and sensations and make dressing changes and other self-care activities difficult. A home-care aide or nurse may be needed to assist the patient achieve the level of activity demonstrated before surgery.

▌ PEDIATRIC PATIENTS

The conditions that require surgery in pediatric patients are not limited to one area of the body or to any one surgical speciality, but several procedures are exclusive to this patient population. Many of the principles discussed in other chapters of this text are pertinent for pediatric patients and need only to be "scaled down" to meet the needs of a child. For example, the principles of positioning and preventing pressure areas are the same for adult and pediatric patients, but the size of positioning aids is scaled down for smaller patients. A guiding principle, however, for the perioperative nurse in caring for a pediatric patient is: *The pediatric patient is not a small adult.* The physiological and psychological responses of children are different from those of adults.

A pediatric patient is a unique human being who has age-specific developmental needs that must be addressed by the nurse. Table 15–3 lists the levels of achievement, by age group, in developing physical/motor, sensory, language, and social interaction skills. Not all the milestones occur according to this chronological scale. This information, therefore, is used as a guide in developing an individual plan of care for a pediatric patient. The ages of pediatric patients range from that of fetus to adolescent, ages 12 through 16. Commonly used terms and chronological ages are:

- Fetus—in utero
- Neonate—0 to 28 days
- Infant—28 days to 18 months
- Toddler—18 to 30 months
- Preschool—2-1/2 to 5 years
- School age—6 to 12 years
- Adolescent—12 through 16 years

Physiologic Concerns

Unique physiologic characteristics make children different from adults and can affect surgical outcomes. Many of these differences are evident in Table 15–4: Pediatric Values By Age Groups.

As shown in Table 15–5, major areas of physiologic concern with neonates can be grouped into five areas: thermoregulatory, integumentary, respiratory, metabolic, and fluid and electrolyte balances. A disturbance in one area often may be the result of abnormal symptoms in others. For example, if cold stress, hypoglycemia, hypovolemia, and sepsis occur, the young child is susceptible to respiratory arrest.

Respiratory Management

Airway management in children is a priority because they have small nares, a relatively large tongue, and the diameter of the trachea is small, resulting in a disproportionate narrowing of the airway. This narrowing of the trachea provides an anatomic cuff whenever tracheal intubation is required. For this reason, cuffed endotracheal tubes are not generally used in children before they are 9 years old, because the tubes place pressure within the subglottic area and could result in stenosis if intubation is traumatic or use prolonged.

TABLE 15–3. AGE-SPECIFIC DEVELOPMENTAL NEEDS OF THE INFANT TO 4-YEAR-OLD

Age	Physical/Motor	Sensory	Social	Vocalization
1 month	No head control Hands closed Grasp reflex strong	Fixates on moving objects Quiets when hears a voice	Watches faces intently	Cries to express displeasure

3 months	Holds small objects
	Able to lift head 45° off table
		Locates sound by turning
		  head
		Begins to coordinate
		  different stimuli
			Interested in surroundings
			Shows awareness of
			  strange situations
			Ceases crying when parent enters
			  room
				Squeals, coos, babbles
				"Talks" when spoken to

6 months	Birth weight doubles
	Teething may begin, chewing,
	  biting
	Rolls back to abdomen
	Bears weight when held
		Looks up and down
		Prefers complex stimuli
		Can localize sounds made
		  above ear
			Fear of strangers
			Holds arms out to be picked up
			Mood swings from crying to laugh-
			  ing with little provocation
				Begins to imitate sounds
				Vocalized to toys, mirror
				  image
				Laughs aloud

1 year	Birth weight tripled
	6–8 teeth
	Anterior fontanel almost closed
	Walks with support
	Sits without help
	Turns pages in book
		Can follow rapidly moving
		  object
		Controls and adjusts
		  response to sound; lis-
		  tens for sound to recur
			Shows emotions
			May have "security" blanket, or
			  favorite toy
			Fearful in strange situations; clings
			  to parent
				Says two or more words
				Understands meaning of
				  several words and can
				  follow directions
				Recognizes objects by name
				Imitates animal sounds

2 years	Beginning daytime
	  bladder/bowel control
	Goes up and down stairs
	Turns door knobs, unscrews
	  lids
		Accommodation well
		  developed
			Increased independence from par-
			  ents
			Sustained attention span
				Uses 2–3 word phrases
				Understands directional
				  commands
				Verbalized need for
				  toileting, food or drink
				Talks incessantly

3 years	Jumps off bottom step
	Stands on one foot
	May try to dance but balance
	  not adequate
		Builds towers with blocks
		Copies a circle, names
		  what is drawn
			Dresses self
			Knows own sex
			Talks to toys
			May have fear of dark
			Increased ability to separate from
			  parents for short periods
				Talks incessantly
				Asks questions constantly

4 years	Skips and hops on one foot
	Walks down stairs using alter-
	  nate feet
		Can lace shoes
		Draws; can copy square,
		  adds three parts to
		  stick figure
			Very independent, tends to be
			  selfish and impatient
			Has mood swings
			Identifies strongly with parent of
			  opposite sex
			Many fears
				Tells stories, can count

Cartilage development before muscle growth also makes the airway more prone to collapse than an adult's airway.

At birth the number of saccules and primitive alveoli is 8% of the number in adults. Alveolar maturation continues until 8 to 10 years of age. To satisfy increased oxygen demands, alveolar ventilation among children is twice that of adults. The respiratory rate increases faster than the volume of air. This leads to decreased respiratory reserves related to

TABLE 15–4. PEDIATRIC VALUES BY AGE GROUPS*

	Neonate 0–28 days	Infant 4 wk–18 mo	Toddler 18–30 mo	Preschool 2 1/2–5 yr	School 5–12 yr	Adolescent 12–16 yr
Blood pressure	78/47	95/60	96/56	102/60	112/72	125/81
Pulse (per min)	70	120	110	100	100	80
Respirations (per min)	30–40	32	30	25	22	20
Temperature (degrees)	36–37.7 C 97–100 F	37.7 C 99.8 F	35.8–37.7 C 96.5–99.8 F	35.8–37.2 C 96.5–99 F	36.7 C 98.1 F	36.6 C 97.8 F
Blood volume (ml/kg body wt)	75–85	75–80	75	75	75	70
Hemoglobin (g/dL)	16.5–19.5	15.6–>11.6	9.2–15.5	9.6–15.5	11.5–15.5	12.0–16.0
Hematocrit (mL/dL)	49–54	45–>35	35–36	35–37	35–45	36–49
White blood count (mm)	20,000	4,500–11,000	7,000–10,000	7,000–13,000	7,000–13,000	7,000–10,000

*Values represent averages for the age group.

functional and structural immaturity and increased anesthetic requirements in relationship to size. The uptake of anesthesia is faster in children because of increased alveolar ventilation and cardiac output.

The neonate is transported in an isolette to the OR. The isolette has a blend of oxygen and air to prevent retrolental fibroplasia or retinopathy of prematurity. Transport is completed quickly to prevent the infant from receiving the dry isolette air any longer than is necessary. High humidity is desired to liquefy viscid pulmonary secretions and thereby decrease the potential for respiratory complications.

Thermoregulation

Maintaining body temperature is difficult for neonates and infants. They have a relatively greater body surface and a thinner subcutaneous fat layer than adults. Therefore, heat loss may be four times that of the adult. Neonates and infants tend to become hypothermic during anesthesia and surgery. A body temperature registering below 35°C represents the potential for other problems, such as respiratory depression, hypoglycemia, acidosis, and sepsis.

The greatest risk of hypothermia is usually during postanesthesia recovery. During surgery the temperature in the OR is lower than the body temperature. Consequently, body temperature drops. Hypothermia is associated with decreased oxygen consumption as long as the thermoregulatory mechanism is abolished by the drugs producing anesthesia. When, however, anesthesia is discontinued, oxygen consumption increases rapidly to correct the hypothermia. The increase is metabolically very expensive. High oxygen consumption during the interval when respiratory and cardiac responses are depressed can result in severe hypoxia, acidosis, and cardiorespiratory failure.

TABLE 15-5. SPECIFIC PHYSIOLOGIC CONCERNS IN NURSING CARE OF THE NEONATE PATIENT

Metabolic	Fluid & Electrolyte	Thermoregulatory	Integumentary	Respiratory
Glucose is rapidly depleted	Hemorrhage can occur as Vitamin K is not present for prothombin formation until after 4 days of age Glomerular filtration rate and renal tubular function not well developed; can result in fluid overload Dehydration can occur rapidly	Large body surface relative to body weight Difficulty in producing heat Poor thermal insulation Ability to shiver not developed General anesthesia dilates cutaneous blood vessels and disrupts central thermoregulatory mechanism	Skin is thin and delicate Thin subcutaneous layer of fat	Decreased ventilatory compliance due to inadequate surfactant causing atelectasis, pneumothorax, pulmonary fibrosis or edema Cartilage not well developed/prone to collapse Alveolar ventilation increased to meet demands for oxygen Respiratory muscles not well developed

Nursing Implications

Preop fluid management to include: *-6 hrs clear liquids* *-4 hrs NPO* *Breastfed up to 4 hrs* *Procedures scheduled as first case* *Oral intake resumed ASAP postop* *Sugar nipple may assist to keep patient comforted and quiet*	*Check to see that Vitamin K was given at birth* *Type and cross match* *IV microbore tubing with 30-ml drip chamber to prevent fluid overload* *Remove all air from IV tubing* *Use rubber band as tourniquet* *Protect IVs from dislodgement* *Weigh all sponges immediately* *Attach specimen trap directly to suction tip to collect and accurately calculate blood loss*	*Use isolette for transport* *Maintain isolette temperature:* *34° C (93.2° F)* *Monitor temperature* *Implement measures to prevent heat loss:* *Keep neonate covered* *Increase temperature of OR* *Use radiant warmer/warming lights: 27" from child* *Use warming mattress with two baby blankets to prevent skin burns* *Plastic bubble pack placed on mattress and covered with baby blankets* *Use plastic baggies/cotton cast padding to wrap arms, legs, top of head* *Apply knitted stockinet thermodrape cap* *Warm water for prep* *Warm solutions for sponges and irrigation* *Plug isolette in to keep warm for PO transportation* *Prevent pooling of prep solutions*	*Apply tape carefully to avoid pressure sores* *Dispersive electrode of appropriate size placed on back* *Gauze used to secure legs* *Prevent pooling of solutions/blood* *Absorbable subcuticular suture for skin closure with adhesive spray or collodion*	*Have bulb syringe available for aspiration* *Anesthetic gases heated and humidified* *Proper size BP cuff and EKG pads* *Assist with intubation* *Have Doppler ultrasound available* *Tape pulse oximeter probe to palm or mid-foot to avoid pressure*

The four basic mechanisms of heat transfer in the neonate include:

- *Radiation:* loss of heat from the body surface to cooler solid surfaces not in direct contact, such as cold metal equipment and cold walls in the OR suite
- *Convection:* flow of heat from the body surface to cooler ambient air, such as that in the cold operating room
- *Conduction:* loss of heat from the body surface to cooler surfaces in direct contact, such as a cold operating room bed
- *Evaporation:* loss of heat when a liquid is converted to a vapor, such as cold prep and irrigating solutions

Metabolic Concerns

Neonates and infants have a greater need than adults to minimize their loss of body protein. They develop metabolic imbalances more rapidly than adults.

The primary mechanism for heat production in a neonate is metabolizing brown fat, a process referred to as nonshivering thermogenesis. Brown fat is a specialized adipose tissue located in the posterior neck along the interscapular and vertebral areas; it also surrounds the kidneys. It has a greater capacity for heat production than ordinary adipose tissue.

Infants undergoing surgery may have an increased risk of hypoglycemia. Cold stress, sepsis, and hypoxia add metabolic and energy requirements for the young child. Anesthesia, surgical trauma, and sepsis may also increase energy requirements by 10% to 15% up to 3 weeks postoperatively.[12]

As noted in Table 15–5, neonates and infants do not have the ability to shiver, and have a decreased ability to produce heat. By 3 hours after birth all hepatic glycogen may have been used; muscle glycogen stores are completely utilized by 48 hours.[13] During surgery, it is essential to replace glucose in an infant and a young child, as hypoglycemia compounds cold stress and oxygen and fluid requirements subject the pediatric patient to septic risks.

Fluid and Electrolyte Balance

Children have a larger percentage of their body weight in extracellular water than do adults. Infants can have 70% to 90% of their body weight in water. Increased metabolic rate also increases the need for fluids as does the use of radiant heat warmers, and ventilators. A crying child may double the loss of fluid.

Dehydration can be evaluated by determining body weight, vital signs, urinary output, and skin turgor, and assessing mucous membranes, neurologic status, eyeballs, and fontanels.

Limited renal function contributes to the need for increased surveillance to prevent fluid overload in the pediatric patient. Postoperatively, until capillaries begin to heal and lymphatic function returns, children may require 1-1/2 to 2 times more maintenance fluids to sustain fluid volume and blood pressure. Fluid delivery chambers and intravenous infusion devices help prevent accidental fluid overload. By 24 to 48 hours after surgery, the kidneys, if they have been well hydrated, begin the process of diuresis, and fluid administration can be decreased. Renal function improves during the first 2 months of life and approaches adult levels by 2 years.

When surgery is performed on a neonate, it is important for the nurse to verify that vitamin K was given after delivery. Vitamin K catalyzes the synthesis of prothrombin in the liver. An adult's vitamin K is synthesized by intestinal bacteria, but a newborn's intestinal tract is sterile. Consequently, vitamin K is not present for prothrombin formation until the newborn's intestinal flora is established, which usually takes about 4 days.[14] If vitamin K was not given the neonate could hemorrhage.

Accuracy in weighing sponges and measuring blood loss (see Chapter 13) is an essential responsibility of the perioperative nurse, as some anesthesiologists will replace blood loss at 10% of the body weight.

Cardiovascular Concerns

Cyanosis and tachypnea may be signs of impending respiratory failure; they may also be important indications of cardiovascular compromise and possible hemodynamic instability. Assessing the cardiovascular status of neonates, infants, and toddlers is based on the understanding that the heart rate is normally unstable and fluctuates. After age 5 the cardiopulmonary response to stress is similar to that of a young adult.

Hypothermia induces pulmonary vasoconstriction and results in right-to-left shunting in the ductus arteriosus and atrium, thus increasing hypoxia and acidosis. Shock and cardiac arrest may result.[15]

Psychological Support

Psychological support and preparation for surgery are important in reducing stress levels in children and their families. Educational activities and communication are based on the child's level of development.

Little research has been conducted on the specific fears of children undergoing surgery. Many children report that the events they most remember about their surgical experience are riding to the operating room, receiving injections, waking up in pain, and not being allowed to eat or drink. They most fear injections and the anesthesia mask.

As discussed in Chapter 5, family support and involvement in patient care are associated with successful patient coping and crisis resolution. This is particularly true among pediatric patients. The parents of a neonate born with a congenital defect often feel guilty and inadequate and perceive themselves as failures. They may reject the child and have mixed emotions regarding the outcome of surgical intervention. A sick child may represent a financial burden and create yet another stressful situation for the parents.

The perioperative nurse may note many verbal and nonverbal symptoms of family stress during this period. The nurse should accept and be supportive of the behavioral reactions of the family, and when indicated refer the family to a social worker.

The parents are kept informed of the status of the surgical procedure and any significant findings. Postoperatively, the parents are allowed into the PACU as soon as the child's condition is stable, and they are incorporated into their child's care.

■ References

1. Polk S. Anesthesia for the morbidly obese patient: Proceed with care. *Welcome Trends in Anesthesiology.* 1988; 6(6):3–9.
2. National Institute on Aging. *Special Report on Aging.* Washington, DC: Department of Health and Human Services; 1987.
3. Jackson M. High risk surgical patients. *J Gerontol Nurs.* 1988; 14(1):8.
4. Stotts N. Impaired wound healing. In Carrieri-Kohlman V et al., eds. *Pathophysiological Phenomena in Nursing: Human responses to Illness,* Philadelphia: W. B. Saunders; 1993: 443–444.
5. Collinsworth R. Determining nutritional status of the elderly surgical patient: Steps in the assessment process. *AORN J.* 1991; 54(3):622–631.
6. Nestle M. *Nutrition in Clinical Practice.* Greenbrae, CA: Jones Medical Publications; 1995:157.
7. Murdock B. Recent developments in short term memory. *Br J Psychol.* 1967; 58:421–433.
8. Ciocon J, Potter J. Age related changes in human memory: Normal and abnormal. *Geriatrics.* 1988; 43(10):43–48.
9. Botwinick J, Arenberg D. Disparate time spans in sequential studies of aging. *Experimental Aging Research.* 1976; 2:55–61.
10. Slevin O. Ageist attitudes among young adults: Implications for a caring profession. *J Adv Nurs.* 1991; 16:1197–1205.
11. Moore L, Proffitt C. Communicating effectively with elderly surgical patients. *AORN J.* 1993; 58(2):350.
12. Rowe M. *Critical Care of New Born and Infant Surgical Patient.* St. Louis: C. V. Mosby; 1991:55.
13. Rowe M et al. *Essentials of Pediatric Surgery.* St. Louis: C.V. Mosby; 1994:5–15.
14. Wong D. *Essentials of Pediatric Nursing,* 4th ed. St. Louis: C. V. Mosby; 1993:178.
15. deLorimier A et al. *Pediatric Surgery.* In Way L, ed. *Current Concepts in Surgery;* 1994:1190.

Ambulatory Surgery

Ambulatory surgery is an organized process whereby patients have surgery, recover, and are discharged home the same day. The process is referred to as outpatient surgery, same-day surgery, one-day surgery, in-and-out surgery, come-and-go surgery, or ambulatory surgery. In 1993, 22.8 million surgeries were performed in the United States; 55% were done on an outpatient basis.[1] When the first ambulatory surgery programs were established in the 1960s, patients were primarily young and healthy. With advancements in anesthetic and surgical techniques in the 1970s and 1980s, however, ambulatory surgeries expanded to include complex procedures and medically compromised patients. One such technological advance included minimally invasive techniques, such as endoscopic procedures, angioplasty, and lasers. In addition, new rapid-acting anesthetic agents metabolize more rapidly than traditional agents and allow patients to return to consciousness with fewer side effects, such as nausea and vomiting.

The growing practice of ambulatory surgery was also influenced by government and other third-party payers. They have increased pressure to perform invasive procedures in the most cost-effective setting by reducing or eliminating payment for surgical procedures associated with a hospital stay.

As pressure increased from third-party payers and consumers, two additional concepts developed. One concept is the 23-hour admission, or the observation, unit, which addresses the needs of patients who require a longer period of recovery, yet meets the criteria for ambulatory surgery.

A second concept is that of AM admits (A.M. Admissions, also called TCI—To Come In). With this program patients enter the hospital on the morning of major surgery with a planned hospital admission to follow the procedure. In some instances, patients are admitted and cared for preoperatively in ambulatory surgery units. In other facilities a separate unit may be designated to admit and prepare the patient for surgery.

As the process of ambulatory surgery has evolved, the nursing practice has also changed to meet the needs of the patient. AORN has adopted a position statement on perioperative nursing practice in ambulatory surgery (Appendix F). The statement recognizes that while changes have occurred in health care to move from "the highest quality care at any price" toward "the best care at the lowest price," the perioperative nurse who is clinically and professionally competent to provide care to the ambulatory surgery patient is an essential member of the care team.

The same standards of patient care to meet the expected patient outcomes apply, whether the procedure is performed on an outpatient basis or during a traditional inpatient hospital stay. The approaches to achieve the outcomes, however, may vary. Many of the processes developed for ambulatory surgery patients are now used for all patients requiring surgery. These processes include preadmission telephone calls, postdischarge telephone contact to evaluate patient outcomes, preoperative tours of the facility, and patient education in the form of discharge protocols that emphasize self-care and prevention of illness.

■ AMBULATORY SURGERY SETTINGS

Ambulatory surgery occurs primarily in five locations:

- *Hospital-based dedicated unit.* Self-contained unit within or attached to a hospital. It is physically separate from the inpatient operating rooms.
- *Hospital-based integrated unit.* A unit where outpatients and inpatients share the same operating rooms but where dedicated areas are established for preoperative preparation and postoperative recovery.
- *Hospital-affiliated satellite surgery center.* An ambulatory surgery center owned and operated by the hospital, but physically separated from it.
- *Freestanding ambulatory surgery center.* An independent facility that is privately owned and operated for the purpose of providing surgical care.
- *Office-based practice.* One or more physicians equip an area within their office to perform surgery and recover the patient.

Ambulatory surgery performed in any of the above settings is subject to state licensure requirements, standards set by the Accreditation Association for Ambulatory Health Care and/or the Joint Commission for the Accreditation of Health Care Organizations. Therefore, they require the same mechanical and electrical support systems that are discussed in Chapter 2. In addition to the areas defined in an inpatient operating room, a business office, examination rooms, toilet facilities, laboratory, x-ray room, and admission area are also needed.

Patients who elect to use an ambulatory surgical facility should be provided with adequate waiting areas and with privacy in the treatment and consultation rooms. Easy access to the facility is essential, as is adequate parking and clearly marked entry points. Sensitive use of building materials, room finishes, color, lighting, furniture, artwork, and plants contributes greatly to an atmosphere that promotes patient confidence and well-being.

■ PATIENT SELECTION FACTORS

Several approaches may be used in screening patients for ambulatory surgery:

- The patient may visit the facility prior to the day of surgery
- The patient may visit the office prior to the day of surgery, when a nurse practitioner or physician will conduct preadmission screening and testing
- The patient may be interviewed on the telephone without an office visit

- The patient may complete a health questionnaire at home and return it by mail or fax to the facility
- The patient may complete a computerized health questionnaire that can be accessed by the facility via modem
- Preoperative screening may be done the day of surgery

It is advantageous if a patient does not have to make an additional trip to the facility for a workup. This will work well for patients with ASA 1 or 2 physical classifications but may result in a high number of postponed or canceled surgeries when caring for patients in ASA 3 or 4 classification (see Chapter 10).

Many ambulatory facilities have reduced the number of required preoperative tests, depending on the operative procedure and on the patient's age, condition, and medication history. Patients who have a co-existing disease process, such as hypertension, coronary artery disease, diabetes, or obesity, require additional studies, such as EKG, electrolytes, and chest x-rays. They are acceptable candidates for ambulatory surgery if their systemic diseases are controlled at least three months preoperatively.

Outpatient surgery is contraindicated for patients who are physically unstable, morbidly obese, or acute substance abusers. Patients who do not have an adequate support system at home may also be unacceptable candidates for an ambulatory surgery program. In addition, some patients may refuse to participate.

Some facilities have identified a list of procedures that can be performed for outpatients. While a list may suffice as a short-term answer, the procedures may be misinterpreted as those that can *always* be done safely without hospitalization. As a consequence, the appropriateness of a procedure for an individual patient may be forgotten. The American College of Surgeons (ACS) and the American Society of Anesthesiologists (ASA) have indicated that developing such lists may lead to categorizing certain procedures as ambulatory cases without taking into account patient suitability or giving proper weight to physician judgment. Those organizations have also indicated that the patient's unique medical, social, and psychological needs should be specifically evaluated by physicians.[2]

The patient's willingness and ability to participate in the ambulatory surgery program are important prerequisites to this type of surgery. In addition, the patient must be discharged to a responsible adult and may require help in getting assistance at home. In a research study of 76 adults having ambulatory surgery for the first time, patients identified a number of concerns when asked, "What is it that has concerned you, or is concerning you, most about having surgery on an outpatient basis?" The six areas of concern were:

1. the availability of professional care following discharge
2. the need for information
3. the process of surgery (waiting preoperatively or being discharged too early)
4. the final outcome in relation to health status
5. the recovery process, including complications, pain, and integration back into home responsibilities
6. personal vulnerability[3]

The findings of this study identify the need to have a well-planned patient education program.

■ PATIENT EDUCATION

Patient education is a continuous process integrated into every phase of the outpatient surgical experience. Patient and family education is a key component in the experience of all surgical patients, but is especially relevant for ambulatory surgery patients. As identified in Chapter 5, preoperative assessment is related to preparing the patient for the surgical experience. Patient information booklets may assist with the preoperative instructions and discharge routines. The booklets describe such preoperative routines as:

- when to refrain from eating or drinking
- medications to take and not take
- who should accompany the patient home from the facility
- what to wear to the facility
- what to bring
- when and where to arrive
- what to expect on the day of surgery: preoperative and postoperative routines
- whom to call with questions

The interactions between the perioperative nurse and patient are brief and may be overshadowed by the patient's anxieties about the impending surgery. Consequently, interactions must be reinforced with additional resources that the patient can refer to following discussions with the nurse. Written material or a video will permit the patient to review the information after the anticipatory anxiety associated with surgery has passed. The information in the surgical booklet or video may be used as a point of reference during the preadmission screening visit or the preoperative telephone call.

It is important that the nurse talk one on one with the patient prior to the day of surgery to implement appropriate teaching strategies and to establish realistic parameters for evaluating the success of the educational program. During this time the patient's questions may be answered and concerns addressed. During this brief encounter it is also important to motivate the patient toward self-care and prevention of illness. Because this may require a change in lifelong behaviors, it may necessitate the involvement of other health care providers, such as a dietician, physical therapist, or respiratory therapist.

Discharge teaching begins during the first nurse-patient contact after surgery is decided on. Early discharge planning gives the nurse time to identify patients at risk for self-care deficit and noncompliance.

Discharge instructions should include information about the following topics:

- diet
- pain control
- wound care/dressings
- activity limitations
- what to do should questions or an emergency arise

Instructions are explicit and written so that they may be easily understood. The form should have a space for the signature of the person receiving the instructions and the person giving the instructions. One copy of the instructions is placed in the patient's medical record. If the patient is not fully alert or appears to have difficulty comprehending the information, the discharge instructions should be given to a person accompanying the patient. That person signs the form indicating that he or she has received the information on behalf of the patient. If the protocols are specific to the procedure, they should also include information about self-care and preventing recurrence of the disease or illness that required surgical intervention.

∎ INTRAOPERATIVE CARE AND DOCUMENTATION

The plan of care for a patient is developed from the information obtained during the preadmission screening visit or the preadmission telephone call. The intraoperative care of an ambulatory surgery patient is consistent with the information presented previously in this text. The same standards of nursing care, principles of aseptic technique, and other operating room routines apply.

The American Society of Anesthesiologist has established guidelines specifically for ambulatory surgical facilities. Strong emphasis is placed on the need for ambulatory facilities to be equivalent to hospital operating room areas. The anesthetizing location must be staffed and equipped to handle emergencies. Anesthesia Practice Standards have been published by the ASA and include recommendations for checking equipment and for basic intraoperative monitoring that should be practiced throughout the administration of all general, regional and monitored anesthesia care.[4]

Balanced anesthesia and continuous intravenous anesthesia are the two techniques most often employed for ambulatory surgery. One essential goal is a short recovery period for the patient, including rapid return to appropriate status for ambulation with little or no nausea and vomiting (Chapter 10).

Forms designed specifically for ambulatory surgery are frequently used for documentation. They must meet the guidelines identified in Chapter 5, but frequently consist of check-off boxes or fill-in-the-blank lines. The brevity expedites documentation of short surgical cases and decreases the turnover time between cases. Some of these forms are included in this chapter (Fig. 16–1 through Fig. 16–5). The patient's medical record must be complete and reflect all the care provided during surgical intervention and the immediate postoperative period.

∎ REFERENCES

1. SMG Market Letter. SMG Marketing Group Inc. 1994; 8(6): 1.
2. American College of Surgeons, Socioeconomic Affairs Department. Issues and perspectives: ambulatory surgery. Chicago: American College of Surgeons, March 1988.
3. Caldwell, L. Surgical outpatient concerns; what every perioperative nurse should know. *AORN J.* 1991; 53(3): 761–767.
4. ASA standards of basic intraoperative monitoring. Chicago: American Society of Anesthesiologists, October 21, 1993.

ACU NURSING ADMISSION ASSESSMENT RECORD

DATE		TIME			

☐ AM ☐ PM

IMPRINT AREA

Patient perception of admission _____

Admission diagnosis _____

ORIENTATION TO UNIT

	YES	NO	NA		YES	NO	NA
Nurse call system	☐	☐	☐	Visitor policy	☐	☐	☐
Emergency call light	☐	☐	☐	T.V.	☐	☐	☐
Siderails	☐	☐	☐	Family waiting room	☐	☐	☐
No smoking policy	☐	☐	☐				

From: ☐ Home   ☐ Clinic   ☐ Other (specify) _____

Via: ☐ Ambulatory ☐ Wheelchair ☐ Gurney ☐ Ambulance

Primary language: _____ Interpreter needed? ☐ No ☐ Yes

Advance directive/patient rights:
1. Do you have an advance directive?   ☐ No ☐ Yes
2. Do you want your advance directive to be
   followed during this hospitalization?   ☐ No ☐ Yes
3. Do you have a copy of your patient rights?   ☐ No ☐ Yes
4. Do you have any questions regarding your rights? ☐ No ☐ Yes

CURRENT MEDICATIONS

DRUG	DOSE	FREQUENCY	INDICATIONS	DATE/TIME/LAST DOSE

Age _____ Wt. _____ Ht. _____ RA O$_2$ SAT _____ BP _____ RR _____ HR _____ T _____
R/L   ADEQ/SHALLOW/   APICAL/   TYMP/
LABORED   RADIAL   ORAL

Allergies: ☐ NKA   ☐ Yes (specify) _____ Reaction _____ History of latex sensitivity? ☐ No ☐ Yes
Food (notify dietitian if A.M. ADMIT): ☐ None ☐ Yes (specify) _____

Psychosocial: ☐ Anxious ☐ Nervous ☐ Talkative ☐ Relaxed ☐ Cooperative ☐ Uncooperative ☐ Crying ☐ Lethargic
☐ Demanding ☐ Other _____

Cultural/Spiritual: Religious preference _____ Clergy _____
Do you have any religious/cultural/spiritual requests or concerns about your hospitalization? ☐ No ☐ Yes
Describe _____

Social: Tobacco? ☐ No ☐ Yes Number of packs/day _____ Alcohol use? ☐ No ☐ Yes Number of drinks/day _____
Recreational drugs? ☐ No ☐ Yes (specify) _____
Comments _____

Neurosensory: Loc ☐ Alert ☐ Not alert (specify) _____
☐ No complaints ☐ Visual impairment ☐ Glasses ☐ Contacts ☐ Blind: ☐ Right ☐ Left
☐ Speech impairment ☐ Speech not clear
☐ Hearing impairment ☐ HOH ☐ Deaf: ☐ Right ☐ Left ☐ Uses hearing aid: ☐ Right ☐ Left
☐ Headache ☐ Seizures ☐ Vertigo/fainting ☐ CVA ☐ Numbness/tingling (location) _____

Pupils: ☐ PERLA Size: ● ● ● ● ● · R _____ L _____ ☐ NA
7 6 5 4 3 2

Reaction: Right: ☐ Brisk ☐ Sluggish ☐ No reaction Left: ☐ Brisk ☐ Sluggish ☐ No reaction
☐ Cataracts: ☐ Right ☐ Left

Musculoskeletal: ☐ Hand grasps equal: ☐ No (describe) _____
☐ No complaints ☐ Arthritis (describe) _____ ☐ Spasms ☐ Amputation (describe) _____
Mobility status: ☐ Ambulatory ☐ Ambulate with assistance ☐ Bedrest ☐ Transfer with assistance
☐ Ambulation status recently changed   Patient tires easily? ☐ No ☐ Yes (explain) _____
☐ Crutches ☐ Cane ☐ Walker ☐ Wheelchair ☐ Other _____
Artificial prosthesis or implants? ☐ No ☐ Yes (location) _____

Fall risk assessment: **Scale (check box based**

Criteria:	Points:	Score:
Over 65 years of age	1	_____
Prior Hx of falls	5	_____
Impaired vision	3	_____
Confusion/disorientation	17	_____
Restricted mobility (cane/walker)	4	_____
Unsteady gait	5	_____
Hx of drug abuse	4	_____

on total score at right):
☐ No to low risk (0-8 pts)
☐ Moderate risk (9-16 pts)
☐ High risk (>17 pts)

Total _____

Limitations: ☐ Weakness: ☐ Right ☐ Left Location _____
☐ Decreased ROM: ☐ Right ☐ Left Location _____

☐ **Pain/☐ Discomfort:** Location _____
Rate on scale of 0-10 _____ Describe _____
☐ No pain/discomfort ☐ Educ. on pain scale done Precipitating factors _____
How is pain controlled? _____
Previous pain experience/control _____
Patient's desired postoperative comfort zone on pain scale of 0-10 _____

01734-2 (REV. 5-95)

Figure 16–1. Ambulatory surgery assessment record. *(Courtesy Kaiser Permanente.)*

CV:
☐ No complaints

☐ Chest pain ☐ MI ☐ CHF ☐ Arrythmia   Pain discomfort location and ratio _____

☐ Syncope ☐ Palpitations ☐ Hypertension ☐ Pacemaker   How is pain controlled? _____

Heart rate: ☐ Regular ☐ Irregular ☐ Gallop ☐ Rub ☐ Murmur ☐ Implanted defibrillator _____

Extremities: ☐ Warm and pink ☐ Cool ☐ Cyanotic ☐ Other _____

Edema location _____ ☐ Non-pitting ☐ Pitting _____

Peripheral pulses: Radial ☐ Present and strong bilaterally ☐ Other (describe) _____

Pedal ☐ Present and strong bilaterally ☐ Other (describe) _____

Capillary refill: ☐ Brisk ☐ Prolonged

Comments _____

Respiratory:
☐ No complaints

☐ Asthma ☐ Emphysema ☐ Apnea ☐ Chronic cough ☐ Shortness of breath: ☐ At rest ☐ With activity

☐ Night sweats ☐ COPD ☐ Tracheostomy: Size _____ Type _____ ☐ Use of home O_2: ☐ ___ L/min.

Respirations: ☐ No distress ☐ Labored ☐ Shallow ☐ Other _____

Cough: ☐ Nonproductive ☐ Productive

Sputum: Color _____ Amount _____ Consistency _____

Breath sounds: ☐ Clear ☐ Crackles ☐ Wheezes ☐ Location _____

☐ Fine ☐ Coarse ☐ Inspiratory ☐ Expiratory

Comments _____

GI/Endocrine:
☐ No complaints

Last BM _____ Normal pattern _____ ☐ Constipation ☐ Laxative use: Frequency _____ Type _____

☐ Change in bowel habits ☐ Nausea ☐ Diarrhea ☐ Difficulty swallowing ☐ Unable to swallow

☐ Vomiting ☐ Ulcers ☐ Heartburn ☐ Mouth sores ☐ Hemorrhoids ☐ Hiatal hernia ☐ Incontinence

☐ Blood in stool ☐ Abdominal pain ☐ Change in appetite ☐ Recent weight loss (>12 lbs wt loss/6 mo)

☐ Thyroid disorder (describe) _____

☐ Diabetes: How long? _____ ☐ Insulin dependent ☐ Non-insulin dependent

Time _____ ☐ A.M. ☐ P.M. Fasting blood sugar _____

Bowel sounds: ☐ Normal ☐ Hyperactive ☐ Hypoactive ☐ Faint ☐ Absent

Abdomen: ☐ Soft ☐ Large ☐ Distended ☐ Firm ☐ Tender (location) _____

Bowel diversions: ☐ NG tube ☐ Gastrostomy ☐ Jejunostomy ☐ Ileostomy ☐ Colostomy ☐ Other

Bowel prep compliance: ☐ No ☐ Yes ☐ NA

Comments _____

GU:
☐ No complaints

☐ Frequency/urgency ☐ Hematuria ☐ Change in bladder habits ☐ Dysuria ☐ Burning ☐ Incontinence

☐ Renal problems (stones, failure, dialysis)(describe) _____

☐ Hx. of voiding problems (describe) _____

Urine: ☐ Clear yellow to amber ☐ Unable to assess ☐ Other _____

Urinary diversion: ☐ Catheter (type) _____ ☐ Other _____

Genitoreproductive:
☐ No complaints

Female: LMP (date) _____ Pregnant, EDD _____ Last pap smear (date) _____

Last mammogram (date) _____ ☐ Vaginal discharge ☐ Breast self-exam performed

☐ Change in menstrual cycle ☐ Breast changes ☐ Hormonal disorders

Male: ☐ Penile discharge ☐ Testicular pain or swelling ☐ Testicular self-exam performed

☐ Prostate problems _____

Comments _____

Hematologic: ☐ No complaints ☐ Blood disorders ☐ Sickle cell ☐ Hemophilia ☐ Transfusion history

Comments _____

Skin Integrity: ☐ At risk (Initiate the Prevention of Pressure Ulcer Protocol)
☐ No complaints

1. Draw area on diagram. Use code below. Note grade of Pressure Ulcer in comments.

Stage I: Nonblanchable erythema of intact skin.

Stage II: Partial thickness skin loss involving epidermis and/or dermis. The ulcer is superficial and presents clinically as an abrasion, blister, or shallow crater.

Stage III: Full thickness skin loss involving damage or necrosis of subcutaneous tissue that may extend down to, but not through, underlying fascia.

Stage IV: Full thickness skin loss with extensive destruction, tissue necrosis, or damage to muscle, bone, or supporting structures.

DIAGRAMMING CODE:

A = Abrasion E = Erythema/rash

B = Burn L = Laceration

C = Contusion/bruise P = Pressure Ulcer

D = Draining wound/incision

List/describe/indicate site of any visible injuries and/or pressure ulcer (include size and grade). Measure in cm. _____

BRADEN SCALE FOR PREDICTING PRESSURE ULCER RISK

Friction and Shear	Mobility	Activity	Sensory Perception/LOC	Nutrition	Moisture/Incontinence
1. Actual problem (mod to max assist)	1. Completely immobile	1. Bedfast	1. Completely limited/unresponsive	1. Very poor (<30%)	1. Constantly moist
2. Potential problem (min assist.)	2. Very limited (requires assist.)	2. Chairfast	2. Very limited/resp. to painful stimuli	2. Inadequate (30-50%)	2. Moist (linen change q shift)
3. No apparent problem	3. Slight, limited movement (no assist)	3. Walks occasionally	3. Slightly limited/slow to respond	3. Adequate (50-80%)	3. Occasionally moist (linen change 2x/day)
	4. No limitations	4. Walks frequently	4. No impairment	4. Excellent (90-100%)	4. Rarely moist (linen change 1x/day)

Circle a number for each area. Add them to get the patient's Braden Scale total score _____ ☐ High risk/potential for skin breakdown.

(Prevention of Pressure Ulcer Protocol must be initiated whenever the score is 16 or less. Also initiate a nutrition consultation.)

Figure 16–1. *(Continued)*

DISCHARGE PLANNING

Destination: ☐ Home   ☐ AM ADMIT   ☐ Other (specify) _____

Living situation: ☐ Alone   ☐ With spouse   ☐ Family   ☐ Skilled nursing facility   ☐ Other _____

If you need assistance at home, is there someone who can help you? ☐ No   ☐ Yes
   Comments _____

Do you anticipate problems caring for yourself after discharge? ☐ No   ☐ Yes   ☐ Unknown at this time
☐ Financial concerns regarding your illness   ☐ Mobility problems

Are you a caregiver for another person?   ☐ No   ☐ Yes   For whom _____
                              Type of care given _____
                              Who is providing care while you are in the hospital? _____

Do you have emotional family concerns that need to be addressed during your hospitalization?   ☐ No   ☐ Yes
   Comments _____

Patient will be on crutches post-op? ☐ No   ☐ Yes   Have you attended crutch training classes? ☐ No   ☐ Yes

Stairs to climb at home? ☐ None   Number of flights _____

Home needs: ☐ None anticipated   ☐ Needs exist (specify) _____

Does home health need to be notified? ☐ No   ☐ Yes   Explain _____
      Notified (ext. 4465):   ☐ Verbal referral   Time _____   ☐ AM ☐ PM
                        Name of person contacted _____
      Fax number: 4885   ☐ Faxed referral with orders and patient chart information
                        Time _____   ☐ AM ☐ PM
      Signature _____, R.N.

Does Social Services need to be notified? ☐ No   ☐ Yes   Explain _____
      Notified (ext. 3530):   ☐ Verbal referral   Time _____   ☐ AM ☐ PM
                        Name of person contacted _____
      Fax number: 3001   ☐ Faxed referral   Time _____ ☐ AM ☐ PM
      Signature _____, R.N.

PATIENT/FAMILY PREOPERATIVE EDUCATION AND ASSESSMENT

RN (please initial):

	INITIALS	SIGNATURE	TITLE
__ Perioperative experience			
__ Estimated length of perioperative process			
__ Pain control measures			

Procedures (check only if applicable):

___ IV	___ Tourniquet	___ Cough & deep breathe
___ Foley catheter	___ O$_2$ mask	___ Incentive spirometer
___ Skin prep	___ Drains/tubes	___ Exercises
___ Monitors	___ Wound dressing	___ Crutch training
___ Review D/C instructions	___ Positioning/restraints	

In the Assessment of the Ability to Learn, the following entries are noted:
   Educational level, Literacy, Care giver/decision maker, Knowledge base, Biological variations, Anxiety level, and Cultural
   considerations ☐ No   ☐ Yes   Comments _____

Prior to the Teaching/Learning Process, the following were addressed:
   Patient medicated which will alter participation: ☐ No   ☐ Yes
   Will illness interfere with participation? ☐ No   ☐ Yes

Patient's willingness to participate in the Teaching/Learning Process at this time:
   ☐ Active   ☐ Passive   ☐ Refused   ☐ Unable due to medical condition

☐ Knowledge verbalized by patient/family   ☐ Return demonstration adequate
☐ Need further reinforcement, repeat learning activity   ☐ Further education needed

Name of person who will transport you home _____ Relationship _____

Patient contact phone number _____

Profile information obtained from: ☐ Patient   ☐ Other _____

Patient disposition: To: ☐ Pre-op area   ☐ OR   ☐ PACU   ☐ P.R.   ☐ Other _____

TIME OUT	SIGNATURE OF ADMITTING NURSE	
☐ AM ☐ PM		R.N.

01734-2 (REV. 5-95) REVERSE

Figure 16–2. Discharge planning. *(Courtesy Kaiser Permanente.)*

DATE OF SERVICE	LOCATION	STATION
LAST NAME	FIRST NAME	INITIAL

PLEASE BRING THIS FORM WITH YOU
TO YOUR NEXT APPOINTMENT

BIRTH DATE MO. DAY YEAR	HEALTH INSURANCE CLAIM NUMBER	
MEDICAL RECORD NUMBER		CHECK DIGIT

SEX	COVERAGE	GROUP NUMBER	ACCOUNT NUMBER	SUB GROUP

DISCHARGE SUMMARY/PATIENT INSTRUCTIONS

I. DISCHARGE DIAGNOSES: _____

_____

_____

Discharge Date: _____

Operations & Procedures : _____

_____

II. DIET: ☐ Resume Normal Diet   ☐ Special Dietary Instructions: _____

III. All medications are listed on Discharge Prescription Order Sheet (Form #09362).

Medication(s) to **AVOID:** _____
Including these medications to
which patient had adverse reaction: _____

IV. ACTIVITIES

☐ *Restrictions   ☐ No Restrictions

☐ Shower: _____

☐ Tub Bath: _____

☐ Climb Stairs: _____

☐ Housework: _____

☐ Resume Sex: _____

☐ Sports: _____

☐ Drive a Car: _____

☐ Lift up to: _____ lbs. _____

☐ Other: _____

*Check appropriate box to indicate activities for which specific advice given, then summarize in space provided.

V. SPECIAL INSTRUCTIONS (include wound care, home care, equipment provided at discharge if applicable)

_____
_____
_____
_____
_____

VI. PROBABLE RETURN TO WORK DATE:

VII. FOLLOW-UP APPOINTMENT(S) (include home care, if applicable)

M.D. or NURSE	LOCATION	PHONE #	TIME	DATE
		202-		
		202-		

VIII. If you need further assistance call 202-2000 to reach your physician or advice nurse. The Emergency Department phone number is 202-3300.

IX. HOSPITAL COURSE (include pertinent diagnostic findings, treatment, and outcome)

_____
_____
_____
_____
_____

I have received and understand my instructions for discharge from the hospital:

SIGNATURE OF PATIENT OR RESPONSIBLE FAMILY MEMBER OR FRIEND	DATE

SIGNATURE OF PHYSICIAN	DATE	SIGNATURE OF NURSE	DATE

Figure 16–3. Generic discharge instructions. *(Courtesy Kaiser Permanente.)*

POSTOPERATIVE INSTRUCTIONS
FOLLOWING LAPAROSCOPIC HERNIA REPAIR

IMPRINT AREA

1. **Activity:** Do not lift more than 10 lbs, for the first two weeks, or drive a car for three days. You may perform other activities as soon as you feel able. You may have some discomfort at the incision sites at first but his should only last 1-2 days.

2. **Diet:** Start with light meals (soup, small portions of well cooked meat and vegetables without seasoning, rice) and resume your regular diet as your appetite returns. Take all your usual medications unless given specific instructions by your surgeon.

3. **Dressing:** Remove the dressing on the second day after the operation unless your surgeon gives you other instructions.

4. **Shower/Bath:** You may shower on the third day after the operation.

5. You should notify your surgeon at 202-3385 during normal clinic hours (9 a.m. -5 p.m., M-F) if you observe any of the following:
   a. Temperature 100° F or higher
   b. Blood leaking from under the dressing
   c. Nausea, vomiting or hiccups lasting more than one hour
   d. Increasing pain in the abdomen and shoulders

6. If problems arise at night or on the weekends, call the hospital operator at 202-2000 and ask for the advice nurse. If necessary you will be referred to the Emergency Room or the on-call surgeon.

7. **Work:** Your surgeon advises you to return to work in _____ days.

8. Return to clinic for follow-up appointment on _____

   with _____ Phone _____

MEDICATIONS/SPECIAL INSTRUCTIONS

1. ☐ Resume Previous Medications.

2. ☐ Discharge Medications: _____
   _____

3. ☐ Special Instructions: _____
   _____

   _____, M.D.

This is to verify that I have been released with all of my personal belongings and that I have received and understand my postoperative instructions.

DATE	PATIENT'S SIGNATURE
WITNESS	

09238-5 (10-93)   DISTRIBUTION: WHITE = CHART • CANARY = PATIENT

Figure 16–4. Postoperative instructions following laparoscopic hernia repair. *(Courtesy Kaiser Permanente.)*

**AMBULATORY SURGERY POST-OP ASSESSMENT/
DISCHARGE ASSESSMENT**

IMPRINT AREA

TIME RECEIVED_____ FROM   ☐ OR ☐ PACU ☐ CCL ☐ RADIOLOGY ☐ P.R. ☐ OTHER_____

TIME	B.P.	P	R	T	DRSG PULSE	TIME	B.P.	P	R	T	DRSG PULSE	TIME	B.P.	P	R	T	DRSG PULSE

Procedure: _____   Drsg site: _____

Nursing observations:_____

_____

_____

_____

ALLERGIES (LIST):				IV SOLUTION	AMOUNT REMAINING
☐ NKA ☐ UNCHANGED FROM PRE-OP					
DRUG DOSE ROUTE		TIME GIVEN INIT.			
			FLUID TOTALS	**TOTALS**
			IV:	
			PO:	
			URINE:	
			EMESIS:	

MEDICATIONS

04142-4 (REV. 9-90)   (OVER)

Figure 16–5. Ambulatory surgery postoperative assessment and discharge criteria. *(Courtesy Kaiser Permanente.)*

HOSPITAL AMBULATORY SURGERY DISCHARGE CRITERIA

PATIENT ASSESSMENT INTERPRETATION		SCORE	NURSING ASSESSMENT (CON D)
Res. = Respiration	SCORE 2 – Respirations appear adequate. Deep breaths – coughs – adequate gas exchange – adequate rate/rhythm/depth.		
	SCORE 1 – Impaired respiratory exchange. Rate – fast/slow, intermittent rhythm – regular/irregular, depth – shallow/depressed.		
	SCORE 0 – No spontaneous exchange.		
Cir. = Circulatory	SCORE 2 – B/P stabilized and within patient's normal limits Pulse – rate, rhythm, quality – within normal limits		
	SCORE 1 – Blood pressure fluctuating. Pulse – irregular, fast, weak, thready, slow.		
	SCORE 0 – Unable to palpate blood pressure or pulses. Circulation checks of an affected extremity as indicated will be recorded on face sheet.		
Col. = Color	SCORE 2 – Normal skin color and condition		
	SCORE 1 – Any change in skin color and/or condition Color – pale, jaundiced, dusky, flushed.		
	SCORE 0 – Frank cyanosis		
Loc. = Level of consciousness	SCORE 2 – Alert, coherent, responds appropriately to verbal stimuli, return of reflexes.		
	SCORE 1 – Arouses to name, responsive to verbal stimuli, partial return of reflexes.		
	SCORE 0 – No response to stimuli, Neuro checks recorded on face sheet if necessary.		
Act. = Activity	SCORE 2 – Purposeful movement of extremities.		
	SCORE 1 – Moves extremities involuntarily or on request.		
	SCORE 0 – No movement of extremities.		
Dress. = Dressing	SCORE 2 – Dressing dry/scant amount of drainage or incision undressed but clean, dry and intact.		
	SCORE 1 – Dressing saturated/moderate c̄ sanguineous drainage.		
	SCORE 0 – Dressing continuously saturated/incision dehisced.		
Pain	SCORE 2 – Complains of no pain or very mild, tolerable pain in operative site.		
	SCORE 1 – Definite pain in operative or unrelated site causing obvious discomfort.		
	SCORE 0 – Severe, uncontrollable pain.		
Nausea	SCORE 2 – No complaints of nausea in either supine or vertical position – can take ice chips, progressing to sips of water and carbonated beverages without nausea.		
	SCORE 1 – Has mild nausea and occassional vomiting controlled by staying supine and taking antiemetic medication – tolerates progressive elevation of head.		
	SCORE 0 – Has wretching and vomiting uncontrolled by supine positioning and antiemetic medication.		
Voiding	SCORE 2 – Voiding.		
	SCORE 1 – Voiding small amounts.		
	SCORE 0 – Unable to void.		

DISCHARGED BY _____ , R.N. _____ , M.D. | TOTAL | SIGNATURE _____ , R.N.

DISCHARGE PREPARATION

Pt. discharge c̄ personal belongings ☐ Yes ☐ No ☐ N/A

Discharge medication(s) / prescription(s): (w/instructions) ☐ Yes ☐ No ☐ N/A

Sent home with equipment or materials: ☐ Yes ☐ No ☐ N/A

DISCHARGE PATIENT TEACHING

☐ Pre-printed self-care instructions provided to patient

☐ Other topics discussed (list)

FINAL DISCHARGE NOTE

Mode of discharge:

Discharge destination:

Accompanied by: Time:

☐ Patient/Family verbalizes understanding of instruction:

Comments: _____

84448-4 (REV. 9-90) REVERSE

Figure 16–5. Ambulatory surgery postoperative assessment and discharge criteria. *(Courtesy Kaiser Permanente.)*

Postoperative Care
of Patients

Immediate Postoperative Nursing Care

Lillian H. Nicolette

The role of the perioperative nurse in the immediate postoperative phase of surgical intervention is to facilitate the safe transfer of care from the surgical suite to the postanesthesia care unit (PACU). The immediate postanesthesia phase presents many complex challenges that require special clinical interventions and nursing expertise. The patients are quite vulnerable at this stage, and their return to a homeostatic state is imperative. The postoperative phase of care begins with the transfer and admission of the patient to the PACU and ends with the resolution of postoperative sequelae. The perioperative team members should work together with the postanesthesia care providers to gather information received during the preoperative assessment and planning phases. The recognition of postanesthesia care nursing as a critical specialty is well established and documented in the literature. Because practice settings differ, the role and involvement of the perioperative nurse in postoperative care also varies. Postanesthesia nursing is a specialty requiring that the practitioner have an in-depth knowledge of the process of anesthesia, anesthesia types and actions, emergency drugs, potential complications, and emergency treatment for complications. The medical director of the PACU is usually an anesthesiologist; however, in some circumstances it may be a surgeon.

The significant increase in ambulatory surgery procedures has greatly increased the patient acuity levels in the PACU. Consequently, patients that are admitted to the health care facility for inpatient stays are generally of a higher acuity level. This increase further presents a number of complex clinical situations that need to be handled by skilled professional nurses. Many of these patients have chronic obstructive lung disease, diabetes mellitus, and chronic cardiac conditions. The American Society of Post Anesthesia Nurses (ASPAN) has published a formal "Scope of Practice" document, which identifies the core issues, dimensions and boundaries for postanesthesia practice. In ambulatory surgery centers and some rural health care institutions, the perioperative nurse may serve a dual role, also acting as the postanesthesia nurse. This chapter offers very basic information on providing quality care and services for the perioperative patient.

The perioperative nurse should accompany the patient to the PACU, where relevant patient data is given to the PACU nurse (Fig. 17–1). Data that the perioperative nurse should relay includes the patient's medical, social, and psychological status; allergies to medications or drug abuse; physical disabilities; status prior to the induction of anesthesia; type of surgical intervention; location of incisions, tubes, drains, catheters, packing, dressings; condition and color of the skin; actual or potential impairment of skin integrity; primary language (if the patient's first language is not English); respiratory function or dysfunction, including whether the patient has a history of smoking; any special requests the patient may have verbalized preoperatively (for example, replacement of prosthetic devices, warm blankets, location of family and spouse, wedding rings); and all pertinent intraoperative occurrences and complications.

The anesthesiologist's responsibility includes reporting the type and extent of the surgical procedure; the anesthetic agents used (type of anesthesia technique—fluid therapy, location of IV/CVP lines, type and amount of solutions infused, including blood); estimated blood loss; level of consciousness; level of comfort; muscular response; and any complications occurring intraoperatively. "Standards of Post Anesthesia Nursing Practice" appears in Appendix C.

∎ THE PACU ENVIRONMENT

Achieving the ideal physical design for a PACU is not always possible or cost effective. The PACU should be located as close to the surgical suite as possible to allow uninterrupted transfer of patients and direct access to the services of perioperative practitioners, anesthesiologists and surgeons.

The size of the PACU needed in each health care facility must be based on the volume of surgery and the types of surgery performed, and it must be directly related to the number of operating rooms. The norm is one to two recovery areas per surgical suite. The primary objective should be to seek a balance among maximizing the staff efficiency, ensuring patient safety, and maintaining adequate privacy and respect for the patients' physical and psychosocial needs.

The PACU is typically designed as one large room with cubicles; there should be at least 4 to 5 feet of maneuvering space on both sides of each patient bed and a stretcher ra-

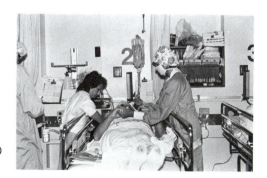

Figure 17–1. The perioperative nurse accompanies the patient to the PACU where a report is given to the PACU nurse.

dius of approximately 38.5 square feet in the open areas.[1] A separate PACU area should be allocated for isolation patients (such as burn patients) or for loud or combative patients. A large, clean storage area and utility room with a sink adjacent to or within the PACU are also recommended.

The provision of quality care in the PACU requires strong, knowledgeable leadership and excellent management skills. Particular attention must be paid to developing the organizational structure of the unit and maintaining the best possible professional nursing care providers.

▮ POSTANESTHETIC CONSIDERATIONS

When a patient is brought to the postanesthesia care unit, the immediate concerns of the nurse evaluating the patient include respiration, circulation, and neurologic status. A postanesthesia score sheet appears in Table 17–1.

TABLE 17–1. POSTANESTHESIA RECOVERY SCORING (PARS)

Activity

0 = Unable to lift head or move extremities voluntarily or on command
1 = Moves two extremities voluntarily or on command and can lift head
2 = Able to move four extremities voluntarily or on command. Can lift head and has controlled movement. *Exceptions:* patients with a prolonged IV block such as bupivacaine (Marcaine) may not move an affected extremity for as long as 18 hours; patients who were immobile preoperatively

Respiration

0 = Apneic; condition necessitates ventilator or assisted respiration
1 = Labored or limited respirations. Breathes by self but has shallow, slow respirations. May have an oral airway
2 = Can take a deep breath and cough well; has normal respiratory rate and depth

Circulation

0 = Has abnormally high or low blood pressure: BP 50 mm Hg of preanesthetic level
1 = BP 20–50 mm Hg of preanesthetic level
2 = Stable BP and pulse. BP 20 mm Hg of preanesthetic level (minimum 90 mm Hg systolic). *Exception:* Patient may be released by anesthesia provider after drug therapy

Neurologic Status

0 = Not responding or responding only to painful stimuli
1 = Responds to verbal stimuli but drifts off to sleep easily
2 = Awake and alert; oriented to time, place, and person. *Note:* After ketamine anesthesia, the patient must have no nystagmus when released

Color

0 = Cyanotic, dusky
1 = Pale, blotchy
2 = Pink

IV = intravenous; BP = blood pressure.
Modified from Aldrete J and Kroulik D. A post anesthetic recovery score. Anesth Analg. 1970;49:924–933.

Respiratory Function

As soon as the patient arrives in the PACU, the nurse should check for airway patency and an adequate respiratory exchange. A simple process for determining the patient's respiratory exchange is to place the hand lightly over the nose and mouth. The nurse should check the rate and depth of respiration, symmetry of chest expansion and excursion, breath sounds, color, mucous membranes, and the presence of respiratory stridor. Assessing the need for position changes in the jaw, head, and neck to facilitate adequate respiratory exchange is also critical. The administration of oxygen to the patient in the PACU is an important facet in the emergent phase of anesthesia. Oxygen is given postoperatively because of the respiratory depressant side effects of volatile anesthesics, IV narcotics, and sedatives. It is critically important that when a patient has received a general or spinal anesthetic, oxygen should be administered.

A patent airway must be maintained throughout the administration of oxygen. The patient should be encouraged to cough, breathe deeply if possible, and to perform the sustained maximal inspiration (SMI). Oxygen should be administered, according to the patient's needs: for a nasal catheter system, 6 liters per minute; for a full mask, 10 liters per minute. The patient should be observed for the following signs of anoxia:

- Color of the skin, lips, and nail beds (if pigmentation prevents an accurate evaluation of skin color, inspection of the oral mucosa would be done)
- Rapid, shallow breathing, rhythm of breathing, respiration with intercostal/diaphragmatic effort
- Rapid apical and radial pulses
- Capillary filling of the fingers and toes
- Restlessness and apprehension

It is essential when obtaining a history to note whether the patient chronically retains carbon dioxide, as in chronic obstructive pulmonary disease. The patient with CO_2 retention who is receiving oxygen should be closely monitored for signs of hyperventilation, confusion, or becoming semi-comatose.

If a partial airway obstruction occurs, it may be the result of muscle relaxants, narcotics, mucous accumulation, or the patient's position intraoperatively or on the PACU bed. When the patient's tongue falls toward the back of the mouth and prevents the free passage of air, the head can be hyperextended and the chin brought forward, or the patient can be positioned laterally on the bed to facilitate appropriate respiration/breathing.

Pulse Oximetry. The use of pulse oximeters is the current standard of practice in the surgical suite and the PACU. Pulse oximetry provides a diagnostic display of the trend in a patient's oxygenation and helps detect states of hypoxia more quickly than subjective signs, such as skin color, blood color, and respiratory and cardiac rates.[2] In many health care facilities, the perioperative nurse assists anesthesia personnel in attaching the oximeter probe and monitoring the display readout. In the PACU, the pulse oximeter supplements subjective assessment data when caring for the patient.

If pulse oximetry equipment is used, the PACU nurse must be able to interpret the data from the monitoring equipment. How to deduce PO_2 (oxygen partial pressure) from the pulse oximeter is important (Fig. 17–2).

The percentage of oxygen saturation is not a measure of arterial PO_2. There is no straight correlation between the two figures. When plotted on the oxyhemoglobin dissociation curve, minor changes in O_2 saturation may result in significant changes in PO_2 levels (Fig. 17–3). Clinically, the nurse should be aware that an SaO_2 of 90 percent may be considered to be hypoxemia, and severe hypoxemia occurs when the PO_2 is less than 30 torr or the SaO_2 is 75 percent. The PACU nurse needs to know the specific patient's pulse oximeter measurement and what it means in terms of the patient's clinical status.[2] The nurse also needs to know the patient's baseline O_2 saturation to decide the appropriate and acceptable lower limits. The PACU nurse always needs to collaborate with the postanesthesia care provider in assessing the patient's status.

Caution must be taken with patients having ventilatory depression, chronic obstructive pulmonary disease, and other pulmonary pathologies. If the patient is positioned laterally, a decrease in ventilation will occur. However, patients may be turned from side to side in short intervals. If a patient remains supine, the head should always be turned to one side to avoid aspiration of secretions. This process should also be used when suctioning a patient. If the air exchange does not improve, the administration of reversal agents for narcotics and muscle relaxants may be indicated. In some patients, the insertion of a nasopharyngeal or an oropharyngeal airway may be indicated.

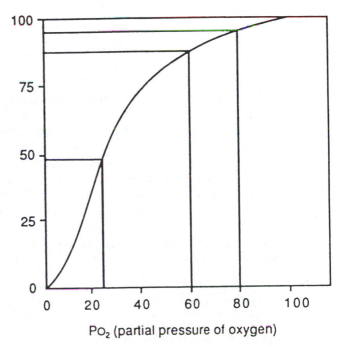

A molecule of hemoglobin (Hb) may bind up to 4 oxygen molecules. If a hemoglobin molecule is binding 4 oxygen molecules, it is 100% saturated; if it is binding 3 oxygen molecules, hemoglobin is 75% saturated; and so on. saturation in the blood is determined by averaging the O_2 saturation of all the Hb molecules. The oximeter measures O_2 saturation.

The partial pressure of oxygen (PO_2) is derived from the oxygen saturation curve. The graph at the right illustrates how the PO_2 is determined: From an oxygen-saturation value (indicated on the vertical axis) a line is drawn to the oxygenation curve, then extended down to the horizontal axis. The line intersects the axis at teh PO value.

Oxygen saturation is not equal to the partial pressure of oxygen. As seen on the graph, a small drop in oxygen saturaion, from 96% to 90%, yields a bid drop in the PO_2—from 80 to 60 mm Hg.

PO_2 (partial pressure of oxygen)

Figure 17–2. Oxygen saturation curve. Demonstrates the relationship of oxygen saturation and partial pressure of oxygen. (*From Schultheis AH. When and how to extubate in the recovery room. Am J Nurs. August, 1989; 1042, with permission.*)

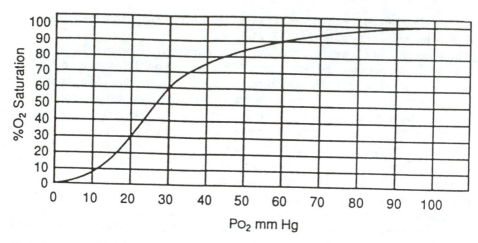

Figure 17–3. The oxyhemoglobin dissociation curve. Changes in oxygen saturation are seen here as significant changes in PO₂ levels. *(From Jones M. Pulse oximetry: The numbers behind the numbers. Point of View. 1988; 25(3):10, with permission.)*

If patients are responsive, they should be encouraged to breathe deeply and cough to promote gas exchange and assist in the elimination of the anesthetic agents used intraoperatively.

Cardiovascular Function

The PACU nurse needs to be constantly aware of the signs of patient anxiety, arrhythmias, shock, left ventricular failure, pulmonary embolism, and systemic embolism.[1] Pain and apprehension may be relieved by the administration of antianxiety and/or narcotic agents. Vital signs should be checked every 10 to 15 minutes and compared to the preoperative and intraoperative baseline data. Continuous cardiac monitoring should be immediately initiated in a quiet, controlled environment. Medications such as atropine, lidocaine, digitalis, quinidine, sodium nitroprusside (SNP), phentolamine, and nitroglycerin should be readily available. Fluid therapy and urinary output must be monitored to prevent fluid overload. A Swan-Ganz catheter or central venous pressure (CVP) device may be utilized to identify and monitor fluid replacement in specific patients with reduced intravascular volume and hypotension. If large variations exist, the anesthesiologist and surgeon should be immediately notified, so that a medical evaluation can be accomplished.

Postoperative patients should be observed for shock. Shock indicates the inability of the circulatory system to meet the oxygen demands of the body. The most common postoperative causes of shock are:

- Vasomotor collapse caused by deep anesthesia or overdoses of narcotics
- Hypovolemia caused by excessive loss of blood or plasma
- Toxemia due to infection

The signs and symptoms of shock are restlessness; pallor; rapid, thready pulse; cyanosis of lips and fingernails; low blood pressure; cold, moist skin; rapid, shallow respiration; decreased body temperature; and decreased urinary output.

The treatment for shock depends on the cause. For example, in the case of hypovolemic shock, the treatment is to restore the blood volume by administering crystalloids, plasma, or plasma substitutes to restore low volume status. Oxygen is always administered to increase the oxygen saturation of the blood and the tissues.

Fluid and Electrolyte Balance

The evaluation of a patient's fluid and electrolyte status involves the total process of body assessment.[1] Fluid and electrolyte imbalances may occur rapidly and are caused by any of a number of factors, including fluid and food restrictions preoperatively, fluid loss intraoperatively, or surgical stress. The main patient goals for maintaining fluid and electrolyte balance are to correct previous fluid and electrolyte problems/deficits, replace fluid loss due to the surgical intervention and associated tubes or drains, and maintain the patient's blood pressure and urinary output. Each patient must be assessed and evaluated to determine the baseline requirements and the associated fluid replacement for the abnormal loss. The normal adult who has been NPO (nothing by mouth) requires approximately 2000 to 2200 ml of water per day to replace both urinary output and insensible body loss. If a patient has experienced a significant blood loss, a plasma expander (such as Plasmanate, Dextran 40, Dextran 70, Albumin, Hespan) or a blood transfusion may be required, depending on the patient's problem. The patient who is fluid restricted should always be regulated by an automated fluid administration device.[1]

Obviously, the accurate measurement and documentation of both intake and output is essential to the overall assessment of each patient's fluid and electrolye status. The PACU nurse should always be alert to signs and symptoms of fluid and electrolyte imbalance and the associated nursing interventions (see Table 17–2).

TABLE 17–2. CLINICAL STATES AFFECTING FLUID AND ELECTROLYTE BALANCE IN THE POSTOPERATIVE PATIENT

Clinical Status	Effect on Fluid Balance
Pain	Heightened response to a stressor state and, H_2O and Na retention
Anesthetic Agents	
Trauma	
Fear of the Unknown	
Acute renal failure	Impaired Acid-Base Balance
Blood loss	Circulatory impairment due to fluid loss
Immobilization	
Drains	Excessive fluid loss by created surgical means
Suction-GI	K^+ and Na loss and deficit
Bleeding	
Vomiting	
External Drainage Devices (automated and gravity)	
Thyroidectomy procedures	Ca^{++} deficit
Treatment of acidosis	
Excessive administration of citrated blood	

Adapted from Drain CB. The Post Anesthesia Care Unit, 3rd ed. Philadelphia: W. B. Saunders; 1994:284.

Neurologic Status

The patient's level of consciousness should be assessed and documented every 5 to 10 minutes while the patient is in the PACU. During emergence from general anesthesia, the patient will first react to painful stimuli, such as pinching the earlobe, and to motor or reflex activity if the nurse touches the eyelashes or an eyelid. A semiconscious patient may respond to verbal stimuli but may easily drift off to sleep. During this phase, the patient may respond to commands more slowly. The conscious patient may be drowsy, but is usually awake and alert, and is oriented to time, place, and person. The exception is the patient who has had a ketamine anesthetic; such a patient must have *no* nystagmus when released.

Nausea and Vomiting

One of the most difficult problems for the PACU nurse is the management of postoperative nausea and vomiting. Nausea and vomiting may occur following the administration of a general or regional anesthetic agent, although, with the introduction of new agents and adequate prophylaxis, the problem is diminishing. Nausea and vomiting can be initiated by stimulating the vomiting center in the medulla by autonomic afferent nerve fibers from the gastrointestinal tract and mediastinum. The vomiting center can become excited by chemicals through the blood stream. Medications such as apomorphine, morphine, and meperidine react in this fashion and subsequently excite the vomiting center. For example, propafol (Diprivan), an injectible anesthetic, was found to be associated with a significantly lower incidence of nausea, retching, and vomiting during postanesthesia recovery than other types of injectible anesthetics.

Several studies have concluded that the incidence of nausea and vomiting is higher in women than in men. Furthermore, additional studies have revealed the incidence of vomiting postoperatively has been reported to decrease with age for both sexes. The incidence of postoperative nausea and vomiting appears to increase with certain types of surgical procedures, such as open appendectomy, ENT procedures, uterine procedures, and strabismus surgery in children. Additionally, the patient's medical status, the type of analgesia administered, and the technique used to ventilate the patient intraoperatively may influence this symptomatology.

When patients experience nausea, the nurse should encourage them to perform SMI, cough, and if possible perform deep breathing exercises. Oxygen should be administered if there is any indication of hypoxemia. Placing a cold cloth on the patient's forehead may assist in eliminating the feeling of nausea. The nurse's primary responsibility in assisting the patient with this complication is to focus on airway management. The nurse needs to remain with the patient to assess for the possibility of aspiration and airway obstruction.

If the symptoms of nausea and vomiting persist, the most common agents given to patients are Zofran (ondansetron hydrochloride), Inapsine (droperidol), or Emete-con (benzoquinamide), as ordered by the surgeon or anesthesia care provider. Other nursing interventions could include placing the patient in a head down position to drain vomitus away from the lungs. If airway obstruction occurs, the patient should be placed in a head down position, the head turned to one side, and any foreign material removed by suctioning it or removing it with a gloved finger. The nurse should always remain with the patient during these types of crises.

■ POSTOPERATIVE WOUND ASSESSMENT AND MONITORING

To adequately understand wound complications, the perioperative nurse needs to be aware of the stages of surgical wound healing (see also Chapter 18). Table 17–3 summarizes the stages of healing.

Postoperative dressings need to be checked every 10 to 15 minutes in the PACU for the type of drainage (if any), amount, color, consistency, and odor. The uncomplicated wound should appear:

- pink (free from necrosis and inflammation)
- flat (free from serum fluid buildup and/or hematoma)
- intact (all edges sealed)
- dry (free of drainage)
- soft (free from induration)

With the widespread use of endoscopic surgical approaches, many patients will simply have a small incision covered with a Band-Aid or a small bandage. In the case of larger incisions, many surgeons will use a spray, such as Nu Skin Spray, that seals off the surgical site from outer materials. Documentation of all wound assessment and management should be noted on the PACU record.

All surgical drains, such as hemovacs, sump drains, J-vacs, and Pleura-vacs, should be connected to the appropriate drainage apparatus. They should be checked for patency every 15 minutes, from immediately postoperatively until discharge from the PACU. Materials excreted into the drainage apparatus should be noted for:

- amount
- color
- consistency
- odor (if present)

TABLE 17–3. STAGES OF SURGICAL WOUND HEALING

Stage	Time	Event	Cells
Inflammation (0–4 d)	0–2 h	Hemostasis	Platelets Erythrocytes Leukocytes
	0–4 d	Phagocytosis	Neutrophils Macrophages
Proliferation (2–22 d)	1–4 d	Epithelialization	Keratinocytes
	2–7 d	Neovascularization	Endothelial cells
	2–22 d	Collagen synthesis	Fibroblasts
	2–20 d	Contraction	Myofibroblasts
Maturation (21 d–2 y)		Collagen remodeling	Fibroblasts

Adapted with permission from AORN J. 1989;49:506.

Casting materials that are used for patients undergoing orthopedic or podiatric procedures should be assessed every 10 to 15 minutes for signs of circulatory impairment. Clinical manifestations of circulatory impairment may include swelling and a decreased return of color after pressure has been applied to the exposed distal portion of the extremity. The patient's skin may also "feel cold" and appear cyanotic in color. If circulatory impairment is imminent, the surgeon should be notified immediately. If during the physical assessment, the nurse identifies blood seeping through the cast from the incision, the boundaries need to be identified and the time noted so that excessive bleeding can be readily determined and treated accordingly.

∎ POSTOPERATIVE PAIN MANAGEMENT

Postoperative pain is so common that we expect the patient to experience this process as part of the normal course of surgical treatment. Pain is often considered a protective mechanism, but subjectively speaking, postoperative pain serves no useful purpose and can be a difficult problem both for the patient and the PACU nurse. Although there are many sophisticated pain relief modalities available, postoperative pain continues to be undertreated and underrated, while patients suffer the consequences related to the lack of understanding. Thus, one of the most critical nursing activities of the PACU nurse is the management of postoperative pain.

Postanesthesia patients experience altered respiratory functions, so the concern needs to be to maintain an adequate gas exchange. The "stir up regimen" is aimed at preventing complications by arousing patients; primarily this regimen is directed toward preventing atelectasis and venous stasis as a result of poor gas exchange and immobility from surgery.

Pain is a complex phenomenon and many times is difficult for the nurse to assess due to the subjective nature of the problem. Pain postoperatively usually is stimulated by the fact that tissue damage has occurred and could be an effect of the anesthetic agent and the anesthesia technique employed.

There are many factors that affect postoperative pain. Some of these include:

- Type and duration of the surgical procedure (invasive versus noninvasive techniques)
- Anesthetics administered before and during surgery
- Patient age, physiologic and psychosocial status
- Patient preparedness for pain
- Complications related to surgery
- Patient care following the surgical experience

Nurses are the primary practitioners who assess pain in the surgical patient. An accurate physical and psychosocial assessment of the patient's pain will form a baseline for the selection of the appropriate medical and nursing interventions.

The major goal for the surgical experience and, subsequently, for the nurse is to prevent pain and promote patient comfort postanesthetically. Attention to utilizing comfort as a modality can reduce stimulation and support the patient's tolerance for pain. There are many types of modalities that can be employed. Sensory stimulation, such as noise and bright lights, should be reduced to eliminate excessive sensory overload. This type of intervention can promote a sometimes tolerable level. It is also essential that the PACU nurse continually reassure patients to allay their anxiety and fears related to the surgical experience and the subsequent pain.

A large number of pharmacologic agents have been used for the relief of pain in the PACU. The most commonly used agents are listed in Table 17–4. There are many side effects of narcotic analgesia and these types of side effects should be considered prior to prescribing or administering analgesia. Some of these side effects include:

- Respiratory depression
- Cardiovascular depression
- Nausea
- Vomiting
- Clouding of sensorium
- Drowsiness

Table 17–5 and 17–6 identify suggested doses for nonsteroidal anti-inflammatory drugs (NSAIDS) and for opioid analgesics.

Patient-controlled analgesia (PCA) has become a popular method of pain relief. This method allows the patient to determine the timing of opioid doses. A computer-controlled PCA pump is triggered by pushing a button and is programmed to deliver incremental doses of the analgesic via the patient's intravenous line. Although the nursing

TABLE 17–4. TYPES OF ANALGESIC AGENTS USED FOR POSTOPERATIVE PAIN RELIEF

Generic Name	Trade Name
Non-Narcotics	
Aspirin	Various
Acetaminophen	Tylenol, Tempra, Datril, Panadol
Ibuprofen	Motrin, Nuprin
Fenoprofen	Nalfon
Phenacetin	Various
Narcotics	
Codeine	Codeine
Oxycodone	Percocet
Pentazocine	Talwin
Meperidine, Pethidine	Demerol
Morphine	Morphine
Hydromorphone	Dilaudid
Methadone	Dolophine
Levorphanol	Levo-Dromoran, Levorphan
Fentanyl	Sublimaze

TABLE 17–5. SUGGESTED DOSES FOR NONSTEROIDAL ANTI-INFLAMMATORY DRUGS (NSAIDS)

Drug	Usual Adult Dose	Usual Pediatric Dose[1]	Comments
Oral NSAIDS			
Acetaminophen	650–975 mg q 4 hr	10–15 mg/kg q 4 hr	Acetaminophen lacks the peripheral anti-inflammatory activity of other NSAIDs
Aspirin	650–975 mg q 4 hr	10–15 mg/kg q 4 hr[2]	The standard against which other NSAIDs are compared. Inhibits platelet aggregation; may cause postoperative bleeding
Choline magnesium trisalicylate (Trilisate)	1000–1500 mg bid	25 mg/kg bid	May have minimal antiplatelet activity; also available as oral liquid
Diflunisal (Dolobid)	1000 mg initial dose followed by 500 mg q 12 hr		
Etodolac (Lodine)	200–400 mg q 6–8 hr		
Fenoprofen calcium (Nalfon)	200 mg q 4–6 hr		
Ibuprofen (Motrin, others)	400 mg q 4–6 hr	10 mg/kg q 6–8 hr	Available as several brand names and as generic; also available as oral suspension
Ketoprofen (Orudis)	25–75 mg q 6–8 hr		
Magnesium salicylate	650 mg q 4 hr		Many brands and generic forms available
Meclofenamate sodium (Meclomen)	50 mg q 4–6 hr		
Mefenamic acid (Ponstel)	250 mg q 6 hr		
Naproxen (Naprosyn)	500 mg initial dose followed by 250 mg q 6–8 hr	5 mg/kg q 12 hr	Also available as oral liquid
Naproxen sodium (Anaprox)	550 mg initial dose followed by 275 mg q 6–8 hr		
Salsalate (Disalcid, others)	500 mg q 4 hr		May have minimal antiplatelet activity
Sodium salicylate	325–650 mg q 3–4 hr		Available in generic form from several distributors
Parenteral NSAID			
Ketorolac	30 or 60 mg IM initial dose followed by 15 or 30 mg q 6 hr Oral dose following IM dosage: 10 mg q 6–8 hr		Intramuscular dose per day not to exceed 150 mg Intravenous dose (over no less than 15 seconds) 30 mg

Note: Only the above NSAIDs have FDA approval for use as simple analgesics, but clinical experience has been gained with other drugs as well.
[1]Drug recommendations are limited to NSAIDs where pediatric dosing experience is available.
[2]Contraindicated in presence of fever or other evidence of viral illness.
Reprinted from U.S. Department of Health and Human Services.[4]

time required for patient monitoring is shortened with the use of a PCA pump compared to conventional drug administration, careful assessment still needs to be a nursing priority.

Epidural opioids have also been proven in recent years to be an effective approach to managing postoperative pain. The efficacy of an epidural approach depends on the ability of the drug to interact with opiate receptors in the dorsal horn of the spinal cord, where

TABLE 17–6. SUGGESTED DOSES FOR OPIOID ANALGESICS

Drug	Approximate Equianalgesic Oral Dose	Approximate Equianalgesic Parenteral Dose	Recommended Starting Dose (Adults More Than 50 kg Body Weight)		Recommended Starting Dose (Children and Adults Less Than 50 kg Body Weight)[1]	
			Oral	Parenteral	Oral	Parenteral
Opioid Agonist						
Morphine[2]	30 mg q 3–4 hr (around-the-clock dosing) 60 mg q 3–4 hr (single dose or intermittent dosing)	10 mg q 3–4	30 mg q 3–4 hr	10 mg q 3–4 hr	0.3 mg /kg q 3–4 hr	0.1 mg/kg q 3–4 hr
Codeine[3]	130 mg q 3–4 hr	75 mg q 3–4 hr	60 mg q 3–4 hr	60 mg q 2 hr	1 mg/kg q 3–4 hr[4]	Not recommended
Hydromorphone[2] (Dilaudid)	7.5 mg q 3–4 hr	1.5 mg q 3–4 hr	6 mg q 3–4 hr	1.5 mg q 3–4 hr	0.06 mg kg q 3–4 hr	0.015 mg/kg q 3–4 hr
Hydrocodone (in Lorcet, others)	30 mg q 3–4 hr	Not available	10 mg q 3–4 hr	Not available	0.2 mg kg q 3–4 hr[4]	Not available
Levorphanol (Levo-Dromoran)	4 mg q 6–8 hr	2 mg q 6–8 hr	4 mg q 6–8 hr	2 mg q 6–8 hr	0.04 mg /kg q 6–7 hr	0.02 mg/kg q 6–8 hr
Meperidine (Demerol)	300 mg q 2–3 hr	100 mg q 3 hr	Not recommended	100 mg q 3 hr	Not recommended	0.75 mg/kg q 2–3 hr
Methadone (Dolophine, others)	20 mg q 6–8 hr	10 mg q 6–8 hr	20 mg q 6–8 hr	10 mg q 6–8 hr	0.2 mg/kg q 6–8 hr	0.1 mg/kg q 6–8 hr
Oxycodone (Roxicodone, others)	30 mg q 3–4 hr	Not available	10 mg q 3–4 hr	Not available	0.2 mg/kg q 3–4 hr[4]	Not available
Oxymorphone[2] (Numorphan)	Not available	1 mg q 3–4 hr	Not available	1 mg q 3–4 hr	Not recommended	Not recommended
Opioid Agonist-Antagonist and Partial Agonist						
Buprenorphine (Buprenex)	Not available	0.3–0.4 mg q 6–8 hr	Not available	0.4 mg q 6–8 hr	Not available	0.004 mg/kg q 6–8 hr
Butorphanol (Stadol)	Not available	2 mg q 3–4 hr	Not available	2 mg q 3–4 hr	Not available	Not recommended
Nalbuphine (Nubain)	Not available	10 mg q 3–4 hr	Not available	10 mg q 3–4 hr	Not available	0.1 mg/kg q 3–4 hr
Pentazocine (Talwin, others)	150 mg q 3–4 hr	60 mg q 3–4 hr	50 mg q 4–6 hr	Not recommended	Not recommended	Not recommended

Note: Published tables vary in the suggested doses that are equianalgesic to morphine. Clinical response is the criterion that must be applied for each patient; titration to clinical response is necessary. Because there is not complete cross tolerance among these drugs, it is usually necessary to use a lower than equianalgesic dose when changing drugs and to retitrate to response.

Caution: Recommended doses do not apply to patients with renal or hepatic insufficiency or other conditions affecting drug metabolism and kinetics.

[1] Caution: Doses listed for patients with body weight less than 50 kg cannot be used as initial starting doses in babies less than 6 months of age. Consult the *Clinical Practice Guideline for Acute Pain Management: Operative or Medical Procedures and Trauma* section on management of pain in neonates for recommendations.

[2] For morphine, hydromorphone, and oxymorphone, rectal administration is an alternate route for patients unable to take oral medications, but equianalgesic doses may differ from oral and parenteral doses because of pharmacokinetic differences.

[3] Caution: Codeine doses above 65 mg often are not appropriate due to diminishing incremental analgesia with increasing doses but continually increasing constipation and other side effects.

[4] Caution: Doses of aspirin and acetaminophen in combination opioid/NSAID preparations must also be adjusted to the patient's body weight.

Reprinted from the U.S. Department of Health and Human Services.[4]

nociceptive signals are processed. The complications associated with the use of epidural opioids include respiratory depression. Consequently, the PACU nurse needs to continually check the rate and depth of respiration, along with the patient's general status and level of consciousness.

Regional anesthesia techniques have been used postoperatively to reduce pain in an effort to avoid the risk of opioid-induced respiratory depression. Epidural anesthetic blockade causes an interruption in the transmission of the pain receptor by the spinal cord. Epidural nerve blocks can be an especially effective technique in patients with lung disease who are at risk for postoperative pulmonary complications.[3]

The Agency for Health Care Policy and Research published "Clinical Practice Guidelines on Acute Pain Management" in 1992, which addresses the care of patients with acute pain after surgery or medical procedures, and the care of trauma victims. The guidelines have four major goals:

1. To reduce the incidence and severity of the patient's postoperative or postraumatic pain
2. To educate patients regarding the need to communicate unrelieved pain so they can receive prompt evaluation and effective treatment
3. To enhance patient comfort and satisfaction
4. To contribute to fewer postoperative complications, and in some cases, shorter stays after surgical procedures

These clinical guidelines include overall strategies for pain control as well as for site-specific pain control. The health care institution's quality assessment and improvement procedures should be used to assure that pain management practices are always implemented.[4]

Management of Analgesia by Catheter Techniques

A registered nurse may manage the care of patients with catheters or devices for the delivery of analgesia to alleviate acute postsurgical pain, pathological pain, or chronic pain, including reinjection of medication following establishment of appropriate therapeutic ranges or adjustments in drug infusion rate. These activities should be implemented in conjunction with the anesthesia care provider's or the physician's patient-specific written orders.[5]

It is within the scope of practice for the RN to manage the care of patients receiving analgesia by catheter, as defined by the "Position Statement on the Role of the RN in the Management of Analgesia by Catheter Techniques" (Appendix G).

The following criteria should be utilized when performing this technique:

- Management and monitoring of analgesia by catheter techniques, including reinjection and/or alteration of infusion rate by nonanesthetist RNs, is allowed by state laws and institutional policy, procedure, and protocol.
- The qualified anesthesia care provider placing the catheter or infusion device, or the attending physician, selects and orders the drugs, doses, and concentrations of opioids, local anesthetics, steroids, alpha-agonists, or other documented, safe medications or combinations thereof.

- Guidelines for patient monitoring and drug administration and protocols for dealing with potential complications or emergency situations are available and have been developed in conjunction with the anesthesia or physician provider.

The RN providing care for patients receiving catheter or infusion-device analgesia for acute or chronic pain relief or for women during labor should be able to:

- Demonstrate the acquired knowledge related to analgesia techniques and medications
- Assess the patient's total care needs during analgesia
- Utilize monitoring modalities, interpret physiological responses, and initiate nursing interventions to insure optimum patient care
- Anticipate and recognize complications of the analgesia
- Recognize emergency situations and implement interventions according to guidelines and orders
- Demonstrate cognitive and psychomotor skills necessary for use of the analgesic catheter or mechanical infusion devices
- Demonstrate knowledge of the legal ramifications of managing and monitoring analgesia by catheter technique

A nurse using an epidural catheter must understand intravascular injections and associated signs and symptoms. All emergency equipment must be at hand and fully functioning prior to injection. All personnel need to be trained in cardiovascular resuscitation as complete cardiovascular collapse may quickly ensue.

▌ PHYSICAL AND EMOTIONAL SAFETY AND COMFORT

Physical and emotional safety are always important aspects of the plan of care, specifically when the patient is either semiconscious or in an unconscious state. The nurse's responsibility includes ascertaining that all bed or stretcher rails are in the upright position and that the bed or stretcher is in the locked position. It is recommended that an armboard or arm protector devices be used to ensure that IV and arterial lines do not become dislodged, uncapped, or cause a patient injury.

Frequently after anesthesia, patients develop excessive restlessness. The perioperative nurse in the PACU needs to assess the underlying factors that might cause this restlessness, which may be hypoxia, carbon dioxide retention, hemorrhage, discomfort due to a full bladder, or pain. The application of restraints should only be applied to protect the patient from self-injury and only after nursing interventions related to restlessness have been implemented. A thorough nursing assessment and formulation of a nursing diagnosis related to possible injury should be made and documented on the care plan and nursing record.

Providing emotional support is an important aspect of PACU care. A warm, quiet environment should be provided so that the patient can emerge from anesthesia without obtrusive external stimuli. After patients are fully conscious, they may want to discuss the surgical procedure. The nurse should allow them to express their feelings and should provide the emotional support necessary.

▌ DOCUMENTATION

The nursing process is the essential component in documenting nursing care provided during the postanesthetic period. Assessment, planning, implementation and evaluation phases of the nursing process should be documented. The patient's outcome also needs to be recorded. In many institutions today, patient records are fully computerized. A computerized record may begin during the preoperative phase and follow the patient through the surgical experience. The advantage of a computerized system is that it is time efficient for the nurse and cost efficient for the institution.

Development of a comprehensive nursing record should be the objective of each PACU, and a record should be kept on every patient admitted to the PACU. The American Society of Post Anesthesia Nurses suggests a formalized system of reporting and documenting the care provided to each anesthetic patient.[6] The record should include but not be limited to assessment of the following:

Preoperative status including ECG, vital signs, radiology findings, laboratory values, allergies, disabilities, drug use and abuse, physical or mental impairments, mobility limitations, and prosthetic devices (dentures, hearing aides, contact lenses)
Anesthesia techniques (general, regional, local, IV)
Anesthetic agents used
Length of anesthesia time (including preoperative, induction, and emergence)
Type of surgical procedure (invasive/minimally invasive)
Estimated fluid/blood loss and replacement therapy
Complications occurring during anesthesia course of care

Documentation should include the following:

Respiratory rate (patency and types of artificial airways, mechanical ventilators)
Blood pressure (cuff and/or arterial line)
Pulse (apical-peripheral and cardiac monitor patterns)
Temperature (oral, rectal, or axillary)
Pressure readings (CVP; arterial lines; pulmonary wedge)
Patient position
Condition and the color of skin
Circulation (peripheral pulses and sensation of extremities as applicable)
Assessment of and condition of the wound and associated dressings
Condition of suture line, if applicable
Type and patency of drainage devices and catheters (amount and type of drainage)
Muscular strength
Fluid replacement therapy (location of lines, type and amount)
Level of consciousness
Level of comfort

See Figure 17–4 for an example of postanesthesia nursing notes.

DATE: _____

PROCEDURE: _____

ALLERGIES: _____

TIME IN: __a.m.__ __p.m.__ TIME OUT: __a.m.__ __p.m.__   Addressoplate

TEMPERATURE _____

VS TIME								
BP								
P								
R								
O₂ Saturation								
SCORE ACTIVITY								
RESP								
BP								
CONSCIOUS								
COLOR								
TOTAL								

GENERAL ☐   MAC ☐   BLOCK ☐
☐ Patent   ☐ Oral
AIRWAY ☐ Tracheal ☐ Nasal

CARDIAC MONITOR

MEDICATIONS
Time   Med.   Dose   RT.   Site   Initials
_____
_____
_____
_____
_____
_____

DRESSING SITE:
ADMISSION   ON DISCH

INTAKE

IV SOLUTIONS: IN OR ON ADM. PACU START PACU _____

DsRL _____

OTHER _____

RATE _____ CC/HR _____

OUTPUT IN PACU

urine _____

other _____

total _____

COMFORT LEVEL ON:

admission _____

discharge _____

DISCONTINUE ON TRANSFER

O₂   Time On _____ MASK _____ %

Time Off _____ Cannula _____ 1/min.

T Tube _____ %

_____ M.D.

TOTAL IV _____ OR _____ PACU _____ TOTAL

D/C to Phase II _____ M.D.

NSG. Signature: _____   Initials:

_____ R.N. _____

_____ R.N. _____

_____ R.N. _____

Wheelchair ☐   Carried ☐

Ambulated ☐   To Phase II _____ R.N.

NURSING NOTES:

Figure 17–4. PACU record. (Courtesy Thomas Jefferson University Hospital, Philadelphia, PA.)

▌DISCHARGE FROM THE PACU

When the patients are conscious and ready for discharge to the nursing unit, they should be accompanied to the unit by the PACU nurse and an assistant. A full report on each patient's perioperative course of care is given to the unit nurse, including:

> the surgical procedure performed
> the type of anesthesia used
> vital signs
> surgical wound assessment (including dressings and exudate, if present)
> drains and tubes
> urinary output
> fluid therapy and replacement
> results of laboratory values, radiology reports, ECG interpretations
> levels of consciousness
> medications administered in the PACU
> any emotional responses the patient may be experiencing

When ambulatory surgical patients are discharged to the home environment, discharge criteria should be developed, including the following:

> pain control
> nausea control
> patient is tolerating fluids sufficiently
> patient is ambulatory consistent with the procedure and preoperative status
> responsible adult is available to escort the patient back into the home and community environment

Discharge criteria should always meet the appropriate standards of care for the PACU practice environment. Fig. 17–5 is an example of discharge documentation.

▌QUALITY ASSESSMENT AND IMPROVEMENT ACTIVITIES IN THE PACU

Each PACU practice setting needs to have an established quality improvement program to assess and evaluate the overall improvement of a system, which also includes the consumer in the process. The Joint Commission on Accreditation of Health Care Organizations has established criteria and standards that specifically focus on the role of the professional nurse in Continuous Quality Improvement (CQI). The common focus for CQI activities in the PACU and in the surgical environment should be quality patient care and services. The discussion of CQI in Chapter 19 further addresses this process.

▌REFERENCES

1. Drain CB. *The Post-Anesthesia Care Unit: A Critical Approach to Post-Anesthesia Nursing,* 3rd ed. Philadelphia: W. B. Saunders, 1994.

2. Jones M. Pulse oximetry: The numbers behind the numbers. *Point of View*. 1988; 25(3): 10, 11.
3. Crischieri RJ, Morran CG, Howie JC et al. Post-operative pain & pulmonary complications—a comparison of three analgesic regimens. *Br J Surg*. 1985; 72:495–498.
4. Agency for Health Care Policy and Research. *Clinical Practice Guideline—Acute Pain Management:* Operative or medical procedures and trauma. Rockville, MD: US Department of Health and Human Services. 1992; 1–14: 110–113.
5. Vender JS, Spiess BD. *Post Anesthesia Care*. Philadelphia: W. B. Saunders; 1992.
6. ASPAN. Guidelines for standards of care. In Drain. *Post-Anesthesia Care Unit: A Critical Approach to Post-Anesthesia Nursing,* 3rd ed. Philadelphia: W. B. Saunders; 1994.

DISCHARGE INSTRUCTIONS

1. Limit your activities for 24 hours.

   - Do not drive a car or operate hazardous machinery.
   - Do not drink alcoholic beverages.
   - Do not make any important personal or business decisions.

2. Drink as much water or clear liquids (cola, 7- UP, apple juice, etc.) as you can tolerate.

3. Eat light foods (jello, soup, broth).

4. Restrict your work and activities as directed by your surgeon.   (See written instructions below.)

5. Report the following signs to your surgeon immediately:

   - Bleeding which soaks through your bandages.
   - Excessive redness or swelling of or around the wound area.
   - Temperature of 100 F or above.
   - Excessive pain.

Special Instructions and Medications:

_____
_____
_____
_____

Level of Activity:

_____
_____
_____
_____

If you experience medical problems, call your physician at the number listed below.

Follow - Up Appointment	**Instructions Given By:**
Your physician would like to see you in _____ days.	_____ M.D./R.N.
To schedule an appointment, call:	Date: _____
(Phone Number) _____	**Patient Acknowledges Receipt and Understanding of Discharge Instructions:**

_____	Date	_____	Date
Surgeon's Signature		Patient/Guardian	

Figure 17–5. Discharge instructions. *(Courtesy Thomas Jefferson University Hospital, Philadelphia, PA.)*

EIGHTEEN

Wound Healing and Dressings

■ WOUND HEALING

The healing of a wound means restoring the continuity in the tissue after injury or surgical intervention by replacing dead tissue with viable tissue. Wounds are considered open if the skin has been divided, and closed if the continuity of the skin is uninterrupted. Several factors affect wound healing:

- infection
- presence of a foreign body
- starvation (protein depletion)
- oxygenation and perfusion
- hypovolemia
- diabetes mellitus
- uremia
- obesity
- medications (steroids and chemotherapeutics)
- radiation therapy
- age

Open Wounds

Abrasion. An *abrasion* is an injury confined to the epidermis or the mucous membrane. It is usually caused by a glancing blow in which varying amounts of the epidermis or mucous membrane are scraped off, leaving defects in the surface. Frequently, the defects are filled with small particles of dirt or other foreign material. If not removed, those particles retard healing and may result in a "tattoo" that remains following healing.

Treatment consists of irrigating the abrasion with copious amounts of saline to remove any foreign particles; washing the area with an antiseptic solution; applying a mild antiseptic or antibiotic ointment; and applying a dressing if appropriate (depending upon the location and the extent of the injury).

Incised and Lacerated Wounds. In *incised* and *lacerated* wounds the skin is divided with exposure of or possible injury to the underlying structures. Incised wounds are caused by sharp cutting objects, and the edges are smooth and even. These wounds may be either

401

aseptic or infected, depending upon the circumstances that caused them. A surgical incision is an aseptic wound; healing will occur without incident if the patient's condition is not compromised and if pathogenic organisms or foreign material do not enter the wound and contaminate it.

A laceration results from the application of force that tears or splits the skin, leaving the edges ragged. This wound is not clean, as it is usually caused by an implement that may be contaminated with pathogenic bacteria. This wound is cleaned with an antiseptic solution and the ragged edges trimmed; the wound is frequently left open to heal by secondary intention.

Puncture. A *puncture* wound is made by piercing the skin with a sharp object such as a needle, nail, bullet, or an ice pick. These wounds are characterized by a small surface opening that gives no clue to the depth or extent of internal damage. Treatment frequently involves surgical exploration of the wound to assess internal damage.

Compound Fracture. In a *compound fracture* of a bone an external wound leads down to the site of the fracture. Before treating the fracture, hemostasis is achieved, and the wound is cleaned with an antiseptic solution. The fracture is then treated, the soft tissue sutured, and a cast applied.

Closed Wounds

Blister. A *blister* is a superficial closed wound that occurs following chemical, thermal, or frictional irritation of the skin. The damaged epidermis is raised and separated from the dermis by an excessive collection of serum. If blisters become extremely painful due to pressure of the fluid, they can be aseptically punctured and then treated as open wounds.

Contusion. A blow of adequate force on the skin produces a *contusion*. The blood vessels beneath the skin rupture, causing discoloration and edema. If the extravasated blood becomes encapsulated, it is termed a *hematoma;* if it is diffused, an *ecchymosis.* Treatment consists of cold compresses, rest, and elevation of the affected area.

Sprain. A *sprain* is the forcible wrenching of a joint, with partial rupture or other injury to the tendons or ligaments at the joint. Bones are not dislocated. The signs of a sprain are rapid swelling, heat, discoloration, and limited function. Treatment consists of applying cold compresses, bandaging and elevating the joint.

Dislocation. The temporary displacement of a bone out of its normal position in a joint is termed a *dislocation*.

Simple Fracture. A *simple fracture* is a broken bone without an external wound. Treatment consists of reducing the fracture and then immobilizing the bone until union takes place.

Forms of Healing

Open wounds may heal in three different ways: primary, or first intention; secondary, or second intention; and tertiary, or third intention.

First Intention. First intention healing occurs when the tissue is cleanly incised and accurately approximated, and contamination is minimal. In these wounds, functional and cosmetic results are optimal.

Second Intention. Healing by second intention differs from first intention in that wound edges are not approximated and healing occurs through the formation of granulation tissue (red, granular, moist tissue that appears during the healing of open wounds), which is finally covered by epithelial cells.

Most infected wounds, traumatic wounds with excessive loss of tissue, and burns heal by secondary intention. Initially, these wounds may seep serosanguineous drainage. If infection does occur, the drainage is purulent with a color characteristic of the dominant invading organism. In burns, the open area becomes covered with dried plasma proteins and dead cells called *eschar*. To maintain cleanliness and promote epithelialization, these wounds may require debridement at frequent intervals. As healing progresses, the appearance changes to that of granulation tissue.

Fine-mesh gauze is the preferred dressing for these wounds because the fineness of the mesh inhibits the interweaving of granulation tissue into the gauze. Large-mesh gauze allows the interweaving to occur and may result in a hemorrhage when the dressings are changed.

Healing by second intention is prolonged, the wound is susceptible to further infection, and the scar is excessive. The consequence of this scarring is a contracture with loss of function and limited movement.

The nursing assessment should include observation for signs and symptoms of generalized infection and fluid and electrolyte imbalance. Attention should also be directed at a psychological assessment, as the patient may be concerned with altered body image or lifestyle. When patients require lengthy hospitalization and/or multiple operations, they will need a support system. Consistently assigning the same circulating nurse to a patient will help to fulfill this need.

Third Intention. Healing by third intention, usually called delayed primary closure, is a combination of primary and secondary healing. It occurs when the wound is left open to heal by secondary intention. After 4 to 6 days, the granulation tissue covers the surface of the wound; the wound is then sutured closed. This procedure is used when the risk of infection is high, as the wound is less likely to become infected while open. The closed wound is most susceptible to infection in the first 4 days.

Healing of Incised Wounds

Wound healing begins immediately after injury and is the same process for all wounds. Variations in the process, however, result from differences in the location, the severity, and the duration of the injury; the presence of pathogenic bacteria; and the regenerative capacity of the cells. The healing process has three phases that are interdependent and overlapping. They are referred to as the 3Rs of wound healing: reaction, regeneration, and remodeling.

Reaction. The reaction phase (also called the inflammation, substrate, exudative, defensive, or lag phase) starts at the time of injury and lasts 4 to 6 days. This phase, as discussed in Chapter 6, prepares the wound for healing through hemostasis, inflammation, and biologic cleansing of the wound. During this phase, the tissues are held together by fibrin from blood clots and serum. The inflammatory reaction increases in degree and duration with the severity of the injury, the presence of foreign bodies, or contamination by bacteria. A prolonged inflammatory phase delays the formation of new tissue and results in the retarded development of strength in the wound.

Regeneration. The regeneration phase (also called fibroplasia, healing, connective tissue, or proliferative phase) starts on the third or fourth day and continues for approximately 2 weeks. During this phase, the epithelial cells migrate along the cut edges of the wound to the base of the clot and form capillaries and lymphatics. The capillaries give a red appearance to the tissues and provide the blood flow for the delivery of oxygen and nutrients to the granulation tissue.

Fibroblasts synthesize a protein substance called *collagen*. The signals that direct fibroblasts are growth factors and cytokines. Growth factors are a class of peptides that signal cells to proceed through their replicative cycle.[1] Collagen is the chief constituent of connective tissue and influences the tensile strength and the pliability of the wound. As the collagen content increases, so does the tensile strength.

Wounds in highly vascular areas, such as the head and neck, may regain sufficient tensile strength by the fourth day so that skin sutures can be removed. Wounds of the abdomen heal more slowly; therefore, skin sutures are removed about the seventh day.

Remodeling. The remodeling phase (also called regeneration, or maturation, phase) may last as long as 2 years. During this phase the strength of the scar increases despite a decrease in the number of fibroblasts and a net loss of collagen. Wound strength increases due to restructuring of the collagen fiber network. Tensile strength is usually adequate to withstand normal activity in 3 to 4 weeks; however, wounds do not regain the strength of uninjured tissues. For example, the skin and the fascia achieve only about 80% of their normal strength. The suture line continues to contract and decrease in size, and the color diminishes during the ensuing months.

Complications of Wound Healing

Wound Dehiscence. Wound dehiscence is the partial or total separation of the wound edges and occurs most often between the fifth and the tenth postoperative days. Total dehiscence of an abdominal wound, for example, results in *evisceration*—a protrusion of the viscera through the abdominal incision. Abdominal wound dehiscence may be preceded by excessive coughing, vomiting, or straining. The patient may state, "Something gave way." The contour of the abdomen may change with marked bulging and the dressing becomes saturated with serosanguineous drainage. Other causes of dehiscence may be infection, distention, malnutrition, poor surgical technique, improper selection or placement of suture, and poorly tied knots.

In the event of abdominal dehiscence, nursing actions include covering the abdomen with a sterile towel moistened with saline, monitoring vital signs, and providing emotional support to the patient until he or she can be returned to the operating room.

Incisional Hernia. An incisional hernia occurs most frequently in a lower abdominal incision and is the result of a defect in the posterior fascia sheath located beneath the rectus muscle. This is similar to a wound dehiscence, but the peritoneum and the skin remain intact and the viscera protrudes through the defect in the fascia. Incisional hernias become apparent usually 2 to 3 months after surgery, and the defect must be treated surgically to avoid bowel strangulation.

Fistula and Sinus. During the regeneration phase of wound healing, a fistula or sinus may develop. A fistula is a tract between two epithelium-lined surfaces. It is open at both ends, whereas a sinus is open at only one end. This complication occurs most frequently among patients having surgical procedures that involve the bladder, bowel, or pelvic organs. The primary symptom is abnormal drainage arising from a particular cavity. For example, in ureterovaginal or vesicovaginal fistulas, urine constantly drips through the vagina. With a rectovaginal fistula, flatus and fecal material constantly escape through the vagina. Surgery to repair fistulas may not be performed until the inflammation and induration have subsided; this may take 3 to 4 months.

Poorly Absorbed Sutures. On rare occasions suture material may cause complications. Surgical gut does not always absorb appropriately; and nonabsorbable sutures, especially silk and cotton, may be a source of irritation and inflammation. When this occurs, the suture knots encapsulate and are surrounded by a serous fluid. The suture then migrates through the incision and is rejected from the body. This is usually referred to as "spitting." If the suture is not rejected, a sinus tract may eventually develop around the suture, and surgical removal of the suture may be required.

Keloid Scars. When the metabolism of collagen is altered during the fibroplasia (regeneration) phase, a keloid or hypertrophic scar may develop. This dense, fibrous tissue grows outside the original incision. These scars may be revised; however, the condition tends to recur. In most patients, injections of corticoids directly into the scar will reduce its size. Keloids are mainly found in persons with dark skin.

Hemorrhage. Hemorrhage is a serious complication that may occur during the first few days postoperatively. The bleeding may be evident or concealed. Fresh blood on the dressing or in the drainage device should be closely observed, as it may indicate active bleeding within the wound. Skin discoloration suggests the accumulation of blood in the interstitial spaces and formation of a hematoma.

Internal hemorrhage is accompanied by a fall in blood pressure; a weak, rapid pulse; rapid, deep respirations; restlessness; apprehension; thirst; cold, clammy skin; and cyanosis or pallor. Postoperative hemorrhage may result from a suture sloughing off a vessel, a blowout of clots from a vessel, or faulty tying of a ligature. Any sign of active postoperative hemorrhage or of hematoma formation should be immediately reported to the surgeon.

Infection. Some degree of bacterial contamination occurs in all open wounds; however, only a small percentage become infected. Infection is the unfavorable result of the following equation: the dose of bacteria multiplied by the virulence divided by the resistance of the host. Wound infection prolongs the inflammatory stage, causes additional tissue destruction, delays collagen synthesis, and prevents epithelialization.[2]

Many causes of wound infection are in the direct control of the perioperative nurse and have been discussed in previous chapters. There are, however, nonmicrobial factors that influence the invasiveness of the bacteria in the wound and that often cannot be controlled by the nurse. These factors are important in determining if an infection develops.

Unhealthy, irritated, or dead tissue, for example, encourages the growth of bacteria because it is unable to resist bacterial invasion. Precautions should be taken to keep tissue moist and to handle it as gently as possible. Excessive use of the electrosurgical machine or tieing sutures too tightly results in necrotic tissue and increases the likelihood of infection.

Foreign bodies such as dirt, gravel, glass, and metal harbor microorganisms. Every attempt should be made to rid the wound of such particles prior to closing the wound.

The location, nature, and duration of the wound are significant factors in the development of an infection. Infection rates are relatively high in wounds that involve large masses of tissue, gunshot wounds, compound fractures, or crushing injuries. Wounds of the abdomen, calf, thigh, buttock, and perineal area also have a high incidence of infection, whereas wounds of the head and the neck tend to heal with a few complications. Wounds that are not treated within 6 to 10 hours of the injury are more susceptible to infection. A twofold to threefold increase in wound infection has been noted in surgeries that exceed 3 hours, occur at night, or are emergencies.[3]

Dead spaces due to the inadequate approximation of wound edges trap air or serum between the layers of tissue and delay healing. This predisposes the wound to infection.

Hemostasis is important to preventing postoperative wound infections. Accumulated secretions or hematomas distend the tissue and compress surrounding capillaries, resulting in devascularization and impaired oxygen diffusion to the repairing cells. A favorable environment is thereby created for the invasion and growth of microorganisms.

Use of Drains

Drains can expedite the healing process and prevent deep wound infections. They are used to remove serosanguineous fluid, blood, and purulent material; to obliterate dead spaces; and to drain anticipated secretions such as bile and intestinal contents. Drains function by gravitational flow or capillary action or are attached to a suction system.

Drains in closed-wound suction maintain a constant negative pressure and are effective when pressure dressings cannot be applied. The system consists of plastic tubing with multiple perforations connected to a portable self-contained suction unit, which is compressed fully to create a negative pressure. The negative pressure evacuates tissue fluids and blood, promotes healing by reducing edema, prevents hematoma formation, and eliminates a medium for bacterial growth. The system is frequently used following radical mastectomy, radical neck dissection, total hip replacement, and in the pelvic cavity after abdominoperineal resection.

If the patient with closed-wound suction is ambulatory, the drainage device is placed dependent to the drainage site and free of tension on the wound. The excess tubing is coiled to prevent inadvertent dislodging.

Drains do not exit from the incision site, but from a separate stab wound. They are taped or sutured into place to prevent excessive movement. The number of drains, their locations, and any drainage collected intraoperatively are documented on the intraoperative nurse's notes.

Systemic Factors Affecting Wound Healing

During the preoperative assessment, perioperative nurses have the opportunity to identify many significant factors that may alter and/or impact the postoperative course of wound healing. The use of alcohol or self-prescribed medications, smoking, diet and nutrition habits are influential. Uremia, uncontrolled diabetes mellitus, malignancies, and cirrhosis make a wound more vulnerable to infection and abnormal healing. Anemia produced by hypovolemia can also delay healing. Documentation of observations and evaluation of factors related to intraoperative care are essential in developing the individual plan of care for the patient. This information will also be used by the surgeon in prescribing postoperative therapies and for the care givers providing care postoperatively.

Nutrition. Adequate nutrition and balanced electrolytes are essential to the healing process (Table 18–1). Wound healing is significantly impaired in surgical patients who eat less than 50% of their usual food intake for 1 week prior to an operative procedure. This is true even though there is no difference in percentage weight loss, body composition analysis, or other nutritional indices when compared with patients who eat normally.[4] Therefore, maintenance of normal food or nutritional intake prior to surgery is important in preventing impaired wound healing. Essential nutrients are proteins, carbohydrates, fats, vitamins, and minerals.

Nutritional deficiencies may occur as a result of inadequate intake, absorption, and/or utilization of nutrients (Table 18–2). Mild to moderate nutritional deficiencies do not affect healing. Major nutritional depletion, however, does retard healing; collagen formation is impaired, and development of wound tensile strength is delayed. In addition, the incidence of infection related to reduced formation of white blood cells and antibodies increases.

Laboratory values that assist in determining malnutrition include serum albumin, serum transferrin, and total lymphocyte counts. A serum albumin level less than 3 g/dL, serum transferrin levels less than 150 mg/dL, or a total lymphocyte count less than 900n/mm indicates a high probability for impaired wound healing.[5,6]

Protein and amino acids are essential for protein synthesis and cellular multiplication. Protein aids in revascularization, fibroblastic proliferation, collagen synthesis, and lymphatic formation. Enzymes function in all steps of collagen synthesis.[7]

Carbohydrates and fats are the major energy sources, and they are essential in preventing gluconeogenesis, which deprives the viscera of essential amino acids and decreases

TABLE 18–1. KEY NUTRIENTS AFFECTING WOUND HEALING

Nutrient	Specific Component	Contribution to Wound Healing
Proteins	Amino acids	Aids revascularization, lymphocyte formation, fibroblast proliferation, collagen synthesis and wound remodeling
	Albumin	Prevents wound edema secondary to low serum oncotic pressure
	Cystine	Cofactor in collagen synthesis
	Glutamine	Synthesis of purines and pyrimidines
Carbohydrates	Glucose	Energy source for cell proliferation and phagocytic activity
Fats	Essential unsaturated fatty acids	Serve as building blocks for prostaglandins that regulate cellular metabolism, inflammation and circulation
	a. Linoleic b. Linolenic c. Arachidonic	Constituents of triglycerides and fatty acids contained in cellular and subcellular membranes
Vitamins	Ascorbic acid	Hydroxylates proline and lysine in collagen synthesis Enhances capillary formation and decreases capillary fragility A necessary component of complement that functions in immune reactions and increases defenses to infection
	B complex	Serve as cofactors for enzyme systems
	Pyridoxine, pantothenic and folic acid	Required for antibody formation and white blood cell function
	A	Enhances epithelialization of cell membranes Enhances rate of collagen synthesis and cross-linking of newly formed collagen Antagonizes the inhibitory effects of flucocorticoids on cell membranes
	D	Necessary for absorption, transport, and metabolism of calcium Indirectly affects phosphorus metabolism
	E	Important if there is a fatty acid deficiency
	K	Required for synthesis of prothrombin and clotting factors VII, IX, and X Required for synthesis of calcium-binding protein
Minerals	Zinc	Stabilizes cell membranes Needed for cell mitosis and cell proliferation in wound repair
	Iron	Needed for hydroxylation of proline and lysine in collagen synthesis Enhances bactericidal activity of leukocytes Secondarily, deficiency may cause decrease in oxygen transport to wound
	Copper	An integral part of the enzyme, lysyloxidase, that catalyzes formation of stable collagen crosslinks
	Calcium	Cofactor for collagen synthesis

lean body mass. In addition, fatty acids are required for normal cell membrane function. Essential fatty acid deficiency has been shown to impair wound healing.[7]

Vitamins A, B, and C are also necessary for repair. Vitamin A accelerates the healing of skin incisions and the formation of granulation tissue. It promotes the inflammatory response by inhibiting glucocorticoids. The supplementation of vitamin A in steroid-

TABLE 18–2. A COMPARISON OF HEALTHY AND MALNOURISHED BODY AREAS

Body Area	Normal Appearance	Signs of Malnutrition
Hair	Shiny, firm	Lack of natural shine; hair dull, dry, thin, sparse. Can be easily plucked
Face	Skin color uniform, smooth pink, not swollen	Loss of skin color, skin dark over cheeks and under eyes, flakiness of skin of nose and mouth, face swollen, scaling of skin around nostrils
Eyes	Bright, clear, shiny; no sores at corners of eyelids, membranes healthy pink and moist. No prominent blood vessels or mound of tissue on sclera	Conjunctiva pale or red; redness and fissuring of eyelid corners, eye membranes dry, cornea has dull appearance, cornea is soft
Lips	Smooth, not chapped or swollen	Red and swollen mouth or lips, especially at corners of mouth
Tongue	Deep red color, not swollen or smooth	Swollen, scarlet and raw; smooth tongue, swollen with sores
Teeth	No cavities, no pain	Missing or erupting abnormally, gray or black spots, cavities
Gums	Healthy, red, no bleeding	Spongy, bleed easily, recession of gums
Skin	No signs of rashes, swellings, dark or light spots	Skin dry, flaky, petechiae, lack of fat under skin; excessive lightness and darkness of skin
Nails	Firm, pink	Nails spoon shaped, brittle, ridged nails
Musculoskeletal	Good muscle tone, some fat under skin, can run or walk without pain	Muscles appear wasted, open fontanel on infant, knock-knees, bleeding into muscle, cannot walk properly
Skeletal	Can run or walk without pain	Painful, tender, swollen, open fontanel on infants
Cardiovascular	Normal heart rate and rhythm, no murmurs or abnormal rhythms; normal blood pressure for age	Rapid rate, enlarged, abnormal rhythm, elevated blood pressure
Gastrointestinal	No palpable organs or masses	Enlarged liver and spleen
Neurologic	Psychological stability; normal reflexes	Apathy, lethargy, paresthesia, disoriented, memory loss, irritability, confusion, decrease and loss of ankle and knee reflexes

dependent patients prior to surgery may promote a rapid healing response and reduce the incidence of wound dehiscence.[8]

Vitamin B is necessary for carbohydrate metabolism. Vitamin C (ascorbic acid) enhances capillary formation and permits collagen formation. Ascorbic acid deficiency can occur rapidly in critically ill, surgical, or severely malnourished patients, because the body does not store vitamin C.[7]

Other vitamins and minerals that have an impact on wound healing are thiamine, vitamins K and E, calcium, and trace amounts of copper, iron, and magnesium. Thiamine is required to strengthen collagen. Vitamin K is necessary for blood coagulation; its deficiency results in prolonged bleeding times and hematoma formation. Wound infection and dehiscence may then result. Vitamin E deficiency can cause impaired collagen synthesis and can retard wound healing. Calcium is necessary both as a cofactor in the action of various collagenases during remodeling and also as a cofactor in normal coagulation.[7]

Zinc is necessary for the synthesis of nucleic acids, including RNA. It is also essential in a number of enzymatic actions. Zinc deficiency can occur rapidly in patients with malnutrition, chronic diarrhea, and chronic steroid use. Urinary losses also increase with stress and weight loss.[5]

The caloric intake needed to correct and maintain a nutritional balance may be as high as 4,200 calories a day. Oral feedings are high in calories and proteins and supplemented with vitamins. Nasogastric feedings can be used to supplement the oral feedings, and intravenous hyperalimentation of amino acid glucose solutions is used when oral and nasogastric feedings are inadequate.[5]

Oxygenation/Perfusion. Oxygen, which is necessary for basic cellular processes, is a prime component in wound healing. It promotes collagen formation and fibroblast synthesis. With inadequate oxygen, new tissue is compromised and wound healing delayed.[9]

In addition to having adequate supplies of oxygen, efficient perfusion into the tissues is essential to promote the healing process. Poor perfusion prevents oxygen from reaching the damaged tissues and decreases delivery of leukocytes and other immune substances. The outcome of decreased systemic perfusion, as seen with hypovolemia or sepsis, is poor healing. Therefore, any respiratory dysfunction that results in an inadequate delivery of oxygen to the tissue will impair wound healing.

An increased supply of oxygen can accelerate healing and appears to be effective in open, poorly healing, nonnecrotic wounds where an impaired blood supply is the major reason for inadequate healing.[2] Intraoperatively, the use of warm saline for wound irrigations supports this information, as tissue oxygen tension increases with local hyperthermia. In addition, irrigation can reduce bacterial contamination by serving as a lavage and if the solution is warm, it assists in relieving pain and swelling that occurs in the tissues.

Smoking has an impact on wound healing; it reduces functional hemoglobin by 10% to 15%. Hemoglobin is the oxygen-carrying component of the red blood cell; if less is functional, less oxygen is delivered to tissues, prolonging wound repair.

Hypovolemia. How low a patient's hemoglobin may fall during surgery is controversial. The concerns about hepatitis, cytomegalovirus, and acquired immunodeficiency syndrome (AIDS) transmission, however, have led to continuing investigation into intraoperative blood replacement. The consensus appears to be that in relatively healthy patients, hemoglobin levels may fall significantly lower than the long-accepted value of 100 g/L with no reduction in oxygen-carrying capacity. Replacement of volume with crystalloid maintains adequate tissue perfusion. In addition, as the red blood cells become more dilute, the viscosity of the blood is reduced and blood flows more easily.[10]

Diabetes Mellitus. The regeneration and remodeling healing phases in patients with diabetes mellitus are affected during healing mainly because of impaired perfusion. The inflammatory response is also impaired due to hyperglycemia. In addition, all aspects of leukocyte function are impeded, particularly phagocytosis. Management of wounds in patients with diabetes must include measures to maximize tissue perfusions, as well as strict control of blood glucose levels.[2]

Obesity. During surgery for a patient who is obese, a thick layer of subcutaneous fat requires vigorous retraction, which frequently causes trauma to the abdominal wall. Excessive abdominal fat makes wound closure technically more difficult for the surgeon.

Obese patients tend to breath shallowly due to thick, heavy chest walls and increased intraabdominal pressure on the diaphragm. Therefore, oxygen delivery to the tissues is diminished, and wound repair extended. Moreover, because fatty tissue is relatively avascular, patients are vulnerable to microbial invasion. Wound dehiscence is not uncommon in obese patients.

Drugs. Antiinflammatory steroids suppress the inflammatory response in wound healing. They have their greatest impact when given during the first 3 days following injury. After 4 or 5 days, the effect is reduced; however, wound contraction and collagen synthesis will be delayed no matter when steroids are started.

In renal transplant patients who are taking steroids, primarily closed wounds heal in a reasonable time. If, however, the wound is left open or opens up, the steroid effect becomes vastly more significant. The open wound requires more circulation and more energy expenditure for healing than does the primarily closed wound.

Chemotherapeutic drugs such as actinomycin D, 5-fluorouracil, and methotrexate also retard wound repair. When the wound is healing by primary intention, these drugs arrest cell replication, suppress inflammation, and inhibit protein synthesis during the period of maximum cellular response—the second to tenth days. Healing impaired by inadequate inflammation may be accelerated by administering vitamin A systemically or locally. In some cases, the growth factors have had an effect. Both growth factors and vitamin A increase the number of inflammatory cells in a wound.[1]

Radiation Therapy. A small dose of radiation given 24 hours before surgery has little effect on wound repair. When larger doses are required preoperatively, surgery is usually delayed for 4 to 8 weeks, because by that time, inflammation from the radiation has subsided and the blood supply remains good. If more time were allowed to pass, the blood supply to irradiated tissue is decreased and the risk of poor repair is increased.

Aging. Wound healing is delayed in elderly patients. The wounds contract more slowly, and incised wounds gain strength more slowly. Clinically, wound failure is more frequent in elderly patients; they are more at risk for wound dehiscence, evisceration, and formation of fistulous tracts.[11]

The three cellular responses that are reported to account for delayed wound repair are the increased number of autoantibodies; mutation in lymphocytes and fibroblasts with production of altered proteins; and decrease in the synthesis of collagen, elastin, and structural glycoproteins by cells within the connective tissues.[11]

Decreased pulmonary function is another factor that compromises wound healing in elderly patients. Forced vital capacity, inspiratory reserve volume, and maximum breathing capacity decrease progressively with age.[12] Preoperative instruction in coughing and deep breathing exercises to facilitate lung expansion will assist in improving gaseous exchange.

Whenever possible, the elderly patient's nutritional status must be evaluated preoperatively and nutritional deficiencies corrected prior to surgical intervention.

Hyperbaric Oxygen Therapy

Hyperbaric therapy is the therapeutic application of selected gases at pressures in excess of the standard sea level pressure of 14.7 lb/inch. The use of hyperbaric oxygen combined with antibiotics and surgical debridement has increased the survival rate of patients with complicated infections and wounds.

Hyperbaric oxygen therapy involves the intermittent administration of 100% oxygen via inhalation in a compressed air chamber. The high oxygen tension may be toxic to certain infectious organisms, especially anaerobic organisms such as *Clostridium perfringens*. Some fungal infections, such as botriomycosis and mucormycosis, which were nearly 100% fatal in the past, are also susceptible to hyperbaric oxygen.[13]

Contraindications for hyperbaric therapy include a history of asthma or chronic obstructive pulmonary disease, a history of pneumothorax, and unstable cardiac status, particularly congestive heart failure.

Nursing care may include transporting the sedated patient to the hyperbaric chamber. A specific consent form must be signed for treatment in the chamber. If the patient is to be sedated or anesthetized, a myringotomy is performed to equalize pressure in the middle ear during descent into the chamber. In addition, the patient's skin is cleansed of all petroleum-based products to eliminate them as an ignition source for the oxygen line. To prevent the forcing of air or debris into the patient during ascent from the chamber, an in-line filter is put in place.

Claustrophobia is a major issue for some patients to cope with while in the chamber. Anti-anxiety medications may relax the patient enough to tolerate the procedure.

∎ DRESSINGS

The choice of dressing for an open wound depends on several factors, including the color of the wound, the amount of drainage, wound depth, and the color and condition of the surrounding skin. Regardless of the type of dressing, it is applied after the surgeon's gown and gloves are removed. Dressings have several functions:

- protect the incision from contamination
- absorb drainage
- support the incision
- provide pressure to reduce edema
- assist in achieving hemostasis
- maintain an optimal (moist) environment
- allow free exchange of gases
- serve as an esthetic measure

Nearly all surgical wounds are covered with a dressing for the first 24 to 48 hours for optimal resurfacing and more rapid healing. Closed wounds may be infected by surface contamination of bacteria within the first 2 to 3 days.[14] In addition, occlusive and semiocclusive dressings protect exposed cutaneous nerve endings, and thereby relieve pain. A dressing is designed so that it may be removed without disrupting viable cells necessary for healing.

Generally, a moist environment promotes the best epithelial migration and protects the wound from invading microorganisms. On a moist surface, new cells can slide easily from the edge of the wound where they are produced to create "islands" of epithelial covering. In dry wounds, new cells cannot move as readily and the body uses energy attempting to move them. The dry environment also damages or destroys many of the cells.

Currently, there are several dressings designed for specific purposes, each with its own advantages. For example, alginate dressings, for which seaweed is the source of alginic acid, are designed to provide a controlled wound environment and thereby enhance the body's own natural defenses against infection. Various polyurethane dressings may be used for a one-layer dressing. Optimal resurfacing of superficial wounds occurs when a polyurethane dressing is applied within 2 hours after the incision is made and left in place for at least 24 hours.[15]

Alginate and polyurethane materials maintain a moist wound environment, inhibit crust formation, decrease pain and inflammation, prevent bacterial contamination, and produce epithelialization of superficial wounds 30% to 45% faster than wounds exposed to air.[15]

The three-layer technique of wound dressing is used for primarily closed wounds that may have drains, for secondary or tertiary healing wounds that are full thickness and have moderate to heavy drainage, and for wounds that require the dressing to remain in place longer than 48 hours. The three-layer dressing consists of a contact layer, an absorbent or intermediate layer, and a securing layer.[16]

The surface of the material in contact with the wound may be occlusive, semiocclusive, or nonocclusive. Occlusive dressings prevent drying of the wound and are impermeable to air and water. Semiocclusive dressings include hydroactive dressings such as those used for chronic wounds. Nonocclusive dressing material facilitates removal of excessive drainage and should be nonadherent for painless removal.

The layer beneath the surface dressing must be absorbent and easily molded to the contour of the body. It is held in place with tape or a binder. Before the tape is applied, the area, including the incision site, must be clean, dry, and free of soaps, chemicals, oils, blood, and other body fluids. Residues of any of these fluids will prevent the tape from sticking and may cause a chemical burn. Tincture of benzoin should be avoided. A chemical injury is a common reaction caused by the entrapment of irritating chemicals under the adhesive. If necessary, a skin protector may be applied to the skin to allow it to dry before using tape. For patients allergic to tape, hypoallergenic porous tape or self-adherent wraps are available.

Tape is applied without tension from the center of the dressing outward, with at least one inch of tape allowed on the skin around the dressing edges. Maximum adhesion can be achieved by firmly rubbing or pressing on the tape. For large or bulky dressings and dressings on areas of high movement or friction, a stretchy tape or dressing cover is best. Either will allow for some swelling and skin movement with minimal possibility of skin trauma. When compression or pressure dressings are needed, stretch may be applied to the tape over the dressing area, but it is relaxed on the ends where applied to the skin. If swelling, edema, or distention occurs, the tape is repositioned or replaced to avoid the formation of blisters.

For proper placement of tape over bony prominences, the joint is positioned in maximum flexion, and then the dressing and tape are applied. If repeated taping is anticipated, porous tape is recommended.

Whenever possible, tape is removed in the direction of hair growth. The tape is kept close to the skin surface and as it is pulled back, the skin immediately adjacent to the tape being removed is supported. If adhesive residue remains on the skin after the tape is removed, it can be removed by firmly rubbing another piece of fresh tape over the affected area and peeling the tape back slowly. This process can be repeated if necessary.

Pressure dressings are used to obliterate dead spaces and prevent capillary oozing, serum accumulation, and hematoma formation. It is necessary to check the area around a pressure dressing for adequate circulation. Any discomfort or change in sensation around the dressing may indicate that the dressing is too tight. Pressure dressings may be made of fluffed gauze, bulk dressing, cotton rolls, foam rubber, or abdominal pads. Elastic bandages may be used to provide pressure and hold bulky dressings in place.

For burns and large pressure sores, biologic dressings may be used. Biologic dressings include cadaver skin, pigskin, and human amniotic membranes. The dressings reduce fluid loss, minimize local bacterial growth, and facilitate granulation tissue formation. These actions ensure that the wound will be in the best possible condition for retaining an autograft.

■ ADVANCES IN WOUND HEALING

Research is being conducted to improve wound healing. A new technique being used stimulates the growth of tissue, capillaries, and skin, thereby promoting rapid healing of infected sites. The therapy, which works by using growth factors derived from the patient's own blood, is called *platelet-derived wound healing*. The platelets are applied directly to the wounds of diabetic patients with nonhealing foot ulcers, patients with rheumatoid arthritis who have developed chronic wounds from steroid therapy, and patients who have deep wounds or ulcers resulting from peripheral vascular disease.[17]

Microskin grafting has been developed for the treatment of severe burns. The procedure involves mincing skin autographs into tiny skin particles, evenly dispersing the skin particles using a piece of silk cloth and saline, transferring the skin particles to the dermal surface of an allograft, and transplanting the allograft to the excised wound. The skin particles grow larger until they coalesce with each other and resurface the whole area. Then the allograft is rejected.[18]

■ REFERENCES

1. Hunt T, Mueller R. Wound healing. In Way L, ed. *Current Surgical Diagnosis and Treatment.* Norwalk, CT: Appleton & Lange, 1994: 80–93.
2. Cooper DM. Acute surgical wounds. In Bryant R, ed. *Acute and Chronic Wound Nursing Management.* St Louis: Mosby Year Book; 1992: 91–104 (31–68).
3. Culver D et al. Surgical wound infection rates by wound class, operative procedure, and patient risk index. *Am J Med.* 1991; 91: 152S–157S.
4. Windsor J et al. Wound healing response in surgical patients: recent food intake is more important than nutritional status. *Br J Surg.* 1988; 75: 135–137.
5. Souba W, Wilmore D. Diet and nutrition in the care of the patient with surgery, trauma and

sepsis. In Shils M et al, eds. *Modern Nutrition in Health and Disease,* 8th edition. Philadelphia: Lea & Febiger; 1994: 1210.

6. Nelson R, Franzi L. Nutrition and aging. *Med Clin North Am.* 1990; 73: 1531–1549.
7. Johnson L. Nutrition and wound healing. *Sem Periop Nurs.* 1993; 2(4): 239.
8. Winkler M, Mandry M. Nutrition and wound healing. *Support Line.* 1992; 13(3): 1–4.
9. Cooper D. Optimizing wound healing. *Nurs Clin North Am.* 1990; 25: 165–180.
10. Gordon B, Newman S. Factors influencing surgical wound healing and their anesthetic implications. *Sem Periop Nurs.* 1993; 2(4): 223.
11. Latz P, Wyble S. Elderly patient: perioperative nursing implications. *AORN J.* 1987; 46: 238–250.
12. Walters J, McClaron J. The elderly surgical patient. *Scientific American.*
13. Shafer M. Use of hyperbaric oxygen as adjunct therapy to surgical debridement of complicated wounds. *Sem Periop Nurs.* 1993; 2(4): 259.
14. Cuzzell J. Choosing a wound dressing: a systemic approach. *AACH Clinical Issues.* 1990; 566–576.
15. Eaglstein W et al. Optimal use of an occlusive dressing to enhance healing. *Arch Dermatol.* 1988; 124:393–394.
16. Wysocki A. Surgical wound healing. *AORN J.* 1989; 49(2): 511–514.
17. New developments in healing wounds. *AORN J.* 1989; 50(3): 622.
18. Fang C. Burn treatment. *AORN J.* 1989; 49(2): 528.

PART

SIX

Organizational Concerns in Perioperative Nursing

Improving Organizational Performance

One of the first individuals to express concern regarding the adequacy of medical and nursing care was Florence Nightingale. She compared the mortality experience in the British Armed Forces during the Crimean War with the mortality experience in the civilian population. In her *Notes on Matters Affecting the Health, Efficiency and Hospital Administration of the British Army,* published in 1858, Nightingale brought to the attention of the government and the public the atrocious standards of care for military personnel. Although by today's standards the data were crude, the report was instrumental in bringing about basic reforms in the living standards and the health services for the armed forces.

Again, in 1863, Nightingale proposed keeping a log of circumstances surrounding surgical procedures for the purpose of improving the morbidity and mortality of surgery.

Little emphasis was given to assessing quality in health care until the early 1970s. Since that time, the concept of ensuring quality has gained momentum from governmental agencies, accrediting bodies, and consumers. Through the various media, consumers have become more knowledgeable about health care and the increasing cost of that care. As a result, consumers are demanding that the health care profession be more accountable for the quality and the quantity of the services delivered.

Historically, one method of increasing accountability by the health care profession was through the development of quality assurance programs. A quality assurance program is a systematic process of measuring the quality of care against standards, and ensuring that the patient receives the necessary level of care. Variations were reviewed, deficiencies corrected, and the issues reevaluated. The goal of quality assurance programs was to improve patient care.

▪ STRUCTURE, PROCESS, AND OUTCOME MEASURES

Donabedian[1] and Bloch[2] defined three major criteria for assessing the quality of care: structure, process, and outcome. Each measures a different aspect of patient care.

Structure. Structure standards and criteria concern the physical facilities; equipment; philosophy and objectives; organizational characteristics; management of human, material, and fiscal resources; and the status of certification, accreditation, and licensure of the hospital, department, and staff. Subjects for structure issues may include an assessment of turnover time between surgical procedures, or a random sampling of patient charges to determine their appropriateness. Examples of standards might be that all local cases must have two circulating nurses or that electrical safety is monitored regularly by the biomedical technician and is consistent with the institutional and national standards.

The structure of the hospital or department may meet the designated standards, but since structure is only one of three criteria, the quality of the care delivered may still be suboptimal.

Process. Process standards and criteria concern all the activities performed by the nurse in the delivery of nursing care. Of critical importance is how the activities are performed and in what sequence.

Outcome. Evaluation of outcome is the most reliable means of measuring patient care. Outcome standards and criteria focus on what happens to the patient as a result of nursing intervention. In identifying patient outcomes, the nurse must predict before delivering care what the desired outcome is and then measure results against that criterion. Failure to meet the desired outcome results in examining the process and performance standards to identify areas of deficiency. Because the patient and family have input in the assessment, this method has the most relevance in measuring the quality of care delivered. The following is an example of an outcome statement with specific criteria:

> Integrity of the patient's skin is maintained
>> No allergy or sensitivity to the prep solution
>> No allergy or sensitivity to adhesive agents
>> No redness related to use of electrosurgical machine
>> No disruption or destruction of skin surface

■ BACKGROUND OF QUALITY PROGRAMS

One of the first proponents of the concept of quality assurance in health care was the federal government. As part of the 1972 amendments to the Social Security Act, the government required that a Professional Standards Review Organization (PSRO) be created. The PSRO was designed to involve practicing physicians in the ongoing review of the quality and the cost of care received by clients of Medicare, Medicaid, and maternal and child health programs.

All facilities receiving these funds were to have state and local PSROs developed by July 1, 1978. The legislation was based on two concepts: health professionals are the most appropriate people to evaluate the quality of health care services, and an effective peer review at the local level is the soundest method for ensuring appropriate use of health care resources and facilities.

In 1973 the Joint Commission on Accreditation of Healthcare Organizations (JCAHO) included medical and nursing audits as a requirement for accreditation. The standard directed the professions to formulate criteria and to implement a systematic evaluation system to ensure that optimal quality care is delivered.

During the 1980s the focus of JCAHO evolved from requiring a specific number of audits that focused on retrospective chart reviews to a standard that promoted the monitoring and evaluation of the quality and appropriateness of care.

Each institution was required to establish, maintain, and support an ongoing quality assurance program that included an effective mechanism for reviewing and evaluating patient care as well as for documenting appropriate responses to the findings. It was required that the plan be defined in writing and include a mechanism for ensuring the accountability of the medical and other professional staffs for the care they provide.

In 1986 the JCAHO introduced the "Agenda For Change," which identified a ten-step model by which monitoring and evaluation was to occur in all health care institutions:

1. Assign responsibility for monitoring and evaluation activities.
2. Delineate scope of care provided by the organization.
3. Identify the most important aspects of care provided by the organization.
4. Identify indicators and appropriate clinical criteria for monitoring the important aspects of care.
5. Establish thresholds for the indicators to trigger evaluation of the care.
6. Monitor the important aspects of care by collecting and organizing data for each indicator.
7. Evaluate care when thresholds are reached to identify opportunities to improve care or correct problems.
8. Take actions to improve care or to correct identified problems.
9. Assess the effectiveness of the actions and document the improvement in care.
10. Communicate the results of the monitoring and evaluation processes to relevant individuals, departments, or services, and to the organization-wide quality assurance program.

One individual was responsible for administering or coordinating the program. Each clinical discipline was responsible for developing a quality assurance program and for reporting the findings through a designated mechanism. To the extent that integration was possible, multidisciplinary audits were encouraged. It was thought that this would minimize duplication, enhance communication, and potentially save costs for the institution. Experience with this model identified that quality could not be assured, but that it could be continuously monitored and effectively improved through efforts by individuals caring for the patient and by those managing the resources.

In 1995 the JCAHO identified a link between organizational performance and judgments about quality by introducing an evolutionary move from "Quality Assessment" to "Continuous Quality Improvement" (CQI) (Table 19–1). The premise of this shift was that every plan, every effort and every process can always be made better. Instead of striving to achieve an arbitrary end point or to solve only one problem, organizations must make every effort to improve constantly. In addition, the primary focus shifted from department-specific programs to an organizational perspective that emphasizes improving performance across the entire organization. The goal of improving organizational performance (Fig. 19–1) is to design processes and systematically measure, assess, and improve the organization's performance. Measurements include:

TABLE 19–1. COMPARISON OF QUALITY ASSESSMENT AND QUALITY IMPROVEMENT

Quality Assessment	Quality Improvement
Externally driven	Internally driven
Narrow in scope (focus on one discipline)	Broad in scope
Few people involved in process	Many people/departments involved in process
Focuses on individuals	Focuses on processes
Process has end point	No end point
Analysis divided	Analysis integrated
Stands alone; no integration of information and functions required	Requires integration/coordination of information and functions
Department based; no support or involvement from upper management	Upper managers involved and may lead process

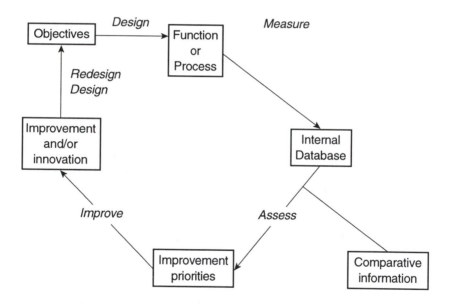

The performance-improvement cycle depicted in this flowchart has no beginning and no end. An organization may start its improvement effort at any point: by designing a new service; by flowcharting an existing clinical process; by measuring patient outcomes; by comparing its performance to that of other organizations; by selecting specific areas for priority attention; or even by experimenting with new ways of carrying out current functions.

Figure 19–1. Flowchart for improving organizational performance. *(Reprinted with permission from* Comprehensive Accreditation Manual for Hospitals. *Oakbrook, IL: JCAHO; 1995.)*

- *Performance of clinical activities (service/care)*: What is done to and/or for the patient? How well it is done?
- *Outcomes of clinical activities*: What are the results of clinical activities? What is the cost of the service/care? Is the customer satisfied with the results and how service was delivered?
- *Judgments regarding clinical activities*: Does the customer believe that the quality of the service delivered is acceptable? What is the value of the service to the customer and is it appropriate?

▌ FACTORS THAT AFFECT PERFORMANCE

Continuous quality improvement requires valuing the internal and external consumer and a commitment to critical thinking and innovation.

External Factors

Several external factors that interact and influence how a facility designs and delivers its services are reviewed to improve their performance. These factors include political, social, and economic issues as they impact the health care delivery system, professional standards, new regulations, new payor mandates, and revised expectations of consumers for the quality and value of the health care they receive.

Internal Factors

The internal environment refers to functions inside an organization that influence how the organization performs. Most important are leadership, management of information, management of human resources, and improvement of organizational performance.

Leadership. The leadership of a facility in collaboration with staff members identifies the mission, vision, and values of the facility, and creates a strategic plan with goals and objectives to accomplish the plan. The leadership empowers, or enables, staff to make decisions and act on improving processes and services within defined parameters (such as fiscal resources) without obtaining the approval of the leadership team. Overriding all of this must be a commitment by the leaders to be champions of the facility's program for continuous quality improvement.

Information. Organizations must have timely, valid, and reliable information regarding:

- individual patient records to identify care/service delivered and the outcomes of that service
- administrative and business functions of the facility
- department-specific performance
- performance of the organization as a whole
- other organizations' performance
- current data regarding the science of health care delivery

Access to this information will allow a facility to coordinate, integrate, assess, and improve its services.

Human Resources. Facilities must have an adequate number of competent staff, whose performance is assessed upon employment and regularly thereafter, with improvement identified through continuing education and training opportunities. Feedback must be routine and consistent with personal and professional development occurring continuously. Performance appraisal systems should include assessment by peers and leaders, as well as a self-assessment. Information obtained in the appraisals should reflect the quality of performance based on observation of that performance, and an action plan for improvement and/or further development.

Improvement of Organizational Performance. The fourth important internal function is an organization's ability to evaluate itself and generate improvements. The performance being measured can be any interaction or event that impacts patient care, the manner in which the interaction or task is executed, and the final outcome of the interaction or event. The performance of these events is multidimensional. Specifically, the nine interdependent dimensions of performance codified by JCAHO are:

- Appropriateness of care
- Efficacy of care
- Safety of environment as it affects patient, family and staff
- Continuity of care
- Timeliness of care delivery
- Effectiveness of care
- Efficiency of care delivery, delivered in a caring and respectful manner
- Availability of care when it is required
- Patient satisfaction

An effective organization will create well-designed processes, measure the performance of existing processes, assess processes based on measurement data, and improve

---

∎ CLINICAL INDICATORS AND CONTINUOUS QUALITY IMPROVEMENT

1. Identify a clinical area requiring assessment/improvement
2. Determine what the objective of the study will be
3. Identify relevant practice guidelines or standards
4. Evaluate practice parameters
5. Select and modify the practice parameters
6. Develop clinical indicators to measure compliance to guidelines
7. Assess current practice
8. Evaluate and communicate results
9. Assess modified practice and outcomes

outcomes through the redesign of existing processes or by designing new processes when appropriate.

In addition, leadership must be committed to the process of quality improvement as evidenced by personal involvement and consistent attention to the program. Quality must be acknowledged and rewarded, as should small improvements. Leadership should build incentives into every role in the organization to indicate support of quality improvement.

JCAHO does not require any specific management style or a specific process. The Joint Commission, however, has developed a guide that may be used for quality improvement: the Plan, Do, Check and Act Model (see the PDCA Model below).

What is essential is that all the improvement teams in a facility use the same approach. Irrespective of the model, certain major concepts underlie quality improvement. They all focus on the internal factors identified earlier, the collection and interpretation of data, and finally a plan of action. The following needs must be addressed:

- measurement on a continuing basis to understand and maintain the systems and processes throughout the facility (coordination and collaboration are necessary among departments, services, and disciplines; multifunctional and multidisciplinary groups are essential, as many of the opportunities to improve quality are outside the normal department work groups)
- measurement of outcomes to help determine priorities for improving systems and processes
- assessment of individual competence and performance

▌ THE STANDARDS TO FOLLOW

Although an organization has flexibility in designing its program, five processes are identified in the standards: plan, design, measure, assess, and improve.

▌ THE PDCA MODEL

- Plan
  - Identify customers
  - Develop product/service to meet customer needs
- Do
  - Deliver product or service
- Check
  - Continuously measure and analyze product/service
  - Compare results to customer needs/expectations
- Act
  - Refine/improve the product/service

Plan

An institution must have a planned, systematic, organization-wide approach to designing, measuring, assessing, and improving its performance. The plan is implemented collaboratively and must include all the appropriate departments and disciplines. Although a written plan is not required, it will assist in the planning and monitoring of activities.

Design

The design standard is relevant to either new, improved, or redesigned processes. The design process must be based on the organization's mission, vision, and plans and on the needs and expectations of patients, staff, and other interested parties. Essential to design is a review of current literature regarding the process being designed or redesigned. This review should include professional standards of practice, recommended practices, regulatory guidelines, and best practices or benchmarking. Benchmarking involves comparing the organization's performance with performance outside the organization where consistently good outcomes are achieved. Benchmarking is most often associated with a standard of excellence. Finally, a review is conducted of available databases that provide information about how other organizations have addressed the process, function, or service that is currently being reviewed.

Measure

An organization must have a system in place to collect data for designing and assessing new or important existing processes. The goal of measurement is to provide data that objectively describe how a function or process is operating and what the results or outcomes are. Specifically what must be measured is whether care is efficacious, appropriate, available, timely, effective, safe, efficient, continuous, respectful, and caring. This requires that departments quantify their performance through patient outcomes, patient satisfaction, and resource consumption.

The process of review includes measures of both outcomes and processes—outcomes to understand the results, and processes to understand the "causes" of the results. The JCAHO indicates that the outcomes of many clinical processes are not evident or measurable at discharge, or they vary considerably due to patient variables. It is important, therefore, to measure the processes that have the greatest impact on the anticipated outcomes as surrogate measures of the outcomes.

Data should be collected for issues that need improvement as well as for those that do not currently present problems or concerns. Sources of data include:

- patient and family satisfaction questionnaires
- patient records
- unusual occurrences
- infection control reports
- staff concerns
- log books
- committee reports/meetings
- direct observation of staff and patients

Measuring an issue that is not currently a problem is an opportunity to evaluate the stability of a particular process and to predict outcomes. In addition, when a decision is made to improve a process and the new process is put into place, it is important to measure the results of the change.

In assessing organizational performance, it is essential to realize the needs, expectations, and perceptions of patients, families, and staff. The data thus gained are important in the assessment and design of new processes. Data sources may be expanded to include community residents and local businesses who can be questioned about their needs and about their expectations of the organization's performance and the scope of services provided. The information can be used to develop the strategic plan and to set the goals and objectives for the following year.

The processes of patient care functions and organizational functions identified by the JCAHO are measured routinely (See Table 19–2).

Additional priorities for measurement include important patient care functions, such as situations involving a large percentage of patients (high volume); situations when the availability, effectiveness, and timeliness of the treatment place the patient at serious risk; and patient care situations that include "problem prone" activities.

Functions and processes of specific concern to patients and staff also need to be measured. Satisfaction surveys of patients and staff can assist in identifying areas that need attention.

The processes, identified by JCAHO, as specifically relating to the use of operative and other invasive procedures include the following:

- selecting the appropriate procedure
- preparing the patient for the procedure

TABLE 19–2. IMPORTANT PATIENT CARE AND ORGANIZATIONAL FUNCTIONS

Care of Patient Functions

- Patient rights and organizational ethics
- Assessment of patients
- Care of patients (including care planning, anesthesia care, medication use, nutritional care, operative and other invasive procedures, and special treatment procedures)
- Education
- Continuum of care, including entry to setting or service, continuity, coordination and discharge planning

Organizational Functions

- Leadership
- Management of information
- Management of human resources
- Management of the environment of care
- Surveillance, prevention, and control of infection
- Inproving organizational performance

- performing the procedure and monitoring the patient
- providing postprocedure care
- using medications
- using blood and blood components

When high-volume cases are sampled, it is recommended that at least 5% of the cases be reviewed. However, if the average number of cases per quarter is fewer than 600, at least 30 cases must be reviewed.[3] Surveyors will inquire about the sample's rationale and adequacy when the sample size is less then 5% of the average number of cases occurring quarterly or less than 30 cases, whichever is greater.

Quality Improvement Techniques for Measuring Patient Care. Concurrent monitors are accomplished during the patient's hospitalization and may result in improved outcomes. This method of monitoring care includes mechanisms other than the patient's record, such as interviews and discussions with the patient, family members, and members of the health care team. Data obtained from the patient or the patient's environment are more reliable in assessing the quality of care than a health record, which is a secondary source.

Sources of information for concurrent evaluations are observations of the staff while performing patient care activities (process monitor), physical assessment of the patient, open-chart audits, staff interviews, patient interviews, or surveys and group conferences that include patient, family, and staff.

Retrospective monitors measure the outcomes of nursing care either before or after the patient is discharged. Closed-chart reviews, patient care plans, postcare interviews, or questionnaires are used.

One of the disadvantages of the retrospective chart review is that what may be assessed is the quality of the record rather than the actual care that was delivered. Skillful recording may give a false impression of quality. Conversely, if information is omitted from the record, it may be assumed that that care was not delivered. In either situation, a false assessment of the quality of care may result.

Interviews and Questionnaires. Interviewing the patient and family is an excellent way to gain information regarding their perception of the care delivered. The interview can be used with a wide variety of patients, and the interviewer can minimize misunderstandings by probing or clarifying a topic. The interview may be structured—the interviewer asks routine questions of all patients; or it may be unstructured—the interviewer asks random questions that are directed by the patient's responses.

The interview method is expensive and time-consuming. Also, it may elicit answers that the patient thinks the interviewer wants to hear. To minimize subjectivity, the nurse conducting the interview should not be the one who delivered care to the patient.

Surveys and questionnaires are less time-consuming; also, because the patient feels a sense of anonymity, the responses are less pressured. These tools require that the patient be literate, that no health care jargon be included, and that the questions not be written at a reading level higher than sixth grade. In addition, the text should be translated for the major ethnic cultures served within the facility.

Each question should be short and present only a single idea. Before a questionnaire is implemented, it is field tested with an appropriate sample size. Routinely, only a small percentage of questionnaires are returned. A personalized covering letter that explains the project and a self-addressed return envelope or postcard frequently result in an increased rate of return.

Risk Management and Quality Improvement. Data collected for risk management functions can provide an important link to improving organizational performance. Analyzing unusual occurrence reports and committee findings related to both individual safety and clinical care may help in identifying problems that require additional assessment activities. For example, if the infection control committee notes an increased incidence in urinary tract infections, all the processes that occur before, during and after bladder catheterization should be assessed.

Measurement Process. When a decision is made to measure a specific process, the nature of the process will determine who performs the measurement. The measurement may be delegated to an individual or to a specific work group assigned to study the process and to recommend changes. The type of indicator selected should be sensitive to the process or outcome being monitored or measured. The product of the measurement will create a data base that aggregates information about process performance, outcomes, satisfaction, and cost, as well as judgments about quality.

Examples of data that are appropriate for the phases of the perioperative period are presented in Figures 19–2, 19–3, 19–4, and 19–5, which illustrate continuous quality improvement screens for the preoperative, intraoperative, and postoperative periods as well as for ambulatory surgery.

Assess

Following data collection, the information is sorted and interpreted by a work group, which includes the process's owners, customers, suppliers, and additional "expert" assistance as needed. As a result, the organization is able to determine:

- whether design specifications for new processes were met
- the level of performance and stability of important existing processes
- possible improvement of existing processes
- appropriateness of suggested actions to improve the performance of processes
- if changes were made, whether the changes resulted in improvements
- priorities for improvement opportunities

The assessment process is strengthened by the use of statistical techniques. For example, statistics may be collected to identify the number and reasons for surgery cancellations occurring less than 8 hours prior to the scheduled time.

The performance being reviewed may be compared with the organizations's historical performance, other institutions' performance, facility-specific practice guidelines/parameters, desired performance targets, standards from professional associations (such as AORN and ASPAN), and with best practices.

Date _____ Procedure _____ Surgeon _____

Medical Record Number_____ Reviewer_____

Incomplete Health Data   ___ Adverse Medication Reaction
 ___ H & P
 ___ X-Ray   ___ Incomplete Nursing Documentation
 ___ Lab
 ___ EKG   ___ Blood Availability Delays
                                              reason: _____

Consent
 ___ Incomplete   ___ IV size/site inappropriate
 ___ Incorrect
 ___ Missing   ___ Allergies not documented

Inadequate Patient Preparation   Patient Prep
 ___ Pre op instructions not followed   ___ Wrong prep
 ___ Medication instructions not followed ___ Inadequate
 ___ Nursing assessment   ___ Abrasions noted

Surgery   Personnel delays:
 ___ Postponed   ___ Nursing staff
 ___ Rescheduled   ___ Surgeon
 ___ cancelled   ___ Anesthetist
                                           ___ RNFA
Reason: _____

Comments:

Figure 19–2. Continuous quality improvement screen: preoperative period.

Date: _____ Procedure: _____ Surgeon: _____

Medical Record Number: _____ Reviewer: _____

___ No problems/deviation noted

Surgery delay > 15 minutes   Equipment or instrumentation
 ___ anesthesia   ___ surgeon   problem during surgery
 ___ OR staff   ___ radiology   ___ missing   ___ broken
 ___ lab results   ___ other   ___ improperly cleaned
 ___ case not scheduled properly*   ___ improperly set up
 ___ transportation   ___ not available

Surgery cancelled*   Incorrect counts
 ___ after patient in room   ___ sponge
 ___ after induction   ___ instrument
                                           ___ sharps

Room not cleaned   Specimen
 ___ floor   ___ equipment   ___ lost
 ___ furniture   ___ walls   ___ mislabeled
 ___ lights   ___ suction canister   ___ mishandled*
                                           ___ placed in wrong solution

Critical Events:
Intraoperative injury to patient
 ___ disruption in skin integrity   ___ Wrong patient taken into OR*
 ___ burns
 ___ falls   ___ Break in aseptic technique*
 ___ transfer/positioning injury

___ Cardiac or respiratory arrest   ___ Death

Comment: (all items* require comment)

Figure 19–3. Continuous quality improvement screen: intraoperative period.

```
Date _____ Procedure _____    Surgeon _____

Medical Record Number: _____     Reviewer: _____

___ No problems/deviation noted

___ Blood loss requiring transfusion          Thermoregulation
                                               ___ < 96 F
                                               ___ > 101 F
___ Pulse oximetry < 90 on admission
                                               ____ Medication error
___ O2 required > 30 minutes after admission
                                               ____ Unplanned ICU admission
___ Chest pain
                                               ____ Ventilator required, unplanned
___ Narcotic antagonist required
                                               Equipment
___ Complications from invasive procedure*     ___ unavailable
                                               ___ malfunctioning
                                               ___ other*

Returned to OR within 24 hours for:
___ second procedure
___ control of bleeding

___ Cardiac/respiratory arrest                 ____ Death


Comments: (all items* require comment)
```

Figure 19–4. Continuous quality improvement screen: postoperative period.

The assessment process is continuous. To assist, JCAHO is developing a data base, the *Indicator Measurement System*, or IM System. The system will use uniform indicators to provide organizations the opportunity to compare their performance on specific indicators with other facilities of like size and similar patient populations.

Immediate and intensive assessment is triggered by the occurrence of a *sentinel event*. An example of such an event in the perioperative area is a retained foreign body or impaired skin integrity following surgical intervention. These events are so important that

```
Date _____ Procedure _____   Surgeon _____

Medical Record Number: _____       Reviewer: _____

___ No problems/deviation noted

___ Discharge > 2 hours after procedure         Discharge delayed
                                                ___ postop instructions not
___ Unplanned admission*                              understood
                                                ___ postop teaching not
___ Discharge criteria not met                        completed
                                                ___ Adult not available
___ No MD response > 30 minutes                       to accompany patient home



Comments: (all items* require comment)
```

Figure 19–5. Continuous quality improvement screen: ambulatory surgery.

every effort is directed at resolving the issue, finding the cause for the event, and developing a plan of action to prevent a recurrence.

To assist in analysis, various tools can be used to graphically display results. These include Pareto charts, histograms, scatter diagrams, flow charts, cause and effect, run charts, and stratification of data.

The findings of the assessment process may identify opportunities for changing existing processes or establishing new ones in order to improve expected outcomes. Defects in the system may be changed after reviewing departmental policies and procedures, correcting communication problems, and redistributing staff, supplies, and equipment.

Individual Performance Deficiencies. Occasionally, behavior or performance deficiencies may be identified through the assessment process. The deficiencies are corrected through coaching and counseling, and are documented in the individual's personnel or credentials file. The plan of action should include the opportunity for education and training to bring the performance to the desired level. Institutional policies and procedures should address the issue of failure to meet the required job competencies (see the section on credentialing and assurance of quality at the end of this chapter).

Improve

The next phase in the cycle for improving organizational performance is to establish priorities for improvement. Setting the priorities is an important link between the assessment and the actions required to improve performance. Managers have an important role in this activity as they keep the process focused on the organization's strategic goals, provide the appropriate resources required to address improvement opportunities, and maintain an organizational perspective on the effects of changes in process and outcomes.

Priorities for improvement are not static. The list will need to be updated as necessary based on occurrence of sentinel events, changes in the facility's goals and objectives, and feedback from customers. Periodic review of the facility's quality programs is essential to maintain the strength of the program and to integrate new approaches, themes, and ideas.

Criteria for setting priorities is specific to the facility's goals and objectives, the resources required, the potential impact on patient care and services, the importance of the improvement opportunity (whether regulatory, high volume, high risk, or problem prone), and the potential impact of savings of resources.

The systematic approach to improving performance includes identifying a potential for improvement, testing the strategies for change by setting up a control group, and assessing the data from this trial to identify whether the change produced the desired improved performance. If the desired changes occurred, then the strategy is ready for implementation throughout the facility.

Prior to any change being implemented, the expected impact of the change must be evaluated by involving the appropriate stakeholders. These are the individuals and departments who will be affected by the design or improvement activity. Together the group should set performance expectations for the newly designed or improved process and identify mechanisms to measure the performance after the changes have been implemented.

Unit-Based Committees. To assist with the process of organizational improvement, a unit-based committee should focus on coordinating the department's quality efforts by using the most appropriate measurement tools and techniques to analyze and improve care or services. This committee could serve as a work group for the department's program and serve as a link to the facility's quality improvement steering committee. Membership in a departmental committee should consist of a cross section of departmental personnel and physicians. The chairperson should be committed to the concept of continuous quality improvement and to facilitating progress toward developing an awareness of the process with other members of the staff. The committee also has a responsibility to communicate the activities of the departmental and hospital committees via staff meetings, departmental newsletters, and communication book. Identification of serious existing problems, potential high-risk problems, or related concerns in the care of the patient should be directed through this work group.

Specific objectives of the committee may include:

1. To review current standards of nursing practice
2. To identify actual or potential patient problems
3. To collect and assess data regarding the outcomes of care delivered
4. To report findings to appropriate individuals (such as the director of department, supervisor, or the facility committee)
5. To make recommendations to eliminate identified problems and to test solutions
6. To assess the effectiveness of the interventions
7. To maintain documentation regarding quality improvement activities
8. To annually assess the effectiveness of the committee

Committee members should review the literature to assess "the state of the art" and to develop an understanding of performance improvement mechanisms. Other concepts and methods of current interest include total quality management (TQM), continuous quality improvement (CQI), and systems thinking.

Such a review will assist the committee in identifying the methods that have been developed by other facilities and national associations. Using established methods encourages identification with national standards of practice and thereby with nursing as a profession.

■ CREDENTIALING AND ASSURANCE OF QUALITY

As a profession matures, it recognizes the need to be accountable and to ensure the competence of the practitioners. Credentialing and its components of accreditation, certification, and licensure are formal methods of recognizing professional and technical competence. The purpose of credentialing in nursing is to assure the consumer that quality care is being provided by identifying the members qualified to practice through the issuing of a license. This process controls the practice by establishing parameters of practice and minimal standards of performance for all members of the profession. Therefore, the consumer is protected against performance by unqualified individuals. In addition the JCAHO standard indicates that each institution should have processes designed to ensure that the competence of all staff members is assessed, maintained, demonstrated, and improved on an ongoing basis.

AORN developed a "Perioperative Nursing Credentialing Model" to assist with the credentialing of nurses practicing in the operating room (see Fig. 19–6). Files should be maintained on each individual that include the following information:

1. Educational preparation
2. Verification of licensure
3. Certification
4. Professional development
   a. Professional associations
   b. Continuing education
   c. Research, publications, seminars
5. Institutional requirements
   a. Verification of orientation
   b. Job description
   c. Performance appraisal
   d. Verification of skill level by surgical specialty that includes technology
   e. Regular verification of competency by surgical specialty to include appropriate technology

To maintain clinical competency by surgical specialty, the number and type of cases should be defined for each service; the staff should then be responsible for scrubbing and

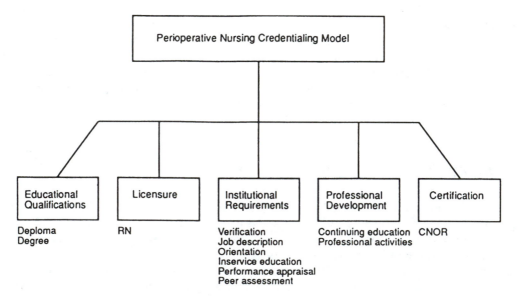

Figure 19–6. The AORN perioperative credentialing model. *(Reprinted with permission from Perioperative credentialing model. AORN J. 1986; 43(1):262.)*

circulating on these cases throughout the year. Failure to meet this requirement should result in a "mini rotation" through that service. If individuals are not able to meet these responsibilities, coaching, counseling, education and assignment changes must be considered and acted upon. It is the director of perioperative services' responsibility to ensure competency of all personnel on the nursing staff.

The accreditation component assures the consumer that the institution or program of study meets certain predetermined criteria or standards (for example, those of the JCAHO and the NLN, whose focus is on accrediting educational programs for nurses).

The process of certification in nursing was developed as a mechanism to provide formal recognition for excellence in the practice of nursing. The ANA and the AORN are currently certifying individuals who achieve a level of performance based on predetermined standards relating to an area of specialty practice.

Accountability for improving the quality of care delivered at an affordable cost is no longer a philosophic concept. It is demanded by consumers of all health care services. It is required by legislation and by regulatory agencies and is mandated by the profession.

Nursing has the opportunity and is faced with the challenge to demonstrate that it can control its practice by delivering professional nursing care, assessing the care delivered, and changing the practice that does not meet the desired outcomes of care. Self-regulation is the authentic hallmark of a mature profession.[4]

▌ REFERENCES

1. Donabedian A. Evaluating the quality of medical care. *Melbank Memorial Fund Q.* 1966; 44:166–206.
2. Bloch D. Evaluation of nursing care in terms of process and outcome: Issues in research and quality assurance. *Nurs Res.* 1975; 24(1):256–263.
3. Comprehensive Accreditation Manual for Hospitals. Oakbrook, IL: Joint Commission on Accreditation of Healthcare Organizations; 1995.
4. Phaneuf MC. *The Nursing Audit: Profile for Excellence.* Foreword by Donabedian A. New York: Appleton-Century-Crofts; 1972:5.

Developing Perioperative Clinical Education Programs

Traditionally, the operating room experience was part of the basic educational preparation for professional registered nurses. As ideologies in nursing education underwent modification, the hospital apprenticeship type programs began to disappear. Concurrently, nursing education has moved out of these schools and into the mainstream of higher education.

Movement of nursing education from the diploma school to the collegiate environment has resulted in elimination of the operating room experience, and therefore, in a lack of qualified entry-level nurse practitioners for this specialty. In an effort to ensure that there are qualified practitioners in the operating room, perioperative training programs have been instituted. These programs are more cost effective than the time-consuming, one-on-one orientation many institutions, by necessity, were forced to implement.

The focus of this chapter is on developing clinical education programs for professional registered nurses. The concepts and examples may be utilized to structure a perioperative training program or a competence-based orientation program to ambulatory surgery centers or operating rooms.

The Joint Commission for the Accreditation of Healthcare Organizations (JCAHO) defines competence as "capacity equal to requirement."[1] Competence is the ability to perform the task or process effectively by applying the appropriate knowledge and skills at the appropriate time and place. The elements of a competency assessment system include a policy and procedure to define competency, and processes that:

1. assess an individual's initial competence
2. maintain competence during employment
3. develop competence in new clinical techniques, practices, and equipment
4. validate competence in accordance with policy/procedure

Knowledge is an organized body of information, usually of a factual nature or a procedural nature, which, if applied, makes the performance of a job possible. Skill is the manual, verbal or mental manipulation of data, people or things (see Table 20–1).[2]

The orientation programs are the means by which new nursing staff are introduced to the philosophy, goals, policies, procedures, role expectations and other factors needed to function in a specific work setting.[3] Orientation socializes the new staff member to the or-

TABLE 20–1. KNOWLEDGE AND SKILL COMPETENCIES

Knowledge	Skills
describe the psychosocial influences affecting the patient's response to surgical intervention	assess the pathophysiological and psychosocial influences affecting the patient's response to surgical intervention
demonstrate knowledge necessary to implement the peroiooperative nursing role	demonstrate the knowledge and skills needed to implement the perioperative role
discuss principles of asepsis used in providing patient care during the perioperative period	apply principles of asepsis in providing patient care during the perioperative period
define the theoretical basis of role function as an interdisciplinary team member in the delivery of care to the perioperative patient	function as a member of the interdisciplinary perioperative team
plan nursing interventions that reflect the nursing process in providing care to the perioperative patient	demonstrate application of the nursing process to perioperative patient care
relate nursing, legal and ethical boundaries in the practice of professional perioperative nursing	

From *Bray C et al. Perioperative nursing internship: Designing, implementing a collaborative program. AORN J. 1990; 52(4): 792*, with permission.

ganization's culture and is provided at the time of employment or when changes in roles and responsibilities occur in a specific work setting.

The outcome of an orientation program is to identify and clarify role expectations for new staff members and to socialize the staff member to norms, practices, attitudes and values of the profession as it is implemented at a specific institution. Tables 20–2, 20–3, and 20–4 illustrate types of criteria and checklists that can be used with an orientation program.

Table 20–2 is an example of measurable criteria for orientation to the gynecology service. Table 20–3 is an example of skill checklists utilized to support the orientation to a service and the annual competency assessment. Table 20–4 identifies equipment required for staff members to maintain a competent performance on the gynecology service. During the orientation phase the skills lists are utilized by the preceptor and the preceptee. During the annual competency review the same checklist can be used to validate skills required for functioning in the service.

■ COMMUNITY REVIEW

Before the decision to design a training program is made, the programs currently available should be reviewed. Is there a need for a training program? What is the supply and demand for operating room nurses in the community? How is the current supply being met? Is there a college or university in the area interested in collaborating in the development of such a program?

If the didactic aspects of the course are to be offered outside the hospital premises, the clinical faculty must be identified. However, this should occur only after the hospital and departmental philosophy, objectives, and goals have been carefully reviewed, and the names of the individuals responsible for implementation of the contract identified. In most

TABLE 20–2. OPERATING ROOM ORIENTATION OUTCOME CRITERIA: GYNECOLOGIC SURGERY

Aspect of Care: Nursing Process: Care of the patient undergoing gynecologic surgery

Competency: Demonstrate the knowledge and skills necessary to provide safe, comprehensive care to the patient undergoing gynecologic surgery

1. Describe the anatomy of the normal female reproductive tract
2. Describe the common gynecologic disorders including:
   a. Cervical carcinoma
   b. Endometrial carcinoma
   c. Infertility
   d. Leiomyomata
   e. Ovarian carcinoma
   f. Tubal carcinoma
   g. Vaginal carcinoma
   h. Vulvar carcinoma
   i. Enterocele/rectocele
   j. Dysfunctional bleeding
3. Identify the nursing considerations and functions specific to the intraoperative care of gynecologic patients
4. Develop nursing care plans that reflect consideration of the patient's specific needs
5. Locate the special supplies and equipment required for GYN surgery as listed on the Gynecologic Supply and Equipment List
6. Perform effectively the preoperative assessment and admission of an ambulatory surgery patient
7. Demonstrate the ability to circulate effectively and independently on the procedures identified in #2 above utilizing the Standard of Care for the specific procedure
8. Demonstrate the ability to scrub effectively and independently on the procedures identified in #2 above
9. Demonstrate the use and processing of the special supplies and equipment required for GYN surgery, according to established procedures
10. Evaluate the outcomes of care provided during the perioperative experience by making postoperative phone calls to outpatients
11. Describe the use, dosage and location of drugs used routinely in GYN surgery
12. Locate and use, as necessary, appropriate resource materials and personnel to assist in providing safe, effective patient care

settings, this will be the operating room manager and a representative of the educational institution. Once established, the relationship of the affiliated constituents is ongoing.

▮ INSTITUTIONAL REVIEW

In surveying characteristics of an institution as a resource for the clinical experience, several factors must be considered:

1. Size of the hospital or ambulatory surgery center
2. Number of operating rooms available for student assignments
3. Turnover rate of departmental staff
4. Hiring policies regarding:
   a. Experienced versus inexperienced RNs
   b. Clinical competence criteria

TABLE 20–3. SKILL INVENTORY CHECKLIST: GYNECOLOGICAL ROTATION

Operative Procedure	Scrub	Circulate	Skill Observed Date/Name
Hysterectomy			
Radical hysterectomy			
Tuboplasty			
Tuboplasty with microscope			
Adnexal surgery			
Hysterectomy, vaginal			
Anterior-posterior repair			
Cervical conization			
Radium insertion			
Laparoscopy/ Laparotomy			
Pelvic exeneration			
Construction of vagina			
Radical vulvectomy			
Endometrial ablation			
Pelviscopy with laser			
Hysteroscopy			

Competency Codes: C = Competent   S = Skill development required   I =Improvement required

Comments: (Employee/Student)   Comments: (Preceptor)

_____   _____
Signature/Date   Signature/Date

TABLE 20–4. SPECIAL EQUIPMENT AND SUPPLY LIST: GYNECOLOGY SURGERY

Item	Purpose	Location	Method of Sterilization	How to Assemble and Check
Laparoscope Insufflator				
Laparoscope cart				
Fetuscope				
Argon Beam Coagulator				
CO2 Laser				
GYN Resectoscope				
Nezart Irrigation System				
Allen Stirrups				
Kleppinger Bipolar				
Video Systems Stryker Olympus				
Hyskon Irrigation Pump				
Uterine Manipulators				

Competency Codes: C = Meets competency standards
                      S = Skill development required
                      I = Improvement needed

Evaluation Method Code: P = Direct patient care
                         D = Discussed/described
                         RD = Return demonstration
                         DR = Document review

5. Ratio of professional registered nurses to operating room technicians
6. Departmental commitments to existing programs (i.e., nursing, medical students)
7. Willingness of the professional nursing staff to participate actively as preceptors

In conjunction with the cited appraisal, a comprehensive census analysis depicting predominant trends and characteristics of the surgical case load must be prepared. Inclusive features are case consistency, variety, and the scope of technical complexity.

Following the community and institutional survey, a decision should be reached regarding the level of skill the practitioner is expected to exhibit at the end of the program. Will it be an entry-level practitioner able to function in a community facility or ambulatory surgery center where less complex and routine procedures are performed? Or, will it be a practitioner whose intraoperative skills are more advanced due to clinical experience in the highly complex surgical specialities?

Deciding the desired competence level of practitioners will influence the length of the program and will assist in determining course objectives. A 3-month course in a hospital or a surgery center with a routine surgical case load may produce an acceptable entry-level practitioner; however, 6 months, or longer, may be required in the hospital where extremely technical and involved procedures dominate the surgical schedule.

▌FINANCIAL IMPLICATIONS

It is essential that the financial resources for a training program be identified and confirmed by the appropriate individuals early in the planning stage. Those concerned should include the surgical services manager, the perioperative educator and, when pertinent, a representative of the affiliating educational institution.

Paramount to this discussion is the determination of the kind of credit the program will grant. The choices are nondegree academic credit, degree academic credit, continuing education unit (CEU) contact hours, or a certificate.

A community-college or university-affiliated program may grant nondegree academic credit that, in some institutions, may be used to satisfy elective requirements. Hospital-based programs may award continuing education units, according to the American Nurses' Association guidelines, or a certificate attesting to satisfactory completion of a course. In states requiring continuing education for relicensure, continuing education courses must be approved by the State Board of Nursing.

Determining the type of credit to be awarded will assist in resolving the financial issues. Four possible options for fee structures are:

1. The student pays a fee consistent with the rate per hour of course instruction established by the academic institution.
2. The student receives a stipend from a grant procured by the educational institution or the hospital.
3. The hospital establishes an internship program that provides a portion of the entry-level practitioner's salary for the duration of the course.
4. The student neither pays a fee for the course nor receives any monies for the training period. At the program completion, however, the student is committed to remain on the departmental staff for a specific period of time.

Following the resolution of the economic issues, emphasis should be focused on developing the philosophy and objectives for the program.

■ RESPONSIBILITY FOR THE CLINICAL EDUCATION PROGRAMS

The success of clinical education programs is predetermined by the caliber of the associated educational institution and the individual selected as the course coordinator. It follows, therefore, that extreme care should be exercised in establishing appropriate criteria for the process. The minimal basic educational requirement should include credentials as a registered nurse, preferably with a master's degree, and extensive experience in and knowledge of perioperative nursing. Individuals selected should be articulate and enthusiastic, and demonstrate excellent professional, technical, and interpersonal skills. It is preferable that they have knowledge of the principles of adult learning, curriculum development, methods of program evaluation, and the methods of testing.

One of the most important factors in the adult learning process is how the educator views the learner. Table 20–5 illustrates key differences in the education of children and adults in five areas.

TABLE 20–5. CONCEPTS OF EDUCATION: ADULTS COMPARED WITH CHILDREN[4]

	Assumptions			Process Elements		
	Children	Adults			Children	Adults
1. Self-concept	Dependence	Increasing self-directiveness		Climate starts with first contact	Authority oriented	Mutuality
				Quality is influenced by each contact	Formal Competitive	Respectful Collaborative Informal
2. Experience	Of little worth	Adults are a rich resource for learning		Planning	By teacher	Mechanism for mutual planning
3. Readiness	Biological development Social pressure	Developmental tasks of social roles		Diagnosis of needs	By teacher	Mutual self-diagnosis
4. Time perspective	Postponed application	Immediacy of application Need to cope with person centered		Formulation of objectives	By teacher	Mutual negotiation
5. Orientation to learning	Subject centered	Problem centered		Design	Logic of the subject matter Content units	Sequenced in terms of readiness Problem units
				Activities	Transmittal techniques	Experiential techniques (inquiry)
				Evaluation	By teacher	Mutual rediagnosis of needs Mutual measurement of program

Courtesy Malcolm S. Knowles, Boston University, with permission.

If the educator views the teaching-learning process as participative, the student will have a greater commitment to the process. Collaboration and mutual goal setting allow the student to become actively involved in this process. The educator must be sensitive to those individuals who will require a judicious combination of the process elements in teaching children and adults.

■ CANDIDATE SELECTION

There are three groups of nurses who will be seeking a training program. They are:

1. Professional nurses with minimal or no previous operating room experience
2. Professional nurses who are reentering the work force and require updating before obtaining a position
3. Professional nurses who want to change their area of specialization

Specific criteria should be developed for the selection of the candidates and should be confirmed during the interview process. Areas of consideration are:

- Graduate of an accredited school of nursing
- Current state licensure
- Good physical and emotional health
- Desire to attain competence in perioperative nursing

■ PROGRAM DESIGN

The philosophy of the clinical education programs should be developed collaboratively with members of the perioperative management staff and closely aligned with the philosophy of the clinical setting. The program philosophy should be reviewed annually and revised to reflect changes as they occur in perioperative nursing, the philosophy of the educator, and concepts of teaching and learning.

Program Objectives

An objective is a statement that is measurable and includes a specific time frame for achieving the objective. Objectives may be classified as cognitive, psychomotor, and affective.

Cognitive objectives are concerned with the perception of factual knowledge and focus on the understanding of new material or ideas. *Psychomotor* objectives concern actions proceeding from mental activity, ranging from the simple reflex to the performance of highly complex skills. *Affective* objectives are the most difficult to measure due to their emotional basis, which is reflected through intangible attitudes and feelings.

Objectives are necessary because they describe the program and/or the clinical experiences in objective, measurable terms. Well-designed objectives can be utilized to measure performance and progress throughout the program. An example of objectives follows:

▌PERIOPERATIVE TRAINING PROGRAM: OBJECTIVES

Learning experiences selected collaboratively throughout the program will enable the clinician to competently:

1. Assess the physiological and psychosocial health status of the patient
2. Formulate a nursing diagnosis based on assessment data
3. Identify expected outcomes unique to the patient
4. Develop a plan of care that prescribes interventions to attain expected outcomes
5. Implement interventions identified in the plan of care
6. Demonstrate a repertoire of clinical skills and knowledge pertinent to defined surgical specialties
    a. Demonstrate progressive skills in performing these functions
    b. Demonstrate ability to safely use the equipment associated with these specialties
7. Apply principles of aseptic technique and maintain sterile fields
8. Identify the implications of changes in anatomical and physiological functioning that may occur following an operative procedure
9. Provide information to the patient, family, and significant others in relation to the perioperative period
10. Utilize available resources to assist the patient postoperatively (for example, home health or social work)
11. Identify the legal responsibilities involved in administering care to patients undergoing surgical intervention
12. Identify behavioral manifestations of individuals under stress
13. Evaluate patient outcomes
14. Measure effectiveness of nursing care

Course Content

The content of the course should be consistent with the list of objectives and its predetermined length. Accordingly, the educator must determine the magnitude of theory required to achieve the anticipated assimilation of student knowledge as well as the most appropriate sequence for presentation of the material.

If the participants differ in background and experience, they should be required to submit a current self-assessment of clinical practice. This will assist the educator in ascertaining individual and collective levels of competence. An analysis of the submitted data will provide the educator with valid documentation for adjusting the course content within the scope of a structured course curriculum.

The program content should include:

1. Introduction
   a. Course structure and process
   b. Clinical experiences
   c. Educator expectations
      1) Attendance
      2) Assignments
      3) Method of determining competency
2. Institutional-departmental
   a. Philosophy
   b. Organizational structure
   c. Personnel policies
3. Perioperative nursing—a historical perspective
4. Operating room design and construction
   a. Environmental orientation
   b. Standard OR equipment
   c. Hazards/emergencies
   d. Safety measures
   e. Maintenance-environmental services
   f. Related hospital departments
5. Identification of the roles of the team members
   a. Introduction
   b. Job descriptions
6. Perioperative role
   a. Nursing process
   b. Documentation
7. Principles of operating room technique
   a. Asepsis
      1) Microbiology
      2) Infection control
      3) Sterilization
      4) Disinfection
      5) Preparation of the skin
      6) Surgical hand scrub
      7) Gowning and gloving
   b. Anesthesia
      1) Types
      2) Methods of administration
      3) Complications
      4) Cardiac arrest and resuscitation
      5) Monitoring local/conscious sedation patient
      6) Care of anesthesia equipment
   c. Positioning
   d. Draping
   e. Methods of maintaining homeostasis
      1) Sutures

      2) Electrosurgery
      3) Synthetic agents
      4) Tourniquets
      5) Counts
   f. Wound healing
   g. Terminal cleaning
      1) Operating room
      2) Instruments
      3) Supplies
      4) Equipment
 8. Care of the patient during the immediate postoperative period
 9. Review of basic sciences and operative procedures
10. Professional responsibility
   a. Personal attitudes and attributes
   b. Hygiene
   c. Ethics and legal responsibility
   d. Continuing education
   e. Current issues affecting nursing
   f. Legislative action
   g. Nursing research
   h. Professional accountability
11. Operating room management
   a. Functions of the nurse manager
      1) Fiscal
      2) Interpersonal
      3) Technical

▮ TEACHING METHODOLOGIES

There are many teaching methods available to the educator. The method selected should meet the identified objectives, be compatible with the resources available, and be able to be used effectively by the educator.

Lecture

The lecture is a formal discourse of facts usually presented by a member of the nursing staff or another provider. In addition to members of the surgical team, a wide variety of resource people are available in the health care facility and in the educational setting who can contribute in this capacity, such as infection control nurse, hospital attorney, chaplain, dietician, and social worker. Use of these resources adds interest and depth to the educational experience.

Demonstration

The demonstration is the best method for students to learn psychomotor skills. In this method, the educator identifies the objective of the procedure, describes each step while demonstrating it, and relates each step to a relevant principle. The student repeats the demonstration to verify comprehension and dexterity. Evidence of student error during the repeat demonstration is an indication for corrective instructional measures.

Observation

Identification of specific objectives followed by observation in the clinical setting can be an asset to the teaching-learning experience. For instance, following a lecture on stress, the specific objective for observation might be, "Observe interactions of surgical team members to identify the symptoms of stress."

Role Playing

Role playing is the method of choice to build skills in learning to use interviewing techniques or in using effective listening skills. In this method, a situation is described and the students are assigned parts without a script. Role playing provides for trial use of interventions in a nonthreatening environment. A discussion follows the dramatization and culminates in a critique by the observers. This method is useful in teaching preoperative assessments.

Programmed Instruction

The educator may develop programmed instruction modules to teach a variety of subjects such as the principles of aseptic technique, patient prepping, and draping. This method allows the student to progress at his or her own rate and may be in a written or audiovisual format.

The programmed instruction:

1. Presents information and requires frequent responses from the student
2. Provides immediate feedback to the student with information on whether or not the response is appropriate
3. Allows students to work individually and adjust their own rate of progress to personal needs and capabilities

Educational Media

There is a wide variety of educational media available to aid in the teaching-learning process. Those used most frequently are:

- Audiotape recorders
- Direct circuit television
- Educational television
- Videos
- Slides
- Transparencies
- Interactive computer

A number of videos are available for rent or purchase. They require advance scheduling and preplanning to integrate them into the course at the appropriate time.

The educator must always preview the selected media and make certain that the content is consistent with the desired learning activities. Immediately prior to the class, the appropriate equipment must be checked to make sure it is functioning properly. An extra bulb should always be available for all projectors.

Independent Study

In independent study, the student selects a topic or problem of personal interest and seeks out information on the topic or solves the problem independently of the educator.

Clinical Conferences

Clinical conferences with case presentations guide the student to identify experiences and, through analysis, to associate them with previous knowledge gained from didactic material. Criteria for case presentations should include the following patient data:

1. Review pathophysiology of surgical procedure
2. Discuss psychosocial aspects influencing patient's response to surgical experience
   a. Social history
      1) Culture and ethnicity
      2) Family organization
      3) Language
      4) Religion
      5) Socioeconomic status
   b. Mental status
   c. Teaching and learning needs
   d. Pertinent laboratory data
   e. Emotional reaction of patient and significant others
   f. How patient and significant others cope with stress
   g. Nonverbal communication
3. Identify components of nursing diagnosis and patient care plan for intraoperative period
4. Discuss implementation of patient care plan
5. Discuss postoperative outcome, including interpreting impact of surgical intervention

Additional Resources

Additional resources are the course syllabus, bibliographies, and textbooks. The bibliography must be revised annually to reflect the latest concepts regarding the perioperative role.

Feedback regarding the participant's progress is an important component of the teaching-learning process. Feedback can come from a variety of sources. Clinical conferences, checklists, tests, and evaluations supply the students with information as to their progress toward the objectives. Frequent feedback also helps the students and the educators to measure the quality of the experience and collaboratively to create an environmental of mutual respect and concern.

The educators must remain informed of new approaches to teaching and include in their repertoire a wide variety of methods with which they are comfortable and that will best achieve the desired outcome.

∎ USE OF PRECEPTORS

Preceptors are an important component of all clinical education activities. The preceptor provides one-on-one teaching in the clinical area and is responsible for reinforcement of theory content during the student's clinical experience. The goal of preceptorship is to improve the clinical experience.

Whereas a buddy system has the same goal, it is not as effective as a preceptorship. The difference in the two concepts relates to the definitions of the words *preceptor* and *buddy*.

- Preceptor: Teacher, mentor, consultant
- Buddy: Fellow soldier, partner

A buddy system merely provides someone with whom the student can work, someone to show the student how to do tasks. There is no specific accountability or responsibility inherent in being a buddy.

A preceptor is one who makes certain that the student translates theory content into departmental policies and procedures. The preceptor serves as a role model and stimulates the learner to identify with an appropriate reference group in developing his or her professional practice. The attitudes, philosophies, and skills of the preceptor are eventually reflected in the student and the new employee. Therefore, explicit criteria for preceptors should be established and discretion must be exercised in the choice of these individuals.

Criteria for Preceptorship Appointments

1. Minimum of 1-year experience at current institution
2. Demonstrated clinical competency substantiated consistently with above-average or outstanding performance evaluations
3. Demonstrated leadership skills (e.g., problem-solving skills)
4. Demonstrated communication skills, as evidenced in positive interpersonal relationships through tactful, direct, and sensitive interactions
5. Demonstrated interest in personal professional growth
6. Demonstrated comprehension of the theoretical concepts of adult learning through application to appropriate practice situations
7. Willingness to participate in the program, meet identified responsibilities, and provide feedback to the learner

Prior to the selection of preceptors, the specific responsibilities of the role must be defined and conveyed to qualified candidates. These responsibilities include:

1. Cognizance and affirmation of the purpose and objectives of the course
2. Competence to impart course content in theory and practice
3. Capability to develop the clinical experience collaboratively with the student
4. Accessibility to the student, at least once per week, to discuss clinical progress and establish future goals
5. Attendance at regularly scheduled preceptor meetings
6. Attendance at weekly student clinical conferences

7. Submission of written evaluations on designated students at the end of a clinical rotation
8. Attendance at prescheduled conferences to evaluate clinical experience and submit recommendations for program revisions

A workshop covering all aspects of preceptorship should precede assumption of responsibilities by selected individuals. Material for a workshop should include:

1. The role and responsibilities of the preceptor
2. Presentation of the individual and collective needs of the learners and formulation of plans to meet them
3. Advantages and disadvantages of andragogy and pedagogy, and their applications
4. Hypothetical problem situations: how to handle them; how to cope with feelings; and how to evaluate the outcome

After the preceptors have been designated, it is important that their work schedule coincide with that of the learner's clinical experience. If there are unavoidable scheduling problems, the preceptor must make specific arrangements for a substitute preceptor from among the selected individuals, appraising him or her as to the clinical skills that the student is capable of performing.

Together, the preceptor and the learner should develop objectives for the clinical experience by surgical service, and the student should maintain a clinical experience record. The objectives and the clinical experience record are effective tools for evaluating the student's performance in the clinical setting. The final evaluation of the clinical experience is outcome based. The outcomes are the changes in the practice of the learner who participated in the learning activity.

Preceptorship is a rewarding experience for both participants. Such a collegial relationship enhances the student's clinical experience while providing increased job satisfaction for the preceptor. Through the experience, preceptors have an opportunity for professional growth as they develop their teaching, planning, and supervisory skills.

∎ EVALUATION OF THE COURSE

Evaluation is a systematic process by which judgment is made about the consequences, results, effects, or merits of an education activity in order to make subsequent decisions.[3] There are five stages of evaluation: process, content, outcome, impact, and program.[5]

- Process evaluation: measure of the participant's overall feelings about the educational activity
- Content evaluation: measure of change in knowledge, attitude, or skill as a result of participating in the educational activity
- Outcome evaluation: measure of identifying whether participants really changed their behavior following participation in an educational activity
- Impact evaluation: measurement of the outcome of the educational activity on either the departmental, organizational, or health care system within which a person is employed

- Program evaluation: measure and summary of all the other components of evaluation.

The nurse educator will design a tool that will effectively assess these areas and will reflect his or her philosophy of education and views about the participants. If the educator has set a climate of mutual respect and open exchange of ideas and suggestions, the participants will willingly provide feedback. Table 20–6 is an example of a form used by participants to assess the content of a program.

The educator then uses the feedback from students to implement changes in the

TABLE 20–6. PARTICIPANT ASSESSMENT: PERIOPERATIVE CLINICAL EDUCATION PROGRAM

	(1) Strongly Agree	(2) Agree	(3) Undecided	(4) Disagree	(5) Strongly Disagree
1. Course has clearly stated objectives.					
2. Stated goals/objectives are consistently pursued.					
3. Lecture information is highly relevant to course objectives.					
4. Course material is pertinent to my professional training as an OR nurse.					
5. The course contributed significantly to my professional growth.					
6. I can apply clinical skills and theory learned in this course.					
7. There was sufficient time in class for questions and answers.					
8. Bibliographies for this course are current and extensive.					
9. The content of the clinical experience is a worthwhile part of this course.					
10. In general I learned a great deal from this course.					

Other Comments:

course objectives or in the clinical experience. Evaluation of the course should be a continuous, ongoing process that reflects changes in perioperative nursing practice and in principles of adult education.

∎ REFERENCES

1. Joint Commission on Accreditation of Healthcare Organizations. *Manual.* Oakbrook, IL: JCAHO, Inc; 1995.
2. Bray C et al. Perioperative nursing internship: Designing, implementing a collaborative program. *AORN J.* 1990;52(4):790.
3. American Nurses Credentialing Center. *Standards for Continuing Education in Nursing.* Washington DC: ANA; 1994.
4. Knowles MS. *The Adult Learner: A Neglected Species.* Houston, TX: Gulf Publishing; 1978:110.
5. Abruzzese R. *Nursing Staff Development: Strategies for Success.* St. Louis: Mosby-Year Book; 1992.

APPENDIXES

APPENDIX A

■ STANDARDS OF PERIOPERATIVE ADMINISTRATIVE PRACTICE*

Standard I
A philosophy, a purpose and objectives shall be formulated to guide operating room services.

Standard II
An organizational plan for the operating room shall be developed and communicated.

Standard III
A registered nurse shall be authorized with administrative accountability and responsibility for the operating room services.

Standard IV
The registered nurse administrator shall be accountable and responsible for developing mechanisms that ensure optimal patient care.

Standard V
The operating room management team shall develop and manage the budget for operating room services.

Standard VI
The operating room services shall have written standards of nursing practice.

Standard VII
The operating room services shall have written policies and procedures that serve as operational guidelines.

Standard VIII
The operating room management team shall be responsible for establishing staffing requirements, selecting personnel, and planning for appropriate utilization of human resources.

*Adapted with permission from AORN Standards and Recommended Practices, 1995, pp. 99–105. Copyright © AORN, Inc. 2170 Parker Road, Suite 300, Denver CO, 80231.

Standard IX

Staff development programs shall be provided for operating room personnel.

Standard X

A safe operating room environment shall be established, controlled, and consistently monitored.

Standard XI

The operating room management team shall promote the discovery and integration of new knowledge by encouraging development of and use of nursing research.

Standard XII

The operating room staff shall maintain appropriate documentation related to OR activities.

Standard XIII

The operating room management team shall recognize professional responsibility to promote, provide, and participate in a learning environment for students in health care disciplines.

Standard XIV

There shall be a quality assurance program for operating room services.

APPENDIX B

▮ STANDARDS OF PERIOPERATIVE PROFESSIONAL PERFORMANCE*

Standard I: Quality of Care
The perioperative nurse systematically evaluates the quality and appropriateness of nursing practice.

Interpretive statement. The perioperative nurse engages in the evaluation of care delivery through a systematic quality assessment and improvement process. This systematic approach uses specific steps to promote patient care quality.

Criteria
1. The perioperative nurse participates in quality of care activities as appropriate to the individual's position, education, and practice environment. Such activities may include
   - identifying and assigning responsibility for monitoring and evaluation activities,
   - delineating the scope of patient care activities or services,
   - identifying aspects of care,
   - developing quality indicators for each identified aspect of care,
   - establishing thresholds for evaluation of the quality indicators,
   - collecting data related to the aspects of care and indicators,
   - evaluating care based on the cumulative data collected,
   - taking actions to improve care or services,
   - assessing the effectiveness of the action(s) taken and documenting the outcomes, and
   - communicating data organization-wide.
2. Knowledge gained via the quality assessment and improvement process is used to initiate change in nursing practice.

Standard II: Performance Appraisal
The perioperative nurse evaluates his or her practice in context with professional practice standards and relevant statutes and regulations.

*Adapted with permission from AORN Standards and Recommended Practices, 1995, pp. 111–113. Copyright © AORN, Inc. 2170 Parker Road, Suite 300, Denver CO, 80231.

Interpretive statement. Performance appraisal is a process that includes defining and evaluating professional practice behaviors. The perioperative nurse is responsible for self-evaluation as well as receiving constructive feedback from health care team members.

Criteria

1. The perioperative nurse
    a. identifies the behaviors that support the level of performance desired within the role(s) of perioperative nursing practice;
    b. assesses perioperative practice behaviors on a regular basis, seeking constructive feedback;
    c. identifies areas of personal and professional development;
    d. develops and initiates an action plan to achieve professional development goals identified during the appraisal process;
    e. periodically monitors and evaluates the progress of goal achievement; and
    f. participates in peer review when appropriate.

Standard III: Education

The perioperative nurse acquires and maintains current knowledge in nursing practice.

Interpretive statement. The purpose of professional development is to build on varied educational and experiential bases for the enhancement of perioperative nursing practice. The perioperative nurse has primary responsibility for his or her ongoing education and professional development. The practice setting may provide the support needed for this development.

Criteria

1. The perioperative nurse
    a. completes an orientation based on individualized learning needs that have been identified for the performance description and practice setting in which the individual will perform;
    b. identifies learning needs based on performance behaviors that include critical thinking, interpersonal, and technical skills;
    c. seeks experiences to meet established goals for professional development; and
    d. demonstrates accountability for maintaining competency within the performance description, and participates in ongoing education activities relevant to professional issues and trends in perioperative nursing practice.

Standard IV: Collegiality

The perioperative nurse contributes to the professional growth of peers, colleagues, and others.

Interpretive statement. The perioperative nurse has an obligation to support and advance the speciality and the profession by sharing his or her knowledge and expertise. The perioperative nurse assists colleagues in building and maintaining the competencies necessary to provide safe, effective care to patients. This obligation may be fulfilled informally through role modeling, acting as a resource, and mentoring, or formally by serving as a preceptor or instructor in the clinical setting.

Criteria

1. The perioperative nurse shares knowledge and skills. This is accomplished through a variety of methods, including, but not limited to,
   - inservices, programs, seminars, and workshops,
   - preceptoring and mentoring,
   - role modeling in the clinical setting,
   - publishing,
   - participation/service in professional organizations,
   - consultative services, and
   - problem-solving or issues groups.
2. The perioperative nurse provides peers with constructive feedback regarding their practice. Feedback may be provided through
   - the peer review process,
   - quality improvement activities,
   - committee participation, and
   - one-on-one discussions.
3. The perioperative nurse uses appropriate communication techniques to avoid defensive responses and resistance to changing practice.
4. The perioperative nurse contributes to a positive environment conducive to education of novice perioperative practitioners.
5. The perioperative nurse is a role model for perioperative nursing competencies and correct implementation of policies, procedures, and protocols.

Standard V: Ethics

The perioperative nurse's decisions and actions on behalf of patients are determined in an ethical manner.

Interpretive statement. The basic human rights of individual patients are not forfeited when the patient enters the health care system. Care and services must be delivered without impeding these basic rights. The perioperative nurse is accountable to patients to safeguard these rights while providing appropriate nursing care or services in the perioperative setting. Nursing practice is guided by the *Code for Nurses with Interpretive Statements* of the American Nurses Association.

Criteria

1. The perioperative nurse acts as a patient advocate.
2. Patient confidentiality is maintained.
3. Care is delivered in a nonjudgmental and nondiscriminatory manner that is sensitive to cultural, racial, and ethnic diversity.

4. Care is delivered in a manner that preserves and protects patient autonomy, dignity, and rights.
5. The perioperative nurse uses available resources to help formulate ethical decisions.

Standard VI: Collaboration

The perioperative nurse collaborates with the patient, significant others, health care providers, and others in providing care.

Interpretive statement. Care of the perioperative patient requires cooperative efforts from many internal and external customers in order to achieve optimum outcomes. The perioperative nurse demonstrates accountability, flexibility, and communication skills when collaborating.

Criteria

1. The perioperative nurse
   a. communicates pertinent information relative to perioperative care,
   b. consults with health care providers and others, and
   c. makes referrals, including provisions for continuity of care, as needed.

Standard VII: Research

The perioperative nurse uses research findings in practice.

Interpretive statement. Perioperative nursing practice is supported by research. The perioperative nurse uses research to demonstrate the relationship between nursing interventions and patient outcomes. The perioperative nurse, regardless of position, education, or practice environment, participates in various aspects of the research process.

Criteria

1. Perioperative nurses participate in research by involvement in one or more of the following activities:
   - identifying clinical problems,
   - participating in data collection,
   - sharing research activities with others,
   - reading and critiquing research for application to practice,
   - participating on a research committee, and
   - using knowledge gained through research findings to initiate change.

Standard VIII: Resource Use

The perioperative nurse considers factors related to safety, effectiveness, efficiency, environmental concerns, and cost in planning and delivering patient care.

Interpretive statement. Human and material resources in the perioperative setting are costly and sometimes scarce. The perioperative nurse identifies and promotes the most efficient and economical method of providing safe and effective patient care in accordance with established standards.

Criteria.

1. The perioperative nurse
   a. evaluates factors related to safety, effectiveness, efficiency, environmental concerns, and cost when two or more practice options would result in the same expected outcome;
   b. assigns tasks or delegates care based on the needs of the patient and the knowledge and skill of the provider selected;
   c. and assists the patient or significant others in identifying appropriate services available to address perioperative patient needs.

APPENDIX C

■ STANDARDS OF POST ANESTHESIA NURSING PRACTICE*

Standard I: Patient Rights and Ethics

Standard. Post anesthesia nursing practice is based on philosophic and ethical concepts that recognize and maintain the autonomy, dignity and worth of individuals.

Rationale. Each individual has dignity and worth, deserves respect and recognition, and has the right to quality health care services. Patient and family have the right to explore health care alternatives and to make choices regarding their care. Consideration of social and economic status, culture, personal attributes and the nature of the health care problem must be given when working with patient, family and community.

Standard II: Environment

Standard. Post anesthesia nursing practice promotes and maintains a safe, comfortable and therapeutic environment for patients, staff and visitors.

Rationale. The intrusion of anesthesia and surgery has significant impact on motor and sensory functions that necessitates a safe, supportive environment. Individuals may be exposed to infectious organisms, hazardous materials and other environmental risk factors.

Standard III: Personnel Management

Standard. A sufficient number of qualified nursing staff with demonstrated competency in the provision of nursing care during all phases of post anesthesia are available to meet the individual needs of patients and families.

Rationale. Nursing is a unique and separate discipline that contributes positively to the patient's health and wellness. Nursing care in post anesthesia settings is directed toward provision of direct patient care, supervision of care given by others, health teaching and pa-

---

*The American Society of Post Anesthesia Nursing Practice. Thorofare, NJ, 1992.

tient advocacy. The expertise of professional registered nurses is necessary to implement and supervise the care provided to patients in all post anesthesia settings.

Standard IV: Continuous Quality Improvement

Standard. Post anesthesia nursing practice is monitored and evaluated on an ongoing basis. Identified problems are resolved in order to assure the quality and appropriateness of patient care.

Rationale. Evaluation of the quality of patient care through examination of the clinical practice of nurses is one way to fulfill the profession's obligation to ensure that consumers are provided excellence in care.

Standard V: Research

Standard. Post anesthesia nurses participate in research designed to improve patient care by initiating and conducting studies, utilizing results and incorporating findings into practice.

Rationale. Each professional has accountability for continuing development and refinement of knowledge in the post anesthesia field through development of new and creative approaches to practice, use of relevant research findings and participation in research. The professional nurse assumes responsibility for this at a level appropriate to his/her educational and experiential knowledge base.

Standard VI: Interdisciplinary Collaboration

Standard. Nursing personnel facilitate continuity of care by assuring that the needs of patients and families are recognized and addressed through coordination with other health team members within the health system and the community.

Rationale. Post anesthesia practice involves multiple disciplines. The professional nurse is responsible for coordination of patient care through collaboration with those disciplines.

Standard VII: Assessment

Standard. Post anesthesia nursing practice includes the systematic and continuous assessment of the patient's condition. The nurse assures that the data are collected, documented, and communicated. The professional nurse analyzes the data to determine appropriate nursing interventions.

Rationale. Assessment and data collection provide a clinical and legal basis for nursing actions and accountability.

APPENDIX D

▌ STANDARDS FOR BASIC ANESTHETIC MONITORING*

These standards apply to all anesthesia care although, in emergency circumstances, appropriate life support measures take precedence. These standards may be exceeded at any time based on the judgment of the responsible anesthesiologist. They are intended to encourage quality patient care, but observing them cannot guarantee any specific patient outcome. They are subject to revision from time to time, as warranted by the evolution of technology and practice. They apply to all general anesthetics, regional anesthetics and monitored anesthesia care. This set of standards addresses only the issue of basic anesthetic monitoring, which is one component of anesthesia care. In certain rare or unusual circumstances, 1) some of these methods of monitoring may be clinically impractical, and 2) appropriate use of the described monitoring methods may fail to detect untoward clinical developments. Brief interruptions of continual† monitoring may be unavoidable. *Under extenuating circumstances, the responsible anesthesiologist may waive the requirements marked with an asterisk (*); it is recommended that when this is done, it should be so stated (including the reasons) in a note in the patient's medical record.* These standards are not intended for application to the care of the obstetrical patient in labor or in the conduct of pain management.

Standard I
Qualified anesthesia personnel shall be present in the room throughout the conduct of all general anesthetics, regional anesthetics and monitored anesthesia care.

Objective. Because of the rapid changes in patient status during anesthesia, qualified anesthesia personnel shall be continuously present to monitor the patient and provide anesthesia care. In the event there is a direct known hazard, e.g., radiation, to the anesthesia personnel which might require intermittent remote observation of the patient, some provision for monitoring the patient must be made. In the event that an emergency requires the temporary absence of the person primarily responsible for the anesthetic, the best judgment of the anesthesiologist will be exercised in comparing the emergency with the anesthetized patient's condition and in the selection of the person left responsible for the anesthetic during the temporary absence.

---

†Note that "continual" is defined as "repeated regularly and frequently in steady rapid succession" whereas "continuous" means "prolonged without any interruption at any time."

*Reprinted with permission of the American Society of Anesthesiologists, 520 N. Northwest Highway, Park Ridge IL, 60068-2573.

Standard II

During all anesthetics, the patient's oxygenation, ventilation, circulation and temperature shall be continually evaluated.

Oxygenation Objective. To ensure adequate oxygen concentration in the inspired gas and the blood during all anesthetics.

Methods

1. Inspired gas: During every administration of general anesthesia using an anesthesia machine, the concentration of oxygen in the patient breathing system shall be measured by an oxygen analyzer with a low oxygen concentration limit alarm in use.*
2. Blood oxygenation: During all anesthetics, a quantitative method of assessing oxygenation such as pulse oximetry shall be employed.* Adequate illumination and exposure of the patient are necessary to assess color.*

Ventilation objective. To ensure adequate ventilation of the patient during all anesthetics.

Methods

1. Every patient receiving general anesthesia shall have the adequacy of ventilation continually evaluated. While qualitative clinical signs such as chest excursion, observation of the reservoir breathing bag and auscultation of breath sounds may be adequate, quantitative monitoring of the CO_2 content and/or volume of expired gas is encouraged.
2. When an endotracheal tube is inserted, its correct positioning in the trachea must be verified by clinical assessment and by identification of carbon dioxide in the expired gas.* End-tidal CO_2 analysis, in use from the time of endotracheal tube placement, is strongly encouraged.
3. When ventilation is controlled by a mechanical ventilator, there shall be in continuous use a device that is capable of detecting disconnection of components of the breathing system. The device must give an audible signal when its alarm threshold is exceeded.
4. During regional anesthesia and monitored anesthesia care, the adequacy of ventilation shall be evaluated, at least, by continual observation of qualitative clinical signs.

Circulation Objective. To ensure the adequacy of the patient's circulatory function during all anesthetics.

Methods

1. Every patient receiving anesthesia shall have the electrocardiogram continuously displayed from the beginning of anesthesia until preparing to leave the anesthetizing location.*

2. Every patient receiving anesthesia shall have arterial blood pressure and heart rate determined and evaluated at least every five minutes.*

3. Every patient receiving general anesthesia shall have, in addition to the above, circulatory function continually evaluated by at least one of the following: palpatation of a pulse, auscultation of heart sounds, monitoring of a tracing of intra-arterial pressure, ultrasound peripheral pulse monitoring, or pulse plethysmography or oximetry.

Body Temperature Objective. To aid in the maintenance of appropriate body temperature during all anesthetics.

Methods. There shall be readily available a means to continuously measure the patient's temperature. When changes in body temperature are intended, anticipated or suspected, the temperature shall be measured.

APPENDIX E

▮ PATIENT OUTCOMES: STANDARDS OF PERIOPERATIVE CARE*

Standard I
The patient demonstrates knowledge of the physiological and psychological responses to surgical intervention.

Standard II
The patient is free from infection.

Standard III
The patient's skin integrity is maintained.

Standard IV
The patient is free from injury related to positioning, extraneous objects, or chemical, physical, and electrical hazards.

Standard V
The patient's fluid and electrolyte balance is maintained.

Standard VI
The patient participated in the rehabilitation process.

*Adapted with permission from AORN Standards and Recommended Practices, 1995, pp. 125–126. Copyright © AORN, Inc. 2170 Parker Road, Suite 300, Denver CO, 80231.

APPENDIX F

■ AORN POSITION STATEMENT ON PERIOPERATIVE NURSING PRACTICE IN AMBULATORY SURGERY

A combination of legislative trends, changes in technology, a more knowledgeable society, and greater professional sophistication has created a climate for change in health care in which the focus is moving from "the highest quality care at any price" toward "the best care at the lowest price." Ambulatory surgery, as an established component of surgical patient care, is one outcome of these changes. As AORN assumes a leadership role in the care of all surgical patients, dynamic, creative, proactive strategies are essential. Perioperative nursing must be practiced in all surgical settings.

Perioperative nursing, of a distinctive nature, is practiced in ambulatory surgery settings. Because of a wellness orientation, teaching, self-care, and responsibility and inclusion of family and support people are emphasized. Our belief is that professional nursing competencies are essential during all three phases of the ambulatory surgery patient's experience. Because of the compressed nursing time frame, technical proficiencies, assessment, judgement, and organizational skills must be highly refined and sophisticated. Ambulatory surgery nurses must also be flexible, accepting of change, and willing to become functional in all patient care areas. Mechanisms to achieve desired patient outcomes may be different from those in the inpatient setting but are equally important. The ambulatory surgery setting serves as a model for perioperative nursing practice and as an ideal clinical laboratory for visualizing the total nursing process in a few hours.

We recognize that today's patient population expects to participate in their own care and that their rights must be respected regardless of practice settings. We believe that ambulatory surgery patients, as well as all surgical patients, should expect to receive:

1. cost-effective, convenient, efficient care,
2. care consistent with accepted standards of practice, recognizing the patients' rights to be active participants in their plans of care, and
3. succinct perioperative education involving. family and significant others.

From Standards and Recommended Practices. *Denver: AORN, 1995: 23. Reprinted with permission.*

APPENDIX G

■ POSITION STATEMENT ON THE ROLE OF THE RN IN THE MANAGEMENT OF ANALGESIA BY CATHETER TECHNIQUES*

Placement of a catheter or infusion device, administration of the test-dose or initial dose of medication to determine correct catheter or infusion device placement, and establishment of analgesic dosage parameters by written order for patients who need acute or chronic pain relief or for the woman during labor should only be done by licensed professionals who are educated in the specialty of anesthesia and physicians in other specialties who have been granted clinical privileges by the institution.

Management and Monitoring

A registered nurse may manage the care of patients with catheters or devices for analgesia to alleviate acute post-surgical pain, pathological pain, or chronic pain, including reinjection of medication following establishment of appropriate therapeutic range or adjustment of drug infusion rate in compliance with the anesthesia provider's or physician's patient-specific written orders.

For the woman in labor who is receiving epidural analgesia, a qualified anesthesia provider must be immediately available as defined in institutional policy. The RN may monitor the mother and fetus, replace empty infusion syringes or bags with new pre-prepared solutions, stop the infusion, initiate emergency therapeutic measures under protocol if complications arise, and remove the catheter. For the woman in labor, only those RNs with advanced education in obstetric analgesia may administer subsequent bolus doses or adjust the drug infusion rates in compliance with the anesthesia provider's or physician's patient-specific written orders.

It is within the scope of practice of the RN to manage the care of patients receiving analgesia by catheter as defined above only when the following criteria are met.

1. Management and monitoring of analgesia by catheter techniques, including reinjection and/or alteration of infusion rate by non-anesthetist RNs, is allowed by state laws and institutional policy, procedure, and protocol.
2. The qualified anesthesia provider placing the catheter or infusion device or the attending physician selects and orders the drugs, doses and concentrations of opioids, local anesthetics, steroids, alpha-agonists, or other documented safe medications or combinations thereof.
3. Guidelines for patient monitoring and drug administration and protocols for deal-

*Adapted with permission from AORN J. 1992;55:209–210.

ing with potential complications or emergency situations are available and have been developed in conjunction with the anesthesia or physician provider.

4. The RN providing care for patients receiving catheter or infusion-device analgesia for acute or chronic pain relief or for the woman during labor is able to:

- Demonstrate the acquired knowledge of anatomy, physiology, pharmacology, and complications related to the analgesia technique and medication.
- Assess the patient's total care needs during analgesia.
- Utilize monitoring modalities, interpret physiological responses, and initiate nursing interventions to insure optimal patient care.
- Anticipate and recognize potential complications of the analgesia in relationship to the type of catheter/infusion device and medication being utilized.
- Recognize emergency situations and institute nursing interventions in compliance with the anesthesia provider's or attending physician's guidelines and orders.
- Demonstrate the cognitive and psychomotor skills necessary for use of the analgesic catheter or mechanical infusion devices.
- Demonstrate knowledge and skills required for catheter removal.
- Demonstrate knowledge of the legal ramifications of managing and monitoring analgesia by catheter techniques, including the RN's responsibility and liability in the event of any untoward reaction or life-threatening complication.

5. An educational/competency validation mechanism is developed, and the institution documents the successful demonstration of knowledge, skills, and abilities related to the management of the care of persons receiving analgesia by catheters or pain control infusion devices for all nurses who will be providing such care. Evaluation and documentation of competence occurs on a periodic basis.

Removal of Catheter

When educational criteria are met and institutional policy allows, the RN may remove the catheter that has been used for analgesia upon receipt of a specific order from a qualified anesthesia or physician provider.

Developed July 25, 1991 by:
American Association of Critical-Care Nurses (AACN)
American Association of Nurse Anesthetists (AANA)
American College of Nurse Midwives (ACNM)
American Nurses Association (ANA)
AORN
Association of Pediatric Oncology Nurses (APON)
American Society of Post Anesthesia Nurses (ASPAN)
American Society of Pain Management Nurses (ASPMN)
Emergency Nurses Association (ENA)
Intravenous Nurses Society, Inc (INS)
The Organization for Obstetric, Gynecologic and Neonatal Nurses (NAACOG)
National Association of Orthopaedic Nurses (NAON)
Nursing Pain Association (NPA)
Oncology Nursing Society (ONS)

APPENDIX H

■ COMPETENCY STATEMENTS IN PERIOPERATIVE NURSING*

Competency Statements	Measurable Criteria	Examples
Assessment		
1. Competency to assess the physiological health status of the patient	1. Verifies operative procedure	1.1 Consent form 1.2 Patient's statement 1.3 Surgeon's verification
	2. Notes condition of skin	2.1 Rashes 2.2 Bruises 2.3 Lesions 2.4 Previous incisions 2.5 Turgor
	3. Determines mobility of body parts	3.1 Patient's statement 3.2 Range of motion
	4. Reports deviation of diagnostic studies	4.1 Laboratory values 4.2 Radiology imaging 4.3 Other diagnostic imaging
	5. Checks vital signs	5.1 Blood pressure 5.2 Temperature 5.3 Pulse 5.4 Respiration
	6. Notes abnormalities, injuries, and previous surgery	6.1 Loss of extremity or body part 6.2 Congenital anomalies
	7. Identifies presence of internal and external prostheses/implants	7.1 Pacemakers 7.2 Harrington rods 7.3 Joint prostheses 7.4 Lens implant
	8. Notes sensory impairments	8.1 Hearing deficit 8.2 Visual deficit 8.3 Tactile deficit 8.4 Speech deficit

(Continued)

*Adapted with permission from AORN Standards and Recommended Practices, 1995, pp. 76–84. Copyright © AORN, Inc. 2170 Parker Road, Suite 300, Denver CO, 80231.

COMPETENCY STATEMENTS IN PERIOPERATIVE NURSING

Competency Statements	Measurable Criteria	Examples
	9. Assesses cardiovascular status	9.1 Pulse alteration 9.2 Arrhythmias 9.3 Edema 9.4 Electrocardiogram 9.5 Hemodynamics parameters
	10. Assesses respiratory status	10.1 Skin color 10.2 Breath sounds 10.3 Oxygen saturation 10.4 Arterial blood gases
	11. Assesses renal status	11.1 Intake and output 11.2 Urinalysis 11.3 Renal function studies
	12. Notes nutritional status	12.1 Nothing by mouth 12.2 Weight 12.3 Skin tugor
	13. Verifies allergies	13.1 Medication 13.2 Food 13.3 Chemical
	14. Screens for substance abuse	14.1 Skin changes 14.2 Patient's statement
	15. Communicates physiological data relevant to planning patient's discharge	15.1 Patient/family Services 15.2 Home health service 15.3 Community service
	16. Communicates/documents physical health status	16.1 Verbal reports 16.2 Patient record
II. Competency to assess the psychosocial health status of the patient/family	1. Elicits perception of surgery	1.1 Patient's statement 1.2 Behavioral responses
	2. Elicits expectation of care	2.1 Perceived outcomes
	3. Determines coping mechanisms	3.1 Patient's statement 3.2 Acceptance/denial
	4. Determines knowledge level	4.1 Well-informed 4.2 Lack of relevant information
	5. Determines ability to understand	5.1 Language barrier 5.2 Level of comprehension
	6. Identifies philosophical and religious beliefs	6.1 Blood transfusions 6.2 Sacrament of the sick 6.3 Symbols 6.4 Disposition of limbs
	7. Identifies cultural practices	7.1 Family member in constant attendance 7.2 Cultural/ethnic requirements
	8. Communicates psychosocial data relevant to planning	8.1 Support group 8.2 Counseling service 8.3 Social service

COMPETENCY STATEMENTS IN PERIOPERATIVE NURSING

Competency Statements	Measurable Criteria	Examples
	9. Communicates/documents psychosocial status	9.1 Verbal reports 9.2 Patient records
III. Competency to formulate nursing diagnosis based on health status data	1. Interprets assessment data	1.1 Selects pertinent data 1.2 Sets priorties for data
	2. Identifies patient problem/nursing diagnosis pertinent to surgical procedure	2.1 Actual patient problems 2.2 Potential patient problems
	3. Supports nursing diagnosis with current scientific knowledge	3.1 Theoretical base 3.2 Rationale for diagnosis
	4. Communicates/documents nursing diagnosis to health care team	4.1 Verbal reports 4.2 Written records
Planning		
IV. Competency to establish patient goals based on nursing diagnosis	1. Develops outcome statements	1.1 Patient is free from infection 72 hours postoperatively 1.2 Maintenance of skin integrity
	2. Develops goals that are congruent with present and potential physical capabilities and behavioral patterns	2.1 Realistic 2.2 Attainable 2.3 Measurable
	3. Develops criteria for measurement of goals	3.1 Signs and symptoms 3.2 Laboratory data
	4. Sets priorities for goals based on needs	4.1 Mutually set 4.2 Maslow's hierarchy of needs
	5. Communicates/documents goals to appropriate persons	5.1 Verbal reports 5.2 Patient record
V. Competency to develop a plan of care that prescribes nursing actions to achieve patient goals	1. Identifies nursing activities necessary for expected outcomes	1.1 Positioning 1.2 Patient teaching
	2. Establishes priorities for nursing actions	2.1 Immediate 2.2 Long term
	3. Organizes nursing activities in logical sequence	3.1 Dispersive pad placement before draping 3.2 Functional suction before induction
	4. Coordinates use of supplies and equipment for intraoperative care	4.1 Instrument availability 4.2 Scheduling conflicts
	5. Coordinates patient care needs with team members and other appropriate departments	5.1 Patient transfer 5.2 Equipment needs
	6. Controls environment	6.1 Temperature/humidity 6.2 Sensory stimuli 6.3 Traffic 6.4 Clean, safe environment

(Continued)

COMPETENCY STATEMENTS IN PERIOPERATIVE NURSING

Competency Statements	Measurable Criteria	Examples
	7. Assigns activities to personnel based on their qualifications and patient needs	7.1 Categories of personnel 7.2 Demonstrated competencies 7.3 Acuity
	8. Prepares for potential emergencies	8.1 Crash cart available 8.2 Tracheostomy tray available
	9. Participates in planning for discharge	9.1 Patient/family education 9.2 Referral services
	10. Communicates/documents patient's plan of care	10.1 Verbal reports 10.2 Patient record
Implementation		
VI. Competency to implement nursing actions in transferring the patient according to the prescribed plan	1. Confirms identity	1.1 Patent's statement 1.2 Identification bracelet
	2. Selects personnel for transportation as determined by need	2.1 Sufficient number 2.2 Patient acuity
	3. Determines appropriate and safe method according to need	3.1 Stretcher/bed 3.2 Support measures 3.3 Monitoring devices
	4. Provides for the emotional needs during transfer	4.1 Comfort measures 4.2 Touch 4.3 Verbal communication
	5. Communicates/documents transfer	5.1 Verbal reports 5.2 Patient record
VII. Competency to participate in patient/family teaching	1. Identifies teaching needs	1.1 Surgical routines 1.2 Coughing/deep breathing techniques 1.3 Discharge instructions
	2. Assesses readiness to learn	2.1 Attention span 2.2 Anxiety level
	3. Provides instruction based on identified needs	3.1 Postanesthesia recovery routine 3.2 "Splinting" techniques 3.3 Coughing and deep breathing 3.4 Postoperative pain management instructions
	4. Determines teaching effectiveness	4.1 Return demonstration 4.2 Patient verbalization
	5. Communicates/documents patient/family teaching	5.1 Verbal reports 5.2 Patient record
VIII. Competency to create and maintain a sterile field	1. Uses principles of aseptic practice in varying situations	1.1 Skin scrub for colostomy 1.2 Clean vs. sterile field
	2. Initiates corrective action when breaks in technique occur	2.1 Changing gown and gloves 2.2 Surgical conscience

COMPETENCY STATEMENTS IN PERIOPERATIVE NURSING

Competency Statements	Measurable Criteria	Examples
	3. Inspects sterile items for contamination before opening	3.1 Intact package 3.2 Sterile indicator
	4. Maintains sterility while opening sterile items for procedure	4.1 Delivery to field 4.2 Pouring solutions
	5. Functions within designated dress code	5.1 Hair covered 5.2 Scrub attire
	6. Communicates/documents maintenance of sterile field	6.1 Verbal reports 6.2 Patient record
IX. Competency to provide equipment and supplies based on patient needs	1. Anticipates the need for equipment and supplies	1.1 Electrosurgical equipment 1.2 Prosthetic devices 1.3 Positioning devices
	2. Selects equipment and supplies in an organized and timely manner	2.1 Preoperative 2.2 Intraoperative
	3. Assures all equipment is functioning before use	3.1 Mechanical equipment checked 3.2 Pressure-powered equipment checked 3.3 Implants
	4. Operates mechanical, electrical, and air-powered equipment according to manufacturer's instructions	4.1 Tourniquet 4.2 Electrosurgical unit 4.3 Video equipment
	5. Removes malfunctioning equipment from OR	5.1 Light sources 5.2 OR bed 5.3 Electrosurgical unit
	6. Assures emergency equipment and supplies are available at all times	6.1 Defibrillator/monitor 6.2 Emergency drug and supply cart
	7. Uses supplies judiciously and in a cost-effective manner	7.1 Lost charge 7.2 Excess suture use
	8. Communicates/documents provision of equipment and supplies	8.1 Verbal reports 8.2 Patient record
X. Competency to perform sponge, sharps, and instrument counts	1. Follows established policies and procedures for counts	1.1 Sponges/sharps/instruments 1.2 Hospital's policies and procedures
	2. Initiates corrective actions when counts are incorrect	2.1 Surgeon notification 2.2 Risk management
	3. Communicates/documents results of counts according to facility policy	3.1 Verbal reports 3.2 Patient record
XI. Competency to administer drugs and solutions as prescribed	1. Administers medication according to hospital policy	1.1 Patient identification 1.2 Drug reaction 1.3 Dosage 1.4 Administration route 1.5 Complications/contraindications
	2. Communicates/documents administration of drugs and solutions	2.1 Verbal reports 2.2 Patient record

(Continued)

COMPETENCY STATEMENTS IN PERIOPERATIVE NURSING

Competency Statements	Measurable Criteria	Examples
XII. Competency to physiologically monitor the patient during surgery	1. Assists/monitors physical symptoms	1.1 Skin color 1.2 Electrocardiogram 1.3 Oxygen saturation
	2. Assists/monitors behavioral changes	2.1 Restlessness 2.2 Level of consciousness
	3. Calculates intake and output	3.1 Fluid intake 3.2 Blood loss
	4. Operates monitor equipment according to manufacturer's instruction	4.1 Automatic blood pressure monitor 4.2 Temperature probe 4.3 Pulse oximeter
	5. Initiates nursing actions based on interpretation of physiological changes	5.1 Surgeon notification 5.2 Crash cart
	6. Communicates/documents physiological responses	6.1 Verbal reports 6.2 Patient record
XIII. Competency to monitor and control the environment	1. Regulates temperature and humidity as indicated	1.1 Patient need 1.2 Staff need
	2. Adheres to electrical safety policies and procedures	2.1 Hazard identification 2.2 Line isolation monitor
	3. Monitors sensory environment	3.1 Noise levels 3.2 Noxious odors
	4. Maintains traffic patterns	4.1 Hospital's policies and procedures 4.2 Unobstructed corridors
	5. Adheres to sanitation policies and procedures	5.1 "Confine and contain" 5.2 Waste disposal 5.3 Universal precautions
	6. Communicates/documents environmental controls	6.1 Verbal reports 6.2 Patient record
XIV. Competency to respect patient's rights	1. Demonstrates awareness of the individual rights of the patient	1.1 American Hospital Bill of Rights 1.2 American Nurses' Association Code for Nurses 1.3 Patient Self-determination Act
	2. Provides for privacy through maintaining confidentiality	2.1 Communication 2.2 Documentation
	3. Provides for privacy through physical protection	3.1 Examination 3.2 Positioning
	4. Identifies ethnic and spiritual beliefs	4.1 Pastoral counseling 4.2 Communion
	5. Communicates/documents provisions for patient's rights	5.1 Verbal reports 5.2 Written records

Evaluation

XV. Competency to perform nursing actions that demonstrate accountability	1. Exercises safe judgment in decision making	1.1 Thorough assessments 1.2 Past experience

COMPETENCY STATEMENTS IN PERIOPERATIVE NURSING

Competency Statements	Measurable Criteria	Examples
	2. Demonstrates flexibility and adaptability to changes in nursing practice	2.1 Change agent 2.2 Professional associations
	3. Responds in a positive manner to constructive criticism	3.1 Self-evaluation 3.2 Peer review
	4. Demonstrates tact and understanding when dealing with patients, team members, members of other disciplines, and the public	4.1 Team negotiation 4.2 Family interaction 4.3 Consumer awareness
	5. Practices within ethical and legal guidelines	5.1 Nurse Practice Act 5.2 Legal statutes 5.3 American Nurses' Association Code for Nurses
	6. Seeks opportuinty for continued learning	6.1 Continuing education 6.2 Inservice education
	7. Communicates/documents nursing actions	7.1 Verbal reports 7.2 Patient record
XVI. Competency to evaluate patient outcomes	1. Develops outcome criteria for goal measurement	1.1 Signs and symptoms 1.2 Laboratory data
	2. Measures degree of goal achievement	2.1 Nurse's observation 2.2 Patient's responses
	3. Communicates/documents degree of goal achievement	3.1 Verbal reports 3.2 Patient record
XVII. Competency to measure effectiveness of nursing care	1. Establishes criteria to measure quality of nursing care	1.1 Quality improvement 1.2 Peer review
	2. Assesses the patient postoperatively	2.1 Patient interview 2.2 Questionnaire 2.3 Physical examination
	3. Compares results of nursing actions to desired patient goals	3.1 Appropriateness of nursing actions 3.2 Realistic goals
	4. Communicates/documents results of nursing care	4.1 Verbal reports 4.2 Patient record
XVIII. Competency to continuously reassess all components of patient care based on new data	1. Reassess health status	1.1 Physiological 1.2 Psychological
	2. Refines nursing diagnosis	2.1 Changes in health status
	3. Reestablishes goals	3.1 Changes in signs and symptoms 3.2 Changes in laboratory data
	4. Revises plan of care	4.1 Revised priorities
	5. Implements revised plan of care	5.1 Revise nursing actions
	6. Reevaluates outcomes	6.1 Patient responses 6.2 Outcome criteria
	7. Communicates/documents reassessment process	7.1 Verbal reports 7.2 Patient record

APPENDIX I

■ ADVANCED PRACTICE COMPETENCIES*

Competency Statements	Measurable Criteria	Examples
1. The perioperative advanced practice nurse (APN) is competent to manage client health/illness status.	1.1 Manages comprehensive and individualized care through the perioperative continuum using in-depth knowledge from the natural and behavioral sciences with clinical experience as the foundation for perioperative care.	1.1.1 Assesses, diagnoses, monitors, coordinates, and manages complex care of perioperative clients.*
		1.1.2 Uses advanced analytical skills to assess data, symptomatology, and other measures as related to pathophysiologic processes to formulate diagnostic hypotheses.
		1.1.3 Incorporates strategies of risk analysis and reduction, lifestyle change, screening, and disease prevention and detection into all aspects of perioperative care.
		1.1.4 Collaborates with nursing and other disciplines in planning, implementing, and evaluating client care.
		1.1.5 Selects, recommends, coordinates, and/or orders diagnostic, therapeutic, and pharmacologic interventions to meet multiple client needs.
		1.1.6 Performs and interprets selected therapeutic and diagnostic procedures and tests that may include physical examination, laboratory tests, electrocardiograms, and radiological tests.
		1.1.7 Evaluates the appropriateness of intervention strategies and articulates factors to be considered in alternative decisions.
		(Continued)

*Adapted with permission from AORN Standards and Recommended Practices, 1995, pp. 87–92. Copyright © AORN, Inc. 2170 Parker Road, Suite 300, Denver CO, 80231.

ADVANCED PRACTICE COMPETENCIES

Competency Statements	Measurable Criteria	Examples
		1.1.8 Executes the principles of surgery during the perioperative continuum as permitted by statute and/or licensure. Surgical principles may include those related to tissue handling, wound healing, hemostasis, surgical asepsis, and surgical instrumentation as determined by curricular content.
		1.1.9 Selects and initiates referrals for clients' needs.
		1.1.10 Evaluates postoperative outcomes and plans for continuing recovery and rehabilitation (e.g., schedules postoperative evaluations, arranges for discharge needs, identifies and contacts community resources).
		1.1.11 Manages rapidly changing and complex client situations.
2. The perioperative APN is competent in the helping/healing role.	2.1 Uses selected interpersonal theories and strategies to promote positive client interactions and outcomes by establishing a healing environment.	2.1.1 Identifies contributions of self in creating and maintaining positive client interactions while respecting clients' social/cultural values in therapeutic relationships.
		2.1.2. Creates relationships that acknowledge and support clients' rights to self-determination.
		2.1.3 Applies the principles of counseling, therapeutic communication, group process, and teaching/ learning in client interactions.
		2.1.4 Creates a climate for and establishes a commitment to healing.
	2.2 Operationalizes the concepts of caring, support, advocacy, and ethics in interpersonal transactions.	2.2.1 Demonstrates caring behaviors by recognizing and attending to clients' expressed and unexpressed concerns.
		2.2.2 Respects cultural and psychosocial value systems while considering clients' developmental stages.
		2.2.3 Protects and enhances human dignity and clients' rights.
		2.2.4 Provides culturally and spiritually sensitive care.

ADVANCED PRACTICE COMPETENCIES

Competency Statements	Measurable Criteria	Examples
3. The perioperative APN is competent to teach and/or coach disease prevention and health promotion.	3.1 Demonstrates knowledge of learning theories, human behavior, change theory, stress and coping mechanisms, crisis management, human family development and interactions, and health issues.	3.1.1 Elicits an understanding of clients' interpretations of health and illness. 3.1.2 Provides anticipatory guidance for expected and potential situational changes. 3.1.3 Provides an interpretation of conditions and gives rationale for procedures to clients. 3.1.4 Assists in developing, coordinating, and implementing educational programs for clients and families. 3.1.5 Organizes and participates in interdisciplinary educational programs for health care professionals and the community.
	3.2 Evaluates the effectiveness of education/counseling interventions.	3.2.1 Assesses outcome data to determine effectiveness of education/counseling. 3.2.2 Minimizes barriers to client education and/or health behavior changes by modifying teaching methodologies based on evaluation results. 3.2.3 Solicits formal and informal evaluation from peers and clients to modify educational program content and delivery.
	3.3 Provides staff education in area of expertise.	3.3.1 Acts as a resource person in relationship to area of clinical expertise. 3.3.2 Provides educational programs to professional and paraprofessional personnel in area of expertise. 3.3.3 Mentors nursing personnel in all levels of clinical practice.
4. The perioperative APN is competent in the organizational and work role.	4.1 Collaborates with other disciplines to facilitate the delivery of client care.	4.1.1 Functions in a variety of role dimensions: provider, educator, consultant, researcher, and manager. 4.1.2 Serves as a nursing expert and colleague member of the multidisciplinary team planning care for perioperative clients. 4.1.3 Encourages creativity in the development of innovative health care delivery systems. 4.1.4 Minimizes role conflict and territoriality.

(Continued)

ADVANCED PRACTICE COMPETENCIES

Competency Statements	Measurable Criteria	Examples
	4.2 Contributes to the advancement of nursing practice, particularly as it pertains to the perioperative role.	4.2.1 Interprets and markets the APN role to the public and other health care professions. 4.2.2 Publishes scholarly works. 4.2.3 Serves as a role model, preceptor, or mentor to perioperative practitioners. 4.2.4 Participates in scientific inquiry, including theory building and nursing research.
	4.3 Provides leadership in professional activities.	4.3.1 Participates in professional activities at local, state, and/or national levels. 4.3.2 Evaluates implications of contemporary health policy on health care providers and clients. 4.3.3 Participates in legislative and policy-making activities that influence health services/practices. 4.3.4 Attends professional educational activities.
5. The perioperative APN is competent to monitor and promote the quality of perioperative practice.	5.1 Evaluates quality of practice in relation to established professional and legal standards.	5.1.1 Uses knowledge of therapeutic regimens and client reponses for evaluation of care. 5.1.2 Participates in peer and colleague review. 5.1.3 Confronts incompetent care practices.
	5.2 Analyzes appropriateness of research to perioperative practice.	5.2.1 Participates in the use, dissemination, and/or generation of research. 5.2.2 Applies research findings pertinent to client care management. 5.2.3 Interprets research findings and makes recommendations to clients. 5.2.4 Guides colleagues in understanding research findings.
	5.3 Analyzes ethical dilemmas in perioperative care.	5.3.1 Articulates both sides of ethical dilemmas. 5.3.2 Requests consultation from expert resources for selected situations. 5.3.3 Participates in resolution of ethical dilemmas.

*The term client is used throughout these guidelines to denote an individual and his or her family or significant others.

APPENDIX J-1

■ MODEL OF PATIENT CARE: LITHOTOMY POSITION

Nursing Diagnosis	Patient Outcome	Nursing Actions	Schedule for Evaluation
1. Risk of contamination of surgical site related to shedding of epidermis from feet	1a. Shedding of epidermis contained b. No symptoms of wound	1. Place cotton or flannel boots over paitent's feet	24–48 hours postoperatively
2. Risk of peripheral vascular compromise related to improper positioning of legs	2. No symptoms of peripheral vascular compromise	2a. Apply antiembolectomy stockings as needed b. Position stirrups to prevent excessive pressure on popliteal space	24–48 hours postoperatively
3. Risk of musculoskeletal discomfort and/or hip dislocation related to improper position of legs	3a. No musculoskeletal discomfort b. No dislocation of hips	3a. Use two people when positioning legs in stirrups to facilitate simultaneous placement b. Check sacrum and pad with foam if appropriate c. Use two people to remove legs from stirrups	24–48 hours postoperatively
4. Risk of nerve damage related to improper positioning of legs or pressure of instruments	4. No nerve damage	4a. Check pressure areas and pad if appropriate b. Position stirrups properly c. Position footboard at right angle to OR table to serve as work surface for surgeon as needed d. Remind surgeon that instruments should not be placed on the patient	24–48 hours postoperatively

(Continued)

MODEL OF PATIENT CARE: LITHOTOMY POSITION

Nursing Diagnosis	Patient Outcome	Nursing Actions	Schedule for Evaluation
5. Risk of damage to digits when lowering foot of OR table	5. Digits intact	5a. Place arms or armboards positioned parallel to the table when allowed by surgical procedure b. Before lowering end of table check location of digits	Recovery room
6. Risk of loss of dignity related to excessive exposure	6. Dignity maintained	6a. Pull shades on doors	Intraoperatively
7. Risk of damage to skin related to pooling of antiseptic solution under the patient	7. No skin damage	7a. Place "prep" pad under buttocks prior to prepping b. Remove "prep" pad when prep is complete and check for wet linen	Intraoperatively 24–48 hours postoperatively
8. Risk of circulatory compromise related to pooling of blood in lumbar region	8. Signs and symptoms of circulatory compromise prevented or controlled	8a. Raise and lower legs slowly with anesthesiologist's knowledge	Intraoperatively

APPENDIX J-2

▌ MODEL OF PATIENT CARE: 2- TO 3-YEAR-OLDS

Nursing Diagnosis	Patient Outcome	Nursing Actions	Schedule for Evaluation
1. Risk of anxiety related to fear of separation	1. Minimal anxiety	1a. Request that parents accompany child to the OR b. Encourage child to bring familiar object to the OR (i.e., toy, blanket) c. Communicate level of anxiety to recovery room	Preoperatively
2. Risk of fear of being transported in crib	2. Transported to operating room without fear	2a. Allow parents to carry patient b. Instruct hospital assistant to use wagon to transport child	Immediately preoperative
3. Inability to express fears	3. Express fears	3a. Allow child to express feelings (i.e., crying, anger) b. Use terminology and examples child can understand c. Organize activities to be able to stay with patient prior to induction d. Request additional circulator if needed	Preoperatively Postoperatively 24 hours
4. Risk of fear of being immobilized related to restraints being applied	4. No feelings of immobility	4a. Hold or touch patient b. Speak softly c. Apply restraints after patient is anesthetized	Intraoperatively
5. Risk of loss of dignity related to clothes being removed	5. Preserve dignity	5a. Remove clothes after patient is anesthetized b. Reapply clothes prior to patient going to recovery room	Intraoperatively

(Continued)

MODEL OF PATIENT CARE: 2- TO 3-YEAR-OLDS

Nursing Diagnosis	Patient Outcome	Nursing Actions	Schedule for Evaluation
6. Risk of alteration in body temperature	6. Body temperature maintained within normal limits	6a. Turn temperature of room up to 70° 30 minutes prior to bringing patient into room	Preoperatively
		b. Instruct hospital assistant to place K-Pad on OR bed	
		c. Insert temperature probe and connect to monitor	Intraoperatively
		d. Warm soutions for prepping	
		e. Place warm blankets on child	Postoperatively
		f. Know procedure for malignant hyperpyrexia	Intraoperatively
7. Risk of skin burn related to use of electrosurgical unit	7. Integrity of skin maintained: No burns No blisters No redness	7a. Use proper size ground plate	Intraoperatively
		b. Cover plate evenly with conductive substance	
		c. Place plate as close as possible to incision site	
		d. Check connections of inactive cord to plate and electrosurgical unit	
		e. Set controls on appropriate setting	
8. Patient size	8. No delay in surgical procedure	8a. Instruct hospital assistant on appropriate selection of instruments consistent with size of child	Preoperatively
		b. Select supplies consistent with size of child	
9. Risk of impaired circulation related to use of restrains	9. Circulation monitored	9a. Wrap arms and legs with Webril prior to applying restraints	Intraoperatively
		b. Check circulation in extremities every 30 minutes during procedure	
10. Risk of imbalance of fluid volume related to n.p.o. and loss of body fluids	10. Body fluids maintained within normal limits	10a. Instruct hospital assistant to obtain sponge scale when setting up OR	Preoperatively
		b. Weigh sponges for blood loss; communicate to anesthetist as they are handed off the field	Intraoperatively
		c. Use pediatric suction container	
		d. Monitor amount of irrigating solution used	

MODEL OF PATIENT CARE: 2- TO 3-YEAR-OLDS

Nursing Diagnosis	Patient Outcome	Nursing Actions	Schedule for Evaluation
		e. Provide 1000-cc bag with Buretrol and minidrip administration set	
11. Risk of musculoskeletal discomfort, nerve damage, or circulatory and respiratory compromise related to improper positioning	11a. No musculoskeletal discomfort b. No nerve damage c. No compromise in circulation or respirations d. Skin integrity maintained	11a. Place safety strap above knees b. Pad all boney prominences c. Align extremities anatomically and support if necessary d. Provide anesthesia with free access to airway and IV lines	24–48 hours postoperatively
12. Anxiety of parents related to separation from the child, unknown diagnosis, or surgical treatment	12a. Ability to verbalize feelings of depression, helplessness, fear, anger b. Ability to verbalize realistic understanding of proposed surgery and activities of day of surgery c. Ability to cope with anxiety	12a. Encourage parents to verbalize concerns and to ask questions b. Assess level of knowledge regarding surgical procedure c. Give clear, succinct information appropriate to the parent's level of education d. Reinforce surgeon's explanation of surgical procedure e. Explain sequence of events on day of surgery (i.e., n.p.o., transportation to OR, recovery room location and length of stay, anticipated catheters, tubes, drains, casts, or dressings) f. Inform parents of waiting area	Preoperatively
		g. Communicate with parents at time of incision and on completion of surgical intervention	Intraoperatively
		h. Explain child's reaction to impending surgical intervention	Preoperatively
		i. Communicate to surgeon any unresolved concerns or questions parents may have	Preoperatively Postoperatively

APPENDIX J-3

■ MODEL OF PATIENT CARE: LOCAL INFILTRATION

Nursing Diagnosis	Patient Outcome	Nursing Actions	Schedule for Evaluation
1. Risk of anxiety related to unfamiliar environment and/or impending surgery	1. Ability to cope with anxiety	1a. Explain preoperative and intraoperative activities b. Encourage patient to verbalize questions and concerns c. Stay with patient and provide support d. Provide nonverbal support by touching patient	Preoperatively Intraoperatively 12–24 hours postoperatively
2. Risk of fear of pain	2. Pain controlled	2a. Encourage patient to verbalize discomfort b. Discuss with patient availability of pain medication	Intraoperatively
3. Risk of altered sensory perceptions related to preoperative medication	3. Able to respond appropriately and to follow directions	3a. Maintain quiet atmosphere b. Post sign on door "Patient Awake" c. Turn off auditory intercom	Intraoperatively 12–24 hours Postoperatively
4. Risk of loss of dignity related to excessive exposure and lack of personal care	4. Dignity maintained	4a. Limit exposure of patient only to area required for surgical procedure b. Call patient by name c. Only pertinent team members permitted in room	Intraoperatively 12–24 hours Postoperatively
5. Possible discomfort related to position	5. Comfortable position	5a. Position patient anatomically b. Flex table slightly at knees to reduce strain on back muscles c. Place pillow under knees d. Pad all bony prominences	Intraoperatively 12–24 hours postoperatively

(Continued)

495

MODEL OF PATIENT CARE: LOCAL INFILTRATION

Nursing Diagnosis	Patient Outcome	Nursing Actions	Schedule for Evaluation
		e. Pad wrists with Webril prior to restraints being applied f. Ask patient about position	
6. Risk of contamination of wound related to patient inadvertently touching wound	6. No wound contamination	6. Apply padded clover leaf hitch arm restraints	Intraoperatively
7. Risk of alteration in body temperature related to temperature of operating room	7. Body temperature maintained within normal limits	7a. Apply warm blankets b. Use warm solutions c. Limit skin exposure to area required for surgical procedure d. Ask patient about body temperature	Intraoperatively
8. Possible adverse reaction to local anesthetic agent	8. Avoid or minimize cardiovascular and respiratory compromise	8a. Two nurses assigned to circulate b. Check chart for allergies c. Obtain baseline vital signs before surgery d. Use electrocardiograph to monitor patient for cardiac arrhythmias e. Monitor and record vital signs as indicated or at least every 15 minutes before and after medication f. Communicate changes to surgeon	Intraoperatively
9. Risk of lack in continuity of care related to patient returning to primary care nurse/inpatient unit	9. Continuity of care maintained	9a. Inform primary care nurse what procedure was performed b. Vital signs c. All medications administered d. Amount of intravenous fluids infused e. Estimated blood loss f. Location of any drains or packs g. Type of dressing h. How the patient tolerated the procedure	Immediately postoperative and 12–24 hours postoperative
Ambulatory Patients Only			
10. Risk of latent adverse reaction or side effects to local anesthesia or surgical procedure	10. Adverse reaction or side effects treated appropriately	10a. Observe patient for minimum of 30 minutes postoperatively prior to discharge	Immediately postoperative

MODEL OF PATIENT CARE: LOCAL INFILTRATION

Nursing Diagnosis	Patient Outcome	Nursing Actions	Schedule for Evaluation
		b. Alert patient and significant others to signs and symptoms of adverse reaction and how to respond appropriately	
		c. Validate postoperative instructions by requesting verbal feedback	
		d. Give patient and significant others telephone number of operating room surgeon and emergency room. Instruct patient to call regarding any questions or concerns	
		e. Obtain telephone number where patient can be reached for postoperative phone call in 24 hours	24 hours postoperatively

Index

Obese patients
  anesthesia management in, 346
  nursing implications for, 346–347
  postoperative concerns for, 347
  surgical techniques for, 346
  and wound healing, 410–411
Objectives, 444
Occupational Safety and Health
    Administration, 71
  and rule on bloodborne pathogen exposure,
    138
  guidelines for TB, 126
  regulations for ETO exposure, 180, 181,
    181t
  regulations for ozone sterilization, 185
  standards on clothing, 140–141
Ochsner clamp, 279
Open gloving technique, 216f, 217
Operating room
  hazards in, 36–37
  sales representatives in, 74
  tables. *See Operating room tables*
  television cameras in, 29
  ventilation in, 25–26
  See also Surgical suite
Operating room supervisor, 42
Operating room tables, 3f, 30–31, 32f,
    256–257
  accessories for, 256–257
Operating room technicians, 9, 54
Opioid analgesics, 392, 393t, 394
Orderly, 55
Orders, verbal, 73–74
Organizational performance. *See* Performance
Orientation programs, 437–438
OSHA. *See* Occupational Safety and Health
    Administration
Osler, Sir William, 3
Outcome criteria, for gynecologic surgery,
    439t
Outcomes
  formulation in preoperative phase, 104–
    105
  measurement of, 426–427
  standards of care, 420, 471
  See also Patient outcomes
Outlets, location of, 28
Oxidized cellulose, 305, 306

Oxygen
  saturation, 385, 385f
  and wound healing, 410
Ozone sterilization, 185

Packaging, protective, 170
Packaging systems
  nonwoven, 169
  sterility of, 167–168
  types of, 168–170
PACU. *See* Postanesthesia care unit
Pain
  agents for relief of, 391, 391t, 392t
  factors affecting, 390
  guidelines for control of, 394
  standards for management of, 5t
Panic, symptoms of, 97
Pare, Ambroise, 121
Pasteur, Louis, 121
Pathogens, 126
  and infections, 130–132t
  occupational exposure to, 138
  protection against, 145–147
Patient care
  aspects of, 48–51t
  assessment of, 428–431
  model for abdominal hysterectomy,
    107–109t
  model for lithotomy position, 489–490t
  model for local infiltration, 495–497t
  model for pediatric patients, 491–493t
  models of, 106, 107–109
  plan for regional anesthesia, 246–248t
  quality of, 419–420, 428
  standards of, 48
Patient bill of rights, 105
Patient education, 49t, 370–371
Patient outcomes
  formulation of, 104–105
  postoperative evaluation of, 110
  standards for, 71, 471
  See also Outcomes
Patient rights, 105, 465
Patient Self-Determination Act, 76–77
Patients
  admission procedure for, 199–200
  comfort of, 395–396
  diabetic, 357–358